HISTORY OF
THE SECOND WORLD WAR

The author of this, as of other official histories of the Second World War, has been given free access to official documents. He alone is responsible for the statements made and the views expressed.

BRITISH
FOREIGN POLICY
IN THE
SECOND WORLD WAR

BY

SIR *Ernest* LLEWELLYN WOODWARD

Fellow of All Souls College
and formerly Professor of Modern History
in the University of Oxford,
Professor Emeritus at the Institute for
Advanced Study, Princeton, N.J.

Volume II

LONDON: 1971
HER MAJESTY'S STATIONERY OFFICE

First published 1971

© *Crown copyright* 1971

Printed and published by
HER MAJESTY'S STATIONERY OFFICE

To be purchased from
49 High Holborn, London WC1V 6HB
13a Castle Street, Edinburgh EH2 3AR
109 St Mary Street, Cardiff CF1 1JW
Brazennose Street, Manchester M60 8AS
50 Fairfax Street, Bristol BS1 3DE
258 Broad Street, Birmingham B1 2HE
80 Chichester Street, Belfast BT1 4JY
or through booksellers

Printed in Scotland

SBN 11 630068 x

FOREWORD

THE main subjects dealt with in the second Volume of the *History of British Foreign Policy in the Second World War* are Anglo-Russian relations from the opening of the German attack on the U.S.S.R. to the end of 1943, with a chapter on Great Britain and Russo-Polish relations during this period; Anglo-French relations (General de Gaulle and the Vichy Government) from February, 1941, to the recognition of the French Committee of National Liberation in August, 1943; the surrender of Italy, and relations with the Italian Government to June, 1944; relations with China and Japan from September, 1939, to the Japanese entry into the war; the signature of the Atlantic Charter and the Declaration of the United Nations. I have not given separate treatment to relations with the United States, since they come, directly or indirectly, into every chapter of the volume.

In plan and method this volume does not differ from Volume I; that is to say, it is written primarily from the archives of the Foreign Office and Cabinet Office, and, where necessary, the archives of other British Departments. I have printed in footnotes additional material from British, Allied or enemy sources, and not included in the original version (or the shorter published version) of the *History*.

I want to say once more how grateful I am to those who helped me in writing this *History* for official use, and how much I owe to the continued collaboration of Miss J. Dawson B.Litt., of the Cabinet Office Historical Section, in revising the work and preparing it for publication.

LLEWELLYN WOODWARD

Oxford, November 1968.

CONTENTS

A*

KEY TO REFERENCES

FOREIGN OFFICE RECORDS

The great majority of the references quoted in this book are to Foreign Office files. These references are always preceded by a letter, indicating the department responsible for the file in question. Thus, A indicates the American department, E the Eastern, N the Northern etc.

CABINET OFFICE RECORDS

ASE	Allied Supplies Executive
CA	Confidential Annex (or Secretary's Standard File) to Cabinet Conclusions
CCS	Combined Chiefs of Staff
Churchill Papers. .	Sir Winston Churchill's personal files in the custody of the Cabinet Office
COS . . .	Chiefs of Staff Committee
COS(W) . . .	Telegrams from Chiefs of Staff to J.S.M., Washington
DO	Defence Committee (Operations)
FAN . . .	Telegrams from Combined Chiefs of Staff to Allied Commander-in-Chief, North Africa
Hist (F), (G) . .	Cabinet Office printed series of Middle East telegrams
JIC	Joint Intelligence Committee
JSM	Joint Staff Mission, Washington
NAF . . .	Telegrams from Allied Commander-in-Chief, North Africa, to Combined Chiefs of Staff
PMM . . .	Printed series of Prime Minister's minutes
P.M.. . . .	Prime Minister's registered files
SIC	Special Information Centre files
T	Prefix to the Prime Minister's personal telegrams
WM	War Cabinet Conclusions
WP	War Cabinet Papers

PRINTED SOURCES

D.B.F.P. . . .	*Documents on British Foreign Policy*
D.G.F.P. . . .	*Documents on German Foreign Policy*
F.R.U.S. . . .	*Foreign Relations of the United States*
Parl. Deb., H. of C. .	*House of Commons Debates*

NOTE

Throughout these volumes, footnotes are indicated in the text by numerals, [1], [2], [3], etc. The marginal notes in brackets, (a), (b), (c), etc., indicate references to sources which are printed at the foot of each page.

CHAPTER XIX

The first month of the German attack on Russia: the
Anglo-Russian declaration and agreement of July 12:
exchanges of messages between Mr. Churchill and
Stalin (June 22-July 24, 1941): relations with Turkey:
Anglo-Russian action in Iran

(i)

*The German attack on Russia: despatch of British Military and Economic
Missions to Russia: questions of Anglo-Russian co-operation (June 28–July
7, 1941).*

IN the light of after knowledge the German attack on Russia
appears as an act of presumptuous folly.[1] It is indeed impossible
not to see in it yet another example of the over-confidence which
the Greeks described in terms of impiety. The Germans, not for the
first time, and not Hitler alone, had lost through too much success
a sense of the limits set to human action. Their 'new warfare', or
rather their application of time-old tactics to new conditions, had
won them victories in the west which they took to be decisive. A less
headstrong direction of the war would have asked whether these
methods could be applied in the immense spaces of Russia and against
a people known throughout modern history for their powers of
endurance and, one might almost say, for their indifference to suffering. Calamity, confusion, anarchy, death by violence and death by
starvation were familiar to Russians; the Soviet Government were
unlikely to collapse through sudden failure of nerve—no one without
strong nerves ever reached the central junta of power in Moscow.
The Russian masses were unaccustomed to political questioning;

---

[1] In telling Mussolini on June 21 (by letter) of his intention to begin his attack on
Russia, Hitler brought forward his usual arguments (the need to deprive Great Britain
of her last hope, and to free the air and land forces which he would otherwise have to
keep in the East, etc.). He concluded by saying that, since he had made his decision, he
felt 'spiritually free' again. His partnership with the Soviet Union had seemed to break
with his whole origin, concepts, and former obligations. He was 'happy now to be relieved
of these mental agonies'. (*Documents on German Foreign Policy*, Series D, XII (H.M.S.O.,
1962), No. 660. Hereafter referred to as *D.G.F.P.*)

foreign propaganda could hardly touch them. They resisted invasion as their ancestors had resisted it, without reasoning about alternatives. There might be a limit to this resistance, but it would not be reached at the early stage at which resistance had collapsed in France. Moreover, the Germans could not reckon that Russian resistance would be unaided. They had not yet defeated Great Britain; their failure to win the war in 1940 ought to have shown them the measure of British power as well as of British determination. The greatest weakness of the Allies in 1939—their military unpreparedness—was slowly being overcome, not only by the immense resources of the United States, but by the organisation of manpower and production in Great Britain and the Dominions. A more careful estimate of his enemies' resources would have suggested to Hitler that, even if the German armies reached Moscow before the winter of 1941–2, the Russians could still obtain supplies from their own distant factories and from the democratic Powers on a scale sufficient at least to keep large armies in being, and that meanwhile the drain on German war production—not to speak of German military manpower—and the respite allowed to Great Britain might ultimately change the situation in the west. Finally, the Germans—and Hitler in particular—overrated the political distrust of Russia, as a Communist state, in Great Britain and the United States. From this point of view the immediate response of the Prime Minister, and the lead given to American opinion by President Roosevelt were of great importance. Hitler, and the German people behind him, could reckon now only on the support of Japan (Italy already counted for little), and every step which bound Japan more closely with Germany increased the probability of American participation in the war. The Atlantic Charter was the significant answer to Hitler's 'crusade' against 'bolshevism'.

These things are seen now in the light of after events. They were not so clear at the time. With few exceptions, the leading military authorities in Great Britain and the United States shared the German view that Russian large-scale resistance would not last long. The Germans first supposed that they could reach Moscow in about three weeks and finish the campaign in two months. Even those German generals who regarded the campaign as a mistake thought that their armies would break the enemy before the end of the year. In mid-July the 'average' British estimate was that the German armies would be in the Caucasus at the end of August or early in September; the British military experts suggested an offer of assistance in demolition work at the Caucasian oil-fields. At the end of July the Germans were still confident, though the strength of Russian resistance had surprised them. Nevertheless they thought the Russians were making a mistake in counter-attacking fiercely rather than in withdrawing their troops, since by these expensive tactics the Russian armies would soon be annihilated.

The German plan was, roughly, to make a three-fold advance: one army moved through southern Poland with Kiev, the Ukraine and the industrial area of the Donetz basin as its objective; a second was directed through White Russia on Smolensk and Moscow, and a third through the Baltic States towards Leningrad. The Finns collaborated in the north, and the Roumanians in the south. In less than two months these three armies has made great progress, especially in the south, where Odessa and Kiev were threatened. In the centre the Germans had reached Smolensk and the northern thrust had come to Lake Peipus on the Estonian border. Nevertheless the three main objectives, Leningrad, Moscow and the Donetz basin, had not been reached, and the Russian armies, after their huge losses of men and material in the first weeks of the war, were becoming more skilful in counter-attacking and harassing the enemy while avoiding as far as possible large-scale 'encounter battles'. The Germans did not allow sufficiently for the great distances in Russia which enabled the Russian forces to withdraw after defeat and then to reappear behind the German line of advance. The Germans also underestimated the number of divisions which the Russians could put into the field, and the extent of new industrial development in the east of the country. Hitler now decided, against the advice of his generals, to suspend temporarily the drive towards Moscow and to concentrate on the southern advance which would give him, in addition to the food of the Ukraine, the minerals of the Donetz basin, and open the way to the Caucasian oilfields.[1]

The change of plan caused delay, and although the Germans came through the Ukraine to the line Kharkov–Stalino–Tagenrog and occupied the whole of the Crimea except the fortress of Sebastopol, they had not broken Russian resistance. The northern armies had also advanced, but had not taken Leningrad. When the offensive in the direction of Moscow was resumed early in October the Germans again made large captures; by the end of the month they were within 65 miles of Moscow. The position now seemed critical. The Soviet Government withdrew their main administrative departments and the diplomatic corps to Kuibyshev. The Germans made another effort to reach Moscow in November, but they were too late.[2]

Even without this series of German victories and Russian retreats, the relations between Russia and Great Britain, and also between

---

[1] On August 28, Hitler for the first time approved a review of future plans on the hypothesis that the German forces had not reached their main objectives in Russia before the winter.

[2] See below, p. 41.

Russia and the United States, would not have been easy. The Russians had not come into the war through sympathy with the democratic Powers. They were fighting only because they had been attacked, and the fact of this attack did not change their fundamental hostility to Great Britain and the United States as the leading States of the capitalist world. The Russian leaders regarded their own defensive war against Germany as an episode in a vaster and longer struggle. Unlike the British and Americans, they did not look forward to victory over the Germans as the beginning of a new era; they were not fighting for the 'freedom' of western civilisation—still less for the reestablishment of a powerful western coalition—and never expected to remain on friendly terms with their Allies; they were hardly less concerned with protecting themselves against these Allies than with winning the war against Germany. They had watched with malevolent neutrality the British fight for survival. They now feared that Great Britain might let them and the Germans fight to mutual exhaustion. Stalin and Molotov bargained with Great Britain and the United States just as they had bargained with Germany in 1939; their methods remained those of manoeuvre, lacking imagination or sympathy or any attempt to see questions as they appeared to non-Russians. It is not possible to distinguish between the Russian leaders as far as concerned the essentials of policy, but there was a special hardness and rigidity about Molotov which exasperated those who negotiated with him. This stubborn refusal to consider the interests or even the convenience of others made day to day collaboration more difficult than it would have been anyhow owing to the Russian habits of secrecy and of centralised control. Discussions at lower levels than those of the directing group in the Kremlin were disliked by the Russians partly because they required a certain latitude of judgment and decentralisation of authority. Furthermore, although the war showed that the allegation of inefficiency in every branch of Russian organisation was exaggerated, there were grave faults, and these faults were displayed at many points of contact between the Russians and their Allies.

During this early stage the Russian demand for a second front was less imperious than it became after the entry of the United States into the war. The demand was made, and in fairly strong terms, within a month of the German attack, but the British answer was clear and convincing enough to satisfy the Russians at least for the time, though they very soon raised the question again. It is doubtful whether, even with their ignorance of conditions in the west, the Russians believed it practicable for the British to land and maintain an army in France. Indeed, although the case was not put directly in such terms, the British themselves had been fighting alone for a year largely because the Russians had left the Germans free in 1939–40 to use their whole striking force in the west. The situation in the summer and autumn of 1941 was thus due in some part to the mistakes and miscalculations of Russian policy. On the other hand, if the Russians could not reasonably ask for a second front in the west, they used the alleged 'inaction' of Great Britain as an excuse for demanding material of war on an impossibly large scale, and for assistance, especially in the air at the northern and southern ends of their immense battle-front, which Great Britain could not give.[1]

The political history of Anglo-Russian relations in the first year of the German attack is thus largely a history of increasing friction; the Russian claims upon their Allies came more and more into the foreground; the claims were increasingly embarrassing because they could not be met either in the field of military action or by promises to accept the Russian views about a post-war settlement in eastern and central Europe. Until December 1941, Great Britain had the main task of dealing with these exigencies. British policy aimed at doing everything possible, within the available resources, to maintain Russian resistance, and to satisfy Russian suspicions about the post-war settlement. Even so, the Russians were not satisfied, and, although an Anglo-Russian political agreement was signed in July 1941, and a treaty in May 1942, not one of the main subjects of dispute was really settled. The Allies had not opened a second front; the Russians had not withdrawn the territorial claims which, in the Anglo-American view, conflicted with the principles for which the democracies were fighting.

The first question put by M. Maisky to Mr. Eden on the morning of the German attack showed his suspicions that Great Britain might (a) treat Russia as Russia had treated Great Britain in 1939. M. Maisky came to the Foreign Office on the morning of June 22 with the information that the Germans had begun to bomb Russian cities and that the German Ambassador had called on M. Molotov to say that a state of war existed between Germany and the U.S.S.R.; M. Maisky expected a reply within a few hours to our suggestion that we should send military and economic missions to Russia.[2] Meanwhile he asked whether he could tell the Soviet Government that our position and policy were unchanged. He felt sure that Germany would try to combine war against Russia with a peace move towards the Western Powers. Could he say that our war effort would not slacken?

---

[1] Even if the munitions and other supplies of war which Great Britain was able to send could have arrived in time (which was improbable) they would have made little or no difference to the issues in the first catastrophic period of Russian defeats. The Russians on their part took no account (and could hardly have been expected to do so) of the fact that the material of war sent to them was most urgently needed for the defence of the Middle East and of Singapore.

[2] See Volume I, page 621.

(a) N3056/3014/38.

Mr. Eden answered that, so far from slackening our war effort, we should increase it. We had already undertaken successfully an air action against the Germans in France in order to ease the pressure against Russia and another similar action was even now taking
(a) place.[1] Meanwhile Mr. Baggallay[2] had seen M. Vyshinsky on the morning of June 22. Mr. Baggallay said that obviously he had received no instructions since the opening of the German attack, but that M. Vyshinsky would probably agree that the position between Great Britain and the U.S.S.R. had changed, since, whether we liked it or not, we now had a common interest in defeating Germany. M. Vyshinsky gave a cautious assent. Mr. Baggallay then reminded him of Mr. Eden's offer to M. Maisky, and said that he assumed that the Soviet Government were now studying this offer even if they had not done so before the German attack. M. Vyshinsky answered that he would bring the matter to the notice of the Soviet Government. Mr. Baggallay thought that M. Vyshinsky was extremely nervous, and that this nervousness might account for the 'over-caution'.

On June 23 Mr. Eden told the War Cabinet that the Soviet
(b) Government were ready to receive a Military Mission if we accepted the principle of reciprocity. This stipulation did not mean that the Russians wanted to send a Military Mission to Great Britain, but that they wished to give help as well as to receive it. The War Cabinet decided that the British Mission should be in charge of an officer of high rank and outstanding personality. This officer need not be a technician, but would have technicians at his disposal from each of the fighting services. The members of the Mission were chosen without delay. They arrived[3] in Moscow on June 27. At the suggestion of the War Cabinet, Sir S. Cripps returned with them.

On June 28 Sir S. Cripps reported that after consultation with
(c) Stalin, M. Molotov had sent for him on the previous night in order to clarify the attitude of the British Government. He wanted to know (a) what degree of co-operation we proposed, (b) whether we intended political co-operation, (c) whether we would conclude a

---

[1] At the end of the interview M. Maisky said that he felt some anxiety about opinion in the United States. Mr. Eden suggested that he (M. Maisky) should see Mr. Winant. (Mr. Winant had been appointed on February 6, 1941, to succeed Mr. Kennedy as United States Ambassador in London. He arrived in London on March 1.)
[2] Mr. Baggallay was Chargé d'Affaires at Moscow. Sir S. Cripps had been recalled for consultation on June 2. He left Moscow on June 6.
[3] I have dealt with the work of the military mission and of other technical and economic assistance to Russia only to the extent necessary to explain the course of Anglo-Russian diplomatic relations. The Foreign Office archives contain a large number of telegrams on technical subjects sent by or through the military mission; these subjects are best dealt with apart from the general history of Anglo-Russian diplomatic relations. Lieutenant-General F. N. Mason-Macfarlane was appointed head of the military mission.

(a) N3018/3/38.   (b) WM(41)62, N3138/3014/38.   (c) N3231/3/38.

political agreement to define the basis of our co-operation. This last point was of the greatest importance.

Sir S. Cripps replied that (a) our economic co-operation would be as full as possible within the limited means of transport available to us; (b) our military co-operation would take the form of advice and technical help; we could not spare men or material; (c) political co-operation would be highly desirable in the Middle and Far East, where our common aim should be the exclusion of the Axis Powers; (d) we had not contemplated a political agreement at the present stage. Our common hostility to Hitler was a sound basis for military and economic co-operation, but it was not a satisfactory basis for a political agreement. The new relationship between Great Britain and the U.S.S.R. had existed only since June 22. It might therefore be better to wait for the growth of mutual trust over a period of military and economic co-operation before we attempted to put our political relations into the form of a written agreement. Sir S. Cripps hoped that such an agreement would follow at a future date, probably at the Peace Conference. M. Molotov said that he would report Sir S. Cripps's views to the Soviet Government and let him have an answer on June 28.

On June 29 Sir S. Cripps telegraphed that he might find it (a) necessary to ask for an interview with Stalin within a day or two in order to learn how the Soviet Government regarded our co-operation. They were very suspicious of us, and would not treat us frankly for some time. Hitherto their attitude was that it was 'more blessed to receive than to give'. Sir S. Cripps said that if he had instructions he could secure an interview and introduce the subject of co-operation.

Shortly after sending the telegram suggesting a message to (b) Stalin, Sir S. Cripps was called (11.30 p.m.) to see M. Molotov. M. Molotov said that, according to a report from M. Maisky of a conversation with Lord Beaverbrook, we might be prepared to assist Russia by means of (a) increased air activity over western Germany and France, (b) a landing in northern France, (c) naval activity off Petsamo and the Murmansk coast. M. Molotov explained that there were intense German attacks by mechanised forces and aircraft over the whole of the front and that action under (a), (b) and (c) would be of the greatest value; (c) was more urgent than (b). Sir S. Cripps gathered that the military situation was very grave, especially in the Baltic provinces and around Minsk.

Sir S. Cripps replied that he could say nothing about (b) and (c) since they were a matter for the Military Mission. Unfortunately, however, the Mission had as yet made little real contact with the Russian military and naval chiefs. Sir S. Cripps suggested an immediate meeting. M. Molotov agreed with this proposal, and (c)

(a) N3302/3/38. (b) N3260/78/38. (c) N3278/78/38.

asked General Mason-Macfarlane to see him at 3 a.m. He then repeated his suggestions under (a), (b) and (c) with particular emphasis on (c). General Mason-Macfarlane asked for more information about the Russian front and said that we were far more likely to come to a rapid decision if they were fully informed than if we had only vague reports. He also pointed out that it was impossible to decide upon action at Petsamo without more detailed local knowledge.

M. Molotov replied that time was being wasted and that he would take up the question in London. He would not give any recent facts about the military position. Finally, in order to avoid a deadlock, General Mason-Macfarlane undertook to let the Chiefs of Staff know M. Molotov's requests. M. Molotov said that, until we had undertaken to carry out an operation at Petsamo, no details in connection with this operation could be discussed. General Mason-Macfarlane explained that Sir S. Cripps had asked for a meeting with the Russian General Staff in order to obtain information for the guidance of the British Government in deciding upon possible action to relieve the pressure on the Russian armies. No meeting had taken place, and the British Mission had been given practically no information. M. Molotov said that he would arrange better co-operation. General Mason-Macfarlane thought that the Russians were anxious about Murmansk and that they genuinely felt that we had an opportunity to take advantage of the relative German weakness in the west.

(a)   On June 30 Sir S. Cripps telegraphed that he thought M. Molotov was trying to bring off a personal or party triumph by getting us into some specific commitment in order that he might re-establish his own position, and that of the Communist party, in view of their past failure. Meanwhile Stalin was awaiting events and keeping himself free to throw in his lot with the army or the party. Sir S. Cripps asked that no arrangements should be made through M. Maisky, and that M. Maisky should be told firmly that, unless we had real co-operation and a full exchange of information we could not leave the distinguished heads of our Mission wasting time in Moscow, and that we could not act without proper advice of an expert kind from them.

Sir S. Cripps said that as soon as he received an answer about his proposal for a message to Stalin, he would take a similar line. He also suggested that the Prime Minister should see M. Maisky. He thought that the critical moment had come in our relationship with the Soviet Government and that the latter must co-operate fully or we should have to leave them alone. We had already done much for them on the economic side; the 'hold-up' was in military matters.

(a) N3279/78/38.

A few hours later Sir S. Cripps withdrew his suggestion that the Prime Minister should speak to M. Maisky. He telegraphed that this move was now unnecessary in view of developments in the contacts of the Mission, but that the rest of his telegram was still valid.

In view of this later telegram Sir S. Cripps was instructed on July 1 that it would be better, before sending a personal message, to see (a) how matters developed as a result of his own and General Mason-Macfarlane's interviews with M. Molotov. If the position were satisfactory, it would probably be unwise to ask for an interview with Stalin in order to urge closer co-operation. Sir S. Cripps should therefore not apply for this interview unless he were convinced that for ulterior reasons M. Molotov was working against a policy of co-operation and that an appeal to Stalin was the only way of countering him. It was also doubtful whether Stalin would be greatly impressed by a message from the Prime Minister unless it were accompanied by definite promises of military help, but in present circumstances we could not give such help.

Sir S. Cripps telegraphed on July 2 that he and General Mason-Macfarlane had again seen M. Molotov. M. Molotov had asked (b) whether an answer had been received to his urgent requests. Sir S. Cripps explained once again that we had already taken the political decision, i.e. we had decided to give all possible aid to the U.S.S.R. We could decide upon practical measures only with full knowledge of the facts. The practical decision would have to be taken in London on the basis of information from the Military Mission in Moscow. We needed the fullest and most frank disclosures of the military situation and our co-operation, if it were to be successful, must rest on a basis of action by both parties without reserve. Sir S. Cripps said that he was not sure whether there was not still some reserve even between M. Molotov and himself.

M. Molotov answered that, in the past, the interests of his Government had compelled him to show reserve since Russia had wanted to postpone the danger of war. He had never felt hostility to Sir S. Cripps, and could now deal with the British Government frankly and without reserve. The Russian military, naval, and air authorities had been instructed to do likewise.

In a second telegram Sir S. Cripps hoped that we would consider (c) active help on one of the lines suggested by M. Molotov. The Russians were standing up magnificently against tremendous pressure, and some gesture of active help would do much to reinforce their determination. A landing even on a small scale in northern Norway or France would be of great help. Sir S. Cripps said that he could not overstate the importance of immediate action. He asked

---

(a) N3301/78/38. (b) N3351/78/38. (c) N3352/78/38.

that Mr. Dalton should be informed and should give some response in terms of action on the various suggested cargoes. M. Mikoyan had enquired whether any replies had been received, and seemed disappointed at a negative answer.

(a)　　Meanwhile Mr. Eden had seen M. Maisky during the afternoon of June 30. M. Maisky said that the Soviet Government were grateful for our prompt action in sending the Missions to Moscow. Their speedy despatch, however, made it more necessary to define the scope of their work. M. Maisky thought that at present they had perhaps too little authority. They asked questions about Russian action, but when they in turn were asked about our plans and the action we proposed to take, they said that they had to refer home. The Soviet Government wanted a definition of the collaboration which we had in mind e.g. was it to be military or military and economic or military and economic and political? M. Maisky thought that the Soviet Government wanted this threefold collaboration.

Mr. Eden said that on military and economic matters the position was clear from the Prime Minister's broadcast and his own speech in the House of Commons. The question of political collaboration was more difficult. Did the Soviet Government suggest an alliance or some less far-reaching agreement? M. Maisky thought that the Soviet Government wanted to know whether we would discuss our respective policies in those parts of the world where we both had interests e.g. the Middle and Far East. Mr. Eden said that there would be no difficulty about such an exchange of views. He had indeed asked some time earlier for the views of the Soviet Government about the Middle East. He promised to raise the question in the Cabinet and to speak about it again to M. Maisky.

(b)　　On July 7 Sir S. Cripps was given the text of a message for Stalin from the Prime Minister in the following terms:

> 'We are all very glad here that the Russian armies are making such strong and spirited resistance to the utterly unprovoked and merciless invasion of the Nazis. There is general admiration of the bearing and tenacity of the soldiers and people. We shall do everything to help you that time, geography, and our growing resources allow. The longer the war lasts, the more help we can give. We are making very heavy attacks both by day and night with our Air Force upon all German occupied territory and all Germany within our reach. About 400 daylight sorties were made overseas yesterday. On Saturday night over 200 heavy bombers attacked German towns, some carrying 3 tons apiece, and last night nearly 250 heavy bombers were operating. This will go on. Thus we hope to force Hitler to bring back some of his Air power to the west and gradually take some of the strain off you.

(a) N3304/3/38. (b) N3539/78/38.

Besides this the Admiralty have at my desire prepared a serious operation to come off in the near future in the Arctic, after which I hope contact will be established between the British and Russian navies. Meanwhile by sweeps along the Norwegian coast we have intercepted various supply ships which were moving north against you.

We welcome the arrival of the Russian Military Mission in order to concert future plans.

We have only got to go on fighting to beat the life out of those villains.'

(ii)

Sir S. Cripps's interview of July 8 with Stalin: Stalin's proposal for an Anglo-Russian political agreement: acceptance of this proposal by His Majesty's Government: Russian acceptance of the British draft text: signature of the agreement, July 12, 1941.

Sir S. Cripps delivered this message to Stalin at 1.30 p.m. on July 8. He saw Stalin alone for an hour. He reported that the talk (a) was frank and easy. In reply to a question from Sir S. Cripps about the progress of the war, Stalin answered 'very frankly and seriously' that there was nothing pleasant to report. The strain all along the line was very great. Minsk had fallen. The position in the south was rather better, but the Russians were still withdrawing. The thrust towards Leningrad was very strong at Pskov. Murmansk had not yet fallen. The 'element of surprise' was still operating in that the Russians had not yet been able fully to deploy their forces.

Stalin raised the questions of Afghanistan and Iran.[1] He regarded those questions as important. He said that there were 6–7,000 Germans in Iran[2] and too many in Afghanistan. Stalin thought that the Germans and Italians would attempt a *coup* against Baku and against us in Iran. We ought therefore to take some action. Sir S. Cripps said that we were aware of the danger and had made representations accordingly in Teheran. He suggested a joint Anglo-Russian *démarche*. Stalin agreed with this suggestion.

Stalin discussed the question of an agreement between Great Britain and the U.S.S.R. He answered Sir S. Cripps's references to the British efforts to secure an agreement in the autumn of 1940 by saying that Russian acceptance of the offer at that time would have been tantamount to an attack on Germany. He now felt, however, very strongly that an agreement was necessary in order to clarify our

---

[1] See below, section (v) of this chapter.
[2] The British estimate was much lower.

(a) N3528, 3529/3/38; N3527/78/38; E3691/3551/65.

respective positions and to create a basis for our joint co-operation. His idea was an agreement of a purely general nature under two heads: (i) mutual help without precision as to quantity or quality; (ii) neither side to conclude a separate peace. Without such an agreement Russia felt isolated in view of all the agreements which Germany had against her.

Sir S. Cripps said that he had misunderstood M. Molotov's proposal and had thought that Stalin wanted something more specific with regard to our political interests *vis-à-vis* other countries. Sir S. Cripps pointed out that, although we were wholly determined on both points raised by Stalin, we should not necessarily find it easy or advisable to reduce them to a formal agreement at this early stage. There were still elements of opinion in Great Britain and in the United States which needed to be convinced.

Sir S. Cripps said that he would recommend to the British Government an exchange of notes covering Stalin's headings. Stalin answered that an agreement would be far more valuable but that an exchange of notes would be 'something'. He also asked whether the negotiations could take place in Moscow.

(a)   On July 9 the Prime Minister sent to Mr. Eden the draft of a reply to Stalin's proposal. The draft was in the following terms:

'Ambassador Cripps having reported his talk with you and having stated the terms of a proposed Anglo-Russian agreement under two heads, namely (1) mutual help without any precision as to quantity or quality and (2) neither country to conclude a separate peace, I have immediately convened the War Cabinet, including Mr. Fraser (Prime Minister of New Zealand) who is with us now. It will be necessary for us to consult with the self-governing Dominions of Canada, Australia and South Africa, but in the meanwhile I should like to assure you that we are wholly in favour of the agreement you propose. We think it should be signed as soon as we have heard from our Dominions and published to the world immediately thereafter. The details will fall naturally into their places in later discussion.

You will of course understand that at the victorious Peace Conference in which the United States will certainly be a leading party, our line would be that territorial frontiers will have to be settled in accordance with the wishes of the people who live there and on general ethnographical lines, and, secondly, that these units, when established, must be free to choose their own form of government and system of life, so long as they do not interfere with the similar rights of neighbouring peoples.'

Mr. Eden suggested to the Prime Minister that it would be better to leave the matter to be dealt with by Sir S. Cripps himself rather than to send a personal message to Stalin. Mr. Eden thought that

(a) N3607/3/38.

messages from the Prime Minister should be left for occasions of capital importance, and that the Prime Minister should not become involved in the day to day business of diplomacy. Mr. Eden also said that, in view of Catholic opinion in the United States, it was necessary to carry the United States Government with us in any step such as a political agreement with Russia. Mr. Eden saw Mr. Winant (a) on July 9 about the proposed agreement. Mr. Winant said that, from the point of view of opinion in the United States, it would be desirable that the agreement should not take the form of a treaty. Owing to the procedure under the United States constitution a treaty had a 'specially serious sound' to American opinion.

The War Cabinet considered Sir S. Cripps's report on July 9. They agreed to meet Stalin's proposal with 'an immediate and (b) generous response'. In a discussion on the form of the agreement it was decided that something more was needed than an exchange of notes, while an agreement in treaty form might have an unfavourable reaction on public opinion in certain countries. Moreover Stalin had not asked for a treaty but for an agreement and an agreed declaration was in substance as binding as a treaty. The War Cabinet considered that the best form of response would be a message from the Prime Minister to Stalin accepting the proposal. They also thought that it might be unwise to include in the message any reference to the Peace Conference after the war and the right of ethnographical units then established to choose their own form of government and system of life. Such a reference might cause difficulties for the Poles in their negotiations with the Russians. It was decided therefore to limit the reply to the two points covered by Stalin's proposal and to delete from the draft of the Prime Minister's message to Stalin the sentences following the words 'published to the world immediately thereafter'.

The Prime Minister's message as thus amended[1] was telegraphed (c) to Sir S. Cripps on the night of July 9–10. Sir S. Cripps was also told, for his own information, that His Majesty's Government had in mind an agreement as follows:

'His Majesty's Government in the United Kingdom and the Government of the U.S.S.R. have agreed and declare as follows:

(i) The two Governments mutually undertake to render each other assistance of all kinds in the present war against Germany.

(ii) They further undertake that during the present war they will neither negotiate nor conclude an armistice or treaty of peace except by mutual agreement.'

---

[1] There were two other small amendments to the first paragraph. The word 'self-governing' was omitted before the words 'Dominions of Canada', etc. and the word 'the' substituted for 'our' before the words 'Dominions and published'.

(a) N3603/3/38. (b) WM/41/67. (c) N3561/3/38.

(a)   Sir S. Cripps reported on the evening of July 10 that he had seen
Stalin at 2 p.m. Stalin was 'most pleased' with the Prime Minister's
message. Sir S. Cripps said to him that, in order to save time, he had
prepared a draft of an agreement. He then read out a translation of
the draft which he had received. After some discussion Stalin agreed
to the following terms:

> 'Agreement for joint action between His Majesty's Government in
> the United Kingdom and the Government of the U.S.S.R. in the war
> against Germany.
>
> His Majesty's Government in the United Kingdom and the
> Government of the U.S.S.R. have concluded the present agreement
> and declare as follows:
>
> (i) The two Governments mutually undertake to render each other
> assistance and support of all kinds in the present war against Hitlerite
> Germany.
>
> (ii) They further undertake that during this war they will neither
> negotiate nor conclude an armistice or treaty of peace except by
> mutual agreement.'

Sir S. Cripps reported that Stalin wished the agreement to be
signed in Moscow; he insisted on some form of title for it, and wanted
the signature to take place as soon as possible because some Communists in Russia were speaking in a pro-German sense and the
publication of the agreement would enable him to put a stop to their
(b)   activities. Sir S. Cripps was instructed during the night of July 11–12
that His Majesty's Government agreed with the draft text which
Stalin had approved and that the declaration could be signed at
once. Sir S. Cripps communicated the acceptance of the draft to
(c)   Stalin on the morning of July 12, and the declaration was signed in
the afternoon. M. Molotov, who signed on behalf of the Soviet
Government, asked for the addition of a protocol to the effect that
the agreement between the two Governments should enter into
force at once and not be subject to ratification.

(iii)

*Russian appeals for military action by Great Britain: Stalin's message of
July 19 to the Prime Minister and the Prime Minister's reply of July 21,
1941.*

The signature of the Anglo-Russian declaration did not solve the
difficulties of the Military Mission. The members of the Mission

---

(a) N3565/3/38. (b) N3565/3/38. (c) N3659/3/38.

still found it hard to secure information from the Russian military authorities and to persuade them that we were doing everything in our power to help Russian resistance. On July 14 the Chiefs of Staff telegraphed to General Mason-Macfarlane that they were disturbed (a) at a suggestion recently made by him that the Russians were convinced that we were not pulling our weight. This view would doubtless result in demands for action which we could not possibly carry out. Our present difficulties were largely due to the attitude of the U.S.S.R. in 1939. For twelve months we had been fighting alone against heavy odds. We had overcome great difficulties and, with ever increasing American aid, were confident that in time we should defeat Germany. All our forces were devoted to that object. Our main strategy was to weaken Germany by air, naval and economic action and to maintain our position in the Middle and Far East. This strategy was indirectly of very great help to Russia; direct aid was a different question. We were considering certain diversions, but from a military point of view nothing beyond the action which we were already taking could affect the operations of the main Russian armies and air forces. They must save themselves as we had saved ourselves in the Battle of Britain and in the Atlantic. The vital question was for the Russians to try to keep their armies and air forces intact and to try to hold some front next winter and spring. Our own resources and American armaments would then allow us seriously to weaken Germany by air, naval and economic action, and in 1942 we should hope that Germany would be thrown on the defensive.

On July 19 M. Maisky told Mr. Eden that he had a personal (b) message from Stalin for the Prime Minister. Mr. Eden arranged that M. Maisky should see the Prime Minister in the country at 5 p.m. Stalin's message to the Prime Minister was in the following terms: (c)

'Let me express my gratitude for the two personal messages which you have addressed to me.

Your messages were the starting point of developments which subsequently resulted in agreement between our two Governments. Now, as you have said with full justification, the Soviet Union and Great Britain have become fighting allies in the struggle against Hitlerite Germany. I have no doubt that, in spite of all the difficulties, our two States will be strong enough to crush our common enemy.

Perhaps it is not out of place to mention that the position of the Soviet forces at the front remains tense. The consequences of the unexpected breach of the Non-Aggression Pact by Hitler, as well as of the sudden attack against the Soviet Union—both facts giving advantages to the German troops—still remain to be felt by the Soviet armies.

(a) N3729/78/38. (b) C8096/3226/55. (c) N3955/3955/38.

It is easy to imagine that the position of the German forces would have been many times more favourable had the Soviet troops had to face the attack of the German forces not in the regions of Kishinev, Lwow, Brest, Kaunas, and Viborg, but in the region of Odessa, Kamenets Podolsk, Minsk and the environs of Leningrad.

It seems to me, therefore, that the military situation of the Soviet Union, as well as of Great Britain, would be considerably improved if there could be established a front against Hitler in the west—northern France, and in the north—the Arctic.

A front in north France not only could divert Hitler's forces from the East, but at the same time would make it impossible for Hitler to invade Great Britain. The establishment of the front just mentioned would be popular with the British Army, as well as with the whole population of southern England.

I fully realise the difficulties involved in the establishment of such a front. I believe, however, that in spite of the difficulties it should be formed, not only in the interests of our common cause, but also in the interests of Great Britain herself. This is the most propitious moment for the establishment of such a front, because now Hitler's forces are diverted to the east and he has not yet had the chance to consolidate the position occupied by him in the east.

It is still easier to establish a front in the north. Here, on the part of Great Britain, would be necessary only naval and air operations, without the landing of troops or artillery. The Soviet military, naval and air forces would take part in such an operation. We would welcome it if Great Britain could transfer to this theatre of war something like one light division or more of the Norwegian volunteers, who could be used in north Norway to organise rebellion against the Germans.'

The Prime Minister replied to this message on the night of
(a) July 20–1 as follows:

'I am very glad to get your message, and to learn from many sources of the valiant fight and the many vigorous counter-attacks with which the Russian Armies are defending their native soil. I fully realise the military advantage you have gained by forcing the enemy to deploy and engage on forward westerly fronts, thus exhausting some of the force of his initial effort.

Anything sensible and effective that we can do to help will be done. I beg you however to realise limitations imposed upon us by our resources and geographical position. From the first day of the German attack upon Russia, we have examined possibilities of attacking occupied France and the Low Countries. The Chiefs of Staff do not see any way of doing anything on a scale likely to be of the slightest use to you. The Germans have 40 divisions in France alone, and the whole coast has been fortified with German diligence for more than a year, and bristles with cannon, wire, pill-boxes and beach mines.

(a) N3955/3955/38.

The only part where we could have even temporary air superiority and air fighter protection is from Dunkirk to Boulogne. This is one mass of fortifications with scores of heavy guns commanding the sea approaches, many of which can fire right across the Straits. There is less than 5 hours' darkness, and even then the whole area is illuminated by searchlights. To attempt a landing in force would be to encounter a bloody repulse, and petty raids would only lead to fiascos doing far more harm than good to both of us. It would all be over without their having to move or before they could move a single unit from your front.

You must remember that we have been fighting all alone for more than a year, and that although our resources are growing and will grow fast from now on, we are at the utmost strain both at home and in the Middle East by land and air, and also that the Battle of the Atlantic, on which our life depends and the movements of all our convoys in the face of the U-Boats and Focke-Wolf blockade, strains our naval forces, great though they be, to the utmost limit.

It is therefore to the north we must look for any speedy help we can give. The Naval Staff have been preparing for three weeks past an operation by sea-borne aircraft upon German shipping in the north of Norway and Finland, hoping thereby to destroy enemy power of transporting troops by sea to attack your Arctic flank. We have asked your staff to keep a certain area clear of Russian vessels between July 28 and August 2 when we shall hope to strike. Secondly we are sending forthwith some cruisers and destroyers to Spitsbergen, whence they will be able to raid enemy shipping in concert with your naval forces. Thirdly we are sending submarines to intercept German traffic on the Arctic coast, although owing to perpetual daylight this service is particularly dangerous. Fourthly we are sending a minelayer with various supplies to Archangel. This is the most we can do at the moment. I wish it were more. Pray let the most extreme secrecy be kept until the moment when we tell you publicity will not be harmful.

There is no Norwegian light division in existence, and it would be impossible to land troops, either British or Russian, on German occupied territory in perpetual daylight without having first obtained reasonable fighter air cover. We had bitter experiences at Namsos last year and in Crete this year of trying such enterprises.

We are also studying as a further development the basing of some British fighter air squadrons on Murmansk. This would require first of all a consignment of anti-aircraft guns, in addition to ground staff and equipment, then the arrival of the aircraft, some of which could be flown off carriers, and others crated. When these were established our Spitsbergen squadron might possibly come to Murmansk. As soon as our Naval forces are known to be in the north, we are under no delusion but that the Germans will immediately follow their invariable practice of opposing our forces with a strong force of dive-bombers, and it is therefore necessary to proceed step by step. All this, however, will take weeks.

B

Do not hesitate to suggest anything else that occurs to you, and we will also be searching earnestly for other ways of striking at the common foe.'

The Prime Minister read Stalin's message and his own reply to
(a) the War Cabinet on July 21. Mr. Eden said that M. Maisky expected the Soviet Government to be disappointed with the reply and to ask whether we could not send material supplies to Russia if we were unable to make a diversion in France. It was pointed out that M. Maisky had also given us large demands for aircraft. Although we could not meet these demands, we might make a limited number of American aircraft (on our order) available to Russia. The United States Government were about to send some aircraft and other supplies via Vladivostok, but they would take many months to arrive. The War Cabinet thought that it would be advisable for us to have joint discussions with the Soviet and United States Governments on the question of supplies to Russia.[1]

Sir S. Cripps gave the Prime Minister's message to Stalin on the
(b) night of July 21–2. Stalin said to him, 'I understand the difficulties of operations. I have no questions and no reproaches.' Sir S. Cripps also asked whether it was yet possible to arrange for a visit of the Military Mission to the front. Stalin said that their visit had been agreed in principle but that the time was not expedient. He hoped that the matter would be arranged shortly. There was no great secret about the Russian operations, but if the Military Mission went to the front now, the United States would ask for the same privilege and American journalists would also want to go. Furthermore, the Russian General Staff were planning certain operations which they wished to put into effect before any visits were made to the front.

(c)   On the day after the delivery of Stalin's message to the Prime Minister, the Foreign Office asked Sir S. Cripps whether he could confirm reports that measures were being taken to evacuate Moscow and that a number of Government Departments had already been moved, possibly to Sverdlovsk. Sir S. Cripps replied on July 22 that
(d) he could not confirm the reports. There had been evacuation of women and children on a considerable scale during the first days of the German attack on Russia. There was also a plan for the evacuation of Government Departments in case of need, and certain steps had already been taken. On the other hand there were no signs of

---

[1] The Prime Minister sent a message to Stalin, after the reply of July 21, that we were sending to Russia 200 aircraft which we had just received from the United States. These aircraft had been intended partly as a reinforcement for the Middle East.

(a) WM(41)72, N3978/78/38.   (b) N4024, 3988/78/38.   (c) N3929/2823/38.
(d) N4004/78/38.

evacuation in the few departments with which His Majesty's Embassy was in contact. M. Molotov and M. Vyshinsky had promised Mr. Baggallay that they would give him ample warning before 'the Government' left Moscow. Sverdlovsk was an obvious seat for the Government with Kazan as a half-way point. Sir S. Cripps thought that the report might be due to the fact that the American Embassy had sent a small staff with much baggage to Kazan. Sir S. Cripps himself had sent a smaller party with the indispensable heavy gear which he might not be able to transfer from Moscow after heavy bombing had begun.

Sir S. Cripps was also told on July 22 that, according to informa- (a) tion received by His Majesty's Government, the Turkish Ambassador in Moscow had reported to his Government that the fall of Smolensk[1] had made a deep impression in Moscow, and that open criticism of the Government had begun, and a feeling was spreading that the war was lost, although the outcome was awaited with resignation. The authority of the Government was complete and there were no signs of a break-up in the army.

Sir S. Cripps replied[2] on July 24 that, in spite of a most friendly (b) atmosphere since the German attack, the contacts of the British Embassy with the civil population were and would probably continue to be 'practically non-existent'. The same conditions applied in a large measure to all the diplomats in Moscow, including the Turkish Ambassador. From his very few contacts with the Russian 'intelligentsia', Sir S. Cripps thought that the vagueness of the military communiqués, which nevertheless implied a rapid German advance, had a depressing effect. It was, however, unsafe to generalise. There were no visible signs of panic after the third heavy raid on Moscow. Rationing was fairly stringent but the population was used to it and even more severe restrictions were unlikely to affect morale. The re-appointment of the Political Commissars would not be popular, although there probably were good reasons for the step. It might be said, therefore, that the attitude of the Moscow population towards the war was one of calm resignation, without enthusiasm or defeatism, but with reasonable determination. If, as the Soviet Government had announced 'categorically', the German advance on Moscow was being held up, the attitude of the population would become more positive.

---

[1] The Germans reached Smolensk on July 16, but the Russians did not evacuate it until nearly four weeks later.

[2] Sir S. Cripps thought that the Turkish Ambassador was personally and politically defeatist, since his Government wanted Russia to be defeated. He therefore welcomed any sign of difficulty.

(a) N4019/78/38. (b) N4043/78/38.

(iv)

Anglo-Turkish relations after the German attack on Russia.

The German attack on the U.S.S.R. was regarded in Turkey with
(a) mixed feelings. From one point of view a war between the Germans
and the Russians meant that the two Powers whose collusion might
have been of the gravest danger to Turkey were now fighting each
other. Turkey was thus freed from the nightmare of a Russo-German
agreement at her expense. On the other hand the complete victory
of Russia or Germany would only increase the danger to Turkish
independence. Meanwhile, whatever the issue, the area of fighting
might now spread from the Balkans to the north shores of the Black
Sea and even to the Caucasus. The Turks feared that they might
have to face very strong German demands for the passage of German
troops across their territory, and also that their ally, Great Britain—
to whom they could not be said to have given much positive support
—might make concessions at their expense in return for a military
alliance with the U.S.S.R.

Mr. Churchill's broadcast on the night of June 22–3 was indirectly
an answer to Turkish hints that the best policy would now be to
avoid intervention in the war between Germany and Russia. One
(b) passage, however, in the broadcast caused the Turks to suspect that
they might have avoided a Russo-German bargain to their detriment
only to be faced with an Anglo-Russian arrangement of a similar
kind. Mr. Churchill had recalled the days of the First World War
when the Russian armies had 'helped to gain a victory from a share
in which, alas, they were, through no fault of ours, utterly cut out'.

Owing mainly to a delay in communications, an official British
assurance that the Turkish interpretation of this passage was entirely
unfounded did not reach Ankara until July 3. On the other hand
the Turks noticed, again with concern, that in the House of Commons
on June 25 Mr. Eden had spoken disapprovingly of the Turkish-
German agreement.

(c)   Meanwhile the War Cabinet had decided that the best way to
reassure the Turkish Government would be through an exchange of
notes on the situation arising out of the German attack on Russia. On
(d) June 30 the Foreign Office instructed Sir H. Knatchbull-Hugessen
to offer an undertaking that His Majesty's Government would
respect the territorial integrity of Turkey and regard the Anglo-
Turkish treaty of 1939 as the basis of their relations with Turkey, and

---

(a) R6399/1934/44; R6532/236/44. (b) N3087/78/38; R6581/236/44. (c) WM(41)64.
(d) R6532/236/44.

therefore would not make with any country engaged in the struggle against Germany an agreement detrimental to essential Turkish interests. In return for this declaration the Turkish Government would be required to give an undertaking that they also regarded the Treaty of 1939 as the main foundation of their foreign policy, and that they would not do anything likely to be detrimental to essential British interests. The declaration would thus be a counter-move to the agreement which Turkey had made a few days earlier with Germany.

After they had received the assurance that Mr. Churchill's speech (a) did not foreshadow any action against the territorial integrity of Turkey, the Turkish Government agreed to consider an exchange of notes, and perhaps to include in it a promise (which Sir H. Knatch-bull-Hugessen had been unable hitherto to obtain) that they would not allow the transit of enemy troops or war material across their territory. A month passed, however, without any declaration on the Turkish side. It was therefore clear that the Turkish Government were intending to let the matter drop. On the other hand, in view of their own proposals for action in Iran,[1] the British and Soviet Governments now thought it desirable to take the initiative in giving assurances to Turkey even though the Turks would not commit themselves to any more promises.

Mr. Eden had suggested to M. Maisky on July 19 that the Soviet Government should exchange assurances with Turkey on the lines of (b) our own proposed declaration. M. Maisky thought that the Soviet Government would agree to the suggestion. Sir S. Cripps was therefore instructed to propose a statement on the lines that the U.S.S.R. would confirm the Montreux Convention and, like His Majesty's Government, would undertake to respect the territorial integrity of Turkey. Sir S. Cripps considered that, in return for a Soviet declara- (c) tion, Turkey should give an undertaking to the U.S.S.R., but on August 7 the Soviet Government accepted the plan for a unilateral (d) declaration to be made simultaneously by the British and Soviet Ambassadors at Ankara; they also suggested the addition of a promise of assistance to Turkey if she were attacked by a European Power.

The assurances were delivered on August 10. The Turkish Government welcomed them, and asked that they should be published. The Foreign Office, however, still doubted whether a statement in general terms would really remove Turkish suspicions about Anglo-Russian action in Iran. Turkish mistrust of Russian designs

---

[1] See below, section (v) of this chapter.

(a) R6658, 6703, 6721, 6747, 6955, 7288/236/44. (b) R7248/112/44. (c) R7312/112/44. (d) E4524/3444/34; R7516/112/44.

in the Caucasus—where Turkey had acquired territory from Russia after the war of 1914–18—was hardly less than the mistrust of Russian aims with regard to the Straits. At the British suggestion, therefore, the British and Russian Ambassadors at Ankara re-affirmed on August 16—the day of the Anglo-Russian *démarche* at

(a) Teheran—that their respective Governments had no designs against the independence or territorial integrity of Iran. Even so Turkish suspicions continued. Furthermore the Turks were hardly less nervous of the consequences of a complete Russian defeat. The speed of the German advance gave the impression that the German armies might reach the Caucasus by the winter or even that the Russians might surrender. In either case the Germans could threaten Turkey with heavy air attack.

(b)   On Sir H. Knatchbull-Hugessen's advice, the Turkish Govern-ment were informed that we could give them very considerable support in the air, but the immediate German demands on Turkey turned out to be economic rather than political or military. On September 6 a German trade delegation came to Ankara, and began to press Turkey to readjust her trade to suit German needs. The principal object of negotiations was the supply of chrome. Early in 1940 Great Britain and France had secured an agreement guarantee-ing to them the whole of the Turkish chrome output for two years, with the offer of purchase for a third year.[1] The British Government

(c) held that the collapse of France did not invalidate this pact as far as Turkey and Great Britain were concerned. Hitherto the Turkish Government had accepted this interpretation, and, as late as July 1941, had given assurances that they would not allow Germany to purchase any of their chrome.

Under German pressure, however, they now began to say that the

(d) renewal of the agreement after January 1942, depended upon notification by the French as well as by the British Government. The British Government protested against this view and pointed out that we had continued to fulfil our promise to send supplies and that to sell chrome to Germany was to provide means for killing Allied

(e) troops. After more than a month's negotiations with the Germans, the Turkish Government held out against supplying Germany with chrome until January 1943, i.e. after the expiry of the original Anglo-French agreement. They promised a certain quantity (less than the amount for which the Germans asked) in and after January 1943, but only in return for deliveries of material which—on the British estimate—Germany would find it difficult or even impossible

---

[1] See Volume IV, Chapter L, note to section (iii).

(a) E4524/3444/34; E4830/3326/34.   (b) R7899, 7914/1934/44; R8036/236/44.
(c) R1901, 6846, 7073, 7135, 7852, 7912, 8254/179/44.   (d) R8500, 8503, 8537, 8597, 8639/179/4 .   (e) R8686, 8710, 8711, 8781, 8839, 8927, 8935, 8965, 8966, 9093/179/44.

to supply. The Foreign Office therefore thought that, in the circumstances, the Turks had given away very little, and that, as after the political agreement with Germany in the previous June, we should continue our support to Turkey.

(v)

Anglo-Russian demands on Iran, July–August 1941.

Iran was of economic interest to Great Britain as a source of oil, and was of strategic importance owing to its geographical position between the Caspian Sea and the Persian Gulf, with frontiers touching Iraq, Turkey, the U.S.S.R., Afghanistan and the outposts of British India. Anglo-Iranian relations, however, in the recent past had not been close or friendly. The nationalism of the Iraqi Arabs was as sensitive as that of the Iranians, but Iraq had at least been liberated by Great Britain from the old Ottoman Empire; the Iranians, on the other hand, associated Great Britain with the partition of their country under the Anglo-Russian agreement of 1907 into two spheres of influence. After the first World War, in spite of British efforts to remove Russian control, the Soviet Government had been able to re-establish their position. They had secured a treaty with Iran in 1921 whereby, in return for a guarantee of Iranian sovereignty and territorial integrity, they had the right to send troops into the country if any other Power attempted to usurp authority in Iran or to use it as a base for an attack on the U.S.S.R.

The Russians were able to exercise greater pressure than the British because they could march across their own frontiers into Iran. For these same reasons of proximity, they had always been the most important purchasers of Iranian goods. Here again the Soviet Government continued in a new form, and by a series of trade agreements, the policy of the Tsarist Government, and also sent engineers and technicians to Iranian industries. In the years before the war their most important rivals were German rather than British. The Iranian Government had welcomed German interest in the country as a set-off against Russian control, and to a lesser extent, against British control. Furthermore, the 'Government' of Iran in 1939 was in fact the Shah, and the Shah was trying to modernise his kingdom in a headlong way without regard either to the susceptibilities of his subjects or the dislocation caused by his grandiose schemes. The Germans were more willing and able than the British— or the Russians—to supply him with aircraft, railway material and other symbols of modernity which he demanded.

At the outbreak of war, therefore, the Foreign Office was concerned both with Russian and with German influence in Iran. After the defeat of France, the Germans increased their hold on the country. Iranian opinion generally was much impressed with the scale of the German victories, and thus inclined even more to regard Germany as the potential deliverer of Iran from Russian and British domination. In the spring and early summer of 1941 the German successes in the Balkans gave increased scope for anti-British propaganda, but Iran was not within the sphere of active military operations either for Germany or for Great Britain, and—as the Shah well knew—there were no British forces available to compel Iran to put a curb on German activities; even if there had been troops to spare, a British move against Iran would at once have brought strong opposition from the U.S.S.R.

The German attack on Russia changed the situation. The Russians were now more interested than the British in getting the Germans out of Iran. The German 'fifth column' which had previously menaced Iraq might threaten the Caucasian oilfields, and might damage the new railway from Teheran to the Persian Gulf. This railway was one of the shortest and safest routes by which British and American supplies could reach the U.S.S.R. On December 31, 1940,
(a) the Foreign Office had instructed Sir Reader Bullard, British Minister at Teheran, to speak strongly to the Iranian Government about the number of Germans—some 2,000—in the country. Six
(b) months later—after the opening of the German attack on Russia—the Soviet Government made similar representations. Sir R. Bullard supported their demands; so did Mr. Eden in conversation with the Iranian Minister in London. On July 8, at his first meeting with
(c) Sir S. Cripps, Stalin approved of a joint Anglo-Russian *démarche* at Teheran; two days later M. Maisky raised the matter at the Foreign Office. M. Maisky thought that, if the Shah argued that the services of the Germans were indispensable, we should threaten Iran with economic sanctions. Sir S. Cripps went further, and suggested Anglo-Russian military demonstrations on the northern frontier of Iran.

Mr. Eden, on the advice of Sir R. Bullard, thought it better first
(d) to try the effect of diplomatic action, and to ask for the removal of Germans known to be engaged in political activities. The Soviet Government agreed to this plan. Sir R. Bullard, therefore, told the Iranian Foreign Minister on July 19 that, while we wanted to maintain the independence of Iran, we could continue to do so only if the Iranian Government took precautions to preserve their own freedom from foreign control. To this end we asked for the expulsion

---

(a) E44/44/65; E3801/3551/65. (b) E3801/3551/65. (c) E3691, 3801/3551/65; E3707, 3844/3444/34. (d) E3780, 3844/3444/34; E4071/42/34.

of certain specified Germans. Sir R. Bullard hinted that if these Germans were not turned out, we might withhold goods and services which we would otherwise supply. The Soviet Ambassador made a similar request on the same day.

The Iranian Government agreed that a reduction in the number (a) of Germans in the country was desirable, and said that they were keeping a watch on them. They could not, however, expel a large number at once without acting contrary to their neutrality and bringing themselves into conflict with Germany. Early in August Sir R. Bullard reported that the German Minister had threatened to break off diplomatic relations if the Germans were expelled. In fact, only a few had left the country by mid-August.

Before this date the Foreign Office and the Chiefs of Staff came to the view that economic sanctions without a threat of force would be (b) useless, and indeed harmful to ourselves, since the Iranians would reply by cutting off our oil supplies. On the other hand they would be unable to resist a demand backed by the threat of a Russian invasion from the north and a British invasion from the south. The Soviet Government agreed on July 28 to a joint move of this kind if (c) our demands were refused.

M. Maisky now suggested for the first time that the demands should include the right of passage for Russian troops and war material across the trans-Iranian railway. Mr. Eden pointed out that this demand could hardly be reconciled with the argument that Iran was acting in an unneutral way by allowing so many Germans to remain in the country.[1] M. Maisky said that we could quote as a precedent the transit facilities given by Sweden to Germany, but the War Cabinet felt that at first at all events our demands (d) should be limited to the expulsion of the Germans. The whole question of Russian pressure on Iran raised serious difficulties with Turkey and an Anglo-Russian request for passage might well be followed by a demand from Germany for similar rights in Turkey. In any case we did not want to let the Russians into northern Iran.

The anxiety of the Turks was quieted to some extent by the joint Anglo-Russian declaration[2] that neither Great Britain nor the U.S.S.R. had designs on Iranian independence, but there was no way of getting the Shah and his Ministers to accept the Allied demands except by force. The British and Soviet Ministers made a (e)

---

[1] In view of the doubts in London at this time about the duration of Russian resistance, the development of the supply route through Iran (which would have taken a good many months) did not seem immediately practical, especially when we were finding it difficult to supply our own forces in the Middle East. There was a change of view on the question of the supply route before the end of August.

[2] See above, p. 21.

(a) E4135, 4428, 4244/42/44.   (b) E4141/3444/34; E4179/1682/34; E4295/933/34. (c) E4306/933/34.   (d) WM(41)75, E4277/933/34.   (e) E4597, 4720/1682/34; E6301/3326/34.

B*

new approach to the Iranian Government on August 16. They asked 'in the most formal and emphatic manner' for the expulsion of the Germans, with certain minor exceptions. They did not mention the question of transport facilities or make an open threat of forcible action if the demands were refused. They also repeated that neither Great Britain nor the U.S.S.R. had designs against the neutrality, independence or territorial integrity of Iran.

(a)   The Iranian Government replied on August 21 that the Germans were being closely watched and their numbers reduced, but that the question of their expulsion was solely an Iranian concern, and that they (the Iranian Government) could not put into effect against the nationals of one State measures incompatible with the neutrality of Iran.

The British and Soviet Governments thought this reply unsatisfactory. Sir R. Bullard indeed considered that the Iranians—probably at German prompting—were merely trying to gain time. Hence on August 25—without further warning—British and Soviet forces crossed respectively the southern and northern frontiers of Iran, and

(b)   and on the same day the Ministers of the two Powers presented notes in Teheran to the effect that the Iranian Government appeared to attach more importance to keeping the Germans in the country than to meeting the wishes of the Allies. The Allies therefore had to take military measures, but these measures were designed solely against the Axis Powers and not against the Iranian people or the integrity of their country.

(c)   The Iranian resistance collapsed within three days, and on August 29 the British and Soviet Governments agreed upon terms to be presented to the Shah. They required (i) the withdrawal of Iranian forces from the areas under British and Russian occupation, i.e. south-west of a line from Khanikin through Kermanshah to Bandar Dilam on the Persian Gulf—including the oilfields area—and north of a line running from the Turco-Iraqi frontier to the southern shore of the Caspian Sea, and eastwards as far as the port and railway terminus of Bandar Shah (but excluding the Meshed area); (ii) the expulsion of all Germans except the Legation staff; (iii) an undertaking on the part of the Iranian Government to facilitate the transit across their territory of supplies and war material. In return for the fulfilment of these demands, the Allied Governments would continue to pay oil royalties, and to meet the economic needs of Iran. They would also halt the advance of the troops, and withdraw them as soon as the military situation allowed them to do so.

(d)   The Shah and his Government accepted these terms on September 2,

---

(a) E4927/1682/34; E6301/3326/34.   (b) E4812, 5004, 5005, 6301/3326/34.   (c) E5114/3326/34; E5060, 5162, 5201, 5204, 5320, 6301/3326/34.   (d) See also E6135/103/34 of 1945.

but delayed over carrying them out. The Allies then decided to advance on Teheran. They entered the suburbs of the city on September 17, and secured the abdication of the Shah. The Allied forces were withdrawn on October 17 to the agreed lines after the Germans had been rounded up (a few—including the leading German agent—managed to escape). Negotiations for an Anglo-Russo-Iranian treaty were begun, and, after delays caused mainly by Iranian obstructiveness, the treaty was accepted by the Majlis on on January 26, 1942, and ratified three days later.[1]

---

[1] See below, pp. 56–7.

CHAPTER XX

Russian demands for a second front: the Moscow Conference: correspondence between Mr. Churchill and Stalin: proposal for a visit by Mr. Eden to Moscow: British declaration of war on Finland, Hungary and Roumania.

(i)

Russian demands for the establishment of a second front or for the transfer of 25–30 British divisions to the eastern front, September, 1941.

WHILE the Germans were winning great, though indecisive, victories, and advancing on the whole length of the front, the relations between the Russians and their western Allies would in any case have been difficult. The Russians knew little about shipping problems, and the extent to which British resources were strained to the limit; they exaggerated the possibilities of large-scale help and consequently attributed the lack of such help to deliberate selfishness and ill-will rather than to the physical necessities of the situation. The difficulties of liaison were greater owing to this intense suspicion on the Russian side. The Russian authorities refused to treat the British representatives with confidence or even to supply them with the information required for the provision of assistance. Sir S. Cripps reported on September 15, that is to say, two months after the conclusion of the Anglo-Russian agreement, that it was 'impossible to have any contacts with any Russians and thus to obtain any reliable information as to what is going on in the country. The most that one can get is an occasional piece of gossip through the Russian chauffeurs or *dvorniks*, or possibly through foreign journalists.'

The service Missions were not better treated. General Mason-Macfarlane complained again and again of the lack of proper liaison.
(a) Sir S. Cripps wrote that even when the Mission had important information to communicate, there would be delays, amounting to forty-eight hours, in arranging a meeting. The contacts on air matters were not on an operational basis, but only with the Director of the

---

(a) N4070/3014/38.

Research Institute. The British Government had sent an air raid precautions mission to Moscow; the Russians took no notice of it for eleven days. They gave no explanation of such delays, and, although from time to time there was an improvement, matters soon fell back again into an unsatisfactory state. The Foreign Office inclined to think that Sir S. Cripps and General Mason-Macfarlane made too much of the lack of co-operation. Mr. Eden noted on one of their complaints: 'I am doubtful if we ought to make too much fuss. We are not giving all that amount of help.'

Complaint was indeed useless, and led only to counter-remonstrances on the Russian side. On September 19 Sir S. Cripps gave Stalin a memorandum on the treatment of the Military Mission. He (a) mentioned the delays in arranging meetings, the inability of the most senior Russian staff officers to decide even the smallest questions without reference to higher authority, the failure to provide information of practical value, and the lack of reciprocity with regard to the exchange of operation details and technical military secrets. Sir S. Cripps realised the preoccupation of the Russian staff with the conduct of the war, but even so the failures of liaison were so serious that he could account for them only as the result of unwillingness on the part of individual officers or as the consequence of a definite political directive from the Soviet Government. Stalin replied that the Soviet Government wanted full co-operation. He said that the Staff in Moscow were greatly overworked, and that Russian lack of method was a contributory cause of the trouble. He then complained that 'not all of the members of the British Military Mission conducted themselves as they should'. As an example he mentioned reports that one member—subsequently the charge was made against three members—had spoken 'in an anti-Soviet sense'. These officers cleared (b) themselves completely of the charge made against them; in Sir S. Cripps's view, the difficulties lay with M. Molotov, who was Stalin's (c) main channel of information, and remained anti-British.

There would probably have been less friction if the Russians had not become increasingly disquieted about the extent of British assistance. It is difficult not to avoid the conclusion that they were afraid that the British would do just what the Russians themselves had done before they were attacked, i.e. sit back and allow someone else to bear the brunt of resisting the Germans. In any case the Russians could hardly have failed to raise their demands for help as their position became more serious. The Prime Minister and Mr. Roosevelt at their meeting in mid-August sent a joint message to Stalin promising the maximum help in supplies and suggesting a conference in Moscow to discuss the best apportionment of 'our joint

---

(a) N5458/78/38. (b) N5679, 6901/78/38. (c) N5542/78/38.

resources'.[1] The message referred to the need of a long-term policy, since the war already extended to many fronts, and other fronts might yet be developed. Stalin was assured that, pending the decisions of the conference, American and British material would continue to be sent to him as rapidly as possible. From the Russian point of view this proposal for a conference was concerned with a distant future. The signature of the Atlantic Charter was of no direct and immediate military value, and indeed even caused some suspicion.[2] On August 26 M. Maisky spoke in lukewarm terms about

(a) the Charter, and complained that the Soviet Government had not been consulted about it. He also said that the Soviet Government were dissatisfied at our failure to give any important measure of help. If we could not open a second front in France or the Low Countries, we might at least supply more armaments, and, in particular, more aircraft.

(b) Mr. Churchill sent another message to Stalin after his return to London. He undertook to provide 200 more Hurricanes in addition to the aircraft already promised.[3] He spoke of the improved position in Iran and the possibility of developing the railway from the Persian Gulf to the Caspian. Stalin replied in a message of thanks on

(c) September 4, and also pointed out the extreme gravity of the Russian military situation. He said that the aircraft would not arrive in time to effect a real change owing to the immense length of front, and, above all, owing to the deterioration in the position in the Ukraine and before Leningrad.

The Germans now realised they could move all their forces to the east, and that, since there would be no second front in the west, they could deal with their enemies singly. Stalin considered that there was 'only one means of egress' from the existing situation, the establishment of a second front somewhere in the Balkans or France capable of drawing away 30–40 divisions from the eastern front, and the provision of a monthly minimum of aid to Russia amounting to 400 aircraft and 500 tanks.[4] Without these measures the U.S.S.R. would 'either suffer defeat or be weakened to such an extent that it would lose for a long period any capacity to render active assistance to its Allies by its actual operations'.

(d) M. Maisky enlarged on the danger when he gave Stalin's message

---

[1] Mr. Hopkins, whom President Roosevelt had sent to Moscow at the end of July to get the facts (which the British Military Mission had been unable to discover) about the Russian situation, had suggested to Stalin 'unofficially' that a conference of representatives of the three Governments should be held. Stalin had accepted the suggestion.
[2] See below, Chapter XXV, part (2).
[3] In addition two squadrons (with 40 aircraft) were already on their way to Murmansk. Thus the total sent from Great Britain would be 440 aeroplanes.
[4] Stalin also asked for 30,000 tons of aluminium by October.

(a) N4840/78/38. (b) N4880/3084/38. (c) N5105/78/38. (d) N5096/78/38.

to Mr. Churchill on September 4. Mr. Churchill agreed that Russia was bearing the brunt of the German attack. This situation, however, had not come about through lack of effort on our part. We had studied the possibility of invading France or Norway, but did not think it practicable with the limited forces at our disposal. Mr. Churchill described the German defences and the lessons we had learned from operations undertaken without sustained air support. If we could have relieved the pressure on the Russian front, we should have been willing to face great risks and losses, but it would be foolish to delude ourselves that we could bring any relief. Action in the Balkans would be equally impracticable. In the spring we had taken seven weeks to land two divisions and an armoured brigade although we had no opposition at the ports. Mr. Churchill said that he realised the gravity of Stalin's message. He would examine the situation again, but we had already done so often with the sole desire to help Russia.

> 'As regards winning the war . . . we should continue to fight in this island and wherever we could until victory was won. Great Britain and the United States would do all they could to help in the way of supplies and we were considering ways of increasing the capacity of the Trans-Persian railway to guarantee a warm-water channel for the passage of American supplies to Russia. Meanwhile there seemed no alternative but for Russia to hold on through the winter; we could do nothing to affect events in Russia during the next two months.'

Sir S. Cripps had been given a copy of Stalin's message. He telegraphed on September 4 that in his view Stalin's statement was (a) not exaggerated, and that it showed the result of our inability to create a diversion. Unless now at the last moment we could make 'a superhuman effort', we should 'lose the whole value of any Russian front, at any rate for a long time, and possibly for good'.

We had unfortunately considered the Russian war as no direct responsibility of ours, but merely as a war we wanted to help in any way we could without unduly endangering our own position. Sir S. Cripps thought it was now almost too late to keep an effective Russian front in being unless we were prepared to 'throw everything in'. During the last three weeks the task of sending supplies had become much greater and more difficult, yet, if we were to do anything effective, we must envisage large and immediate help. Otherwise it was doubtful whether it would be much use doing anything at all.

The Prime Minister answered this telegram on September 5. He (b) pointed out that Sir S. Cripps's sentence 'we had unfortunately considered the Russian war . . .' was unjust, and that Sir S. Cripps did

---

(a) N5105/78/38. (b) N5105/78/38.

not know the practical and technical facts. If we could make a diversion in France or the Low Countries which would bring back German troops from Russia, we should order it even at the heaviest cost. All our generals, however, thought that we should get only a bloody repulse or at most small lodgements which would have to be withdrawn after a few days. The French coast was fortified to the limit. The Germans had more divisions, with formidable air support, in the west than we had in Great Britain. We had not the shipping to transport a great army to the Continent unless the operation were spread over many months. A diversion of flotillas for a Continental landing would mean 'a paralysis of the support of the Middle East armies and the breakdown of the whole Atlantic traffic. It might mean the loss of the battle of the Atlantic, and the starvation and ruin of the British Isles. Nothing we could do or could have done would affect the struggle on the Eastern front.'

With regard to the Balkans, even with the shipping then available in the Mediterranean, the placing of two divisions and an armoured brigade in Greece had taken seven weeks, and after we were driven out, the whole of the mainland and many of the island airfields had been occupied by Germans and Italians and were outside the range of our fighter protection.

The Prime Minister continued:

'I wonder that the losses sustained by our shipping and the fleet in the evacuations of Greece and Crete have been forgotten. The conditions are far more adverse now than then, and our naval strength is reduced. When you speak of a "superhuman effort", you mean, I presume, an effort rising superior to space, time and geography. Unfortunately those attributes are denied us.

The situation in the West would be entirely different if the French front were in being, for then I have no doubt the invasion of Russia would have been impossible because of the enormous counter-attacks that could be immediately launched. No one wants to re-criminate, but it is not our fault that Hitler was enabled to destroy Poland before turning his forces against France or to destroy France before turning them against Russia.

The 440 fighter aircraft which we have taken from our seriously diminished reserves are no doubt petty compared to the losses sustained by the Russian Air Force. They constitute, however, a painful and dangerous sacrifice on our part. The attacks by the Royal Air Force both by day and night are maintained with our utmost strength, and the even character of the fighting above the French coast shows the high degree of air power still possessed by the Germans in the West.

Nothing we could do or could have done can affect the terrible battle proceeding on the Russian front. Arrangements can still be made to provide for the campaign of 1942. The route established through Persia will be opened to the full, and whatever can be found and shipped from British resources and from American resources which would otherwise have come to Britain will be sent as fast as possible. I am pressing President Roosevelt to send Mr. Harriman here at the earliest moment in order that the Russians may know what aid to expect in 1942 to compensate for the losses sustained by their munitions industry and make their plans accordingly. Meanwhile I am replying to Stalin's telegram today and this telegram is solely for your own guidance.

I sympathise keenly with your feelings as you watch the agony of Russia at close quarters, but neither sympathy nor emotion will overcome the kind of facts we have to face.'

Mr. Churchill's reply on the night of September 5–6 to Stalin (a) repeated the facts which he had explained to M. Maisky and Sir S. Cripps. Mr. Churchill began by a plain statement: 'Although we should shrink from no exertion, there is in fact no possibility of any British action in the West, except air action, which would draw the German forces from the East before the winter sets in. . . . There is no chance whatever of a second front being formed in the Balkans without the help of Turkey. . . . Action, however well-meant, leading only to costly fiascos would be of no help to anyone but Hitler.' Mr. Churchill went on to discuss supplies and gave a promise that the Russians would receive from British production one half of the monthly total of aircraft and tanks for which Stalin had asked.[1] He hoped that the United States would be able to supply the other half. Mr. Churchill also sent to Mr. Roosevelt a copy of Stalin's message and of his reply. He told Mr. Roosevelt that we could not exclude from M. Maisky's statements the possibility that the Russians might be thinking of a separate peace.

Sir S. Cripps saw Stalin on September 7. He found him 'very (b) depressed and tired', with 'some return of the old attitude of suspicion and distrust'. Sir S. Cripps asked whether the Russians could hold out until the spring if they had the supplies foreshadowed in the Prime Minister's reply. Stalin answered that it was 'difficult to say'; He could not foresee what the Germans would do, since they had no need to take a western front into consideration. In any case the U.S.S.R. would not make a separate peace. He explained that if the Russians lost the Donetz basin with its coal and metallurgical works, and Moscow and Leningrad, they would be deprived of two-thirds

---

[1] Stalin had used the word 'sale' with regard to the additional 200 fighter aeroplanes which Mr. Churchill had promised to send. Mr. Churchill referred to this word in his message. He said that 'we had not viewed the matter in such terms and have never thought of payment. Any assistance we can give you had better be put upon the same basis of comradeship as the American Lend-Lease Bill, of which no formal account is kept in money.'

(a) N5105/78/38. (b) N5113/78/38.

of their war industries. They would then be compelled to withdraw from active fighting, and to dig in and wait on a defensive front, perhaps beyond the Volga.

(a) A week later M. Maisky received Stalin's answer to the Prime Minister. The answer was in the following terms:

> 'In my last message I stated the viewpoint of the Soviet Government that the establishment of a second front was the most fundamental remedy for the improvement of the situation with regard to our common cause. In reply to your message, in which you stress once more the impossibility of a second front at the present moment, I can only reiterate that the absence of a second front simply favours the designs of our common enemy.
>
> I have no doubt that the British Government desires to see the Soviet Union victorious and is looking for ways and means to attain this end. If, as they think, the establishment of a second front in the West is at present impossible, perhaps another method could be found to render the Soviet Union active military help.
>
> It seems to me that Great Britain could without any risk land in Archangel 25–30 divisions or transport them across Iran to the southern regions of the U.S.S.R. In this way there could be established military co-operation between Soviet and British troops in the territory of the U.S.S.R. A similar situation existed during the last war in France. The arrangement just mentioned would constitute a great help. It would be a serious blow against the Hitler aggression.
>
> I thank you very much for your promise to render us assistance by the monthly deliveries of aluminium, tanks and aircraft.
>
> I can only welcome the intention of the British Government to render this assistance in aluminium, tanks and aircraft not on the usual commercial basis but on the basis of comradeship and collaboration. I hope the British Government will have ample opportunity of being convinced that the Soviet Government understands how to appreciate the help received from its Ally . . .'

(b) In the afternoon of September 16 M. Maisky came to see Mr. Eden in order to emphasise the importance of Stalin's message. He said that the Soviet Government understood that a second front in the west might not be possible, but they hoped that we might move part of our Middle East forces into Russia and also send troops (e.g. Canadians who were used to a similar climate) to Archangel. M. Maisky asked in particular for something more than a token force of one or two divisions for south Russia.

(c) Mr. Churchill replied on September 18. He mentioned the forthcoming conference in Moscow for the study of supplies to Russia and the preliminary work which was being done in London with the

---

(a) N5421/78/38. (b) N5397/78/38. (c) N5421/78/38.

American mission under Mr. Harriman.[1] He said that all possible spheres of military co-operation had been examined, but we had neither the men nor the ships available for an expedition in the north, and in the south we needed the co-operation of Turkey.

M. Maisky thought that Mr. Churchill's reply would have a 'disheartening effect' because he rejected the possibility of assistance in south Russia. M. Maisky asked whether he could say that Mr. Churchill was examining the plan. Mr. Churchill explained once again that the situation was governed by shipping. We could study any plan, but we ought not to encourage the delusion that we could send large armies to fight in Russia.

(ii)

The Moscow Conference, September 28–October 4, 1941.

When Mr. Churchill and Mr. Roosevelt had proposed a conference in Moscow to discuss the delivery of supplies to Russia, they had (a) not intended that the meeting should be held before the latter part of September, since they thought it impossible before that date to know where the Russian front would be stabilised, or even whether it would be east or west of Moscow. In view of the gravity of the situation on the Russian front[2] the Foreign Office thought it desirable to try to hold the conference sooner. Mr. Eden had raised the question with the Prime Minister on August 22 and the War (b) Cabinet had discussed it on August 25 and the following days, i.e. before the series of telegrams from Stalin. Mr. Eden suggested September 15 as the date, although it was uncertain whether the American representatives would be available so soon. The War Cabinet agreed that Mr. Eden should explain to Mr. Winant that the Russians were pressing for the date to be fixed. It appeared at this time that the Americans would not be ready before October 15. Mr. Churchill thought this date too late and suggested September (c) 30. The War Cabinet finally authorised Mr. Eden to tell Sir S. Cripps that the decision depended on the United States.

On September 1 the Prime Minister proposed to the War Cabinet (d) that Lord Beaverbrook, Minister of Supply, should represent the British Government at the conference, and that an announcement to

---

[1] I have not dealt with these discussions. See J. M. A. Gwyer, *Grand Strategy*, III, Pt. I (H.M.S.O., 1964), 146–55.
[2] A telegram of August 19 from the Military Mission described this situation in serious terms.

(a) N4781/3084/38. (b) WM(41)86. (c) WM(41)87; N4920/3084/38. (d) WM(41)88; N5057/3084/38.

this effect should be made in the near future. We should also say that our delegation was ready to go to Moscow as soon as the United States delegation had arrived in Great Britain.

(a)   On September 7 Stalin asked Sir S. Cripps about the meeting of the conference. Sir S. Cripps enquired whether Stalin thought the conference would be of value even though the Prime Minister was unable to fulfil the Russian request for a second front. Stalin said that the usefulness of the conference would depend on the attitude of the British and (more particularly) the United States Government. Sir S. Cripps thought that Stalin was 'distrustful and suspicious' about the plan.

(b)   Mr. Eden also talked over the question with M. Maisky on September 8. M. Maisky was most anxious for an announcement of the date of the meeting. He mentioned the discussion of wider strategic plans and said that, in his reply to Stalin's message of September 4, the Prime Minister had agreed to such discussion. M. Maisky had also understood from Lord Beaverbrook that General Ismay would go with the British representatives. Did we intend General Ismay to discuss strategic plans with the Soviet Government? Mr. Eden said that he would refer these questions to the Defence Committee, but that, if General Ismay were going to the Conference, it would no doubt be possible to open up strategic matters with him. Methods of continuing the discussion, if necessary, could then be considered.

The conference was in fact held at the end of September. The British and American representatives arrived in Moscow on September 28 and left on October 4. The directive given to the British representatives dealt in the first place with the question of supplies,
(c)   and then considered the general strategic situation in the following terms:

> 'The Conference must proceed upon the basis that the United States is not a belligerent. The burden upon British manpower is already heavy and the strain will be intense during 1942 and onwards. Apart from the help we get from Dominions, India and the Colonies, our manpower is fully engaged. We have to feed ourselves and keep alive by maintaining vast merchant fleets in constant movement. We have to defend the British Isles from invasion, for which the Germans can at any time gather a superior army, and also from the most danger-ous forms of air attack by the main strength of the enemy Air Force, which can rapidly be transferred from East to West at the enemy's convenience. We have to maintain our armies in the Middle East and hold a line from the Caspian to the Western Desert. We hope to develop on this front during 1942 approximately 25 divisions, British, Indian, and Dominion, comprising, with all the exceptional rearward

---

(a) N5114/3084/38. (b) N5156/3084/38. (c) N5540/3084/38; DO(41)12; DO(41) 62nd Mtg.

services needed in these undeveloped regions and strong proportionable Air Force, about a million men. The strain on shipping of supplying these forces largely round the Cape, and the time taken in the turn-round of available ships, should be explained, if necessary, in detail.

For the defence of the British Isles we have an army of slightly over two million men, backed by about one-and-a-half million armed Home Guard. We possess only about three-and-a-half million rifles and can only get 100,000 or so in the next year. Of this army of two million men, 900,000 constitute the Field Force, comprising 20 mobile infantry divisions, 9 less mobile county or beach divisions, and 6 armoured divisions, 3 of which are only partly formed, together with 5 Army tank brigades, of which only one is as yet complete. Nearly a million men will be required for the enormous Air Force we are creating; 750,000 are already enrolled. The Navy already absorbs half a million sailors and marines. When to this is added the shipbuilding, aircraft production and munitions industries, and the need of food production at home and other domestic civilian industries all cut to a minimum, it will be seen that the manpower and available women-power of a population of 44,000,000 is, or will soon be, engaged to the limit.

Out of the eleven hundred thousand men behind the Field Army at home, the Air Defence of Great Britain, the Coastal Defence, the garrison of Northern Ireland, the draft-producing units and training schools, the defence of aerodromes and vulnerable points, leave only a small margin.

It will not be possible to increase the Field Army at home beyond the number of divisions—less than forty—already mentioned, and great efforts will be needed to maintain the existing strength at home while supplying the drafts for the Middle East, India, and other garrisons abroad, e.g. Iceland, Gibraltar, Malta, Aden, Singapore, Hong Kong.

We could not allow the force needed in Great Britain to repel invasion to fall below 25 infantry and 4 or 5 armoured divisions. It must be noted that troops can be transferred by the enemy across the main lateral railways of Europe incomparably quicker than any of our divisions could be recalled from abroad. The number of divisions available for offensive oversea action is therefore small.

Apart from the 25 British and Imperial divisions proposed to be built up in the Middle East during 1942, an Expeditionary Force of 6 or 7 divisions, including 2 armoured divisions, is the maximum that can be conceived. This is being prepared. Even if more were available, the shipping does not exist to carry larger forces and maintain them overseas. All ideas of 20 or 30 divisions being launched by Great Britain against the western shores of the continent or sent round by sea for service in Russia have no foundation of reality on which to rest. This should be made clear.

We have every intention of intervening on land next spring if it can be done. All the possibilities are being studied, including action on the northern and southern flanks of the Russian front. In the north an expedition into Norway would raise a serious revolt and might if it succeeded win the Swedish Government with its good army to our cause. This has been studied in detail. It is not, however, seen how the Russian forces could help, in fact their intervention would antagonise Sweden beyond all hope; the hostility of Finland is already declared.

At any moment we may be called upon to face the hostility of Spain and the penetration of the Germans into Morocco, Algeria and West Africa. Should the French resist in Africa, our available force might be sent to help them there. In both these cases the sea routes are short and not comparable with the vast distances round the Cape.

In the Middle East on the southern flank of Russia we shall deploy the strong forces mentioned above. Once the Western Desert and Cyrenaica have been cleared of the German and Italian armies now active there, our Middle Eastern forces would have a choice of action. If they increasingly give their right hand to the Russians, either in the Caucasus or east of the Caspian, it must be realised that their supply will choke the rail and road connection from the Persian Gulf. On the other hand Turkey, if she could be gained, is the great prize. Not only would the German road to Syria and Egypt be barred by powerful Turkish armies, but the Black Sea naval defence could be maintained with great advantages, thus helping the defence of the Caucasus. The action of Turkey one way or the other may be determined in the near future by the promises, should she become involved, of help in troops and modern equipment, including especially aeroplanes, tanks, anti-tank and anti-aircraft artillery, etc. It should be made clear to the Russians that much of this equipment and the greater part of the troops would, of course, be withdrawn from the contributions available for Russia which are all we can give. In order, however, to induce Turkey to come in on our side, especially in the near future, it would be well worth Great Britain and Russia revising their arrangements.

We are much interested in the development of the Polish and Czech armies in Russia, the latter being only small, and we should be glad to help in their equipment. It should be pointed out that the Poles and Czechs have influential communities in the United States. If a proportion of our equipment could be earmarked for the Poles and Czechs, it would have a good effect.

The Russians will no doubt ask how you propose to win the war, to which our answer should be: "By going on fighting till the Nazi system breaks up as the Kaiser's system broke up last time". For this purpose we shall fight the enemy wherever we can meet them on favourable terms. We shall undermine them by propaganda; depress them with the blockade; and, above all, bomb their homelands ceaselessly, ruthlessly, and with ever-increasing weight of bombs. We could not tell last time how and when we should win the war, but by not giving in and by not wearying we came through all right. We did not hesitate to face Germany and Italy alone all last year, and the determination of the British masses to destroy the Nazi power is inflexible. The phrases "Nazi tyranny" and "Prussian militarism" are used by us as targets rather than any implacable general condemnation of the German peoples. We agree with the Russian Government in hoping to split the Germans, and to isolate the criminal Nazi régime.

Of course, we cannot predict what action the United States will take. The measures already sanctioned by President Roosevelt and his Government may at any time in the near future involve the United States in full war, whether declared or undeclared. In that case we might look forward to a general offensive upon Germany in 1943. If German morale and unity were seriously weakened, and their hold upon the conquered European countries relaxed, it might be possible to land large numbers of armoured forces simultaneously on the shores of several of the conquered countries, and raise widespread revolts. Plans for this are now being studied by the British Staffs.'

The Moscow Conference was concerned primarily with questions (a) of supply; no official record was kept of informal conversations on other subjects.[1] Mr. Harriman, however, made some notes of these conversations, and gave a copy of his notes to Lord Beaverbrook. From the notes, which were shown to the War Cabinet, it appears that Lord Beaverbrook on September 28 told Stalin that General Ismay would be ready to hold 'strategic discussions'.[2] He also invited Stalin to send a mission to Great Britain 'to consider the British problem and advise on what might be done' and to explain what the Russians had learned in recent battles. Lord Beaverbrook said that the British were building up in Iran divisions which might join the Russians in the Caucasus. Stalin answered: 'There is no war in the Caucasus, but there is in the Ukraine'. Lord Beaverbrook said that 'this might be taken up too'. He asked whether Stalin thought that the British could invade France. Stalin said that he did not know enough about the situation but that he had confidence in Mr.

---

[1] A protocol of the Conference signed on October 1, 1940, listed the material which Great Britain and the United States would supply to Russia before June, 1942. This material would be 'made available at British and American centres of production'. The British representatives gave an undertaking that Great Britain would help in transporting it to Russia. In fact 90 per cent of the ships used to transport the material were British or American or under the control of these Powers. The British and, to a lesser extent, the United States navies, provided most of the naval escorts. In spite of appeals to them for more minesweeping, anti-submarine escorts, etc. the Soviet Government gave little assistance. For Stalin's complaint in July 1942, that in postponing the convoys for some months owing to very heavy losses (23 out of 34 ships in one convoy) the British Government was eluding a 'contractual obligation', see below, p. 264.

[2] See also below, p. 45, note 2. It is impossible, from the notes of these conversations, to say whether Lord Beaverbrook actually made clear to Stalin the reasons why 25–30 British divisions could not be sent to the Russian front. At all events Stalin did not take up the suggestion for a meeting with General Ismay to discuss the strategic situation. There is no evidence to show whether Lord Beaverbrook pressed for such a meeting.

(a) N6148/3084/38; N6267, 6312/3/38.

Churchill's judgment: on the other hand, why did we not send a force to Archangel or the Ukraine?

Stalin asked about our peace objectives. Lord Beaverbrook spoke about the 'Eight Points' of the Atlantic Charter and then talked of the importance of the United States and urged Stalin to use the American press for the purpose of building up a better understanding of Russia in the United States. Stalin asked whether the 'Eight Points' would satisfy us. Lord Beaverbrook gave a 'non-committal' answer. Stalin said: 'What about getting the Germans to pay for the damage?' Lord Beaverbrook evaded the question with 'We must win the war first'.

No political questions were discussed on September 29. On September 30 Lord Beaverbrook talked of help to Turkey and explained that some of the munitions which Stalin did not want might make the difference in Turkey's decision. Stalin agreed, but said that Turkey did not behave like an ally, and that we must be sure that our supplies to her would not be lost. Lord Beaverbrook thought that our assistance might re-establish the alliance. Stalin said that Turkey was afraid of Bulgaria on account of the Bulgarian alliance with Germany and the help which the Germans might provide.

Stalin asked Lord Beaverbrook whether the Anglo-Russian military alliance and agreement not to conclude a separate peace might be extended to a treaty covering not only the war but the post-war period. Lord Beaverbrook said that he was in favour of such an extension. Stalin added that all the officials of the Soviet Government wanted it.

(iii)

Further Russian demands for the despatch of 25–30 divisions to the eastern front: Stalin's message of November 11, 1941, to Mr. Churchill.

In spite of the Moscow Conference Anglo-Russian relations in October and early November became worse. At this time the situation of the Russian armies was extremely grave; an article in
(a) *Pravda* on October 9 admitted for the first time the danger to Moscow. In the south the German advance was not less serious. Sir
(b) S. Cripps telegraphed on October 15 that the Soviet Government and the diplomatic corps were leaving Moscow forthwith for Kuibyshev. A week later there was some improvement; M. Molotov

---

(a) N5895/78/38. (b) N6013/78/38.

said that the move for Kuibyshev had been decided on after a (a)
German break-through near Mozhaisk on October 14. The Germans
were now held and had advanced only a few kilometres at the
cost of great and continuing losses. On October 28 M. Vyshinsky told (b)
Sir S. Cripps that the position at Moscow was 'quite sound' and that
the Germans had been unable to advance beyond the positions held
on October 15. Winter came early both on the central front and in
the Crimea. The Germans were unable to take Sebastopol; they
made another attempt in the third week of November to capture
Moscow. They were too late; they came within thirty miles of the
city, but in the first week of December the Russians began to push
them back on a wide front. In spite of the huge Russian losses in men
and material, Hitler's attack had failed at all events of its chief
objective, the final defeat of Russia in 1941. The Germans had
occupied Russia's best agricultural land—in the Ukraine—and many
of her industrial centres, but Russian military and political resistance
was unbroken, and the Germans, who had themselves suffered
heavily, were committed to an immense military undertaking in
eastern Europe at the moment when they added the United States
of America to their enemies.

Early in October Mr. Churchill offered to take over the responsi- (c)
bility of maintaining the supply route through northern Iran if the
Russians wished to withdraw the five or six divisions stationed there.[1]
Mr. Churchill explained that British interests in Iran were limited
to the use of the country as a barrier to German penetration eastward, and as a route for supplies to the Caspian basin. He gave a
promise that we should not 'seek any advantages for ourselves at the
expense of any rightful Russian interest during the war or at the end'.

Sir S. Cripps was unable to see Stalin, but gave the Prime
Minister's message to M. Molotov. M. Molotov did not much like (d)
the suggestion about Iran; he thought that it would be better to
send British troops to fight the Germans in the Caucasus.[2] In reporting the conversation Sir S. Cripps gave his own view that the
despatch even of a small British force to the Caucasus would have a
great moral effect. On October 16 Mr. Eden repeated to M. Maisky (e
the proposal about Iran, and said that, if the Russians insisted, we
might be able to send a token force to the Caucasus. M. Maisky
suggested that we should send a larger force. Mr. Eden explained
the obvious difficulty of maintaining such a force, even if we could

---

[1] For the Anglo-Russian negotiations with Iran, see below, section (v) of this chapter.
[2] As Stalin had pointed out, there was no fighting in the Caucasus (although there was
at this time some fear on the British side that the Germans might get there). Sir O. Sargent
thought that the word 'Caucasus' in Sir S. Cripps's telegram should read 'Ukraine'. The
term 'Caucasus' was however used in these discussions with considerable vagueness.

(a) N6102/78/38. (b) N6235/78/38. (c) N6026/78/38. (d) N6132/78/38. (e) N6029/78/38.

(a) spare the men. M. Molotov continued to ask why we could not send an army to Russia. He complained on October 23 that neither he nor Stalin had been given an answer to their request of September 14 for the despatch of 25–30 divisions to the Russian front. Sir S. Cripps said that, although the documents were not available in Kuibyshev, he believed that we had replied that we could not send 25–30 divisions anywhere, but that we would keep the matter under constant review and send a smaller force if we were able to do so. He promised to enquire from London whether his answer was right.

The Prime Minister replied that the idea of sending so large a
(b) force was a 'physical absurdity'. We had taken eight months to build up ten divisions in France across the Channel when shipping was plentiful and U-boats were few. We had sent one division to the Middle East in the last few months with great difficulty and were sending another 'only by extraordinary measures'. All our shipping was fully engaged and could be diverted only at the expense of our maintenance convoys to the Middle East or the transport of supplies to Russia. Any troops sent to Murmansk at this time of year would only be frozen in darkness for the winter. We were willing to relieve the five Russian divisions in Iran. Surely it would be better for these divisions to defend their own country rather than for us to choke one of the two supply lines to Russia with the maintenance of a British force north of Iran. To put two fully armed British divisions into the Caucasus would take at least three months, and the two divisions would then 'only be a drop in the bucket'.

This message crossed a telegram of October 25 from Sir S. Cripps
(c) setting out his views at length. He reported that there was very strong feeling indeed in the Soviet Government about the lack of armed help from us. Informed soldiers shared this feeling and, in view of official publicity, the attitude of the population as a whole was similar. Hence relations between the two countries were getting worse. It was clear 'to us here' (i.e. Kuibyshev) that, if we could not relieve the pressure on the Russians by action elsewhere, the only way of improving matters would be to send troops to their country. Until something was done we should find increasing difficulties in the way of co-operation other than arranging for supplies which were accepted 'most ungraciously and without a word of thanks'.

The Russians were obsessed with the view that we were 'sitting back and watching them'. M. Molotov and others were emphasising this view for reasons of policy, but it was already widely held. If the sense of isolation continued, there might be a break in morale during the winter when conditions would inevitably be very bad throughout most of the country. Already, and after the harvests,

---

(a) N6135/78/38. (b) N6135/78/38. (c) N6169/78/38.

there were reports of a serious food shortage. We could not exclude the possibility that disappointment and disillusion might affect morale 'to such an extent as to count Russia out of the war'. The Soviet Government were determined to fight on, but might not be able to do so. Although Sir S. Cripps realised the military difficulties in sending a force, he thought that the promise of not less than an army corps, with Royal Air Force support, was probably our only hope to checking the dangerous deterioration not only in the Russian will to resist but also in our relations with the Soviet Government. He added that the Military Mission agreed with his view but considered that his suggestion would be only a temporary remedy because, whatever we sent, the Russians would press for more.

Sir S. Cripps sent another telegram on October 26 to the Prime Minister in reply to the latter's message of October 25. He con- (a) sidered that the Soviet Government had not yet been given a full explanation of our difficulties because no interview had been arranged between Stalin and General Ismay at the Moscow Confer- ence. The Russians were not familiar with the difficulties of fighting overseas and the matter could be explained to them adequately only by someone who had all the necessary information. Neither Sir S. Cripps nor anyone else could give the explanation without first returning to England.

Sir S. Cripps thought that the Russians, in view of their highly suspicious outlook, were likely to find confirmation of their own fears in the suggestion that we should send more troops to Iran. They would think that we wished to take advantage of their difficulties in order to gain control of the whole of Iran and that, if we could afford troops to replace the Soviet divisions in Iran, we could spare them to fight the Germans on one of the active fronts.

The Russians were obsessed with the idea that we were prepared, as German propaganda suggested, 'to fight to the last drop of Russian blood'. If we attacked in Libya, they would say that we were taking our chance of conquering Africa while they were holding the Germans for us. Finally, Sir S. Cripps suggested that a special representative should come to Moscow or that he or General Mason-Macfarlane should return to London.

The Prime Minister replied to Sir S. Cripps on October 28. Meanwhile on October 27 Sir S. Cripps was informed that M. (b) Maisky had spoken unfavourably to Mr. Eden about the proposal to offer a token force. M. Maisky suggested that we should put forward a plan to send 'X' troops at the end of the year, and more as they became available. We should not offer merely to send them to the Caucasus; otherwise we were likely to arouse the suspicions

---

(a) N6583/3/38. (b) N6230/78/38.

of the Soviet Government. There had been conflicts in the past in this area between British and Russian troops and the Soviet Government would not welcome a proposal limited to military co-operation in the Caucasus.

The Prime Minister thought it desirable to send a full reply to (a) Sir S. Cripps. The reply summed up the attitude of the British Government at this time to the Russian demands:

> 'I fully sympathise with you in your difficult position, and also with Russia in her agony. They certainly have no right to reproach us. They brought their own fate upon themselves when by their Pact with Ribbentrop they let Hitler loose on Poland and so started the war. They cut themselves off from an effective second front when they let the French Army be destroyed. If prior to June 22 they had consulted with us beforehand, many arrangements would have been made to bring the great help we are now sending them in munitions earlier. We did not however know till Hitler attacked them whether they would fight or what side they would be on. We were left alone for a whole year while every Communist in England, under orders from Moscow, did his best to hamper our war effort. If we had been invaded and destroyed in July or August 1940, or starved out this year in the Battle of the Atlantic, they would have remained utterly indifferent. If they had moved when the Balkans were attacked, much might have been done, but they left it all to Hitler to choose his moment and his foes. That a Government with this record should accuse us of trying to make conquests in Africa or gain advantages in Persia at their expense or being willing to "fight to the last Russian soldier", leaves me quite cool. If they harbour suspicions of us it is only because of the guilt and self-reproach in their own hearts.
>
> We have acted with absolute honesty. We have done our very best to help them at the cost of deranging all our plans for rearmament and exposing ourselves to heavy risks when the Spring invasion season comes. We will do anything more in our power that is sensible, but it would be silly to send two or three British or British-Indian divisions into the heart of Russia to be surrounded and cut to pieces as a symbolic sacrifice. Russia has never been short of manpower, and has now millions of trained soldiers for whom modern equipment is required. That modern equipment we are sending and shall send to the utmost limit of the ports and communications.
>
> Meanwhile we shall presently be fighting ourselves as the result of long-prepared plans, which it would be madness to upset. We have offered to relieve the five Russian divisions in Northern Persia, which can be done with Indian troops fitted to maintain internal order but not equipped to face Germans. I am very sorry that Molotov rejects the idea of our sending modest forces to the Caucasus. We are doing all we can to keep Turkey a friendly neutral and prevent her being tempted by German promises of territorial gain at Russia's expense.

(a) N6583/3/38.

Naturally we do not expect gratitude from men undergoing such frightful bludgeonings and fighting so bravely, but neither need we be disturbed by their reproaches. There is of course no need for you to rub all these salt truths into the Russian wounds, but I count upon you to do your utmost to convince Russians of the loyalty, integrity and courage of the British nation.

I do not think it would be any use for you and Macfarlane to fly home now. I could only repeat what I have said here, and I hope I shall never be called upon to argue the case in public.[1] I am sure your duty is to remain with these people in their ordeal, from which it is by no means certain that they will not emerge victorious. Any day now Hitler may call a halt in the East and turn his forces against us.'

On November 2 Sir S. Cripps was also sent Mr. Harriman's record (a) of Lord Beaverbrook's talks with Stalin during the Moscow Conference. Sir S. Cripps was greatly surprised that these conversations had (b) not been reported to him earlier and that little notice appeared to have been taken of them. He thought that Stalin's suggestion for an extension of the Anglo-Russian military alliance was of particular importance. He complained that he had been put in a false position because M. Molotov had been present at the discussions, but, at Lord Beaverbrook's request, and since the conversations were to deal only with supply, he (Sir S. Cripps) had not been present. This fact probably explained why, in answer to a statement from him that he was 'urging a certain course of action' on His Majesty's Government, M. Molotov had replied recently that he was afraid Sir S. Cripps 'had no power of persuading them'. M. Molotov had evidently taken the 'quite natural view' that Sir S. Cripps was now 'excluded by His Majesty's Government from political discussions about the U.S.S.R.'[2]

Sir S. Cripps added: 'in these circumstances I can see no use in my remaining here to act as an occasional postbox (for messages to Stalin about the formulation of which I am not consulted and which I am not instructed to discuss with him) unless I can do something to contribute to winning of (*sic*) the war or assisting in the post-war settlement'. Sir S. Cripps asked to be relieved of his post if he were not authorised at once to take up Stalin's proposals for the extension of the Anglo-Russian alliance. The basis of a new treaty should be

---

[1] Mr. Churchill at this time thought that Sir S. Cripps was considering an attack in Parliament on the policy of the British Government with regard to aid to Russia.

[2] Sir S. Cripps also thought that there must have been misunderstanding about the offer of strategic discussions made by Lord Beaverbrook to Stalin. He (Sir S. Cripps) had tried to persuade Lord Beaverbrook to let him arrange a meeting between General Ismay and Stalin. Neither he nor the head of the Military Mission knew of the offer made by Lord Beaverbrook, and he was sure that General Ismay was also unaware of it.

(a) N6312/3/38. (b) N6544/78/38.

that Great Britain, the United States and the U.S.S.R. would negotiate 'subsequently, and before the Peace Conference, an agreement covering the broad lines of a European settlement, and that we undertake to enter consultations with the Soviet Government in this matter at an early date'. The treaty should also include an undertaking of mutual assistance in post-war reconstruction and an agreement by the parties not to interfere in 'one another's internal affairs'. Sir S. Cripps asked for a decision as soon as possible since he could not 'remain long in the present unsatisfactory situation'.

In reply to this telegram Sir S. Cripps was told on the night of (a) November 10–11 that, according to Lord Beaverbrook, Stalin did not attach much importance to the 'diplomatic' discussions incidental to the main business of the Moscow Conference. Meanwhile we were dealing with those of the points raised by Sir S. Cripps which were open to immediate treatment, but at a time when the position at the end of the war could not be foreseen it was impracticable to formulate our peace objectives for discussion with our Allies more definitely than had been done in the Atlantic Charter. We should certainly be ready to continue collaboration with the Soviet Government after the war for the purpose of working out the terms of the new settlement of Europe. We did not know, however, what Stalin meant by his proposal for a post-war alliance. 'The important thing is surely that the Russians should know that we are prepared to carry forward our collaboration with them into the peace and beyond.' We had explained to M. Maisky our general attitude, and Sir S. Cripps was instructed to explain it to Stalin and Molotov. We could not commit ourselves now 'to an undertaking to enter into early consultations with a view to an agreement covering the broad lines of a European settlement. Nor have the Soviet Government asked for any such engagement.' Nevertheless, we hoped that, as the war situation improved, we should find more frequent opportunity of discussing future plans of Anglo-Russian collaboration. This 'gradual and tentative procedure' would be 'safer and more profitable' than any premature attempt to define our collaboration in treaty form. 'In a treaty we should both have to introduce so many provisos and conditions to safeguard our position in the unforeseeable future that the result might well be to arouse suspicions and misgivings on both sides which might injure rather than improve relations between our two countries.' Even if we did not embark on negotiations at once, Sir S. Cripps's services as Ambassador in Russia would be of the greatest value in preparing the ground. Mr. Eden added that, if an opportunity offered, he hoped to come to Russia 'at a not too distant date'.

(a) N6544/78/38.

The Russian demands became more insistent, and began to cover a wider field in the last critical weeks of the German thrust towards Moscow. On November 4 Mr. Churchill sent a message to Stalin that if he would like to see them, General Wavell and General Paget[1] (a) would go to Russia in order to explain the British position. Mr. Churchill referred to the tanks and aeroplanes which we were sending through Archangel at the risk of weakening our own resources. Finally he asked Stalin to consider whether it was good policy for the British Government to declare war on Finland, Roumania and Hungary. This last question had been under consideration for some time. The Soviet Government had asked for a British declaration of (b) war on Finland early in September. The Foreign Office, however, held that a declaration would be inexpedient. We should lose the use of twenty-eight Finnish ships and their crews, and might drive (c) the Finns completely to the German side. Hungary and Roumania were acting under German constraint; we could not declare war only on one of them, since we should be supporting one of two sets of conflicting territorial claims. The Prime Minister (as he told Stalin) thought we should take account of the large body of pro-Finnish opinion in the United States, and that, if occasion offered, Hungary and Roumania might well come back to our side. The War Cabinet decided to take no action against Hungary or Roumania, but to (d) warn the Finns that, if they continued to invade Russia, they would be at war with us.

The warning had no effect, and in the third week of October M. Maisky brought a message from M. Molotov asking that, as a (e) gesture of solidarity, we should declare war on the three countries. The War Cabinet still thought a declaration of war undesirable on (f) practical grounds, since it would fix the three countries on the German side and enable the Germans to use three more armies (g) against us. If, however, the Russians insisted, we should give way. The War Cabinet consulted the Dominions and the United States. The Dominions were divided in opinion, but were prepared to leave the decision to the United Kingdom. The United States Government (h) would not make a definite statement but seemed on balance to be (i) against a declaration of war.

Mr. Eden showed the Prime Minister's message of November 4 to M. Maisky. M. Maisky did not like it. He was disappointed at our

---

[1] General Wavell was now Commander-in-Chief in India, Iran and Iraq, and would have been concerned with a British force sent to the Caucasus. He also knew Russian. General Paget had been designated Commander-in-Chief, Far East, though this designation remained secret. He was previously Chief of Staff, Home Forces, and could explain the reasons why the opening of a second front or the despatch of a large force to the Russian front was militarily impracticable.

(a) N6585/3/38. (b) N5096/78/38. (c) N5347/185/56; WP(41)219. (d) WM(41)93; N5348/185/56. (e) N6161/185/56. (f) WM(41)104; WP(41)245; WM(41)150. (g) N6353/201/56; WM(41)108. (h) N6309/185/56. (i) N6373/78/38.

hesitation to declare war against Finland. He asked whether the two
generals could discuss future plans, and whether the discussions
might cover the despatch of British forces to the southern front in
Russia. He complained that we had not answered Stalin's request
that we should send an army to Russia.

Mr. Eden said that on the latter point there should be no misunderstanding. Stalin had spoken of 25–30 divisions, and Mr.
Churchill had explained how impossible it was to send them. We
had offered to relieve the Soviet forces in northern Iran and to send
a small force to the Caucasus; the Soviet Government had refused
our offer. We could discuss the despatch of a force, but the difficulty
was that troops could be sent only at the expense of the delivery of
material to Russia.

A week later M. Maisky brought Stalin's reply to the Prime
(a) Minister. The tone of the reply was less friendly than that of previous
messages. Stalin wrote:

'Your message received on November 7.
    1. I fully agree with you that clarity should be established in the
relations between the U.S.S.R. and Great Britain. Such a clarity does
not exist at present. The lack of clarity is the consequence of two
circumstances: (a) There is no definite understanding between our
two countries on war aims and on plans of the post-war organisation
of peace: (b) There is no agreement between the U.S.S.R. and Great
Britain on mutual military assistance against Hitler in Europe.

As long as there is no accord on both these questions there can be
no clarity in the Anglo-Soviet relations. More than that: to be quite
frank, as long as the present situation exists, it will be difficult to secure
mutual confidence. Of course, the agreement on military supplies to
the U.S.S.R. has a great positive value, but it does not settle neither
does it exhaust the whole problem of relations between our two
countries. If the General Wavell and the General Paget, whom you
mention in your message, will come to Moscow with a view to conclude
agreement on two fundamental questions referred to above I naturally
would be happy to meet them and to discuss with them these questions.
If however the mission of the Generals is confined to the questions of
information and to the consideration of secondary matters, it would
not be, I think, worth while to intrude upon the Generals. In such a
case it would be also very difficult for me to find the time for the
conversations.

It seems to me an intolerable situation has been created in the
question of the declaration of war by Great Britain to Finland,
Hungary and Roumania. The Soviet Government raised this question
with the British Government through the secret diplomatic channels.
Quite unexpectedly for the U.S.S.R. the whole problem—beginning
with the request of the Soviet Government to the British Government

---

(a) N6540/3/38.

and ending with the consideration of this question by the U.S.A. Government—received wide publicity. The whole problem is now being discussed at random in the press—friendly as well as enemy. And after all that the British Government informs us of its negative attitude to our proposal. Why is all this being done? To demonstrate the lack of unity between the U.S.S.R. and Great Britain?

You can rest assured that we are taking all the necessary measures for speedy transportation to the right place of all the arms coming from Great Britain to Archangel. The same will be done with regard to the route through Iran. In this connexion may I call your attention to the fact—although this is a minor matter—that tanks, planes, artillery are arriving inefficiently packed, that sometimes parts of the same vehicle are loaded in different ships, that planes because of the imperfect packing reach us broken.'

Stalin's dissatisfaction with the British attitude seemed also to be shown in a speech which he made on November 6 (the twenty-fourth anniversary of the establishment of the Red Army). In this speech he said that the absence of a second front eased the German position; (a) the appearance of this front, 'and such a front must[1] unquestionably appear in the near future', would make the Russian position easier.

On November 12 Mr. Eden gave M. Maisky an interim reply from the Prime Minister to Stalin's message as follows: 'M. Stalin's (b) message is being considered. I am not at present in a position to give Your Excellency any reply to it as it raises such very large issues. At the same time I cannot conceal from you that the Prime Minister and the Cabinet were surprised and pained at the tone and the contents of the message.'

Mr. Eden also told M. Maisky that Lord Beaverbrook regretted that the part of the message dealing with supplies had not been sent to him. Mr. Eden said that he had nothing to add to the interim message except that he also regretted the contrast in tone between Stalin's message and those which he had previously sent.

After a long pause M. Maisky asked whether Mr. Eden had anything to suggest. Mr. Eden said 'No'. M. Maisky then said that he would like to speak 'off the record'. He implied that the tone of Stalin's message was unhappy, although the proposals in the message were not unreasonable. Stalin was under great strain. He also took the view that the war would be over in 1942 and this view might account for his wish for early consultation about the post-war period. M. Maisky knew that we expected the war to last much longer.

---

[1] This word was used in the translation of the speech issued by the Tass Agency in London. In the translation telegraphed from the Embassy at Kuibyshev the word used was 'ought'.

(a) N6468, 6473/78/38. (b) N6586/3/38; Churchill Papers 395/17.

C

Mr. Eden—also speaking 'off the record'—said that at times we thought that the Soviet Government believed it possible to affect our decisions by means of their political influence in Great Britain. M. Maisky said that this was not the case. He referred to the statement in Stalin's speech that after the war there must be States with many different forms of government. Russia did not want to try to set up a Communist State in Great Britain. Stalin had not mentioned a second front until his latest speech, and M. Maisky himself had been careful not to say anything on the subject.

Mr. Eden said that the Cabinet did not like the linking of an acceptance of the visit of the generals with the condition that there should be a discussion of post-war policy. This latter question would obviously be outside the scope of the generals' instructions. M. Maisky said that the discussions 'need not be limited to generals', and might be held in London. Stalin might be unenthusiastic over the visit of the generals because we had not decided whether we would send troops to Russia. We had not answered Stalin's request for troops. M. Maisky thought that the Soviet Government would be content if we said that in principle we would agree to send troops and that the generals could go to discuss the matter. They could put forward the difficulties about the maintenance of the troops and the interference with the flow of supplies to Russia. The Soviet Government might then say that they would rather have the supplies than the troops, but until we had come to a decision on the principle military conversations could not have a decisive result.

Mr. Eden said that he had already suggested that the Soviet Government could raise the question of our troops going, for example, to Rostov. M. Maisky replied that this suggestion was not a decision to send troops to Russia. Earlier in the conversation M. Maisky had emphasised that before the war many people in Great Britain advocated a free hand for Germany in the East. The Russians knew this, and therefore when, possibly for good reasons, we did not form a second front, their suspicions were revived. Hence there were very important political reasons for sending troops to Russia, apart from their military value.

(iv)

Further exchanges of messages with Stalin: decision that Mr. Eden should visit Moscow for discussions with Stalin.

On November 18 a discussion was held in the Foreign Office on the main political question raised by Stalin, i.e. what progress could be made towards an Anglo-Russian understanding on war aims and post-war organisation. Meanwhile Sir S. Cripps had also written (a) criticising our policy in terms which the Prime Minister and the Foreign Office regarded as not wholly reasonable. Sir S. Cripps considered that we should agree to discuss with Stalin questions of post-war collaboration and planning, and that the longer we left Stalin in uncertainty about these matters the more readily would he believe (as M. Molotov believed) that we were 'not prepared to go in whole-heartedly with Russia on his terms,[1] but that our only object is to keep her fighting the Germans as long as we can'. Sir S. Cripps proposed that Mr. Eden and the Chiefs of Staff should come to Russia for discussions with Stalin or that he (Sir S. Cripps) should be given detailed instructions to deal with the matters. Otherwise he would have to resign his post as ambassador. A reply was sent to Sir S. Cripps on November 17 explaining that we had no (b) intention of excluding all discussions with the Soviet Government on peace objectives and post-war collaboration, but it was difficult in present circumstances to define at all precisely the lines of this collaboration. We could not go beyond the principles laid down in the Atlantic Charter without bringing the United States into the discussions, and the United States Government had asked us repeatedly not to undertake during the war commitments which would bind us at and after the peace negotiations.

Sir S. Cripps was also told that, if possible, Mr. Eden would come to Russia within the next few weeks. He replied on November 20 (c) that in these circumstances he would stay at his post. On the same day M. Maisky explained to Mr. Eden that Stalin, in his message to (d) Mr. Churchill, 'had only practical and businesslike questions in view'. He had not intended to cause offence. M. Maisky said that Stalin was very busy and had practically no chance to think of anything but affairs at the front.

The discussions in the Foreign Office may be summarised as (e) follows: Stalin's wish for an understanding on war aims and plans for the post-war organisation of peace probably came from the suspicion that we wanted to see the U.S.S.R. weakened at the end of the war and to make an Anglo-American peace from which the U.S.S.R. would be largely excluded. Stalin had doubtless hoped to see Great Britain and Germany fight each other to a standstill with the result that Russia would have played a predominant rôle at the

---

[1] The Foreign Office pointed out to Sir S. Cripps that we could not 'go in whole-heartedly' on Stalin's terms without even knowing what they were. Sir S. Cripps replied that his text had been wrongly received, and that he had said 'on equal terms'.

(a) N6605, 6574, 6575/3/38.   (b) N6575/3/38.   (c) N6750/3/38.   (d) N6704/3/38.
(e) N6839/3/38.

peace settlement. He therefore wished to carry further the agreement of July 12 and to commit us to co-operation after the war when Russia might be greatly weakened and Great Britain and the United States much stronger. Stalin might ask for a treaty or a bilateral declaration. The Russians were very reticent about their war aims and their ideas for a post-war settlement. They would probably want access to warm-water ports and the preservation of their interests in the Black Sea and the Baltic. Hence they would ask for access to the Persian Gulf, the revision of the Montreux Convention, and possibly the establishment of Russian bases in Norway, Finland and the Baltic States. Their chief aim would be the security of the U.S.S.R. These demands could therefore be revised more easily if an efficient scheme were produced for disarmament and an international police force.[1] We also had not made up our minds about 'war aims' and had promised the United States that during the war we would not undertake commitments binding us at the peace settlement and were thus at a disadvantage. The Russians might agree to a general resolution about post-war co-operation. If they asked for more, they would have to define their ideas to us and to the United States. We should make it clear to them that they were being treated on an equality and that the peace settlement would be dictated largely by the three Powers. We might find it desirable in our discussions with the United States to bring in Russia.

On November 21 Mr. Churchill sent another message to Stalin:

(a)　　　'Many thanks for your message just received. At the very beginning of the war I began a personal correspondence with President Roosevelt which led to a very solid understanding being established between us and has often helped in getting things done quickly. My only desire is to work on equal terms of comradeship and confidence with you.

2. About Finland, I was quite ready to advise the Cabinet to declare war upon Finland when I sent you my telegram of September 5. Later information has made me think that it will be more helpful to Russia and the common cause if the Finns can be got to stop fighting and stand still or go home, than if we put them in the dock with the guilty Axis Powers by a formal declaration of war and make them fight it out to the end. However if they do not stop in the next fortnight and you still wish us to declare war upon them we will certainly do so. I agree with you that it was very wrong that any publication should have been made. We certainly were not responsible.

---

[1] i.e. if Russian security were safeguarded in other ways the Soviet Government might find it unnecessary to go on with the policy which had led them to the partition of Poland, the absorption of the Baltic States and the establishment of bases in Finland.

(a) N6799/3/38.

3. Should our offensive in Libya result as we hope in the destruction of the German-Italian army there, it will be possible to take a broad survey of the war as a whole with more freedom than has hitherto been open to His Majesty's Government.

4. For this purpose we shall be willing in the near future to send the Foreign Secretary, Mr. Eden, whom you know, via the Mediterranean to meet you at Moscow or elsewhere. He would be accompanied by high military and other experts, and will be able to discuss every question relating to the war including the sending of troops not only into the Caucasus but into the fighting line of your Armies in the south. Neither our shipping nor the communications will allow large numbers to be employed, and even so you will have to choose between troops and supplies across Persia.

5. I notice that you wish also to discuss the post-war organisation of peace. Our intention is to fight the war in alliance with you and in constant consultation with you, to the utmost of our strength and however long it lasts, and when the war is won, as I am sure it will be, we expect that Soviet Russia, Great Britain and the United States will meet at the Council table of the victors as the three principal partners and agencies by which Nazism will have been destroyed. Naturally the first object will be to prevent Germany and particularly Prussia breaking out upon us a third time. The fact that Russia is a Communist State and Britain and the United States are not and do not intend to be, is not any obstacle to our making a good plan for our mutual safety and rightful interests. The Foreign Secretary will be able to discuss the whole of this field with you.

6. It may well be that your defence of Moscow and Leningrad, as well as the splendid resistance to the invader along the whole Russian front, will inflict mortal injuries upon the internal structure of the Nazi régime. But we must not count upon such good fortune, but simply keep on striking at them to the utmost with might and main.'

Stalin's reply was received four days later. The reply was in friendly terms:　　　　　　　　　　　　　　　　　　　　　　　(a)

'Many thanks for your message. I sincerely welcome your wish as expressed in your message to collaborate with me by way of personal correspondence based on friendship and confidence. I hope this will contribute much to the success of our common cause.

2. On the question of Finland the U.S.S.R. never proposed anything else—at least in the first instance—but the cessation of the military operations and the *de facto* exit of Finland from the war. If, however, Finland refuses to comply even with this in the course of the short period you indicated, then I believe the declaration of war by Great Britain would be reasonable and necessary. Otherwise an impression may be created that there is no unity between us on the question of war against Hitler and his most ardent accomplices and that the accomplices of Hitler's aggression can do their base work

(a) N6888/3/38.

with impunity. With regard to Hungary and Roumania we can perhaps wait a little while.

3. I support by all means your proposal of an early visit to the U.S.S.R. by the Foreign Secretary Mr. Eden. I believe our joint consideration and acceptance of an agreement[1] concerning the common military operations of the Soviet and British forces at our front as well as speedy realisation of such an agreement would have a great positive value. It is right that consideration and acceptance of a plan concerning the post-war organisation of peace should be founded upon the general idea to prevent Germany and in the first place Prussia once more to (*sic*) violate peace and once more to plunge peoples into terrible carnage.

4. I also fully agree with you that the difference of the State organisation between the U.S.S.R. on the one hand and Great Britain and the United States of America on the other hand should not and could not hinder us in achieving a successful solution of all the fundamental questions concerning our mutual security and our legitimate interests. If there are still some omissions and doubts on this score I hope they will be cleared away in the course of the negotiations with Mr. Eden.

5. I beg [you] to accept my congratulations on the successful beginning of the British offensive in Libya.

6. The struggle of the Soviet armies against Hitler's troops remains to be (*sic*) tense. In spite however of all the difficulties the resistance of our forces grows and will grow. Our will to victory over the enemy is unbending.'

In view of this message the War Cabinet decided to transmit to (a) the Finnish Government through the United States Government a warning that, unless the Finns ceased military operations against the U.S.S.R., we would have to declare war on them. The Finns continued to collaborate with the Germans in the attack on Russia, and His Majesty's Government declared war against them on December 5. They also declared war on Hungary and Roumania.

(v)

Negotiation of an Anglo-Russian treaty with Iran (September 1941–January 1942).

The surrender of the Shah and his Government at the beginning of September 1941, to the Anglo-Russian demands[1] was very far from (b) solving the problem of British policy towards Iran. The Chiefs of Staff wanted to go beyond the terms accepted by the Shah on

---

[1] See above, Chapter XIX, section (v).

(a) N6834/185/56. (b) E5183, 5395/3326/34.

September 2 and to ensure that we and the Russians had full control of Iranian communications and the right to take all the necessary measures to secure Iran against German attack. The Chiefs of Staff were considering the present emergency; the Foreign Office thought in terms of the ultimate effects of the proposed measures, and agreed with Sir R. Bullard that the Russians would be only too ready to (a) bring the whole of northern Iran, including Teheran, directly or indirectly under their rule. The Government of India also looked at (b) the matter from the point of view of immediate defence, and considered that the Foreign Office policy of respecting Iranian neutrality was impracticable; the Viceroy of India telegraphed to Mr. Amery (Secretary of State for India) on September 3 his surprise that the staff of the German Legation were to be allowed to remain in the country. The British press also argued for stronger measures against the Germans.

The Prime Minister was not afraid of Russian encroachments on Iran; he thought that the Russian interest would be to get supplies (c) through the Iranian route as quickly as possible, and that we ought to concentrate on developing this route. The Prime Minister suggested that Sir R. Bullard might use the 'leverage' of a possible Russian occupation of Teheran to obtain Iranian consent to our requirements.

On September 6 Sir R. Bullard and the Soviet Ambassador delivered notes asking for the removal of all the Legations at (d) Teheran under German control, and the internment of all Germans. The Iranian Government agreed to these demands, and thus made it more difficult for the British and Soviet Governments to justify their further military advances into the country. At this time, however, the British Government had come to the conclusion that they could not get a real change in Iranian policy without deposing the Shah, and that his removal would be welcomed by Iranian opinion.

The Shah, in fact, gave the Allies an opportunity to get rid of him. In spite of his promise to turn the Germans out of Iran within (e) forty-eight hours, he and his Government were either unwilling or unable to do so.[1] On September 17, therefore, British and Russian forces entered the outskirts of Teheran. The Shah now abdicated (f) in favour of his eldest son, Mohammed Reza Pahlavi.

The way thus seemed clear for a tripartite treaty of alliance between Iran, Great Britain and the U.S.S.R. The War Cabinet

---

[1] At the time of the Anglo-Russian move into Iran the Shah had appealed to President Roosevelt to intervene in order to 'put an end to the acts of aggression'.

(a) E5271/3326/34. (b) E5308/3326/34. (c) E5396/3326/34. (d) E5411, 5487, 5518, 5519, 5372, 6301/3326/34. (e) E5611/3326/34. (f) E5724/3326/34.

(a) agreed on September 22 to a draft for submission to the Soviet Government. The draft included an undertaking by the Allies to protect the independence and territorial integrity of Iran, in return for full Iranian co-operation and the unrestricted Allied use of communications in the country. The Iranian Government were also required to allow the presence of Allied forces in Iran subject to their withdrawal on the conclusion of peace with Germany, or within a year after the signature of an armistice,[1] and to maintain relations only with Powers in diplomatic relations with the Allies.

The treaty was not signed until the end of January 1942. The delay was due partly to the Russians, and partly to hesitation on the Iranian side as the German armies drew nearer to the Caucasus. The Russians took a long time to reply to the British proposals, or even to agree to joint administrative measures in order to avoid friction and confusion in Iran. They accepted, however, on October

(b) 8, a suggestion from Sir R. Bullard that the Iranians would find it easier to accept the treaty if the Allied troops withdrew from the neighbourhood of Teheran. This withdrawal took place on October 17. Even so the Iranian Government began to ask for more con-

(c) cessions. Sir R. Bullard thought that they were in fact justified in saying that public opinion in Iran would disapprove of the treaty, and particularly of an alliance with the U.S.S.R. The Iranian Government complained of the behaviour of the Russian forces of occupation. Although Sir R. Bullard thought that these complaints were exagger-

(d) ated, he also wrote that 'if the Russians have treated the Persians as Allies, the Persians have not noticed it'. One of the objections

(e) was to the clause allowing Allied troops to remain in the country for a year after the armistice unless a treaty of peace was signed earlier. Sir R. Bullard considered that 'the retention of the Russians in Persia for one day beyond the strict minimum should be avoided'.

The Iranian Government continued to be afraid of Russian encouragement of separatist movements in the north of the country; they wanted the period of occupation to be reduced to three months, but Sir R. Bullard was informed that we could not concede more than an alteration of the time-limit to read 'as soon as possible and in any case not later than a year'. We were also unwilling to agree

(f) that the treaty should be one of 'association' rather than of alliance. The Iranian Prime Minister explained that this change of words would help to allay the fear that Iran might be drawn into military operations and that it would also be welcomed by public opinion which disliked an 'alliance' with the U.S.S.R. The Foreign Office

---

[1] This period was reduced to six months in the final treaty (Cmd. 6335, Persia no. 1, 1942).

(a) WM(41)95. (b) E6283, 6450/3444/34. (c) E6880/3444/34. (d) E6960/3444/34. (e) E7303, 7390/3444/43. (f) E7265/3444/34.

replied that the treaty was on the lines of our treaties with Iraq and Egypt, and that in giving a promise of protection we were in fact assuming the responsibility of an ally.

The Iranian Government could not refuse to sign the treaty, or the Majlis to ratify it. The ratification took place on January 29, 1942. At this time the German attack on Moscow had been held; the United States had come into the war, and in spite of the Japanese successes in the Far East, the chances of a German victory were much less than they had appeared only two months earlier. The Iranian Government had asked that the United States should accede to the treaty; they were unable to obtain this protection for themselves, but on February 6 President Roosevelt telegraphed to the Shah that the United States had taken note of the assurances in the treaty with regard to Iranian independence and the ultimate withdrawal of British and Russian troops.

Note to Chapter XX. Anglo-Russian action in Afghanistan, September–October, 1941.

It was natural that the success of the Allies in securing the expulsion of the Axis colonies from Iran should suggest dealing with the Afghan Government after the same fashion. In Afghanistan also there was a German potential fifth column, although on a far smaller scale than in Iran—it was estimated that there were about 100 adult male Germans in the country. Neither the threat constituted by the German colony nor the need to secure Anglo-Soviet communications were nearly so pressing as in Iran, but in early September the Foreign Office and the (a) India Office thought it would be opportune, while the lesson of Iran was fresh, to bring pressure also to bear on the Afghan Government. The press too were drawing attention to the question.

The Government of India and Sir F. Wylie (the British Minister at Kabul), however, pointed out that there were important differences (b) between the cases of Afghanistan and of Iran. In Afghanistan we had no stakes such as oilfields, and no immediate strategic need to secure cover for our flank. In Iran the personal unpopularity of the Shah had helped to shield us from hostile reactions amongst the Shiah Muslims, but measures to coerce Afghanistan might have repercussions throughout the Sunni Moslem world, and might seriously impede India's war effort. To give up Axis nationals who might throw themselves upon the Government's protection would run counter to the Afghan code of hospitality. Finally, while in Iran we had been prepared to back up our demands by force, in Afghanistan it would be a grave mistake to become involved in armed conflict. The armed tribesmen, aided by difficult terrain, would be adversaries very different from the demoralised Iranian army. We could not afford to tie up India's forces on and beyond the North-West Frontier. Our policy now as always should be the maintenance of the

(a) E5454, 5607/144/97. (b) E5717, 5794/144/97.

C*

Afghan buffer, and it would be unwise to take action in concert with Russia which would lead even temporarily to the disruption of Afghanistan. The continued presence of the Germans would indeed be preferable to a Russian occupation.

(a) By September 24 it had been agreed that we could not go to the length of demanding the closing of the Axis Legations; our request for the expulsion of non-official Axis nationals should avoid specifying particular individuals, which would flout Afghan conventions of hospitality; all but the really dangerous of those expelled should be offered a safe-conduct home via India. We should assure the Afghans that we had no wish to open up an Anglo-Russian supply route via Afghanistan; and that, although the offer of a treaty of alliance similar to that under negotiation with Iran had some attractions, it would on balance be unwise to make the suggestion at this stage;[1] we should proceed in the first instance by persuasion, but should be prepared to threaten, and if need be to apply, economic sanctions to gain our end. Finally it was agreed that while we might hint to the Afghans of possible Russian pressure in case of refusal, we should not in this case act jointly with the Russians. We should explain to the Soviet Government why we thought unilateral action more advisable.

(b) Already it seemed to the Foreign Office that the psychological opportunity offered by the Iranian incident was passing. When Mr. Eden informed the Soviet Ambassador of our proposed action, and explained that in the first instance we thought it might be wiser for us to make the representations alone, M. Maisky replied that he must consult his Government. On September 29 he reported that the Soviet Government desired to be associated with us from the outset in representations to the Afghan Government. Sir F. Wylie's instructions were thereupon revised

(c) in this sense, since 'it would obviously be undesirable to oppose the clearly expressed wishes of the Soviet Government in this matter', and in view of the delay that had occurred a 'concerted Anglo-Soviet approach at the first stage might now perhaps be more effective'.

(d) It was not until October 11 that the Soviet Ambassador in Kabul received his instructions. Sir F. Wylie had decided that he could not wait any longer, and had seen the Afghan Prime Minister on October 10. The British representations were on the lines previously agreed: the Soviet note was more brusque in tone. It referred to several of the German agents by name and complained that they were engaged in subversive activities in direct contravention of the Soviet-Afghan treaty of 1931. It also required that the Afghan Government should guarantee adequate supervision of the German and Italian diplomatic missions.

(e) The Afghan Government submitted with little protest to the Allied demands. By the end of October the final batch of non-official Axis nationals had left the country.

---

[1] The Government of India thought it would overstress the parallel with Iran, and that a treaty with Russia, whose early defeat the Afghans both hoped for and expected, could hold little attraction for the Afghans.

(a) E5936/144/97. (b) E6001/144/97. (c) E6143/144/97. (d) E6319, 6449, 6451, 6536, 6542, 6572, 6607, 6752/144/97. (e) E6649, 6748, 6803, 6822, 7033, 7097/144/97.

CHAPTER XXI

Anglo-French relations in 1941

(i)

The Vichy Government and the British blockade: British attitude towards American relief measures (February–May 1941).

AT the end of the year 1940, there had seemed to be some chance of reaching at least an economic agreement with the Vichy Government but the negotiations soon faded out and the political relations with Marshal Pétain and his colleagues became worse. The Foreign Office thought that the French trade demands bore little relation to reality. Sir S. Hoare had therefore been instructed on January 24, 1941, to tell the French Ambassador at (a) Madrid that we could make no concessions with regard to imports into unoccupied France other than those already granted with regard to the relief of children, and that, for the time, the talks on a possible agreement should be limited to Morocco.[1]

The Vichy Government replied on February 5 with an *aide-mémoire* asking for the immediate delivery of 8 million quintals of (b) wheat, and repeating their previous denials (which the British Government knew to be untrue) that a large part of the supplies brought into French Mediterranean ports passed into German hands. Finally they threatened that, if necessary, they would escort and defend their convoys, with the consequent risk of 'incidents' which they as well as the British Government wished to avoid.

The question of supplies to unoccupied France was complicated by the general divergence of view between the British Government and the State Department on the policy of concessions to Vichy. The two Governments did not differ in aim; each wanted to minimise the advantages which Hitler had gained from the defeat of France, and in particular to prevent the Vichy Government from handing over the fleet to the Germans or allowing them the use of bases in unoccupied France or North Africa. Each also hoped that the spirit of resistance would revive in France and North Africa as soon as Frenchmen realised that their defeat was not final and that in the end the Germans were going to lose the war.

---

[1] See Volume I, pp. 431–2.

(a) Z252/87/17. (b) Z971/87/17.

The Americans, however, were much more hopeful about an immediate reaction. Unlike the British, they had not experienced the full measure of Vichy treachery and defeatism. They were not at war, and hardly realised the gravity of the dangers which would follow French capitulation to more German demands. They also underrated the psychological effect upon French opinion of the German victories, or the mood of apathy which dominated France— a mood which accepted and even respected Marshal Pétain as head of a French Government. Marshal Pétain himself had made it clear that he wanted France to keep out of the war. He was trying stubbornly not to go beyond the armistice terms in concessions to Germany and Italy, but he seemed equally convinced of the impossibility of a British victory.[1] Since he thought a British attempt to win such a victory futile and foredoomed to failure, he was unlikely to do anything to stimulate resistance in France or in the French possession overseas. Meanwhile Marshal Pétain regarded the Free French movement merely as a form of high treason, an act of civil and military disobedience which could only anger the Germans and lessen the chances of a favourable peace. This hope of a 'favourable peace' dominated French policy in the spring and summer of 1941.

(a) There is written evidence, in a statement which came into British hands, that the Vichy Ministers viewed the situation as follows: they had regarded the régime established by the armistice as something temporary which would last only until the war ended. Nearly a year had passed, however, and the chances of an early peace had receded. The only hope of escaping from the prolongation of an unduly rigorous régime was to try to shift Franco-German relations from a basis of '*diktat*' to one of collaboration. Collaboration meant further concessions to Germany; in return for them the Vichy Government hoped not only for an immediate alleviation of the harsh armistice terms but for assurances with regard to the future. In particular they counted upon a German promise to leave intact the French colonial Empire if the French would defend it against attack.

In any case, even if he had held a more robust view of the prospects of the war, and a more realist view of German promises, Marshal Pétain was old, tired, and surrounded by men who were pushing him always towards more concessions. Laval was more than a defeatist;

---

[1] Marshal Pétain seems to have given a different impression to Señor Suñer, the Spanish Foreign Minister, who went with General Franco to meet Pétain and Darlan at Montpellier on February 13, 1941. Señor Suñer told the German Ambassador in Madrid that Marshal Pétain (who obviously wanted to discourage Franco from committing himself completely to Germany) behaved in a pro-German way 'only when it was necessary. . . . At heart he hoped for England's victory.' Marshal Pétain seems to have said to Señor Suñer that he 'did not believe in the complete victory of Germany'. British and American resources were too great, and the result after a very long war would be a compromise. Darlan, however, had taken a decidedly opposite view. (*D.G.F.P. XII*, No. 62).

(a) Z4527/12/17.

he welcomed Franco-German collaboration as a desirable end. (a)
Admiral Darlan was perhaps even more dangerous, partly because
he was less unpopular than Laval in France, and less suspected of
complete subservience to Hitler, partly also because he was personally anti-British, and might sacrifice French interests to his own
resentment.[1] Laval and Darlan were known to be rivals for Pétain's
place. In mid-January Marshal Pétain met Laval on the frontier
between occupied and unoccupied France. The purpose of this meeting was ostensibly to 'clear up misunderstandings'; it was likely that
the Germans were putting pressure on the Marshal to bring back
Laval into his Government and to dismiss the Ministers who had
been most active in getting rid of him. For the time, however,
Admiral Darlan more than held his position. Flandin resigned on
February 9 and Darlan became Vice-Premier as well as Foreign
Minister and successor to Marshal Pétain as Chief of the State if the
Marshal were unable to fulfil his duties. Thus there was nothing to
hope from Vichy. Hence the British view that an alleviation of the
conditions of life in unoccupied France would improve the internal
position of the Vichy Government but would fail to bring them or
to bring French opinion any nearer to resisting their German
conquerors. Furthermore the humanitarian argument which was
being used in the United States by Mr. Hoover and others as a
reason for relaxing the British blockade seemed to the British Government to be dangerously unreal. There was, of course, no doubt about
the legal position. The legal responsibility for feeding the countries
which they had captured and occupied lay with the Germans. Unoccupied France was, in fact, conquered territory which could be
occupied at any moment. There were conflicting reports about the
food situation in unoccupied France; even if it were established that
the position was as desperate as the Vichy Government alleged it to
be, the relief of France could only mean an addition to German
resources, and therefore a prolongation of the war and of the misery
of other peoples under German occupation.

Mr. Hoover's proposals for European relief covered a wider area
than unoccupied France. It was easy to point out that on the scale
suggested by Mr. Hoover and his friends real control of the supplies

---

[1] Darlan, even before the fall of Laval, had been trying to get a relaxation of the
armistice terms relating to the French navy in full knowledge that the result might be
war with Great Britain. The German Naval Staff was in favour of concession in order to
be able to use the French fleet for the defence or recovery of French African colonies.
(*D.G.F.P., XI, No.* 432). On December 1, 1940, Darlan told the Germans that he expected
activity by the French navy off the coast of Africa to result in a state of open warfare with
Great Britain at sea, and that, in view of the British shortage of capital ships, 'a concentrated operation by the French fleet would seem to have good prospects of success'.
(*ib.* No. 434.)

(a) Z968/13/17.

sent to Europe would have been impossible and that the plan would have benefited the Germans and prolonged the war at the expense of the very people whose sufferings it was intended to relieve. Moreover a good deal of the support for proposals involving relaxation of the blockade was suspect, since it came from elements in the United States known to be working for a compromise peace.

On the whole, Mr. Hoover's general proposals failed to convince the American people. The State Department realised the force of the British argument that the maintenance of the blockade was the least harmful course from the point of view of Germany's European victims since, if it had any effect, it must contribute towards shortening the war. On the American view, however, the question of supplies to unoccupied France and North Africa was a different matter. Here the possibility of control was greater, and indeed in the case of North Africa American control could be used as a means of getting information and counteracting German and Italian influences. In the case of unoccupied France the humanitarian and the political arguments worked together. If the Vichy Government, and French opinion in general, saw the advantages of 'keeping in with' the United States, they would be less inclined to give way to German demands, and public opinion, realising that further submission to Germany meant the end of American supplies, would thus support a policy of resistance.

For reasons already stated the British Government did not agree with this view. American help merely allowed the Vichy Government to avoid the unpleasant consequences of collaboration with the Germans, and to play with both sides. The Germans would see to it that they were not the party to be tricked, and the total result would be to prolong the war. On the other hand, the British Government did not think it possible to go beyond a certain point in refusing the American proposals. At the beginning of December 1940, Lord Lothian had asked that consent should be given to a proposal from the American Red Cross for the distribution of relief in unoccupied France. After some discussion the War Cabinet agreed to refuse their consent unless they were very strongly pressed in the matter. They were pressed, however, by the President himself, and, on January 3, the Prime Minister considered that it was expedient to give way. The question of Lend-Lease had been propounded to the American people at this time, and it was undesirable to give the supporters of relief an occasion for joining the opponents of Lend-Lease. In any case the matter was at this time a little unreal owing to the incompleteness of the British blockade of unoccupied France.

Here—with the despatch of one relief ship—matters remained in regard to unoccupied France. The United States Government insisted in February on fairly substantial provisions for North Africa in return for the introduction of American control officers to ensure that the terms of distribution were kept. Early in March, the question of relief ships to unoccupied France was again raised. The Vichy Government themselves appealed for American help to tide (a) over the months before the 1941 harvest. The Americans proposed to send two shiploads of wheat and maize.

The War Cabinet again felt bound to agree. In view of a public threat by Admiral Darlan to escort French convoys across the Atlantic the British Government decided to suggest that we should agree to the passage of the two ships, but that otherwise we should not relax our blockade, and that we should ask the United States Government not to try to make us change our policy. We should also make our agreement in the case of the two ships subject to assurances that no more Germans would be permitted to go to North Africa, that the activities of the Armistice Commission in North Africa should be limited, and that certain British Consular Officers should be allowed to return to unoccupied France.

Mr. Churchill telegraphed to Mr. Roosevelt on March 12 that (b) in view of Admiral Darlan's attitude, it might be desirable for Mr. Roosevelt to try to bring about a working arrangement on the general question of supplies to France. In addition to the conditions laid down by the War Cabinet Mr. Churchill also suggested that the French should agree to move more of their warships from Toulon to Casablanca or Dakar.

On March 20 Mr. Churchill told the War Cabinet that the President had confirmed his general agreement with our policy, but (c) that we should have to allow the passage of the two ships. We should make it clear, by intercepting another convoy in the near future, that we were not abandoning our blockade.[1]

The pressure on the American side was lessened at the end of March when it became known that Admiral Darlan had concluded a barter arrangement whereby the Germans would supply the Vichy Government with 800,000 tons of wheat in return for the (d) export of livestock from unoccupied France. In any case American

---

[1] On March 30, after H.M.S. *Sheffield* had been fired on by coastal guns (and later bombed) while stopping a French convoy, and after the French had bombed Gibraltar, Lord Halifax was instructed to ask the United States Government to warn the Vichy Government that, if these attacks continued, we should bomb Vichy. On April 2 the Prime Minister telegraphed to Mr. Roosevelt that the Admiralty had received reports that the *Dunkerque* was being moved from Oran to Toulon for repairs. The President replied that he would 'understand' if we attacked the *Dunkerque*. On April 5 the President telegraphed that the *Dunkerque* would not be moved for at least ten days. See *Foreign Relations of the United States*, 1941, II, 143. (Hereafter referred to as *F.R.U.S.*) On April 8 the French Government told Admiral Leahy that the ship would not be moved until an agreement had been reached with the United States about its transfer. *F.R.U.S.*, id., 146–7. See also below, p. 289, n.1.

(a) Z1458/54/17; Z1373/380/17; Z1902, 1903, 1593, 1704/54/17; WM(41)23.
(b) Z1575/27/17. (c) Z2080, 2317/54/17; WM(41)30. (d) Z2400, 2401/54/17.

opinion was coming to realise that measures which had the appearance of acts of mercy might cause more suffering in Europe than they would relieve. Mr. Welles informed Lord Halifax on March 30 that the United States Government would probably send the two ships but in fact they waited for assurances from Vichy about a consignment of oil to Italy and a cargo of rubber which had been unloaded at Casablanca.

(a)   A month later, however, the State Department told Lord Halifax that they had agreed in principle to send two more wheat ships as soon as possible, and at the latest by early July, on condition that they had complete control of the disposal of the wheat, and facilities for appointing observers to exercise this control. The State Department appeared to be planning further shipments—two at a time—on similar lines if the distribution of the first two cargoes were satisfactory.

(b)   The War Cabinet decided that, although these plans were inconsistent with the previous negotiations, we should be unwise to take a stiff line about them. Owing to the demands on our naval forces we could not maintain an effective blockade of unoccupied France or North Africa, and the French were known to be importing supplies on a large scale. Thus they had imported enough ground nuts to provide the German and Austrian margarine ration for six months.

(c)   Lord Halifax was therefore instructed to say only that we hoped that the two ships would not be sent at once, and that we attached great importance to the appointment of 'controllers' as a means of introducing observers into unoccupied France.

The British Government agreed to the despatch of supplies—including oil—to North Africa on condition that American observers went with the cargoes. They were prepared to agree to similar measures on similar terms in West Africa, but they asked that, in the latter case, assistance should also be given to the colonies in West Africa which had joined the Free French. These colonies, in contrast to the apathy of the rest of the French Empire, had decided to go on fighting at our side. They had cut themselves off from all their associations with France and were bound to feel a certain isolation. It would be unfair, and politically dangerous, for them to see American assistance going to the Vichy-controlled colonies which were hindering our war effort, while they received nothing. On the other hand, if the Free French colonies were treated more generously than the Vichy-controlled colonies, the latter would see that their best hopes of getting more help lay in co-operation with us.

The United States Government agreed to provide supplies for the Free French colonies. In view of Marshal Pétain's strongly collabora-

---

(a) Z3470/54/17. (b) WM(41)47, Z3667/54/17. (c) Z3470/54/17.

tionist broadcast of May 15,[1] they suspended the proposed monthly shipments of wheat to unoccupied France, though they were prepared to continue them to North Africa if they had satisfactory (a) assurances from General Weygand.

Note to Section (i). The case of M. Chartier.[2]

The divergencies between British and American policy were also shown in a minor matter affecting the representation of Great Britain in unoccupied France, and vice versa. On April 19, 1941, the Foreign Office asked the United States Embassy in London to transmit a message to the Vichy Government that His Majesty's Government desired the withdrawal of M. Chartier, the French consular agent in London. This action was taken after the Vichy Government had demanded the withdrawal of a former British Vice-Consul temporarily attached to the (b) American Consulate-General at Marseilles, but there were also wider reasons for the action, notably in the inexcusable delays of the Vichy Government over the repatriation of British soldiers certified unfit for further service.

The United States Government were much concerned at this step and asked that it might be reconsidered. The Foreign Office therefore (c) pointed out that we had to make the Vichy Government realise our displeasure at their consistently unfriendly attitude towards our representation in their territories and their treatment of British civilians and service personnel. We had not cut off the official representation of Vichy in Great Britain. After the withdrawal of the French Embassy we had agreed to an exchange of diplomatic agents. M. Paul Morand, who was in London as head of a French economic mission, stayed on, mainly to clear up the affairs of the mission. M. Morand was then recalled to Vichy, and left M. Chartier in London. After much delay, the French let it be known that they could not receive a British agent. Nevertheless we allowed M. Chartier, whom M. Morand had designated as his assistant, to remain in charge of the French Consulate-General. We also permitted other French consuls (except those found to be engaging in anti-British activities) and a nucleus staff of the French missions which had collaborated with us before the armistice to stay in Great Britain.

On the French side there had been no reciprocity. All British Consuls in North and West Africa had been expelled and not allowed to return. When we suggested sending back some of our consuls to unoccupied France we were told that they would not be allowed in any port, and when, later, in response to a suggestion from the Vichy Government, we proposed to establish a Treasury representative at Vichy to help in the settlement of the many outstanding financial questions between the two countries, we had a blunt refusal.[3]

---

[1] See below, p. 70.
[2] See also Volume I, p. 405.
[3] See also Volume I, pp. 405-6.

(a) Z4285/54/17. (b) Z3348/92/17. (c) Z3349/92/17.

We had done our best to repatriate all French citizens who wished to go back to France and our efforts had failed only because the Armistice Commission would not allow a ship come to to fetch them. We had sent back French sailors and soldiers who did not wish to join the Free French. On the other hand the Vichy Government had forbidden all British civilians of military age to leave unoccupied France and had interned all British soldiers. The French put the responsibility on the Germans, but this fact did not alter the position that we had been treating them in a way in which they did not treat us.

(a) Although the State Department again stated their regret at the British decision, they agreed to transmit a communication to the Vichy Government. The Foreign Office authorised them to say that the British Government would be willing to receive a successor to M. Chartier. M. Chartier left England on May 7, but the Vichy Government did not suggest a successor.

(ii)

Attempts to prevent further concessions by the Vichy Government to the Germans (February–May 1941).

Throughout the first half of 1941 the evidence of French political subservience to German demands seemed to support the British rather than the American view about the possibility of stiffening the attitude of the Vichy Government. The dismissal of Laval in December 1940 had been followed by very strong German protests. Laval had been put under arrest, but the Germans secured his release almost at once. On December 24 Marshal Pétain sent a message to Hitler explaining that the attitude of France in international affairs was unchanged. He continued in January 1941 to make statements that France intended loyal co-operation in the organisation of the European continent and the establishment of a solid and enduring peace.

At the beginning of February the Foreign Office view was that
(b) the Germans intended to put an end to Marshal Pétain's 'delaying tactics' and to face the French sharply with demands for the return to office of Laval, the surrender of Bizerta, the right of passage for German troops through unoccupied France to the Mediterranean ports, and the use of the French fleet. It was impossible to say how far the Germans would get what they wanted. They had very strong means of pressure. They had a million French prisoners of war; they could take over physical control of unoccupied France, or starve it. Above all, they were dealing with a defeatist Government which

(a) Z3673/92/17. (b) Z793/12/17, WP(41)25.

remained convinced of the hopelessness of resistance. In fact, the Vichy Government were making concessions. They had allowed Germans to infiltrate into North Africa; in spite of his assurances to the United States, Marshal Pétain had permitted the numbers of Germans on the Armistice Commission in French Morocco to be more than doubled, and it was known that other Germans were being sent quietly into Morocco and elsewhere in order to undertake espionage and propaganda.

On April 18 the United States Government instructed Admiral Leahy to tell Marshal Pétain that unless his Government could give (a) satisfactory assurances that they were not going back on their promises to hold out against further German infiltration into North Africa, the United States would be obliged to give up their programme of relief for North Africa and Metropolitan France. The Foreign Office at first thought it undesirable at least for the time to (b) lose the advantage of establishing American observers in France, but the sinister increase in the number of Germans sent to North Africa and Admiral Darlan's increasing truculence about the blockade made it necessary for the British Government to give yet another warning to the Vichy authorities.

On April 28 Mr. Eden told the War Cabinet that the position in Syria was serious. We were trying to discover what General Dentz (c) would do if German airborne troops landed in Syria.[1] If he agreed to resist, we would help him. If he said that he would have to obey orders from Vichy, we should have to decide what action to take. Mr. Eden thought that we should make it clear to the Vichy Government that if they allowed German airborne troops to land in Syria, or the Germans to occupy Morocco or to be given a passage through unoccupied France, we should be free to take whatever military action we thought fit, e.g. bombing lines of communication in France, and that we should no longer be bound by our undertaking to restore the greatness and independence of France. On the other hand if the French resisted, we should do all that we could to help them.

The War Cabinet decided to ask the United States Government to transmit a message from His Majesty's Government to Marshal (d) Pétain. The message pointed out that, if the French did not refuse the German demands, they would have been driven 'from capitulation to collaboration, and from collaboration to participation in the war' and would 'suffer from both sides and gain nothing'.

'Such participation would constitute a departure from the condition of passive capitulation in which France received from us our guarantee

---

[1] See also Volume I, Chapter XVII, section (ii).

(a) Z3075/132/17. (b) Z3063/132/17. (c) WM(41)44. (d) Z3420/92/17.

to restore her independence and greatness. It would be impossible for us to maintain in any respect the distinction we have hitherto drawn between unoccupied and occupied France in the execution of our military and economic plans. If, on the other hand, the French Government would effectively resist these encroachments, we should give them the utmost assistance in our power. It should be possible to hold Syria against any forces which the Axis could bring against it in the near future. The French and British fleets acting together in the Eastern Mediterranean could cut Axis communications with Africa, and invaluable bases would be available to us. French resistance and renewed Franco-British collaboration would go far to prevent the dangers which the French at present fear.'

Lord Halifax was asked to explain to the United States Government that the message represented all that we ourselves were able to do to arrest the deterioration in the French situation, and that we should much value anything which the United States Government could say from themselves and any step which they could take. Mr. Churchill also sent a message to Mr. Roosevelt summing up the

(a) position in the words: 'I feel Hitler may quite easily now gain vast advantages very cheaply, and we are so fully engaged that we can do little or nothing to stop him spreading himself'.

Lord Halifax saw Mr. Welles[1] on the evening of April 29. Mr.

(b) Welles began by doubting whether it was wise to give a written message to Marshal Pétain who was 'fighting a lone hand against Darlan, de Brinon and company'. The Germans would hear of the message, and decide to force the issue. In any case we were asking the French to abandon the armistice and resume the fight. They could not do this in present circumstances, and Marshal Pétain's policy was to stand on the armistice terms.

Lord Halifax said that we were appealing to the French to refuse demands outside the armistice terms and, if necessary, to resist them by force. If they adopted this line, we would help them; otherwise they must take the consequences of refusal. Mr. Welles, however, continued to think that the message would nullify everything that the United States and Great Britain were trying to do in North Africa. Lord Halifax agreed to the suspension of the message for the time on condition that Admiral Leahy should speak at once to Marshal Pétain in the general sense of the message. Mr. Welles said that Mr. Murphy was leaving for North Africa by air and would offer General Weygand supplies of munitions and the despatch of American ships to Dakar and Casablanca.

Lord Halifax was instructed on May 1 that the American proposal was satisfactory, and that we would not press for the message to be

---

[1] Mr. Hull was not available for an interview.

(a) T123/1. (b) Z3421/92/17.

delivered, but that we were telling Generals Dentz and Weygand of Admiral Leahy's representations. We also thought it desirable that the proposed offer to General Weygand should be made at once.

Admiral Leahy saw Marshal Pétain on May 3. A report of the interview was sent by Lord Halifax to the Foreign Office on the night (a) of May 5–6. Marshal Pétain, as the Foreign Office expected, maintained his usual position. He said that there had as yet been no German pressure to allow more troops in North Africa or a passage through unoccupied France to Spain, and that no demands had been made for French assistance against Great Britain. Marshal Pétain expected more requests for collaboration but would not go beyond the armistice terms. He refused to comment on the offer of British help in resisting demands beyond the armistice terms; he repeated that these terms bound him not to allow the use of the French fleet against the Axis.

Admiral Leahy thought that there was no hope of French resistance until a British victory had shown that the Germans could be defeated. Events in Greece and North Africa had seriously damaged British prestige at Vichy and discouraged the pro-British minority. There was a tendency to accept the German thesis that co-operation would bring generous terms, while a refusal to recognise the facts of German victory would only increase the calamities of France. Admiral Leahy had told Marshal Pétain that the United States would withdraw their practical assistance—i.e. food supplies—and moral support if the French Government went beyond the armistice terms in giving assistance to Germany. He did not, however, mention the statement in the proposed British message that, in the event of the French Government agreeing to action amounting to participation in the war on the German side, the British Government could no longer maintain their guarantee to restore the independence and greatness of France and could not continue to distinguish in their military and economic plans between occupied and unoccupied France.

In view of the information about increasing collaboration the Foreign Office thought it necessary that a plain statement should be made. Mr. Eden therefore spoke very clearly in the House of Commons on May 15 in relation to the position in Syria and German support of the Iraqi revolt.[1] He said that the French authorities in Syria were allowing German aircraft to use Syrian aerodromes as ports on their flights to Iraq in support of the rebels.[2]

---

[1] See Volume I, p. 565.
[2] See note at end of section (iii).

(a) Z3633/12/17; Z3837/92/17.

We had therefore given full authority for action to be taken against these German aircraft on Syrian aerodromes. The French Government could not escape responsibility for this situation, since their action under German orders in permitting such flights was a clear breach of the armistice terms and inconsistent with their undertakings.

Meanwhile Admiral Leahy had seen Marshal Pétain again on May 12 to deliver a message from Mr. Roosevelt. Admiral Leahy (a) asked whether he might tell the United States Government that Marshal Pétain would not give military assistance to Germany. Marshal Pétain answered that he would not give 'voluntary active military aid'. Admiral Leahy once more said that Great Britain would go on fighting until she defeated Germany, but Marshal Pétain and General Huntziger, who was with him, were sceptical of this, and asked how long it would take.

On May 15 Marshal Pétain delivered a short broadcast in which he approved of the meeting between Admiral Darlan and Hitler and described it as 'lightening the path of the future' and 'continuing the present conversations with the German Government'. Marshal Pétain appealed to the French people to follow him 'without any mental reservation in the path of honour and national interest. If within the strict discipline of our public spirit we are able to bring to a successful conclusion the present negotiations, France will be able to overcome her defeat and retain in the world her rank as a European and colonial Power.'

The United States Government regarded this broadcast, with (b) good reason, as showing that there was little hope of French resistance to any German demands. President Roosevelt at once issued a statement that Marshal Pétain had given the United States Government assurances that he would not agree to any collaboration with Germany which exceeded the terms of the armistice: 'this was the least that could be expected from a France which demanded respect for its integrity'. The President continued:

> 'It is inconceivable that [the French people] will willingly accept any agreement for so-called "collaboration" which will in reality imply their alliance with a military Power whose central and fundamental policy calls for the utter destruction of liberty, freedom and popular institutions everywhere. The people of the United States can hardly believe that the present Government of France could be brought to lend itself to a plan of voluntary alliance, implied or otherwise, which would apparently deliver up France and its colonial Empire, including the French African colonies and their Atlantic coasts, with the menace which that involves to the peace and safety of the western hemisphere.'

(a) Z3903/12/17. (b) Z3993/368/17.

Within a short time after Admiral Leahy's interview with Marshal Pétain there were more reports indicating a French surrender to German demands. On the night of May 23–4 Lord Halifax was instructed to tell the State Department that a new Franco-German (a) agreement appeared to be under signature. The terms of this agreement included military co-operation and the provision of naval and air bases in French North Africa. The Germans expected that the agreement would bring France into the war on the German side. Admiral Darlan had paid a visit to Hitler and in return for the French concessions the Germans had promised the release of 200,000 prisoners and a modification of the line of demarcation between occupied and unoccupied France.

According to information received by the Foreign Office the French decision was extremely sinister. At a meeting of the Vichy (b) Ministers at which General Weygand was present it had been made clear that naval and air bases in North Africa would be given to the Germans. General Weygand had protested strongly, and had left the meeting, but the Ministers had nevertheless decided that France had gone so far along the road to collaboration that she must continue on it. After a pressing appeal from Marshal Pétain General Weygand had decided that his loyalty to the Marshal required him to obey. He was said to be trying to obtain some public statement justifying the grant of bases as necessary to preserve the French Empire.[1] The French source of this information feared that, if suitably presented, a statement of this kind might win general acceptance in France. The French High Commissioner in Syria actually broadcast a statement on the night of June 5–6 that the French Government had decided to modify its policy towards Germany in order that France, which was starving under the blockade, might live. In these circumstances the Foreign Office telegraphed to Lord Halifax on June 6 that it was desirable to bring the facts of the new policy before the French people, but that the Vichy Government had taken care to give no information, and we could not publish without American consent the information which we had received from the United States. We hoped therefore that the State Department would make public as soon as possible the facts about the grant of air and naval bases. We assumed also that the United States would now give up their policy of assistance to North Africa, and announce that they would assist the Free French colonies which were now in danger.

Further American information showed that Admiral Darlan was still convinced that Great Britain could not possibly defeat Germany. (c)

---

[1] This information about General Weygand's action was not correct. See below, p. 78.

(a) Z4172, 4254/12/17. (b) Z4714/12/17. (c) Z4765/12/17.

Marshal Pétain was afraid that, if the war continued, the whole of Europe would be destroyed and fall under Communism. On June 4, 1941, Admiral Leahy assured Marshal Pétain and Admiral Darlan that the United States was determined on the defeat of Hitler, and that he would be defeated. Pétain and Darlan 'both immediately asked,"When?" '. Darlan, with the Marshal's agreement, said that if the war went on, 'and it may last for years, it will mean only the destruction of all concerned and the United States itself will end in social revolution. Communism alone will prevail throughout Europe.'[1] Admiral Darlan also felt that the perpetual enmity between France and Germany should come to an end. He told Admiral Leahy that he had found the Germans more honest and reliable than the British in his dealings with them in the last ten years. He did not know what action the British in their stupidity might now be led to take, but the limit of French patience had been reached. Neither Marshal Pétain nor Admiral Darlan would explain the scope or extent of their policy of collaboration, but Admiral Leahy had the impression that the Marshal completely accepted Admiral Darlan's policy and that he would approve any commitment that he (Admiral Darlan) might make in the future.

(iii)

The Vichy Government and the Germans in the autumn of 1941: the dismissal of General Weygand: Marshal Pétain's assurances in December 1941.

The German attack on Russia was unlikely to change the defeatist attitude of the Vichy Government. Marshal Pétain indeed told Admiral Leahy on June 27 that in his opinion Hitler was doing a service to the world in attacking the Communists and that the German army would meet with no difficulty. At the beginning of November—when this military forecast had turned out to be wrong —Marshal Pétain was still sure that the Germans would be in Moscow and Rostov by the end of the month and that they would return to an attack on Great Britain or North Africa. For a time indeed the confidence of Marshal Pétain and Admiral Darlan in a German victory seems to have been shaken, but the continued German advance appears to have convinced them that, unless they could get a peace treaty out of the Germans soon, the British might anticipate them by agreeing to a 'compromise' peace at the expense of France.

---

[1] *F.R.U.S.*, 1941, II, 185.

Rumours of new Franco-German negotiations reached the Foreign Office during August. Although Marshal Pétain denied that there was any change in his policy towards Germany, there were reports that the German terms would secure for the Axis Powers the control or use of the ports of Cette in France and Oran, Bizerta and Algiers in Africa. Admiral Darlan was said to have given a definite promise about Bizerta, but Marshal Pétain had refused to agree, and had brought General Weygand to Vichy to support him in opposition.

On August 18 Mr. Eden suggested to Mr. Winant that the State (a) Department might warn the Vichy Government about the dangers of a peace treaty. The Department had already sent a warning on August 2—after the French acceptance of the Japanese demands in (b) Indo-China—that the attitude of the United States towards Marshal Pétain's Government would be determined by the effectiveness with which France defended her territories against the aggression of the Axis Powers. It was therefore unlikely that the State Department would want to repeat their warning, and Mr. Winant does not seem to have transmitted Mr. Eden's suggestion.

The reports of French concessions, however, continued; in the third week of September the Foreign Office decided once again to (c) raise the question of a warning. Meanwhile the President had sent another message to Marshal Pétain urging him to maintain French sovereignty in North Africa. Marshal Pétain replied that he did not (d) intend to cede any bases but that France was a conquered country and that the Germans might enforce concessions. Sir R. I. Campbell[1] spoke to Mr. Welles on October 1. Mr. Welles did not think that (e) another warning was desirable or that Marshal Pétain would give way. He also repeated the American view that a complete break with the Vichy Government would not be to the advantage of Great Britain since it would mean the withdrawal of Admiral Leahy who was doing a good deal to keep the French from giving way to the Germans.

Throughout this time the United States Government had maintained their contact with General Weygand, and had sent a certain amount of supplies—including two tankers of oil—to North Africa. On November 18, however, Marshal Pétain announced the dismissal of General Weygand. He told Admiral Leahy that the Germans had compelled him to take this step under threat of sending troops into (f) unoccupied France. Marshal Pétain had already recalled General Weygand to Vichy, but the actual date of the dismissal is significant since it was the opening day of the British offensive in Cyrenaica. The Prime Minister at once asked Mr. Roosevelt whether he could

---

[1] Minister in the British Embassy in Washington.

(a) Z7066/92/17. (b) Z6645/368/17. (c) Z7919/92/17. (d) Z7971, 8431/4353/17.
(e) Z8440/92/17. (f) Z9813/132/17; Z9892/1374/17.

try to secure the retention of General Weygand in his command or at all events the appointment of 'some friendly figure'—for example General Georges—as his successor.

The Prime Minister thought that nothing more could be done until we knew the upshot of the fighting in Cyrenaica. If we won an important victory, we could ask President Roosevelt to say to Marshal Pétain that now or never was the time when he should tell North Africa to assert its independence and freedom, and that we should give all the aid in our power. If the French accepted the German demand for the use of Bizerta, we should take the line that the United States would never help them again and we should put on a merciless blockade.

Meanwhile before Mr. Churchill's message reached the President (a) the United States Government announced that they were suspending supplies to French North Africa until it was seen to what further extent Hitler would 'attempt to take over by force or threat of force the sovereignty and control of the French Empire'. This suspension was only temporary. General Weygand himself asked that there should be no change of policy; Mr. Hull continued to hope much from the French and to support the policy of keeping in contact with Vichy. Mr. Murphy, the chief American representative in North Africa, also recommended the continuance of supplies. The United States Government therefore decided to tell Marshal Pétain that they would resume shipments if they were assured that General Weygand's dismissal did not imply a change in policy with regard to North Africa.

Admiral Leahy made a statement to this effect to Marshal Pétain (b) and Admiral Darlan on December 11. He pointed out that the United States was now at war with Germany—the Marshal and the Admiral said how much they regretted this fact—and Franco-American relations were on a changed basis since French help to Germany would be of direct harm to the United States. In reply Marshal Pétain said that the Germans had not requested the French Government to alter their relations with the United States, but that, if this request were made, it would be difficult to reject it because the Germans could threaten to starve France. Later the French Government gave Admiral Leahy three memoranda stating that (i) the (c) French fleet would not be used against Great Britain except in the event of hostile British action, (ii) the recall of General Weygand did not mean a change in the status of the French territories in North Africa, (iii) the French would not allow Germany to use French territory as bases for hostilities, (iv) France would remain neutral in the war between the United States and Germany and

Italy. The French Government therefore hoped that with these assurances the United States Government would resume their programme of supplies for North Africa.

The Foreign Office regarded these French statements as most unsatisfactory since they implied that France would continue a policy of benevolent neutrality towards Germany. The promises about bases did not apply to their use for supplies, and the reference to retaliation in the event of hostile British naval action was ominous in view of the evidence that the French were trying to build up a case against us in order to justify the use of their fleet for convoy purposes. Even if Marshal Pétain's assurance about North Africa was technically correct, the departure of General Weygand meant that there was no one of sufficient authority there to gather round him the forces of resistance to Germany.

The Prime Minister, before leaving England for his visit to Washington, had considered the possibility of a joint Anglo-American note to Vichy requiring the Vichy Government to show by some act, e.g. sinking the French fleet, or handing it over to the United States, or starting a revolt in North Africa, that they were on our side. We would then reaffirm our promises to France, and these promises would also have American backing. If the Vichy Government refused to give this evidence of their allegiance, we should tell them that Great Britain and the United States refused to recognise them as the legitimate Government of France. We should not declare war on them, but we should regard ourselves free to take any action against them which we might think necessary.

The Foreign Office thought it unlikely that Marshal Pétain would go as far as removing the fleet or starting a revolution in North Africa, or indeed that he would do anything until he was sure that we were winning the war. Since we did not want to risk bringing the whole of the French fleet into the war against us our best policy would be to avoid putting the sharp alternative of 'for' or 'against' to the Vichy Government; we should try to keep Admiral Leahy at Vichy and to press Marshal Pétain to resist German demands, and at the same time to accept a barter agreement over North Africa which would prevent American supplies for this area reaching the Germans.

At the end of December the Vichy Government sent a message through the French Naval Attaché at Madrid that there was no truth in the report of the cession of bases or of the fleet. Marshal Pétain was determined never to give way on these points, and Admiral Darlan would never act against the Marshal's wishes. Thus, on the information available to the British Government, the year ended as it had begun with the Vichy Government uncertain of the issue, indifferent to the sufferings and the endeavours of their former Ally, and still hoping that by skilful measures they might avoid Hitler's worst vindictiveness in the event of a German victory, while by a kind of underhand reinsurance they might also keep a certain measure of American good-will.[1] The most sinister fact in the situation was that, next to, and even above, their complaints against Great Britain, the greatest anger felt by the men of Vichy was towards General de Gaulle and those Frenchmen who had refused to accept the defeat of France and the predominance of Nazi Germany as a final event in European history.

Note to Sections (ii) and (iii). Information from German sources on the negotiations with the Vichy Government in 1941 over French concessions (beyond the armistice terms) in Syria and North Africa, and French collaboration in the war against Great Britain.

On April 28, after earlier negotiations for the sale and transfer of 13,000 French lorries from occupied France, Darlan agreed with the Germans on behalf of the French Government to the sale of lorries in North Africa for the German forces. A week later he brought to the German Ambassador in Paris the assent of the French Government to the transfer for the use of the Iraqi rebels of stocks of French arms under the control of the Italian Armistice Commission in Syria, and to the use of Syrian airfields by German aircraft bound for Iraq. Darlan accepted agreements to this effect on May 7 in return for German permission for the rearming of seven French torpedo boats, certain relaxations of controls between the occupied and unoccupied zones of France, and a reduction in the costs of occupation. The Germans themselves were surprised at the extent of the French willingness to go 'far beyond the stipulations of the armistice treaty'.[2]

These transactions were followed by agreements on a larger scale. Darlan met Hitler and Ribbentrop on May 11,[3] and on the next day had another interview with Ribbentrop. Ribbentrop said that France had to make a choice, and that this choice implied war against England. Darlan answered that he was entirely willing to make the choice, and resolved to go with Germany. Ribbentrop then said that the war would be fought almost wholly by Germany and that France 'would merely have to render a certain kind of assistance', especially on the naval side. Darlan answered that the French navy was ready, but that it had to ask

---

[1] In November, 1941, Admiral Darlan, who must have realised that the Germans did not intend to make the concessions for which he had asked in return for active French collaboration in the war against Great Britain, appears to have made a secret and tentative approach to the British Government with the question whether, at the end of the (a) war, the British would refuse to treat with a French Government of which he (Darlan) was a member. The Prime Minister's answer was that it would be a matter of the first order if the French fleet would sail for North and West Africa and would be prepared to resist German attack. Whoever commanded and effected such a service would be entitled to an honoured place in the Allied ranks. No reply was received from Admiral Darlan.

[2] *D.G.F.P.*, XII, Nos. 417, 459 and 475.

[3] *ib.* No. 491.

(a) COS(41)430th Mtg.; S.I.C./D/France/2, f.15A.

for several concessions. The German record of the conversation summed up the position on both sides as completely clear, i.e. 'Darlan was resolved to take the clear course of entering the war against England in the near future'.[1]

On May 15, after his return to Vichy, Darlan described the agreement as the last chance of a *rapprochement* with Germany. If France supported England she would be utterly destroyed as a nation. If she attempted a policy of balance, Germany could cause her great embarrassment in the exercise of her sovereignty, and the final peace treaty (Darlan assumed a German victory) would be disastrous. If France collaborated with Germany without actually making war on England, French losses would be reduced to a minimum and an honourable future would be secured. Marshal Pétain agreed with Darlan's action, and on the following day made a broadcast in support of it. On May 21 Darlan went to Paris for further negotiations. These negotiations resulted in the signature oi Franco-German protocols on May 27-8. The first of these protocols confirmed the agreements already made with regard to (i) the transfer to the Germans for use in Iraq of three-quarters of the French war material stored in Syria; (ii) the use of Syrian ports, roads and railways for the transmission of material to Iraq; (iii) the availability of Syrian aerodromes and the provision of a special base for German aeroplanes in Syria. The French also promised to defend Syria and Lebanon against attack. The second protocol dealt with North Africa. Bizerta was to be made available as a port for the supply of German forces in Africa. The French would also provide shipping and naval escorts for these supplies from Toulon, and railway transport from Bizerta to Gabes. The third protocol related to West and Equatorial Africa. Dakar was to be open to German ships and aircraft; the French would be allowed reinforcements to defend their African possessions and to regain the territories which had recognised General de Gaulle. A supplementary protocol was agreed (on which Darlan insisted to the annoyance of the Germans) to the effect that the French Government 'must expect that the utilisation of the port of Bizerta and the protection of convoys for the supplies of the German Afrika Corps . . . can lead to an immediate armed conflict with England or the United States'. The German naval and military concessions would make possible the 'immediate' assumption of the risks attending the French promises regarding Bizerta, but the engagements under the third protocol made it necessary to grant political and economic concessions which would enable the French Government 'to justify before public opinion' in France 'the possible outbreak' of war with England and the United States.[2] Darlan had told Hitler on May 11 that the further concessions for which France would ask needed less to go very deeply than to be outwardly apparent ('des avantages plus spectaculaires que profonds').[3]

Before his acceptance of these agreements for active collaboration, Marshal Pétain summoned General Weygand to Vichy. Weygand

---

[1] ib. No. 499.
[2] ib. No. 559.
[3] ib. No. 491.

arrived on June 2. He opposed, absolutely, military collaboration, the grant of African bases to the Axis Powers, and war with England. Marshal Pétain, who had accepted the protocols, now began to hesitate. It was already clear that the French were likely to lose Syria. They might also—as Weygand thought—have to meet an English attack on Dakar. Weygand suggested, as a way out of the position into which the French Government had been placed by Darlan, that the Germans should be asked for much greater political concessions than they would be willing to grant.[1] Darlan himself seems to have agreed with this plan. The Germans made it easier for the French to adopt it because they did not produce any important political or economic concessions. Keitel indeed wrote to Ribbentrop on June 15 asking that concessions should be made quickly and on a generous scale. Keitel pointed out that it was 'entirely out of the question' for the Germans 'now or in the future' to seize the French bases by force.[2] A month later, on July 12, Abetz was given a note from the French Government that it was impossible to carry out the protocol relating to North and West Africa until the political concessions had been agreed. These concessions were to include an assurance that France would retain her territorial possessions in Europe as they had been in 1914, and, subject to changes for which she would receive compensation, her colonial Empire.[3]

Ribbentrop, with Hitler's approval, ordered Abetz to return the French note with an 'oral comment' that it was based on complete misconception of France's position as a nation defeated by Germany.[4] From this time the Germans seem to have realised that their plans to bring the French into war with Great Britain had failed. The Chairman of the German Armistice Commission told Admiral Michelier plainly on July 26 that Germany could not recognise the French attempt to link the Paris Protocols with political negotiations and that further German concessions would depend upon a change in the French attitude over Bizerta.[5] Hitler said to Abetz on September 26 that he did not want any alteration in the 'tactical treatment of the French' until the campaign in the East had been 'wound up', but that in the course of the winter he would increase the occupation troops in France by fifty divisions. 'Then he could and would do some plain talking to the people in Vichy.'[6]

In fact the German treatment of France was already harsher; savage reprisals were taken after the assassination of Germans; Marshal Pétain was so much distressed by the shooting of 600 hostages that he considered giving himself up as a prisoner[7] and even Abetz suggested a temporary suspension of the death sentences against another 100 hostages. Pétain addressed a short letter to Hitler on October 21—the anniversary of the Montoire meeting—regretting that Franco-German collaboration

---

[1] For Weygand's attitude, see his memoirs, *Recalled to Service* (trans. E. W. Dickes, Heinemann, 1952), 320–43.
[2] *D.G.F.P.*, XII, No. 633.
[3] *id.* XIII, Nos. 100 and 113.
[4] *ib.* No. 113.
[5] *ib.* p. 232, n. 1.
[6] *ib.* No. 327.
[7] *ib.* No. 422.

had not produced the expected results.[1] Hitler made a long, rambling reply on November 10 that the responsibility for lack of co-operation lay entirely with the French.[2] On November 18 Pétain—at German insistence —agreed to remove General Weygand from his command in North Africa. A fortnight later Pétain had a meeting with Göring. Pétain had drawn up a memorandum explaining the need to get the approval of the French people for a policy of collaboration, and therefore to make clear to them what they were to gain from it in alleviation of their sufferings. Göring assumed that this memorandum must have come not from Marshal Pétain but from the French Government. He therefore told Darlan, who was present at the interview, that he could not understand why such a document had been submitted, since it assumed that Germany, not France, had been conquered, etc.[3]

The Germans made no attempt to meet Marshal Pétain's requests. A hundred more hostages were put to death in Paris during the second week of December. The Italians had told the German General Staff that they could not do without the use of Bizerta and that Ciano intended to raise the question at a meeting with Darlan in Turin; the Germans warned the Italians that a premature demand for the harbour might lead to British intervention before the Luftwaffe and German submarines had restored Axis mastery of the sea and air in the Central Mediterranean.[4] The Turin meeting had no result. On December 20 Göring told General Juin, who had succeeded General Weygand as French Commander-in-Chief in North Africa, that the Germans would make no concessions over the occupation of France unless the French agreed to their demands about Bizerta and promised to fight with Rommel against the English forces in the event of an Axis retreat into southern Tunisia. The French reply was to approve once again the principle of collaboration, and to agree to the two German demands subject to conditions which they knew to be unacceptable.[5]

(iv)

Relations with General de Gaulle (August 1941–January 1942): the Brazzaville interview: the Free French occupation of St. Pierre and Miquelon.

During the months when relations between Great Britain and the Vichy Government had reached open war in Syria, and were near to general hostilities elsewhere, the collaboration between Great Britain and the Free French had not been easy. At the beginning of August, 1941, indeed, there was serious danger of an open breach between General de Gaulle and the British Government. Neither party was without blame for this increasing friction. General de Gaulle was not easy to deal with. He was a soldier unused to

---

[1] *ib.* No. 417.   [2] *ib.* No. 460.
[3] *ib.* No. 529. For the French memorandum, see *ib.* No. 531.
[4] *ib.* Nos. 532 and 552.
[5] Hitler told Mussolini on 29 December 1941, that he did not think France would ever be won over to active and real collaboration. Id. Ser. E., No. 62.

political negotiations. He inclined to express his views, publicly as well as in his correspondence with the British Government, in an authoritarian form which could easily be misinterpreted. His attitude, as a Frenchman, towards the Vichy Government was bound to be even more severe than that of English critics. He was almost absurdly suspicious of British motives, especially in the Levant. He was not always a good judge of his own countrymen and included in his London headquarters some Frenchmen who were of no value to his cause. Since the autumn of 1940 the Free French Movement had gained little ground; a few notable individuals joined it, and the Free French had acquitted themselves well in action, but they were far from becoming the great military force for which the General had hoped. In these circumstances General de Gaulle was inclined to blame the British Government for ignoring, as he put it, the 'moral side' of his movement (as for example the fact that France was still the enemy of Germany) and thinking of it solely in terms of the number of units it could put into battle.

On the British side there were also faults of tact and consideration. The military liaison with the Free French was unsatisfactory, and General de Gaulle had some reason to complain that he and his staff were not brought sufficiently into the confidence of their Ally or even treated in minor matters on the same terms as the officers of other Allied Governments in London. It is probable that the larger grievances would have lost at least some of their importance if more sympathy and understanding had been shown for the position of the French who had cut themselves off from their country, and had refused, in a period when this refusal meant taking the gravest risks not only for themselves but for their families, to follow the Vichy Government in its policy of surrender and collaboration.

The Syrian affair only added to the causes of discord, and in an unguarded moment General de Gaulle gave an angry interview to
(a) an American newspaper correspondent at Brazzaville. This correspondent telegraphed a summary of the interview to the United States where it was published on August 27. General de Gaulle apparently did not realise that his words would be published, but he was too late to prevent publication. The interview was strongly anti-British in tone, and also revealed that the General had offered to the United States the use of the principal ports in Free French West Africa on long-term lease as bases against the Germans.

The Prime Minister greatly resented General de Gaulle's allegations, and the more so because the anti-British tone of the interview was exaggerated in the summarised form in which it was telegraphed to the United States. At the time of publication General de Gaulle

(a) Z7383/114/17.

was on his way to England; the Prime Minister gave instructions that he and the Free French should be treated with extreme reserve (a) until the matter had been explained.

On September 12 the Prime Minister invited General de Gaulle to meet him at No. 10 Downing Street. The Prime Minister said that he had been very sorry to see a deterioration in General de (b) Gaulle's attitude towards the British Government; he felt that he was no longer dealing with a friend. General de Gaulle said that it could not seriously be maintained that he was an enemy of Great Britain. He regretted any remarks which must have sounded disparaging towards the Prime Minister or the British Government, but complained that the Free French were not being properly treated in Syria.

The purpose of this meeting was not only to deal with the question of the newspaper interview but also to suggest the formation of a Free French National Committee (or Council as it was first called) with which the British Government would deal in matters affecting their relations with General de Gaulle and his movement. The trouble was increased by difficulties within the movement itself; in particular, there were serious differences between General de Gaulle and Admiral Muselier.[1] An agreement between them was patched (c) up with the help of British mediation; one reason for the establishment of the proposed Committee was that it might reduce the chances of these personal disputes. General de Gaulle wanted to go beyond the British suggestion, and to give portfolios to the members of the Committee. The Committee would thus have the appearance of a Government. The list of members was, however, very satisfactory, and the War Cabinet agreed on September 25 to an announcement in the press that the Committee had been set up. (d) General de Gaulle therefore made the announcement and Mr. Eden wrote to him that His Majesty's Government would be prepared to regard the Free French National Committee as (e) 'representing all Free Frenchmen, wherever they may be, who rally to the Free French Movement in support of the Allied cause', and to treat with the National Committee on all questions involving British collaboration with the Free French Movement and with the French overseas territories which placed themselves under its authority. Mr. Eden added a *caveat*—on the lines of the Prime Minister's letter of December 24, 1940,[2]—that His Majesty's Government were not to be taken as expressing any views about the

---

[1] In March 1941 General de Gaulle had wished to put another officer in command of the Free French Navy.

[2] See Volume I, p. 423, note 2.

(a) Z7481, 7574/3725/17, WM(41)88. (b) Z7883/3725/17. (c) Z8037, 8038, 8084, 8133, 8187, 8188, 8189, 8190/3725/17. (d) WM(41)97, Z8281/8098/17. (e) Z8210, 8280/8098/17.

D

various constitutional and judicial considerations expressed in General de Gaulle's *ordonnance* and in the decrees establishing the Committee. In particular, Mr. Eden referred to a phrase referring to diplomatic representation; he pointed out that we could not accredit a diplomatic representative to General de Gaulle or receive such a representative accredited by him since in doing so we should be recognising him as head of a Sovereign State.

Although Mr. Eden did not publish his letter to General de Gaulle, he took the opportunity, in answer to a parliamentary question on November 26, to state the British attitude towards the Free French National Committee.[1] The British Government at this time also decided to give wider publicity throughout the Dominions as well as in Great Britain to the achievements and importance of the Free French, but the difficulties of relationship—almost inevitable in the special circumstances—were not removed by these changes in organisation.

At the end of the year 1941, while Mr. Churchill was in the United States, General de Gaulle unexpectedly took action which brought about a fresh crisis in his relations with the British and American Governments. The trouble arose over the islands of St. Pierre and Miquelon off the coast of Newfoundland. These islands were under the official jurisdiction of Admiral Robert, French Governor of Martinique, who was an obedient supporter of the Vichy Government. During November and December 1941 the British, Canadian and American Governments had been discussing (a) what to do about a powerful wireless station on St. Pierre which could be used to guide German submarines.

The British Government thought the best course would be to (b) allow Free French forces to take and control the islands. The United States Government refused to accept this plan, partly owing to their general policy of giving no cause of offence to Vichy, partly because they were pledged with the Latin American States to allow no transfer of sovereignty or of possession or control of territory in the western hemisphere.[2] In view of the American objections the British Government agreed that the Free French should not make a move against the islands. General de Gaulle understood the position, but disregarded it and ordered Admiral Muselier to land on the islands, arrest the Governor and rally the islanders to the Free French Movement.

Admiral Muselier, though not approving what he was told to do,

---

[1] *Parl. Deb.* 5th Ser., *H. of C.*, vol. 376, col. 727.
[2] The United States Government were willing to allow action by the Canadian Government to secure control of the wireless installations.

(a) Z8948, 10285, 10810/93/17. (b) Z10591, 10592, 10701/93/17.

carried out General de Gaulle's order on December 24. The British
Government immediately disclaimed responsibility for this breach
of faith on the part of General de Gaulle, but they now had to try (a)
to save the General from the consequences of his own mistake.
These consequences seemed at first likely to be extremely serious for
the Free French. Mr. Hull felt very strongly in the matter, and
issued a statement in which he referred to the action of three (b)
'so-called Free French ships'. A later explanation that 'so-called'
meant only 'supposedly belonging to the Free French' was not convincing, since there had never been any doubt about the identity of
the ships. It was now more difficult for General de Gaulle to withdraw from the islands, where the inhabitants had voted in favour of
joining the Free French, and for the British Government, especially
since they disagreed with Mr. Hull's views on the extent to which it
was expedient to conciliate the Vichy Government, to put pressure (c)
on General de Gaulle and to restore Vichy authority in the islands
at the expense of the supporters of the Free French. Mr. Hull went (d)
as far as a threat to turn out the Free French by force, but the
Foreign Office realised that British public opinion would be most
strongly opposed to any such action.

The Prime Minister discussed the matter with the President
during his visit to Washington. He suggested as a compromise that (e)
the British, United States and Canadian Governments should agree
to regard the islands as demilitarised and out of the war and to
withdraw from them all armed forces including the Free French.
The Vichy administrator would also be withdrawn, and the administration of the islands would be placed under a Consultative Council.
The Canadian and United States Governments would continue
economic assistance to the islands, and would send observers to
supervise the use of the wireless stations. The War Cabinet, however,
thought that the State Department greatly overrated the reaction of (f)
the Vichy Government and that, after the behaviour of the Vichy
authorities at Dakar and in Syria, it would seem incomprehensible to
British public opinion not to allow General de Gaulle to occupy
French territories which welcomed him. The War Cabinet therefore
agreed to an attempt to persuade General de Gaulle to accept the
proposed terms, but were unwilling to compel him to do so.

General de Gaulle at first refused to accept the proposal that the
islands should be regarded as out of the war. He said that he regarded (g)
it as an essential point of principle to bring French territory back
into the war, and that, if he made an exception in the case of St.
Pierre and Miquelon, he might be asked to treat other French
territories in a similar way.

(a) Z10885, 10947/93/17. (b) Z10885/93/17. (c) Z10940, 10956/93/17. (d) Z162, 275/3/17 (1942). (e) Z372/3/17. (f) WM(42)4, Z372/3/17. (g) Z521, 531/3/17.

(a) After discussion with Mr. Eden, however, General de Gaulle was willing to agree to a compromise on the lines suggested by the Prime Minister to Mr. Roosevelt. He asked for a secret understanding that the Free French Administrator should remain as a member of the Consultative Council; that the Council should be under the orders of the Free French National Committee, and that, although the French ships would be withdrawn, a detachment of Free French marines should stay in the island. The Prime Minister then agreed with President Roosevelt that on his return to England he should try to get General de Gaulle to drop his reservations.

(b) The Prime Minister saw General de Gaulle on January 22. He made it clear that the United States would not accept his suggestion that, in addition to a published arrangement about the islands, there should be a private agreement. The State Department, however, might acquiesce tacitly in some of the points raised by General de Gaulle, if he would raise them informally. After considerable argument, General de Gaulle agreed to recommend the Free French National Committee to drop the demand for a formal secret agreement.

(c) Nonetheless Mr. Hull, who apparently had not seen the terms agreed between the President and Mr. Churchill, objected to the compromise on the grounds that it would be unacceptable to the Vichy Government, and make it less possible for the United States to put pressure on Vichy to refuse more concessions to Germany. He said that Admiral Darlan had hinted that, unless the question of the islands was settled in a way satisfactory to the Vichy Government, American Consuls in France and observers in North Africa might be asked to leave and an arrangement might be made with the Japanese on the lines that they should occupy the French islands in the central Pacific.

(d) The War Cabinet thought that Mr. Hull was being unduly influenced by representations from Vichy.[1] Lord Halifax was instructed to point out that Mr. Hull was not taking sufficient account of American means of pressure on the Vichy Government. The United States, if necessary, could retaliate by occupying the French possessions in the West Indies, cutting off French trade with them, and seizing all the French gold. In fact the United States Government accepted the proposed compromise and the question of the islands receded into the background during the months in which much larger issues were being decided.

---

[1] Mr. Hull, however, spoke strongly to the French Ambassador in Washington on December 30 about the attitude of the Vichy Government. *F.R.U.S.*, 1941, II, 565–8.

(a) Z532, 521, 1186/3/17. (b) Z766, 786, 810, 854, 911/3/17. (c) Z923, 1063, 1257/3/17. (d) WM(42)17; Z1063/3/17.

CHAPTER XXII

The Far East in 1939-40

(i)

Relations with Japan and China at the outbreak of war in Europe.

IN September 1939 the Japanese had been at war[1] with China for more than two years. The war had become a test of endurance in which the Japanese were trying to cut off Chinese supplies from abroad and the Chinese were hoping to wear down the Japanese forces in the field and indirectly to break the internal economy of Japan. Each side could claim a certain measure of success. The Chinese armies, although ill-trained, badly equipped, and often badly led, were still in being, and could still win local successes. Chinese guerrillas harassed the Japanese everywhere and only a small minority of the population 'co-operated' with the 'puppet governments' under Japanese control. There was also 'unofficial' fighting between Japanese and Soviet forces in Outer Mongolia. In August 1939, the Soviet forces inflicted heavy losses on the Japanese in this region. An armistice was concluded at Moscow on September 15, but the Japanese High Command realised that their defeat had been due largely to the superiority of the Russian mechanised columns; they therefore wanted to spend money on the mechanisation of their army as an insurance against attack by Russia.

The economic situation of Japan, however, was already strained. The circulation of paper money at the end of 1939 was double that of 1937; the gold reserve had diminished. There were shortages of important manufactures and of consumer goods. During the latter part of 1939 the wholesale price of rice rose almost by a quarter. On July 26, 1939, the United States Government had given notice of termination in six months' time of the Commercial Agreement of 1911 with Japan; American-Japanese trade relations, which were far more important to Japan than to the United States, would therefore continue only on a 'good behaviour basis'. Thus the Japanese Government were looking for a way out of the war without loss of face. They could not have for long illusions about the puppet régimes which they were able to set up; they regarded them merely

---

[1] In fact, though not in name. Japan had never declared a state of war, and therefore, technically, and on her own interpretation, had not violated the Kellogg pact and her other engagements.

as a possible mode of extrication. In words attributed to Baron Shidehara, a former Minister of Foreign Affairs, 'how can Japan expect peace in China by shaking hands with herself there? It is China with whom she must shake hands.'

On the other hand, the Japanese had reason to think that the test of endurance might end in their favour. Their own people equalled the Chinese in capacity for self-sacrifice and surpassed them in readiness to accept the strongest discipline. Japanese armies occupied vast areas of China, and were, in fact, cutting off the Chinese sources of supply. The invasion of Kwangsi and the capture of Nanning in December 1939, brought the railway line between Yunnan and Indo-China within easy bombing range. In any case the European situation, even before the outbreak of war, made it unlikely that China could obtain munitions on a scale likely to change the military balance. Within the provinces still under the control of General Chiang Kai-shek the political and economic position was much worse than in Japan. The Kuomintang was not a united body; dependence upon Russian aid weakened the government in relation to the Communists. The mismanagement of the finances was an even greater source of public discontent; the Japanese might hope, therefore, that if they held on long enough, the Chinese Government would disintegrate or at least become so weak that it would be forced to accept terms which would give Japan a lasting hold in China.

Earlier in 1939 the Japanese Government, under pressure from the military extremists, had been considering whether they should accept the transformation of the Anti-Comintern pact into a military alliance. The Russo-German agreement for a time put an end to these proposals. This pact was so disconcerting a surprise to the Japanese that on August 28 the Government of Baron Hirahuma resigned, and General Abe formed a new Cabinet.

The change of ministers did not alter the policy of trying to end the war with China or suggest a *rapprochement* with Great Britain and France. There was indeed some support among the military extremists for an understanding with Russia as a means of getting British and other foreign influence out of China, but the conflict of interests between Russia and Japan was too serious to allow any real and lasting agreement between them. The Japanese might be willing to co-operate with Russia to the extent of supplying raw materials to Germany which would be used to weaken Great Britain; they were unlikely to lose their distrust of the Soviet Government or their fear of Communism. The Soviet Government were unlikely to give the Japanese a free hand in China or strengthen a possible enemy; Russian aid to China brought the Soviet Government a return out of proportion to its cost.

On the Chinese side a small party wanted neutrality towards the European belligerents or even an improvement of relations with Germany, but opinion generally was in favour of the Allies. If Great Britain and France could have provided China with the supplies which she was receiving from Russia, General Chiang Kai-shek would have been willing to declare war on Germany. The Allies could not provide these supplies, and did not wish to risk war with Japan. They did not expect Japan to take the initiative against them or against the Dutch East Indies (in the event of a German invasion of the Netherlands) while the war in China remained unsettled. The lead in Allied policy was taken by Great Britain; the aim of British policy was to restore friendly relations with Japan and to assist in a settlement with China which would not injure Chinese interests. Such a policy was, obviously, dictated by circumstances as well as by considerations of principle. British opinion would not have tolerated the abandonment of China; in any case an act of this kind would have lost American goodwill. On the other hand Great Britain could not fight Japan without American help. America was unprepared for war, politically and materially, and even if the military aid of the United States had been certain, the Allies needed American productive capacity for themselves in order to supplement their own armaments.

If, however, Great Britain was bound to attempt a 'middle' line, the chances of success for a policy of conciliation were slight. Japanese policy was likely to be cautious, but there would be the strongest pressure from the army, and from public opinion in general, to take advantage of the preoccupation of Great Britain (and, indirectly, of the United States) and to establish Japanese predominance in China so firmly that the victors in the European war could not overthrow it. Thus, at least until the issues in Europe were clear, Japan would not accept a settlement with China which left Chinese interests uninjured, and would not discontinue the 'step by step' methods of edging out all foreign influences.

The plan to secure a *fait accompli* in China, and, for this purpose, to extrude British influence, directed the first measures taken by the Japanese after the outbreak of war. The Japanese Government proclaimed their neutrality and also issued a statement that they would not intervene in the European war, but would concentrate upon ending the China 'incident'. In a note given to Sir R. Craigie (and to the representatives of other belligerent Powers) on September 5 the Japanese Government invited the belligerents not to do anything to prejudice the position of Japan in regard to China, and offered 'friendly advice' that they should withdraw their naval and military forces from parts of China occupied by the Japanese.[1] The

---

[1] *Documents on British Foreign Policy*, Ser. Vol. III, (IX H.M.S.O., 1955), Nos. 617–9. Hereafter referred to as *D.B.F.P.*

British land forces concerned were in Tientsin and Peking and in the International Settlement of Shanghai.[1] These garrisons had already been reduced; their withdrawal would take place in any event when the Sino-Japanese war had come to an end.

(a)   The War Cabinet thought it best to leave the Japanese 'advice' unanswered until they knew the views of the French and American Governments. President Roosevelt told Lord Lothian that the United States intended to keep American forces in the Far East, and hoped
(b) that we should do the same. In view of the American decision, the War Cabinet agreed on October 23 to leave a token force of a company, instead of a battalion, in Tientsin.

Apart from our attitude towards the Japanese 'friendly advice' we had to consider the possibility of settling serious outstanding differences at Tientsin. The actual questions in dispute at Tientsin concerned the surrender of certain Chinese nationals alleged to be guilty of terrorist acts against the Japanese, and the disposal of a large sum of silver lodged in Tientsin banks. The Chinese Government claimed that the silver belonged to them; the Japanese disputed their title. Since April 1939 these questions had become matters of great difficulty in Anglo-Japanese relations. The British refusal to comply with Japanese demands had led to a blockade of the British concession in Tientsin; the blockade was enforced with much hardship and British subjects were treated with indignity under the pretext of search for arms or for anti-Japanese documents. To some extent the personal maltreatment of individuals was due to the crude and overbearing habits of the local military authorities who would have shown a similar uncivilised arrogance towards their own countrymen. There was also some cause for complaint about the misuse (against the wishes of the British authorities) of the 'neutral' concession at Tientsin by Chinese terrorists. The real reason, however, for the persistence of the Japanese in magnifying small local disputes was that they dared not let their own people know the truth about the failure of their Chinese policy and that they were driven to use every method of placing the blame upon others. The foreign powers least able to retaliate were thus obvious scapegoats.

On the other hand, if the Japanese on general grounds found it worth while to improve their relations with Great Britain, there was nothing to prevent a settlement at least of these local issues. Before the outbreak of war in Europe, the British Government had agreed to hand over to the Japanese the alleged terrorists. They had also suggested that the silver should be sealed in a neutral bank until the

---

[1] These forces had been stationed at Peking and Tientsin since 1901, and at the International Settlement at Shanghai since 1927. The War Cabinet decided early in 1939 that the garrisons should be retained for the time being.

(a) WM(39)8, F10253/4027/61. (b) WM(39)57, F11242/3918/10.

end of the Chinese war. The Japanese would not accept this solution, and continued a violent anti-British campaign in their press.

The Russian attack on Finland increased Japanese suspicions oᵢ the Soviet Government and appeared likely to have a favourable effect upon Japanese willingness to end the Tientsin dispute. Sir R. Craigie, British Ambassador at Tokyo, believed, after informal con- (a) versations in Tokyo, that he could obtain agreement for a proposal to seal the silver in a neutral bank under joint Anglo-Japanese control and possibly to use some of it to relieve the suffering caused by recent floods in the province of Hopei. On December 4 the War Cabinet authorised instructions to Sir R. Craigie to reopen discussions on this basis, with the condition that the Japanese would also stop their anti-British activities.

(ii)

The Asama Maru *incident: Japanese reactions to the German attack on the Netherlands: signature of the Tientsin agreement.*

On January 14, 1940, General Abe's Cabinet fell, mainly because it had failed to meet the difficult economic situation. A new Government, under Admiral Yonai, took office with Mr. Arita as Foreign Minister. Sir R. Craigie described Mr. Arita as 'well known for anti-Soviet views, and, unlike some Japanese leaders . . . probably sincere with regard to the anti-Comintern pact, which he signed in the first place'. Mr. Arita himself, in a statement of foreign policy, (b) explained that the aims of the Government were two-fold; the 'disposal of the Chinese affair' and 'the readjustment of relations with third Powers'. He said that there was no change in the friendly relations between Japan, Germany and Italy; he hoped that these relations would become even closer, and that there would also be an improvement of Anglo-Japanese relations as a result of a British 'awakening'. This language did not imply a change in policy. The new Government was strong enough to meet a storm of patriotic excitement over the British exercise of belligerent rights at sea. A British warship stopped a Japanese ship, the *Asama Maru*, and took off 21 Germans travelling as passengers. All the Germans were technicians; 13 of them were ship's officers. On January 22 the (c) Japanese Vice-Minister for Foreign Affairs gave to Sir R. Craigie

---

(a) F12288, 12289, 12359, 12360/6457/10.   (b) F385/17/23; F435/66/23.   (c) W1205, 1220, 1253/31/49.

D*

a strong note of protest against this action. The Japanese Government maintained that a belligerent was entitled to take from a neutral ship only 'those actually embodied in the armed forces'. The British action was 'a great shock to public opinion in Japan', especially as it had occurred in waters near Japan.[1] The Japanese Government asked for the return of the 21 men.

In spite of the language of the note, and of an outburst of anti-British feeling in Japan, the Japanese Government seemed willing to accept a compromise settlement if their prestige were not affected.

(a) The War Cabinet therefore agreed to a proposal from the Foreign Office that we should offer to return some of the detained Germans if the Japanese would agree not to carry Germans of certain pre-scribed categories in their ships. After considerable bargaining over the number of Germans to be returned, the Japanese Government accepted this proposal.

The settlement of this dispute led to a certain reaction of opinion outside extremist circles. The Germans were not winning the war, and time did not appear to be on their side. It might therefore be in Japanese interests to back the more probable winners, and to use Anglo-American mediation to end the war in China while the Allies and the United States were likely to accept a settlement more favourable to them than would be the case after a German defeat. In March 1940, the Japanese inaugurated a new puppet government under Wang Ching-wei, a deserter from the Chinese Government at Chungking. Wang Ching-wei had no influential support, but it was not impossible that, in the course of time, the people of the occupied areas would accept his government. For the time, however, the Japanese themselves found Wang Ching-wei unexpectedly difficult in his negotiations for a treaty of peace; throughout the spring and early summer they seem to have made indirect overtures to General Chiang Kai-shek. These overtures failed; the Japanese then extended their attacks. On June 11 they took Ichang. Their bombers were thus within 320 miles of Chungking; the Chinese army supply routes were disorganised and the import of oil through Ningpo was cut off.

Meanwhile the heavy defeats of the Allies in Europe had given a new turn to Japanese opinion. At first, during the German successes in Scandinavia, Japanese policy remained cautious. When a German invasion of the Netherlands appeared probable, the Japanese

---

[1] Off Cape Noshima within 35 miles of the Japanese coast.

(a) W1397/31/49; WM(40)22, W1443/31/49; WM(40)23, W1470/31/49; W1467, 1537, 1547, 1643, 1644, 1709/31/49; WM(40)28, W1811/31/49; WM(40)29, W1920/31/49; W1806, 1862, 1864, 1944/31/49; WM(40)32, W2062/31/49; WM(40)33, W2106/31/49; W1960, 2060, 2061/31/49.

Government announced that the interests of Japan required the maintenance of the *status quo* in the Dutch East Indies. Since Mr. Cordell Hull spoke on similar lines about American interests to the (a) press in the United States, the Foreign Office thought it unnecessary for Great Britain to make any statement. They suggested, however, that the United States Naval Attaché in London might be told (in answer to an informal approach on his part) that, if the United States Government should order the American fleet to the Philippines, all facilities at Singapore would be open to them.

After the Germans had invaded the Netherlands the Japanese Government showed some concern over the British action in sending (b) forces to the Dutch West Indies.[1] The Foreign Office issued a statement that Great Britain had no intention of changing the status of the Dutch colonies and authorised the Dutch Foreign Minister to assure the Japanese that we should not interfere with their oil supplies from the Dutch East Indies. These assurances seemed to satisfy the Japanese Government; at all events Mr. Arita repeated previous statements that Japan intended to remain neutral.

The Japanese Ambassador stated on June 11 that there would be no change in the policy of 'non-involvement' even if there were a new government in Japan. The Japanese would therefore leave the Dutch East Indies alone, since otherwise the war would spread to the Pacific. He suggested that we might possibly enter upon wider conversations about the question of peace in the Far East, and said that the Japanese Government had 'greatly modified their ambitions in China'. He agreed, however, that there was not yet sufficient basis for any conversations.

The Tientsin agreement was finally concluded during this period of Japanese hesitation. It was initialled on June 12 and signed six days later.[2] The terms of the agreement were that £100,000 worth of the silver coin and bullion in dispute should be employed for famine relief in north China and that the remainder of the sum should remain under joint Anglo-Japanese seal in the Bank of Communications in Tientsin. In other circumstances the settlement of this local dispute might have been regarded as a favourable sign. Within a week, however, there was a rapid change for the worse.

---

[1] See Volume I, p. 336.
[2] The agreement was arrived at with the knowledge and consent of the Chungking Government.

(a) F2828/2739/61. (b) F3264/66/23.

(iii)

Japanese reactions to the collapse of France: demands for the closing of the Burma Road: the Anglo-Japanese agreement of July 17, 1940: Chinese protests against the agreement.

It was indeed hard to expect the Japanese military party to continue a policy of caution after the collapse of France. Hitherto the extremist sections of the army had been held in check to some extent by the aristocracy, the capitalists and the intelligentsia. Japan had remained at least in name a democratic state; she was not wholly committed to the Axis Powers. The extremists now claimed that events had justified all their forecasts. They expected the collapse of Great Britain to follow that of France; they also regarded the military defeats of the Allies as proof of the failure of democratic institutions and suggested that the internal troubles of Japan were due to those very weaknesses which had been fatal to democracy in Europe. There was no time to be lost. If Japan were to extend and even to retain her position in Asia she must abandon the way of liberalism and remodel Japanese institutions on totalitarian lines. Meanwhile, although it was still necessary to avoid war with the United States, there was no longer any reason for delaying drastic action against Great Britain. On the other hand, from the Japanese point of view there appeared to be some danger that unless Japan came into the war on the Axis side Germany might dictate peace in Europe, and dispose of the Dutch East Indies and other Asiatic possessions of the defeated Powers, without reference to Japanese interests.

The first demands were made bluntly and with menace through a military channel, and were then presented more politely by the Japan-
(a) ese Foreign Office. Sir R. Craigie reported on June 19 a statement to the British Military Attaché by the Director of Military Intelligence that the hostility of Great Britain towards Japanese aspirations in China had driven Japan to the side of Germany. The overwhelming majority of the Japanese people, and especially the fighting forces, were anti-British. With the collapse of France and the powerlessness of Great Britain in the Far East, the Japanese felt that 'they would earn the obloquy of their descendants' if they did not seize the opportunity offered to them. There was nothing to prevent them from occupying French Indo-China, the Netherlands East Indies and Hong Kong. The United States could not stop them from taking any action they pleased. Hence Great Britain now had her last chance. The Japanese military authorities would insist upon a declaration of war unless Great Britain complied at once with

(a) F3432/23/23.

requests for closing the Burma-Chinese frontier and the frontier at Hong Kong, and for withdrawal of British troops from Shanghai. On the following day, Mr. Arita said that this message from the (a) General Staff need not be taken too seriously and that any communication would be made through himself. He had intended to raise the matters discussed by the military representative, but the substance of his communication would be entirely different.

In effect Mr. Arita made the same demands. He was more polite (b) about them; he admitted that Japan had no legal case for asking that the Burma Road should be closed, but he explained that, if the road were not closed, he would be unable to control the Japanese extremists. This argument was not mere bluff; the military party at this time seem to have hoped for a British refusal which would have given Japan a pretext for war.

It was impossible to answer these demands at once. The War Cabinet were fully occupied with the critical situation resulting from the French collapse. In any case they could not decide upon their policy without consulting the Dominions and the United States. They had already agreed that it would be advisable to try to induce the United States Government to announce that they would not tolerate an attempt to change the *status quo* in the Far East or the Pacific. Lord Lothian was instructed on June 18 to put this proposal (c) to the United States Government. We would leave the terms of the announcement to the United States, but these terms would have to be of wide application if they were to deter Japan. There was a danger that the Japanese might bring about the return of Indo-China to China by handing it over to the puppet Government of Wang Ching-wei. On June 19, after hearing from Sir R. Craigie of the (d) Japanese military demands, the Foreign Office telegraphed to Lord Lothian that an American declaration was even more urgent.

On the night of June 20–1 Sir R. Craigie was instructed to bring (e) forward in discussion with the Japanese Ministry for Foreign Affairs the argument that Germany was trying to get Japan into war with America and obviously hoped that this result would come about through Japanese action in territories outside China. German assurances that Japan would recover and retain her share of the spoils of a common victory were worthless. Germany really wanted Japan to be weakened by a war with the democracies. Furthermore the stoppage of all communications between the democracies and the National Government of China would drive General Chiang Kai-shek into dependence upon Russia. The Russians would take full advantage of this situation to the detriment of Japan.

(a) F3432/23/23. (b) F3479/43/10. (c) C7278/65/17. (d) F3432/23/23. (e) F3432/23/23.

(a)   On June 21 Lord Halifax used similar arguments with the Japanese Ambassador. The Ambassador tried to minimise the importance of the General Staff statement. He repeated the Japanese complaint that we were not neutral towards their war in China as they were neutral in the European war, but he said once again that the Japanese Government would continue their policy of keeping
(b) out of the European war and trying to get peace with China. Sir R. Craigie telegraphed on June 22 that our arguments did not carry weight with the extremists. The latter thought that Japan would be able to hold in permanence any territory which she might seize and that General Chiang Kai-shek's position would be untenable if he lost all seaborne sources of supply. They also thought the United States unable to do anything effective to oppose a further Japanese advance in the Pacific area.

On June 25 Lord Lothian was instructed to explain the position to
(c) the United States Government. In our view the American policy of refusing to negotiate a new trade treaty with Japan and of withholding supplies would no longer be effective. Japanese pressure was being exerted solely against Great Britain and France. This pressure was now severe enough to weaken our position in the West; since we could not carry on a war in both spheres alone and unaided, it was surely in the interests of the United States to try to prevent an attack on us in the Far East. We therefore considered that two courses of action were open to the United States: they could risk war by establishing a full economic embargo against Japan or by sending ships to Singapore, or they could try to keep Japan from aggression by reaching agreement on the lines that the United States would assist in bringing about a peace with China based on a restoration of Chinese independence and territory. Japan would undertake to remain neutral in the European war and to respect the integrity of British, French, American and Dutch possessions in the Far East; the question of the future status of settlements and concessions in China would be left temporarily in abeyance. In return for these promises by Japan, the United States and the members of the British Commonwealth would give Japan all possible financial assistance now and in the period of post-war reconstruction. Meanwhile the War Cabinet had to decide on a reply to the Japanese demands. The most difficult problem was that of the Burma Road. We wanted to refuse the Japanese demand that the road should be closed. We had to recognise that they could enforce the demand, and that most of the traffic on the road was American.[1] Were we to incur American

---

[1] The so-called 'Burma Road' ran from Lashio, the terminus of the railway running north from Rangoon, to Kunming in the Chinese province of Yunnan. Only about a sixth of the road was in Burmese territory.

(a) F3432/23/23. (b) F3432/23/23. (c) F3465/23/23.

and Chinese displeasure by closing the road, or could we face without American support the consequences of refusing to close it? We should resist to the best of our powers if we had to fight in the Far East, but the United States Government already knew how slender our resources were, and what would be the effect upon operations in Europe of the severance of communications and loss of shipping and supplies resulting from war in the Far East. Finally, if the alternative of conciliation were adopted, the weakness of our position made it undesirable for us to take the initiative.[1]

Owing to mischance this telegram did not reach Lord Lothian until June 26. He then saw the Australian Minister, and arranged to (a) go with him to see Mr. Hull on the morning of June 27. Lord Lothian left with Mr. Hull an *aide-mémoire* on the lines of his instructions. Mr. Hull promised an early answer. He gave Lord Lothian a written reply in the afternoon of June 28 to the effect that the United States (b) Government could not accept either of the alternatives submitted to them. Mr. Hull thought that they had gone as far as possible in their attempts to restrain Japan by diplomatic pressure and economic threats and by keeping the American main fleet in the Pacific. They might have to move the fleet to the Atlantic; it was therefore impossible for them to do anything which might involve them in war with Japan. They had also been exploring continuously the possibility of a general settlement in the Far East; their information showed, however, that the Japanese leaders felt confident of their opportunity and that they would pursue their objectives wherever they were not actually stopped by material opposition. Hence they could not be 'weaned away' from aggression.

Mr. Hull therefore fell back on the view that it was better to acquiesce in retreats under *force majeure* in the expectation of the turn of the tide, while refusing surrenders which would be irrevocable. He suggested that perhaps the British Government might care to explore on their own initiative the possibility of a settlement with Japan. The United States Government would welcome such a settlement on terms acceptable to China and consistent with their own principles.

Lord Lothian told Mr. Hull that we realised that we could not by our sole action resist Japanese moves to cut off supplies to China through Hong Kong, Indo-China and, probably, the Burma Road. If the United States also could not go to war, was it not better for China that the United States and Great Britain should try to get a settlement even though it meant concessions of a non-fundamental

---

[1] Since the Governments of the Commonwealth of Australia and New Zealand were concerned in the matter, Lord Lothian was instructed to associate the Australian Minister at Washington with his action.

(a) F3465/23/23. (b) F3465/23/23.

kind to Japan? Mr. Hull said that hitherto all suggestions for compromise had been at the expense of China. If we could sugggest other
proposals, the United States Government would be willing to
consider them, although for political reasons it would be easier for
them to conduct parallel rather than joint negotiations.

(a)   In view of this American reply the Foreign Office drew up on
June 29 a memorandum for the War Cabinet on the Japanese
demands. The memorandum explained that the United States would
promise diplomatic but not armed support if we kept our garrisons
in China. We had asked the United States Government whether
they would take the initiative in proposing a general settlement in
the Far East, but so far they were unwilling to do so, since they did
not think the Japanese in a mood to give up their policy of aggression.
Lord Lothian considered that the United States would not use force
in defence of British or French interests in the Far East or indeed in
defence of anything west of Hawaii.

The memorandum dealt with the three Japanese demands as
follows: (i) The garrisons at Tientsin and Peking had already been
reduced.[1] The complete withdrawal of the garrisons would be unwelcome to the Chinese but was not an essential matter for them.
We might therefore agree to withdrawal if the Italian garrison at
Shanghai were also withdrawn and if we were assured that British
lives and property would be respected and that the Japanese would
not attempt to alter the terms of the Concession at Shanghai except
in consultation with the parties concerned. (ii) The Japanese had
cut off Hong Kong from direct access to China in January 1939. It
was not clear what they were asking us to do. They might be thinking
of the entrepôt trade or of the presence of certain Chinese customs
officers in Hong Kong. (iii) The closing of the Burma Road would
cut the last main route of communication to China other than the
Sinkiang route from Siberia. The supplies carried on the Burma
Road were mostly American; they amounted only to 21,965 metric
tons in 1939. The political effect of closing the road, however, might
be much greater than the actual economic effect. General Chiang
Kai-shek might even be compelled to come to terms with Japan or
to rely on Russia. Our action would affect opinion in the United
States adversely and reduce the chances of an American embargo
on the export of war supplies to Japan. Sir R. Craigie, who was
strongly in favour of giving way to the Japanese demand, thought
nevertheless that other demands would follow.

(b)   The War Cabinet agreed in general on July 1 with these conclusions. They considered the possibility of rationing supplies on the

---

[1] See above, p. 88.

(a) WP(40)234, F3444/23/23. (b) WM(40)189 , F3444/23/23.

Burma Road at the level attained during the past twelve months. They also decided to consult the Governments of Australia and New Zealand. The War Cabinet considered the matter again on July 5. Meanwhile the Chiefs of Staff had submitted a memorandum that, (a) in their view, we were not in a position to hold out against the Japanese demands and that it was of the utmost importance to avoid war with Japan at a time when we were unable to send a fleet to the Far East. Sir R. Craigie had also repeated his views about the risk (b) of a refusal to close the road and the Secretary of State for Burma had pointed out the impracticability of rationing supplies, since this plan would lead to difficulties with the exporters, most of whom were American.[1]

The general view of the War Cabinet was against taking action which might involve us in war with Japan. If, however, we had to (c) accept the Japanese demand for the closure of the road, it would be better to do so on the basis of yielding to *force majeure*. Lord Halifax, however, proposed trying to see how far the Japanese really intended to push their demand. The War Cabinet agreed that Sir R. Craigie should be told to gain as much time as possible in exploring with the Japanese the reasons for all their demands, and the chances of reaching a settlement without full acceptance of these demands.

On July 6 therefore Sir R. Craigie was instructed to make no reply (d) for the moment on the question of the garrisons except to say that the local commanders were making arrangements which would avoid incidents. On the question of Hong Kong Sir R. Craigie was to point out that the Japanese demands appeared to have been met. On the Burma Road he would explain that the traffic figures did not support the view that this route of supply was contributing much to Chinese military resources. For some time past little material from Great Britain had been carried; a change in this respect was unlikely. We therefore could not agree that the supply of war material by Great Britain to the Chinese National Government was a direct cause of the prolongation of hostilities.

We did not understand the basis upon which the Japanese were asking for the stoppage of supplies of oil, lorries, and railway material. Some of these commodities came from Burma, and, as far as the Burma Road was a legitimate trade route, we could not take action contrary to our obligations to the Burmese and Indian peoples. Other goods passing over the route into China came from third Powers and, if the trade of these Powers were not to be dislocated, the stoppage of supplies should be made at the source. If we complied

---

[1] Owing to the interlocking marketing arrangements between the oil companies, the position with regard to oil was especially complicated.

(a) WP(40)249, F3565/23/23. (b) F3544/43/10; WP(40)242, F3565/23/23. (c) WM(40) 194, F3565/23/23. (d) WM(40)195, F3565/23/23; F3544/43/10.

with the Japanese request, we should be departing from neutrality
and discriminating against China. In strict neutrality a decision to
cut off materials from China would also involve cutting off supplies
to Japan, but we had no intention of doing this. On the other hand
we had been trying to get Japanese assent to the stoppage of certain
supplies to Germany; the Japanese Government had refused any agreement except in regard to the re-export of certain goods purchased in
the British Empire and had also been unwilling even to discuss the
limitation of the export via Siberia of goods produced in Japan and
Manchukuo.

For all three reasons we could not close the Burma Road, but we
were anxious to see the termination of the dispute with China in 'a
just and equitable peace acceptable to both parties' and to this end
were ready to offer our co-operation.

Sir R. Craigie was told to add that our reply was friendly and left
the way open for counter-suggestions from the Japanese Government. We were willing to meet the latter on questions which seemed
in our view of greater importance to them. Thus we had shown our
desire to understand and make provision for Japanese economic needs.

(a)   Before the War Cabinet considered the question again the Foreign
Office submitted, on July 9, another memorandum giving reasons
for thinking that the alternative to yielding to the Japanese demands
would not necessarily be 'total war' with Japan. (i) The Japanese
could not be sure that the United States would not come to our
assistance. (ii) The Japanese army and a portion of the navy were
occupied in China. (iii) In the event of war Japan would lose all
trade with the British Empire except in territories which she could
seize: she might also have to meet an American embargo. (iv) The
Japanese extremists were unlikely to give up the cautious methods
of 'probing' for weak points, amd withdrawing if resistance were
offered. The reaction to a refusal to close the Burma Road would
probably be in the first instance something in the nature of a
blockade of Hong Kong, and renewed pressure on our economic
interests in China. More forcible action would develop slowly, if at all.

The effect upon China of a decision to close the road would be
most unfavourable. Material supplies, especially from the United
States of America, helped to maintain Chinese resistance, but our
own moral support was even more important. The closing of the
road would appear as a withdrawal of this support and would lead
either to a great increase in Russian influence or to peace with
Japan at the expense of foreign interests. In either case the attitude
of China towards Great Britain would become very hostile. The
United States Government might understand our action; American

(a) WP(40)256, F3565/23/23.

public opinion, which was of particular importance in the pre-election period, would be critical of us, and therefore less disposed to help us. If we gave way on the Burma Road, we should certainly get other demands from the Japanese which it would be more difficult and more humiliating to concede. The Foreign Office thus continued to think that we ought not to give way at least until we had tried to bring about a comprehensive settlement in the Far East.

Sir R. Craigie, on the other hand, thought that there was a real (a) danger of Japanese entry into the war, and that any means of countering such a move would have to be immediate. Mr. Arita wrote to Sir R. Craigie on July 9 that our latest offer was unacceptable; the Japanese Government intended to insist on the closing of the road and further delay might have deplorable effects on Anglo-Japanese relations. Sir R. Craigie suggested to the Foreign Office that we might agree to suspend the transport of war material on the road for three months (i.e. during the rainy season) on the understanding that during this time special efforts would be made to bring about a 'just and equitable peace' in the Far East. If these efforts failed, His Majesty's Government would be free to reopen the road to war material at the end of the three months.

On July 10 the War Cabinet agreed to this suggestion. Sir R. (b) Craigie was therefore instructed that, although we preferred a system of limitation on the basis of the traffic of the previous year, we were prepared to negotiate on the lines of his proposal for a three months' closure of the road to war material. The United States and Chinese Governments were also informed of our action.

The Japanese Government accepted Sir R. Craigie's plan on (c) July 12, though they tried to secure the omission of any public reference to the fact that the closure was for three months only. In the agreement finally reached on July 17 the Government of Burma, at the instance of His Majesty's Government in the United Kingdom, promised to suspend for a period of three months beginning on July 18 the transit through Burma to China of arms, ammunition, lorries, railway material, and petrol other than that required by lorries transporting non-prohibited goods to China, and by aircraft operating the Rangoon–Chungking air mail service. Export of arms and ammunition from Hong Kong had been prohibited since January 1939; none of the war material to which the Japanese Government attached importance was being exported. The categories of material prohibited in Burma were also to be prohibited in Hong Kong.

In a confidential memorandum His Majesty's Government stated that they were making these arrangements on the express condition

---

(a) F3569/43/10. (b) WM(40)199, F3565/23/23; F3569/43/10. (c) F3584, 3597, 3606, 3617, 3943/43/10.

that during the period of three months special efforts would be made to bring about a just and equitable peace in the Far East. At the end of the period His Majesty's Government would remain free to continue or discontinue the closing of the road according to the conditions of the time. The Japanese Foreign Minister on his part stated that the Japanese Government had made, and would make every effort to bring about a peace of the kind desired by His Majesty's Government.

The terms of the agreement were announced on July 18;[1] the text of the confidential memorandum was communicated by the Foreign Office only to the United States Government. On the same (a) day the Prime Minister sent a personal and confidential message to General Chiang Kai-shek: 'I am sure you understand our action about the Burma Road only too well. We shall never press you to any peace against your interests or your policy.'

The Prime Minister's message was not enough in itself to convince the Chinese National Government or to prevent the dismay of Chinese opinion over the closing of the road, and the reasons which had dictated British policy were less understood in China than in the United States. In June the French had given way to Japanese demands for the closing of the Indo-China–Yunnan railway. Thus, apart from the uncertain help of the U.S.S.R., the closing of the Burma Road meant that the Chinese armies were practically isolated from outside supply. On July 16 both the Chinese Ministry of (b) Foreign Affairs and General Chiang Kai-shek had issued statements on the question of the Burma Road. General Chiang Kai-shek stated that he did not believe that Great Britain would do anything contrary to international law, and that to link the Burma Road issue with the question of peace would amount in practice to assisting Japan to bring China to submission. In so doing Great Britain would lose Chinese friendship and also sacrifice her own position in the (c) Far East. On July 17 Mr. Broadmead, Chargé d'affaires at Chung-king, was told by Mr. Han Li Wu,[2] that there could be no question

---

[1] The announcement on the British side was made in the House of Commons in answer (d) to a question by private notice. See below, pp. 101–2. On July 16 Mr. Hull described the closing of the Burma Road as an unwarranted interposition of obstacles to world trade. This statement was the more surprising since Mr. Hull had known of the line we were about to take and had agreed that the United States Government had no cause for complaint since they were unwilling to take a hand in Far Eastern affairs.

[2] Secretary-General of the Sino-British Cultural Association. Mr. Han Li Wu was one of the few men in General Chiang Kai-shek's confidence, and acted as a liaison between the General and the British Embassy. In answer to a question what would happen if the Burma Road were not reopened after three months, Mr. Wu said that the Chinese had enough small arms ammunition to last for a year, but that they needed eighteen months' supply in order to maintain the morale of the army in six months' time when otherwise supplies would begin to run out.

(a) F3617/43/10. (b) F3617/43/10. (c) F3617/43/10. (d) F3606/43/10.

of a secret meeting between a Chinese and a Japanese representative to discuss the general lines of peace. Such a meeting would become known and would have a bad effect on Chinese morale. It would be necessary to use an intermediary, and if the British Government were to act as such the association of the United States would be desirable. General Chiang Kai-shek refused at present to consider mediation.

The Chinese authorities continued their protests. The Prime Minister explained the position personally to the Chinese Ambassador (a) on July 25. Mr. Quo asked what would happen after the three months' period had expired. The Prime Minister said that our action must depend upon the situation three months hence, and that he could make no forecast. He repeated the assurance given to General Chiang Kai-shek that we should put no pressure on him 'to consent to terms or negotiations against his will and policy.'

On July 29 General Chiang Kai-shek replied to the Prime (b) Minister's message as follows:

'I appreciate your kind and reassuring message. I feel confident that China's interests will not be sacrificed under your premiership, who know better than anybody else what we are fighting for. I understand your difficulties, but the policy of appeasing Japan is, as I have said on several occasions, dangerous to the British Empire. Only with a victorious and independent China can British interests in the Far East be preserved. I therefore most earnestly urge you to reopen the Burma route for your own as well as for our benefit.'

Two days later Mr. Quo presented a memorandum from the (c) Chinese Government to the effect that, since the closure of the Burma Road was 'admittedly contrary to international law and the provision of Sino-British treaties, the rule of strict interpretation should be applied in the definition of the five classes of goods' coming within the temporary restrictions of traffic.

(iv)

Consideration of British policy towards the Konoye Government in Japan: question of reopening the Burma Road (July 18–September 18, 1940).

In announcing the agreement to the House of Commons the Prime (d) Minister spoke of the wish of His Majesty's Government to 'see assured to China a free and independent future' as well as 'to improve our relations with Japan'. To achieve these objectives two things were essential—time and a relief of tension. On the one hand

---

(a) F3657/43/10. (b) F3657/43/10. (c) F3657/43/10. (d) F3617/43/10.

it was clear that the tension was rapidly growing owing to the Japanese complaints of the passage of war material by the Burma route. 'On the other hand, to agree to the permanent closure of the route would be to default from our obligations as a neutral friendly Power to China. What we have therefore made is a temporary arrangement in the hope that the time so gained may lead to a solution just and equitable to both parties to the dispute, and freely accepted by them both. . . .'

The initiative in the discussion of peace terms thus rested with Japan, but the chances of reaching a settlement were lessened by the fall of the Japanese Government at the moment when the agreement was signed. A new Government representing more definitely the views of the pro-Axis party took office under Prince Konoye, and Mr. Matsuoka succeeded Mr. Arita as Minister for Foreign Affairs.[1]

(a)   On July 27 Sir R. Craigie called on Mr. Matsuoka. He quoted Mr. Churchill's speech in the House of Commons as evidence of the wish of His Majesty's Government to continue friendly methods of settling outstanding disputes with Japan. Mr. Matsuoka gave a guarded answer that the new Cabinet was considering the whole question of Japanese policy and that he could say nothing about it until these deliberations were completed. He reminded Sir R. Craigie of a conversation several months earlier in which he had said that on his return from Geneva he had realised that Japan could no longer remain isolated. He had therefore strongly advocated the conclusion with Germany of an agreement which later took the form of the anti-Comintern pact. He had then stated that he hoped for the accession of Great Britain as a third party to this pact, but 'fate had decreed otherwise'. There was now little choice:

> 'Scientific inventions which were completely changing war and industry forced peoples like Japan into new paths, and it was useless to seek to arrest, by antiquated diplomatic methods, terrific impulses which such peoples were obeying. The fundamental difficulty between our two countries was that, while Japan was determined—and in fact compelled by circumstances—to set up a new order in the Far East, Great Britain was resisting these new tendencies with every means at her command and would only yield a modicum of ground from time to time when forced by circumstances. . . . It was therefore difficult to see how this fundamental clash of interests and purpose could be avoided.'

Sir R. Craigie pointed out that Mr. Matsuoka was ruling out methods of friendly discussion before they had been tried, and that

---

[1] Prince Konoye had been Prime Minister at the time of the Japanese invasion of China in July 1937: Mr. Matsuoka had been the leading Japanese delegate at Geneva in 1933, at the time of the Japanese withdrawal from the League of Nations.

(a) F3671/23/23.

'the alternative of the application of force was so dangerous for everyone, including Japan', that every other way of settlement should first be tried. At the end of the conversation Sir R. Craigie put certain points which he regarded as relevant to the deliberations of the Japanese Cabinet. He said that Great Britain would win the war; 'the Japanese Cabinet would make a fatal mistake if they based their calculation on any other assumption'. Furthermore, Great Britain was not unwilling to see changes in the world as long as they were not brought about by force. Hence there was room for a general Anglo-Japanese settlement, particularly in the economic field, which would take account of mutual needs and avoid any clash of principle.

On August 1, 1940, the new Japanese Government issued an announcement on national policy.[1] The announcement began by (a) explaining that the world stood 'at a great historic turning point' and was 'about to witness the creation of new forms of government, economy, and culture, based upon the growth and development of sundry groups of States'. It was therefore essential for Japan to 'grasp the inevitable trends in the development of world history, effect speedily fundamental renovations along all lines of government, and strive for the perfection of a state structure for national defence'. Then followed a summary of the 'renovations' which were required in Japanese domestic and foreign policy. In the latter field the aims of Japan were described as 'ultimately . . . the construction of a new order in Greater East Asia', and 'first of all . . . a complete settlement of the China affair'.[2]

Mr. Matsuoka also made a statement on August 1 that the 'mission of Japan' was to proclaim and demonstrate the *Kodo* throughout the world. The *Kodo*, or 'Imperial Way' meant 'a great East Asian chain of common prosperity with the Japan-Manchukuo-China groups as one of the links'.

Behind this verbiage there was a clear warning of another step in Japanese policy. 'East Asia' had become 'great' or 'greater' Asia; the ideograph used in the Japanese version of Mr. Matsuoka's statement might mean 'great, 'greater' or even 'greatest'. The term now appeared to include the Netherlands East Indies. Japan assumed not merely the military success of the totalitarian states but the failure of democratic ideas and methods everywhere. The programme of the government was a 'total' adaptation to the new

---

[1] A copy of this announcement was given—in Japanese—to the Foreign Office by the Japanese Embassy, with an English version of the statement by Mr. Matsuoka.
[2] Mr. Arita had made a statement on June 29 in somewhat similar terms. He said that the destiny of regions of East Asia and the South Seas, 'any development in them, and the disposal of them, is a matter of grave concern to Japan in view of her mission and responsibility as a stabilizing force in East Asia'.

(a) F3552/66/23.

conditions. The proposed changes were immense. They meant more than the suppression of all that remained of a liberal parliamentary régime. Seventy to eighty per cent of Japanese foreign trade was with the United States and the British Empire; it was therefore necessary to recast the whole structure of Japanese economy to fit the framework of a 'self-sufficient' *bloc* in the China-South East Asia area under the control of Japan. Moreover, once the policy of avoiding definite commitments to the Axis had been given up, there could be no 'reinsurance'. The logical consequence of Mr. Matsuoka's policy was the 'tripartite pact' of September 27 with Germany and Italy;[1] a treaty concluded on the assumption of the defeat of Great Britain at the very time when in the west the Battle of Britain had shown that a German victory was very far from certain.

The significance of this turn in Japanese policy was realised at once by the Foreign Office, although they expected no immediate (a) move. In a telegram of August 19 Sir R. Craigie gave his view that internally the movement for more totalitarian control was likely to succeed. The prestige of the extremists had gained from the French collapse. There had been a violent swing of popular sentiment towards the Axis, and the moderates had lost all influence. Hence it was probably useless for us, unless we could secure full American support, to continue the conciliatory policy by which we had tried to strengthen the moderate party. We should now have to face the extremists although these latter would probably not risk an open breach with the United States and ourselves until the China incident had been settled or the Axis Powers had won more successes. In a despatch[2] of which this telegram was a summary, Sir R. Craigie (b) wrote that as long as we had to depend on our own resources and could count only on the moral support of the United States, our policy should be 'to fight a rearguard action giving away as little as possible until the stage is reached where really vital interests are threatened. . . . Any further attack by Japan against British interests should be met with resistance and retaliation in so far as they can be effectively employed.' The absence of a really strong reaction to the recent arrests of Japanese subjects in British territory[3] had shown that as yet the Japanese Government were not prepared to go to extreme lengths.

The Chiefs of Staff agreed generally with Sir R. Craigie that the (c) Japanese would probably limit themselves to their customary policy

---

[1] See below, section (v).

[2] The despatch was sent by bag on August 6 and received on September 20.

[3] These arrests were made at the end of July in retaliation for the arrest of 16 British subjects in Japan on trumped-up charges of espionage.

(a) F3970/66/23. (b) F4320/66/23. (c) WP(40)302, 308; WM(40)222; F3765/193/61.

of a cautious advance 'step by step' until they saw more clearly the position in Europe. Japan could not stand the economic strain of a long war with the British Commonwealth and the United States since she depended on these countries for markets and raw materials. In a survey of August 7 the Chiefs of Staff estimated that Japan had at least six months' supply of all raw materials essential for military purposes. After six months the problem of replenishing stocks, and the general disorganisation of the Japanese economy, even with the Netherlands East Indies in Japanese possession, would create increasing difficulties which might lead to commercial ruin and very serious social repercussions at the end of twelve months.

Nevertheless, even if the Japanese did not at once make a grand attack, their ultimate aim was certain. If they were to exclude western influences from the Far East and to control Far Eastern resources of raw material, they must hold Singapore. Herein lay the critical factor for Great Britain. In a consideration of British military policy in the summer of 1937 it had been assumed that any threat (a) to Singapore would be seaborne, and that within a period of three months from the outbreak of war we should have been able to send to the Far East a fleet of sufficient strength to protect the Dominions and India and to cover our communications in the Indian Ocean. In the summer and autumn of 1940 it was impossible to spare a fleet for the Far East, and the assumption that Malaya would be threatened only from the sea was no longer valid. All we could hope for was to play for time and to cede nothing until we were compelled to do so. In the last resort we could try to retain a foothold from which we might retrieve the position when our forces were stronger.[1]

It was then clear during the first three weeks of August that the Japanese Government were not likely to be willing even to discuss a settlement with China of a kind acceptable to Great Britain. On the other hand they tried to give the agreement about the Burma Road a wider interpretation than was justified by the terms. They asked (b) that goods in Hong Kong addressed to the Chinese Government should not be forwarded even to Rangoon: an official of the Japanese Ministry of Foreign Affairs sent to Rangoon suggested that goods which under the terms of the agreement could not be carried on the road should not be sent into the interior of Burma, and that an alleged anti-Japanese movement among the Chinese in Burma should be suppressed. The Japanese also continued their policy of minor attacks upon British prestige and interests in the Far East.

(c) [1] On August 6 the War Cabinet decided, subject to the views of the Dominion Governments, to withdraw the two British battalions at Shanghai, and the smaller detachments elsewhere in North China.

(a) COS 551 (1937). (b) F3631, 3657, 3954, 3992, 4003/43/10. (c) WM(40)220, F3722/16/10.

(a)   The Foreign Office therefore thought it necessary towards the end of August to raise the question of British policy at the expiry of the three months' period. Lord Lothian discussed the matter in a tele-
(b) gram of August 21. In his view the world position would have changed by the middle of October if we had won the Battle of Britain and Hitler had failed to invade the country or to establish an effective blockade. Our prestige in the Far East would have increased; the Japanese would realise that during the winter months, and as new ships became available, we could reinforce Singapore. It would also be clear that the United States would not be compelled to take their fleet from the Pacific into the Atlantic. Lord Lothian therefore thought that we should open the Burma Road if we could get sufficient American support. During the period of the elections the United States Government could not enter into commitments which might involve war but they still had formidable means of economic pressure.

The Foreign Office considered that Lord Lothian had over-simplified the position. The Middle East situation might be the more serious factor in October. In any case, however, we should prepare the way for a refusal to renew the agreement with Japan in October.
(c) A Foreign Office memorandum for the Cabinet on September 2 suggested that we should emphasise, both in Tokyo and to the Japanese Embassy and Japanese correspondents in London, the temporary nature of our agreement and the fact that it was not unconditional but required the fulfilment of an obligation on the part of Japan. Otherwise we might be manoeuvred into a position in which the Japanese would try to make it appear that the reopening of the road was a breach of an undertaking to them. Japanese opinion could easily be convinced by their Government in this matter since the public in Japan had never been informed of the condition in the confidential memorandum that the three months' period was to be used to secure a just and equitable peace.

On the other hand we should try to avoid publicity about our policy. If we decided to open the road, we should want to attract the least possible attention to the fact. We might secure Chinese co-operation by pointing out that, if too much attention were drawn to our proposed action, we might not be able to carry it out. We should have to tell the Japanese that, as they had not fulfilled the conditions of the agreement, we felt obliged to resume our liberty of action. If we checked publicity, the Japanese might not feel compelled to undertake counter-measures to the extent which they would think necessary to meet a widely-advertised reopening of the road. We also knew that President Roosevelt and Mr. Hull were

---

(a) F4009, 4074/43/10. (b) W9717/9160/49. (c) WP(40)348, F4115/43/10.

interested in discussing the question with us. We could not let their (a)
hints pass without notice even if the United States could not do
much until after the election.

The War Cabinet accepted on September 4 the general con- (b)
clusions of this memorandum. They considered that the factor most
likely to influence the Far Eastern situation in our favour would be
a successful end to the Battle of Britain. In the meantime we should
refuse an extension of the existing agreement with Japan and should
emphasise the temporary nature of the agreement, and the fact that
it involved the fulfilment of an obligation by Japan. The War
Cabinet also suggested that the United States Government should
be sounded about the possibility of sending a cruiser squadron on a
ceremonial visit to Singapore.

Sir R. Craigie was therefore instructed on September 4 to ask the (c)
Japanese Government what they were doing to fulfil their part of the
Burma Road agreement and to say also that before we could make
an approach to the Chinese Government or decide on our own
contribution to a general settlement we should want to know precisely the basis on which Japan was prepared to treat with China.

Sir R. Craigie mentioned to the Japanese Foreign Office on
September 5 that he wished to enquire from the Minister of Foreign (d)
Affairs what steps the Japanese Government were taking to implement their part of the agreement. On September 17 Sir R. Craigie
put this question to the Minister. Mr. Matsuoka said that the (e)
Japanese Government were trying to bring about an agreement with
the government of Wang Ching-wei and that this agreement would
be a contribution towards a general peace with China. Sir R.
Craigie doubted whether the negotiations with Wang Ching-wei
would facilitate the conclusion of peace with General Chiang
Kai-shek. Mr. Matsuoka then said he had been also doing his best
to reach an understanding with General Chiang Kai-shek through
a Chinese intermediary. He realised that no permanent peace was
likely on a basis of domination and exploitation by one side. He
thought that there was some 'slight hope' of a settlement. He did
not consider that there were any other steps which could usefully
be taken or that in present circumstances the British Government
could be of any assistance.

On September 5 the Japanese Government announced the
signature of an agreement with the Vichy Government allowing the
passage of Japanese troops through northern Indo-China and recognising the predominance of the political and economic interests of
Japan in the Far East. Mr. Matsuoka tried to maintain to Sir R. (f)
Craigie that this agreement had been freely negotiated and that it

(a) F4038/43/10; F4020/23/23. (b) WM(40)241, F4115/43/10. (c) F4074/43/10.
(d) F4217/43/10. (e) F4334/43/10. (f) F4126/3429/61.

was not an interference with the *status quo* in the Far East. The British Government refused to accept this view. Sir R. Craigie (a) pointed out to the Vice-Minister for Foreign Affairs on September 18 that the measures contemplated in Indo-China appeared to mean an attack from a new quarter on the Chinese. We could not regard such measures as consistent with a sincere effort to conclude a just peace or as compatible with the spirit of the Burma Road agreement.

The Vice-Minister asked whether Sir R. Craigie meant that, if a Japanese offensive took place through Indo-China, the British Government would repudiate the agreement. Sir R. Craigie would not commit himself on the question. The Vice-Minister then asked whether, if the Japanese did not begin an offensive through Indo-China, the Burma Road agreement would be renewed. Sir R. Craigie said that the question of the continuance of the agreement did not depend solely on Japanese action in Indo-China. He mentioned the possibility of a more extensive Franco-Japanese agreement and the continuation of the anti-British campaign and persecution of British subjects in Japan. In fact the Japanese made further demands on (b) the French. They threatened to invade Indo-China on September 22 if the Vichy authorities did not allow them to occupy Hanoi, Haiphong and five airports. The Vichy Government gave way to (c) these demands. On September 16 Lord Lothian and Mr. Casey, the Australian Minister at Washington, had discussed with Mr. Hull the question of preventing a Japanese occupation of Indo-China. Mr. Hull did not think that Japan would come into the war at this time; on the other hand he regarded it as impracticable to give any military help to Indo-China. Neither the British nor the Dutch could do much in the Far East, while if the United States entered the war the result would be that fewer supplies would be available for Great Britain. Mr. Hull wanted to gain time, and thought that the British success in resisting a German attempt at invasion would have a very great effect on the policy of Japan.

(a) F4328/43/10. (b) F4308/3429/61. (c) F4290/193/61.

(v)

Announcement of a three-Power pact between Germany, Italy and Japan, September 27, 1940: decision of His Majesty's Government not to renew the Burma Road Agreement, October 2: announcement of the decision, October 8: American proposal for staff discussions.

On September 27 the German wireless announced the conclusion in Berlin of a pact to create a new order in Asia and (a) Europe. The pact was signed by Ribbentrop, Ciano, and the Japanese Ambassador in Berlin. The terms included promises of mutual aid if any one of the parties were attacked by a Power not already taking part in the European war or in the hostilities in China. The pact appeared to be directed against the United States; it might therefore have the object, or certainly the result, of accelerating the entry of the United States into the war. This was indeed the first view taken by the Foreign Office. Sir R. Craigie reported, however, on October 1, from a good source, that the initiative had (b) come from Germany and was due to German fears of attack by Russia. Japan also wanted the alliance, not merely owing to fear of American action but also in order to avoid the risk of isolation if she had not made an arrangement with Germany and Italy before the end of the war.[1]

This development, following the Japanese entry into northern Indo-China, made it very difficult to justify to public opinion at home and in the United States a renewal of the three months agreement about the Burma Road. The Foreign Office therefore drew (c) up on October 2 another memorandum on the subject for the War Cabinet. The memorandum considered three possible courses: we could merely refuse, without discussion, to renew the agreement; we could announce at once our intention not to renew it; we could cancel the agreement forthwith on the general ground that Japanese policy had clearly ceased to permit the hope that the agreement would achieve the object for which we had concluded it. Sir R. Craigie thought that the third course might lead to some reprisals, but that (d) it would not in present circumstances lead to war. He considered

---

[1] On October 5 Mr. Matsuoka invited the United States Ambassador to his house in order to give him the Japanese text of a 'statement to the United States' concerning the Tripartite Pact. The statement was on familiar lines. The alliance was described as a (e) contribution to world peace. Japan was intending to develop a 'sphere of mutual prosperity' in Greater East Asia, and to do so 'as far as possible by peaceful means and with the least undesirable change in the *status quo*'. Then followed the usual complaints against British and American encouragement of China. The motive of this action in China was to weaken Japan; Japan had therefore made a defensive alliance with Germany and Italy. If the United States understood the Japanese argument, the new treaty would not make a change in the relation of Japan with America.

(a) F4457/626/23. (b) F4469/626/23. (c) WP(40)400, F4519/43/10. (d) F4485/626/23. (e) F4633/626/23.

(and the Foreign Office agreed with him) that a Japanese decision to go to war would be based on wider grounds. He therefore recommended the denunciation of the agreement, subject to the approval of the United States.

There was no doubt that American opinion was in favour of re-

(a) opening the Road. On September 16, before the conclusion of the Japanese pact with Germany and Italy, Lord Lothian had reported that Mr. Hull 'greatly hoped that we would reopen the Burma Road'. The United States had since granted a new loan to China and had announced, as from October 16, a ban on the export of scrap

(b) metal to Japan.[1] On the other hand Mr. Hull thought that the cancellation of the agreement before October 17 would be needless provocation. The best course would be to notify the Japanese Government at once that the agreement would not be renewed.

The Foreign Office thought that an announcement of non-renewal would have a good effect in China. The Japanese appeared to hope for direct German intervention in Chungking, and the Chinese had twice during the previous week asked us about our general attitude towards Japan. General Chiang Kai-shek had also requested that the Burma Road agreement should not be renewed.

If we decided against renewal, the procedure suggested by Mr. Hull was not altogether appropriate, since the agreement did not contain a provision for renewal, and a statement to the Japanese Government might only exacerbate matters. The Foreign Office considered that the best mode of procedure would be a statement in answer to a parliamentary question on October 8. The answer would be that the agreement was for a definite period and did not include a provision for renewal, and that, in any case, owing to recent developments, His Majesty's Government would have felt unable to renew it.

The Foreign Office suggested that General Chiang Kai-shek should be told at once, in strict confidence, of our intention, and that, on the day before our announcement, Sir R. Craigie should inform the Japanese Government of the parliamentary question and our proposed answer. We might also give short advance notice to the Soviet Government.

(c) On October 3 the War Cabinet accepted this view, and decided to adopt the procedure recommended by the Foreign Office, subject to the concurrence of the Dominion Governments. The Dominion

---

[1] On July 26, 1940, the United States Government had subjected to license all exports to Japan of aviation fuel and certain kinds of scrap metal. This was not an 'embargo' and, in fact, the value of oil exports to Japan in August, 1940, was greater than that of the previous six months of 1940. The value of scrap exports in August was about equal to that of the previous six months. On September 26 the order had been extended to all grades of iron and steel scrap.

(a)F4290/193/61. (b) F4495/626/23. (c) WM(40)265, F4519/23/10.

Governments agreed with the decision. Sir R. Craigie therefore (a) made an oral statement to the Japanese Foreign Minister on October 8 at 10 a.m. (Japanese time). He explained that the purpose of the agreement of July 17, as far as His Majesty's Government were concerned, had been to allow time during which a genuine effort might be made to reach an all round settlement. This purpose had not been achieved. On the other hand the Japanese Government had obtained facilities for sending troops into Indo-China in order to launch a fresh attack on China, and had concluded a political, military, and economic pact with the Axis Powers. The agreement of July 17 provided that at the end of three months His Majesty's Government would be free to continue or discontinue it according to conditions existing at the time. In the circumstances His Majesty's Government regretted that they did not see their way to renew the agreement.

In answer to this statement Mr. Matsuoka said that the Japanese Government were most anxious to secure an early peace with the whole of China, i.e. with General Chiang Kai-shek as well as with Wang Ching-wei. They had not succeeded so far with General Chiang Kai-shek but they were still not without hope of success. Mr. Matsuoka thought that our decision would make a settlement more difficult. He had done his best to damp down anti-British agitation; although there would now be a new outburst, he would do what he could to prevent demonstrations likely to exacerbate matters.

The decision not to renew the Burma Road agreement did not bring immediate Japanese reprisals. It seemed clear that, for the time at least, the Japanese were acting with some caution and that they had been impressed, not only by the American economic counter-measures but also by the British successes over the German air force and by the failure of the Germans to invade Great Britain. Sir R. Craigie had reason to think that opinion in the Japanese Foreign Office was not unanimous in believing that Germany would win the war, and that some members of the office even welcomed the conclusion of the pact with the Axis Powers on the grounds that this pact was a gross mistake of the military party which would ultimately lead to their fall. Sir R. Craigie also heard that the pledge (b) for mutual aid under the pact would come into effect only if such attack were entirely 'unprovoked'. Mr. Matsuoka himself had told Sir R. Craigie that the first step in invoking the article in question would be consultation between the signatory Powers, each of whom would then be free to decide whether an 'attack' within the meaning of the article had taken place.

Sir R. Craigie thought the omission of any public reference to this

---

(a) F4589, 4596, 4624/43/10. (b) F4603, 4663/626/23.

point meant that the Germans needed the pact for 'window-dressing' purposes. He also regarded it as not impossible that by skilful diplomacy Japan might be kept neutral if and when the United States entered the war. The Foreign Office were less confident of avoiding war but agreed that we should keep Japan to neutrality only if we acted firmly and at the same time without provocation in resisting further encroachments on our rights and interests.[1]

It was of great importance, therefore, that British policy should be co-ordinated with that of the United States. The United States Government had in fact been consulted at every point.[2] Lord Lothian had discussed the question of the Japanese-German-Italian pact on

(a) September 30. Mr. Hull had then said that he had long been convinced of the existence of an underground agreement between the three 'aggressor' Powers; the signing of the pact would not change the 'fundamentals' of the position and would make no difference to the policy of the Administration in giving all possible help to Great Britain. In this respect indeed the effect of the pact had been to lead the Administration to the conclusion that they must build up American armament production so that supplies available for Great Britain should, if possible, be larger and available sooner than had been expected. The United States had already cut off the export of scrap to Japan and would now need all the output of machine tools to meet the demands of American defence.

Mr. Hull could give no pledge in answer to a question from Lord Lothian about American support if the reopening of the Burma Road led to a Japanese attack, but he said that the United States intended to maintain opposition to Japanese aggression especially by economic means. He asked whether Great Britain, Australia and the Netherlands would be willing to hold staff conversations with the United States on the technical problems involved in common action for defence. These conversations would not be concerned with political matters.

---

[1] Sir R. Craigie had asked on October 2 whether he was right in assuming that the United States, if involved in war with Japan, would be obliged to cease sending war material to Great Britain. The Prime Minister considered that Sir R. Craigie should be told at once that 'the entry of the United States into war either with Germany and Italy or

(b) with Japan is fully conformable with British interests' and that 'if Japan attacked the United States without declaring war on us, we should at once . . . declare war upon Japan.' The Foreign Office, however, decided not to send to Sir R. Craigie the second part of the message in view of the need first to consult the Dominions. Instead Sir R. Craigie was informed that, in Mr. Churchill's words, 'nothing in the munitions sphere can compare with the importance of the British Empire and the United States being co-belligerent'.

[2] In October 1940 the War Cabinet set up a Far Eastern Committee, with inter-depart-
(c) mental representation, to keep under review Far Eastern policy with special regard to co-operation with the Dominion Governments, the Governments of India and Burma, and the United States and Netherlands Governments.

(a) F4495/626/23. (b) F4634/60/23. (c) WM(40)264, F4432/103/23.

Lord Lothian reported on October 4 that Mr. Welles had described the proposal for staff talks as important and far-reaching. (a) Lord Lothian had said that we should probably have to consult the Dominions before giving a reply. He asked Mr. Welles for his views on the form which the talks would take. Mr. Welles thought that they should be held in Washington, but that there would be difficulty about getting a Dutch expert there soon enough. Lord Lothian thought that preliminary talks might be held in London with Admiral Ghormley,[1] and that an inner technical committee might meet afterwards, as soon as possible, in Washington. Lord Lothian commented to the Foreign Office that Washington was certainly the right place for the talks, if only because the fact that they were being held would certainly become known.

On October 5 Lord Lothian was told that we should welcome such (b) conversations. Lord Lothian telegraphed during the night of October 7–8 that instructions had been given to the American (c) Consuls in China and Japan that American women and children should leave both countries. American forces in China (including Shanghai) were being withdrawn. Mr. Hull thought this was the best way of bringing home to Japan that the United States 'meant business'. He asked what progress had been made towards the staff talks, and said that the talks should take place quickly.

The War Cabinet accepted Lord Lothian's suggestions. They had (d) intended, before the receipt of Lord Lothian's telegram of October 4, to propose conferences in the United Kingdom and in the United (e) States for the study of broad general considerations, while particular problems might be studied locally in the Far East. A Defence Conference was being arranged in Singapore between British representatives and representatives of Australia, New Zealand, India, Burma and, possibly, of the Netherlands.[2] His Majesty's Government therefore invited the United States to participate in this conference, or, if they thought that such a move would be too public, to arrange for representatives to be present without actually attending formal meetings.

The War Cabinet on October 9 also proposed that representatives (f) of Australia, New Zealand and Canada should attend the meetings in London and Washington. Lord Lothian found, however, on October 9 when he went to discuss the general subject with Mr. Hull, that the latter's attitude had changed to one of extreme (g)

---

[1] Admiral Ghormley had been sent to London as the United States naval representative for staff talks in August 1940, and had stayed on in London as a special naval observer.
[2] See J. R. M. Butler, *Grand Strategy*, II (H.M.S.O., 1957), chap. XXI.

(a) F4556/193/61. (b) F4556/193/61; F4495/626/23. (c) F4615/193/61. (d) F45341/193/61; WM(40)265. (e) F4615/193/61. (f) WM(40)268, F4615/193/61. (g) F4627/4601/61; F4732/193/61.

E

caution. Lord Lothian thought that the change was due to reasons of domestic politics. The Administration wanted to prevent its opponents from using the crisis in the Far East to support their thesis that the President was deliberately provoking war. Mr. Hull therefore did not favour a conference in Washington or in London or in Singapore since the press would certainly find out about it and exaggerate its importance. He also thought that the Dutch would not wish to enter into formal defensive arrangements with the United States and Great Britain. Lord Lothian believed that Mr. Hull would suggest that the naval authorities should collect all the necessary information about the naval, military and air resources of the five democratic Pacific Powers and discuss problems of common defence arising out of this information and that the Netherlands
(a) Government should be told of the discussions. On October 10 Mr. Hull told Lord Lothian that Admiral Ghormley had already had a good many conversations on Pacific problems with the Admiralty and that it was unnecessary for the moment to send him further instructions. Mr. Hull suggested that we might privately consult the Netherlands Government. Lord Lothian thought it now clear that anything like a conference could not be held until after the presidential election.

The Foreign Office accepted this view, though with some disappointment. Lord Lothian was told on October 14 that we wished to emphasise both the need for keeping the Japanese aware of Anglo-American vigilance and for bringing the Dutch into the staff discussions. Lord Lothian was instructed to suggest that after an exchange of information had taken place, British and Dutch representatives should go 'unobtrusively' to Washington to continue the exploration of the problems on a technical level.[1]

(vi)

General Chiang Kai-shek's proposals for closer co-operation between Great Britain and the United States and China: Foreign Office memorandum of November 10, 1940.

The Chinese National Government welcomed, for obvious reasons, the decision to reopen the Burma Road. Mr. R. A. Butler made a

---

[1] After the election the President agreed to secret Anglo-American Staff conversations in Washington. These conversations began at the end of January 1941 and continued until the end of March.

(a) F4627/4605/61.

formal statement on the subject to the Chinese Ambassador on (a)
October 7. Mr. Quo, in conversation at this time, confirmed recent
messages from General Chiang Kai-shek that the real Japanese aims
were Malaya and Singapore. Mr. Quo pointed out that the country
in the north of Indo-China was extremely mountainous, whereas
the Japanese forces could move more easily to the south. General
Chiang Kai-shek followed a letter of thanks to the Prime Minister (b)
by an approach through the Ambassador at Chungking for closer
co-operation between Great Britain and the United States and China.
Sir A. Clark Kerr was authorised to give a friendly reply and to ask
for more detailed proposals. General Chiang Kai-shek submitted
his proposals to Sir A. Clark Kerr on November 2.

The Foreign Office drew up a memorandum on the proposals for (c)
the War Cabinet on November 10. General Chiang Kai-shek had
asked that (i) China, Great Britain and the United States should
reaffirm the 'Open Door' principle in China, and the maintenance
of Chinese sovereignty and territorial and administrative integrity.
(ii) Great Britain, the United States and China should declare their
opposition to the Japanese attempt to secure 'a new stabilisation' in
'greater East Asia' and also say that they intended to carry out their
obligations under the Nine-Power treaty.[1] (iii) Great Britain and
China should conclude a treaty of alliance and invite the adherence
or at least the approval of the United States. (iv) Great Britain and
the United States should make joint or separate loans to China of
£50–75 million for the maintenance of the Chinese currency and
foreign exchange. (v) The United States should lend to China
500–1,000 aircraft a year, of which 200–300 would be supplied in
1940. (vi) Great Britain and the United States should send military,
economic and communications missions to China. General Chiang
Kai-shek had also said that, if Great Britain and the United States
became involved in war with Japan, the Chinese army would
participate in hostilities, and all Chinese aerodromes would be placed
at the disposal of the Allied forces. General Chiang Kai-shek, in
putting forward his proposals, had indicated that the effects of
Japanese air raids during the summer and of price inflation had
been so serious that without British and American help he would be
unable to maintain resistance to Japan beyond the end of the
year.

---

[1] This treaty, which related to 'the principles and policies to be followed in matters
concerning China', was signed in Washington on February 6, 1922. The signatories were
Belgium, China, France, Italy, Japan, the Netherlands, Portugal, the United Kingdom
and the United States.

(a) F4649, 4859/43/10. (b) F4817, 4826, 4997, 4998, 4999/57/10. (c) WP(40)436;
F5088/174/10.

The Foreign Office assumed that, in view of the increasing pressure of Japan on Indo-China and of other signs of preparations for a move southwards against British and Dutch territory, the continuance of Chinese resistance was of vital interest to us. We should therefore wish to help China as far as we could do so without provoking Japan to go to war with us. General Chiang Kai-shek's needs could be summed up as a demonstration of Anglo-American solidarity with China as a means of reviving morale, financial and economic help, and technical advice.

The memorandum then commented on General Chiang Kai-shek's proposals in detail:

(i) (ii) and (iii): We could not at present expect the United States to undertake a definite commitment: hence a tripartite alliance was out of the question. An Anglo-Chinese alliance would not serve the same purpose, and its reactions in Japan would be out of proportion to its utility. The declarations proposed by General Chiang Kai-shek might be arranged, but, except in regard to giving the utmost help to China, they dealt with matters already covered in various statements by the British and United States Governments. It seemed better, therefore, that more practical help should precede the consideration of any more declarations. (iv): Loans on the scale suggested could be made only if the greater part were provided by the United States. We could, however, provide a currency stabilisation loan if we could secure satisfactory arrangements about the use to which the sterling credits might be put. Export credits from the United Kingdom were difficult owing to our own needs: we might obtain material from the Empire and from Allied countries within the sterling area. (v): We could not supply aircraft, and the most modern production of the United States was absorbed either by American or by our own requirements. Less modern aircraft might be supplied from the United States. (vi): A military mission would be undesirable at present. We might improve our military co-operation by replacing the Military Attaché to China by a more senior officer and expanding his staff. We might also prepare plans for a full military mission in the event of war with Japan. It would be a mistake to send out economic or communications missions until arrangements had been made for the provision of material help. Finally, while we should want Chinese participation against Japan, we ought not to overrate the support which the Chinese army could give us. It was unlikely that they could undertake more than guerrilla warfare.

The Foreign Office proposed that, subject to the approval of the Governments of the Dominions and India, we should offer China a loan for currency purposes, and a credit to cover exports from the sterling area. We should make these offers at once, and without waiting for possible Anglo-American declarations.

The War Cabinet agreed that it would be better to concentrate (a) on measures of immediate assistance to China rather than to put out more declarations of policy. The United States Government had also made their attitude clear and were disinclined to say more. They repeated, however, in a public statement that they continued to recognise the National Government in Chungking as the Government of China. A similar statement was made in Great Britain on December 4 in answer to a parliamentary question.

Six days later His Majesty's Government announced that they would make an additional contribution of £5,000,000 to the Chinese Currency Stabilisation Fund and a grant of export credits to China up to a maximum of £5,000,000;[1] the United States Government gave a currency loan of $50,000,000 (American), with a promise of another $50,000,000. General Chiang Kai-shek was told that Great Britain could not spare arms or military personnel, but that, in order to increase military contacts with China and to examine the ground for possible future military co-operation, the status of the Military Attaché to China would be raised, and his staff increased.

Major-General L. E. Dennys, Indian Army, was sent to Chungking as Military Attaché. After his arrival in January 1941, he began talks with General Chiang Kai-shek, and, as a result, recommended that arrangements should be made to operate British air squadrons from Chinese aerodromes in the event of war between Great Britain and Japan, and that a *corps d'élite* of Chinese guerrillas should be formed under British leadership to assist the Chinese to contain the Japanese in China after the outbreak of war.

The question of increasing supplies to China again brought up the problem of getting them into the country. The shortest line of communication lay through Burma, but, even if the Burma Road were used to its full capacity (and it was most unlikely that the Chinese could organise or conduct an efficient service), this single channel of communication was not enough to meet the needs of a large army. The Chinese Goverment were considering other routes, e.g. roads from Szechuan and Yunnan to Assam, air freight services between China and Assam and India or Burma, and, particularly, the building of a railway between Burma and Yunnan. This latter project had been suggested earlier; the Burmese Government had then been unfavourable to it. The Chinese had now begun construction at the Yunnan end, and were pressing the Burmese Government to start work in Burma. The Burmese Government were willing to send an official mission to

---

[1] These contributions were subject to certain restrictions to prevent unfavourable reactions on sterling.

(a) WM(40)288, F5088/174/10.

Chungking to discuss the whole question of communications, if on their side the Chinese Government would agree to the demarcation of the southern section of the boundary between Burma and Yunnan. The mission reached Chungking early in 1941, settled the boundary question, and agreed to provide facilities for railway and road construction.[1]

---

[1] Construction work continued on this railway until early in 1942, when the project was given up.

CHAPTER XXIII

Japanese policy in 1941 to the fall of Prince Konoye's Government on October 16

(i)

Reports of an imminent Japanese move: warning to the Japanese Government: exchanges with the United States: Mr. Matsuoka's memorandum of February 15 and the Prime Minister's reply of February 24, 1941.

THE 'rhythm' of Japanese policy was now clear. In retrospect it is easy to see the fundamental error behind this policy even though it won very great temporary successes. The Japanese army, the politicians who supported the military extremists, and Japanese public opinion in general, knew too little of the outside world. They underrated, first, the latent power of recovery in Great Britain, and then the defensive strength of Russia; above all, they miscalculated the immense resources of the United States. There was, from the Japanese point of view, a time-lag in all their judgments. They did not realise the strategic significance of the military failure of the Germans to invade Great Britain in the autumn of 1940 or the consequences of the German political failure to establish their 'new order' in Europe after the French collapse. In other words, Japan continued to act in 1941 as though the world situation was that of the summer of 1940.

The nemesis of Japanese miscalculation, however, lay in the future. For Great Britain, and increasingly for the United States, the immediate situation was one of great danger. There was now no doubt that Japan had decided upon a southward move, even if she were thereby involved in war. The danger was not less because Japanese policy, though the extremists continued to be reckless and blind in the largest issues, remained cautious in detailed execution. The Japanese naval and military chiefs knew their business. They would not act without premeditation and preparation; each step, carefully chosen and planned for the right moment, would bring them nearer to the fulfilment of their plan. British policy therefore continued to aim at deterring Japan as long as possible from entering the war, and increasing the difficulties of her task if she did so. As in 1940, this policy required close collaboration with the United States.

At the end of January 1941 there was evidence that the southward move would be resumed at once. Here again the opportunity was given by the collapse of France. The Government of Thailand, with encouragement from Japan, had taken the obvious chance to bring forward claims against French Indo-China for the return of territory which, for the most part, Thailand had been compelled to surrender at various times during the past half-century. Thailand had concluded a non-aggression treaty with Great Britain in June 1940, and had been on the point of concluding a similar treaty with France. The French treaty, however, was not ratified. Even if it had been ratified, the Thai demands would still have been made. The Vichy Government refused to consider the demands and local fighting

(a) broke out between Thai and Indo-Chinese forces. Great Britain was unable to put pressure on the French and the United States Government were unwilling to do so. Hence the Thais turned to Japan who already had *de facto* political and economic control of Indo-China.

The Japanese Government insisted that France should accept
(b) Japanese mediation, and on January 31, 1941, an armistice was signed at Saigon on board the Japanese cruiser *Natori*.[1] It seemed likely that the Japanese intended to use this mediation as a means
(c) of getting a naval base at Camranh Bay, air bases in southern Indo-China and control of the Indo-Chinese customs. There was also reason to suppose that they were considering a military agreement with Thailand for action against British and Dutch territories. A crisis might therefore develop within a few weeks or even sooner.

Sir R. Craigie telegraphed on January 27 that there was a general
(d) feeling among the Japanese that this crisis was imminent. It was thought that a Japanese move would synchronise with a German attempt to invade Great Britain; that the increased tension in Japanese-American relations could not continue without a break, and that some hint of action might have been given during the recent secret sessions of the Japanese Diet. At all events the Germans were tightening their hold on Japanese policy. Sir R. Craigie telegraphed
(e) again on February 3 that our only chance of preventing Japan from establishing herself in Thailand was through American co-operation, and that it was urgently necessary to represent to the United States Government the importance of maintaining our position in the Indian Ocean. The control of Thailand would allow the Japanese not only to attack Singapore in the most favourable conditions, but to by-pass it and also to starve out Malaya by cutting off supplies of Thai rice. The Foreign Office agreed with this view, and Mr. Eden raised the matter in the War Cabinet on February 5. The

---

[1] A peace agreement was signed in Tokyo on May 9, 1941.

(a) F79, 142, 307, 328/5/40. (b) F394, 396, 420, 457, 517/5/40. (c) F1208/210/40. (d) F458/9/61. (e) F540/9/61.

Prime Minister thought that rapid developments were unlikely, and (a) that for the moment we wished the United States Government to concentrate upon the passage of the Lend-Lease bill.

The War Cabinet decided, however, to invite the Chiefs of Staff to consider the strategic implications of Japanese control over Indo-China. The Chiefs of Staff extended their study to include the results of a Japanese move into Thailand and the Dutch East (b) Indies. They considered that the Dutch East Indies would be the first Japanese objective after the securing of bases in Indo-China. The control of Indo-China would bring the threat of attack on British possessions nearer but would not in itself directly threaten our vital interests. It would lead, however, almost certainly, and in accordance with the Japanese 'step by step' methods, to the requisition of bases in Thailand as a result of which Singapore might be threatened and the defence of Burma and Malaya would become more difficult.

The establishment of Japanese bases in the Dutch East Indies would directly threaten our vital interests. Finally, the loss of Singapore would throw upon the United States the whole responsibility for the control of Japanese expansion and the safeguarding of American interests in the Far East.

It was therefore of the greatest importance that the United States should try to prevent any further southward move on the part of Japan by making it clear that such a move would lead to war with America. The Chiefs of Staff suggested a joint Anglo-American declaration that any attack on our possessions in the Far East or on the Dutch East Indies would involve Japan in war with the United States and the British Empire.

Mr. Eden spoke in strong terms of warning to the Japanese Ambassador on February 7. He described the course of events since (c) Prince Konoye's Government had taken office, and reminded the Ambassador that Mr. Matsuoka had then given the impression that there was no hope of a general settlement between Great Britain and Japan, and that Japan had no alternative to strengthening her connexion with the Axis Powers. It now seemed possible that a Japanese move would take place in the next few weeks. We could not ignore the accumulating evidence of Japanese intentions. We were not prepared to give way to Japanese claims to sole domination in the Far East, and would defend ourselves in the event of Japanese attack. We were now sure that, with our own resources and the increasing amount of help which we were obtaining from the United States, we should win the war. With this conviction, we wished to try to prevent our relations with Japan from getting worse.

(a) WM(41)13, F669/9/61. (b) F677/17/23. (c) F648/17/23.

E*

(a)   Lord Halifax discussed the Far Eastern position with Mr. Roosevelt on February 8. Mr. Roosevelt said that our information about the imminence of Japanese action coincided with information received by the United States, and that the date might be February 10 or 18. Mr. Roosevelt realised that we could not at the moment send an adequate force—which should include not less than seven battleships—to the Far East. The United States would declare war on Japan if the latter attacked American possessions, but public opinion would be unlikely to approve of a declaration of war if the Japanese attack were directed only against British or Dutch territories. Moreover, if the United States were involved in war with Japan, an active campaign in the Pacific would be a dangerous diversion of forces and of material from the main theatre of operations, i.e. the Atlantic and Great Britain. Mr. Roosevelt thought that the United States would have to limit operations in the Pacific to a 'holding war'.

Mr. Roosevelt had been considering what he could do to deter Japan. He felt that he was 'through with bluffing' and that the Japanese well knew the limitations of possible American action. He might issue a further warning to American nationals to leave the Far East, or he might send six or eight more submarines to Manila or tell the new Japanese Ambassador, who would be arriving in a few days, that he hoped that the rumours about forthcoming Japanese action were untrue, since it would be a pity if the Ambassador had to leave Washington almost at once. He might also ask why the Japanese appeared to be establishing themselves permanently on the Spratley Islands.[1]

Lord Halifax was instructed on February 11 to point out to the
(b)   United States Government that if Japan, under German pressure, forced us into war and threatened to invade Australia or New Zealand, we might have temporarily to move our fleet from the Mediterranean to the Indian Ocean. This move would have the result of lengthening the war with Germany, and making ultimate success improbable without full American participation. The initiative lay with Japan; we alone could not keep her from aggression. The indirect danger to American interests was thus very great. We considered that the proposed joint declaration would be the best deterrent, but that the United States Government would hardly go as far as a statement on these lines. Mr. Hopkins (to whom Mr.

---

[1] In the South China Sea, and near Borneo and Indo-China. The Japanese occupied the islands in 1939. The French claimed that they had annexed the Spratley Islands in 1930. The Japanese counter-claim was that they had been in continuous commercial occupation since 1917. The Japanese seem to have withdrawn for a time, and to have returned after the collapse of France.

(a) F709/523/23. (b) F677/17/23.

Eden had spoken on the matter in London) thought, however, that Mr. Roosevelt might see the Japanese Ambassador and make plain 'in words of one syllable' American interests in the Far East. Lord Halifax was instructed to explain to Mr. Roosevelt the extreme seriousness of the position, and the need for some statement or warning to Japan. Finally, Lord Halifax was told that the Chiefs of Staff also hoped that the United States would strengthen their naval forces at Manila and send a detachment to Singapore. Although it would be unwise for us to try to suggest any specific strategic action by the United States, the most effective check to Japan would be a move on the part of the United States fleet, for example, manoeuvres over an unusually wide range.

Lord Halifax had already spoken to Mr. Hull on February 10 on the general lines suggested by the Foreign Office. Mr. Hull had not (a) ruled out the possibility of sending a cruiser force to Manila. Lord Halifax therefore sent him a private letter summing up the situation (b) as it appeared to the British Government and repeating the suggestion about the despatch of cruisers.

On February 12 Mr. Ohashi, Japanese Vice-Minister for Foreign Affairs, told Sir R. Craigie that he was sorry that the latter had (c) thought it necessary to send home alarmist reports on the situation. Sir R. Craigie pointed out that Japan had allied herself with our enemies and that we might therefore find ourselves at war with her independently of our volition. We had therefore to make our preparations. There were also increasing signs that Japan was accelerating the tempo of her advance southwards.

The Vice-Minister stated, with some emphasis, that Japan did not intend to take 'aggressive action in South-East Asia unless she were forced to do so through acts of others'. Sir R. Craigie pointed out that a State engaged in carrying out a policy of expansion might well regard as 'aggressive' the most 'elementary precautions' taken by others. His general impression of the interview was, however, that the Vice-Minister was personally very friendly and unaware of a plan to synchronise a Japanese attack on us with a German move elsewhere. This was not of itself evidence against the existence of such a plan, since the German General Staff would make their arrangements for it directly with the Japanese army. In any case the Vice-Minister's statement did not exclude action (which seemed more likely) to secure bases and facilities in Thailand and Indo-China.

On the evening of February 15 the Prime Minister sent a personal message through the Foreign Office to Mr. Roosevelt reinforcing the (d)

(a) F741/17/23. (b) F929/17/23. (c) F895/17/23. (d) F1068/17/23.

arguments used by Lord Halifax to bring home the seriousness of the position. The message was in the following terms:

'Many drifting straws seem to indicate Japanese intention to make war on us or do something that would force us to make war on them in the next few weeks or months. I am not myself convinced that this is not a war of nerves designed to cover Japanese encroachments in Siam and Indo-China. However I think I ought to let you know that the weight of the Japanese Navy, if thrown against us, would confront us with situations beyond the scope of our naval resources. I do not think that the Japanese would be likely to send the large military expedition necessary to lay siege to Singapore. The Japanese would no doubt occupy whatever strategic points and oilfields in the Dutch East Indies and thereabouts that they covet, and thus get into a far better position for a full scale attack on Singapore later on. They would also raid Australian and New Zealand ports and coasts, causing deep anxiety in those Dominions which have already sent all their best-trained fighting men to the Middle East. But the attack which I fear the most would be by raiders including possibly battle-cruisers upon our trade routes and communications across the Pacific and Indian Oceans. We could by courting disaster elsewhere send a few strong ships into these vast waters, but all the trade would have to go into convoy and escorts would be few and far between. Not only would this be a most grievous additional restriction and derangement of our whole war economy, but it would bring altogether to an end all reinforcements of the Armies we had planned to build up in the Middle East from Australasian and Indian sources. Any threat of a major invasion of Australia or New Zealand would of course force us to withdraw our Fleet from the Eastern Mediterranean with disastrous military possibilities there, and the certainty that Turkey would have to make some accommodation for re-opening of the German trade and oil supplies from the Black Sea. You will therefore see, Mr. President, the awful enfeeblement of our war effort that would result merely from the sending out by Japan of her battle-cruisers and her twelve 8-inch gun cruisers into the Eastern Oceans, and still more from any serious invasion threat against the two Australasian Democracies in the Southern Pacific.

Some believe that Japan in her present mood would not hesitate to court or attempt to wage war both against Great Britain and the United States. Personally I think the odds are definitely against that, but no one can tell. Everything that you can do to inspire the Japanese with the fear of a double war may avert the danger. If however they come in against us and we are alone, the grave character of the consequences cannot easily be overstated.'

(a) Meanwhile earlier on February 15 Lord Halifax had discussed the situation with Mr. Hull in the light of Sir R. Craigie's interview with the Japanese Vice-Minister for Foreign Affairs. Mr. Hull said that

---

(a) F1001/17/23.

Mr. Roosevelt had seen Admiral Nomura, the new Japanese Ambassador, and used 'friendly but very straight' terms in telling him that the Government and people of the United States were firmly opposed to the methods of aggression and seizure of other people's property by which Japan had created a situation of tension and uncertainty in American-Japanese relations. Mr. Roosevelt made it clear that another Japanese move might lead to war with the United States.

There was, however, from this date a temporary relaxation. Mr. Matsuoka gave Sir R. Craigie on February 15 a memorandum (a) which the Japanese Ambassador had been instructed to communicate to the British Government. This memorandum stated that Japanese policy continued to be on the lines publicly explained, i.e. that the Tripartite Pact aimed at preventing the extension of the European war and bringing about its termination as soon as possible. The Japanese Government were therefore concerned at the preparations which were being made by Great Britain and the United States to meet 'supposed contingencies in the Pacific and the South Seas'.

The memorandum included a personal message to Mr. Eden from Mr. Matsuoka asserting that the aims of Japanese policy were 'no conquest, no oppression, no exploitation'. Mr. Matsuoka could see no good reason for prolonging a war which might lead to the collapse of civilisation. Japan was deeply concerned with the early restoration of peace and was prepared to act as mediator 'not only in Greater East Asia, but anywhere the world over'.[1]

Mr. Matsuoka, in presenting the memorandum, discussed the situation with Sir R. Craigie. Sir R. Craigie produced a résumé of some of Mr. Matsuoka's own statements[2] and of press comments which had caused anxiety about Japanese intentions. Mr. Matsuoka admitted that, in a speech of January 30 to the Diet, he had said that, as a matter of argument, it could be maintained that the passage of the Lend-Lease bill and action thereunder by the United States might constitute 'an attack' within the meaning of article 3 of the Tripartite Pact, but that such an interpretation would require to be very carefully considered before it could be accepted. Mr. Matsuoka explained that he had used these words in order 'to hint at what he could not say publicly, namely, that any such claim on

---

[1] See also below, p. 196.
[2] One example of these statements may be quoted: In a general review of foreign affairs given on January 20, 1941, to the Japanese Diet, Mr. Matsuoka spoke in the following (b) terms of the British victories in Cyrenaica: 'Incidentally, reference may be made to Italy's military operations. There appear to be various species of malicious propaganda circulated on this head, but I have no doubt that our ally Italy will attain her object before long.'

(a) F1009/12/23. (b) F390/12/23.

the part of the Axis would undoubtedly be rejected by the Japanese Government'.

Mr. Matsuoka also denied that Japan would expect a price for her mediation between Thailand and Indo-China. Again he admitted in confidence that there was some justification for Anglo-American anxiety in that a strong current of Japanese opinion demanded that every possible advantage should be taken of present opportunities. He and the Prime Minister were firmly opposed to schemes of adventure or aggression, and, if necessary, would ask the Emperor to support them in their opposition. If this step were insufficient, they would resign.

Sir R. Craigie explained our need, as a belligerent Power, to make preparations in British territory for every eventuality. Mr. Matsuoka agreed, but said that any overt or provocative Anglo-American action would play into the hands of the extremists and that he might not be able to prevent countermeasures by the Japanese army and navy. Finally he accepted Sir R. Craigie's suggestion that the best plan would be for each side to inform the other of any action or report likely to cause concern.

The Japanese Ambassador gave Mr. Matsuoka's memorandum,
(a) in Mr. Eden's absence from London,[1] to Mr. R. A. Butler in the afternoon of February 17. The Ambassador wanted Mr. Eden to be told of the memorandum at once. Mr. Butler therefore promised to show it during the evening to the Prime Minister.

On February 20 Mr. Matsuoka again spoke to Sir R. Craigie
(b) about the effect on Japanese opinion of public mention of the despatch of reinforcements to the South Seas area. Sir R. Craigie replied that it was absurd to regard these measures as a threat to Japan. He reported to the Foreign Office that he believed Mr. Matsuoka to be restraining the army and navy,[2] and that it would be wise to discontinue press references to our preparations. These references had served their purpose and the situation was now easier, but we still needed to be most cautious. In a later telegram Sir R. Craigie said that by describing the situation as 'easier' he meant that the chances of a direct Japanese attack synchronising perhaps with a German attack in the west were less than they had been a few weeks earlier. The chances of a Japanese seizure of southern Indo-China

---

[1] Mr. Eden had just left on a mission to the Eastern Mediterranean with Sir J. Dill, Chief of the Imperial General Staff. See Volume I, Chapter XVI.

[2] The American view (reported by Lord Halifax) at this time was that the firm line taken by the United States and Great Britain had strengthened the position of the moderates in Japan, but that the army was still pressing for a forward policy, while the navy was holding back.

(a) F1069/17/23. (b) F1159/17/23.

had not diminished; the Japanese believed that they could carry out this move without serious risk of war, at least with the United States.

The Foreign Office agreed with Sir R. Craigie that the German- (a) Japanese plans had been deferred. There was no reason to think that the plans had been abandoned. We were certain of Mr. Matsuoka's insincerity, and we had to assume that at any time we might be faced with an attack by Japan.[1] Sir R. Craigie was instructed on February 25 to tell Mr. Matsuoka that we were surprised at his (b) latest complaints. We could not allow any other Power to question our right to defend territories committed to our charge. If 'some jubilation' had appeared in the British press at the arrival of reinforcements in Malaya, the reason was a sense of 'relief in the face of the actions of Japanese forces outside the territories of the Japanese Empire, and of the threatening speeches of responsible persons in Japan'. Mr. Matsuoka had said that reinforcements had not been sent recently to Indo-China, but the question was not whether it was a fortnight since more troops had gone to Indo-China, but why Japanese forces were being concentrated at all in Formosa, Hainan, Indo-China and the South China Seas. These southward moves by Japan compelled neighbouring territories to look to their defences.

Meanwhile on February 24 the Prime Minister gave the Japanese Ambassador a note in reply to Mr. Matsuoka's memorandum. The (c) reply was on firm lines; it rejected the Japanese offer of mediation, and stated that there could be no 'compromise or parley' with the Nazi régime. In conversation the Prime Minister said to the Ambassador that the Tripartite Pact had been 'a very great mistake for Japan. Nothing had done them more harm in their relations with the United States, and nothing had brought Great Britain and the United States closer together.' We could not believe that 'a Pact so much in favour of Germany and so little in favour of Japan had not got some secret provisions'.

Mr. Matsuoka's answer to the Prime Minister's note disclaimed any suggestion that he had offered Japanese mediation and reaffirmed (d) that the Tripartite Pact aimed at 'preventing a third Power from

[1] At this time the Germans were trying to get Japan to attack Singapore. (See *D.G.F.P.*, XII, Nos. 78 and 100.) Ribbentrop in a long and bombastic disquisition to General Oshima, Japanese Ambassador to Germany (who returned to Berlin in February 1941), said that the Axis Powers had won the war. He also hinted strongly that, if Russia intervened, the result would be a gigantic German victory. The Japanese reply was that they would be ready to launch an attack on Singapore by the end of May, but must secure themselves against a move in the north by Russia (*Ibid.* No. 209).

(a) F1307/17/23. (b) F1159/17/23. (c) F1239/17/23. (d) F1575/17/23.

participating in the European War or Sino-Japanese conflict, thus limiting the participants and dimensions of the war' and contributing towards 'bringing about peace at the earliest possible date'.

(ii)

Mr. Matsuoka's visit to Europe: Russo-Japanese neutrality pact: proposed declaration by Great Britain, the United States and the Netherlands: proposed declaration of British interest in the integrity of the Netherlands East Indies.

Behind this diplomatic fencing by Japan the danger of an immediate southward move appeared to have receded for a time.[1] A turn in Japanese policy showed, however, that the recession would not be lasting. On February 20 Lord Halifax telegraphed that the United
(a) States Government had hread that Mr. Matsuoka was shortly going to visit Berlin, Rome and Moscow, and that he hoped to reach a general settlement with the Soviet Government. A week later Mr. Matsuoka explained to Sir R. Craigie the purpose of this visit to
(b) Europe. He said that he wanted to find out for himself what kind of Europe his Allies desired to see established at the end of the war. Sir R. Craigie pointed out that this proposed visit would greatly increase the strain on Anglo-Japanese relations. It would be assumed that Mr. Matsuoka's purpose was to reinforce the Tripartite Pact in a sense still more favourable to his Allies. Mr. Matsuoka denied this intention and repeated the familiar arguments that British and American policy had driven Japan to the German side.

Mr. Matsuoka left Tokyo on March 12. He told Sir R. Craigie
(c) that he was going to Berlin and Rome 'to see and listen'. He might prolong his journey to Paris and Vichy in order to see Marshal Pétain 'whom he greatly admired'. He expected to spend only one day in Moscow on his way to Berlin in order to pay his respects to M. Molotov; he might remain a little longer if Stalin asked to see him. On his way home he might stay a few days in Moscow, 'but he had no definite business there'. He said that the fact that he was expecting to be away for six weeks showed how unfounded were British suspicions of impending trouble in the Pacific.

The Prime Minister decided to send a message to Mr. Matsuoka
(d) during his visit to Europe. The message was to have been delivered

---

[1] Mr. Churchill telegraphed to Mr. Roosevelt on February 20 that he had better news about Japan. He thought that Mr. Matsuoka's proposed visits might be a 'diplomatic sop to cover absence of action against Great Britain'. The postponement of such action was due largely to fear of the United States. Mr. Churchill said that the naval consequences of Japanese aggression would continue to be as stated in his previous message.

(a) F1138/12/23. (b) F1452/137/23. (c) F1871/21/23. (d) F2554/17/23.

by the Japanese Ambassador in London but the arrangements for a meeting in France between the Ambassador and Mr. Matsuoka broke down. The Prime Minister therefore sent the message on April 2 to be delivered through Sir S. Cripps to Mr. Matsuoka in Moscow.

The Prime Minister's message consisted of a series of questions which the Japanese Government might put to themselves: Would Germany, without command of the sea or air, be able to invade Great Britain in 1941 or to prevent American aid from reaching British shores and the United States from transforming its whole industry to war purposes? Did Japanese accession to the Tripartite Pact make American entry into the war more or less likely, and would not British and American seapower enable these countries to deal simultaneously with Japan and with the Axis Powers in Europe? Was Italy a strength or a burden to Germany? Would not the British air force be stronger than the German air force before the end of 1941 and far stronger before the end of 1942? Would the countries held down by Germany learn to like the Germans more or would they like them less as the years passed? Was it true that the Anglo-American production of steel would amount to 90 million tons in 1941, and, if Germany were defeated, would not the Japanese production of 7 million tons be inadequate for a 'single-handed' war?

Mr. Matsuoka did not answer this message at once: indeed an answer was hardly expected. In any case the real purpose of Mr. Matsuoka's visit was not altogether clear.[1] The Foreign Office thought that he hoped to persuade Hitler to put stronger pressure on the U.S.S.R. to come to terms with Japan, and to give up the support of General Chiang Kai-shek. In fact Mr. Matsuoka's success was limited. The Soviet Government would not agree to a non-agression pact on terms which Japan could accept. After hard bargaining they signed a neutrality agreement on April 13.

This pact had an advantage for the U.S.S.R. in leaving the Soviet armies free to meet the increasing German threat from the west, but

---

[1] Mr. Matsuoka's interviews in Berlin are fully reported in *D.G.F.P.*, XII, Nos. 218, 222, 230, 233 and 266. Hitler and Ribbentrop treated Mr. Matsuoka to their usual disquisition that Germany had already won the war. At the same time they produced arguments that the interest of Japan required her to enter the war and to make a surprise attack on Singapore. They assured Mr. Matsuoka that the Japanese need not fear a Russian attack in the north if they were engaged in the south. Hitler and Ribbentrop gave very strong hints to Mr. Matsuoka that Germany might find it necessary to attack Russia and inflict a total defeat on her.

Mr. Matsuoka said that he agreed with the German advice, but that he could not yet bring the opposition in Japan to his point of view. He made it clear that the Japanese were worried about the United States, and that the army and navy thought that a war against the United States and Great Britain might last five years. Mr. Matsuoka explained that he was doing all he could to 'soothe' Great Britain by assuming a friendly manner; he would thereby also mislead pro-British and pro-American elements in Japan until he suddenly attacked Singapore.

(a) the Japanese gain seemed to be greater since they were now free (as far as they could trust the Soviet Government) to make another southward move.[1] In any case the British reverses in Greece and North Africa encouraged the Japanese to make this move. Reports of troop concentrations suggested that the move might take place at once, and that it might be directed against Singapore and coincide with a German-Italian attack to block the Suez Canal.

In these circumstances the British Government decided once again to raise the question of a joint or parallel declaration by Great Britain, the United States and the Netherlands. This plan had been dropped earlier in the year partly because the situation seemed to have eased a little. and also because the United States and the Netherlands had regarded a public statement as inexpedient. Mr. Hull, however, had told Lord Halifax in March that the United
(b) States Government would 'say anything short of an unqualified threat', and the Dutch objections had been only to a public declaration.[2] On April 19, therefore, Lord Halifax was instructed to
(c) suggest, possibly to Mr. Roosevelt, that some kind of declaration was needed at once. The form of words might be that, if the Japanese made any further move to the south, the interests of the United States, the British Empire and the Netherlands would be jointly and individually affected. An alternative would be to declare the vital interests of the Powers concerned in certain areas, and in any activities which might affect those areas.

Lord Halifax thought it better to raise the question with Mr. Hull,
(d) since he had originally discussed it with him. Mr. Hull said that he would consider the proposal but that the United States Government had been 'saying this sort of thing steadily' to Japan. On May 3
(e) Mr. Hull told Lord Halifax that he thought a public declaration too provocative at the moment and that the most useful thing would be some further move by the United States Navy. The Netherlands

---

[1] Mr. Matsuoka's *démarche* obviously disquieted the Germans who did not trust him enough to tell him plainly of their intention to attack the U.S.S.R.

[2] On February 14, after Lord Halifax had been instructed to suggest an Anglo-American declaration (see above, p. 122), the Netherlands Minister gave Sir A. Cadogan a note
(f) saying that the idea of an Anglo-Dutch declaration that the two countries would act together if the Netherland East Indies were attacked had recently been considered at Singapore. The proposal had been rejected, but an Anglo-American-Dutch (and possibly Australian) declaration had been recommended. The Netherlands Government thought that a public declaration might have a provocative effect in Japan; they therefore suggested that we should propose to the United States Government that all three Governments should warn the Japanese through diplomatic channels that further southward aggression would not be tolerated. They considered that any Japanese action against southern Indo-China or Thailand would be an appropriate moment for such a declaration. In view of the decision not to pursue, for the time, the question of a declaration, Lord Halifax was instructed not to raise the Dutch proposal with the State Department.

(a) F3581/421/23. (b) F1627/17/23. (c) F3144/275/61. (d) F3283/17/23. (e) F3682/17/23. (f) F925/17/23.

Government were also still of opinion that a declaration through (a)
diplomatic channels would be less provocative than a public
statement.

For the time therefore the British Government again accepted the
American and Dutch views. The Japanese did not begin a southward
move, but the situation remained uncertain and dangerous. On
April 25 the Japanese Ambassador brought to Mr. Eden a reply (b)
from Mr. Matsuoka to the Prime Minister's letter. The reply was
polite but uncompromising. Mr. Matsuoka stated that Japanese
policy had been settled after the most careful consideration of all
the facts, and in view of the Japanese conception of a universal peace
under which there would be no conquest, oppression or exploitation.
This policy, once determined, would be 'carried out with resolution
but with utmost circumspection, taking in every detail of changing
circumstances'. Although the Japanese Ambassador tried to make
the best of this reaffirmation of his country's intentions,[1] and to
suggest the possibility of improving Anglo-Japanese relations, he had
no answer to Mr. Eden's comment that improvement did not seem
practicable 'while Japan complained about our help for China, and
Mr. Matsuoka prayed for the victory of our enemies'.

On the night of May 17–18 Lord Halifax reported a conversation
with Mr. Hull which led at first to some misunderstanding. Mr. (c)
Hull told Lord Halifax that when Admiral Nomura had come to
Washington as Japanese Ambassador at the end of January 1941,
he had opened the question of reaching an agreement with the
United States and of a settlement with China on terms which did
not appear unreasonable: (i) a recognition of the independence of
China, (ii) the withdrawal of the Japanese forces from China, (iii)
no discrimination. The Ambassador said that he spoke with the
assent of the naval and military chiefs and hoped to get the support
of the Emperor and of all the members of the Cabinet except Mr.
Matsuoka. Mr. Hull had told the Ambassador that he had better
see what he could do with the Emperor and the Cabinet. The
Ambassador had come back later to say that he had obtained their
support.

Mr. Hull did not think that there was much chance of success,
but that, if there were only one chance in twenty-five, he ought to
listen to any further approach which the Ambassador might make.[2]
The Ambassador had implied that the party in Japan which
favoured an agreement had thought it better to begin discussions

---

[1] The Ambassador also had to try to explain the meaning of one important sentence in
the letter where Mr. Matsuoka's English had gone badly wrong.
[2] Mr. Welles, however, told Lord Halifax that he was inclined to attach more importance to Admiral Nomura's talk than he would have done a short while ago.

(a) F3164/54/61. (b) F3424/17/23. (c) F4187/12/23.

with the United States. If anything came of them, they would be extended to include the British and Dutch.[1] Lord Halifax also reported that a suggestion had been made to Mr. Willkie that he should visit Japan as an unofficial intermediary.

(a) This information caused some disquiet in London. Lord Halifax was therefore instructed on May 21 to give Mr. Hull the view of the British Government that the situation had changed since the summer of 1940 when the possibility of a general Far Eastern settlement was discussed with the American Government. It was clear now that Admiral Nomura was acting as the mouthpiece of Mr. Matsuoka in a scheme discussed with Ribbentrop.[2] The plan seemed to be (i) to

---

[1] For the American record of these conversations, see *F.R.U.S., Japan 1931–41*, II, 325 ff, and 1941, IV, 1–729. For a Japanese account of the negotiations to the resignation of Prince Konoye on October 16, see the latter's memoirs (English trans. in the *Report of the U.S. Joint Committee on the Investigation of the Pearl Harbour Attack, pt. 20, exhibit 173*, Washington, 1946).

[2] The Foreign Office view of the origins of these American-Japanese discussions was not correct. The approach through Admiral Nomura was not made at first with Mr. Matsuoka's connivance, but resulted from the initiative of certain Japanese and American private citizens who disapproved of Mr. Matsuoka's policy. These persons presented to the State Department a memorandum on April 9, suggesting as the basis of an agreement that Japan would pledge herself to take only peaceful measures in the south-west Pacific, and (with reference to the Tripartite Pact) would come to the assistance of Germany only in the event of an aggressive attack on the latter by a Power not at present engaged in the war. In return the United States would agree (i) to restore normal trade relations with Japan, and assist her to obtain raw materials which she needed from the south-west Pacific area, (ii) to ask Chiang Kai-shek to make peace with Japan on certain stated terms, and (iii) in the event of his refusal, to give up American aid to China. The Japanese also asked for the friendly and diplomatic assistance of the United States in securing 'the removal of Hong Kong and Singapore as doorways to further political encroachment by the British in the Far East'. (*F.R.U.S., Japan 1931–1941*, II, 398–402.)

Mr. Hull, in discussing these proposals with Admiral Nomura on April 16, put forward four general principles upon which agreement was necessary before coming to details— (i) respect for the territorial integrity and sovereignty of each and all nations, (ii) support of the principle of non-interference in the internal affairs of other countries, (iii) support of the principle of equality, including equality of commercial opportunity, (iv) non-disturbance of the *status quo* in the Pacific, except as the *status quo* might be altered by peaceful means (*F.R.U.S., id.* 406–10).

The Japanese reply of May 11–12 to Mr. Hull accepted generally his four principles, but their answer was worded with adroit vagueness both on the question of Japanese support for Germany in the event of the latter becoming involved in war with the United States and on Japanese policy in China. On the first of these questions the Japanese appeared to be asking the United States to give up action in the Atlantic in the interest of Great Britain. The Japanese did not offer a pledge to take only peaceful measures in the south-west Pacific. After lengthy and inconclusive talks with the Japanese, Mr. Hull handed them a redraft of the proposals on June 21. The redraft explicitly provided for a Japanese statement that the measures which the United States might have to adopt to defend its own security (in other words, war with Germany) would not lead to Japanese entry into the war.

The Japanese did not answer this note until August. Meanwhile they were under strong pressure from the Germans to attack Vladivostok. On July 1 Ribbentrop sent a message to Mr. Matsuoka to the effect that Russian resistance in European Russia would be broken, perhaps in a few weeks, and that the Bolshevik régime would probably collapse. The Japanese ought therefore to seize Vladivostok and advance westwards along the Trans-Siberian railway to meet the Germans (*D.G.F.P.*, XIII, No. 53). General Ott, German Ambassador to Japan, replied on July 3 that Mr. Matsuoka had tried to get Japan to enter the war with an attack on the Russians, but that this was for the present impossible for Japan 'without facing other complications'. Japan would, however, seize

(a) F4187/12/23.

separate the policy of the United States from that of Great Britain; (ii) to enable Japan to withdraw from China with the least possible loss of face, and to retain Manchukuo and the Japanese position in Thailand and Indo-China; (iii) since the Japanese wished the United States not to assist one nation against another in the European War, they were also trying to limit the possibility of American help to Great Britain in the Atlantic as well as in the Pacific. Mr. Matsuoka was personally committed to the policy which had tied Japan to the Axis. He had obtained a pact of neutrality with the U.S.S.R. and now hoped to get an agreement which would free Japan from her commitments in China and from fear of American intervention. Mr. Matsuoka was aiming high, but he could count only on bluffing his way to success. The Japanese economic situation was bad, and the economic restrictions imposed by the United States, Great Britain and the Netherlands were beginning to have some effect. Japan had been restrained from direct action against Great Britain partly by her preoccupation with China and by the knowledge that the British and Dutch defensive position had become stronger. The main deterrent, however, was the possibility of American intervention. Even if the United States became involved in war with Germany, Japan would hesitate before an attack. There were signs that some Japanese were afraid that Mr. Matsuoka's policy would precipitate war with the United States. In our view the best policy would be to encourage these fears and to avoid falling into any trap.

Lord Halifax summarised these arguments in an *aide-mémoire* to Mr. Hull. Mr. Hull did not take kindly to what he termed 'a lecture' (a)

(*continued*)

points d'appui in French Indo-China (*id.* Nos. 63–4). On July 15 Hitler received General Oshima at his headquarters in the East, and again urged Japan to take part in the annihilation of Russia. The Germans had already been disquieted by the fact of Japanese-American negotiations which they regarded as contrary to the terms of the Tripartite Pact and as leaving Germany to deal alone with the United States and Great Britain (*D.G.F.P.*, *id.* Nos. 316 and 324).

The Japanese civil and military leaders, however, were determined to take their own line, and not just to be used by the Germans. At an important conference, held in the presence of the Emperor on July 2, they decided, while not abandoning the Tripartite Pact, at least for the time not to intervene in the Russo-German war. They would, however, reinforce their army in Manchuria, with a view to a possible offensive later on. Meanwhile, they confirmed previous decisions to concentrate upon a southern advance 'no matter what obstacles may be encountered', that is to say, at the risk of war with Great Britain and the United States. They would continue diplomatic negotiations with the United States, and carry forward preparations for war with Great Britain and the United States in the event of a breakdown of the negotiations.

One important factor throughout the Japanese-American negotiations was that the United States Government was able to intercept and decypher Japanese messages to their missions abroad. The decisions at the conference of July 2 were known in this way. See below, p. 152.

(a) F4430, 4570/86/23.

from the British Government, but Lord Halifax explained that we had received information that Mr. Matsuoka himself was sponsoring the approach. Mr. Hull said on May 27 that, while the discussions were continuing, there was only one chance in ten that they would succeed. In fact, the discussions had not produced any result before the Japanese moved into Indo-China;[1] it is unlikely that they failed merely owing to a leakage in Washington that they were taking place.

Meanwhile the War Cabinet were again considering the question
(a) of a public declaration. The reason for raising the matter was that the Netherlands Government wanted an exchange of assurances regarding mutual support in the event of a Japanese attack on the respective possessions of the Netherlands, Great Britain and the United States in the Far East.[2] Hitherto Dutch representatives had been taking part in joint discussions with British and Australian representatives on defence at Singapore,[3] but their participation did not imply a political commitment by Great Britain. The War Cabinet considered that they ought not to enter into such a commitment unless the United States had made a public declaration that they would come into a defence agreement. They felt, however, that they could no longer postpone giving assurances to the Dutch and that, in any case, apart from their alliance with the Dutch, they would have to assist in the defence of the Dutch possessions in order to safeguard their own communications with Australia and New Zealand. Delay was even more difficult after the Netherlands Foreign Minister, M. van Kleffens, had broadcast on May 6 a statement to the people of the Netherlands East Indies (which he had been visiting) that an attack on their territories would be resisted, and that such an attack would affect Great Britain.

Hence the British Government decided, subject to the agreement
(b) of the Dominion Governments, to make a public statement on lines similar to those of M. van Kleffens's broadcast. The statement would welcome the determination of the Netherlands East Indies to resist attack, and emphasise the British interest in any threat to the security of the line running from Malaya to New Zealand through the East Indies; an attack on any part of this line would be regarded by Great Britain as an attack upon the whole line.

Lord Halifax was instructed on May 22 to inform the United
(c) States Government of our proposed statement, but not to ask that

---

[1] See below, p. 139.
[2] See also note (ii) at the end of Chapter XXIV.
[3] These conferences were opened on February 22, 1941. I have not dealt with them since they were concerned primarily with technical problems. American representatives attended as observers.

(a) WP(41)101, F4130/54/61. (b) DO(41)30th meeting. (c) F4130/54/61.

they should take parallel action. We should, however, consider as before a parallel declaration or any endorsement of our action as a decisive contribution to the maintenance of peace in the Far East.

Lord Halifax replied on the night of May 26–7 that, in view of Mr. Hull's treatment of the *aide-mémoire*, it would be better not to (a) tell him that we intended to make the declaration. Lord Halifax suggested that we should explain the situation to Mr. Hull. We should tell him our view that a public statement of our assurances would have the advantage of deterring the Japanese and encouraging the population of the Netherlands East Indies, and ask whether the United States felt it undesirable that our assurances to the Dutch should be public. If the answer was 'yes', we should then make a private communication.

The Foreign Office did not consider that a private assurance would meet the case. Lord Halifax was therefore instructed to say (b) that we proposed to make the public declaration unless the United States Government saw serious objection to it. Mr. Hull saw no objection to the statement if it were not in provocative terms. He (c) pointed out that, whatever the terms, the Japanese extremists would try to read provocation into them. The Dominion Governments also (d) felt doubts about the expediency of a public statement, especially without American participation in it. There was a further difficulty that the deadlock in economic negotiations between the Japanese and the Dutch had excited opinion in Japan. These negotiations had begun in September 1940; they continued throughout the winter and were still in progress during the spring of 1941. The main question at issue was then the export quotas for tin and rubber. No agreement was reached on these matters in the early part of May. On May 22 Mr. Matsuoka asked the British Government to use their good offices to secure a settlement with the Netherlands (e) Government. We refused to interfere in the negotiations on the grounds that we could not put pressure on an independent govern- (f) ment, and that, in fact, we shared the preoccupation of the Dutch in regard to preventing rubber from reaching Germany.

The negotiations came to an end on June 17. In the state of tension thus produced Sir R. Craigie thought that the proposed declaration 'might just touch off an explosion'. He suggested that he (g) might say to Mr. Matsuoka at their next meeting that he hoped Mr. Matsuoka would succeed in preventing a Japanese attack on the Netherlands East Indies, since such an attack would involve Great Britain as an ally of the Netherlands. Sir R. Craigie was authorised to speak informally in this way but not to use words implying that (h) Great Britain would be 'automatically' involved, since so definite a

---

(a) F4529/4366/61. (b) F4529/4366/21. (c) F4883/54/61. (d) F4366, 4724/4366/61; F4703/54/61. (e) F4342/1732/61. (f) F4376/1732/61. (g) F5148/1732/61. (h) F5157/1732/61.

statement could not be made without further consultation with the
Dominions. Before receiving these instructions Sir R. Craigie had
(a) given a personal warning to the Japanese Vice-Minister for Foreign
Affairs that Great Britain must necessarily be concerned with the
outcome of any forcible action by Japan in the Nertherlands East
Indies. The Vice-Minister replied that Japan was well aware of
British concern in the matter.

(iii)

*Japanese policy after the German attack on Russia: consideration by His
Majesty's Government of possible economic action against Japan in the event
of a further Japanese southward move: Japanese occupation of bases in
Indo-China: American and British decision to freeze Japanese assets, July 25,
1941.*

The German attack on Russia brought a new turn in the situation.
(b) Sir R. Craigie telegraphed on the night of June 24–5 that the German
Ambassador at Tokyo was putting very strong pressure on Mr.
Matsuoka, and was offering Japan the Russian Far Eastern Maritime Provinces in return for Japanese assistance. Sir R. Craigie
thought that Japan would maintain a benevolent neutrality towards
Germany and try to obstruct the acquisition of supplies by the
U.S.S.R. from Indo-China and Thailand. He suggested a warning
to the Japanese Government that action of this kind would increase
the restrictions on Japanese imports by the Allies and the United
States.

The Foreign Office view was also that for the time Japan would
remain neutral, and that it was probably better not to try to influence
her decision. There were, however, indications that the plans for a
southward move had not been given up and that this move might
soon take place. From the Japanese point of view, the choice would
appear to be between attacking Russia at once or waiting until
the Russians had been defeated in Europe. The first alternative would
mean giving up plans for a southward advance, with the possibility
that the opportunity for it might not recur. On the second alternative
Japan might secure her objectives in the north as well as in the south.

At the beginning of July the evidence available pointed to a
Japanese move within the next two or three weeks. The Foreign
(c) Office thought that this move would be to secure bases in southern

---

(a) F5245/1732/61. (b) F5537, 5593/12/23. (c) F5868/12/23; WP(41)154, 155;
F5954/18/23; F5953/9/61.

Indo-China.[1] The Japanese were probably influenced by the fact that for the second time in two years Germany had paid no attention to Japanese interests in determining her policy towards Russia. Japan would therefore consider only herself, and would give up the idea of attacking Russia while the Soviet Far Eastern army was intact. The Japanese Government would regard a move against Indo-China as unlikely to cause war with Great Britain or the United States. If the British and American reactions were vigorous, the Japanese might hesitate before their next step. Otherwise they would go at least as far as taking bases in Thailand.

The problem, therefore, was to decide upon measures which would be a warning to Japan without actually provoking her to war. One obvious means of pressure was to restrict Japanese trade. This method had the advantage that the pressure could be increased, if not altogether unobtrusively, at all events without raising, suddenly, the most dangerous political issues. Furthermore economic pressure was already being employed to a very considerable extent; the imposition of new restrictions, therefore, appeared less like a change in policy. This change had come, in fact, at the time of the Tripartite Pact of September 1940. Hitherto, although the attitude of Japan was always suspect, the main interest of the Allies had been to prevent the Japanese from conniving at the supply of goods to Germany and Italy through the Pacific ports of Russia. After September 1940, the emphasis changed; it was necessary to regard Japan not merely as a medium of supply to the enemy but as a potential enemy. One of the duties of the Far Eastern Committee set up in October 1940[2] was to 'concert measures of precaution or pressure against Japan; to facilitate resistance to her, and to diminish her war potential, while bearing in mind the great importance of avoiding action likely to provoke Japan into aggression against our own possessions in the Far East or the Netherlands East Indies'.

On the economic side the committee worked to concert with the Dominions, the United States and the Netherlands East Indies, measures for cutting down trade with Japan. The instrument of this policy in British and Dominion territories was the export licensing system. It was agreed to control exports to Japan by licence and to

---

[1] Sir R. Craigie was instructed on July 5 (i) to call the attention of Mr. Matsuoka to a press report from Shanghai in the *Daily Telegraph* of July 4 that Japan intended to take (a) advantage of Russian pre-occupation and to carry out a long-delayed plan of acquiring bases in Indo-China and Thailand; (ii) to tell Mr. Matsuoka that, if the report were true, a serious situation would arise. Mr. Winant promised to ask the United States Government whether they would make similar representations. Mr. Matsuoka was away from Tokyo, but the Vice-Minister for Foreign Affairs denied categorically and without hesitation the accuracy of the report.
[2] See above, p. 112, note 2.

(a) F5904, 5905/12/23; F5883/17/23.

limit to normal figures the export of all commodities in which Japan—
and Germany and Italy—were known to be deficient. Certain commodities, e.g. jute, had already been restricted below the 'normal'
level: the list was gradually extended. The Netherlands East Indies
were willing to co-operate in imposing quotas on Japan, but during
their long negotiations with the Japanese the Dutch had hesitated
to go very far in practical measures. The United States Government
had inclined towards a different line of action. They thought it
better to impose a full embargo on a few commodities, e.g. scrap-
iron, and to leave the remainder free of control.

In July 1941 there was a change of policy in the United States.
(a) According to statements made by Mr. Welles to Lord Halifax, the
United States Government also had information, at the beginning
of July, that a Japanese move was imminent. Mr. Welles said that
the United States would make no further communication 'of a
minatory kind' to Japan until the Japanese had committed some
'overt act'. As soon as such an act took place, the United States would
impose an embargo on the principal materials imported by Japan,
e.g. lubricants, metals, and cotton, but not necessarily foodstuffs.
The United States would regard as an 'overt act' the acquisition of
bases in Indo-China even by agreement with local authorities. They
would not decide in advance whether the acquisition of bases in
Thailand should be taken as an 'overt act' determining an embargo;
they would certainly impose the embargo if Japan attacked the
U.S.S.R.

The Foreign Office at first understood from Lord Halifax that the
United States Government had in mind a complete economic
embargo. They were afraid that the sudden imposition of a measure
of this kind—i.e. the complete stoppage of Japanese imports and
exports and the freezing of Japanese assets—would compel Japan
to choose between a full reversal of her policy or a rapid advance
southward even to the point of war. The Foreign Office did not
know whether the United States Government were prepared to
force the issue to this extent and whether they were prepared to give
Great Britain and the Netherlands full support if war should result.
It was, however, clear that the United States Government were not
ready to promise this support. After Lord Halifax had telegraphed
that the embargo was not to be complete, there was less objection
on the British side; parallel action by the United States in increasing
pressure short of the breaking point was obviously welcome. In any
case it was essential not to give an impression of holding back when
the United States wanted firm action.

(a) F5868, 5869, 6101/12/23; F5957, 6022/9/61.

Meanwhile the action proposed by the British Government, after (a) consultation with the Dominions, included notice of the termination of the Anglo-Japanese Treaty of Commerce of 1911,[1] and the imposition of defence measures on the Malayan coast. These latter measures prohibited loading at night, and laid down that no vessel above 1,000 tons should be allowed to arrive at anchorages off the east coast of Malaya and the west coast of Johore during the night hours. Such precautions against Japanese landings or 'infiltration' were obviously desirable in themselves; they also had the effect of slowing down by about 50 per cent the export of iron ore from Malaya to Japan.

In the course of discussions with the United States authorities it soon became clear that the American action would in fact be near to a complete embargo. Mr. Welles said on July 19 that the United States might freeze[2] all Japanese assets and thus bring to a standstill (b) all trade with Japan except by special licence. The United States Government did not ask Great Britain to take similar action, but, again after consultation with the Dominions, the British Government decided to follow American policy and to freeze all Japanese assets. (c)

The decision had to be made quickly, since Japan committed the 'overt act' to which the embargo was to be a counter-measure. On July 16 Admiral Darlan told the United States Ambassador at (d) Vichy that the French Government had just learned of the Japanese intention to occupy bases in Indo-China. There would be no ultimatum, but the Japanese would use force if there were any opposition by the French. Admiral Darlan said that the French defence could be only 'symbolic'. In effect the Japanese had asked, on July 14, for eight air bases and two naval bases (Camranh Bay and Saigon) and for freedom of movement and manoeuvre in southern Indo-China for their troops. On July 21 Admiral Darlan (e) informed the United States Ambassador that the Vichy Government had been compelled to accept the Japanese demands. Two days later a public announcement on the subject was made at Vichy, and on July 29 a Franco-Japanese agreement for a joint defence of Indo-China—in other words, a Japanese occupation of the country— was ratified by the Japanese Privy Council at a meeting at which the Emperor was present. It was thus very difficult for the Japanese, even if they had wished to do so, to reverse their policy.

---

[1] The India-Japan Commercial Convention of 1934, and the Burma-Japan Commercial Convention of 1937 were also to be terminated.

[2] At the request of the Chinese Government Chinese assets were also frozen in order to prevent the Japanese from using such assets as were in their control in the areas under their occupation in China.

(a) F6272, 6291/12/23. (b) F6472, 6588/1299/23; F6734/9/61; WP(41)172; WM (41)72. (c) WM(41)73, F6588/1299/23. (d) F6473/9/61. (e) F6621, 6752/9/61.

On July 24 Mr. Welles issued a statement in very strong terms
(a) describing the Japanese action as evidence of determination 'to
pursue an objective of expansion by force or threat of force'. The
State Department brought into effect a freezing order against all
Japanese and Chinese assets as from the morning of July 26. Mr.
(b) Eden spoke equally strongly in the House of Commons on July 25
(c) and on July 26 the British Government announced that they too
intended to apply the freezing order.[1]

(iv)

*Consideration of the possibility of obtaining a promise of American support in
the event of a Japanese attack: reports of a Japanese move into Thailand
(July 26–August 9, 1941).*

The United States Government did not believe that the Japanese
(d) reaction to the freezing order against their trade would go as far as
an attack on British or Dutch possessions. Mr. Welles thought the
Japanese had only twelve months' reserves of oil, and that, as long
as they were occupied in China and had also to make provision
against an attack by Russia, they would not start upon a 'major
adventure' in the East Indies. Nevertheless the British Government
had to consider the possibility that the American decision to force
the issue might result in war, and that Japanese tactics would
certainly be to attack the British or Dutch and not the United States.
We had not wished to increase the risks of attack without at the same
time getting a promise of American support. We had now acted
without this promise, but it would have been difficult to have
attached conditions or reservations to the decision to keep level with
the United States. The constitutional position in the United States
made it impossible for the President to give a definite assurance of
support, and anything less than a clear promise would have been
more embarrassing than helpful. The view of the War Cabinet was
that, if the case arose, American support would be forthcoming, and
(e) that the best time to ask for it would be when war seemed imminent.

The Australian Government agreed in general with this view, but
considered that the question should be raised, in some form, at once.
There was less reason for delay since a state of tension with Japan

---

[1] The Netherlands Government also applied the order. Some confusion arose at first
over the details of the American measure. I have not dealt here with correspondence on
the subject. The freezing of assets did not necessarily cut off all trade with Japan, but
subjected it to the control of the Governments imposing the order, i.e. they could decide
whether or not to release any of the frozen funds.

(a) F6745/9/61. (b) F6834/9/61. (c) F6749/1299/23. (d) F6272/12/23. (e) F7070, 7168,
7169, 7170/1299/23.

existed, and in view of the action already taken, the question could not be regarded as limiting or conditioning the extent to which Great Britain and the Dominions would co-operate with the United States in economic pressure on Japan. Lord Halifax was therefore instructed on the night of August 1–2 that we proposed to approach (a) the United States on the following lines: (i) we hoped that the measures against Japanese trade would deter Japan from any further southward advance. These measures, however, might have an opposite effect. We were aware of the risk when we decided to follow the lead of the United States. We were doing what we could for our defence, but it would be a great relief to us to have the 'clearest indication that the United States feel able to give that we and the Netherlands can count on their armed support if we are attacked by Japan'. (ii) The security of Malaya and the Dutch East Indies— with their immense strategic and economic importance—depended largely on the United States. This fact was realised with special force in Australia and New Zealand. At the risk of their own security and in spite of the danger to their communications, since we had insufficient naval strength in the Pacific and Indian Oceans, these two Dominions had sent important contingents to the Middle East. They now saw the Japanese taking up positions from which they threatened Singapore and the Dutch East Indies. The Dominions had joined in the economic measures imposed on Japan; the dangers involved were the more clearly present to them because they were nearest to the scene of action. The United States Government would therefore understand why they wanted some 'indication that in the last resort the United States would be at their side'. (iii) We recognised the constitutional difficulties in the way of a formal commitment, but might not the President find it possible to intimate to us that in the event of a Japanese attack on British or Dutch possessions in the Far East leading to war, he would ask for the authority of Congress to come to our aid?

The War Cabinet had decided that this approach should be made (b) at once. Mr. Winant, however, said to Mr. Eden during the afternoon (c) of July 31 that it would probably be better not to raise the question of an undertaking with the State Department, but to wait until the Prime Minister had made a direct approach to the President. For this reason Lord Halifax was told not to act upon his instructions (d) until further notice. On the other hand it was necessary to raise another matter without delay. There was evidence that the Japanese were about to make demands upon Thailand similar to those made to Indo-China. Sir J. Crosby, British Minister at Bangkok, had (e)

(a) F7169/1299/23. (b) WM(41)75, 76. (c) F7244/54/61. (d) F7169/1299/23. (e) F6870/246/40.

warned the Thai Prime Minister that we should regard the concession
of bases to Japan as an infringement of the Anglo-Thai Non-
(a) Aggression Treaty of June 1940. Here as elsewhere the key to the
situation was Japanese fear of war with the United States. A public
or private warning from the United States might therefore encourage
the resistance of the Thais. Lord Halifax was asked to suggest that
this warning might be given at once, since the Japanese move against
Indo-China had shown that any warning measure would be effective
only if it were taken before the Japanese had committed themselves
to an overt act.

Lord Halifax had already spoken to Mr. Roosevelt about Thailand
(b) on July 31. Mr. Roosevelt's view was that, if Japan took action in
Thailand on the limited scale of their move into Indo-China—e.g.
landing 40–50,000 men—it would be unwise to send them an
ultimatum. He was considering whether he might say to the Japanese
that the United States Government was disturbed by rumours of
possible Japanese intentions against Thailand; the Japanese Govern-
(c) ment had not replied to proposals made by the United States that
the interested Powers should guarantee the neutralisation of Indo-
China,[1] but the United States now repeated this suggestion in
relation to Thailand.

Mr. Welles had actually made the suggestion on behalf of the
(d) President to the Japanese Ambassador on July 31. He mentioned
the fact on August 2 when Lord Halifax went with the Australian
and South African Ministers to Washington to the State Department.
Mr. Casey then raised directly the question of an American promise
of support. He referred to Mr. Welles's statement to the press about
the threat to American interests by Japanese action in Indo-China.
He said that this statement suggested that, if Japan attacked the
Netherlands East Indies or the British Commonwealth, the United
States would inevitably find themselves involved in the war. The
Australian Government therefore thought that a clear statement by
the United States would be of the greatest advantage. He also
mentioned instructions given in June—but not yet carried into effect
(e) —to Mr. Grew for parallel action in the event of a British warning to
the Japanese Government that an attack on the Netherlands East
Indies would automatically involve Great Britain in war as an ally
of the Netherlands. Mr. Grew had been authorised to say that the
United States were doing everything in their power generally to

---

[1] President Roosevelt had put this suggestion to Admiral Nomura on July 24, but,
according to Mr. Grew, the United States Ambassador at Tokyo, the suggestion had not
reached the Japanese Foreign Minister on July 27. Mr. Grew thought that the delay
might be due to 'deliberate suppression in the Japanese Foreign Office by the extremist
element'.

(a) F7169/1299/23. (b) F7171/210/40. (c) F6884, 7251/9/61. (d) F7212/1299/23.
(e) F5433/1732/61.

keep Great Britain supplied across the Atlantic, and that, obviously, they could not stand by and watch Great Britain's life-line cut in the Pacific through an attack on Singapore or the Netherlands East Indies.

Mr. Roosevelt had said to Lord Halifax that the attitude of the United States remained as summarised in the instructions to Mr. Grew. Mr. Welles also assumed that these instructions held good, but thought that it was necessary to wait for the Japanese reply to the proposal for neutralising Thailand.

The Foreign Office also asked Lord Halifax to raise the question (a) of American economic assistance to Thailand. Apart from technical difficulties the matter was not easy because the United States Government were doubtful about the value of helping a State which had already committed unprovoked aggression against Indo-China, and, in process of doing so, had lost independence of action in relation to Japan. It thus appeared unlikely that Thailand would resist Japan. The British view was that, although the Thais were more afraid of Japan than confident of the ability of Great Britain to give help, the provision of economic support—including the supply of war material—would have some effect in stiffening their resistance.

Meanwhile the Japanese Government showed no open sign of any change in policy. The Japanese Cabinet had resigned on July 16; (b) two days later Prince Konoye formed a new administration in which Admiral Toyoda took the place of Mr. Matsuoka as Foreign Minister. Sir R. Craigie reported the general view that the resignation of the (c) Cabinet had been a means of getting rid of Mr. Matsuoka whose policy had been discredited by the German attack on the U.S.S.R.[1] Admiral Toyoda had been Naval Attaché in London; otherwise he had no experience of diplomacy. His appointment was unlikely to mean a new direction in foreign policy, and the events which immediately followed his appointment showed that the previous Japanese line of advance was being continued.[2] Sir R. Craigie had no general discussion with the new Foreign Minister until August 1. This discussion did not advance matters; Admiral Toyoda merely repeated the usual Japanese complaints and gave the usual explanation of Japanese action.

In these circumstances the Prime Minister left England (in H.M.S. *Prince of Wales*) to meet Mr. Roosevelt off the coast of Newfoundland.

---

[1] This view was correct. See Prince Konoye's memoirs in *op. cit.*, pp. 3996-7.
[2] On July 20 Admiral Toyoda told General Ott that he intended to continue Mr. Matsuoka's foreign policy—*D.G.F.P.*, XIII, No. 130.

(a) F7027/210/40. (b) F6292, 6485/33/23. (c) F6602/33/23.

In the Prime Minister's absence the Defence Committee came to the
(a) conclusion that the position with regard to Thailand required
immediate action. On August 9 therefore Mr. Attlee, Deputy
(b) Chairman of the Committee, sent a message to the Prime Minister
that the only hope of preventing the Japanese from treating Thailand
as they had treated Indo-China seemed to be a plain warning by
ourselves and, *a fortiori*, by the United States that any such move
would lead to war. Neither Great Britain nor the United States
had gone beyond saying that a Japanese move into Thailand would
be a menace to the security of their respective possessions. A blunt
warning that this move would be a *casus belli* would be too direct a
challenge: in any case the United States could not give this warning.
Moreover we should not regard a Japanese move into north or east
Thailand as constituting such a direct threat to ourselves as an
attempt to occupy the Kra Isthmus.

The Defence Committee recommended the delivery of parallel
warnings through diplomatic channels that 'any incursion by
Japanese forces into Thailand would produce a situation in which
we should be compelled to take measures likely to lead to war
between our respective countries and Japan'. They hoped that the
Prime Minister would be able to obtain Mr. Roosevelt's agreement
to this course.

The Committee had also considered whether Great Britain and
the Dominions should give the warning alone if the United States
refused to take parallel action. The decision turned on the question
whether we should fight Japan if she attempted to occupy the Kra
Isthmus. The Chiefs of Staff thought that, as we had not enough
men and ships, we should avoid war with Japan as long as possible
unless we were certain of American support. Without this support
we should have to accept the position even if Japan forestalled us in
the Kra Isthmus. Any warning to Japan would therefore be bluff.
Against this view it was argued that we could not afford to let Japan
occupy the Kra Isthmus, since she would then hold the best jumping-
off ground for a heavy attack on Singapore at the moment most
favourable to herself. The occupation of the Isthmus would have no
other object than to serve an attack on Singapore and the threat
would be so plain that we should have to fight. Opinion in Great
Britain and in Australia and New Zealand would require this course
and our prestige in the east would not survive refusal. A sharp and
bold reaction to the Japanese move would also win sympathy in the
United States, and be more likely than anything to bring the United
States to our aid. In any case, whether a warning was or was not
issued, the Defence Committee agreed that if the Japanese advance

---

(a) DO(41)55th and 56th meetings. (b) F7882/4366/61; Tel. Abbey 23.

were limited to northern Thailand, we should at once advance to Singora in the Kra Isthmus without starting hostilities with Japan. The Defence Committee asked for the Prime Minister's advice in case it might be necessary to act before his return.

(v)

The Prime Minister and the President discuss the Far Eastern question: Mr. Roosevelt's proposed warning to Japan: negotiations between the United States and Japan: Mr. Churchill's broadcast of August 24: suspension of the proposal for a further British warning to Japan: fall of Prince Konoye's second Government, October 16, 1941.

On August 10 the Prime Minister gave Mr. Roosevelt a short memorandum suggesting the possibility of 'parallel' communica- (a) tions to Japan by the United States, Great Britain and the Netherlands. Mr. Churchill proposed (i) that any further encroachment by Japan in the south-west Pacific would produce a situation in which His Majesty's Government (or the United States Government) would be 'compelled to take counter-measures even though these might lead to war' with Japan; and (ii) that if any third Power became the object of aggression by Japan in consequence of counter-measures which it had taken or supported to meet further encroachment by Japan in the south-west Pacific, the President would seek authority from Congress to give aid to such a Power. The British declaration would be on similar lines with the substitution under (ii) of the words that 'His Majesty's Government would give all possible aid' to the third Power.

The President made it clear on August 11 that he could not give assurances that he would ask Congress for armed support. The (b) discussions, however, went beyond the consideration of a formula of warning. It was indeed inevitable that they should do so owing to the informal negotiations for a general settlement which had been taking place between Mr. Hull and the Japanese Ambassador at Washington. These negotiations were broken off after the Japanese move into Indo-China, but, if the Japanese showed signs of a willingness to resume them, the United States Government were unlikely to refuse. In fact the Japanese had already made a move towards reopening the negotiations.

The President showed the Prime Minister copies of two documents given to Mr. Hull by the Japanese Ambassador on August 6. In these

(a) WP(41)202. (b) F7995/86/23.

F

documents the Japanese Government proposed a resumption of discussions on the following terms: (i) Japan would not station troops anywhere in the south-west Pacific area except in Indo-China; (ii) the troops in Indo-China would be withdrawn after the settlement of the 'China Incident'; (iii) Japan would guarantee the neutrality of the Philippines; (iv) Japan would co-operate in procuring for the United States such 'natural resources' as the latter might require; (v) the United States in return would suspend military measures in the south-west Pacific area and advise the Governments of Great Britain and the Netherlands to do the same; (vi) the United States would co-operate in procuring for Japan in the south-west Pacific area, and especially in the Netherlands East Indies, such 'natural resources' as Japan might require, and (vii) would restore normal trade relations with Japan. (viii) The United States would use its good offices for initiation of direct negotiations between Japan and China, and (ix) would recognise the special status of Japan in French Indo-China even after the withdrawal of Japanese troops from that area.

The President said that he proposed to tell the Japanese Government that the United States were interested in these suggestions, and would discuss them on condition that during the discussions the Japanese did not extend their occupation of Indo-China or make Indo-China a base of operations against the Chinese. If the discussions were resumed, Mr. Roosevelt would again put forward his proposals for the neutralisation of Indo-China and Thailand. He agreed to add a warning that 'any further move by Japan would produce a situation in which the United States Government would be compelled to take counter-measures even though this might lead to war between the United States and Japan'.

Mr. Roosevelt told Mr. Churchill that he thought the Japanese conditions 'fundamentally unacceptable', but that it was desirable to get a month's delay by negotiation in order that we might improve our position in Singapore. The Prime Minister pointed out that the Japanese would 'double-cross' the President by trying to attack China or to cut Chinese communications with Burma. The President, however, thought it advisable to reopen the negotiations, and the Prime Minister said that it would be essential to maintain at full pressure the economic restrictions already imposed on Japan. He also suggested that American observers should see that Japan kept the condition with regard to a 'standstill' during the discussions. The President thought that it would be difficult to carry out this condition.

It was agreed that Mr. Roosevelt on his return should himself see the Japanese Ambassador. Mr. Churchill authorised him to say that we had been consulted and were acting in complete accord with the United States Government. Mr. Roosevelt declared that he intended to maintain the economic measures in full force.

The President and Mr. Churchill then considered what part the Soviet Government might play in the procedure. Mr. Roosevelt thought that the Soviet Ambassadors in London and Washington might be informed that the negotiations were being accepted in order to gain time, and that the Soviet Government might tell the Japanese that they hoped a settlement would be reached and that it would be applied to the north Pacific as a whole. The American warning to Japan might include a statement to the effect that, since the U.S.S.R. was a friendly Power, the United States would be similarly interested in any conflict in the north-west Pacific. Mr. Roosevelt asked whether we would give an assurance that we had no designs on Indo-China or Thailand and sought no change in the *status quo*. Mr. Churchill authorised the President to give this assurance.

In a wireless message to the Foreign Office summarising the discussions the Prime Minister hoped that the Dominions would (a) agree to the plan and realise that it meant 'a very great advance' on the American side. The Japanese might refuse the President's conditions or go on with the military action while pretending to accept them. The parallel declarations would then come into effect. On August 12 the War Cabinet endorsed Mr. Churchill's action. (b)

The American plan was not wholly satisfactory to Great Britain or the Dominions since the proposed warning was not in itself an assurance that they or the Netherlands could count on the support of the United States in the event of war with Japan arising out of a Japanese attack on British or Dutch possessions in the Far East. In any case the whole matter became complicated, or rather confused, because the United States Government did not give the warning in the terms agreed with the Prime Minister.

For some days indeed the shift of policy implied in the change of words was not known to the Prime Minister or the Foreign Office. Mr. Churchill came back to London on August 19. He had intended to see the Japanese Chargé d'Affaires and give him the 'warning' in terms similar to those which Mr. Roosevelt had agreed to use. He felt sure at this time that the message would not be toned down. On August 19, however, Mr. Winant sent Mr. Churchill a message (c) from the President that three days earlier the Japanese Ambassador had asked Mr. Hull whether he would resume the unofficial conversations about a basis of negotiations for a settlement in the Pacific area. Mr. Hull repeated what he had said about the develop-

---

(a) Tel. Tudor 19, F7882/4366/61. (b) WM(41)81. (c) F7995/86/23.

ments in the Japanese course of conquest which had led to the break-off of the conversations. On August 17 Mr. Roosevelt had given the Ambassador a statement on the lines agreed with Mr. Churchill. Mr. Roosevelt described this statement as 'no less vigorous than' and 'substantially similar to' that discussed with Mr. Churchill.

Mr. Roosevelt did not indicate the actual words of his statement.
(a) Lord Halifax was instructed on August 20 to ask for them, since we had agreed to follow with a similar warning, and must therefore know exactly what the President had said. Lord Halifax had already
(b) reported that the Japanese Ambassador had suggested a meeting between Prince Konoye and the President, and that the President had agreed to this proposal, although he did not expect much to come of it, and thought that Japanese policy was concerned more with the outcome of the war in Russia than with regard for the United States. Mr. Welles, however, was inclined to rate more highly the chances of 'something coming from the Konoye *démarche*'.[1]

The text of Mr. Roosevelt's 'warning' was telegraphed to London
(c) on the night of August 22–3. After summing up the situation since the negotiations were first opened, the 'warning' concluded:

> 'This [i.e. the United States] Government now finds it necessary to say to the Government of Japan that if the Japanese Government takes any further steps in pursuance of a policy or programme of military domination by force or threat of force of neighbouring countries, the Government of the United States will be compelled to take any and all the steps necessary towards safeguarding the legitimate rights and interests of the United States and American nationals, and towards ensuring the safety and security of the United States.'

These words differed in important respects from those agreed between the President and Mr. Churchill. The word 'war' was not included; the emphasis was laid on the security of the United States, and no reference was made to Great Britain. The area covered by the declaration was not limited to the south-west Pacific, and the term 'neighbouring countries' was introduced to reassure China and the U.S.S.R. Hence it was necessary for the British Government to reconsider the terms of the parallel warning which they had agreed to give. The Prime Minister, in a broadcast on August 24, said that Japanese expansionist activities could not be allowed to go on. He also made it clear that, in the event of failure of the efforts of the United States to bring about an amicable settlement in the Far East, Great Britain would be at the side of the United States if the latter

---

[1] But see below, p. 151, n. 1.

(a) F7995/86/23. (b) F7883, 7985/86/23. (c) F8218/86/23.

were involved in war with Japan. The Prime Minister did not say explicitly that a further southward move by Japan would be followed by counter-measures on our part, even though such measures might lead to war.

Lord Halifax was therefore told on August 27 that we still felt it desirable to warn Japan that, apart from our support of the United (a) States, we should be compelled, in the interest of our own territories, to take counter-measures in the event of further Japanese expansion. Lord Halifax was instructed to ask the United States Government whether they would object to the linking-up of our warning with theirs, since we had no previous negotiations with which we could connect it, and to our use of the words agreed between the President and Mr. Churchill. Two formulae were sent for consideration by the United States. Mr. Hull preferred the second formula, which (b) made no mention of the United States; he thought that, in view of the internal situation in Japan, it would be better to avoid the use of the word 'war'. He also suggested that the objection to Japanese encroachment should not relate to the 'south-west Pacific area', but should be made more broadly in the form of a warning against the continuance of a policy of war and expansion by force. As in the case of the American declaration Mr. Hull wanted to meet the suspicions of Russia and China; the former might think we were trying to divert Japan northwards, and the latter that we might desert China if our own interests were safeguarded.

Mr. Hull said that messages on August 28 from Prince Konoye had made the resumption of negotiations possible. He would tell us if the conversations reached a stage where a basis was found for the negotiation of a general Pacific settlement. He thought that the chances of success were one in twenty-five or fifty, but anyhow we should be gaining time.

Mr. Hull's comments made it necessary to reconsider the whole question of a 'warning'. We had proposed to use the word 'war' because we wanted to make it clear to the Japanese that a further move in the south-west would mean war, and unless we made this point clear, the warning would lose its value. A general warning, which might, for example, appear to apply to any new Japanese move in any part of China, would either be too vague or would commit us to more than we had intended. On the other hand there was considerable force in the American argument that the Far East should be treated comprehensively and that the Japanese should not think that our warning applied only to the south-west Pacific and therefore left them free to attack the U.S.S.R. without risk.

The Foreign Office considered the various possibilities during the (c)

(a) F8218/86/23. (b) F8651/17/23. (c) F8985/1299/23.

first half of September. The general situation seemed a little easier.
The Prime Minister, indeed, thought the situation much less tense,
and did not believe that Japan would risk war against the combination now developing against her. The Japanese had not made a
move against Thailand, and, although the United States Government did not tell us much about their talks it was clear—from
information given to Sir R. Craigie by Mr. Grew—that the Japanese
(a) had undertaken not to make any advance beyond Indo-China and
had also said that they would observe their neutrality pact with the
U.S.S.R. if the pact were kept on the Russian side. On the other
hand Mr. Grew was not certain whether these undertakings (as
communicated to Washington by the Japanese) were not contingent
on the conclusion of a general agreement. In any case Mr. Hull was
not 'appeasing' Japan; he had maintained the economic measures
against Japan and the freezing of Japanese assets was being carried
out more strictly than we had expected. Japanese trade with the
British Empire, the United States, and the Netherlands East Indies
was almost at a standstill. There were indications that some Japanese
had begun to think that the Tripartite Pact had lost its value as a
means of promoting the interests of Japan and that for the time
these interests might be served by a compromise with the United
(b) States and Great Britain. Sir R. Craigie thought at the end of
September that there was some chance that Japan might begin to
move away from a pro-Axis policy, though he gave a warning that a
change of tactics by the Japanese would not imply a change in their
fundamental objectives. The Foreign Office was less hopeful than
Sir R. Craigie about the prospects of the American-Japanese
(c) negotiations, but considered it better, on balance, to give up for the
time being the plan of another warning. A warning in general terms
would add nothing to the Prime Minister's broadcast of August 24,
and might even detract from its force. The broadcast had made
clear our attitude towards Japanese expansion and our full support
of the United States. The Japanese Government had already understood it in this sense.

With the approval of the Dominions Governments, therefore,
(d) Lord Halifax was instructed on October 8 to tell Mr. Hull our views.
(e) Mr. Hull agreed that the declaration should be held over. Mr. Hull
seemed a little more optimistic than the President that his arguments
would convince the Japanese. The President told Mr. Casey on
(f) October 11 that the prospects of gaining anything except time from
the negotiations were not great. The Japanese did not want to go
beyond vague assurances about non-aggression; the United States

---

(a) F8814/86/23. (b) F10117/12/23. (c) F9475/54/61. (d) F9744/17/23. (e) F10886/
1299/23. (f) F11299/1299/23.

Government were insisting on specific undertakings with regard to definite areas. Prince Konoye still suggested a meeting with the President, but Mr. Roosevelt had stipulated that the 'exploratory conversations' must first reach a stage at which they showed promise of a successful conclusion.

Although the United States Government did not give much information about the detailed undertakings for which they were holding out, there was, from the Japanese side, interesting corroboration of the general state of the negotiations. The Japanese Vice-Minister for Foreign Affairs told Sir R. Craigie on September 26 (a) that a meeting between Mr. Roosevelt and Prince Konoye was under consideration. (This proposal had already been mentioned to the press by the Japanese Ambassador in Washington.) The Vice-Minister said that the Japanese Government wanted a meeting to take place as soon as possible in order to strengthen Prince Konoye's position in relation to the extremists in Japan. For the same reason the Japanese also wanted an agreement to be concluded on general principles; the details could then be settled through diplomatic channels. On the other hand the United States Government appeared to be working for a more detailed elaboration before the meeting between the President and Prince Konoye; they also said that the other Pacific Powers must be consulted. The Vice-Minister said that the extremists, with German support, were doing all they could to wreck Prince Konoye's plans.

It appeared that at least on this point the Vice-Minister was right because on October 16 Prince Konoye's Government fell on the issue of the Washington negotiations, and was succeeded by a new administration under General Tojo. For the first time an officer on the active list became Prime Minister. General Tojo had been Minister of War, but had no diplomatic experience. The new Foreign (b) Minister, Mr. Togo, was an official of the Foreign Office,[1] and had been Ambassador to the Soviet Union in 1938–40.[2]

---

[1] Neither President Roosevelt nor Mr. Hull appears to have taken Lord Halifax fully into his confidence over the progress of the negotiations with Japan, and Lord Halifax, from his reports, does not seem to have realised the implications, on the Japanese side, of the approach made by Prince Konoye. The facts were that the decision of the Japanese conference of July 2 had been a defeat for Mr. Matsuoka and the army leaders and a temporary success, if only of a limited kind, for the moderates and for the naval chiefs who feared that Japanese resources (especially in oil) were insufficient for a war against the United States. Prince Konoye, who remained Prime Minister after Mr. Matsuoka had ceased to be Foreign Minister, continued to support the moderate (and naval) view of the danger to Japan of getting involved in war. Prince Konoye, however, knew the almost insuperable obstacles which the army leaders would place in the way of a settlement; he thought that the only hope—a slender hope—of reaching agreement was that

[2] Mr. Togo was married to a German wife.

[continued on page 152]

(a) F9987/86/23. (b) F10937, 10957/33/23.

he should negotiate personally with President Roosevelt. He would return to Japan with the best terms he could get from this negotiation, and secure the Emperor's consent to them. There was a risk that Prince Konoye might be assassinated when the terms, which would appear to the Japanese public as a surrender, were known, but the army leaders would accept the Emperor's decision. It is impossible to say whether Prince Konoye's plan would have succeeded, or even whether his own version of his policy and intentions is to be believed, because a meeting with President Roosevelt did not take place. Mr. Hull, among other reasons because he knew the intercepted Japanese telegrams (see above, p. 133, note), convinced the President that it would be unwise to hold discussions with Prince Konoye before the general heads of a settlement had been negotiated through diplomatic channels.

The resumption of the Japanese-American negotiations did not bring agreement any nearer. The Japanese indeed, for their own reasons, were resisting further German appeals—almost in the form of demands—that they should enter the war against Russia. On August 22 General Ott had reported that in spite of Japanese concern at the shipment of oil from American ports to Vladivostok (when Japan was receiving practically nothing), the Japanese navy still insisted upon concentrating for action in the south, and that neither army nor navy wanted to go to war with the U.S.S.R., the U.S.A. or Great Britain (*D.G.F.P.*, XIII, No. 225). Hitler had to accept the situation that Japan would take advantage of the cover provided by the German attack on Russia, but would follow her own interests. On September 8 the German Foreign Office drew up a memorandum in favour of further pressure on Japan to attack Vladivostok. Hitler was unwilling to do anything because he thought that pressure on Japan would be interpreted as a sign of weakness, i.e. that Germany needed Japanese help (*D.G.F.P.*, *ib.*, No. 291). Early in October General Ott considered that the Japanese-American negotiations were making no headway, but that opinion was hesitant and uneasy about policy. The army would be unable to attack Russia until next year, though an advance in the south was more possible, but, again, the Japanese Government were inclined to postpone it. The Japanese did not draw the optimistic conclusions of Hitler and Ribbentrop that organised Russian resistance was about to come to an end and that the collapse of the Bolsheviks was imminent (*D.G.F.P.*, *id.*, No. 378).

The Japanese Cabinet and the service chiefs, in a conference under the presidency of the Emperor on September 5–6, agreed that, if the United States did not accept their terms of settlement by early October, they would get ready for war. At this meeting the Army chiefs had appeared disinclined to continue negotiations, but the Emperor 'took from his pocket a piece of paper on which was written a poem by the Emperor Meiji: "Since all are brothers in this world, why is there such constant turmoil?" ' (Konoye's memoirs in *op. cit.*, p. 4005). On September 6 Admiral Nomura presented the terms to Mr. Hull. They did not meet the American requirements. The Japanese were ready to promise not to make a further advance from Indo-China and to withdraw their forces from China after peace had been made on satisfactory terms. They would carry on their economic activities in the south-west Pacific by peaceful means in accordance with the principle of non-discrimination. The United States would suspend all military activities in the Far East and the south-west Pacific areas and would do nothing to prevent the Japanese endeavour to settle the 'China Affair'. Japan also declared that, if the United States should enter the European war, 'the interpretation and execution of the Tripartite Pact by Japan' would be 'independently decided' (*F.R.U.S. Japan, 1931–41*, II, 608–9).

No amount of discussion, however, was able to bridge the gulf between the American and Japanese positions. The President and Mr. Hull (to the regret of some of their advisers) continued to think it premature to agree to a visit by Prince Konoye. Thus the time-limit which the Japanese had set for themselves was reached and passed. Meanwhile the American conditions, amounting in the Japanese view to a rejection of Prince Konoye's proposal for a meeting, damaged the latter's position, while the naval chiefs who had wanted to avoid war owing to the inadequacy of Japanese oil reserves were now thinking that for this very reason, if a war were inevitable, it should be fought at once and before stocks were further reduced. Prince Konoye's resignation on October 16 followed the failure of his policy. The idea of a settlement by negotiation was not totally abandoned, but the execution of policy was now in the hands of leaders less willing to compromise and more sure that war—whatever its risks—could not be avoided.

It is clear from German as well as Japanese sources that these risks were not underrated by the Japanese leaders. General Ott reported on October 31 that Japanese policy was still undecided and that Mr. Togo had put to him a number of questions about German plans after the fall of Moscow. General Ott repeated the German view that Russian resistance would be broken before the end of the year and that Germany could then turn with her whole national strength against England (*D.G.F.P.*, XIII, No. 434). Ribbentrop sent further instructions to General Ott on November 9 that Japan was in a most favourable position and could attack anywhere in the East 'without the risk of armed intervention' as long as 'American territories' (the Philippines) were not touched (*D.G.F.P.*, *ib.*, No. 458).

The Japanese did not hold this view, but their decision had now been taken. At a conference of civil and military chiefs with the Emperor on November 5 it was agreed to send two proposals to Washington with Mr. Kurusu as special envoy. If neither proposal was accepted by November 25, the Emperor would be advised to go to war with the United States. Preparations for war—including the attack on Pearl Harbour—were accelerated. The Japanese Government also made sure that, if they took the initiative in attacking the United States and thus were not technically entitled under the Tripartite Pact to German assistance, Germany would nonetheless declare war on the United States. They therefore suggested to the Germans that, since operational co-operation was not possible between Germany and Japan, the best form of mutual support would be, a 'no separate armistice or peace declaration' (*D.G.F.P.*, *ib.*, No. 480). General Ott was instructed on November 21 to reply that Germany would agree to the desired declaration about a 'no separate peace', and indeed accepted it as a matter of course, if Japan or Germany were involved in war with the United States, 'no matter for what reason' (*D.G.F.P.*, *ib.*, No. 487. See also No. 546).

The first of the Japanese proposals—known as 'A'—was presented at Washington by Admiral Nomura (before Mr. Kurusu's arrival) on November 7: the Americans already knew its terms from intercepted telegrams. The Japanese were to withdraw their troops from Indo-China after the 'China Affair' had been settled or an equitable peace established in East Asia. They would keep for a specified time (they had in mind twenty-five years) troops in certain areas of North China, Inner Mongolia and Hainan Island, but would withdraw their forces elsewhere from China within two years of the firm 'establishment of peace and order'. This proposal, as the Japanese knew, had no chance of success, but, while rejecting it, Mr. Hull began to consider the possibility of concessions which might enable the moderates in Japan to show that Japan was not being driven into war in order to live.

Mr. Kurusu and Admiral Nomura on November 18 also suggested the possibility of a temporary *modus vivendi*. Mr. Togo rejected this suggestion and instructed the envoys to present proposal 'B' as agreed at the conference of November 5. (For the text of proposal 'B' and the final breakdown of the negotiations, see below, Chapter XXIV, sections ii–iv.)

CHAPTER XXIV

The last negotiations with Japan

(i)

Anglo-American exchanges on possible action in the event of a Japanese attack on the U.S.S.R., October 16–30: deadlock in the American-Japanese negotiations, November 18, 1941.

FROM the imposition of the freezing order at the end of July, the British Government had left the United States Government the initiative in dealing with Japan. The overriding necessity of keeping in step with the United States had determined British policy, and although there were considerable divergencies in method between the two countries, they agreed in principle upon the importance of gaining time and of avoiding, if possible, any step which would result in war. The British and Dutch were more immediately threatened, but, if their policy remained in line with that of the United States, they could hope for American support in war, although they could not get—and the President could not give—a definite promise of such support.

On the side of Japan there were no more 'overt acts'; the Japanese, keeping as always to their 'step by step' tactics, were consolidating their position in Indo-China. The new Government might bring an increase in the tempo of the Japanese advance. It was therefore necessary for the Foreign Office to review the situation again. The Japanese extremists appeared once more to have strengthened their position in Japan. These extremists might take action very soon, partly owing to the pressure of the economic embargo, partly because the Russian situation seemed critical. The Russian resistance had lasted longer than had seemed likely in the first weeks of the German attack, but the Germans had launched what was intended to be a final offensive against Moscow and had won very considerable success. On October 16 the Soviet Government and the diplomatic corps had left Moscow for Kuibyshev. In the south the Germans were approaching Rostov-on-Don. Although the Japanese had been disconcerted by the German *volte-face* with regard to Russia, they might well think that they ought to profit by the new circumstances; the Germans, obviously, were trying to persuade them that the moment had come for them to do so.

The Japanese might move south-west into Thailand. They knew, however, that this choice was likely to bring them into collision with the British and Americans and Dutch. There was less risk for them in the north, where Japan already had a strong military concentration. We had thus to reckon on the possibility of an attack on Russia in the near future. Even if we could do little to help the Russians, it was desirable to consult the United States at once, and to point out that, as long as our Russian allies were resisting Germany in the west, we ought not to weaken or discourage them by a failure to support them to the best of our ability in the Far East. We had also to consider our Dutch allies, and the effect upon them if we were to fail the Russians.

Still more important was the question whether we could allow Japan to attack her enemies one by one and, after dealing with Russia, to turn against us at the moment which best suited her and which would no doubt coincide with the moment when Germany was free to turn westwards. Indo-China was already lost. Japan had established her bases there, and, if she were allowed by an attack on Russia to remove the present threat to her rear, the danger to us and to the Dutch would be very serious indeed.

Lord Halifax was instructed on the night of October 17–18 to put (a) these arguments to the United States Government, and to add that, hitherto, we had left the handling of the Japanese problem to the United States and had been content to follow them in their policy of maximum economic pressure. The Prime Minister's broadcast of August 24 had made it clear that, if the attempt at a settlement failed, we should support the United States in war. We were still ready to do so. We therefore wanted to know what the United States would do in the event of a Japanese attack on Russia.

This first impression of the new Japanese Government was wrong to the extent that there was no open change in policy. Mr. Hull had thought on October 15—just before the fall of Prince Konoye's (b) administration—that the opposition to an agreement was gaining strength in Japan and that the negotiations could not go on much longer. The Japanese were saying that the Americans were not playing fairly with them, and were merely using the time to co-operate with the British and Dutch in carrying out measures hostile to Japan.

Mr. Hull told Lord Halifax, however, on October 17, that the new Japanese Government wished to continue the conversations. (c) He thought it difficult to find any practical way of strengthening the moderates in Japan who were favourable to a settlement without

---

(a) F10885/86/23. (b) F10885/86/23. (c) F10960/86/23.

causing unfounded anxiety in China and undoing the effect of our firm attitude on economic questions. Mr. Hull thought it vital to avoid this danger.[1] He was considering whether some isolated barter exchange with Japan on a small scale—e.g. cotton for silk—might be possible on condition that the Japanese took no action meanwhile to disturb the *status quo*. He asked for the opinion of the British Government on this possibility.

(a)   A reply was sent on October 21 that in British experience the effect of concessions to Japan was more to stiffen the extremists than to encourage the moderates. We therefore did not think that Mr. Hull's proposal would deflect Japanese policy into a more satisfactory channel. Mr. Hull did not press his suggestion. He made it

(b)   clear to Lord Halifax on October 22 that the United States Government had not decided what to do in the event of a Japanese attack on Russia. He said that his own inclination would be to impose

(c)   further naval blockade measures, but he did not expect an immediate move by Japan. He had recommended to Mr. Roosevelt that, if the Japanese attacked Russia, the United States should take the line of saying that this was further proof of the Japanese desire to dominate the Pacific and that the United States could not stand still and do nothing.

The Foreign Office were uncertain whether Mr. Hull meant by 'further naval blockade measures' naval interception of Japanese

(d)   trade. A week later Mr. Hull referred to the subject. He said that not much progress was being made in the talks with Japan and that he doubted whether the Japanese Government would be able to hold the position much longer against the military extremists. He was inclined to give the warning of which he had previously spoken, i.e. to tell the Japanese that action by them against Siberia 'would be proof of their desire for domination', and that the United States would be obliged to take counter-action. Mr. Hull spoke again of 'long distance blockade measures' and evidently regarded them as a possible retaliation for a Japanese blockade of Vladivostok.

Lord Halifax asked whether Mr. Hull thought it would be of value for us to give a similar warning[2] if the United States Government warned Japan on the lines he had suggested. Mr. Hull said that, if his plan were approved by the President, it would be a matter for

---

[1] Mr. Eden minuted: 'I agree'.

[2] At this time also the War Cabinet considered whether we should accede to the wishes of the Netherlands Government for a guarantee in the event of a Japanese attack on the Netherlands East Indies. The War Cabinet agreed that, in view of the risk that we might thereby be committed to war with Japan, without an assurance of American support, it would be better not to undertake a definite commitment until we had seen how the situation developed: an attack on the Netherlands East Indies would inevitably have an important effect on American opinion. See also note at the end of this chapter.

(a) F10960/86/23. (b) F11204/86/23. (c) F11187/86/23. (d) F11532/1299/23.

consideration whether we should let the Japanese Government know that we were aware of the American warning and agreed with it, or whether we should convey 'more or less simultaneously' our warning that any attack on Russia would be 'a matter of immediate and direct concern' to Great Britain.

On October 29 and 30 Mr. Togo spoke to Sir R. Craigie about (a) the negotiations with the United States. Sir R. Craigie had given Mr. Togo an *aide-mémoire* about Japanese action in Indo-China, and had told him of the warnings he had delivered to Mr. Matsuoka about the serious results likely to follow from a Japanese move into southern Indo-China. The Minister tried to argue that everything done by Japan in Indo-China was in full agreement with the French local authorities, although in fact they had protested against the Japanese action. He then discussed the larger question of the American negotiations. He said that the negotiations had been going on for six months, and that Japanese opinion was now becoming impatient over them. He was surprised that we were taking no part in discussions which concerned us. He thought that the United States Government were deliberately dragging out the conversations: the Japanese therefore could not continue them, and the breakdown might have repercussions on British interests.

Sir R. Craigie thought that this indirect request for British inter-vention was not intended primarily to make trouble between us and the United States; few Japanese now believed it possible to separate the two countries. The Foreign Minister was really anxious about the situation and wanted to try every means of avoiding war. Sir R. Craigie was instructed to say to the Minister that we were aware (b) that the United States Government were trying to get a basis of discussion with Japan with a view to a general settlement in the Far East. We believed such a settlement to be in the interests of ourselves and of Japan, but the concessions could not be all on our side; we saw no advantage in entering upon negotiations unless some basis of discussion had been reached, and the principles of an agreement had been settled. We were therefore content to leave the preliminary part of the discussions to the United States.[1]

Lord Halifax told Mr. Welles on November 12 of the approach (c) made by Mr. Togo and of the reply made through Sir R. Craigie. Mr. Welles agreed with the reply and spoke in some detail about the

---

[1] In a speech of November 10 at the Lord Mayor's Banquet, the Prime Minister said that the United States were 'doing their utmost to find ways of preserving peace in the Pacific'. If, however, they 'became involved in war with Japan, a British declaration of war would follow within the hour'. For the text of the Prime Minister's speech, see Churchill, *The Second World War*, III (Cassell, 1950), 528–9 published in U.S. by Houghton Mifflin Company.

(a) F11592, 11621/9/61; F11651/12/23; F11673/86/23. (b) F11672/86/23. (c) F12186/86/23.

state of the negotiations. Meanwhile, Mr. Kurusu, Vice-Minister for Foreign Affairs, and formerly Ambassador in Berlin, had left
(a) Japan on November 5 to fly to Washington. On November 18 Mr. Hull gave Lord Halifax an account of the latest discussions.[1] Mr. Kurusu had said that opinion in Japan was such that an explosion might occur if agreement could not be reached between the two governments. Mr. Hull had replied that the United States could not abandon certain principles. The United States could not link up any settlement with the Axis, and would have nothing to do with Hitler. Japan must also withdraw her troops from China. Mr. Hull rejected out of hand a suggestion that some Japanese garrisons might remain. Mr. Kurusu argued that opinion in Japan would not allow the immediate withdrawal of all Japanese troops. Mr. Hull said again that without a withdrawal there could be no agreement. Finally the question of 'non-discrimination' in Japanese commercial policy had been discussed without result.

Mr. Kurusu was in 'a great state' about the breakdown on these three points. He asked whether some means could not be found of giving the Japanese Government time to educate their own public opinion towards accepting the American bases of agreement. He suggested a Japanese withdrawal from Indo-China in return for a relaxation of the economic pressure on Japan to the extent of sending small quantities of rice and oil to the country.

(ii)

Japanese proposals and American counter-proposals for a modus vivendi: *Mr. Roosevelt's message of November 24 to Mr. Churchill, and Mr. Churchill's reply.*

The Foreign Office agreed entirely with Mr. Hull's firmness in insisting that nothing should be conceded to Japan except in return for a recognition of the principles laid down by the United States Government and for definite action in accordance with these principles. It seemed unlikely that the Japanese would withdraw from Indo-China on the terms suggested by Mr. Kurusu. If, however, they were willing to do so, their withdrawal would not only benefit the countries—including China—threatened by the presence of Japanese troops in Indo-China, but would also show that Japan

---

[1] It is not altogether clear from the British record whether Mr. Hull spoke to Lord Halifax or to Sir R. I. Campbell.

(a) F12475, 12544/86/23.

was ready to go a considerable way towards meeting the Anglo-American point of view. If the offer to withdraw were not accompanied by unacceptable conditions, it would be worth while responding to it. The response would have to avoid any semblance of abandoning China or of disinteresting ourselves in a Chinese settlement on the basis laid down by the United States. It therefore seemed better not to allow even a limited relaxation of our economic pressure until some understanding had been reached about an ultimate settlement in China. The Foreign Office thought that this view would probably be that of the United States Government.

The United States Government were inclined to go a little further in the direction of concessions. On November 22 Mr. Hull asked (a) Lord Halifax and the Australian and Netherlands Ministers and the Chinese Ambassador to see him. He told them that his main purpose in holding the conversations had been to strengthen the peace party in Japan and to gain time. Mr. Kurusu had emphasised the urgent importance of giving the peace party some evidence of progress, however small it might be, and the United States navy and army were most anxious to gain time for further strengthening of the Philippines. Mr. Hull had therefore tried to keep the conversations going, while standing firm on all 'vital principles'. He now thought that further delay was not possible. On November 20 Mr. Kurusu had brought to him a communication from the Japanese Government.

This document was in the following terms: (i) The two Governments would undertake not to make any armed advance in south-east Asia or in the southern Pacific area except in the part of Indo-China where Japanese troops were already stationed.

(ii) Japan would withdraw her troops from Indo-China either upon restoration of peace with China or upon the establishment of an equitable peace in the Pacific area. Meanwhile Japan would move the troops in south Indo-China to north Indo-China on conclusion of the present interim settlement.

(iii) The two Governments would co-operate in securing commodities needed by them from the Netherlands East Indies.

(iv) The two Governments would undertake to restore their commercial relations to those existing before the freezing of assets. The United States Government would also supply Japan with a required quantity of oil.

(v) The United States would undertake to refrain from action prejudicial to the restoration of general peace between Japan and China.

(a) F12654, 12655/86/23.

Mr. Hull had already made notes on these demands: (i) would leave Japan free to act against Russia and against China; (ii) the United States would require Japan to leave only a few thousand troops in any part of Indo-China; (iii) implied that the United States would be asked to persuade the Netherlands Government to let Japan have more oil, etc.; (iv) the United States would not consider a complete restoration of economic relations; (v) the United States would not agree to stop sending aid to China.[1]

In conversation Mr. Hull said that he was considering an alternative proposal. He might suggest that the United States Government, while maintaining their position on the fundamental points, would be willing to consider a limited agreement. This agreement would give time for wider discussions, but would probably not last for more than two or three months unless progress could be made in settling the larger questions. The basis of the limited agreement might be that Japan should withdraw the bulk of her troops from Indo-China —leaving only a few thousand—and the United States, the British Commonwealth and the Dutch would allow some relief from the present economic pressure on Japan.

At one point Mr. Hull spoke of getting Japan to agree not to make an aggressive move in any other direction. Lord Halifax was not clear whether this promise would be part of the limited agreement. Mr. Hull asked what view we and the Dutch would take of his proposal. He thought that, at best, we should be preparing the way for a wider settlement if the Japanese really wanted to change their policy, and at the worst we should be gaining time. From the Chinese point of view, the removal of the threat to Indo-China would be of value. Mr. Hull was not hopeful, but believed that there was an 'outside chance' of success.

Later in the day Mr. Hull telephoned to ask Lord Halifax whether the British, Australian and Dutch Governments would give their representatives in Washington authority to decide upon the amount of economic relief which should be granted to Japan. Lord Halifax's own view was that it would be wise to take the chance of getting the Japanese out of Indo-China if we could do so without too great concessions. Lord Halifax agreed with Mr. Hull that there was a danger of the extremists seizing control of policy unless the moderates (with whom, according to Mr. Hull, the Emperor agreed) could show some prospect of improved relations with the non-Axis Powers and some economic alleviations. The Chinese Ambassador had agreed upon the advantage of getting Japan out of Indo-China, but had pointed out that Mr. Hull's plan left Japan free to go on with the war in China, and that the Chinese Government thought

---

[1] For Mr. Hull's view, see *The Memoirs of Cordell Hull* (Hodder, 1948), II, 1069–70.

economic pressure on Japan of vital importance and would not wish
to see an important reduction of it.

Mr. Churchill inclined at first to give Mr. Hull the latitude for (a)
which he asked. Our major interest in regard to Japan was 'no
further encroachments and no war'. We could be sure that the
United States would neither throw over the Chinese, nor allow
Japan a free hand against Russia. Subject to these conditions, Mr.
Churchill thought it worth while 'to ease up upon Japan economically sufficiently for them to live from hand to mouth—even if we
only got another three months'.

The Foreign Office considered that the Japanese proposals merely (b)
confirmed the view that they wanted the speedy removal of economic
pressure but not the speedy settlement of anything else. In addition
to the comments already made on the proposals by Mr. Hull, it
might be added that clause (i) related only to 'armed' advances and
would leave the Japanese free to carry on infiltration. The Japanese
might also interpret the clause as precluding further strengthening
of the Philippines and other outposts of the democratic Powers.
Clause (iii) suggested that the Netherlands East Indies could be
looked on merely as a storehouse without much reference to Dutch
sovereignty. Clause (iv) put special emphasis on oil, of which Japan
had no shortage except for war purposes. The Japanese proposals
amounted not only to the withdrawal of the freezing measures but
to the provision of positive assistance to Japan to acquire certain
commodities, while assistance of this kind would cease to be given
to China. The only offer made by Japan was to move her troops
from one part of Indo-China to another. Thus the proposals could
not be accepted, and the question was whether to reject them without
closing the door to a better offer from Japan for a limited agreement,
or to take the initiative in counter-proposals.

Lord Halifax was instructed on the night of November 24–5 to
say that we had complete confidence in Mr. Hull's handling of the
negotiations and thought him the best judge of the next step to be
taken. He would also understand that the Japanese would try to
force a hurried decision by magnifying the danger of delay. If,
however, Mr. Hull considered it desirable to put forward a counter-
proposal, we would support his decision. The State Department,
however, already realised the danger that the Japanese would use
any agreement as a kind of triumph for themselves and make capital
out of it, especially by trying to convince the Chinese that they had
been betrayed.

Furthermore, the Japanese proposals were an opening move in the
process of bargaining, and therefore their demands were put at a

---

(a) M1061/1, F12813/86/23. (b) F12655/86/23.

maximum and their offer at a minimum. If a counter-proposal were made, this process should be reversed. Mr. Hull's counter-proposal did not go far enough to justify a relaxation of economic pressure. The removal of 'the bulk' of Japanese forces from Indo-China was too vague. We ought not to accept or support a proposal in these terms, but should rather frame our conditions in such a way as to prevent the possibility of an attack on Kunming during the period of an interim agreement.

On this basis the Foreign Office suggested that we should ask for the total withdrawal from Indo-China, not merely of Japanese 'troops', but of Japanese naval, military and air forces with their equipment, and for the suspension of further military advances in China. We should also require assurances about other areas in south-east Asia, the southern Pacific and the U.S.S.R. In return, we might offer a partial relaxation of our economic measures by allowing the export from the United States of limited quantities of goods in order to ensure the welfare of the Japanese civilian population. We should not permit the entry of goods of direct importance as war potential (in particular, oil). These relaxations would come into effect as and when the withdrawal of Japanese armed forces took place. We should also have to state publicly—in order to prevent misrepresentation on the Japanese side—that an interim agreement was concluded only to facilitate the conclusion of a settlement of more fundamental issues.

It was difficult to delegate full authority to our representatives in Washington. Our economic structure was very complicated, and we had to consult other members of the Commonwealth. We could not give *carte blanche* to our diplomatic representatives until we had decided more definitely what goods we could allow Japan to import, and whether we should work through the machinery of financial control or by barter.

(a) These instructions had not reached Lord Halifax when he saw Mr. Hull on November 24, again in company with the Australian and Dutch Ministers and the Chinese Ambassador. Mr. Hull showed the draft of a document which he proposed, after revision, to give to the Japanese. The preamble recited the general principles which should govern settlement of the whole Pacific area. These principles were the preservation of territorial integrity and sovereignty, non-interference in internal affairs, equality of economic opportunity, and reliance on peaceful methods for the settlement of disputes. The

(a) F12765/86/23.

document then referred to previous conversations and described the Japanese proposals as containing features in conflict with the fundamental principles upon which the two Governments had agreed. The United States Government, however, wanted to continue discussions towards a general settlement, and therefore put forward a *modus vivendi* as follows: (i) The two Governments would declare that they had no territorial designs in the Pacific area. (ii) The two Governments would reciprocally undertake not to make, from regions in which they had military establishments, an advance by force or threat of force into any area of south-east or north-east Asia or in any part of the Pacific area. (iii) Japan would withdraw, and not replace, her armed forces in southern Indo-China, and reduce the total number of her forces in Indo-China to 25,000. (iv) The United States would allow all imports from Japan, provided that two-thirds per month of such imports were of raw silk. Exports from the United States to Japan would include food, medical supplies, and oil for civilian use.[1] The amount of exports might be increased if it appeared that the agreement was furthering a peaceful settlement in the Pacific area. (v) The United States would approach the British, Australian and Dutch Governments with a view to similar economic concessions on their part. (vi) The United States reaffirmed its fundamental interest that a settlement between Japan and China should be based on the principles of peace, law, order and justice. (vii) The *modus vivendi* would last for three months, and could be extended for a further period.

In answer to questions from Lord Halifax, Mr. Hull said that point (ii) was intended to cover Soviet territory, and that an attack on the Burma Road was covered by point (iii), since 25,000 troops were too few for an invasion of Yunnan. The Chinese Ambassador suggested a figure of 5,000 for the troops to be retained in Indo-China, and asked that point (iii) should be broadened to include troops in transit. Otherwise the Japanese might pass troops through Indo-China to Yunnan while keeping technically within the numerical limit. Mr. Hull did not think it possible to get closer supervision than that provided by the Allied and American consulates in Indo-China.

The Chinese Ambassador also asked that 'south-east Asia' in point (ii) should include China. Mr. Hull thought it impossible to get the Japanese to agree to suspend operations in China. Mr. Hull said that he wanted to present the *modus vivendi* at once. Lord Halifax hoped that he could wait for the views of the British Government, but

---

[1] Mr. Hull (*Memoirs*, II, 1081) also mentions cotton. There is no reference to cotton in Lord Halifax's report, but the President mentioned it in his message of November 25 to the Prime Minister.

that, if he felt bound to go ahead, we would trust his discretion and give him full support.[1]

(a) On the morning of November 25 Lord Halifax spoke to Mr. Hull in the sense of the instructions which he had received during the previous night. Mr. Hull agreed that 'troops' should include all arms; he did not think that he could ask for a total withdrawal from Indo-China or for the suspension of further military advances in China. He agreed also that the Japanese were deliberately withholding oil from civilian use in order to stir up resentment; for this reason he thought it of great importance to give some relief to the civilian population in order to blunt the instrument with which the military extremists were working on public opinion. In any case, in view of the time necessary to bring the oil to Japan, he did not think that much could be supplied in three months. He spoke of the possibility of excluding oil of the highest grade, and pointed out that, although there would be strong feeling about oil concessions, the balance of opinion would be on the other side if negotiations broke down over 'a few barrels of oil' and war followed.

Mr. Hull said that he would probably accompany his communication to the Japanese with some general statement about a wider settlement. Lord Halifax reminded him that the British Government had not seen this statement. Mr. Hull said that, if it became a matter of practical discussion, he would consult the British Government. He repeated that he was being strongly pressed by his technical advisers to gain time, since the whole defensive situation of the United States in the Pacific depended on delay.

(b) The Foreign Office were not reassured by fuller knowledge of Mr. Hull's proposals or by his explanations. During the night of November 24–5 Mr. Roosevelt had sent a message to the Prime Minister explaining the *modus vivendi*. Mr. Roosevelt said that the 'proposition' was a fair one for Japan, but that its acceptance or rejection was 'really a matter of internal Japanese politics'. He was 'not very hopeful', and 'we must all be prepared for real trouble, possibly soon'. The Prime Minister replied on the night of November 25–6 that we left the President to handle the question; we did not want an additional war, but were disquieted by the possibility that the *modus vivendi* might have had a bad effect on Chinese morale. Mr. Churchill thought that General Chiang Kai-shek was 'having a very thin diet' on the American plan, and that a Chinese collapse would be most dangerous.

---

[1] Lord Halifax's account of this interview was received at 4.50 p.m. on November 25.

(a) F12766/86/23. (b) F12818/86/23.

The Dutch also felt doubts about the plan, but the strongest opposition came from the Chinese. General Chiang Kai-shek sent messages in vehement terms to Mr. Roosevelt.[1] Mr. Soong, General (a) Chiang Kai-shek's brother-in-law, who was in Washington, went with the Chinese Ambassador to see the President and Mr. Hull during the afternoon of November 26. Mr. Soong said that the Chinese would rather retain the economic embargo, with the risk of an attack on the Burma Road, than choose the *modus vivendi*. In any case the proposals about Indo-China would not reduce pressure on the Burma Road, since the Japanese could attack it from Kwangsi, and use Indo-China as a supply base. Mr. Soong thought that if the United States now reversed the policy of the embargo, there would be a collapse of morale not only in China but throughout Asia, and that the moral position of the United States would be greatly compromised. According to Mr. Soong, the President said that thirty Japanese transports were reported to have left Shantung for the south. If this report were true, the Japanese were breaking faith while negotiations were taking place, and war might break out at any time.

(iii)

Abandonment of the American proposal for a modus vivendi: *general statement by Mr. Hull to the Japanese Government.*

During the night of November 26–7, Lord Halifax reported that Mr. Hull had given the Japanese the general statement[2] to which he (b) had referred, but that he had not given them the *modus vivendi*. Lord

---

[1] The Chinese Minister for Foreign Affairs expressed concern about the proposals to Sir A. Clark Kerr, but did not ask the British Government to take any steps in the matter. On December 2 the Foreign Office thought of instructing Lord Halifax to tell Mr. Hull that we had received no representations from the Chinese, since Mr. Hull seemed to think that we had been speaking for the Chinese when we mentioned our doubts about the *modus vivendi*.

[2] The statement given to the Japanese envoys on November 26 and headed 'Outline of Proposed Basis for Agreement between the U.S. and Japan' consisted of two parts. Part I was a draft mutual declaration of policy and repeated the principles already laid down by the United States. Part II detailed 'steps to be taken'. The two Governments would (i) conclude a multi-national non-aggression pact with the British Empire, China, the Netherlands, the U.S.S.R. and Thailand, (ii) agree, with the other Governments concerned, to respect the territorial integrity of Indo-China, (iii) agree not to support 'militarily, politically or economically any government in China' other than the National Government temporarily established at Chungking. Japan would withdraw all her forces (including police) from China and Indo-China. The United States and Japan would make a trade agreement and remove the 'freezing' restrictions in force. (*F.R.U.S., Japan, 1931–41*, II, 764–70). It was impossible, without a complete reversal of policy, for Japan to accept these proposals, and the United States Government did not expect her to do so.

(a) F12857, 12858, 12955, 13055/86/23. (b) F12859/86/23.

Halifax concluded that Mr. Soong's arguments, and perhaps the views of the President, had caused the abandonment of the *modus vivendi*: Mr. Hull had felt it necessary to give the Japanese something, and had therefore handed them the general statement. Lord Halifax thought that Mr. Hull ought not to have acted in this way without showing the British Government so important a document, but that no harm would have been done. On the morning of November 27

(a) Lord Halifax asked Mr. Welles whether the idea of a *modus vivendi* had now been abandoned. Mr. Welles said that Mr. Hull felt that, in view of the sharp Chinese reaction and of the little support which he had received from the British Government, he was not inclined to go on with his proposal. Lord Halifax pointed out that we had made comments and suggestions in response to an invitation to do so, but that we had in fact promised our full support to the plan. Mr. Welles said that the Prime Minister's message did not give this impression. Lord Halifax said that the message had expressed doubt only on one point, namely, China.[1]

Mr. Welles said that the Japanese were reported to be moving large numbers of troops in the direction of Indo-China, and that he

(b) expected an early attack on Thailand. On November 28 the United States naval authorities informed the Admiralty of instructions sent to the Commanders-in-Chief of the United States Asiatic, Pacific and Atlantic fleets. These instructions were to the effect that the negotiations had broken down, and that an aggressive move was expected from Japan, possibly within the next few days. Information showed that the Japanese attack might be directed against the Philippines, Thailand, the Kra peninsula or Borneo.[2]

---

[1] Mr. Hull told Mr. Casey on November 27 that he blamed the Chinese principally for the dropping of the *modus vivendi*, but that he would have liked stronger support from the British and Netherlands Governments. He did not stress this latter point, but said that it would have been impossible to implement the *modus vivendi* in the face of strong Chinese opposition. Mr. Casey suggested that further discussion with the Chinese might save the position, but Mr. Hull thought that it was now too late.

[2] The Americans intercepted instructions to Admiral Nomura and Mr. Kurusu on November 28 that the talks would now be ended. A conference of the political and military (army and navy) chiefs in the presence of the Emperor on December 1 accepted the Prime Minister's opinion that attempts at a peaceful settlement had failed and that Japan could wait no longer. Next day the chiefs of the army and navy informed the respective commanders that the war would begin on December 8 (Tokyo time). The Japanese were now sure of German support, but they had not given Hitler any information about their military plans for a surprise attack on Pearl Harbour. General Ott reported on December 5 that the Japanese Foreign Office considered that 'for domestic political reasons a declaration of war against the United States simultaneously with or after the beginning of hostilities (was) inevitable' (*D.G.F.P.*, XIII, No. 545). General Ott had taken the line that the Japanese should avoid a direct attack in order that the United States 'should be saddled with responsibility for war' (*ibid.*). Ribbentrop instructed General Ott not to suggest any course of action to the Japanese but to say that the Axis Powers and Japan must 'fight through together, regardless of the form of the tactical moves taken by one or the other partner in the individual case' (*D.G.F.P.*, *ib.*, No. 551).

Two points are of special interest in the exchanges between Japan and the Axis Powers in the few days before the outbreak of hostilities: (i) the Japanese seem to have been more

(a) F12939/86/23. (b) F13066/86/23.

The Foreign Office had not received a report from Lord Halifax of a breakdown of negotiations, or an account of an interview between the President and the Japanese representatives on November 27.[1] They asked for immediate confirmation, and pointed out the importance of the closest liaison on the political as well as the military level, in order that 'our respective moves may closely conform'. They therefore asked Lord Halifax, at 1.30 p.m. on November 28, whether the negotiations had in fact broken down, and whether the danger was of the scope and imminence suggested in the naval message. Lord Halifax replied at noon (Washington time) that Mr. Hull had told Mr. Casey that nothing of consequence had happened at the meeting between the President and the Japanese representatives. Both sides had merely restated their position. Lord Halifax said that he was trying to find out as soon as possible whether the United States Government considered that the negotiations had definitely broken down. He telegraphed again during the night of (a) November 28–9 that he had been unable to see Mr. Hull, but that Mr. Welles had told him that nothing further had happened since the President had seen the Japanese representatives and Mr. Hull had given the general note to them. The President had left Washington for a rest at Warm Springs, and would not be back until December 4 unless he were recalled earlier. The Navy Department had based its instructions on the expectation—which the State Department shared—that Japan would not accept the communication from the United States.

(continued)

confident of the completeness of the German victory in Russia. On December 6 Mr. Togo told General Ott that Japan regarded the German retirement from Rostov as a temporary setback of no special importance, 'especially if the German offensive against Moscow continued to develop favourably' (*D.G.F.P.*, *ib*, No. 550). (ii) Mussolini was as reckless as Hitler and Ribbentrop in promising Japan support under the Tripartite Pact for an attack against the United States, but other Italian opinion was less confident. Prince Bismarck, Counsellor of Embassy in Rome, reported a conversation on December 3 with the Marquis d'Ajeta, Ciano's Chef de Cabinet. Marquis d'Ajeta described the Japanese Government, who so far had not received an ultimatum from the United States, as asking for 'the firm promise of Germany and Italy in order thereby to get *carte blanche* for its actions without having previously defined how it visualised them'. Japan should be told not to assume 'war-guilt' by a declaration of war on her own initiative, but to leave it to the American Government to reveal itself in its true colours. Marquis d'Ajeta doubted whether the United States would declare war if the Japanese reply to their proposals was delayed. He also said that Italian opinion was divided about the advantages of an immediate Japanese-American war rather than allowing the existing situation to continue; his own view was that American entry into the war would be to the disadvantage of Germany and Italy (*D.G.F.P.*, *ib*, No. 543).

[1] At 9.30 p.m. on November 27 the Foreign Office telegraphed to Lord Halifax that they wanted to know as soon as possible the substance of the general statement given to the Japanese. It was not clear from Lord Halifax's telegram whether it was a mere recital of principles on the lines of the preamble to the *modus vivendi* as in Lord Halifax's telegram of November 24.

(a) F12980/232/23.

Mr. Welles showed Lord Halifax the record of the President's conversation with the Japanese. The conversation had been in general terms. The Japanese had taken the line of regretting that no temporary agreement had been found possible; the President had said that, although the United States wanted peace, they could not hope for it as long as the Japanese followed a policy of aggression in support of Hitler. Japanese actions were incompatible with a substantial chance of improvement in the relations between Japan and the United States. In view of the temper of American public opinion and of the issues at stake in the world, the United States could not make large economic concessions to Japan until there had been on the Japanese side clear evidence of peaceful intentions. If Japan gave such evidence, the United States would respond to it.

Mr. Welles said that, until Mr. Roosevelt's return, he could not say officially what the United States would do if Japan should attack Thailand. His own view was that the time had come for the United States to resist further Japanese aggression. He thought that the Japanese were more likely to move during the next few days than to reinforce Indo-China and then await the British and American reactions.

Lord Halifax saw Mr. Hull on the morning of November 29. Mr.
(a) Hull said that the situation had not changed, but it seemed inevitable that the Japanese would take some early action under the increased pressure of the military extremists. He had been impressing on the American Service Departments that they should be prepared for all eventualities. Mr. Hull did not expect the Japanese to reply to the communication given to them; he also saw no hope of reviving the plan for a *modus vivendi*.

Lord Halifax had meanwhile received a telegram[1] from the
(b) Foreign Office about the British attitude towards the *modus vivendi*. The Foreign Office and the Dominion Governments had approved of the attempt to reach an interim agreement with Japan. They had been unable to judge the urgency of the situation since they had no information suggesting the imminence of a Japanese move. Hence they could rely only on the judgment of the United States Government.

At the same time they had felt uneasy that the terms in the American counter-proposal were so favourable to Japan and left no room for bargaining. These terms also appeared to take too little account of the Chinese position and of the probable Chinese reactions. The Foreign Office hoped that Mr. Hull would now take us fully

---

[1] The telegram was despatched at 5.35 p.m. on November 28.

(a) F12992/86/23. (b) F12859/86/23.

into his confidence and allow time for considering any proposals before they were made to the Japanese. We entirely shared the desire of the United States Government to avoid war in the Pacific, if possible, and in any case to gain time; hence we still thought it right to aim at an interim agreement on the lines we had suggested.[1]

With these instructions in mind Lord Halifax discussed with Mr. Hull the whole question of the *modus vivendi*. Mr. Hull spoke with (a) some bitterness of what he called the 'unbalanced advice' given to General Chiang Kai-shek by Mr. Soong. He thought that the strong line taken by General Chiang Kai-shek on this advice had influenced Mr. Stimson[2] to change his view about the primary importance of gaining time, and had also affected the judgment of the British Government. Mr. Hull gave Lord Halifax an account of the document which he had presented to the Japanese.[3] He also spoke of the importance of the Service Departments preparing themselves for a Japanese war. Lord Halifax said that, while the Staffs could discuss hypothetical developments, it would be necessary, before any general action, for the two Governments to be 'absolutely together' on policy. Lord Halifax again asked what the United States would do if Japan should attack Thailand, but Mr. Hull gave no direct reply.

Lord Halifax thought that the only way to make progress in co-ordinating policy would be for the Foreign Office to tell him exactly what we were prepared to do, and instruct him to put precise questions to the United States Government.[4]

---

[1] The Netherlands Government also agreed generally with the line taken by the British and Dominion Governments.

[2] Mr. H. L. Stimson,. US. Secretary of War, 1940–5.

[3] Lord Halifax asked Mr. Hull whether he could have a copy of this document. Mr. Hull was willing to give him a copy, but could not find the document on his table. Lord Halifax was not given a copy until the afternoon of December 2.

[4] The only other development reported by Lord Halifax on November 30 was that Mr. Casey had seen the Japanese representatives at their request, and after informing Mr. Hull that he was seeing them. The Japanese asked Mr. Casey whether Lord Halifax would receive them. Lord Halifax asked Mr. Casey to say that he was away for the day. (b) He then telegraphed to the Foreign Office to ask whether he should agree to meet the Japanese. He thought it 'unprofitable and dangerous', even if Mr. Hull saw no objection, since the meeting might become known and the fact might cause doubts among certain sections of American opinion, as well as with the Chinese, and might also give the appearance of a difference of view between Great Britain and the United States. The Foreign Office agreed with Lord Halifax but instructed him to tell Mr. Hull before refusing the Japanese request, since we did not wish to lay ourselves open to the charge (c) of unwillingness, at any stage in the negotiations, to give all the help in our power.

(a) F12992/86/23. (b) F13137, 13159/86/23. (c) F13002, 13135/86/23.

(iv)

Final negotiations with Japan: the President's message to the Emperor of Japan and Anglo-American assurances to Thailand: the Japanese attack at Pearl Harbour.

On the night of November 29–30 Mr. Hull thought it necessary for the President to come back to Washington. Mr. Roosevelt reached
(a) Washington on the morning of December 1, and in the early afternoon had a long conversation with Lord Halifax. Mr. Hull was unwell and could not leave his apartment, but Mr. Hopkins was present during the conversation.[1] Mr. Hull had already telephoned to Lord Halifax that he had seen the Japanese representatives. They had no new instructions from Tokyo, and had spoken, presumably on their own responsibility, about the question of an interim agreement.[2] Mr. Hull repeated that the United States could not meet their demands for oil, for stopping aid to China, and for keeping more than a token number of troops in Indo-China.

The President said to Lord Halifax that he had been considering the possibility of a parallel statement by the two Governments to Japan on the movement of reinforcements to Indo-China,[3] but his conclusion was that it would be better to begin by making a communication to Japan in the form of a question. Mr. Welles would present this communication later in the day or in the morning of December 2. The President proposed to refer to the movement of Japanese troops, and to ask (a) where they were going, (b) if they were going to Indo-China, what was their purpose.

Lord Halifax enquired what would be the next step, since the Japanese reply would be either evasive or a lie. Mr. Hopkins said that there was a danger of giving the impression that the Japanese acted while the United States and Great Britain only sent notes. The President agreed. He thought that the two Governments should settle what they would do in the various situations which might arise. In the case of a direct attack on ourselves or the Dutch, Mr. Roosevelt

---

[1] Lord Halifax saw Mr. Welles later in the day.

[2] The President told Lord Halifax that Mr. Hull had said to the Japanese envoys that an interim agreement was not possible on a unilateral basis, i.e. while Japan was continuing to move troops.

[3] Mr. Churchill had already sent to the United States Embassy—in the early hours of
(b) the morning of November 30—a message* for Mr. Roosevelt suggesting that 'one important method remains unused in averting war between Japan and our two countries, namely a plain declaration, secret or public as may be thought best, that any further act of aggression by Japan will lead immediately to the gravest consequences'. We would make a similar declaration or share in a joint declaration with the United States.

*A copy of this message was telegraphed to Lord Halifax at 4.50 p.m. on November 30.

(a) F13114, 13084/86/23. (b) F13053/86/23.

said that 'we should obviously be all together' but he wanted to clear up matters 'which were less plain'. He therefore asked Lord Halifax to find out what were the intentions of His Majesty's Government (i) if the Japanese reply were unsatisfactory, but their reinforcements had not reached Indo-China; (ii) if the reply were unsatisfactory, and the reinforcements had arrived in Indo-China; (iii) if the Japanese moved against Thailand without attacking the Kra Isthmus, or even if they only enforced concessions from Thailand of a kind 'dangerously detrimental to the general position'. Lord Halifax thought that the United States would support whatever action His Majesty's Government decided to take in any of these cases.

Lord Halifax had been instructed to tell the United States Government that we expected a Japanese attack on Thailand and (a) that this attack would include a seaborne expedition to seize strategic points in the Kra Isthmus. We proposed to counter this plan—as soon as we had evidence that escorted Japanese ships were approaching Thailand—by a rapid move by sea into the Isthmus to hold a line just north of Sengora. By this move we should secure the aerodrome at Sengora, the port facilities, the east and west railway, and the only road. Since the Kra Isthmus was waterlogged during the rainy season (November–February), there would be great tactical advantages in seizing the position before the Japanese could reach it. In any case the political disadvantages in allowing the Japanese to get there first—even if they did not at once develop an attack on Singapore—were very dangerous.[1] We therefore wanted to know urgently what view the United States Government would take of this plan, since it was most important for us to be sure of American support in the event of war.

Lord Halifax put the question of American support if this plan (b) were carried out. Mr. Roosevelt said that we could certainly count on American support, though it might take a few days before it was given. He suggested that we might promise the Thai Government that, if they resisted Japanese attack or infiltration, we would respect and guarantee for the future their full sovereignty and independence. The United States constitution did not allow him to give such a guarantee, but we could be sure that our guarantee would have full American support.

---

[1] The wording of this telegram had been a matter of some discussion between the Foreign Office and the Chiefs of Staff. The Chiefs of Staff wished to be certain of American support before taking action. The Foreign Office thought it unlikely that we should get a definite assurance, and that, if we decided to wait for it before moving into the Kra Isthmus, we should never carry out our plan. The Foreign Office suggested that we should say that we intended to carry out the plan unless the United States Government wished to dissuade us from it.

(a) F13116/3906/40. (b) F13114/86/23.

Mr. Roosevelt believed that there was complete understanding between Berlin and Tokyo and that there was no chance of a *modus vivendi*. Finally Mr. Roosevelt said that he was thinking of sending a letter to the Emperor of Japan. He would write in friendly terms but would state clearly that, if the Japanese continued their present policy, the result would be war.

(a) The reply to Mr. Roosevelt's questions—telegraphed to Lord Halifax on the evening of December 3—went into more detail about this proposed final warning. The reply was that Mr. Roosevelt's first question was based on the assumption that Japanese reinforcements had not reached Indo-China. We knew, however, that reinforcements had arrived, and were continuing to arrive. If, therefore, the Japanese reply to the President's question were unsatisfactory, the United States, British and Dutch Governments should warn Japan that, if she used Indo-Chinese territory as a base for further aggression, she would do so 'at her peril'. We should be clear about our action if such warnings were ignored. On the assumption that we should get American armed support against Japan, our plan in the event of a Japanese attack or threat of attack on the Kra Isthmus was to advance along the Isthmus to a point north of Sengora.[1] If we were sure of American support, we should make this advance in the case of a Japanese attack on Thailand elsewhere than in the Kra Isthmus. We had been considering the possibility of an arrangement with the Thai Government whereby our entry into the Kra Isthmus would take place at their invitation. Unfortunately we could not give direct help to the Thais in the protection of the rest of their territory. The proposal that we should occupy a very small part of the Kra Isthmus was therefore unlikely to appeal to the Thais. Similarly we could hardly ask them to resist Japan in return for an undertaking from us to guarantee their ultimate sovereignty and independence; in fact we should be proposing to them 'to accept the virtual certainty of partial extinction in order to ensure their ultimate independence'.

(b) The Thai Prime Minister had already insisted to us that the only hope of saving Thailand was by a public Anglo-American warning to Japan that, if she went to war with Thailand, she would be at war with the United States and Great Britain. If he knew that we were giving a private warning, the Prime Minister might be more ready to resist Japan.

(c) On the morning of December 2 the President had put his enquiry to the Japanese about the purpose of the Japanese reinforcement of

---

[1] The Prime Minister on December 2 regarded a Japanese attack on the Kra Isthmus as unlikely at all events for several months.

(a) F13114/86/23. (b) F12862/9782/40. (c) F13136, 13160/86/23.

their forces in Indo-China. He had not received an answer when, during the evening of December 3, he discussed with Lord Halifax[1] (a) the British reply to his questions. He said that before deciding upon a simultaneous warning he wanted to know whether we meant by 'the use of Indo-China as a base for further aggression' some act of aggression or merely building up a base with the purpose of further aggression. Mr. Roosevelt said on his side that by support he meant 'armed support'; he agreed also with the proposed operations in the Kra Isthmus if the Japanese attacked Thailand: Lord Halifax was sure that we could count on armed support if we undertook the operation. Mr. Roosevelt thought, however, that the Japanese attack would be directed against the Dutch East Indies, and most probably against one of the islands north of Sumatra.

The President saw Lord Halifax again on the evening of December 4. Lord Halifax had been instructed to express our 'very deep appreciation' of the President's response, and to say that we thought the 'warning' should apply to an attack by Japan on Thailand, Malaya or the Dutch East Indies, and also to an attack on the Burma Road through Indo-China.

Mr. Roosevelt was doubtful about including the Burma Road, but otherwise agreed to the proposal for a warning. He thought that the (b) United States, Great Britain and the Dutch should give the warning independently, and that for political reasons the American declaration should come first, since Mr. Roosevelt wanted to convince American opinion he was acting in the interest of American defence, and not just following a British lead.

Mr. Roosevelt had not given up all hope of a temporary agreement with the Japanese. Mr. Kurusu had let him know indirectly that an approach to the Emperor might still secure a truce, and even lead to a settlement between Japan and China. Mr. Kurusu's plan was that the President should try to 'act as an introducer' between China and Japan with a view to their dealing directly with each other. The 'lines of settlement' might be the withdrawal of the bulk of Japanese troops from Indo-China, and a similar withdrawal from north China on a time-table to be agreed between the Chinese and Japanese military authorities, with an American assessor or arbitrator.

The President said that the Japanese would obviously require 'some economic relief'. He did not put too much importance on Mr. Kurusu's approach: on the other hand he could not miss even the chance of a settlement. He also thought that, in the event of war, his own case would be strengthened if he had been in communication with the Emperor. Lord Halifax thought that there was some danger

---

[1] Mr. Welles was also present at the discussion.

(a)F13219/86/23. (b) F13280/86/23.

in postponing the warning. He suggested that the communication to the Emperor might serve as a definite warning. Mr. Roosevelt agreed with this suggestion, and said that he would decide on December 6, after getting the Japanese reply to his enquiry of December 2 about Indo-China, whether he would approach the Emperor. If he made this approach, he would hope that the three-Power warning might be deferred until the Emperor had sent an answer. Finally, Mr. Roosevelt thought that His Majesty's Government should inform the Thai Government that, even if Thai sovereignty were temporarily destroyed, they and their Allies would restore it at the end of the war.

(a) Lord Halifax was instructed on the night of December 5–6 that we agreed with all the President's proposals. The warning was thus held up, but the position with regard to Thailand was complicated (b) because Mr. Roosevelt asked later on December 5 that the assurance to the Thai Government should not be given until he had come to a decision about the communication to the Emperor of Japan.

The Foreign Office regarded the Thai question as of great urgency. They did not consider that a British move into the Kra Isthmus would infringe the non-agression treaty between Great Britain and Thailand, since they had already told the Thai Government that the grant of bases to Japan would be an infringement of the treaty. On the other hand, as Lord Halifax had explained to the President, they could not expect the Thais to make any strong resistance to Japan unless they were promised material help. His Majesty's Government were unable to provide this help. Sir J. Crosby indeed thought on December 1 that in these circumstances (c) it might be better to advise the Thai Government not to attempt physical resistance, but to follow the example of Denmark and protest against an act of aggression without resorting to war. On (d) December 5 Sir J. Crosby telegraphed an appeal from the Thai Prime Minister. The Prime Minister said that Japan had planned an invasion of Thailand for December 3. The attack had been postponed but might come within the next few days. The Prime Minister therefore asked for an immediate declaration that we should go to war with Japan if the latter attacked Thailand. The Thai Foreign Minister, who gave the Prime Minister's message to Sir. J. Crosby, (e) said that there were rumours of a possible British occupation of part of southern Thailand before a Japanese attack. He hoped that these rumours were untrue, since such a move would put Great Britain in the wrong. Sir J. Crosby suggested on December 6 that His Majesty's Government might exchange notes with the Thai Government reaffirming the non-aggression treaty of June 1940. The Thai Prime

(a) F13280/86/23.   (b) F13282/86/23.   (c) F13164/9789/40.   (d) F13279/9789/40.
(e) F13326/9789/40.

Minister would use this exchange of notes as a means of getting a similar assurance from Japan.

Mr. Churchill thought it desirable to give the Thai Government a promise of British assistance. Hence Lord Halifax was instructed at 8.45 p.m. on December 6 to tell Mr. Roosevelt that Mr. Churchill (a) proposed to send a message to the Thai Prime Minister in the following terms: 'There is a possibility of an imminent Japanese invasion of your country. If you are attacked, defend yourself. We shall come to your aid with the utmost of our power, and will safeguard the independence of your country.' Lord Halifax told the President of Mr. Churchill's proposal on the evening of December 6. (b) Mr. Roosevelt agreed with it, though he suggested a change in the wording which would bring it into line with a message which the President himself had decided to send in confidence to the Thai Prime Minister. In this message the President intended to say that the United States would regard as a hostile act a Japanese invasion of Thailand, Malaya, Burma, or the Dutch East Indies, and that, whatever might happen during the war, the United States and Great Britain would aim at the complete restoration of Thai sovereignty unless the Thais aided the Japanese.

During the night of December 6–7, therefore, Mr. Churchill sent a message to the Thai Prime Minister advising the Thais to defend themselves if, as seemed likely, they were attacked.[1] Mr. Churchill said that the preservation of the full independence and sovereignty of Thailand was a British interest, and that we should regard an attack on Thailand 'as an attack upon ourselves'.

As far as Thailand was concerned, the sequel to this message was not unexpected. At 11 p.m. (Thai time) on December 7 the Japanese (c) Minister at Bangkok gave the Vice-Premier an ultimatum with a time-limit of two hours for decision. Japan offered Thailand the choice between two courses: (a) She could join Japan in making war on Great Britain and the United States; in return she would receive all her lost provinces: (b) She could join the Tripartite Pact, and allow the passage of Japanese troops across Thailand for the purpose of attacking Malaya or Burma. In this case, the independence of Thailand would be assured, but she would not receive back her lost provinces.

The Thai Prime Minister was away from Bangkok; the Vice-Premier and the Minister for Foreign Affairs said that in his absence they had no power to give an answer to the ultimatum. During the

---

[1] The message was sent to Bangkok before Lord Halifax's report was received (4.35 a.m. on December 7). A correction giving the terms stated above was sent to Bangkok at 1.40 p.m. on December 7.

(a) F13329/9789/40. (b) F13329/9789/40. (c) F13417, 13492/210/40.

night the Japanese landed at Sengora and elsewhere and were opposed by the Thais, who also opposed a British attempt to seize a railway station in the Kra Isthmus. After the Thai Prime Minister's return at 7 a.m. on December 8, the Thai Government decided that they could not hold out against overwhelming Japanese force. They signed an agreement at noon on December 8 allowing the passage of Japanese troops; in return Japan guaranteed the sovereignty, independence and honour of Thailand and undertook that she should not be disarmed. The Japanese again offered the restoration of the territories lost by Thailand. The Thai Government declined the offer, since they wanted to show that they were acting under duress and were gaining no special benefit from the agreement. The Thai Foreign Minister told Sir J. Crosby that Thailand was not at war with Great Britain and that, if British forces resisted the Japanese on Thai territory, the Thai forces would not oppose them.

(a) These last events in Thailand came after the Japanese attack on the United States fleet in Pearl Harbour. The Japanese reply to the President's enquiry about the purpose of the reinforcements sent to Indo-China was received in Washington on December 6. The answer referred to alleged Chinese reinforcements along the northern frontier of Indo-China bordering on China, against which Japan had been compelled to take military precautions. In view of this unsatisfactory answer the President decided to send a message to be (b) delivered to the Emperor on the morning of December 7 (Japanese time). If he did not receive a reply by the evening of December 8 (Washington time), or if the reply was unsatisfactory, he would send a warning note to the Japanese Government in the afternoon or evening of December 9. The President suggested that His Majesty's Government and the Netherlands Government should send their warnings on the morning of December 10. If the Japanese moved more quickly, the time-table would have to be advanced. The President did not expect an earlier move; Mr. Hull thought otherwise. Mr. Roosevelt said that the Japanese appeared to have about 105,000 troops in Indo-China, and another 20,000 or 30,000 in transports. The President said that there might be an attack by land or sea on Rangoon.

The Japanese, however, delivered their first blow, not directly against the British or the Dutch, but in a surprise attack on Pearl Harbour in the early morning of December 7. The Japanese representatives had been instructed by their Government to present a final note to Mr. Hull just before this attack was delivered. They did

(a) F13303/9789/40; F13330/86/23. (b) F13314, 13333/86/23.

not decode the message in time; consequently the note was brought to the State Department at 2.15 p.m. (Washington time), after the President and Mr. Hull had received word of the attack.[1]

The Japanese note consisted of a long (and distorted) recapitulation of the negotiations, together with the usual charges against (a) Anglo-American 'imperialist exploitation'. The note ended with the words: 'The Japanese Government regrets to have to notify hereby the American Government that in view of the attitude of the American Government, it cannot but consider that it is impossible to reach an agreement through further negotiations.'

A copy of the Japanese note was given to Sir R. Craigie on December 10. On December 8 Mr. Togo had informed Sir R. (b) Craigie that, as from that day, a state of war existed between Great (c) Britain and Japan. On the British side, the Prime Minister had telephoned to Mr. Roosevelt on the evening of December 7. Mr. Roosevelt had said that he proposed to go to Congress on December 8 with a message declaring the opening of hostilities: the Prime Minister had replied that we should declare war immediately after the United States declaration had been made. A later message, however, was received from Tokyo that Japan had declared war against the United States and Great Britain.[2] The War Cabinet therefore authorised the Prime Minister to state in the House of Commons during the afternoon of December 8 that we had declared war on Japan.

Notes to Chapter XXIV. (i) Sir R. Craigie's Final Report.

In a final report, dated February 4, 1943, on the development of (d) events during the six months before the entry of Japan into the war, Sir R. Craigie gave his opinion (i) that the Japanese decision to go to war was taken on or about November 27; (ii) that this decision would not have been taken, or at all events would have been postponed, if the Japanese 'compromise' proposals of November 20 had been taken as a basis of negotiation. Sir R. Craigie had stated this view at the time in telegrams to the Foreign Office. He regarded the Japanese offer as 'the last throw of the Emperor and the moderates' in their efforts to avert war. He considered that the decision on the American side not to proceed with Mr. Hull's counter-proposals was 'crucial' and 'unfortunate', and that the 'final reply' of the United States Government to Japan was in terms which the latter was certain to reject.

---

[1] Mr. Hull commented to Lord Halifax on December 8 that the two Japanese representatives 'had looked like a pair of sheep-killing dogs'. Mr. Roosevelt telephoned the news of the Pearl Harbour attack to Lord Halifax shortly after 2 p.m. on December 7.

[2] On December 8 Mr. Roosevelt asked Congress to declare that, since 'the unprovoked and dastardly attack by Japan' on the previous day, a state of war had existed between the United States and the Japanese Empire.

(a) F13567/86/23. (b) F13510/86/23. (c) F13489/17/23. (d) F821, 2602/751/23.

G

The Foreign Office, as will be seen from the narrative in this chapter, did not accept Sir R. Craigie's view, either at the time or in 1943, that the acceptance of the Japanese proposals of November 20 would have averted or postponed war, or indeed that the United States (or Great Britain) could have agreed to the proposals.

(ii) *Anglo-Dutch collaboration in the Far East.*

As the situation in the Far East became increasingly tense, the Netherlands Government had pressed for some indication of British intentions in the event of a Japanese attack upon the Dutch East Indies. The Dutch had already said, in July 1940, that if Japan attacked Singapore, they would almost inevitably become involved. On August 5, 1940, the
(a) Chiefs of Staff discussed the question of an assurance to the Netherlands Government which would state that we would go to their assistance if the Dutch East Indies were attacked. The Chiefs of Staff, however, took the view that we should not enter into a binding obligation without an indication of United States support. The deciding factor in the opposition to an assurance was the great weakness in our own means of defence.

On November 20, 1940, M. van Kleffens said that the Dutch were surprised at not receiving an indication as to what we should do if the Dutch East Indies were attacked. They did not expect a formal guarantee, but wanted some limited assurance of our support. On January 7, 1941,
(b) the Chiefs of Staff again advised that the matter should be left open. The Foreign Office had hitherto refrained from suggesting any kind of reciprocal assurance because of the difficulty of framing it; they did not want to involve the Dutch in a wider obligation than they could reasonably be expected to undertake. Mr. Eden and the Netherlands Minister,
(c) indeed, agreed on January 13 that any search for formulae should be avoided. Three days later, the Far Eastern Committee recommended that Mr. Eden should seek authority from the War Cabinet to exchange with the Netherlands Government oral assurances of mutual help in the event of a Japanese attack on British or Dutch possessions in the Far East.
(d)   Accordingly, on February 5, Mr. Eden submitted to the War Cabinet a recommendation that a simple oral statement be made to M. van Kleffens promising co-operation. The improbability at that time of a prior assurance of support from the United States made such co-operation more and not less necessary. Our own position would be clarified and assisted if we were to exchange reciprocal assurances with the Dutch to the effect that 'if the Dutch East Indies were attacked we should do our best to help them, on the understanding that the Dutch East Indies would do their best to help us if the attack fell on Burma, Malaya or British territories in Borneo'.
(e)   Mr. Eden subsequently discussed the matter with the Chiefs of Staff, who were still reluctant to exchange assurances with the Netherlands Government until the attitude of the United States was clearer. Lord Halifax approached the United States Government, but obtained no

---

(a) WP(40)302. (b) COS(41)17. (c) F141/141/61; F230/54/61. (d) WP(41)24; F666/141/61. (e) WM(41)14.

response, since the latter did not regard the matter as within the range
of practicability. On February 20 the War Cabinet agreed that the (a)
matter should be left until the Lend-Lease Bill was out of the way.

On March 24 the Netherlands Minister in London pressed that the (b)
question of a guarantee for the Dutch East Indies be considered on the
political plane, and suggested that the United States Government be
again approached. Three days later, Mr. Eden renewed his recommendation to the War Cabinet of February 5, 1941, but the Cabinet again
decided to take no action.

On May 12, Mr. Eden drew the attention of the War Cabinet to the (c)
unilateral statement made by M. van Kleffens in a broadcast of May 6,
that the Dutch were willing to fight if necessary, and to fight in alliance.
After M. van Kleffen's broadcast of May 6, the War Cabinet reconsidered the question of a further statement on the British side (see pp.
134–6). Mr. Eden decided on July 3 that, in view of the changed (d)
situation and especially the breakdown of Japanese negotiations with the
Dutch East Indies, a public declaration was inopportune. A fortnight
later, however, and again on July 30, Mr. Eden pointed out to the War (e)
Cabinet that we ought not to postpone entering into a political commitment with the Dutch. The Netherlands Government was commenting
on our hesitation to exchange some kind of assurances, and the position
with them was rapidly becoming more difficult. We could not withhold
much longer a reply to the Dutch note of June 12 asking us to ratify the
proceedings of the Singapore conferences and declaring their readiness
to do so. Mr. Eden asked for authority to give the Dutch a limited
assurance.

With the assent of the Prime Minister Mr. Eden made an oral statement
to the Netherlands Minister on August 1 that His Majesty's Government (f)
considered themselves 'to have already assumed the duty of safeguarding
and restoring the possessions and rights of the Netherlands to the best of
their ability during war and at peace. It followed, therefore, that an
attack upon the Netherlands East Indies would lead them to do the
utmost in their power to this end. His Majesty's Government must,
however, remain sole judge of what action or military measures on their
part (were) practicable and likely to achieve the common purpose.'
This statement was confirmed in writing in a letter to the Netherlands
Minister, Baron Michiels, on September 5. (g)

Early in October, Mr. Churchill told Mr. Eden that he was in favour
of some more definite assurance. The Foreign Office were asked to (h)
consider urgently what more could be said to the Dutch. Mr. Eden
thought that the time had come to seek a formal defensive agreement
with the Netherlands Government. Each would undertake to co-operate
immediately to the fullest extent of its available resources in the event of
the other being forced to take military action to counter an attack on any
of its territories in the Far East. On October 31, Mr. Eden asked for the

---

(a) WM(41)19; F1233/141/61. (b) F2343/141/61. (c) WP(41)101; F4130/54/61.
(d) F5952/54/61; WP(41)150. (e) F6620/56/61; WP(41)168; WM(41)72.10, C.A.;
WM(41)75.8, C.A.; F7385/54/61. (f) F7214/54/61. (g) F8675/4366/61. (h) F10561/54/61.

(a) authority of the War Cabinet to examine the possibility of such an agreement with the Netherlands Government. At the meeting of the
(b) War Cabinet on November 3, however, no conclusion was reached. The Chiefs of Staff still hesitated to make an agreement with the Dutch. Consideration of Mr. Eden's proposal was deferred.

Mr. Churchill thought it better to wait until the fleet had arrived in Far Eastern waters. The United States Government had made no definite reply to a further approach about an assurance to the Dutch, and a public declaration might be resented as an attempt to involve them.

(c) On December 4, however, the Prime Minister told the War Cabinet of President Roosevelt's remark that, in the event of any direct attack on ourselves or the Dutch, 'we should obviously all be in it together'. In the light of this assurance Mr. Eden was at last able to offer the Dutch, on December 5, an unconditional agreement for mutual assistance in the event of an attack. No such agreement was ever drawn up, as the Japanese attacked Malaya on December 7. The Dutch received no guarantee at
(d) any time from the United States of support in the event of attack.[1]

---

[1] In spite of these political difficulties, secret Anglo-Dutch staff talks were held at Singapore:
(1) at the end of November 1940.
(2) from February 22 to 25, 1941 (a United States observer was present).
(3) from April 21 to 27 (with United States participation).
(4) April 27 (between British and Dutch alone).
In the letter of September 5 to the Netherlands Minister, formal approval was given to the talks under (2) and (4) as the basis for future plans. The talks under (3) were never formally approved in the absence of formal approval by the United States Government.

(a) WP(41)254. (b) WM(41)108.5, C.A.; F11734/4366/61. (c) F13114, 13219/86/23; WP(41)296; WM(41)124.4, C.A. (d) F13254/54/61.

CHAPTER XXV

(1) The refusal to consider German suggestions for a 'compromise' peace, September 1939 to the end of 1941

(2) The definition of Allied war aims: the Atlantic Charter and the declaration of the United Nations, September 1941-January 1942

(1)

(i)

General character of approaches made to His Majesty's Government from September 3, 1939, to the end of 1941.

HITHERTO the chapters in this History have dealt with various stages of the war; the alignment of forces in the first months after the defeat of Poland, the Allied hesitations over Scandinavia, the 'disintegration of the pattern' in May and June 1940, the British fight for survival in the autumn of 1940, the second wave of German successes in the spring of 1941, the German attack on the U.S.S.R. and, finally, the events in the Far East which preceded the Japanese entry into the war by the raid on Pearl Harbour.

The diplomatic record of the war to the beginning of the decisive year 1942 would be incomplete without mention of the proposals for a compromise peace which came from the German side, and without reference to the formulation in general terms of an Allied programme for the political framework of a world of free nations after Hitler had been defeated and the aggressive power of Germany had been broken.

Throughout the war secret approaches were made to the British Government at different times suggesting the possibility of peace with Germany. Most of these 'peace-feelers' were put out at clearly defined periods, and corresponded with the progress of German operations in the military sphere. They fall into three main phases. The first phase lasted from the actual opening of hostilities in September 1939 to the German attack on Russia in June 1941. The second phase covered the next year or eighteen months before the military situation turned openly against Germany; the third phase covers the period of the decline and fall of German military power.

In the period of increasing German success the most substantial
offers came during and after the campaign in Poland when Hitler
and his associates still hoped that the Allies would recognise the *fait
accompli* of the German military victories and come to terms before
serious fighting began in the west. Mr. Chamberlain's speech[1] in the
House of Commons on October 12, 1939, made it clear that we were
unwilling to discuss even the possibility of a compromise on German
lines and at the expense of Poland or to consider peace with a Nazi
Government. Even so, further overtures were received, though in less
definite terms, until the outbreak of fighting in the spring. The
suggestions began again after the collapse of France. The terms,
which, for obvious reasons, were less favourable than those of the
previous autumn, were now represented as a last offer before the
invasion of Britain. After the failure of the German air force to
prepare the way for this invasion, the suggestions continued, at
intervals, and again with the menace that they were an alternative
to the destruction of Great Britain and the British Empire. The last
of the 'peace-feelers' before the German attack on Russia was an
offer of mediation from Japan. This offer appears to have been made
without consultation with the Germans.

In most of the early overtures Göring was alleged to be, if not the
prime mover, an interested party. According to M. Dahlerus[2] in
September 1939, Göring hoped to negotiate an honourable settlement and to replace Hitler as the real ruler of Germany. The other
principal channel was a section of the German army which was said
to fear the outcome of the pact with the U.S.S.R. and to favour a
compromise peace, the removal of Hitler, and the establishment of
a more moderate government in Germany. This military group,
however, never suggested any detailed plan or gave evidence of their
ability to get rid of Hitler.

The Foreign Office could not decide easily how genuine these
approaches were. Before the war there were many highly-placed
German civilians and soldiers who disapproved of Hitler's policy
while continuing to serve him and who considered that German
aspirations might be met on terms which would not involve war with
Great Britain. Others, again, thought that if Germany resorted to war,
at all events in 1939, she would ultimately be defeated and collapse
in ruin. After the war had begun these people, or some of them, may
have believed in the possibility of a peace on terms which Great
Britain could have accepted. The emissaries who approached the
British Government greatly overstated the influence of their party
or group, and their terms, as far as they were ever defined, did not

---

[1] See Volume I, p. 13 for this speech, and for Hitler's peace offer to which the speech
was a reply.
[2] For M. Dahlerus, see below, pp. 185–6.

offer a basis for negotiations. They wanted, or thought it necessary for their success, to keep most of the advantages gained by Hitler's career of aggressive militarism and treaty-breaking; hence their offers amounted to little more than a suggestion that we should buy peace at the sacrifice of the cause for which we were fighting and at the cost of the Allies whom we had promised to defend. Furthermore, it was impossible to judge how far the military approaches, in particular, came from a body of men strong enough, or, for that matter, sufficiently determined to succeed in carrying out a *coup* against the régime. As early as the spring of 1941 the offers, looked at in retrospect, gave the impression—perhaps a distorted impression —that they were part of a propaganda design intended to test the strength of a peace party in Great Britain and to create doubts in our own minds and in those of the less stalwart neutrals through whom in most cases the approaches were made.

British policy towards the approaches made throughout this period was consistent. The less important approaches were ignored; offers which seemed more authentic were answered in terms of Mr. Chamberlain's statement in Parliament on October 12, 1939. There was obviously more readiness to consider—with due caution— approaches made before the opening of the German offensive, i.e. while an opportunity still seemed open for successful political action against Hitler by Germans themselves. Lord Halifax, for instance, was more inclined than most of the permanent staff of the Foreign Office to follow up approaches, not because he believed them likely to succeed, but because he felt bound to take even the slightest chance of avoiding the calamity of total war. Mr. Roosevelt was told in general terms of the approaches and our attitude towards them, in order that there should be no doubt in the United States of our determination to continue fighting until we had won the war.[1] In 1941, when the offers were renewed, instructions were sent to the posts where overtures had been made in the previous months that henceforward all such enquiries should receive no reply. The only exception was the Prime Minister's formal answer to the offer of mediation received from Japan.

---

[1] For Mr. Sumner Welles's mission in Europe in the early spring of 1940, see Volume I, pp. 164 ff.

Mr. Welles while in Germany was told by Dr. Schacht that a movement was being organised by leading generals to supplant the Hitler régime. The one obstacle in their way was a lack of assurance that, if such a movement succeeded, the Allies would give a positive guarantee that Germany would be permitted to regain her rightful place in the world, and would not be treated as she had been treated in 1918. Dr. Schacht said that he could not mention any names. If an offensive took place (on the western front) it would make the movement more difficult, but he (Dr. Schacht) thought that the individuals sponsoring the movement were in a position to prevent or, at all events, delay such an offensive. Dr. Schacht added that it would take a few months, perhaps, even if no offensive took place, before the conspirators were ready to act. *F.R.U.S. 1940*, I, 56–8.

Note to Section (i). The Dutch-Belgian peace appeal of November 7, 1939.

(a)   On November 7, 1939, a joint appeal for peace was made by Queen Wilhelmina of the Netherlands and King Leopold of the Belgians to Great Britain, France and Germany. The appeal took the form of an address to the heads of each of the three States. This public *démarche* was thus unlike the secret 'peace-feelers' put forward through various channels. The Foreign Office did not consider that the Germans had previous knowledge of it; the motives of the two Sovereigns seemed to be fear of immediate German aggression.[1]

The War Cabinet drafted a reply for submission to His Majesty the King with a view to the likelihood that the Germans would try to use the offer for propagandist purposes. The reply repeated the reasons why the peoples of the British Commonwealth had been compelled to resist German aggression, referred to the Prime Minister's speech of October 12, and stated that His Majesty's Government would consider any proposals from Germany which offered real prospects of a settlement on the lines which we had already outlined in our public declarations.

After this formal reply had been sent in the name of His Majesty the King, and an answer of a similar kind had been sent by the French President, the King of the Belgians asked Admiral Sir R. Keyes, as a personal friend, to tell the Prime Minister that he realised that the British and French replies were uncompromising, and that any further approach must come from Germany. The King of the Belgians repeated that his purpose was to avoid 'ruthless and devasting warfare' and that, in any case, he regarded delay as valuable on military grounds both to Belgium and to the Allies.

The Prime Minister asked Sir R. Keyes to reply that he (the Prime Minister) shared King Leopold's desire to avoid useless bloodshed. He also believed that time was on our side, and would welcome any steps taken by King Leopold to avert or even to postpone the outbreak of active warfare. At the same time the Prime Minister felt bound to say that he thought it impossible for Hitler to make proposals which the British Government could consider. Subject to the latter observation he sent King Leopold his best wishes for any further efforts which he might make. At Mr. Churchill's suggestion the terms of the reply were modified by the omission of a reference to further efforts by King Leopold and the inclusion of a phrase that 'there could be no question of any steps being taken by us, or by our wish, to invite negotiations'. Mr. Churchill suggested these changes because he thought that otherwise King Leopold might misunderstand the letter, and take it as an invitation from the Prime Minister to open another channel of negotiations with Hitler. No further approach was made to His Majesty's Government in connexion with the joint Belgian-Dutch offer.

---

[1] See Volume I, pp. 16–17.

(a) C18086, 18280, 18595, 18523, 18920/13005/18.

(ii)

Offers made with reference to Göring: M. Dahlerus's approaches (September–December 1939).

The most important secret channel used by the Germans during the autumn of 1939 was M. Dahlerus. M. Dahlerus, a Swedish business-man, and a friend and admirer of Göring, had been employed by Göring in the period immediately before the outbreak of war as an unofficial channel of communication with the British Government.

On September 5 M. Dahlerus approached Sir E. Monson, British Minister at Stockholm.[1] He said that he still believed in the possi- (a) bility of a settlement. He was convinced that Göring genuinely regretted the outbreak of the war, and that, short of actual disloyalty to Hitler, he would like to see a truce negotiated. The unwillingness of the Polish Government to treat in earnest about Danzig and the Corridor had played into Ribbentrop's hands; Göring would take the lead in a truce aceptable to His Majesty's Government; he could perhaps 'manage' Hitler, who might eventually assume some form of presidential role with the actual power in Göring's hands. M. Dahlerus recalled as proof of Göring's sincerity the fact that with Hitler's reluctant consent he was prepared to fly to London on September 3. Göring had also given him letters from two Royal Air Force prisoners to be forwarded to their families with a personal message that they were being well treated. On September 18 M. Dahlerus reported to Sir E. Monson that the German army were (b) now approaching a position in Poland beyond which they would not go and that the German Government were seeking an early opportunity to make an offer of peace. Göring suggested that a move should come from His Majesty's Government. In contrast to the other members of the German Government Göring was absolutely trustworthy and would stake his reputation on the observance of any terms which he negotiated personally. The German people were tired of war and the field-marshal's influence was increasing to the detriment of Hitler's, despite German successes in Poland. M. Dahlerus's view was that we should not show eagerness to negotiate, but should continue to avoid any form of warfare likely to inflame feeling and at the right moment should let it be known to Göring that we were ready to open discussions.

---

[1] M. Dahlerus also saw Sir G. Ogilvie-Forbes in Stockholm on September 12 and in Oslo on September 24. Sir G. Ogilvie-Forbes was Counsellor in Berlin on the outbreak of war. He was transferred to Oslo on September 4: he stayed for a time in Stockholm on his way to Oslo.

(a) C13916/15/18, C15620/13005/18. (b) C16448/13005/18.

G*

Sir E. Monson informed M. Dahlerus on instructions that Lord Halifax could think of no peace offer likely to come from the German Government that could even be considered by His Majesty's Government or by the French Government. His Majesty's Govern-could not, however, define their attitude to an offer of which they did not know the nature and if M. Dahlerus were willing to ascertain details from Göring they would be able to examine them.[1]

On October 11 M. Dahlerus transmitted through His Majesty's Legation at The Hague certain proposals, which he described as those of the German Government. He explained that, for obvious reasons, the German Government would not allow him to give Sir N. Bland anything in writing from them. The proposals were as follows: (i) A meeting as soon as possible of representatives of France, England and Germany to draw up a basis of agreed points for submission to the three Governments. If the three Governments accepted the points, an armistice would take place. (ii) A conference of the Great Powers should then meet to discuss Poland, guarantees, non-aggression pacts, disarmament, colonies, economic questions, frontiers and the transfer of populations.

The views of the German Government on the subject detailed in (ii) were as follows:

There should be a new Polish State within the German orbit. The extent of territory was to be considered but that in Soviet occupation was not a subject for discussion. Any agreement reached would be endorsed by a national plebiscite in Germany; other countries would obtain national approval in some similar form. Non-aggression pacts would be concluded between the five Great Powers.

Disarmament. All aggressive weapons should first be destroyed and then the armed forces reduced to correspond with the economic and strategic requirements of each country.

Colonies. All the ex-German colonies should be returned, though other territories might in certain cases be substituted. South-West Africa might not be claimed. Germany might consider the payment of an indemnification for improvements effected in the colonies since 1918 and the purchase of the private property of the present owners who might desire to leave.

Economic questions and disarmament would probably require further consideration after the conference had fixed the guiding principles.

---

[1] At the end of September M. Dahlerus came to England for two days. He put forward to Lord Halifax proposals similar to those which he transmitted in October. Lord Halifax told him that, whatever the merits or the demerits of particular proposals put forward by the Germans might be, the trouble was that no one in Great Britain believed a word that Hitler said. If the Germans wanted peace, they would have to think of a way of over-coming this fundamental difficulty.

Frontiers. All countries would guarantee the frontiers of their neighbours and these frontiers would similarly be guaranteed by the Great Powers.

If His Majesty's Government were not prepared to negotiate with the existing régime in Germany, no discussion was possible.

M. Dahlerus himself made certain comments on the German proposals. He explained that the proposed plebiscite would include three questions: Are you in favour of peace? Are you in favour of building up Europe in collaboration with England and France? and Do you, as individuals, guarantee on your honour the boundaries of other nations and non-aggression pacts?

M. Dahlerus said that Hitler had taxed the patience of the German people over the Soviet Union, Czechoslovakia and Poland, and that if Göring, as the chief negotiator, secured peace, Hitler could not risk acting counter to this national [sentiment].[1]

M. Dahlerus added that Göring had expressed the view that Hitler's desire for peace was based on the principle that there should be neither victors nor vanquished. M. Dahlerus stated that Germany would prefer a pact with England rather than with the Soviet Union. Finally, Hitler would be ready to issue an invitation to a conference.

On October 12, however, the Prime Minister made a statement on British war aims in the House of Commons, in which, while affirming that it was not part of British policy to exclude from her rightful place in Europe a Germany which would live in amity and confidence with other nations, he made it clear that His Majesty's Government would not surrender to wrong-doing or agree to an uneasy truce interrupted by further threats. M. Dahlerus subsequently stated that he had been informed by Göring that the (a) German Government could send no reply to Mr. Chamberlain's statement, 'which they regarded as a declaration of war'.

M. Dahlerus again visited Berlin in late October and afterwards communicated to the British Legation at Stockholm further detailed (b) proposals; he also showed them a copy of a letter from Göring thanking him for his activities in the cause of peace. On November 16 he saw Göring again and, with the latter's sanction, suggested to the (c) British Legation at Stockholm that there should be a secret meeting of British, French and German representatives. He visited Göring twice in December, and on the last occasion informed him that there (d) was no chance of British agreement to a secret meeting. At the end of December he came to London and said that Göring was still asking what guarantees the Allies would require. Sir A. Cadogan (e)

---

[1] The text of the telegram was here uncertain.

(a) C16448/13005/18. (b) C18882/15/18. (c) C18883/15/18; C20525/13005/18.
(d) C20198, 20802, 20923/13005/18. (e) C21022/13005/18.

informed him, however, that he had nothing to add to his previous expression of opinion and to the public statements of His Majesty's Government.[1]

(iii)

Approaches made with reference to German military circles: communication through the Vatican (October 1939–March 1940).

Shortly after the outbreak of war, a British official in the Netherlands reported to the Foreign Office a message received by him and purporting to come from a group of German generals (including General von Rundstedt). The general tenor of the first communication was that the German army disapproved of Ribbentrop's policy, and wanted peace, and that the Nazi regime could easily be upset.

The Foreign Office instructed the British intermediary to give a guarded reply that a new situation would be created if they succeeded in overthrowing the regime. The Allies had no wish to wage a vindictive war, and their minimum terms would probably be the overthrow of the Nazis, real autonomy for Czechoslovakia, and the restoration of Poland.

This approach, however, turned out to be a move by German agents, who appear to have been trying to discover whether a German group hostile to the regime was negotiating with the Allies; the exchange of messages ended abruptly after the kidnapping on the German-Dutch frontier of the British intermediary, and another British subject, by German agents claiming to be the spokesmen of the disaffected party.

The suspicions of the German secret police were correct to the extent that a considerable body of opinion in the army thought Hitler's leadership (which had earlier been accepted by the High Command) now so reckless that Germany was risking immense disaster. Some members of this disaffected group made an attempt (a) late in 1939 to secure an approach to the Allies through the Vatican. Mr. Osborne, British Minister to the Vatican, had reported in December that Mgr. Kaas, a member of the papal Curia,[2] had been approached by a person claiming to be a representative of German military circles who hoped to use the Vatican as an intermediary for a 'fair and honourable peace' over the heads of Hitler

(b)   [1] Other approaches about this time claiming to have the support of Göring were made through American and Swedish business men. These approaches had no importance.
[2] Mgr. Kaas was a former leader of the German Centre Party.

(a) C19745/13005/18 (1939); C770/89/18 (1940). (b) C17031, 17219, 17220, 17285/13005/18; C18287/15/18; C1187, 2750/89/18 (1940).

and Ribbentrop. Göring was said to be in sympathy with the German conservative military circles who feared the Russian alliance and possible growth of communism in Germany. The Pope had indeed spoken of the conditions of a peace settlement in an address to the College of Cardinals on December 24, 1939. He believed that responsible men who were watching the trend of events would be prepared at an opportune moment to define precisely the fundamental points of a just and lasting peace and would not reject negotiations when the occasion offered. Although the Pope's own postulates were stated in very general terms, some of them seemed to suggest previous Italian claims. Three days before the address of December 24, the King and Queen of Italy, accompanied by Ciano, had been received at the Vatican. It was not impossible, therefore, that Mussolini was trying to use the Church as a means of securing—with himself as joint peacemaker—a creditable and not unremunerative way out of his uncomfortable position. Two days after the Pope's address Mr. Roosevelt announced that he was sending Mr. Myron Taylor as special Ambassador to the Vatican in order to assist 'parallel endeavours' for peace and the alleviation of suffering made by the Pope and by himself. Nothing came of this mission, and the approach made through the Papacy in January was not connected with any of these moves and was not in any way the result of papal initiative.

On January 12, in a private letter to Lord Halifax, Mr. Osborne wrote that the Pope had had a visit from the emissary who had seen (a) Mgr. Kaas in December. This emissary said that an offensive was planned for the middle of February, but that, if they could be sure of obtaining certain terms, the German generals would insist on making peace and would overthrow the Nazi Government. The terms of peace would include 'restoration' of Poland and Czechoslovakia, and the retention of the *Anschluss* with Austria.

The Pope had passed on this message to Mr. Osborne for the information of the British Government but had made it clear that, while he felt it his duty to agree to transmit the message, his action must not be taken as implying any personal opinion in the matter. Mr. Osborne had said to the Pope that the first step for the generals would surely be to overthrow Hitler, and only then to talk about peace. The Pope did not demur when Mr. Osborne also said that he did not see how we could take seriously such nebulous and uncertain proposals.[1]

On February 7 the Pope asked Mr. Osborne to see him very (b) secretly, and told him that he had again been approached by the

---

[1] Lord Halifax wrote to Mr. Osborne approving of his comments.

(a) C1137/89/18. (b) C2522/89/18.

intermediary. The latter was undoubtedly acting on behalf of a very important German general, whose name, however, His Holiness was unwilling to mention. The intermediary had again stated that a part of the army (he did not say how large or influential a part) desired a change of Government. A military dictatorship of the anti-Hitler party would be necessary for the time, but it would be replaced eventually by 'a democratic, Conservative and moderate Government', decentralised and federal in nature. The Rhineland and Westphalia would remain united to Prussia; Austria would be within the federation, but Poland and non-German Czechoslovakia would be independent. Once this new Government had been established it would hope to negotiate an honourable peace; the Pope was asked to ascertain whether His Majesty's Government would undertake that they would accept the continued existence of the Reich, including Austria, as a basis for negotiations.

As on the previous occasion, His Holiness made no attempt to recommend this proposal, and said that he intensely disliked even having to pass it on. He suggested at one point that Lord Halifax might give an opinion without consulting the French Government. In view of the importance which the Pope clearly attributed to the
(a) German approach, Mr. Osborne was instructed to inform him that we could obviously take no step except in conjunction with France, though for the present we would say nothing to the French Government; but if we could be convinced that the intermediaries who had approached the Pope represented principals in Germany with the intention and also the power to perform what they promised, we should be willing to consider with the French Goverment any enquiries which these principals might make. In considering a German programme we should look above all for security for the future, as well as for the restoration of the wrongs done to Germany's smaller neighbours. The suggestion for a decentralised and federal Germany was of interest, since it might go some way towards solving the security problem. It might therefore be useful if those who made the proposals were to develop this point in concrete terms. Under the federal plan, however, it would be, in our view, right that Austria should be allowed to decide whether or not to participate.

On March 30 His Holiness told Mr. Osborne that he had heard
(b) no more from the German representatives since communicating to them the British views. He had evidently learned meanwhile that similar approaches had been made to the British Government through other channels; he seemed considerably disillusioned and

(a) C2522/89/18. (b) C5286/89/18.

appreciative of the reasons which led us to be sceptical of German intentions.[1]

On various occasions after this date there were rumours that the Pope intended to initiate peace proposals. The rumours proved false; some of them were denied by the Vatican (though a tentative feeler was put out by the Pope in the summer of 1940). The rumours appeared at times to be encouraged by the attitude of certain of the nuncios, in particular the Nuncio at Berne, who made demands for peace after the collapse of France.[2]

(iv)

Approaches before and after the Battle of Britain.

At the end of June 1940, Signor Attolico, Italian Ambassador in Berlin, spoke to the United States Chargé d'Affaires on the import- (a) ance of Great Britain coming to terms with Germany before the grand German attack took place. Signor Attolico thought that this attack was certain to succeed; it was not, however, to the interest of Italy or Germany that Great Britain should be destroyed, but an initiative in suggesting a settlement must come from the British side, and the United States should insist on acting as intermediary. Signor Attolico said that he was not speaking under instructions, but that he knew the general views of the Italian and German Governments. No response was made to this or to other hints on similar lines which were put out, apparently as propaganda, in various European capitals.

In July 1940, the German Chargé d'Affaires in Washington sent to Lord Lothian, through an American intermediary, Mr. Lovell, (b)

---

[1] A large and controversial literature has accumulated around the opposition to Hitler in German military and other circles in the period of the war before the collapse of France. There is little documentary evidence about the messages, and the response to them, transmitted through the Vatican. The British archives do not contain much on the subject (the matter does not seem to have been discussed in the Cabinet); the Vatican publication *Actes et documents du Saint Siège relatives à la deuxième guerre mondiale* (Rome, 1965), I, does not refer to the German approach or to the British reply. H. C. Deutsch, *The Conspiracy against Hitler in the Twilight War* (University of Minnesota Press, 1968) contains a good bibliography, especially of German works.

[2] In September 1940, overtures were received through an emissary of Dr. Wirth, former German Chancellor, and Herr Gessler, a former German War Minister, to the effect that a group of officers formerly on the General Staff (i.e. in the Brauchitsch period) believed that Germany could ultimately win the war, but that a long war would be a disaster to all parties. They thought that, if Hitler did not succeed in his attack on England, there would be a chance for them to open negotiations. Their terms included the retention of the Channel ports from Dunkirk to Boulogne for a period of years and a free hand in the east. No reply was made to their overtures.

(a) C7578/89/18. (b) C8015/89/18.

Executive Secretary of the Quaker Council in New York, a message to the effect that, if it was desired, he could obtain from Berlin a statement of Germany's peace terms. The message explained that Hitler, though entirely confident of success, was still reluctant to destroy the British Empire. The Foreign Office informed Lord Lothian that approaches on similar lines had been made to the British Minister at Berne; that no reply had been returned to them, and that no good could come of answering the present message. Hitler, in a speech to the Reichstag on July 19, had just broken it to the German people that the war might continue for a long period. By suggesting that peace was possible now he might be hoping to create a division of opinion in Great Britain while strengthening the morale of his own people to whom he could say that he had offered terms which had been refused. If the German Government really wished to put terms to us they could find means of doing so. Their present feelers rather suggested that they hoped to entice us into asking for terms in order to weaken our position.

This answer coincided with a public reply by Lord Halifax to the suggestion made by Hitler in his speech that Great Britain should accept the situation and come to terms. Lord Halifax said that we should not stop fighting until freedom for ourselves and for others had been secured. The German Chargé d'Affaires took the line that the speech had made impossible any secret conversation between himself and Lord Lothian.[1]

Another approach at this period came from the King of Sweden. On August 2, 1940, the King of Sweden sent to King George VI, through the Swedish Minister in London, a telegram offering his good offices to the heads of the States of Great Britain and Germany as a channel for the discussion of the possibilities of peace. The King of Sweden undertook that, if his offer were refused, he would maintain the strictest secrecy. In conveying this message on August 2, the Swedish Minister explained that his Sovereign had taken this step solely on his own initiative, and out of no other desire than to stop further bloodshed. The King of Sweden hoped that, if the reply were in the negative, the approach would be kept strictly confidential.

(a)

---

[1] There seems little doubt that the Germans were making use of their own peace feelers as a means of suggesting that the United States would be making a mistake to put any confidence in British resolution. Hence the German Chargé d'Affaires' attempt to insinuate that Lord Lothian had taken the initiative in suggesting a secret conversation. Lord Lothian made it clear to the Foreign Office that there was no truth in this insinuation, and that the German Chargé d'Affaires had been the first person to mention the idea of a secret conversation.

(a) C8974/89/18.

In view of the attitude of the King of Sweden towards the Russian attack on Finland and the German attack on Norway, the Prime Minister and the Foreign Office felt a certain indignation that he should put himself forward as a peacemaker. Nevertheless a long answer, which was concerted with the Dominion Governments, was returned on August 14 to this communication. The reply (in the form of a letter from King George VI) reminded the King of Sweden that the position of the United Kingdom Government had been defined at length in the considered statement made by Mr. Chamberlain in the House of Commons on October 12, 1939. The reply then referred to the fresh crimes which the Nazi Government had committed since that date. There was nothing in the words or the deeds of the present rulers of Germany to warrant a belief that they were prepared to accept or to observe a peace which recognised the right of other people to live in freedom and security. It lay with the German Government to make proposals by which the wrongs they had inflicted on other nations might be redressed, and to give effective guarantees of their intentions.

When this reply was handed to the Swedish Minister, the latter observed that he was not surprised at its tenor, since he could not see what other answer was possible. Information was later received indicating that Hitler's reply to the overture was also in the negative. The President of the United States was informed of the step taken by King Gustav and the British reply.

Other sources, including Dr. Salazar, Prince Max Hohenlohe and the Finnish Prime Minister, repeated the suggestion that Hitler was returning to the view (which he was said to have held in the past) of a working arrangement between Germany and the British Empire, and was therefore hesitating to attack Great Britain. In September ex-King Alfonso of Spain told Mr. Kelly, British Minister at Berne, that he knew 'from sure sources' of Hitler's genuine wish to avoid damaging the British Empire, since he thought its existence necessary in the interests of world stability. King Alfonso also regarded Hitler as much changed personally; the evidence adduced for the change was Hitler's 'recent solicitude for the French civilian population'. The King said that the continuation of the war would bring universal disaster; he urged strongly that, if it shortly became clear that invasion had failed, the opportunity should be taken to establish touch with a responsible intermediary. This intermediary would be forthcoming if the British Government would show greater interest.

Mr. Kelly replied that we had no confidence in Hitler's word or in any Nazi promise. The German idea of a peace was one which would enable them to consolidate their gains and to prepare for a more successful attack. The 'soundings' hitherto made by them showed that they had no serious intention of making concessions. King Alfonso said he was sure that this was not the case; he admitted that it would be difficult to get their agreement to the complete restoration of Poland and Czechoslovakia.

An approach was made in September through M. Ekeberg, (a) President of the High Court of Sweden. The President called on the British Minister at Stockholm on September 5 and gave him the following information: Dr. Ludwig Weissauer, a Berlin lawyer, whom the Finnish Minister at Berlin had introduced to him on a previous visit to Stockholm as a man with very important connexions, had expressed a desire to meet Mr. Mallet very secretly in order to have a purely unofficial and non-commital discussion on the subject of peace. M. Ekeberg understood Dr. Weissauer to be a direct emissary of Hitler, and as such to have visited Finland in the previous month. He was also believed to have been employed in the past on missions to the United States and China. He told M. Ekeberg that he wished the conversation with Mr. Mallet to be known only to the British Government and Hitler, to whom he intimated that he would report directly. Dr. Weissauer realised that peace might not yet be obtainable, but he felt that conversations might be useful. He considered that attempts at mediation by Kings or by the Pope were too conspicuous a form of approach to offer hope of result. Mr. Mallet said that he could see no useful purpose in the meeting, but, on M. Ekeberg's urgent insistence, he agreed to reflect before giving a final answer, and telegraphed to London for instructions.

The President's revelation that Dr. Weissauer had been to Finland suggested strongly that the move was part of a German campaign conducted through the Scandinavian countries. M. Ekeberg assured Mr. Mallet that the Swedish Government were not aware of Dr. Weissauer's visit, but it had already been ascertained that the King of Sweden's approach had not been kept as secret as His Majesty had promised. In fact, it seemed likely that all these so-called independent overtures had been indirectly inspired by Berlin. In any case, our attitude remained as previously declared. Mr. Mallet was therefore instructed not to meet Dr. Weissauer in view of the obvious danger of misconstruction; he was authorised to explain to the President of the High Court that such a meeting would in any case be useless, since he could not enter into discussion and could only receive a message which it was always open to the President to deliver himself.

(a) C9598/89/18.

After receiving this message, M. Ekeberg saw Dr. Weissauer and returned to Mr. Mallet in great excitement, saying that he was convinced that the matter was of first importance; that Dr. Weissauer was acting at the suggestion of Hitler, and that only two men in Germany were aware of his mission. The President then gave Mr. Mallet the proposals which Dr. Weissauer wished to make.

The following were the main points of the proposals:—(i) The world to be divided into two economic spheres: one continental, organised by Germany; the other maritime and colonial, organised by the British Empire.[1]

(ii) The political independence of the European countries occupied by Germany to be restored, including 'a Polish State', but excluding Czechoslovakia. The economic division of Europe, however, was to be brought to an end.

(iii) The British Empire to retain all its colonies and such mandates as were needed for its political and military interests; Germany possibly receiving some compensation elsewhere.

(iv) Questions concerning the Mediterranean, Egypt and the French, Belgian and Dutch colonies to be open to discussion.

This was the 'last chance', and the alternative was the continuance of the war on an intensified scale; special mention was made of the probable loss of Egypt, the Middle East and ultimately India.

Mr. Mallet, in his report, said that he was convinced that M. Ekeberg was completely disinterested in intention. He gave him no encouragement, however, to suppose that a reply could be returned to this last message, although Dr. Weissauer had decided to prolong his stay in the hopes of obtaining an answer and was evidently extremely anxious not to return to Germany empty-handed.

In these circumstances it was decided to return an answer to Dr. Weissauer through M. Ekeberg. The answer was, in somewhat briefer form, the reply given to the King of Sweden earlier in the year. At the same time the exchange of telegrams with Stockholm was repeated to Washington and Lord Lothian was instructed to tell the President in confidence of their contents, and to say to him that His Majesty's Government would have nothing to do with the suggestions made through Dr. Weissauer.

When Mr. Mallet received the reply Dr. Weissauer had just left for Berlin, where the answer was forwarded to him by the President of the High Court. Dr. Weissauer replied from Berlin that he considered the message as a temporary refusal. He had been rather surprised at the solemn language employed and had hoped that more attention might have been paid to the future rather than to

---

[1] Dr. Weissauer gave the impression that the U.S.S.R. should be considered as a potential enemy, and that the British and German groups would be able to resist 'the encroachments of the Yellow Race'.

the past. In the circumstances he did not propose to communicate the message to higher German authorities since he still wished to keep open the channel of communication and hoped that one day Mr. Mallet might be authorised to enter into unofficial and non-committal discussions, for which he could return to Stockholm at any time.[1]

(v)

Mr. Matsuoka's message to Mr. Eden: the Prime Minister's reply (February–March 1941):[2] the Prime Minister's speech of November 10, 1941.

There were no more approaches of any importance from the German side during the winter of 1940–1. On February 17, however, (a) the Japanese Ambassador gave to Mr. R. A. Butler (in Mr. Eden's absence) a memorandum with a personal message to Mr. Eden from Mr. Matsuoka, Japanese Minister for Foreign Affairs. The memorandum was intended mainly to describe the purpose of the Tripartite Pact and the peaceful nature of Japanese intentions in the Far East. With this background Mr. Matsuoka went on to explain his own 'anxiety' about the action of the British and American Governments in 'expediting and enlarging' their 'warlike preparations in the Far East'. Mr. Matsuoka maintained that the prolongation of the war would serve no good purpose. He stated that Japan was 'fully prepared to act as a mediator' not only in 'Greater East Asia' but 'anywhere the world over'.

The Foreign Office regarded this message as designed either to slow up our defence preparations or to provide an excuse for further Japanese inroads upon Indo-China. It was, however, desirable to answer Mr. Matsuoka's offer. Hence on February 24 the Prime (b) Minister sent a reply to Mr. Matsuoka. The reply pointed out that Great Britain had no intention of attacking Japan, and that all the measures we were taking in the Far East were defensive in character. The Prime Minister then gave the reasons why we were fighting Germany and why we hoped to defeat her. In these circumstances there was no possibility of mediation and, 'in a cause not in any way concerned with territory, trade, or material gain, but affecting the

---

[1] Lord Lothian informed Mr. Hull of this approach and of the reply, Mr. Hull said that he had recently refused to see an American who professed to have had interviews with Göring; Mr. Hull though that a meeting with this American would serve no useful purpose and might give rise to a wrong impression that the United States were interested in an early peace on Hitler's terms.

[2] See also Chapter XXIII, section (i).

(a) F1069/17/23. (b) F1239/17/23.

whole of humanity', there could be 'no question of compromise or parley'.

Mr. Matsuoka had indeed retracted his offer—probably owing to German displeasure at it—on February 21, before our reply was sent. On February 27 he addressed a memorandum to the Prime Minister. In this memorandum, which was presented to the Prime (a) Minister by the Japanese Ambassador on March 4, Mr. Matsuoka stated that he had not intended to convey any hint of his readiness to act as mediator between the actual belligerents in the war and that he had not imagined that such a hint could be read into his letter. He was thinking of the Japanese mediation between Thailand and Indo-China—and stating in a general and abstract manner the views he had always held in order to make clear the attitude of Japan towards the problem of peace.

Other tentative suggestions for a compromise peace reached the Foreign Office in 1941. Some of them came indirectly—or were said to come indirectly—from the German Government; others were made by opposition groups of which it was impossible to gauge the potential strength or capacity for action. The general policy, laid down by the Prime Minister, and confirmed by him later in the year, was that these approaches should be totally ignored. The main inference to be drawn from them was that in the autumn of 1941 some at least of the leading German generals and officials were losing confidence in victory, at all events to the extent of showing themselves ready to 'reinsure' their own position, and that Göring shared in the lack of confidence. There were also reports from a good many sources in the late autumn, especially in the early part of November 1941, that Hitler intended to make a new attempt to (b) persuade the nations of Europe to collaborate in his 'New Order', and that for this purpose he was likely to call a conference before the end of the year. He would invite to the conference not only his 'Quislings' and the men of Vichy but also representatives of the few remaining neutral and independent States in Europe; the conference would be required to endorse the idea of a permanent German hegemony over the Continent.

The Foreign Office thought that this plan had not much chance of success. Hitler had no inducements to offer except the possibility that, faced with evidence of the acceptance of a German order in Europe, Great Britain and her Allies might give up fighting. The independent States, however, well knew that a German peace would only be a breathing-space during which the Germans would gather strength for new aggression; the occupied countries, which had

(a) F1136, 1430, 1575/17/23. (b) C610, 9472, 10206, 10207/324/18; C7892/18/18; C12277/324/18.

experienced the brutality of German rule, would be even less inclined to accept it in permanence.

Although nothing seemed likely to come of Hitler's plan, the Foreign Office regarded it as desirable that the British Government should repeat that they were not interested in any peace offer which Hitler might make, and would be uninfluenced by a suggestion that the peoples of Europe would accept the German 'New Order'. The Prime Minister, therefore, in a speech at the Mansion House on November 10, 1941, repeated the British refusal to negotiate on any terms with Hitler.

Within a short time Germany and Italy had declared war on the United States. The German 'New Order' was thus even less attractive to the neutral States; the victims of German domination were encouraged by the new situation, and the Anglo-American declaration of the United Nations offered a programme to which the Axis Powers could not hope to make an effective answer.

(2)

(vi)

The signature of the 'Atlantic Charter', August 1941.

The definition of Allied war aims was in a sense the counterpart to Hitler's offer of a compromise peace on the basis of a 'new Europe' under German control. The fact that these two aspects of a single question can be treated in chronological sequence is an indication of the rise in confidence on the Allied side and also of the patent failure of the Germans to attract opinion to their own 'sham' programme for a United Europe. The Allied declarations followed from the position taken up by Great Britain and France during the first ten months of the war, and maintained by Great Britain after Marshal Pétain's Government had concluded an armistice with Germany, that no peace terms with Hitler were possible. In the early stages of the war the Allies had given a good deal of consideration to the question whether they should make a more positive statement of their own war aims. The Foreign Office resisted as premature an attempt at a precise definition of Allied intentions. There was no doubt about the reasons why Great Britain was at war, or about the determination of the British people to continue the war until victory. On the other hand no one could forecast what the position in Europe and in the world outside Europe would be at the end of the war. It was thus impossible to say what territorial changes would be desirable or practicable. Furthermore questions of territorial change or of the future political regime in Germany affected Italy and other neutrals and the history of the commitments made in the First World War showed how undesirable it was to lay down in advance the conditions of a post-war settlement.

After the collapse of France and the entry of Italy into the war, there was no immediate possibility of a detailed statement of war aims in the sense of a list of stipulations to be included in a treaty. Great Britain was fighting for existence; until victory was much nearer in sight, there would have been something almost ludicrous in laying down the geographical boundaries of a new Europe. At this time also the Prime Minister, in particular, was convinced that the United States would soon come into the war; American opinion would therefore be decisive in the determination of peace terms, and the discussion of such terms was best left until the United States could take part in it as a belligerent.

The failure of the German plans of invasion in the autumn of 1940 allowed Great Britain and her Allies to affirm more con- (a) vincingly to the world at large their intention to fight on until victory. The British Government had considered in November 1940, a proposal for an inter-Allied meeting in London; the meeting was postponed largely because the Greeks, who were then not technically at war with Germany, felt some difficulty about taking part in it. The proposal was revived in the late spring of 1941, and a meeting (b) was held at St. James's Palace in June of that year. The meeting expressed the determination of the Allies to fight on until victory, but did not attempt a precise statement of the form which the peace settlement would take. Once again it seemed enough for the time to make it clear to all the peoples under German occupation that they could look forward to freedom from their oppressors and to a restoration of their political independence.

The initiative in a more definite statement of war aims came, largely for domestic reasons, from the United States, and before American entry into the war. During his meeting in August 1941 with Mr. Churchill on H.M.S. *Prince of Wales* and the American battleship *Augusta* in Placentia Bay, Newfoundland, Mr. Roosevelt said (at dinner on August 9) that he wished to issue, simultaneously (c) with the 'release' of the account of the meeting, a joint declaration of the broad principles 'which animate the United States and Great Britain at this fateful time'. Mr. Churchill gave Mr. Roosevelt a tentative draft[1] of such a declaration on August 10; on the following day Mr. Roosevelt produced a revised draft which was taken as a

---

[1] This draft was drawn up by Sir A. Cadogan on the Prime Minister's instructions.

(a) C11719, 12934/11444/62. (b) C3912, 5899, 6593/344/62. (c) C9509/9245/62; W10151/426/49.

basis of discussion. In a telegram reporting this proposal to the War
(a) Cabinet Mr. Churchill commented that the President's draft was
not free from the difficulties attaching to all such declarations. The
fourth clause, for example, ran: 'They (i.e. the United States and
Great Britain) will endeavour to further enjoyment by all peoples of
access, without discrimination and on equal terms, to the markets
and to the raw materials of the world which are needed for their
economic prosperity'. Mr. Churchill wanted the phrase amended to
safeguard the obligations of Great Britain under the Ottawa Agreement and not to prejudice the future of Imperial Preference. The
clause might fall into its place after the war in a general economic
settlement with a decisive lowering of tariffs and trade barriers
throughout the world, but the matter could not be decided forthwith.
Mr. Churchill considered that the President would accept (i) the
inclusion of the words 'with due respect to their existing obligations'
after 'endeavour', (ii) the omission of the words 'without discrimination and' and (iii) the substitution of 'trade' for 'markets'.

The final paragraph of the draft referred to the disarmament of
the aggressor nations. Mr. Churchill thought that we should also
include a reference to 'the establishment of a wider and more
permanent system of general security'. Mr. Roosevelt would not like
this reference, but would probably accept it because he attached so
much importance to the effect of the joint declaration on American
opinion.

Mr. Churchill asked for the views of the War Cabinet at once. He
had postponed his own departure for twenty-four hours in order to
settle the declaration. He thought it imprudent to raise 'unnecessary
difficulties'. The declaration could be regarded as 'an interim and
partial statement of war aims designed to reassure all countries of
our righteous purpose and not the complete structure which we
should build after victory'.

Mr. Churchill's message was received during the evening of
August 11. The War Cabinet met on the same evening and again
(b) on the morning of August 12 to consider the draft text. After the
first meeting they telegraphed to Mr. Churchill their general agreement, and their approval of Mr. Churchill's suggestion for the last
clause. They wished the clause about access to raw materials to run:
'They will endeavour to further enjoyment by all peoples of access
without discrimination and on equal terms to the raw materials of
the world which are needed for their economic prosperity, and to
promote the greatest possible expansion of markets for the interchange of goods and services throughout the world.'

(a) Tel. Tudor 15 (WP (41) 203). (b) Tel. Abbey 31 (WP (41) 203).

The War Cabinet also wished to insert an additional clause in the following terms: 'They support the fullest collaboration between nations in the economic field with the object of securing for all peoples freedom from want, improved labour standards, economic advancement and social security.' After their second meeting on the morning of August 12 the War Cabinet authorised another telegram to the Prime Minister. They now suggested the inclusion of the (a) words 'with due respect to their existing obligations' before the word 'promote'. They considered that a distinction should be drawn between raw materials and trade or markets. They supported access on equal terms to raw materials, and saw no reason to qualify their support by reserving existing obligations. This reservation was, however, necessary in dealing with trade in order to safeguard Imperial Preference and to prevent British markets from being undercut by countries like Japan with a low standard of living.

The War Cabinet thought that the phrase 'access on equal terms to trade' might be interpreted in terms of extreme *laissez faire*. We could not accept a formula which, for example, might prevent us from continuing exchange control after the war. On the other hand, if necessary, the War Cabinet were willing to accept the President's draft as amended by the Prime Minister. They regarded as of great importance their proposed new clause referring to social security. The substance of the new paragraph had already appeared in a number of previous declarations, notably in Mr. Roosevelt's speech[1] and in the resolutions of the inter-Allied meeting of June 12, 1941. The omission of any paragraph on these lines would have a bad effect on public opinion in Great Britain and the Dominions and on the Allied Governments. Finally Mr. Churchill had explained that, in view of the President's desire for an immediate announcement, there would be no time for consultation with the Dominions. Mr. Churchill had therefore asked the War Cabinet to agree that he should anticipate their concurrence. The War Cabinet agreed that Mr. Churchill should sign the declaration as Prime Minister of the United Kingdom. Since, however, it was necessary for the Dominion Prime Ministers to be shown the text as soon as possible in order that they could sign and publish it, the War Cabinet had telegraphed to them that a short declaratory statement by the British and United States Governments was being made, and that the text would be sent to them as quickly as possible.

This second telegram reached Mr. Churchill after he had agreed upon the final text with Mr. Roosevelt. Mr. Roosevelt had accepted Mr. Churchill's amendments, and Mr. Churchill had not thought it possible to reopen the discussions, but he had put to Mr. Roosevelt the (b)

---

[1] This reference appears to be to Mr. Roosevelt's speech on the 'Four Freedoms'.

(a) Tel. Abbey 35 (WP (41) 203). (b) Tel. Tudor 23 (WP (41) 203).

alternative phrasing about raw materials and markets. The President did not want to make any change, and the Prime Minister thought that the reference to existing obligations was sufficient. The competition of cheap labour did not come into the matter, since all countries kept the right to retain or impose national tariffs 'pending better solutions'. Mr. Roosevelt had also accepted the new clause, though a reference to 'freedom from want' had already been made in an earlier clause.

A few minor changes were made in the final draft before it was issued on August 14.[1] The text as published in a British Command paper read as follows:

> Joint Declaration by the President of the United States of America and Mr. Winston Churchill, representing His Majesty's Government in the United Kingdom, known as the Atlantic Charter. August 14, 1941.

> The President of the United States and the Prime Minister, Mr. Churchill, representing His Majesty's Government in the United Kingdom, being met together, deem it right to make known certain common principles in the national policies of their respective countries on which they base their hopes for a better future for the world.

> First, their countries seek no aggrandisement, territorial or other.

> Second, they desire to see no territorial changes that do not accord with the freely expressed wishes of the peoples concerned.

> Third, they respect the right of all peoples to choose the form of government under which they will live; and they wish to see sovereign rights and self-government restored to those who have been forcibly deprived of them.

> Fourth, they will endeavour, with due respect for their existing obligations, to further the enjoyment by all States, great or small, victor or vanquished, of access, on equal terms, to the trade and to the raw materials of the world which are needed for their economic prosperity.

> Fifth, they desire to bring about the fullest collaboration between all nations in the economic field, with the object of securing for all improved labour standards, economic advancement and social security.

> Sixth, after the final destruction of Nazi tyranny, they hope to see established a peace which will afford to all nations the means of dwelling in safety within their own boundaries, and which will afford assurance that all the men in all the lands may live out their lives in freedom from fear and want.

---

[1] There is no official text of the Charter, in the form of a signed copy in the British and American archives. The President and the Prime Minister accepted a text which was given to the press. Further evidence of the haste and informality with which the declaration was drawn up may be seen in the fact—which was seized upon by hostile opinion in the United States—that there is no mention in it of freedom of conscience or religion. See also below, p. 217.

Seventh, such a peace should enable all men to traverse the high seas and oceans without hindrance.

Eighth, they believe that all of the nations of the world, for realistic as well as spiritual reasons, must come to the abandonment of the use of force. Since no future peace can be maintained if land, sea or air armaments continue to be employed by nations which threaten, or may threaten, aggression outside of their frontiers, they believe, pending the establishment of a wide and permanent system of general security, that the disarmament of such nations is essential. They will likewise aid and encourage all other practicable measures which will lighten for peace-loving peoples the crushing burden of armaments.'

(vii)

Foreign Office comments on the 'Atlantic Charter'.

The eight points of the Atlantic Charter, like President Wilson's Fourteen Points nearly a quarter of a century earlier, had an immediate popular appeal. The appeal was greater in 1941 than it had been in 1918 because the Atlantic Charter marked a definite association of the United States with the post-war settlement. Although the United States were not at war, the issue of a statement of war aims under the signatures of Mr. Roosevelt and Mr. Churchill implied a very close American interest in the results of the war. The Atlantic Charter could not be given practical effect unless the Axis Powers were completely defeated; it was now clear that the United States wanted something more than a 'negotiated peace', a peace without victory, resulting from the exhaustion of the combatants, and failing to secure for the world the aims laid down in the Charter. Since the provision of munitions of war by the United States was unlikely of itself to bring a decisive victory, the Charter carried the unspoken implication of American belligerency, or at all events of 'armed intervention' on a scale sufficient to secure the liberation of the conquered peoples from the Germans and their associates.

The Charter also had a wide popular appeal as an answer to the German (and, one might add, the Russian) propaganda attacking the domestic institutions of the democracies. This propaganda had little positive success in the United States or Great Britain—especially after the German attack on Russia—but it was cleverly framed, and was, in a sense, an irritant and an affront to the accepted values of the British and American way of life. The Atlantic Charter took the offensive against the German propaganda about the 'pseudo-democracies', and asserted the idealist aims which in fact had sustained British opinion throughout the terrible dangers of the months following the collapse of France. Every one of the eight points of the Charter was a challenge to the practice of the Axis Powers, and a challenge to which they could give no effective answer. In this respect the Charter gained in popularity from the clumsy failure of the Germans to organise a 'New Europe' after their victories in 1940. The German promises had come to nothing, or rather had been falsified by German behaviour in all the occupied countries. The Charter reaffirmed the civilised standards which the Germans and Italians had disregarded everywhere in Europe.

On the other hand, it was necessary for Great Britain and the Dominions, and for their Allies, to examine carefully the terms to which they were now committed. The history of Mr. Wilson's Fourteen Points showed the danger of vague and high-sounding phraseology as the basis of a legal document like a treaty. Some time or other the war would come to an end, and the nations of the world would appeal to the terms of the Atlantic Charter. They would try to apply these terms according to their own interests, and the applications might bring serious difficulties and disputes. In any case, whether the United States had or had not entered the war as a belligerent, the Charter recognised American claims to share in the determination of the post-war settlement. In fact, the United States would demand a predominant part in determining this settlement; Great Britain would be unable to refuse the demand, not only because the United States would come out of the war as the strongest and least exhausted Power in the world, but also because American assistance would be essential to the execution and maintenance of a peace treaty.

It was therefore the obvious concern of the Foreign Office to (a) consider the practical application of the Charter with special regard to the view which American opinion was likely to take of it. This examination was made in the late summer of 1941 in a tentative way since there could be no question of forecasting when and how the war would end, and what terms of settlement would be desirable or possible.

The first task was to examine each of the eight points in the declaration. Point One 'Their countries (i.e. the United States and Great Britain) seek no aggrandisement, territorial or other'. It was clear that the United States would be critical of any British suggestion for a 'protection' relationship towards colonial or backward territory, e.g. Eritrea.

(a) W14302/426/49.

Point Two 'They desire to see no territorial changes that do not accord with the freely expressed wishes of the peoples concerned'. Here it was doubtful whether American opinion understood the complexity of the political and geographical problems involved in the question of 'self-determination' in Europe. Similarly with Point Three. If, for instance, the U.S.S.R. decided, after the war, to absorb the Baltic States, we might be compelled to recognise the facts, and, for the sake of the peace of Europe and our own wider interests, to maintain friendly relations with Russia. The United States would also tolerate the facts, but might refuse to give them formal recognition on moral grounds while accusing us of a selfish surrender of principle.

Point Four would certainly involve us in difficulties. This point was drafted with the Ottawa Convention in mind, but also, on the American side, with the determination to return to pre-war conditions of multilateral trading. We might use the saving phrase about 'existing obligations' as a 'let out', but we were likely to meet with the strongest American opposition if, owing to our shortage of gold and dollars, we tried to maintain a policy of discrimination and trading control beyond an extremely limited period after the war.

Point Five would not affect Anglo-American relations, but there were obvious difficulties in the way of obtaining full international collaboration, and American opinion would not accept the domestic controls and extension of governmental activity necessary to make a reality of the phrase.

Similarly with Point Six the problem lay in the contribution which could be expected from the United States. In the autumn of 1941 the Foreign Office did not think it likely that the United States would accept any responsibility for the territorial status of Europe, or be a party to a treaty which would automatically involve America in a war outside the western hemisphere.

Point Seven involved no serious commitments, other than the maintenance of a fleet.

Point Eight. The kernel of this rather vague clause was that, after the war, we should disarm our enemies while ourselves remaining armed. The practical problem, however, would be not to disarm Germany, but to keep her disarmed. It was again doubtful how far America would assist in the solution of this problem.

To these general considerations the Foreign Office was able to add certain large desiderata with regard to Europe. If we could not easily get American assistance in the political settlement, we ought at least to try to avoid a return to isolationism (which would affect the policies of the Dominions) by bringing the United States into close collaboration over economic reconstruction. Incidentally we should thereby prevent a repetition of the mistake of the United States after the First World War in making large loans, without definite conditions, which had led only to extravagant spending and subsequent economic bankruptcy. As far as we could envisage the position after the war, we might well have to convince the Americans that we and our Allies had a better claim to their assistance than the Germans. We should have American support for the restoration of Czechoslovakia as well as of the Netherlands and Belgium, and we should do our best to get similar support for the strengthening of Poland, and for regarding Czechoslovakia and Poland as a counterbalance to the menace of a German revival.

The main consideration, however, was the need of some international organisation which would secure the conditions of the Charter. The minimum requirements were an international labour office, an international bank, and a disarmament commission. The latter would require the backing of armed forces, national or international. There would also be a demand for some kind of international tribunal. It was hardly possible to suppose that these organisations could exist without some kind of political direction and control. We were therefore led to postulate at least an international council, on the lines of the Council of the League, though we might not require an Assembly. American participation in this Council would be essential. Indeed without such participation we should not be able to enforce any settlement in Europe.

It was impossible at this time to go beyond these generalisations. The Foreign Office thought that we should do what we could to bring before the American public the implications of the document which Mr. Roosevelt had signed, and that we should explain, in particular, that the means towards obtaining the desired aims of the Charter required an acceptance by the United States of the responsibilities of greatness.

(viii)

Further comments on the 'Atlantic Charter': the inter-Allied meeting of September 24, 1941.

The fourth point of the Charter did in fact give rise to some exchanges with the United States Government. Mr. Winant told Mr. (a) Eden on August 27 that Mr. Hull had telegraphed to him about the

(a) W10659/426/49.

interpretation of the phrase 'with due respect for their existing obliga-tions'. Mr. Hull wished to describe this phrase as a 'forthright declaration by the British and American Governments to do every-thing in their power, now and in the post-war period, by means of the reduction of trade barriers and the reduction and elimination of preferences and discriminations, to further the enjoyment by all states, great or small, victor or vanquished, of access on equal terms to the trade and to the raw materials of the world, which is needed for their economic prosperity'.

The Prime Minister thought it better to use the phrase 'elimina-tion of vexatious discriminations, as part of a general scheme to further, etc.'. He considered that there could be 'no great future for the world without a vast breaking down of tariffs and other barriers. The United States, which will be more than ever the world-creditor, although hitherto the worst offender in tariff matters' now seemed disposed to promote a policy of reduction. 'If this mood were implemented, it would be natural that the measures which we have been forced to take should also be thrown into the common pot.'

Mr. Churchill put his amendment to Mr. Hull and, although Mr. Hull's views remained unchanged, the question of interpretation (a) remained for the time in suspense. Meanwhile the War Cabinet considered it necessary to make some statement explaining the relationship between Point Three and the declaration already made with regard to constitutional advance in India and Burma. The Charter was directed to the nations of Europe whom we hoped to free from German tyranny; it was not intended to deal with the internal affairs of the British Empire or the relations, for example, between the United States and the Philippines. It was also clear that one party to the Charter could not issue an authoritative interpreta-tion of it. The War Cabinet, however, thought that Mr. Churchill could explain that these internal questions were matters to which Point Three did not refer.

Mr. Churchill made a statement to this effect in the House of Commons on September 9.[1] He said that the Charter did not try to settle the application of the broad principles which it proclaimed, and that it would be unwise 'to be drawn into laborious discussions on how it is to fit all the manifold problems with which we shall be faced after the war'. The Charter did not qualify in any way British statements of policy about the development of constitutional govern-ment in India, Burma, or other parts of the Empire. 'At the Atlantic meeting, we had in mind, primarily, the restoration of the sovereignty,

---

[1] *Parl. Deb. 5th Series, H. of C.*, vol. 374, cols. 67–9.

(a) WM(41)89 and 91.

self-government and national life of the States and nations of Europe now under the Nazi yoke, and the principles governing any alterations in the territorial boundaries which may have to be made.' The 'progressive evolution of self-governing institutions in the regions and peoples which owe allegiance to the British Crown' was a separate problem. Our declarations on these matters were 'complete in themselves, free from ambiguity, and related to the conditions and circumstances of the territories and peoples affected', and in harmony with the terms of the Charter.

Some of the Allies of Great Britain also felt certain misgivings about the wording of the Charter. They had an opportunity in September both to adhere to the general principles of the Declaration and to suggest their own reservations. At the time of the signature of the Charter, Mr. Eden had already considered it desirable to hold another inter-Allied meeting. He had suggested, at the close of the meeting on June 12, 1941, that such meetings—though they could not be held continuously—might 'represent the inauguration of a new phase of collaboration and form part of the machinery through which victory will be won and by which peace will be maintained after victory'.

There was in fact considerable interest in the holding of further meetings. Since the British Government had already stated their intention of promoting measures for the supply of food and raw materials to Europe as soon as it had been freed from German domination, it seemed appropriate that the next inter-Allied meeting should discuss this subject. The subject was also of particular interest to the Allied Governments in London and to their peoples at home, and the mere fact that it was being discussed would be a sign of confidence in victory as well as a practical answer to the German propaganda about a new Europe. There had already been informal consultations about post-war reconstruction both with the Allied Governments, and, from the point of view of supply, with the Governments of the Dominions and the United States.

The United States Government approved of the proposal to hold a
(a) meeting and authorised a statement on their behalf that they regarded the discussions as useful, and wished to be consulted about any plans in which they might co-operate. The War Cabinet agreed with the
(b) proposal that a meeting should be held on August 27 or as soon as possible after this date. They also thought that the meeting should pass a resolution adhering to the Anglo-American declaration.

The meeting was delayed until September 24 mainly owing to the difficulties raised by the question of adherence to the Atlantic

(a) C8388, 9317/14/62. (b) WM(41)83 and 85.

Charter. The Dominion Governments had announced their adherence, but the Czechoslovak, Polish and Russian Governments, and the Free French felt some uneasiness over the wording. The Russian objections were obvious; Stalin and Molotov could accept the terms of the Charter only by a bland disregard of their own acts in domestic and foreign policy. M. Maisky told Mr. Eden on August 26 that, although the Soviet Government did not object to the declaration, they would have altered some of the phrases, and thought that in any case they should have been consulted about it. The other Allies were less embarrassed, but wished to be sure of the interpretation of the vague terms which satisfied American opinion but were not precise enough to form the basis of a peace settlement.

Mr. Eden told General Sikorski on September 15 that we could neither give the Poles a private interpretation of the Charter nor (a) make a gloss on it in public. Mr. Eden said that the Polish Government should explain their position at the inter-Allied meeting, and put forward their reservations. They could then say at the Peace Conference that they had made these reservations. The Polish Government hesitated at first to do this because they were afraid that their action would be criticised by British opinion. They finally agreed to Mr. Eden's suggestion.

The Free French also decided to give their approval in a general statement. They too wanted to address a letter to the British Govern- (b) ment in which they would state certain reservations with regard to the practical application of the Charter. In particular General de Gaulle wished to say that the declaration should not be considered as applying to the territorial status or government of the French colonies. The Foreign Office explained the difficulty in the way of private exchanges about the Charter.

The Soviet Government decided to make what amounted to a declaration of their own. M. Maisky therefore spoke at the inter-Allied meeting before the discussion of the Charter. The Foreign (c) Office accepted his request to speak, although the Soviet statement contained phrases which would reduce the proceedings almost to a farce and give the Germans a chance of ridiculing them (e.g. 'the Soviet Union has applied and will apply in its foreign policy the high principle of respect for the sovereign rights of peoples . . . the Soviet Union defends the right of every nation to the independence and territorial integrity of its country . . . the Soviet Union was and is willing to render all possible assistance to peoples becoming victims of aggression and fighting for the independence of their native land'.)

(a) C10382, 10607/14/62. (b) C10717/14/62. (c) C10410, 10426/14/62.

H

(a) The declarations of the other Allies and of the Free French were more in keeping with political realities. All accepted the Charter with guarded references to the interpretation of particular clauses. The Czechs and the Poles mentioned the special need of guarantees for the immediate neighbours of Germany. The Poles spoke of 'wide access' to the sea as essential to their independence; they assumed that their territory would not be reduced in strength and importance, and that Poland could be sure of an 'economic development in proportion to the numbers of her population'. The Dutch hoped that the phrase in Point Four about 'respect for existing obligations' did not imply that these obligations should be perpetuated.[1]

(ix)

The United Nations Declaration of January 1942.

The Atlantic Charter was the first large general statement of aims to which all the Allies—including, at least nominally, the U.S.S.R.—gave their assent in company with the United States. The next stage came sooner than was expected, and once again took the form of a public declaration on matters of principle. After the entry of the United States into the war the initiative in binding the Allies to a common statement of purpose came from the Americans. The United States Government first made sure that there were no secret commitments on the European side which might embarrass Mr. Roosevelt as the Treaty of London had embarrassed Mr. Wilson. They then prepared for submission to Mr. Churchill, on his visit to Washington shortly after the Japanese attack at Pearl Harbour, a draft declaration which would commit the signatories to the war aims set out in the Atlantic Charter.[2] It is not possible, from the British side, to say how far the implications of the Charter had been studied in the State Department. Nonetheless the association of the United States as a belligerent with a joint declaration based on the ideas set out in August, 1941, was a long step towards American acceptance of the necessity of some international organisation to put these ideas into practical effect.

---

[1] The meeting also discussed and accepted a resolution on the practical steps to be taken in order to provide for the supply of necessities to the occupied territories as soon as the German oppressors had been removed. I have not dealt with this discussion. A record of the inter-Allied meeting was published in Cmd. 6315.

[2] For the origins of the declaration, see *F.R.U.S.*, 1942, I, 1–38.

(a) C10990/14/62.

On Mr. Churchill's arrival in Washington the President gave him two drafts of a proposed joint declaration. Mr. Churchill telegraphed (a) these drafts on December 24 for consideration by the War Cabinet. Mr. Churchill thought that either draft or a combination of both would be satisfactory; he asked for the views of the War Cabinet and suggested that he should be allowed a certain latitude of choice.

In each draft the preamble began: 'The Governments of the United States of America, Great Britain, Australia, Canada, the Union of Soviet Socialist Republics, the Union of South Africa, New Zealand, China, and the Netherlands, having subscribed to a common programme of purposes and principles emdodied in the joint declaration of the President of the United States of America and the Prime Minister of Great Britain, dated August 14, 1941, known as the Atlantic Charter . . .'. The first draft then continued:

'being convinced that the complete and world-wide victory of all of them is essential to defend and preserve life, liberty, and independence as well as the righteous possibilities of human freedom and justice, not only in their own lands but everywhere, against savage and brutal force seeking to subjugate the world, declare:

(i) Each Government pledges itself to employ its full resources against the Axis forces of conquest[1] and to continue such employment until these forces have been finally defeated:

(ii) Each Government pledges itself to the other Governments associated with this declaration to effect a full co-ordination of military effort and use of resources against the common enemies:

(iii) Each Government pledges itself to continue the war against, and not to make a separate peace with the common enemies or any of them.

Other Governments desirous of associating themselves in this declaration are hereby privileged to adhere to this declaration.'

The second draft continued as follows:

'being convinced that complete victory over their enemies is essential to defend life, liberty and independence and to preserve human freedom and justice not only in their own land but everywhere else and that the struggle in which they are now engaged is a common defence against savage and brutal forces seeking to subjugate the world, declare:

(i) Each signatory Government pledges itself to employ its full resources against the Government or Governments which signed the Tripartite Pact on 27th September 1940, with

---

[1] This sentence was wrongly transmitted as 'The Court of Government pledges itself to employ its full resources against the Axis force conquest'.

(a) C14338/14/62; Tel. Grey 78.

which it is or may be at war, and to continue such employment until that Government or those Governments have been
finally defeated:

(ii) Each signatory Government pledges itself to co-operate with
the others to the entire extent of its capacity to effect full co-
ordination of military effort and use of resources against the
common enemies or any of them.'

The War Cabinet considered these drafts in the afternoon of
(a) Christmas Eve. They replied to the Prime Minister that they were in
general agreement but had certain comments:

(i) It was not clear what countries were to sign. The last sentence
of the first draft suggested the possibility of subsequent signatures.
This might be only to 'keep open a door' for the South American
States, but it was difficult, in view of the 'generality' of the declaration, to find a satisfactory 'half-way house' between a declaration
signed by the Prime Minister and the President and one signed by
all the Allies. The Polish Prime Minister had urged very strongly
that, if there were to be a declaration, Poland, as our first ally in the
war, should be a party to it. Other Allied Governments would hold
the same view. Hence the War Cabinet favoured a declaration
signed by all the Allies, and thus giving the necessary emphasis to
the fact that the war was being waged for the freedom of small
nations as well as great. The Allied Governments should be allowed
a chance of signature before the declaration was published, even if
publication was thereby delayed for a day or two.

The War Cabinet then called attention to the mistake in the
transmission of the first sentence of paragraph (i) in the first draft.
They assumed this sentence to read 'Each Government pledges itself
to employ its full resources against the Axis forces of conquest'. They
took the sentence, and the variant in the second draft, to be an
attempt to use a form of words which, without any explicit statement,
recognised the distinctive position of the U.S.S.R. with regard to the
enemy Powers, i.e. the U.S.S.R. was not at war with Japan. Although
this device might be the only one which would secure the signatures
of all the Allies, it gave a certain obscurity to the declaration.

(ii) The War Cabinet thought that the declaration should include
a pledge not to conclude a separate peace. They therefore favoured
the first draft.

(iii) They approved of the reference in the preamble to the
Atlantic Charter, but wished to add something about social security.
They suggested inserting the words 'and social security'[1] after
'freedom and justice'.

---

[1] An original British draft appears to have included the term 'social justice'. I have not
been able to trace this draft.

(a) Tel. Taut 185 (WM (41) 135).

They also suggested that the enumeration of British and Dominion Governments ought to be in the normal form, i.e. the Governments of 'the United Kingdom, Canada, the Commonwealth of Australia, and the Union of South Africa'.[1] At this stage the War Cabinet did not consider that India should be included.

Finally, the War Cabinet assumed that the Prime Minister was consulting the Dominion Governments through their representatives in Washington, and that he would deal with other points of phrasing.

On December 28 the Foreign Office received from Lord Halifax a redraft of the declaration. The President had made the redraft and (a) the Prime Minister had approved it. The Prime Minister realised that the order of mention of the Governments was not in accordance with the wishes of the War Cabinet, but the President had pressed for it. The State Department were giving the text to the foreign Governments concerned, and Lord Halifax, at the Prime Minister's request, was giving it to the Dominion representatives. Lord Halifax had already telegraphed that the Prime Minister and the President wanted to include India.

The new draft opened with a list of signatories: 'the United States of America, China, the United Kingdom of Great Britain and Northern Ireland, the Union of Soviet Socialist Republics, Australia, Belgium, Canada, Costa Rica, Cuba,[2] the Dominican Republic, El Salvador, Greece, Guatemala, Hayti, Honduras, the Netherlands, New Zealand, Nicaragua, Norway, Panama, Poland, South Africa and Yugoslavia'. The reference to the Atlantic Charter was unchanged, and the second part of the preamble followed the lines of the second draft, with minor changes in wording. The declaration then ran:

'(i) Each Government pledges itself to employ its full resources, military or economic, against those members of the Tripartite Pact and its adherents with which such Government is at war;

(ii) Each Government pledges itself to co-operate with other Governments signatory hereto; and to continue the war against, and not to make a separate armistice or peace with the common enemies or any one of them.'

The redraft concluded: 'The foregoing declaration may be adhered to by other nations which are or may be rendering mutual assistance and contributions towards the defeat of members or adherents of the Tripartite Pact.'

---

[1] This list accidentally omitted New Zealand.
[2] 'Czechoslovakia' was included in the redraft, but was accidentally omitted in deciphering. The omission was discovered on December 29 after the Foreign Office had (b) enquired about it from Washington.

(a) C14339/14/62. (b) C14356/14/62.

(a)   This redraft was received at 9.45 p.m. on December 28. The War Cabinet discussed it on the same night, and, with their authority,

(b)   two telegrams were sent to Lord Halifax in the early afternoon of December 29. The War Cabinet referred to the omission of Czechoslovakia and Luxembourg and asked for their inclusion. They also thought it essential that the Free French should sign the declaration, since they had been a party to the resolutions adopted at the inter-Allied meetings in London, and in one of these resolutions had subscribed formally to the Atlantic Charter. The Free French were in every sense an 'Ally'. Their armed forces were collaborating with our own; they controlled territories which were strategically of the highest importance to us. On the outbreak of war with Japan, they had placed at the disposal of the Allies all the facilities offered by the bases in the Free French islands of the Pacific. The U.S.S.R. and the other European Allies had followed His Majesty's Government in establishing relations with the Free French Government and the fact that the United States Government had not done so could not entitle them to veto the inclusion of the Free French in the declaration. If they were included, it would be necessary to add 'the Free French National Committee' at the end of the list of participating Governments, and the words 'or authority' after the word 'Government' in the text of the declaration.

The War Cabinet had also consulted the Viceroy of India on the inclusion of India. The Viceroy considered that India should be included, but that he should obtain the consent of his Council. He was consulting his Council, and the revised text was being telegraphed to him.

The War Cabinet felt strongly that they should not consent to the separation, in the list, of the different States of the British Commonwealth. Hitherto in the inter-Allied declarations these States had been grouped together in view of their common sovereignty. This rule should govern the case of the declaration. In the St. James's Palace declaration the Commonwealth Governments were so grouped, although the declarations were inter-governmental in form. The War Cabinet thought it particularly desirable to emphasise the fact that the separate members of the Commonwealth were acting together; they asked why the President wanted us to change the previous arrangement.[1] They assumed that the Prime Minister would probably inform the Dominion representatives of their view.

---

[1] The War Cabinet pointed out that in the case of international (i.e. not solely inter-Allied) declarations and treaties, the practice was either to recite the Heads of States—in which case the United Kingdom and the Dominions were grouped under his Majesty The King—or to refer to the 'Governments of the United Kingdom, etc.' and to adhere strictly to the alphabetical order of the countries concerned. The War Cabinet did not wish to extend the latter practice to inter-Allied declarations.

(a) C14339/14/62. (b) WM(41)137; C50/4/62 (1942).

Finally the War Cabinet again regretted that there was no reference to 'social security' in the new draft.

On December 30 Lord Halifax was informed that the Viceroy, with the approval of his Council, wished India to be associated with (a) the declaration, and to appear as a separate signatory. The War Cabinet accepted the Council's view and also suggested that the use of the term 'High Contracting Parties' instead of 'Governments signatory thereto' would get over the drafting difficulty about bringing in the Free French, and any question which might arise over the term 'India'.[1]

Mr. Churchill was at this time in Canada. Lord Halifax telegraphed to him at Ottawa the changes proposed by the War Cabinet, (b) and asked that he should propose to the President to associate the Free French in some form with the declaration. Lord Halifax said that he would try to secure the other changes, but that there would be difficulty about the question of alphabetical order.

On the night of December 30–31 Lord Halifax reported that the State Department accepted the inclusion of India and Luxembourg. (c) Mr. Berle had also said that he would try to get the inclusion of the Dominions and India in their proper order directly after the United Kingdom. Mr. Berle thought, however, that the President might object to any change owing to his wish that the U.S.S.R. and China should figure early in the list. Lord Halifax told Mr. Berle that in such case, 'having regard to the importance of Russian susceptibilities', we should be prepared to accept the order laid down in the latest redraft. The President felt 'definitely unable to agree' with the inclusion of the Free French as an original party to the declaration, since he considered this degree of recognition to be incompatible with the continuance of relations between the United States and the Vichy Government which he regarded as 'being in our common interest'. Mr. Hopkins thought that the President might be willing to accept the accession of the Free French 'at an early date' in accordance with the last article of the declaration.

The President had also proposed some drafting alterations, including the substitution of (i) the words 'contributions in the struggle for victory over Hitlerism' for 'contributions towards defeating members or adherents of the Tripartite Pact', and (ii) the words 'each Government pledges itself to co-operate with the Governments of the signatories hereto, and not to make a separate armistice or peace with the enemies' for the phrase in the redraft with regard to a separate peace.[2] Lord Halifax had accepted these alterations. The State Department had obtained Russian agreement to the statement

---

[1] i.e. the question of the Indian princes.
[2] Lord Halifax reported that these changes were proposed by the Soviet Government.

(a) C14374/14/62. (b) C14389/14/62. (c) C14437/14/62.

in this amended form (although the Soviet Government had at first talked of issuing a separate statement) and did not want to reopen the question of wording. Lord Halifax had been unable to secure the reinsertion of the reference to 'social security'. The President sympathised with the suggestion but M. Litvinov[1] could not accept it without referring it to Moscow; the President therefore thought it better to 'leave well alone'. Lord Halifax had included it in a re-draft which he had communicated to the President after getting the suggestions telegraphed on December 25: he had understood the inclusion to be accepted. In the President's view, however, the point was covered by the reference to the Atlantic Charter. In these circumstances Lord Halifax had said that we would not wish to press the matter.

Mr. Berle was afraid that the use of the term 'High Contracting Parties' would convert the declaration into a treaty which, in the terms of the American constitution, would require submission to the Senate. He promised to consider the matter, but Lord Halifax said that we could 'hardly insist' if there were serious difficulties of this kind on the American side.

An answer to this telegram was sent to Lord Halifax at 9.05 p.m. on December 31 with the authority of Mr. Attlee, Mr. Eden and Lord Cranborne, Secretary of State for the Dominions. (i) They considered it 'most regrettable' that the 'prejudices' of the State Department should put us in the false position of signing an inter-Allied document which excluded one of the Allies—the Free French. The suggestion that the Free French should accede later was not feasible since they could not be described as a 'nation'. (ii) They assumed that the original formula with regard to a separate peace had been drafted to leave the United States and ourselves 'at any rate theoretically a loophole to make a peace with Japan'. It therefore put a certain pressure on the Soviet Government to enter the war against Japan in order to make Japan a 'common enemy'. The Soviet redraft 'removed this feature from the declaration and might be misrepresented as binding us not to make a separate peace with Japan without Soviet consent, while not pledging the Soviet Government to treat Japan as an enemy'. (iii) They considered the substitution of the 'vague term "Hitlerism" ' for the adherents of the Tripartite Pact as 'quite inappropriate' to a document which sought to bring together Governments fighting Japan as well as the European Axis. The effect of the amendment might be to enable the Soviet Government to argue that a South American State which rendered material assistance against Japan was not qualified to accede to the declaration since it

(a)

---

[1] M. Litvinov was appointed Soviet Ambassador in Washington in November 1941.
(a) C14437/14/62.

was not rendering such assistance against Germany (i.e. 'Hitlerism').
(iv) They regarded a declaration referring to signatory Governments and containing solemn pledges as 'in any case a document of
treaty character', which would not be affected by the choice
between the terms 'Contracting Parties' or 'Signatory Governments'.
(v) They pointed out that the omission of the term 'social security'
would be 'very much questioned by a large section of opinion' in
Great Britain and also among the Allies. The omission of a reference
to 'freedom of conscience' in the Atlantic Charter had caused trouble
with American opinion. We should now have similar trouble.
(vi) They still attached the highest importance to the grouping of
the United Kingdom and the Dominions, though they did not mind
what place this group occupied in the list. If it would help to meet
Russian susceptibilities, the U.S.S.R. and China might figure before
the British group which could then take fourth place. Lord Halifax
was asked to insist on this compromise. (vii) Finally Lord Halifax
was asked why the urgency was 'so great as to oblige us to accept a
declaration with these defects'.

Mr. Churchill replied to this telegram on January 1 after discussing
with Mr. Roosevelt and Mr. Hull the points raised in it. The tele- (a)
gram did not reach London until January 2—i.e. the day on which
the declaration was published. Mr. Churchill said that there had
been no time to get agreement to the proposed amendments because
Mr. Roosevelt wanted publication on January 1 and M. Litvinov
could not accept any changes without reference to Moscow. Mr.
Churchill had failed to get Mr. Roosevelt's agreement to the
inclusion of the Free French. He had then suggested the inclusion
of the words 'or authorities' after 'nations' in the last paragraph.
The Free French could thus accede to the declaration, or General
de Gaulle could send a letter to all the signatories stating his accession.

Mr. Churchill had not pressed for the amendment of the phrase
about 'Hitlerism' because Mr. Roosevelt thought the phrase of value
in keeping the mind and effort of the United States directed to the
main target, and also because he (Mr. Roosevelt) was convinced
that Stalin could not accept the amendment. Mr. Roosevelt had
said that he could not sign the document without the concurrence of
the Senate if the term 'High Contracting Parties' were used.

Mr. Churchill recognised the difficulty about excluding the
reference to 'social security' but considered that, as the declaration
spoke of human rights, and justice, and referred to the Atlantic
Charter, social security was covered by implication. Mr. Churchill
had therefore signed the declaration and asked for the formal
authorisation of the War Cabinet.

(a) C179/4/62.

H*

(a) On January 3 Mr. Churchill telegraphed that Mr. Roosevelt had chosen the title 'United Nations' since the word 'Alliance' would have raised constitutional difficulties in the United States and the words 'Associated Powers' were too flat. Mr. Churchill also said that M. Litvinov had refused to agree to the proposed inclusion of the words 'or authorities', but that the adherence of the Free French to the declaration could be covered by an exchange of letters. Mr. Churchill described M. Litvinov as an 'automaton' and 'frightened'.

(b) The declaration thus appeared in the form provisionally accepted by Mr. Churchill and Lord Halifax. On January 4 the State Depart-
(c) ment issued a statement that, in order to give 'liberty-loving peoples, silenced by military force, an opportunity to support the principles of the declaration of the United Nations, the Government of the United States, as the depository for that declaration, will receive statements of adherence to its principles from appropriate authorities which are not Governments'.

(d) This statement led at first to some differences of view between the State Department and the Foreign Office. Lord Halifax reported on the night of January 22–3 that as he had heard nothing more from the State Department about the accession of 'Free Movements' to the declaration, he had asked Sir R. Campbell to raise the point with Mr. Berle. We had also previously heard that the Soviet, Belgian, Yugoslav and Greek Governments were afraid that the State Department might be too forthcoming towards some of the so-called 'Free Movements'.

Mr. Berle explained that the President had decided to keep the whole matter in suspense, and not to lay down any definite rules about application. Sir R. Campbell suggested that His Majesty's Government should be consulted in respect of any applications. Mr. Berle was unwilling to give an undertaking, since the President was dealing with the matter himself.

The Foreign Office therefore asked the Prime Minister whether he had made any arrangements with the President about accessions. They pointed out that the American statement had been intended mainly for the Free French, who had not taken advantage of it, but that a number of self-appointed 'authorities'—including Otto Strasser's 'Free German Movement', the Basque and Catalan émigré movements, and King Zog of Albania—had informed the United States Government, and, in some cases, the British Government, of their desire to accede. In view of Mr. Berle's statement, it was desirable that we should be consulted before any applications were accepted; we could not agree to leave the decision solely to Mr. Roosevelt. In any case, the question of the accession of Iran had been raised and that of Ethiopia was to be raised in Parliament.

(a) Tel. Grey 202. (b) C66/4/62. (c) C332/331/17. (d) C907/4/62.

Mr. Churchill told Mr. Eden on February 11 that he had made
no arrangements on the question with Mr. Roosevelt, but that Mr. (a)
Roosevelt would certainly be willing to consult with us. Mr. Churchill
said that he would speak to Mr. Hopkins: meanwhile he asked for a
list of the 'candidates for election'.

The Foreign Office replied that the candidates, or possible
candidates, were the Free French National Committee, Ethiopia,
Iran, Iraq, and Saudi Arabia. The Ethiopians had not yet applied,
but we should welcome their application. The Iranian Government
were at present unwilling to apply. If Saudi Arabia declared war on
Germany and Italy, probably Iraq would follow, and both countries
would therefore accede to the declaration.

At the Prime Minister's request the Foreign Office drafted a (b)
personal message for him to send to Mr. Roosevelt. Mr. Roosevelt
replied on March 4 that he agreed with Mr. Churchill's suggestion (c)
for consultation. He thought that there would be no need for further
question in the case of the Free French, but that other cases should
be considered as they arose.

The Declaration of the United Nations was primarily a manifesto
of military alliance, with a general statement of the principles which
would govern the policy and mutual relations of the Allies after the
war. At the time when Mr. Roosevelt suggested the term 'United
Nations', the Allies were still a long way from victory, and, for that
matter, there were already signs, especially in the Russian attitude
of aloofness and suspicion, that the problem of restoring political
liberty, independence, and a sense of security to the States of Europe
would not be solved merely by the defeat of Hitler; similarly the
future of China as a democratic country could not be secured merely
by the defeat of Japan. On the other hand there was not even a
possibility of attaining, in Europe or Asia, the ideals set out in the
Atlantic Charter until the Germans and the Japanese, and their
associates, had been utterly defeated. At the beginning of the critical
year 1942, even the most hopeful observer, looking at Europe, and
beyond Europe at a whole world of States and peoples thrown into
confusion by the aggression of Germany and Japan, could not have
said more than the words employed by a French stateman nearly a
century earlier in a different context: 'C'est le chaos, et le chaos
stérile. Je n'ai pas cessé à croire à la lumière; elle se fera un jour sur
ce chaos.' Before the year 1942 was out there were signs at least that
a New Order was in sight; it was not the 'New Order' of Hitler and
Germany.

(a) C1727/4/62. (b) C2278/4/62. (c) C2381/4/62.

CHAPTER XXVI

Mr. Eden's visit to Moscow, December 1941: British acceptance of the Russian demands with regard to the Baltic States: the negotiation of the Anglo-Russian Treaty of May 26, 1942

(i)

Mr. Eden's conversations of December 16, 1941, with Stalin.

(a)   ON November 29, 1941, Mr. Eden submitted to the War Cabinet a memorandum, drawn up in the Foreign Office with his approval, on his forthcoming visit to Moscow.[1] The purpose of the visit was to remove the Russian suspicions that we wished to make an 'Anglo-American peace' excluding Russia and ignoring Russian interests, and that we should not take sufficiently drastic measures to render Germany powerless for many years to come. Mr. Eden suggested that we should give Stalin a memorandum and a proposed joint declaration of policy. In the memorandum we should refer to the joint declaration as marking the association of the Soviet and British Governments and as parallel to the Anglo-American association in the Atlantic Charter. Our first objective was the total defeat of Germany: the two Governments might pledge themselves to continue the war until this aim had been attained and not to make peace with any German Government which had not clearly renounced all aggressive intentions. We should also plan to keep Germany disarmed after the war.

For the peace settlement and the planning of post-war reconstruction we should take the Atlantic Charter as a starting-point, and also associate ourselves with Stalin's own definition of the aims of the Soviet Government in a statement of November 6 to the effect that:

> 'We have not, and we cannot have such war aims as the seizure of foreign territory, the subjugation of foreign peoples, whether it concerns the peoples and territories of Europe, or the peoples and territories of Asia, including Persia. Our first aim consists in liberating our territories and our peoples from the German fascist yoke.

[1] See above, Chapter XX, section (iv). The Chiefs of Staff drew up an *aide-mémoire* on military assistance to Russia. I have limited this chapter as far as possible to the political questions raised before and during Mr. Eden's visit.

(a) WP(41)288 Revise.

We have not, and we cannot have, such war aims as the forcing of our will and our regime upon the Slavonic or any other enslaved peoples of Europe who are expecting our assistance. Our aim consists in helping these peoples in their struggle for liberation against Hitlerite tyranny, and later permitting them fairly to settle their own destiny in their own land. No interference in the internal affairs of other people.'

The memorandum to Stalin would then explain that it was premature to attempt a post-war territorial settlement in relation to clause (ii) of the Charter which laid down that territorial changes should accord with the freely expressed wishes of the peoples concerned. We recognised the need to strengthen the smaller countries of Europe so that they could resist German pressure, and we were considering an extension of the idea of federation on the lines which were already being discussed between Poland and Czechoslovakia.[1] We hoped that the Soviet Government would take part in future discussions on economic reconstruction and we would do all we could to assist in the economic rehabilitation of the U.S.S.R. We should also wish to discuss later on the question of compelling Germany to make restitution for the spoliation of which she had been guilty during the war.

The draft declaration set out these terms in formal clauses recognising the Anglo-Russian agreement of July 12, 1941, and the principles of the Atlantic Charter as the basis of Anglo-Russian collaboration, and linking Stalin's statement of November 6 with the statement in the Charter that Great Britain and the United States sought 'no aggrandisement, territorial or other'.

The War Cabinet approved the two drafts before Mr. Eden left (a) for Moscow. They also hoped that Mr. Eden would be able to convince Stalin that it would be a mistake to divert forces to Russia from our Libyan offensive and to choke the lines of communication in Iran through which we planned to send material to Russia.

Mr. Eden held his first conversation with Stalin on December 16. (b) Sir S. Cripps, MM. Molotov and Maisky (as interpreter) were present throughout the meetings. The situation was now different in two important respects from that of mid-November. The German offensive in Russia had been held. The Russians had made important gains in their counter-attacks; in any case the respite of the winter months would be of greater advantage to them than to the Germans.

---

[1] An agreement between the Polish and Czechoslovak Governments was signed on December 3, 1941. See also Volume V, Chapter LXI, note to section (i).

(a) WM(41)124.3, C.A. (b) WP(42)8; N109/5/38 (1942).

The question of the despatch of British forces was thus less urgent. There was even less chance of providing these forces owing to the entry of Japan into the war in circumstances which would obviously put the greatest strain on British resources in manpower and shipping until the United States had recovered from the attack at Pearl Harbour and deployed American resources to their fullest extent.

On the other hand the new situation, which greatly increased the political importance of Anglo-American co-operation, made the Russians even more anxious to commit Great Britain to their plans for a post-war settlement in Europe. It became clear at once that these aims conflicted not only with Mr. Roosevelt's ideas and with the principles of the Atlantic Charter but also with Stalin's own statement of November 6.

At the beginning of the discussions on December 16 Stalin produced drafts of an alliance providing for military assistance during the war and of an agreement with regard to the post-war reconstruction of Europe and the content of the peace treaties. He proposed the addition of a secret protocol to this agreement as follows: (i) East Prussia should be transferred to Poland; Tilsit and German territory to the north of the river Niemen should be transferred to the Lithuanian republic of the U.S.S.R. (ii) Czechoslovakia should be re-established with her pre-Munich frontiers, and with an extension to the south at the expense of Hungary. (iii) Yugoslavia should also be re-established and should be given the Italian islands and certain coastal towns on the Adriatic. (iv) Albania should become an independent State. (v) Turkey should receive the Dodecanese, and the Turco-Bulgarian frontier might be modified in favour of Turkey. (vi) All other occupied countries, including Greece, should be re-established in their pre-war frontiers. (vii) Stalin considered that, if France did not emerge from the war as a Great Power, Great Britain should occupy military and naval bases, such as Boulogne and Dunkirk, and that Belgium and the Netherlands should be in open alliance with Great Britain, and allow her the right to maintain bases, and, if necessary, garrisons on their respective territories.[1] (viii) The Rhineland should be detached from Prussia; Austria should be restored as an independent State, and Bavaria might also become independent. (ix) The U.S.S.R. would not object to British bases in Norway and Denmark. (x) Stalin then outlined his views about the frontiers of the U.S.S.R. He wanted the frontier in Finland and the Baltic 'provinces' to be restored to its position in 1941; the

---

[1] These suggestions with regard to France and the Low Countries were made by Stalin during the discussion of the proposed secret protocol. France was mentioned in the protocol, but only with a query. Stalin asked for Mr. Eden's views.

Curzon line, with slight variations, might serve as the frontier with Poland. Bessarabia and Northern Bukovina would be taken from Roumania and, in return, Roumania would be given an extension of her western frontier against Hungary. The U.S.S.R. wished for alliances with Roumania and Finland allowing the maintenance of Russian military or naval bases on their territories. They also wanted to take back Petsamo from Finland.

Stalin also asked Mr. Eden's views about reparations and the maintenance of peace and order in a reconstructed Europe. He thought that for this purpose some kind of military force would be required and that it should be organised under a military alliance of the democratic powers. Mr. Eden agreed that the military control of Germany would be necessary; he did not exclude partition, but could not commit the British Government to any particular solution of the German problem; they were, however, in favour of the restoration of an independent Austria. Mr. Eden was sure that, after the experience of the last post-war years, Great Britain would not wish to exact reparation in money; reparation in kind—e.g. the restitution of goods taken from occupied territories—was another matter. Stalin said that the U.S.S.R. also favoured reparations in kind.

Mr. Eden showed Stalin the two British drafts, and suggested an attempt to combine the proposed British declaration with the Russian texts. Stalin, however, pointed out that the British draft was a 'kind of declaration', whereas the Russian drafts were 'agreements.' He said: 'A declaration I regard as algebra, but an agreement as practical arithmetic. I do not wish to decry algebra, but I prefer practical arithmetic, and I think that, in the present circumstances, when Hitler is boasting to everyone of all the treaties he has managed to obtain, it would be wiser to have treaties.'

Stalin then asked about the secret protocol. Mr. Eden said that he could not sign it without consulting his colleagues, and that they had not yet applied their minds to the details of a territorial settlement. M. Maisky then intervened: 'Not even the Soviet frontiers?' Mr. Eden said that it would also be necessary to consult the United States and the Dominions. Stalin said that he wanted to establish that Russian and British war aims were identical. 'If our war aims were different, then there would be no alliance.' Mr. Eden agreed, but again insisted that he would have to discuss all the frontier questions with his colleagues.

At this inconclusive stage the political part of the first conversation ended. Before the next meeting Mr. Eden discussed with M. Molotov the two drafts which he had brought with him and the Russian drafts. The discussion ended with M. Molotov's approval of two draft agreements in the following terms:

(1)

AGREEMENT FOR MUTUAL MILITARY ASSISTANCE BETWEEN THE U.S.S.R. AND GREAT BRITAIN IN THE WAR AGAINST GERMANY.

His Majesty's Government in the United Kingdom and the Government of the Union of Soviet Socialist Republics have concluded the following agreement:

Article 1

An Alliance is hereby established between the Soviet Union and Great Britain and the two Allied Powers mutually undertake to afford one another military assistance and support of all kinds in the war against Germany and those associated with her acts of aggression in Europe.

Article 2

The two Contracting Parties undertake not to enter into negotiations with the Hitlerite Government of Germany or any other Government of Germany that does not clearly renounce all aggressive intentions and not to conclude any armistice or peace treaty with Germany except by mutual consent.

Article 3

Each Contracting Party undertakes not to conclude any alliance and not to take part in any coalition directed against the other Contracting Party.

Article 4

The present Agreement enters into force immediately upon signature and is subject to ratification at the earliest possible date.

The exchange of the instruments of ratification shall take place in London.

The present Agreement has been concluded in duplicate in the English and Russian languages.

Both texts have equal force.

(2)

AGREEMENT BETWEEN THE U.S.S.R. AND GREAT BRITAIN FOR THE SETTLEMENT OF POST-WAR QUESTIONS AND FOR COMMON ACTION TO ENSURE SECURITY IN EUROPE AFTER THE TERMINATION OF THE WAR WITH GERMANY.

His Majesty's Government in the United Kingdom and the Government of the Union of Soviet Socialist Republics have concluded the following Agreement:—

Article 1

The two Contracting Parties undertake that, in the settlement of post-war questions connected with the organisation of peace and security in Europe, they will act by mutual agreement.

Article 2

The two Contracting Parties jointly affirm their acceptance of the principles of the declaration made on the 14th August 1941, by the President of the United States and the Prime Minister of the United Kingdom.

Article 3

The two Contracting Parties agree that after the termination of hostilities they will take all measures in their power to render impossible a repetition of aggression and violation of the peace by Germany.

Article 4

The two Contracting Parties undertake to work together for the reconstruction of Europe after the war with full regard to each other's interests and in accordance with the two principles of no aggrandisement for themselves and no interference in the internal affairs of other peoples.

The objectives of this task of reconstruction will include in particular—

(a) The safeguarding and strengthening of the economic and political independence of all European countries either as unitary or federated States.

(b) The reconstruction of the industrial and economic life of those countries whose territories have been overrun by Germany or her associates.

Article 5

The two Contracting Parties agree to render one another all possible assistance after the war.

The present Agreement etc. (as in article 4 of the first agreement).

In accepting these drafts Mr. Eden had acquiesced in the Russian demand for formal agreements rather than a declaration of common policy, but he had not committed himself to a statement about frontiers. The first of the two drafts was positive and simple, since it recorded the conclusion of a military alliance and an agreement between the two Allies not to make a separate peace with Germany. The second draft was, inevitably, much vaguer, since it dealt with an agreement for post-war collaboration. There were references to an acceptance of the 'principles' of the Atlantic Charter, and also to the 'principles' of 'no-aggrandisement' and 'no-interference'. It was, however, already clear that the Russians would not be satisfied with these generalities and that they would try to get British consent to their main territorial demands. Stalin made this attempt in his second conversation with Mr. Eden.

(ii)

Mr. Eden's conversation of the night of December 17–18 with Stalin: Mr. Eden's later conversations with Stalin: failure to reach agreement over the Russian territorial demands.

(a)   Mr. Eden's second conversation with Stalin and M. Molotov[1] took place at midnight on December 17–18. The record of the conversation is worth quoting at length, since it is typical of so many conversations with the Russians between 1941 and 1945, and, indeed, in the general Russian refusal to give consideration to any point of view or interest other than their own, it is typical of the whole course of Anglo-Russian diplomatic relations.

'. . . *M. Stalin:*[2] You will remember that last night we talked of the possibility of doing something as regards the frontiers of the U.S.S.R. apart from the general question of Central and Western Europe frontiers. The Soviet Government is very interested in this question because during the time of the Chamberlain Government in (*sic*) the earlier negotiations they (*sic*) broke down on this very question of the Baltic countries and Finland, and we want to know what is the position on this matter of the present British Government.

Mr. Eden: Of course I was not a member of the Chamberlain Government at that time, so I cannot tell what went on in the Government. I do, however, fully realise that you want security on your north-western frontier, and also I bear in mind that we have signed the Atlantic Charter. I am afraid it is impossible for me to give you any decision on this question because that decision must be a decision of the British Government. All I can do is to report to them what your views are, and then communicate, as I have promised, with you again through diplomatic channels.

M. Stalin: Is it really necessary on this question of the Baltic States to have a Government decision? Surely this is absolutely axiomatic. We are fighting our hardest and losing hundreds of thousands of men in the common cause with Great Britain as our ally, and I should have thought that such a question as the position of the Baltic States ought to be axiomatic and ought not to require any decision.

Mr. Eden: You mean the future of the Baltic States at the end of the war?

M. Stalin: Yes. Would you support the entry of these three States at the end of the war into the Soviet Union?

Mr. Eden: The present position is that we do not recognise the independent existence of any of these States. They have no diplomatic

---

[1] Sir S. Cripps, Sir A. Cadogan, Lieutenant-General Nye, M. Molotov and M. Maisky were also present.

[2] Three introductory and seven concluding paragraphs are omitted. In the latter Stalin forecast that Japan would be beaten within six months.

(a) WP(42)8; N109/5/38(1942).

status with us, but we are committed to the United States of America not to bind ourselves as to any decision upon European frontiers before the end of the war without consultation with them. I am, however, prepared to seek a decision from my Government on this issue and also consult the Americans upon it as soon as I get back to London. I think it is most desirable that all three Governments should come to an agreement on this question.

M. Stalin: In that case I am afraid there will be great difficulty in coming to any agreement on these proposed treaties.

Mr. Eden: This is really quite a new issue which you are raising. You will remember that the Prime Minister has long since stated publicly that we cannot acknowledge, during the war, any changes of sovereignty which have been made since the beginning of the war.

M. Stalin: Last night I put forward the question of your recognising at least the post-war frontiers of the U.S.S.R. We might re-occupy the Baltic States in the near future, and how are we to know that in that event Great Britain will not deny us these frontiers?

Mr. Eden: The Prime Minister made his statement that we would not recognise changes made during the war when Germany was advancing, and that statement was really to the advantage of the U.S.S.R. The statement was made publicly to the whole world, and it is quite clear that I cannot now decide this issue, though, as I have said, I am prepared to take it up when I return to London.

M. Stalin: If you say that, you might well say tomorrow that you do not recognise the Ukraine as forming part of the U.S.S.R.

Mr. Eden: That is a complete misunderstanding of the position. It is only changes from the pre-war frontiers that we do not recognise. The only change in the Ukraine is its occupation by Germany, so of course we accept the Ukraine as being part of the U.S.S.R.

M. Stalin: This seems to be just the same position as was taken by the Chamberlain Government on the question of the Baltic States, and in that event it is difficult to come to any terms on these agreements.

Mr. Eden: I can only say that I am sorry if that is so. Our position is perfectly clear. The Americans have asked us not to agree to any altered boundaries in Europe, but I am prepared to put the question up to my Government and to the Americans and then to give you the answer. I cannot give you that answer now without consulting the Americans. If you wish for it and attach great importance to this point, then I will try and get a favourable answer for you upon it. There is this difference between the present and the earlier negotiations which I should like to make plain. At the time of the earlier negotiations the Baltic States were free and independent States. Since that time those States have ceased to exist as free and independent States, and therefore *de facto* the situation is now a completely different one.

M. Stalin: Where is the evidence of that? You still have their representatives in London.

Mr. Eden: We don't accept them as representatives. We neither accept notes from them nor allow them diplomatic status. The U.S.S.R. is, in fact, recognised as having the *de facto* sovereignty of the Baltic States.

M. Stalin: That seems to be a very curious situation.

Mr. Eden: I agree it may seem curious, but I don't really think that this is a very important political question. The present position is that there are no independent Baltic States and that in fact they do form part of the U.S.S.R. I am prepared to get an answer for you on your question if you wish for it from the British Government.

M. Stalin: I am surprised and amazed at Mr. Churchill's Government taking up this position. It is practically the same as that of the Chamberlain Government.

Mr. Eden: I have tried to explain to you what the difference is. The Baltic States have now ceased to exist as independent States and they are *in fact* part of the Soviet Union. Do you want me to say that they are recognised *de jure* as part of the U.S.S.R.?

M. Stalin: We are in the midst of the greatest war of history and I think these nice formulae about *de jure* and *de facto*, etc., are rather out of place. According to our constitution the three States form part of the U.S.S.R. This is the result of a plebiscite in which the great majority of all the inhabitants voted in favour of coming into the U.S.S.R. If the U.S.S.R. retained these three republics in their Constitution, does the British Government have any objection?

Mr. Eden: Of course we cannot take objection to what the Soviet Government do or do not put into their Constitution.

M. Stalin: If so, and the British Government does not have any objection, then some method of saying that should be found.

Mr. Eden: My difficulties, and I want to be perfectly frank about this, are two-fold. Firstly the Prime Minister has stated publicly that we could not accept any territorial changes made during the war. It may be that this particular change is an exceptional one, and if you wish it I will consult the British Government on that basis and let you have their answer. Secondly, under the Atlantic Charter we have pledged ourselves to take into account the wishes of the inhabitants. It may be that in this case they have been taken into account, but that is a matter that we must check up on before we arrive at a decision.

M. Stalin: Yes; they were taken into account before the war.

Mr. Eden: But not before our war started with Germany.

Mr. Stalin: Then I think we shall have to postpone the signing of the two treaties.

Mr. Eden: That, of course, is for you to decide. I should like to meet you, but I cannot do so without consulting my Government and the United States of America. I should not have thought that that was any good reason for not signing these agreements, which will be of value to both our countries, and which offer greater possibilities for the future of our arriving at an agreement upon this question of frontiers, and certainly do not in any way prejudice it.

M. Stalin: It is not only the question of the Baltic States, but of the whole of the western frontiers of the Soviet Union.

Mr. Eden: I should like you to understand my position in this matter. We promised President Roosevelt, and it was nothing to do with this present visit of mine, indeed before the Russian Government came into the war, not to agree to any changes in the European boundaries without consultation. You will agree that, if I had made such an agreement with you, you would expect me to keep it. There is nothing in these proposed agreements which in any way prevents my putting the question of your western boundaries up to the United States of America.

M. Stalin: I think that the whole war between us and Germany began because of these western frontiers of the U.S.S.R., including particularly the Baltic States. That is really what the whole war is about, and what I would like to know is whether our ally, Great Britain, supports us in regaining these western frontiers.

Mr. Eden: We in this war are fighting for lots of people's frontiers. As you know, we went to war because of the aggression against Poland, but we have never tied ourselves down to any particular frontiers, as you will remember we stated clearly in the Polish-Russan negotia-tions.[1] If, however, you wish us to agree to some specific boundaries now, I will try to get it done, but I cannot do it myself because I am bound by my promise to America.

M. Stalin: We are bound by the provisions of our Constitution.

Mr. Eden: Of course you are and we have no objection whatever to that, but we are not bound by your Constitution. Up to this point I have not agreed to any frontiers anywhere in Europe. I didn't hear of these frontiers which you now propose until I came here last night and I cannot agree to them until I have consulted both my own Government and America.

M. Stalin: This attitude of the British Government towards our frontiers is indeed a surprise to me so I think it will be better to postpone the proposed agreements.

Mr. Eden: There is nothing new at all about our attitude. We should expect, if we were to sign these agreements, to consult with you on questions of European boundaries such as, for instance, the French boundary and the question of Alsace and Lorraine and that is one of the things that this agreement says.

M. Stalin: Tomorrow, perhaps, our troops might occupy the three Baltic States, and then perhaps at the Peace Conference you would take an objection to that occupation.

Mr. Eden: If you were to do so no one would be more delighted than myself.

M. Stalin: I don't understand.

Mr. Eden: This is the position. In your view and according to your Constitution the three States now form part of the U.S.S.R. In our view, at the moment, they are neither within it nor without it. If

---

[1] See below, pp. 612–3.

you wish us to come to a decision on this I can consult the American Government.

M. Stalin: Great Britain and the U.S.S.R. are now allies, and as I understand it an ally must support an ally. If anyone were to come to me and ask me as to the desirability of touching the Irish Free State, I should tell him to get out. If Great Britain wanted air and military bases in Belgium and Holland I should certainly give my support to it, because it affected the safety of Britain and raised the question of their security.

Mr. Eden: This is not a question of loyalty, but we have committed ourselves to America as I have stated, and the Prime Minister has made a public statement to which I have referred. I am sure that you would not respect me if I were to go back upon my arrangement with President Roosevelt. I can get a decision upon this point before the Soviet troops occupy the Baltic States, even if they continue doing as well as they are doing now.

M. Stalin: If you cannot give us your support on this question of our western frontiers, which is the main question for us in the war, perhaps it would be best to postpone these agreements and to fall back on our agreement of July last.

Mr. Eden: That is a matter for you to decide. From the point of view of Anglo-Soviet relations, there would undoubtedly be a great disappointment in our country and in the Dominions. Nothing in these agreements in any way weakens the claims that you have put forward as regards frontiers.

M. Stalin: We, too, have our public opinion here and they would certainly be horrified if they learnt that Great Britain was not prepared to support us on the question of our frontiers in the Baltic States.

Mr. Eden: There is certainly nothing of that sort in the agreements, nor is it in the least necessity the position.

M. Stalin: If our people were to learn that, after all their sacrifices, Great Britain, our ally, was reluctant to support the claim of the U.S.S.R., they would certainly regard these treaties as scraps of paper.

Mr. Eden: I don't think that that is a fair way of putting it. I had never heard of these western boundaries until I got here, and I cannot agree to them without first putting them to my own Government and to the Dominions and to America. But that does not in the least prevent us being loyal allies or from doing all we can to help you to defeat the Germans.

M. Stalin: You were in general informed of the two questions of importance: military collaboration and post-war reconstruction, including the question of frontiers. If the general question of European frontiers is a difficult one to decide upon, at least that of the Soviet frontiers is in a different category.

Mr. Eden: I have always, as you know, been very strongly in favour of promoting good relations between our two countries, but there are limitations to the power of a Minister in our country, and

I cannot commit the country to your propositions without consulting my own Government, the Dominions, and the United States of America.

M. Stalin: I am far from blaming you for your attitude and I know very well of your desire to improve relations between our two countries. I would not like to blame the British Government but I am surprised that upon this question our Allies cannot give us their support.

Mr. Eden: Let me take the case of Canada and the question of the frontier between Poland and Russia. Canada has sent us hundreds of thousands of soldiers to help us in the war and if they were to hear tomorrow that I had agreed upon the Polish-Russian frontier without any consultation with them they would have every right to the strongest complaint. No Minister who did a thing like that could survive for twenty-four hours.

M. Stalin: I certainly do not want to demand the impossible from you and I fully realise the limitations of your powers, but I am addressing myself to the British Government and I am genuinely surprised. I thought that the Atlantic Charter was directed against those people who were trying to establish world dominion. It now looks as if the Charter were directed against the U.S.S.R.

Mr. Eden: No; that is certainly not so. It is merely a question of putting forward certain views as to your frontiers and of my being unable to give you an immediate reply and asking you to allow me time to get the answer.

M. Stalin: Why does the restoration of our frontiers come into conflict with the Atlantic Charter?

Mr. Eden: I never said that it did.

M. Stalin: When you gave your pledges to America we were not then allies of yours and our relations were very different. At that time the British and French Governments were contemplating giving help to Finland against the Soviet Union. Now you are at war with Finland.

Mr. Eden: And we did that in order to please you.

M. Stalin: Yes, I understand that, but the position is now changed.

Mr. Eden: If you were asking for the frontiers which existed in 1939 before the war broke out between us and Germany there would be no difficulty at all but now you are asking for frontiers which differ from those of 1939 in various places. I have taken a note of that and will report it to my Government, but I cannot see how these agreements that it is proposed to sign will make it any more difficult for us to give you the answer that you want.

M. Stalin: It makes it look as if I should have to come cap in hand.

Mr. Eden: Not at all, I don't understand that. These are documents of perfect equality and don't represent the conferring of anything by either party upon the other.

M. Molotov: We are talking of common war aims, of what we are both fighting for. On one of these important aims, our western frontiers, we have no support from Great Britain.

Mr. Eden: It is not a question of support or lack of support. For the first time last night I heard the details of the boundaries which you thought you ought to have. It is a technical question, as M. Molotov will realise in his position as Foreign Secretary, of the consents that we must obtain. No English Foreign Secretary for the last 200 years could have done what you are asking me to do.

M. Molotov: It is a question of the decision of the British Government and not of yourself.

Mr. Eden: If the Prime Minister and myself were both here we still could not give you that decision. It is a question of our meeting the demands of the U.S.S.R. We are fighting as a family with our Dominions and we must consult them.

M. Stalin: Last night when we were discussing the question of the whole map of Europe, it was obviously new and a complicated matter, and I did not insist on your accepting our views, and agreed that they should be referred to your Cabinet, but the western frontier of the U.S.S.R. is in a different category and should surely be an easy matter as between allies.

Mr. Eden: I agree, of course, that it is in a different category, but it is still a question of frontiers in Europe and of some complication since these run from Finland and the Baltic States in the north to Roumania in the south. I cannot say more than that I will report the matter to my Cabinet. How could I agree, for instance, to the Polish-Russian frontier without saying a word about it to the Poles first?

M. Stalin: The Polish frontier remains an open question and I do not insist upon settling that now. What I am most interested in is the position in Finland and the Baltic States and in Roumania. With regard to Poland, I hope that we shall be able to come to an agreement between the three of us. Generally our idea is to keep to the Curzon Line with certain modifications. But it is very important for us to know whether we shall have to fight at the Peace Conference in order to get our western frontiers.

Mr. Eden: I am certainly hoping not. As to Poland, we shall always, of course, be glad to do anything we can to help in reaching an agreement. We want to agree to the frontiers before the Peace Conference, but we have not yet reached that point, and it seems to me to be not unreasonable to ask you to let me consult the necessary persons on these very important proposals.

M. Stalin: I fully appreciate your position, that you cannot give me any definite answers.

Mr. Eden: I am sorry to appear difficult. I certainly don't want to be but under our Constitution that is my position.

M. Stalin: I fully realise that.

Mr. Eden: This is the letter which I promised to let you have as regards accession to the agreements by the Dominions (that I handed to M. Maisky, who explained the position and translated it)[1]

---

[1] I have been unable to find the text of this draft letter in the Foreign Office archives.

Unofficially I can say that, in my own view, I think the Dominions would be very glad to accede. (At this point Stalin for the first time took copies of the agreements before him and started to study them.)

M. Molotov: I am of the opinion that this question of the western frontiers is the major question for us, and if no definite answer can be obtained upon it I think it is better to put off the signing of the agreements.

Mr. Eden: That is for you to decide. I think that my Government would be astonished if that were to happen. I came out here with full powers to sign agreements on the two points you mention, covering all general matters, but I had no previous warning whatever that this matter of the western frontiers was the major question. If I go back without any agreement the effect on all allied opinion will, in my view, be extremely bad.

M. Stalin: Do you think any mention of frontiers could be made in the second treaty. Perhaps it would be desirable to postpone the consideration of this matter until tomorrow.

Mr. Eden: Frankly, and in all friendliness I think it would be a great pity to postpone indefinitely the signature of the treaties. The Germans would be bound to find out about my visit here and if the British Foreign Secretary comes to Moscow especially and then signs nothing as a result it will undoubtedly cause very great rejoicing, but I don't press that aspect of the question.'

Mr. Eden had another conversation with Stalin during the evening of December 18–19. He tried to find a formula which would leave the disputed points open to later discussion but Stalin again insisted on committing the British Government to the acceptance of the 'frontiers of 1941'. Mr. Eden repeated that he could not accept, for any country, an agreement about definite frontiers without consulting the United States and the Dominions. M. Molotov thought that a British acceptance of the Russian demands would 'greatly facilitate the consultations with America'. Mr. Eden said that the American answer would be that they must 'consider the matter'. Stalin replied that, whatever the British reasons might be for refusing to accept the Russian claims, the Russian people would not understand why there could be any bargaining about 'the restoration of our legitimate frontiers'. Finally Stalin said that he must maintain his formula with regard to 'the recognition of the right of the U.S.S.R. to their 1941 frontiers'.

'*Mr. Eden:* I am afraid I cannot possibly accept it.

M. Stalin: That is very regrettable.

Mr. Eden: I have tried very hard to meet you on this and I am prepared to do anything except to agree to definite frontiers, and I cannot do that without breaking pledges I have already made to other people, and I am not going to break pledges.

M. Stalin: It is a pity.

Mr. Eden: I now understand fully what the point of difficulty is, but it is not in my power to resolve it here and now. I will, however, do my best when I get back to solve it in London. If we do not have these agreements it will be a great pity and it certainly will not make my task in London any easier, but that position I shall have to accept. It might be wise to leave the matter over until tomorrow to see if we can find anything by way of a solution during the night, but I am afraid I do not see any prospect of that.

M. Stalin: Very well, I think you should consult your Prime Minister. When he was in a position to do so he attacked the Chamberlain Government very bitterly in 1939 for the course they pursued as to the Soviet Union, and it was just over this question of the Baltic States that negotiations broke down. I do not believe that the Prime Minister would object to signing an agreement on these lines.

Mr. Eden: Unfortunately, the Prime Minister is on his way to America, the Cabinet is in London, and I am here, and it does not make consultation easy. I am certain that the Prime Minister would take the same view that I do. These frontier questions are really a part of the peace treaty, and we have not yet reached the stage of agreeing what should go into it. I am quite certain that the Prime Minister could not be more anxious to get this agreement concluded than I am.'

(a)   Before his conversation with Stalin on the evening of December 18 Mr. Eden had informed the War Cabinet of the situation. The War

(b)   Cabinet decided on the morning of December 19 that His Majesty's Government could not accept an agreement on the terms proposed by Stalin, though a refusal to pledge ourselves to accept the Russian territorial claims 'at this stage' did not mean necessarily that we should oppose them at the peace conference after the war. At the time of the signature of the Atlantic Charter we had assured the United States Government that we had no secret commitments which would tie our hands in the post-war territorial settlement. Apart from this assurance, if we made commitments with one ally about boundaries, we should be forced into similar undertakings in other cases. Hitherto we had no commitments of this kind, except that we had told the Yugoslav Government, shortly before the war spread to the Balkans, that we should be prepared to reconsider the Istrian frontier of Yugoslavia. Mr. Eden could therefore do no more than he had already done in proposing to discuss the Russian demands with the British and United States Governments on his return to London. The War Cabinet agreed that Mr. Eden should

(c)   be informed of their views[1] and that copies of his telegrams should

---

[1] Telegrams were sent to the Prime Minister and to Mr. Eden in the afternoon of December 19, and read by Mr. Eden to Stalin at their meeting on December 20.

(a) N7483/7462/38. (b) WM(41)131.2, C.A. (c) N7483/7462/38.

be sent to the Prime Minister. The Prime Minister telegraphed to (a) Mr. Attlee on December 20 that the Russian demands conflicted with the Atlantic Charter, and that we could not make any agreement 'secret or public, direct or implied' about frontiers without consulting the United States Government:

> 'the time has not yet come to settle frontier questions which can only be resolved at the Peace Conference when we have won the war[1] . . . The mere desire to have an agreement which can be published should never lead us into making wrongful promises . . . The Russians have got to go on fighting for their lives anyway, and are dependent upon us for very large supplies which we have most painfully gathered and which we shall faithfully deliver.'

Mr. Eden had two more conversations with Stalin. In the first (b) of these conversations, on December 20, they agreed to postpone the signature of any agreement, political or military. Mr. Eden said that he would report Stalin's views to the War Cabinet, and 'see what could be done about it'.

The last meeting, therefore, on December 22, dealt only with military matters. Here also the rapid worsening of the position in the Far East made the discussion of plans rather unreal. It had appeared at the beginning of the talks that, from the Russian point of view, Stalin was very hopeful. He said that the worst period of crisis in Russian war production was now over: he expected another German offensive in the spring, but thought the fighting strength of the German armies so much impaired that, if a second front were opened in the west or in the Balkans, the war might possibly end in the autumn of 1942. He had asked, in his conversation of December 18, for British co-operation in an attack on Petsamo 'in a month or six weeks' time'. Mr. Eden had pointed out that we had no troops trained for winter conditions in Russia and that we could not supply a force through Murmansk without interfering with the transit of the increased amount of war material which we had promised to send to the Russian armies. In the conversation of December 20 Mr. Eden referred to the seriousness of the position in Hong Kong and Malaya, and said that it would have been a help if the Soviet Government could have relieved the pressure on us in the Far East. Stalin, however, had already explained that the Soviet Government could not undertake war with Japan. For similar reasons we could not create a second front, and we had been compelled to send to Malaya one of the divisions which might have formed the basis of a British force for south Russia. We would, however, consider, the question for an expedition to Petsamo.

---

[1] The Prime Minister's definite use of these words 'won the war' is of interest.

(a) Tel. Grey 26, Churchill Papers/399; Tel. Grey 28, Churchill Papers/394.
(b) WP(42)8; N109/5/38(1942).

Stalin seemed satisfied with these explanations. He recognised the new situation in the Far East, and said that he did not feel 'in the least hurt or offended' at our inability 'to establish a second front or send troops to the U.S.S.R.' He said that his message of November 8 had been drawn up 'at a time when your situation was better and mine was worse. I do not now insist on your sending troops to the U.S.S.R. and certainly I do not feel hurt about it as it appears to be impossible.'

Thus the conversations ended in a friendly way, although in the absence of evidence from the Russian side there are no means of knowing how far Stalin expected that on Mr. Eden's return the British Government would accept his political demands and how far his willingness to drop the demands for the opening of a second front or the despatch of a large British force to Russia was due to (i) a better understanding of the facts, i.e. the shipping situation, the strain on British manpower and the impossibility of maintaining a British force anywhere in Russia and at the same time increasing the volume of Anglo-American supplies; (ii) greater confidence in the Russian military position; or (iii) a realisation that the Japanese attack in the Far East had changed the situation in the sense that Great Britain and the United States were in fact diverting to themselves an attack which the Japanese might have delivered on the U.S.S.R. in the Far East and that the Soviet Government could hardly make demands on their British ally in Europe while refusing to share in the task of holding the Japanese in the Far East.

At all events for the time there seemed to be an improvement in Anglo-Russian relations. Mr. Eden's visit had brought Stalin into personal and friendly touch with the British Government, and no ill effects seemed to have been produced by the firmness with which he (Mr. Eden) had refused to commit Great Britain to the Russian demand for the '1941 frontiers'.[1]

(iii)

Foreign Office views on the advisability of giving way to the Russian demands with regard to the Baltic States: British approach to the United States Government: Stalin's order of the day of February 23, 1942: Mr. Roosevelt's statement to M. Litvinov: decision of the British Government to accept the Russian demands, April 8, 1942.

In view of the Prime Minister's absence, the consideration of the Russian demands was postponed until his return. Mr. Churchill

---

[1] At the final meeting Mr. Eden expressed a hope that it might be possible 'one day to welcome M. Molotov in London', but there is nothing in the record to suggest that a definite arrangement was made for such a visit in the spring.

arrived back in London on January 17. On January 28 Mr. Eden submitted to the War Cabinet a memorandum on post-war collaboration with the U.S.S.R. suggesting how Stalin's immediate (a) demands could be met. The general conclusions of the memorandum were that we should need to maintain collaboration with Russia after the war since otherwise the latter might turn to Germany. France was likely to remain for some time a weak Power and, apart from Russia, we should not be able to recreate a balance of power against the possibility of a revived Germany. If we wanted the Russians to work with us, we must make it clear that they would find it to their advantage to do so. On the other hand, if we had to choose between Russia and the United States, we should certainly choose the latter, but we ought to try to avoid such a dilemma by trying to harmonise Anglo-American and Anglo-Russian policy, and to do so by means of tripartite consultation. The Russian demand for the Baltic States was particularly difficult since American opinion would regard it as an attempt to 'by-pass' the principles of the Atlantic Charter, even though the Russians claimed that they were asking only for territory which they had lost in the German invasion. The Russians would say that the three Baltic States had voted themselves into the U.S.S.R. in accordance with the principles laid down in the Charter, and that the Finnish and Roumanian territories in dispute had been ceded to the U.S.S.R. by treaty.

Our first step, therefore, should be to ask Mr. Roosevelt for his opinion. If he were unwilling to accept the whole of the Russian demands, we could propose that Great Britain and the United States would support, after the war, either the acquisition by the U.S.S.R. of bases in territories contiguous to the U.S.S.R. and especially in the Baltic and Black Sea regions, or the control by the Soviet Government of the foreign relations and defence of the Baltic States. The question of the absorption of the Baltic States, Bessarabia,[1] and parts of Finland would thus be left for decision at the Peace Conference. The Russians would be free to propose such a measure; we should be free to accept or reject it.

The War Cabinet approved of these suggestions on February 9. (b) Lord Halifax was instructed on the following day to approach the (c) United States Government. He replied on February 20 that he had (d) spoken to Mr. Roosevelt and, more fully, to Mr. Welles. Mr. Roosevelt thought the matter largely one of presentation. Mr. Welles did not like our alternatives. If we did not build our new world on principles, it would crash again, and if we gave way on

---

[1] The memorandum did not mention northern Bukovina, which was included in the Russian demands.

(a) WP(42)48; N563/5/38. (b) WP(42)69; WM(42)18. (c) N798/5/38. (d) N1024/5/38.

principles now, we might have an 'indefinite sequence of further Russian blackmail later'. We should be sowing seeds of trouble if we began to subordinate peoples to a regime which they repudiated. Mr. Welles sometimes thought that a divided Germany would minimise the future dangers for which we were being pressed to make 'sacrifices of principle of doubtful expediency'.

Lord Halifax's telegram continued: 'All this seemed a bit remote, and I told him that nobody could have been more loyal to the principle of self-determination than we had all been at Versailles under the leadership of President Wilson, but that that solution had not stood up against the stress of power politics.' If it were essential 'to keep Russia right now and after the war', we could not ignore the reality of Stalin's exaggerated claims and suspicions. Mr. Welles 'mainly agreed' and thought that the Russian demand for security might be met by the grant of bases. In any case we could not give an entirely negative reply.

Lord Halifax was told by Mr. Welles on February 20 that Mr. Roosevelt intended to approach Stalin through M. Litvinov, the Soviet Ambassador in Washington, and Admiral Standley (who was shortly going to Moscow). In view of Mr. Roosevelt's proposal Mr. Eden drew up a memorandum for Mr. Winant, who was going on a visit to the United States, to show why the British Government thought it desirable to agree to the Russian demands and also why they considered it better to hold tripartite talks rather than to let Mr. Roosevelt negotiate directly with Stalin on an Anglo-Russian treaty. This memorandum was given to Mr. Winant on February 25, and Lord Halifax was instructed to tell Mr. Welles that the British Government hoped that the President would take no action until he had seen Mr. Winant. Mr. Winant did not arrive in Washington until the night of March 9–10. Meanwhile M. Maisky had asked more than once why there was such long delay in answering Stalin's question about the 1941 frontiers. The Foreign Office were also a little concerned over an order of the day issued by Stalin on February 23 to the Red Army. This order made no mention of Anglo-American assistance to Russia, and appeared to define Russian war aims not as the overthrow of the Nazi régime but as the liberation of Russian territory. Although the Foreign

(a) Office did not regard this order as indirect evidence that Stalin was considering a separate peace, or inviting Hitler to offer terms, they could not exclude the possibility that, once the Germans were turned out of Russia, the Soviet Government might take no further active part in the war.

(a) N1155/5/38.

On March 7 Mr. Churchill sent a message to Mr. Roosevelt (a) suggesting that, owing to the gravity of the war situation, 'the principles of the Atlantic Charter ought not to be construed so as to deny to Russia the frontiers which she occupied when Germany attacked her'. Mr. Churchill hoped that Mr. Roosevelt would give the British Government a free hand in signing the Anglo-Russian treaty as soon as possible. The German offensive against the Russian armies would be renewed on an immense scale in the spring, and we could do very little to help 'the only country that is heavily engaged with the German Armies'. In a message to Lord Halifax the Foreign Office pointed out that Stalin's order of the day might be a convenient opening for proposals leading to a separate peace. We did not wish to exaggerate this possibility, but we ought not to assume that the Russians would not come to terms if Hitler on his side thought it worth while to withdraw from Russian territory. We therefore thought it desirable to hold an early discussion with Russia on the whole conduct of the war, but we could not do so until the frontier question was out of the way.

Lord Halifax telegraphed Mr. Roosevelt's views on March 9 (b) before Mr. Winant's arrival. Mr. Roosevelt felt the greatest difficulty about our proposals, and was sure that the Russians would not 'quit the war' on the question of a recognition of their 1941 frontiers. He thought of telling Stalin that we all recognised his need for security but that it was impossible to put anything on paper now, since the result would be a 'dangerously explosive opinion' in the United States. The future of the Baltic States depended on Russian military progress; if during or after the war Russia reoccupied the Baltic States neither the United States nor Great Britain could turn her out.

Lord Halifax reported that Mr. Roosevelt intended to put these views to Stalin through M. Litvinov; Mr. Roosevelt also said that he thought that at the peace settlement East Prussia should be taken away from Germany. Lord Halifax was instructed on March 10 to (c) repeat to Mr. Roosevelt that we did not agree with the method of approach through M. Litvinov. Mr. Roosevelt appeared not to have understood our reason for giving Stalin a satisfactory answer. We regarded it of the highest importance to leave nothing undone now to get into real contact with Stalin on all subjects connected with the conduct of the war, and thereby try to make him pay some attention to our views and those of the United States Government, for example, on the question of Russian participation in the war against Japan. It was most deplorable that we had no real contact

---

(a) T340/2, No. 40 (Churchill Papers/395; N1174/5/38). (b) N1279/5/38. (c) N1279/5/38.

with Russia and most unwise to lose our chance of securing it by a refusal to admit a claim which we could not in fact resist.

Apart from our objections on grounds of procedure, we did not think that Mr. Roosevelt's proposal would meet the case. Stalin wanted to be sure that we supported his minimum war aims. Mr. Roosevelt's proposal amounted to saying that we rather hoped that Russia would not get back the Baltic States but that we could not do anything if she did get them back. Stalin would regard this attitude as uncollaborative and as confirming his suspicions that he could expect no real consideration for Russian interests from us or from the United States and that we wished Russia to go on fighting solely for British and American ends and would not mind seeing Russia and Germany exhaust each other. The Russians would thus be confirmed in their inclination to think only of Russian interests and fruitful collaboration with them would be rendered impossible. We had to face the facts that our relations with Russia were unsatisfactory and a cause of weakness and even of danger to our war effort.

(a)   Mr. Roosevelt persisted in his plan. He saw M. Litvinov on March 12. According to the record of the conversation shown by Mr. Welles to Lord Halifax, Mr. Roosevelt said that he was disturbed by reports from London and Moscow of the Anglo-Russian negotiations. Stalin would appreciate the great importance of public opinion in a country as large as the United States and the desirability in Russian interests that American opinion should favour close co-operation with the U.S.S.R. Mr. Roosevelt was 'somewhat put out' because Stalin had not consulted him directly about a question with which he (Mr. Roosevelt) was vitally concerned. Mr. Roosevelt could not subscribe to any treaty, secret or public, about definite frontiers until the war had been won but he was entirely in favour of facilitating complete Russian security. He asked M. Litvinov to tell Stalin that at 'the appropriate moment' after the war, the United States Government would support the Soviet efforts to achieve measures of legitimate security. The Soviet Union must be guaranteed against being liable to German attack ten or fifteen years after the war.

Mr. Roosevelt called Stalin's attention to the provision in the Atlantic Charter for the disarmament of Germany. In view of the uncertainties of post-war conditions Mr. Roosevelt wanted to give complete assurances with regard to approval by the United States Government of any legitimate steps required for the future security of the Soviet Union. 'What was involved was a basis of confidence and trust between the Soviet Union and the United States.'

(a) N1364/5/38.

M. Litvinov asked what would happen if Mr. Roosevelt were not President at the end of the war. Mr. Roosevelt replied that questions of such permanent and fundamental character as the relations between the U.S.S.R. and the United States could not be discussed on this basis. He might ask in his turn what would happen if Stalin were no longer in control of the destinies of the Russian people.

On March 23 M. Maisky told Mr. Eden that the Soviet Govern- (a) ment had replied to Mr. Roosevelt that they had taken note of his communication. No further answer was needed because the Soviet Government had neither made any communication to the United States Government about the negotiations with us nor asked for their point of view. Hence the Soviet Government regarded Mr. Roosevelt's observations as intended mainly to inform them of the American point of view.

Meanwhile on March 9 the Prime Minister had telegraphed to (b) Stalin that he had sent a message to President Roosevelt 'urging him to approve our signing the agreement with you about the frontiers of Russia at the end of the war'. Stalin replied on March 15 that he (c) still thought it necessary to exchange views regarding the text of a suitable agreement.

The British Government had now to decide whether to give way to Stalin and accept his demands or to give way to Mr. Roosevelt. In view of the military situation they considered it necessary to satisfy the Russians. Hence the Foreign Office telegraphed on the night of (d) March 26–7 to Lord Halifax instructing him to explain the British decision to Mr. Roosevelt. The message stated that the Soviet Government had refused to accept a settlement of the frontier question on the basis proposed by Mr. Roosevelt. We appreciated Mr. Roosevelt's difficulties, but, as a European Power for whom post-war collaboration with Russia was essential, we could not neglect any opportunity of establishing intimate relations of confidence with Stalin. The Russians, however unreasonably, took the view that they could not discuss major questions relating to the conduct of the war until the frontier question had been cleared up. The matter was especially urgent because we and the United States Government had to arrange a renewal of the supply protocol due to expire in June.

We could not let the question drag on or allow Anglo-Russian relations to be left in suspense at this critical moment in the war. Still less could we risk antagonising Russia at a time when the closest

(a) N1526/5/38. (b) T352/2 (Churchill Papers/402; N1300/5/38). (c) T395/2 (Churchill Papers/402; N1395/5/38). (d) N1653/5/38; WM(42)37, C.A.

I

Allied co-operation in Europe was of vital and urgent importance. Therefore 'in the common interest' we must tell the Soviet Government that we were prepared to negotiate a treaty which would include implicit recognition of their claim to their 1940 frontiers other than that with Poland.

We had done everything possible to consult the United States and hoped that Mr. Roosevelt would agree with our action and understand our reasons. The treaty would not be secret and the United States Government would not be asked to subscribe to it. We remembered Mr. Roosevelt's difficulty about American public opinion, but we also had to consider our own public opinion and the position might well become catastrophic if Stalin adopted a policy more or less hostile to our interests and justified it publicly on the grounds that, owing to our obstinacy and short-sightedness, he could not establish a basis of co-operation with Great Britain.

Stalin did not regard the matter only from the point of view of security. There was a psychological aspect to it owing to the fact that for twenty years the U.S.S.R. had not been in relations of equality and confidence with any of the great Western Powers. Stalin's admittedly discreditable deal with Germany did not affect the Russian claim in his eyes. He had chosen the 1940 frontiers as a test of our intentions because at the time we had refused to recognise the Russian annexation of the Baltic States as a strategic necessity and because he could not admit to himself or to the Russian people that the Government with which he was now in alliance maintained their formal disapproval and still refused to acknowledge the right of the Soviet Government to recover from a common enemy territory which they regarded as their own.

Meanwhile the Russians were bearing the brunt of the fighting and, apart from sending supplies, Great Britain could give no direct help in the coming German attack. This unfortunate situation at what might be the crisis of the war made it all the more necessary not to appear to be refusing the one political concession for which Stalin had so far asked.[1] Recognition of the frontiers was no substitute for the material help which we should like to give, but it might be of inestimable value as a gesture.

(a)   Mr. Eden told M. Maisky on March 27 that we wanted to go ahead with the negotiations and to conclude with the Soviet Government a treaty on the lines discussed at Moscow. We had explained the position to the United States Government and hoped soon for an

---

[1] In a later telegram on March 27 this phrase was altered to: 'the political concession which the Soviet Government has at this juncture asked of us'.

(a) N1670/5/38.

answer from them. Meanwhile we wished to know whether Stalin had any more suggestions for revision. We thought it important to decide on the form of words whereby we should make it known that the Russo-Polish frontier was excluded from the terms of the treaty.

Lord Halifax carried out his instructions in an interview with (a) Mr. Welles on March 30. On April 1 Mr. Welles told him that Mr. (b) Roosevelt's opinion remained unchanged and that he (and Mr. Welles himself) thought that concessions on the frontier question would only encourage more demands. Mr. Roosevelt had asked him to say that, from the point of view of the Atlantic Charter and American public opinion, it would be helpful to include in our treaty a stipulation pledging the Soviet Government, on taking over the Baltic countries, to allow anyone who wished to do so to emigrate with their property.[1] This condition should apply also to Finland and eastern Poland and might be on the reciprocal basis of an exchange of populations.

Mr. Roosevelt would have to state in public that he had been told of our action. He would try to say no more, but he could not indicate approval and expected that his silence would be taken to imply disapproval. He had not seen M. Litvinov but was sending a message to Stalin proposing a visit by M. Molotov to the United States.[2]

On April 8 Mr. Eden, with the approval of the War Cabinet, (c) again told M. Maisky that His Majesty's Government were ready to negotiate a treaty on the basis proposed by Stalin. His Majesty's Government suggested that the negotiations should take place in London and invited M. Molotov to come to London for the signature of the treaty. At this time, however, M. Molotov refused the (d) invitation to Great Britain on the grounds that he was too much occupied to leave Moscow.

---

[1] The Prime Minister noted on these words, 'Surely this is right'.
[2] This proposed visit was in connexion with the American plans for a large-scale landing in northern France in 1943 and a possible landing in the autumn of 1942. Mr. Roosevelt sent a message to the Prime Minister on April 2 that he was sending General (e) Marshall and Mr. Hopkins to discuss these plans with him and that, if the Prime Minister approved, he would ask Stalin to send two Russian representatives for discussions in Washington. After general agreement appeared to have been reached in London on the main American plan, the Prime Minister telegraphed to the President on April 17 that (f) he agreed with the proposed invitation to the Soviet Government to send two representatives to Washington. Mr. Roosevelt therefore sent his invitation—apparently mentioning M. Molotov by name. He told Mr. Churchill on April 22 that Stalin had agreed to send M. Molotov and a Russian general. See also below, p. 257, n.1. (g)

(a) N1701/5/38. (b) N1737/5/38. (c) N1861/5/38; WM(42)44. 4, C.A.; WP(42)144. (d) N1944/5/38. (e) T523/2, Churchill Papers/470. (f) T586/2, No. 70, Churchill Papers/333. (g) T607/2, Churchill Papers/399.

(iv)

The negotiation of the Anglo-Russian treaty of May 26, 1942: M. Molotov's visit to London: the Prime Minister's statement of May 22 to M. Molotov with regard to a second front.

The British decision to accept the Russian demands for their 1940 frontiers had been taken for three reasons. There was the immediate risk that a refusal to agree to the demands might lead Stalin to consider a peace offer from Hitler. The Foreign Office were not greatly alarmed in April at this possibility, but could not overlook the fact that in 1939 the Soviet Government had made an agreement with Hitler in return for concessions, especially in regard to the Baltic States, which Great Britain and France had then refused. Russian policy had been to keep out of the war between Germany and the Western Powers. The Soviet Government had maintained this policy until they were forced by the German attack to abandon it. They might return to it if Hitler gave them a chance of doing so, and if they thought that the Western Powers were likely to treat them after the war as they believed themselves to have been treated before the autumn of 1939.[1]

In the second place, the British Government hoped to dispel the suspicions of the Soviet Government and to secure real co-operation, not only during the war but after it. 'Real co-operation' in the war would have included Russian action against Japan, but this could hardly be expected until the Russians had broken the German offensive or at least had come safely through the campaigning season of 1942 and the Allies had been able to open a second front in Europe. 'Real co-operation' after the war meant a willingness to collaborate in the prevention of further German aggression and in the economic and political settlement of Europe after the Germans had been driven out of the countries under their occupation. The British Government believed such collaboration to be possible in spite of the 'ideological' differences between the Russians and themselves, but clearly they could not reckon on getting Russian confidence if, at a time when they were unable directly to attack the Germans on land, or to draw off a large number of German

---

[1] The military position at the end of the severe winter of 1941–2 was that the Russians had regained a good deal of ground on the Moscow front and south of Kharkov. Moscow, however, was still threatened, and the Germans held important centres of communication such as Orel, Kursk and Kharkov from which they might be expected to launch an offensive. On May 12 the Russians attacked in force south of Kharkov. They were at first successful, but were later driven back with heavy losses. Even so this attack probably delayed the opening of the main German offensive until June. According to General Halder the German losses in Russia during the five winter months were 89,000 dead and over 26,000 missing; the losses in the previous five months had been 162,000 dead and 33,000 missing.

divisions from the Russian front, they also refused to recognise the Russian claim to frontiers which the Soviet Government thought essential for defence against future aggression.

Finally, there was the consideration that, if the Russians drove back the Germans—and especially if they drove them back before the establishment of a second front—they would reoccupy all the territories they had lost since 1941. It would then be impossible to turn them out of the Baltic States, and, therefore, impracticable in the long run to avoid recognising the facts of the situation. If there were no means of preventing the Russians from reabsorbing the Baltic States, the best policy seemed to be to accept the situation, and at the same time to use this acceptance as a means of limiting the Russian demands—for example, in relation to their frontier with Poland—and of obtaining Russian consent to conditions which Great Britain was either directly pledged to fulfil or regarded as necessary for the future peace of Europe.

It is thus easy to understand why the British Government decided not to hold without exception to the terms of the Atlantic Charter. Nonetheless this decision was a surrender of principle; and perhaps the most significant element in the surrender, from the point of view of future dealing with the U.S.S.R., was that at least it implied an admission that the Soviet use of democratic terms could be allowed to cover acts which were in fact contrary to the theory and practice of free States. The British Government had rightly refused to recognise the methods by which the Soviet Government had obtained the 'consent' of the Baltic States to the surrender of their independence. Henceforward it would prove more difficult to maintain that such methods were 'undemocratic' or even to assert that the Russian police state was not a 'democracy' as democracy was understood by the free peoples of the world. The political consequences of this surrender to the Soviet Government were not and could not be fully realised in the spring of 1942, but the negotiations, lasting from mid-April to the end of May, for the conclusion of the Anglo-Russian treaty showed that a surrender to Russian demands was followed—as in 1939—not by concessions on the part of the Russians, but by more demands. The negotiations on the Russian side were carried on with the minuteness and stubborn persistence characteristic of M. Molotov. Some of the haggling was over minor points of wording in which it was easy to show that the Soviet Government had failed to understand the reason why the words in question had been chosen or that their doubts about them were ill-founded.

There were, however, certain large differences of view. The Foreign Office considered that there were four essential requirements upon which the British Government were bound to insist: (i) a stipulation that Anglo-Russian collaboration should be within the framework of the United Nations. Without this stipulation it might be assumed that the British Government were making an exclusive treaty with Russia, and departing not only from the principles of the Atlantic Charter but also leaving the circle of the United Nations. The effect on American, Allied, and neutral opinion would thus be very bad. (ii) A joint statement safeguarding the question of the Polish frontier. (iii) Some mention of the proposals for confederations in order to show the British intention to provide for the political, economic and military security of the smaller States of Europe. (iv) A general acceptance of the principles of 'no territorial aggrandisement' and 'non-interference'. Otherwise it might appear that Great Britain and the U.S.S.R. were free to act contrary to these principles outside Europe, e.g. in Turkey, Iran, Afghanistan, China and (in the case of the U.S.S.R.) India.

(a)   The British draft proposals for a political and a military treaty were given to the Soviet Government on April 13. M. Maisky submitted the Russian counter-proposals on May 1. Stalin had suggested that M. Molotov should come to London for discussions.

(b) Stalin telegraphed to Mr. Churchill that the British drafts

'differed in some material respects from the text of the agreements which were under discussion while Mr. Eden was in Moscow. In view of the fact that these drafts reveal fresh divergencies of opinion which it would be difficult to solve by correspondence, the Soviet Government have decided, despite all obstacles, to send M. Molotov to London in order, by means of personal discussion, to dispose of all the matters which stand in the way of the signing of the agreements.' Stalin added: 'This is all the more necessary because [the] question of opening a second front in Europe (which was raised in the last message addressed to me by [the] President of the United States in which he invited M. Molotov to go to Washington to discuss this matter)[1] calls for a preliminary exchange of views between our two Governments.'

(c)   The Prime Minister replied to Stalin on April 24 in general terms welcoming the visit. He also telegraphed to President Roosevelt explaining that M. Molotov might 'even be already on his way', and that he (Mr. Churchill) could not 'now suggest to him a change in the order of his visits. If, and when, therefore, Molotov bears down on us', Mr. Churchill proposed to agree to a discussion of the drafts and hoped to 'clear the main difficulties out of the way.' He would suggest to M. Molotov that he should then go on to Washington and see the President before anything was finally signed.

---

[1] See above, p. 243, note 2.

(a) N1944/5/38. (b) T608/2, Churchill Papers/402. (c) T626/2, Churchill Papers/402.

M. Molotov did not arrive in London until May 20. Meanwhile it (a) was clear that the Russian proposals, as set out and supported by M. Maisky, did not meet the essential British requirements. The Russian draft excluded a reference to the declaration of the United Nations, and implied that the British Government would have nothing to do with the Soviet-Polish frontier negotiations. The draft also omitted a reference to the encouragement of confederations among the smaller States in south-eastern Europe. The Soviet Government refused the proposal that inhabitants of the Baltic States[1] should have the option of leaving these territories. M. Maisky claimed that the question had already been settled in the Baltic States and that plebiscites had been held there. He also made it clear that the Soviet Government would be unwilling to make a declaration to the effect that the Baltic States would be allowed some form of local autonomy.

On the other hand M. Maisky asked that a secret protocol should be attached to the political treaty. This protocol would define the future European frontiers on the lines of Stalin's expression of views to Mr. Eden at Moscow. Mr. Eden said that on principle we could not accept secret protocols. M. Maisky came back in the course of the discussion to the question of a secret protocol setting out the desire of both parties for their joint security. In this protocol His Majesty's Government would state their willingness to agree to Russo-Finnish and Russo-Roumanian pacts of mutual assistance under the guarantee of the independence of Finland and Roumania, and the Soviet Government would agree to similar pacts between His Majesty's Government and (i) Belgium, (ii) the Netherlands.

Mr. Eden said that we could not accept this proposal. Apart from the issues involved, we were opposed in principle to secret protocols. M. Maisky then asked whether we would accept an open protocol. Mr. Eden replied that His Majesty's Government had not considered the question of a pact with Belgium and the Netherlands.

On May 5 the discussions between Mr. Eden and M. Maisky (b) reached a deadlock. M. Maisky made some 'general observations' about the background of the treaty. The Soviet view was that they had been fighting practically alone for eleven months. By a 'superhuman effort' they had repulsed the German attack and had even passed to the offensive. They were now 'on the eve of further great trials'. They were grateful for the material sent by His Majesty's Government and for our air offensive, but hoped that we would relieve them of the burden of 30–40 divisions. They would then be

---

[1] The British Government had suggested the extension of this option to the inhabitants of all territories placed under new sovereignty since January 1, 1938.

(a) N2336/5/38. (b) N2385/5/38.

be able to take the offensive. There was at present no hope of this immediate relief or of a second front before the autumn. Therefore once again the Soviet forces would have to bear the heavy cost of the struggle. M. Maisky understood the difficulties in the way of the creation of a second front, but there was a feeling of resentment and even of bitterness in Moscow. Hence if we could not give military help, it seemed more than ever desirable that we should give political help and agree to the Soviet draft of the treaty.

Mr. Eden answered that owing to the 'background' His Majesty's Government were anxious to sign the treaty. At the same time they had to ensure that the treaty was a positive contribution to the common cause. Therefore they were bound to consider American opinion. Mr. Winant, who was friendly to the treaty, had brought back a pessimistic report about the attitude of the United States. M. Maisky thought it 'quite likely' that American opinion would be unfavourable. Mr. Eden repeated the British argument that we sincerely wanted Anglo-Russian co-operation during and after the war, but that we had to act in concert with the United States, the Dominions, and our other Allies. M. Maisky then asked again for a secret or open protocol and said that, in any case, the Soviet Government would insist on our approval of Russo-Finnish and Russo-Roumanian pacts.

Mr. Eden pointed out that this demand had not been made to him in Moscow. 'It was despairing to negotiate with the Soviet Government when they invariably raised their price at every meeting.' M. Maisky answered that at our request they had waited four months for the conclusion of the agreement and that they were not unreasonable in asking for the inclusion of a statement which seemed to him perfectly harmless. Mr. Eden said that he would report the proposal to the Cabinet, but that he could not hold out hope of their agreement.

(a)   Mr. Eden submitted a redraft of the treaties on previous lines to the War Cabinet. The discussion was adjourned on May 7 (a Thursday) until the following week, but in fact the War Cabinet do not appear to have considered the treaty again until May 25, i.e. after five meetings had been held with M. Molotov. Mr. Eden, however, telephoned to M. Maisky on May 7 that the War Cabinet

(b)   attached importance to the points upon which agreement had not been reached, and that he (Mr. Eden) was unlikely to make any new communication to him.

Meanwhile, in view of the failure to reach agreement, Mr. Eden, at Sir A. Cadogan's suggestion, had in mind a new offer to the Soviet Government. This new offer would take the form of a post-war

---

(a) WP(42)190 and 193; WM(42)58 and 66. (b) N2422/5/38.

alliance against German aggression without mention of frontiers, but safeguarding British collaboration with the United Nations. Mr. Eden (a) minuted on May 17 that he was inclined to show this new proposal to M. Maisky at once, but it was decided to wait for M. Molotov's arrival. The new draft was, however, circulated to the War Cabinet on May 18; on May 22 Mr. Eden circulated a revised version with a (b) note that he intended to submit it to M. Molotov.

M. Molotov held his first meeting with the Prime Minister and (c) Mr. Eden on May 21. He said that he was authorised to conduct negotiations concerning the treaty and also with regard to the opening of a second front in Europe; he thought the latter question of greater importance, and was proposing to discuss it with Mr. Roosevelt.

The Prime Minister suggested a discussion of the draft treaties, followed by a general interchange of views on the question of a second front with a further meeting to discuss the technical aspects of the matter.[1] The Prime Minister explained the grave difficulties in the way of a treaty on the lines proposed by the Soviet Government. It could be argued that the terms contravened the spirit of the Atlantic Charter. In any case Mr. Roosevelt would not endorse either the Russian or the British draft, and American criticism, which would be reflected in England, would certainly lead to serious controversy detrimental to our common effort. Nevertheless, in order to show that our friendship with Russia would continue after the war, we were prepared to sign a treaty which safeguarded our essential requirements, but 'we had to give account of our acts to Parliament' and must secure in the treaty these conditions which would enable the Government to obtain 'the general assent of the great majority of the British nation'.

M. Molotov replied that it was also necessary to consider Russian public opinion, and that the Soviet Government also had its essential requirements. They insisted on recovering the territory violated by Hitler, and they could make no concessions in this respect. Further, it was not sufficient simply to restore what existed before the war: the Soviet Government must secure their territory on their north-western and south-western frontiers. Without some guarantee in this respect (i.e. the proposed pacts of mutual assistance with Finland and Roumania), no one in the Soviet Union would approve the treaty. It would be much to the good if within these limits a draft could be agreed. If, however, it was not found possible to come to terms with His Majesty's Government on this basis, the Soviet Government supported postponing the whole matter. The most

---

[1] See below pp. 252–4 for the discussions dealing with a second front.

(a) N2646/5/38. (b) WP(42)198 Revise; WP(42)218. (c) N2901/5/38.

I*

delicate question was that concerning Poland. The Soviet Government would do their best to come to to terms with Poland on the basis of mutual interests and on the question of frontiers.

The Prime Minister observed that, in accordance with the proposal he had made earlier, he hoped that points of difference might be discussed in the afternoon with the Secretary of State. He would like, however, if he could, to make M. Molotov understand what was the true British objective. We believed that we should win the war, and that after the war Great Britain, Russia and the United States would share the responsibility of guiding the forward movement of the world. Our wish was that the three Governments should work together for that and for their own security and mutual assistance. Therefore, it was important that no document should take a form which tended to emphasise differences between the three countries who were bearing the full weight of the war, and would be accountable to mankind for what was done after the Nazi tyranny had been destroyed. It was that friendship and trustful co-operation that we must have in view. If that were achieved, other matters would easily fall into their place.

(a)   The Prime Minister was not present at any other of the formal meetings with M. Molotov to discuss the treaties. At the second meeting, in the afternoon of May 21, M. Molotov objected to the clause in the British draft of the political treaty dealing with the question of frontiers.[1] He said that Stalin and he had thought that it had been agreed that the Soviet and Polish Governments should reach direct agreement, as between Allies, on the question of the Soviet-Polish frontier, but the British draft now opened a new question. The Soviet Government were prepared to leave the matter open. Mr. Eden pointed out, however, that the Soviet draft appeared to exclude the interest of the British Government arising out of their declaration of July 30, 1941. M. Molotov made it clear that he was not willing to accept a reference to this declaration. He described the British proposal as 'taking sides' with the Poles. He said that the Soviet

---

[1] This draft ran as follows: 'The High Contracting Parties undertake to work for the reconstruction of Europe after the war in accordance with the two principles of not seeking territorial aggrandisement for themselves and of non-interference in the internal affairs of European peoples. In so doing, they will take account of the interests of both parties in their security, and will have full regard to the desire of the Union of Soviet Socialist Republics for the restoration of its frontiers violated by the Hitlerite aggression and of the Government of the United Kingdom for the recovery of British territory occupied by enemy forces.

It is understood that the reference to the frontiers of the Union of Soviet Socialist Republics in the first paragraph of the present article does not affect the frontier with Poland. The position of the two High Contracting Parties in this regard remains as stated respectively in the agreement between the Government of the U.S.S.R. and the Polish Government signed on the 30th July, 1941, and in the communication made by His Majesty's Government in the United Kingdom to the Polish Government on the same date.' For this communication, see below, p. 613.

(a) N2902, 2903/5/38.

Government claimed the restoration of all frontiers violated by Hitler, and that their aim was to recover the line occupied in Poland in 1941. They were prepared to accept the Curzon line with certain modifications in the Russian favour. They thought that Poland should be compensated by receiving East Prussia. If, however, the Soviet Government made the concession of keeping the matter open for further discussion, and thus leaving undecided the greater part of their western frontier, they were entitled to asked for a concession on the British side.

Mr. Eden repeated that the British Government were not taking the Polish side. They thought the proposal to give Poland East Prussia was 'very wise', but that they could not go back on their declaration of 1941. The discussion was continued at the third meeting in the afternoon of May 22, but again without agreement. M. Molotov refused to accept a reference to the British declaration; Mr. Eden refused to give it up. Mr. Eden said that the British Government had not guaranteed any frontier, and did not propose, pending a settlement between the Soviet and Polish Governments, to offer such a guarantee or to advocate any particular frontier line. On the other hand their declaration had played a large part in facilitating the conclusion of the Soviet-Polish treaty of July 1941, and they could not go back on it.

In view of the difficulty of meeting the Soviet demands, and of the unwillingness of the Russians to make any real concessions with regard to them, the Prime Minister and Mr. Eden suggested to (a) M. Molotov at an informal discussion on the evening of May 22 the proposal for an alternative treaty on a new basis. Mr. Eden brought forward this proposal formally on May 23 at the fourth meeting with (b) the Russians. He gave M. Molotov the draft of a treaty containing a pact of mutual assistance for a period of twenty years. He explained that this new draft was 'an attempt to place relations between the two countries on an abiding footing'.

'We had for some time felt the need for an enduring basis of confidence, both now and after the war, and we thought that the proposed twenty-year pact of mutual assistance would show that the two Governments meant to work together for a generation at least. The treaty would not exclude agreement on other points. . . . Such a treaty would secure a very warm welcome here and in America, and indeed everywhere where there was a determination to prevent the recurrence of German aggression. Though the treaty admittedly did not deal with vexed questions such as frontiers, it was obvious that, if we were to offer a twenty-year pact, it must be our desire that Russia, as our ally, be strong and secure.'

(a) WM(42)66, C.A. (b) N2904, 2646/5/38; WP(42)218.

M. Molotov said that he would report the draft to his Government and discuss it with them on his return to Moscow. Meanwhile he wanted to go on with the discussion on the previous drafts while leaving open the question of an alternative treaty.[1]

(a) The discussion of these earlier drafts was continued through a fifth meeting on May 24. At this fifth meeting Mr. Eden asked M. Molotov whether he could not submit the text of the alternative treaty to Moscow for immediate consideration. M. Molotov was (b) unwilling to do so, but after the meeting he again saw Mr. Winant. Mr. Winant emphasised the bad impression which the earlier treaty would be likely to make in the United States.

As a result of this interview and of the insistence of His Majesty's Government upon safeguarding the 'essentials' of their earlier draft, (c) M. Molotov said at the sixth meeting in the afternoon of May 25 that he was ready to discuss the draft of the alternative treaty and that he might receive instructions about it from Moscow on the night of May 25–6 or on the following morning. He asked whether Mr. Eden would be willing to sign the treaty on May 26. Mr. Eden said that the War Cabinet were meeting during the evening of May 25, and that he had little doubt that they would agree to an immediate signature.[2] Various minor points in the alternative draft were then discussed.

Meanwhile M. Molotov had also heard the Prime Minister's views about the question of a second front. When M. Molotov had mentioned this question at the meeting of May 21, he had explained that he considered it primarily a political matter, and that he wanted an exchange of views with the Prime Minister before a technical discussion took place between British and Russian military representatives.

(d) Mr. Churchill therefore asked M. Molotov to meet him on the following day. Mr. Attlee, Mr. Eden and the Chiefs of Staff were also present. M. Molotov said that the question of a second front had been raised nearly ten months ago, and that President Roosevelt had now suggested that he should go to Washington. The Soviet Government, however, thought that M. Molotov should come to

---

[1] M. Molotov also saw Mr. Winant on May 23. Mr. Winant spoke to him about the effect on American opinion of a treaty on the lines originally proposed. He said that the United States Government would welcome a treaty on the new lines.

[2] Mr. Eden had circulated in the morning of May 25 a memorandum discussing the points of difference on the original drafts, and explaining that M. Molotov had now said (e) that he was ready to discuss the new draft. There is no record in the Foreign Office archives of any statement to this effect by M. Molotov to Mr. Eden between the fifth and sixth meetings. The treaty was signed on May 26. For the text of the treaty, see Appendix I to this volume.

(a) N2905/5/38; WM(42)66, C.A. (b) N2717/5/38. (c) N2906/5/38. (d) WP(42)219 Revise. (e) WP(42)220; WM(42)66, C.A.; N2907/5/38.

London before going to Washington because the main task of organising a second front would fall on Great Britain. M. Molotov wanted to know how the British Government viewed the chances of drawing off in 1942 some of the German forces from the U.S.S.R., where the balance of advantage in armed strength seemed to be with the Germans. He asked that the Allies of the U.S.S.R. and, in the first place, Great Britain, should engage at least 40 divisions in Western Europe.

Mr. Churchill explained the military position. He said that the development of air power had deprived Powers with naval predominance of their previous advantage of being able to land at will on a hostile coast; the enemy could now move his air forces within a few hours to meet an invasion, whereas in the past he could not be equally well prepared at every point. We were therefore limited to those coastal areas where our superior fighter forces would give us control in the air; our choice was thus narrowed to the Pas de Calais, the tip of the Cherbourg peninsula, and part of the Brest area. We were studying the problem of landing a force during the present year in one or more of these areas. Once we had destroyed the enemy's air force in battle over the landing area, we could use our sea power to cover landings elsewhere. The key requirement in all our plans was landing craft. Unfortunately we had not enough of the special craft required for success against the very heavy coast defences. In August 1941, Mr. Churchill had impressed upon Mr. Roosevelt the urgent need for the United States to build as large a number of tank landing and other assault craft as possible. It was unlikely that sufficient landing craft would be available this year or that American forces would be ready at least until late in the year. In 1943, however, we should have much greater resources. Meanwhile in 1942 we could hardly expect to draw off large numbers of enemy land forces from the eastern front. We were in fact occupying in France, Libya, Norway and the Low Countries some 44 German divisions. Moreover in the air we were containing about one half of the enemy fighter force and about a third of their bombers. We would do everything in our power to help the Russians but an action which ended in disaster would be of no advantage to them.

After further discussion M. Molotov asked what we thought of the Russian chances of holding out during the summer of 1942. Mr. Churchill said that, without detailed knowledge of the resources and reserves of both sides, he could not easily form a firm judgment, but, in view of Hitler's failure to break Soviet resistance in 1941, he had great confidence in the strength and ability of the Soviet army; Hitler's attack could not be as strong or as dangerous as in 1941. M. Molotov then asked what we should do if the Russians were unable to hold out. Mr. Churchill answered that in such case Hitler would try to invade Great Britain or strike through Baku into Iran. We had not sufficient forces to be confident about meeting a thrust of the latter kind, and our own fortunes were thus bound up with the resistance of the Soviet army. In the event of a Russian defeat we should fight on, and hope with American help to build up overwhelming air superiority which in the course of eighteen months or two years would enable us to make devastating attacks on German cities and industries. We should also 'maintain the blockade and make landings on the Continent against an increasingly weakening opposition. Ultimately the power of Great Britain and the United States would prevail . . . Great Britain had stood alone for a whole year with but a handful of ill-equipped troops.' This fact showed the difficulty of overseas invasion. When we had less than 100 tanks and 200 field guns Hitler could not invade us because he failed to win command of the air. We had now to face similar difficulties in our invasion of Europe.

CHAPTER XXVII

Russian demands for the opening of a second front:
Mr. Churchill's visit to Moscow, August 12-16, 1942:
British complaints about Russian propaganda for a
second front: Russian misinterpretation of the British
attitude towards war criminals.

(i)

Pressure by the Soviet Government for the opening of a second front: the
Washington communiqué: the Prime Minister's aide-mémoire *of June 10,*
1942, to M. Molotov.

THE signature of the Anglo-Russian treaty on May 26, 1942, marked the end of one important phase of the relations between the two countries during the war. Henceforward there was a written agreement of the most formal kind giving to the Soviet Government assurances from His Majesty's Government on the subjects about which Russian suspicions had been strongest. Except, perhaps, with regard to Poland, the Soviet Government had secured in general terms the assent of His Majesty's Government to their demands, while His Majesty's Government had avoided direct commitments in matters where they and, more strongly, the United States Government, thought the Soviet claims excessive or even in conflict with the Atlantic Charter.

The United States Government were extremely satisfied with the (a) turn taken by the negotiations. Mr. Welles told Lord Halifax that he though the change to the new text 'a miracle'. On the British side the results of the negotiations were summed up to Lord Halifax (b) for the general information of Mr. Roosevelt and the State Department as follows: With the disappearance of the provisions with regard to territory and frontiers we had avoided in the treaty the whole question of the Soviet claims and any conflict between these claims and the Atlantic Charter. The preamble to the treaty stated that Anglo-Russian collaboration would be on the basis of

---

(a) N2861/5/38. (b) N2746/5/38.

the Charter. Article V reaffirmed the two principles of 'no territorial aggrandisement and no interference in the internal affairs of other States', and the provisions for material aid were limited to the case of renewed aggression by Germany and her associates. In general the treaty bound the U.S.S.R. closer to us in the prosecution of the European war until victory had been won, provided for the most effective collaboration against future aggression pending the establishment of a more general system of security, and thus secured the first condition of effective economic reconstruction in Europe after the war; it also brought the U.S.S.R. into the circle of the United Nations in the organisation of security and economic reconstruction, and safeguarded in the second sentence of Article V the interests of other States. During the negotiations His Majesty's Government had tried to increase Soviet confidence in their sincerity and also to dispel the suspicions of neutral and Allied States with regard to our collaboration with the U.S.S.R. If we had succeeded, we should have emerged from a somewhat difficult situation with some positive results which might be of great importance in and after the war.

At the time of the signature of the treaty, however, the military situation was changing much to the Russian disadvantage. In spite of their costly failure to finish the Russian campaign in 1941, and in spite also of the sufferings of the severe winter of 1941–2, the Germans were able to recommence their offensive. The Russian counterattacks had not driven them out of the important road and railway junctions behind the front, and the better organisation of the German armies enabled them to recover their striking power more rapidly than the Russians. The Germans replied strongly in May to a Russian attack on the southern part of the central front below Kharkov. At the end of May they had occupied the whole of the Crimea except Sebastopol (which surrendered on July 1). Their main offensive on the southern front opened on June 28 in an area well suited to armoured warfare. By July 23 when Hitler issued a new directive the German armies held the right bank of the Don almost everywhere from below Voronezh (which they failed to capture) to the mouth of the river. Rostov fell on July 23, though the greater part of the defending army escaped encirclement. Hitler could now order the continuation of his plan to advance along the whole of the Eastern Black Sea coast, capture Stalingrad, deprive the Russians of the industrial areas in the south which were still in their possession, and cut the road, rail and river routes—including the Volga—by which their oil was brought from the Caucasus. The final blow— the occupation of the Baku oilfields could wait, if necessary, until 1943. The Germans assumed that, owing to the Japanese successes in the Far East, the Allies would not be able to open a second front in Europe in 1942. The British losses in the Western Desert also made it clear that the Allies would have little or nothing to spare to protect their northern front in the Middle East, still less to interfere with German operations in the Caucasus or beyond.

As the German offensive gathered momentum the Russians intensified their appeals for a diversion in the west. These appeals had an increased bitterness as well as urgency after M. Molotov's return to Moscow. M. Molotov had arranged, before leaving London, that he would come back for further discussions after his visit to Washington and on his way home to Russia. Since the purpose of his visit to the United States was to consider the American plans for a second front, a phrase in a telegram of Stalin to the Prime Minister on May 24 showed that the Russians were trying to secure a binding commitment in the matter. Stalin said that M. Molotov would stop in London 'to complete the negotiations . . . on the questions in which our countries are interested'.[1] A communiqué agreed in

---

[1] At the time of M. Molotov's visits to London and Washington the general Anglo-American position with regard to strategical plans for Europe was as follows:

On his way to Washington in December 1941 Mr. Churchill had drawn up a review of future Allied strategy. This review envisaged an occupation of North Africa as soon as possible (Mr. Churchill had hopes at least of Vichy 'connivance') not merely to forestall the Germans but as the first stage in the Allied return to Europe: the chances of a successful cross-Channel invasion would be very much greater if the Germans had to direct troops to meet a threat from the Mediterranean and to defend Italy. President Roosevelt also thought that this plan was the best way to bring American troops at the earliest possible time into action against the Germans, but his military advisers were less favourable, though they agreed in postponing 'all-out' operations against Japan until after the defeat of Germany. They continued to regard the British proposal not as a means of easing the immense difficulties of a direct attack on the German positions in Northern France, but as an unwise dispersion of effort desired by the British to secure their political interests in the Mediterranean.

Within a short time after Mr. Churchill's return to England, the disasters in the Far East, the failure to inflict a heavy defeat on the enemy in Cyrenaica, and the obvious unwillingness of the Vichy Government to change its attitude showed that the North Africa plan could not be put into effect at all events at an early date. There was, however, no change in the urgent need to look for some way of relieving German pressure on the Russians. Contrary to Russian suspicions there was no feeling on the British side that the Russians could be left to fight the German armies until the latter were so much weakened that an Anglo-American invasion of the Continent could deliver the final blow. In spite of their immense losses on the eastern front the Germans seemed likely to be able to break Russian resistance in the south and ultimately to threaten the indispensable British oil supplies in the Middle East.

Early in April General Marshall, the United States Chief of Staff, and Mr. Hopkins came to London with proposals for the immediate preparation of an invading force of 48 divisions (30 American and 18 British) to be landed in April, 1943, between Le Havre and Boulogne. These preparations, if set on foot at once, would also make possible an emergency landing in the autumn of 1942 in either of two contingencies; a 'sacrifice' landing, if such a measure were necessary to save the Russians from total collapse by drawing off German forces, or an operation to seize the opportunity if Russian resistance were such that the German forces were totally occupied in the East, or if there were evidence of a sudden deterioration of German military power. The Prime Minister and the British Chiefs of Staff agreed upon planning for an invasion in 1943, and did not exclude the possibility of an 'emergency' operation in 1942, but they thought that the Americans did not realise the technical difficulties in the way even of a temporary success likely to draw German forces from the Russian front, or the necessity of safeguarding the

Washington at the end of M. Molotov's visit was thus open to dangerous misinterpretation. This communiqué, which was to be issued after it had received the approval of the British Government, stated that 'in the course of the conversations full understanding was reached with regard to the urgent tasks of creating a second front in Europe in 1942'.

M. Molotov brought the communiqué to London. The British Government had not been consulted about the wording. Otherwise they would have pointed out that the sentence about a second front in 1942 would certainly be taken by the Russians as committing Great Britain and the United States, whereas the Prime Minister had made it clear that no promise could be made on the subject, and that the difficulties in the way of opening a second front in 1942

(a) might be insuperable. On May 28, before M. Molotov had begun his discussions, the Prime Minister had warned Mr. Roosevelt of the 'difficulties of 1942'.

(b)   On M. Molotov's return from the United States, Mr. Eden explained to him that, in view of the statement agreed at Washington, it would be necessary to alter the draft of our own proposed statement about the two visits to London. Obviously there must be a communiqué dealing with the London visit, since the nature of the talks in London and in Washington had been different; a treaty had been concluded in London and there had been none concluded in Washington. We should also have to include some reference to British plans for 1942. It would seem curious if the only reference to action were to be found in the Washington communiqué; the Americans, with the best possible intentions, could not do much in 1942.

(*continued*)

position in the Middle East and the Indian Ocean. (At the time of General Marshall's visit the situation in the Indian Ocean was at its worst. The Japanese bombed Colombo on April 5 and Trincomalee on April 9; two British heavy cruisers and an aircraft carrier were lost.) General Brooke thought that General Marshall had not studied the strategic implications of a cross-Channel operation. 'I asked him to imagine that his landing had been safely carried out, and asked him what his plans would then be. . . . I found that he had not begun to consider any form of plan of action . . . or to visualise the problems that would face an army after landing.' Sir A. Bryant, *The Turn of the Tide* (from Lord Alanbrooke's diaries and autobiographical notes, Collins, 1957), 358–9. After these discussions, and with the Prime Minister's approval (see above, p. 243, n. 2), Mr. Roosevelt invited Stalin to send M. Molotov and a general to Washington to discuss a proposal involving the use of American forces to relieve the pressure on the Russian western front. Stalin did not answer this invitation at once, but when, after the signature of the Anglo-Russian treaty, M. Molotov arrived in Washington on May 29 he tried to get American agreement to a cross-Channel operation in 1942 which would draw off forty German divisions from the Russian front. General Marshall, who regarded transport difficulties as the main obstacle, was unwilling to be committed to 1942, but Mr. Roosevelt insisted on accepting the wording proposed by M. Molotov. (See R. E. Sherwood, *The White House Papers of Harry L. Hopkins* (Eyre & Spottiswoode, 1949), II, 581–2.) The British Government do not appear to have known that the President had acted in this way against General Marshall's advice.

(a) T772/2, Churchill Papers/471. (b) N3000/5/38.

Mr. Eden explained that we did not object to the reference in the Washington communiqué to action in 1942 since it might be useful as a means of worrying and deceiving the Germans. M. Molotov took the hint implied in Mr. Eden's remark. He said that, while he hoped that we might be deceiving the Germans, there should be 'no deception between friends'. Mr. Eden agreed. The text of the communiqué, which was issued in London on June 11, included the phrase accepted in Washington with regard to a second front in 1942. The phrase was quoted by Mr. Eden in a parliamentary statement, without comment on its meaning. The Prime Minister, however, felt it essential to state in writing that the communiqué did not bind the British Government to open a second front in Europe in 1942. He therefore gave M. Molotov on June 10 an *aide-mémoire* (a) summarising the action which we were already taking and would continue to take in order to assist the Russians and relieve pressure on the Eastern front, but warning the Russians that any plans for a Continental landing in 1942 must depend on circumstances which could not be foreseen. In accordance with our promise, we would go on sending supplies of aircraft, tanks and other equipment by the dangerous northern route as well as through Iran. We were already containing about one half of the German fighter strength and a third of their bombers. In order to compel further German withdrawals from their air strength in the East, we should continue our bombing of German cities and industries and our day and night offensive over occupied France. We should continue to reinforce Libya and Malta (where, at the time, the Germans were using 400 first line aircraft in attacks). We should also continue our policy of raids against selected points. These raids would increase in size and scope, and would prevent the Germans from transferring to the Russian front any of their 33 divisions in western Europe. We were preparing for a landing on the Continent in August or September 1942, but, as M. Molotov had been told, on his first visit to London, the main limiting factor was the availability of landing craft. It would be of no help to the Russians or to the Allied cause in general if, 'for the sake of action at any price', we embarked on an operation ending in disaster. We could therefore 'give no promise in the matter but, provided that it appears sound and sensible', we should not hesitate to put our plans into effect. If the Russian Government wished us to do so, we could send 4 fighter and 2 fighter bomber squadrons to Murmansk to relieve Russian air forces for operations elsewhere; we could also consider with the Russians the question which had been raised earlier—of a combined Anglo-Russian operation in the Petsamo area. We were concentrating upon a large-scale Anglo-American invasion of the Continent in 1943, with a

(a) WM(42)73, C.A.

force amounting in the first instance to over a million men. We set no limits to the scope and objectives of this invasion.

(a)   The Prime Minister informed the War Cabinet on June 11 of the *aide-mémoire* which he had given to M. Molotov. He also made a general survey of the military plans for 1942, and for the proposed large-scale operation in 1943. In dealing with the proposals for a landing—other than a raid—in France during 1942 the Prime Minister said that it would be undesirable to attempt a substantial landing i.e. involving six or more divisions, unless we could maintain our force after it had landed, and unless the Germans were demoralised by failure in Russia and their morale showed signs of disintegration. The Prime Minister thought it unlikely that the situation would be such as to make this operation feasible but that since, owing to weather conditions, we could not carry it out after September, and since two months would be required for assembling the shipping, we ought to begin at once to make preparations. The Prime Minister added that, with the agreement of the General Staff, he had recommended that we should give up the project of a 'three or four days' raid following the smaller raid already planned.

(b)   After his return to Moscow M. Molotov told Sir A. Clark Kerr[1] that he appreciated the frankness with which the Prime Minister had explained the whole British position to him. He said a good deal about the second front, and hoped that he had been able to bring home to the British and United States Government the 'immense weight which the Soviet Government' attached to a second front this year. Sir A. Clark Kerr had no doubt that the reference in the communiqués had impressed Russian opinion, and that the Russians were now expecting the second front to be opened.

In spite of the clear statements made by the Prime Minister to M. Molotov in London, the Russians henceforward took the line that they had a pledge which was binding upon Great Britain as well as

(c)   upon the United States. Sir A. Clark Kerr reported on June 28 that he was much impressed by the improvement in the 'atmosphere' since the conclusion of the treaty but still more impressed by the fact that the Soviet Government and people expected the opening of a second front in 1942. He thought that the words in the communiqués would be taken as a pledge to this effect. Furthermore M. Molotov had spoken to him on June 26 and to the American Ambassador as though the matter were settled. He had said much about the 'Anglo-Saxon promises' and the disillusion which would

---

[1] Sir S. Cripps had left Moscow on January 9, 1942. Sir A. Clark Kerr, who was appointed as Sir S. Cripps's successor as British Ambassador to the U.S.S.R., took up his duties in Moscow on March 14, 1942.

(a) WM(42)73, C.A. (b) N3238/5/38. (c) N3385/30/38.

follow if the promises were not made good. He 'swept aside' Sir A. Clark Kerr's suggestion that perhaps no 'fast promise had been given' and said that the test of the treaty would be the establishment of a second front, and that the British and United States Governments must realise this fact. The British Military Mission also (a) telegraphed on June 29 to the Chiefs of Staff that the treaty was regarded in Moscow as a preliminary step to a second front, and that many Russians expected the opening of the front to be a matter of weeks or even days rather than of months. If these hopes were not fulfilled, there would be a serious reaction in Russian opinion.

On June 29 Sir A. Clark Kerr telegraphed that there might be (b) more in the strong desire for a second front than a wish to remove the strain from the Red Army. Apart from the concern over the fuel and food shortage, observers were struck by slight but unmistakable signs of anxiety on the part of the Soviet authorities about the general internal situation (e.g. repeated references to Stalin's claim that the war must be won this year: 'whipping up' of hatred against Germans in the press and in speeches). This anxiety was relatively new. The growing volume of murmurs was probably responsible for the recent exaggerated Russian claims with regard to German losses: a moment's reflection would dismiss these claims if the German army were still the powerful force which the Russians asserted it to be.

The Foreign Office regarded this information as disturbing, though not unexpected. Mr. Eden suggested to the War Cabinet (c) that we should remind M. Molotov of the position as set out in our *aide-mémoire*, Sir A. Clark Kerr was also instructed, in reminding M. Molotov of our 'reasonable reservations', to add that we would do everything possible, or everything that offered a fair measure of success, to lighten the burden on Russia.

The War Cabinet agreed that Sir A. Clark Kerr should tell (d) M. Molotov that the Prime Minister and Mr. Eden were troubled that he might be overrating the probability of an early establishment of a second front in Europe, and that the Prime Minister had pointed out to him the difficulties, especially in regard to the lack of sufficient landing craft. The Soviet Government knew their own business, but we doubted whether they were wise in giving so much publicity to the plans for a second front. We also regretted that M. Molotov had said that, if we did not open a second front in 1942, we should not be fulfilling our promises, and that the Anglo-Soviet treaty would lose its value. Sir A. Clark Kerr was also instructed to ask M. Molotov to give orders to Russian officers not

---

(a) N3532/30/38. (b) N3386/30/38. (c) WM(42)85.4, C.A. (d) Tel. 110 to Moscow (Prisec).

to ask our Military Mission questions about a second front, since the matter was one of high policy.

(a)   Sir A. Clark Kerr saw M. Molotov on the evening of July 4. In the course of a long and not unfriendly discussion M. Molotov explained that he and his colleagues in the Soviet Government understood the position, but that the Russian people anxiously wanted a second front and, not unnaturally fixed their attention on the reference to it in the communiqués after the Washington and London meetings.

(ii)

Russian dissatisfaction over the British decision temporarily to suspend northern convoys to the U.S.S.R.: Stalin's message of July 23: the Prime Minister's visit to Moscow, August 12–16, 1942.

(b)   On July 14 M. Maisky came to see Mr. Eden. He said that the reports from the Russian front were very grave. German progress had been more rapid and serious than had been expected. He asked what news there was about the latest convoy to Russia. Mr. Eden replied that the news was bad. Only five ships had arrived, and although two others might reach Russia, the losses had been very heavy; 100 only out of 600 tanks and not more than 40 aircraft had been brought in.[1] Mr. Eden said that it was obviously of no help to the Russians if we lost nearly all the ships. Mr. Eden said to M. Maisky that the First Sea Lord considered that, if he were on the German side, he could ensure that no ship of the next convoy reached port. No decision, however, had yet been taken about sending this convoy.

M. Maisky repeated that the Russian position was now very serious. Their manpower was not inexhaustible. They were in fact responsible for two fronts because they had to maintain an army against a possible Japanese attack. Meanwhile we could not open

---

[1] This convoy of 36 merchant ships had sailed from Iceland on June 27. Thirteen of the merchant ships reached Archangel: two of the thirteen were rescue ships. The lost cargoes included 3,350 vehicles, 430 tanks, and 210 aircraft.

One fifth of the previous convoy (in May) had been lost. The northern convoy route was especially dangerous during the almost perpetual daylight of the summer months, since the ships were exposed to attacks from shore-based aircraft on the long stretches of Norwegian coast line as well as to U-boat attacks and surface raiders. Moreover, owing to danger from ice, the ships had to keep close to the coast until midsummer. In spite of urgent British requests the Russians provided little air or anti-submarine protection at their end of the convoy routes. See S. W. Roskill, *The War at Sea*, II (H.M.S.O., 1956) especially chs, V, XII and XVI.

(a) Moscow tel. 65 (Prisec). (b) N3692/30/38.

a second front. We seemed to be doing less bombing and, if our convoys ceased, the effect on Russian resistance must be very serious. Mr. Eden said that he knew this, and that M. Maisky also knew the position about a second front. M. Maisky said that he had always thought that the Japanese might attack if they considered the Russians to be in trouble on their western front. He feared that the Japanese might think that such a position had now arisen.

On July 17 Sir A. Clark Kerr reported that M. Vyshinsky had (a) described the situation as grave, but had 'professed to feel quite confident'. Sir A. Clark Kerr 'did not find his confidence contagious'. M. Vyshinsky ended by saying that the dangerous situation could be eased by the opening of a second front. The Red Armies might, of course, be counted upon to fight on to the death, but the time might come when they could not go on and then a second front would be too late. In a second telegram of July 17 (b) Sir A. Clark Kerr assumed that in making their plans for a second front His Majesty's Government were taking this new and disquieting situation into earnest consideration. The Red Army's need of relief was clearly very urgent, and in unofficial circles criticisms of our apparent inaction were very keen. About this time also the Foreign Office received reports from more than one source that there was a possibility of a German peace offer to Russia. The Foreign Office view was that Hitler was unlikely to make such an offer, but that, if it were made, the Russians might accept it as a means of securing a respite until the Allies were able to direct heavier blows against the Germans.

In these circumstances a decision to postpone the sailing of convoys until the winter might have serious political consequences. Nevertheless, the War Cabinet, on the advice of the Admiralty, came to the conclusion that postponement was necessary. Hitherto the Germans, after they had begun to use their heavy surface forces against the convoys, had kept them west of Bear Island. In this area the Home Fleet could be used to protect the convoys. The Germans had now begun the tactics which the Admiralty had most feared, that is to say, they had sent surface ships east of Bear Island. In view of the naval losses in the Far East, the Admiralty was unwilling to send the Home Fleet to escort the convoys east of Bear Island, since the fleet would have been exposed to attack from submarines and shore-based aircraft. The destruction of one or more of the newer battleships or even their withdrawal for repair, while the *Tirpitz* and other strong German units were in service, might have entailed the loss of the command of the Atlantic. On July 17 the Prime Minister sent a message to Stalin explaining why the decision (c)

(a) N3706/30/38. (b) N3707/30/38. (c) T1020/2, Churchill Papers/393.

to suspend the convoys had become necessary, and saying that their passage would be resumed as soon as was practicable, and that some of the ships would be diverted at once to the Persian Gulf ports.[1]

(a)   Stalin replied on July 23 in very strong and unfriendly terms. He stated that Russian naval experts did not accept our reasons for deciding not to fulfil our 'contracted obligations'[2] and to continue the convoys. Obviously regular convoys could not be operated without losses or risks, but these hazards were inevitable in war. Stalin had not expected that we would stop the despatch of war materials at the very moment when the Soviet Union was in greatest need of them. Transport *via* the Persian Gulf could not be a substitute. Stalin also suggested that the question of a second front was not being treated as seriously as it deserved. He regarded it as necessary to 'state in the most emphatic manner', and taking into account the position on the Russian front, that the Soviet Government could not 'acquiesce in the postponement of a second front in Europe until 1943'.

(b)   Mr. Eden told M. Maisky on July 24 that he regretted Stalin's message, not because it would affect our attitude towards our Ally, but because the charges made by Stalin would have 'unhelpful' effects on the Prime Minister and on His Majesty's Government. Mr. Eden thought that perhaps it would be best not to answer the message. M. Maisky agreed, but thought a discussion on the convoy position desirable in order to convince the Russians that future convoys could not take the northern route. M. Maisky feared that, if we postponed a second front until 1943, the Russian armies might have suffered so severely that the Germans would be able to withdraw strong forces to the west and make a landing impossible; there would also be great disappointment in Russia. Mr. Eden replied that we had explained to M. Molotov the difficulties of

---

[1] The Prime Minister told Stalin that he had sent a copy of his message to President Roosevelt.

[2] There was no contractual obligation on the part of Great Britain or the United States to transport the supplies to Russia. The first protocol dealing with supplies was signed at

(c) Moscow on October 1, 1941; it covered a period extending to June 30, 1942. The relevant sentence in the text ran as follows: 'Great Britain and the U.S.A. will give aid to the transportation of these materials to the Soviet Union and will help with the delivery.' All the more important British supplies under this protocol had been made available for transport to Russia, though some had been sunk *en route*, and a great deal of material was always awaiting shipment.

(d) A second protocol covering the period from July 1, 1942, to June 30, 1943, was not signed in Washington until October 6, 1942. It provided for 4,400,000 short tons of supplies, two-thirds of which were to be shipped to north Russia. The undertaking was subject to unforeseen developments in the progress of the war, and to limitations on shipping. In fact the protocol had been in force since the expiry of the first protocol.

For the third protocol, concluded in June 1943, see below, p. 569.

(a) T1031/2, Churchill Papers/393; WM(42)95.2, C.A. (b) N3846/1/38. (c) N5978/3084/38(1941). (d) N6012/178/38.

landing in sufficient force in 1942 to induce the Germans to withdraw any part of their armies from Russia. Mr. Eden agreed that there would be disappointment in Russia, but we could not be blamed for it, since we had been clear about the position.

On July 25 Sir A. Clark Kerr telegraphed that the British press (a) and public opinion should be warned against giving the impression that mass protestations of friendship and admiration for Russian resistance were a substitute for action. The Soviet Government clearly expected military action by us in Europe. They wanted tangible evidence of our realisation that we should have to make great and costly efforts on land in Europe. They were not convinced that we understood this or that we were taking the war seriously. They saw large British armies apparently inactive; they compared their losses with ours and the sudden fall of Tobruk (after the announcement that it would be held) with the prolonged defence of Sebastopol.

Three days later Sir A. Clark Kerr suggested to Sir A. Cadogan that the Prime Minister should come to Moscow in order to explain the reasons why we could not open a second front. M. Molotov had said that he had passed on what had been told him or given to him in writing in London, but he did not appear to have explained to Stalin 'the Prime Minister's mind'. The military situation was very disquieting and a visit from the Prime Minister might turn the scale as regards Russian morale. The Prime Minister had already suggested to the War Cabinet that he should go to Cairo. In view of Stalin's message and Sir A. Clark Kerr's telegram he decided, with the approval of the War Cabinet, to offer to meet Stalin at any place convenient to him.

On July 27 M. Maisky saw Mr. Eden again. He said that the (b) Soviet Government were 'deeply perturbed' at the effect of the German advance on certain of their supplies. They had lost three-quarters of their aluminium and a quarter of their pig-iron; the shortage of machines and machine tools was becoming more and more serious, since the setting up of new factories in areas remote from the battle area obviously made a demand on machine tools. M. Maisky hoped that we should be able to tell him the earliest date on which we hoped to despatch another convoy, and also to give him in detail the aid we required from the U.S.S.R. to secure the safety of the convoy.

On July 31 the Prime Minister sent a message to Stalin. He did (c) not answer Stalin's charges, but said that preliminary arrangements were being made to run a large convoy to Archangel in the first week of September; he also offered to come for a discussion with

---

(a) N3845/30/38. (b) N3861/1/38. (c) T1062/2, Churchill Papers/393.

Stalin at Astrakhan or in the Caucasus or any convenient meeting place between August 10 and 13. The Prime Minister would then be able to tell Stalin of the plans made with the President for offensive action in 1942.[1] Stalin replied on August 1 thanking the Prime Minister for the promise of a convoy and suggesting Moscow as a meeting place.

(a)   The Prime Minister, accompanied by Sir A. Cadogan,[2] General Sir A. Brooke, General Sir A. Wavell and Air Chief Marshal Sir A. Tedder, reached Moscow on August 12. Mr. Harriman, Major-General Maxwell and Major-General Bradley joined him there as representatives of the United States. The position was easier from the British point of view, since the military situation in Egypt was less grave. At the end of June, after their successes in the western desert, the Germans believed that they would soon occupy Egypt.[3] On July 1 Rommel attacked the positions at El Alamein to which the British forces had been driven back. El Alamein, on a narrow front between the Mediterranean and the great Qattara depression in the desert, was the last point at which the Germans could be held. Rommel's attacks were beaten off; by July 4 he was back on the defensive, and at the end of the month the enemy's chances of achieving the seventy miles between El Alamein and Alexandria were very much less. Reinforcements and supplies, including American material, were reaching Egypt on a larger scale than they were reaching Rommel, since, in spite of a much longer sea route, the British had better landing facilities and were nearer to their base.

---

[1] Within a week of the issue of the joint communiqué on M. Molotov's visit the Prime Minister heard that the President was reconsidering the possibility of a landing in North Africa. Mr. Churchill therefore decided to go to Washington to try to get the proposal for a cross-Channel landing in 1942 abandoned in favour of the North African plan. Mr. Churchill began his talks with Roosevelt on June 19. Two days later came the news of the fall of Tobruk. As well as getting timely American help to meet the crisis in the western desert, Mr. Churchill persuaded the President, without actually abandoning the cross-Channel project for 1942, to agree to make preparations for a North African operation. On his return to England Mr. Churchill reinforced his argument by writing to the President that 'no responsible British general, admiral or air marshal' thought the cross-Channel operation feasible in 1942, and reminding Mr. Roosevelt that the North African plan had been his (Mr. Roosevelt's) own idea. General Marshall and his colleagues, however, still believed that a North African operation would be a dispersal of effort which would interfere with the proposed direct, full-scale attack in 1943 (whereas Mr. Churchill thought of it as a necessary weakening of the German ability to concentrate their forces in Northern France). General Marshall, Admiral King and Mr. Hopkins came to London on July 18 for further discussion. In spite of American doubts agreement was reached by July 25 to give first priority to North Africa and to launch the expedition as soon as possible. In these circumstances the Prime Minister undertook the difficult mission of trying to convince Stalin that the North African plan offered the greatest measure of help which the Allies could offer to Russia in 1942 and the best preparation for a larger invasion of Europe in 1943.

[2] Sir A. Cadogan arrived a day late owing to trouble with the aeroplane in which he was travelling.

[3] Mussolini appears to have sent to Libya a white horse on which he proposed to enter Cairo or Alexandria in triumph.

(a) WP(42)373.

In the Far East also the Japanese had lost in the battles of the Coral Sea (May 7–8) and off Midway Island (June 4–7) five aircraft carriers—more important units than battleships in this vast Pacific area—and had already begun to feel the American counter-pressure which was ultimately to drive them out of the islands they had seized.

On the Russian side, however, the situation was at its very worst. The threats to Stalingrad and Baku were increasing; on August 8 the Russians had destroyed and abandoned the Maikop oilfield. The Soviet High Command could not be sure of holding out until the winter of 1942–3, yet Mr. Churchill could give no hope of direct relief in the critical period before winter set in. During the interval between Stalin's acceptance of the proposal for a meeting and the Prime Minister's arrival in Moscow the Soviet Government indeed made matters more difficult by giving prominent place in the Russian press to statements in Great Britain or in the United States urging the immediate opening of a second front. Other articles emphasised the part played, as in the first World War, by Russia in drawing German forces from the west. On August 6 a leading article in the Moscow press asserted that the British Government were bound by their own word to open a second front. They could not renounce their promise owing to the feelings of their own people and of the peoples in enemy-occupied territory. The article concluded that 'it would be fatal for the Government if the British nation concluded that they were incapable of action'. The foreign news columns of the press of August 7, 8 and 9 were filled with accounts of pressure upon the British and American Governments. These reports were continued during the Prime Minister's visit.

At the first meeting with Stalin on the evening of August 12 the Prime Minister explained very frankly the military reasons why it was impracticable to undertake a major operation in Northern France in 1942. The Prime Minister said that he had told M. Molotov, on the latter's visit to London, that we were considering plans to assist Russia by a diversion of German forces to the western front. The Prime Minister had pointed out the difficulties, and had explained that he could make no promises; he had given M. Molotov an *aide-mémoire* to this effect. Since M. Molotov's visit to London, the British and American Governments had made an exhaustive study of the problem; they had decided that a major operation, i.e. an operation which would compel the Germans to bring tanks and infantry to the western front, was not practicable in September—the only month left in 1942 during which the weather could be counted upon.

On the other hand the two Governments were preparing for a very large operation in 1943. After giving particulars of the force which would then be available, the Prime Minister said that he knew that this plan could not help Russia in 1942, but that we could do no more because we had landing craft sufficient only for putting ashore, and maintaining, six divisions. We had considered the possibility of landings on a small scale in the Pas de Calais or in the area east and west of the Pas de Calais, i.e. between Dunkirk and Dieppe. Our purpose would be to compel an air battle, but we should lose our expeditionary force, since the enemy could bring against it a larger land force than we could transport. We should thus merely invite a defeat in which we should lose trained men and material needed for our operations in 1943.

Stalin did not take the Prime Minister's explanations easily. He talked generally about the need to take risks in war, and argued in detail against Churchill's points. He contested the figures about the number of German troops in France, and showed little understanding of the difficulties of providing continuous air cover across the Channel from British bases or of the fact that in the Pas de Calais area, where our fighters could operate with least difficulty, the harbours were small and shallow, and in the area further west, with larger harbours, we could not provide sufficient air cover. Stalin suggested that we could land troops by air. The Prime Minister reminded him that, in 1940, when there were only 20,000 trained men, 200 guns, and 50 tanks in Great Britain, Hitler did not attempt a landing although he had all the necessary material. Stalin said that there was no analogy between the present position and that of 1940 because in 1940 the British people would have resisted a German landing, whereas in the case of a British landing in France, the French people would be on the side of the landing force. The Prime Minister pointed out that it was important not to expose the people of France to the vengeance of Hitler after the expeditionary force had been compelled to withdraw. Stalin finally said that, although he did not agree with Mr. Churchill, he could not insist upon his demand for a landing.

Stalin became less gloomy when the Prime Minister talked of plans for increasing our air attacks on German centres of industry. Stalin said that he disagreed with those military experts who were inclined to discount the importance of bombing. He thought that the population of Germany as well as the factories should be bombed, since there was no other way of breaking German morale. The Prime Minister said that we regarded the destruction of German morale as a military target, and that, if need be, we would destroy almost every house in almost every German city.

These words obviously cheered Stalin. At all events he gave a much better reception to Mr. Churchill's exposition of the plan for an Anglo-American landing in North Africa in the autumn of 1942.

He asked whether the plan would not mean war with Vichy France and Spain. Mr. Churchill said that Spain was unlikely to go to war and that, in any case, we could land troops more easily in Spain than in France. Mr. Churchill then pointed out that the operation should be considered in connexion with the proposed landing in northern France in 1943.[1] Mr. Harriman added that there was complete acceptance of the plan on the American side, and that the President would support it to the full.

In the course of the discussion Stalin realised the strategic advantages of the plan and summed them up as taking the enemy in the rear in Africa, making the Germans and French fight each other in France, putting Italy out of action, and keeping Spain neutral. On the other hand, until the end of the discussion, Stalin seemed doubtful about the political aspect of the plan. He suggested that the French might be more willing to co-operate if, for example, General de Gaulle were put in charge of the operation, or at all events if it were made clear that the operation was being undertaken in the interests of France and not in the interests of the United States.

At the conclusion of the meeting Stalin seemed to be satisfied on the political side. Mr. Churchill met Stalin again on the night of August 13–14. Earlier in the day he had an inconclusive conversation with M. Molotov. M. Molotov was very cautious in all his comments. He said that the situation on the eastern front was far worse than in May or June and that the Russians wanted something to be done to relieve the pressure on their armies. He suggested that, while it was now clear that a second front in Europe would not be formed in 1942, there was no certainty that the proposed operation in North Africa would take place. The Prime Minister said that the matter was not at all in doubt, and that the time-table for it might even be accelerated. He also explained that, although he foresaw no political difficulties in Great Britain resulting from the decision, it was undesirable to give the Germans any chance of learning even indirectly that there would be no second front in Europe in 1942. The articles in the Russian press (and for that matter, the propagandist activities of M. Maisky) were not mentioned, but the implication was clear that nothing but harm would be done by attempts to stir up a movement in Parliament or elsewhere which would force the British Government into a declaration of policy.

During this conversation M. Molotov gave no hint of a change in Stalin's attitude towards the North African plan since the discusssion

---

[1] At this point Mr. Churchill drew a picture of a crocodile and said that we intended to attack the 'soft belly' as well as the 'hard snout'. After Mr. Harriman had spoken of Mr. Roosevelt's support to the limit of American resources, Stalin exclaimed: 'May God help this enterprise to succeed.'

of the previous night. Stalin, however, opened the second meeting on the night of August 13–14 by communicating to Mr. Churchill and Mr. Harriman an *aide-mémoire* in which he restated the urgent Russian need of a second front. He claimed that the decision to open this front had been taken during M. Molotov's visit to London and that it was implied in the Anglo-Soviet communiqué. The Russian High Command had planned their summer and autumn operations on the assumption that the second front would be formed. The refusal of the British Government therefore prejudiced the Russian military plans and would be a 'moral blow' to Russian public opinion: the military difficulties would also have grave repercussions in the position of Great Britain and other Allies.

The Prime Minister said that he would make a written reply to the *aide-mémoire;* he repeated that his statement of the previous day represented the conclusions reached by the British and American Governments after the most careful consideration. He pointed out later in the discussion that we wanted to do all we could for Russia and realised the ordeal through which she was passing; we ourselves had fought alone for a year. We were certain of ultimate victory, but it would be of no assistance to Russia if the United Nations merely undertook an operation which ended in disaster. We had to accept as facts the existence of the oceans and the need to move over them in ships. Mr. Churchill made a strong appeal for friendship and understanding, and Mr. Harriman supported the Prime Minister's statement.[1]

Stalin then said that the North African project did not directly concern the U.S.S.R. The decision about a second front, however, showed that there was a difference of view about the importance of the Russian front. He (Stalin) regarded this front as of first-rate importance; the British and American Governments regarded it as only of secondary importance. Mr. Churchill protested that this was not the case, and the whole matter was again discussed. Stalin also said that he felt bound to point out that, owing to the abandonment of a good many plans, the Soviet Government had in fact obtained little in the way of supplies from Great Britain and America. Mr. Churchill said that the British Government were doing their utmost to get convoys through to Russia, but that the North African plan would affect the convoy position. Mr. Churchill could not say to what extent the position would be changed; he felt it his duty not to conceal the facts from Stalin.

After further discussion, which included a short survey of the Russian plans with regard to the Caucasus, Mr. Churchill suggested that Sir A. Cadogan and M. Molotov should draw up a draft

---

[1] Mr. Churchill rejected with anger a suggestion by Stalin that British reluctance to undertake a cross-Channel invasion was due to fear of the German army.

communiqué in general terms about the meeting. Mr. Churchill's disappointment at Stalin's change of attitude was clear from the fact that he even doubted whether it would be wise to issue any communiqué. In response, however, to a question from Stalin, he said that he was ready to stay for another day in Moscow if any good purpose could be served thereby.

Mr. Churchill sent a written reply to Stalin's *aide-mémoire* on August 14. He restated the arguments (i) that an attack with six or eight divisions on the Cherbourg peninsula or the Channel Islands would be a futile waste of effort and would not bring back a single German division from the Russian front, (ii) that the North African plan had the advantages which Stalin himself had observed and that it would prepare the way for a second front in Europe in 1943, (iii) that no promise had been made on the British or American side to open a second front in 1942; here Mr. Churchill was able to quote from his *aide-mémoire* of June 10, and to refer Stalin to his conversations with M. Molotov, (iv) that in view of these oral and written reservations the Russian High Command had no grounds for altering their plans as a result of the conversations with M. Molotov.[1] Mr. Churchill also said that the talk about an Anglo-American invasion of France in 1942 had been useful in misleading the enemy and thereby holding large air forces and considerable military forces on the French Channel coast. Hence it would do harm, especially to Russian interests, if any public controversy arose in which the British Government were compelled to state the reasons why they could not undertake a landing in northern France. The best plan would be to employ this operation as a 'blind' to deceive the Germans about the North African plan. Mr. Harriman also wrote to Stalin stating his agreement with the Prime Minister's *aide-mémoire*, and repeating that no promise had been broken with regard to the opening of a second front in Europe.

Little progress was made on August 14 towards a more friendly atmosphere. Sir A. Cadogan saw M. Molotov on this day and told him of the Prime Minister's disappointment at the sudden change in Stalin's attitude. M. Molotov was friendly but professed to see no signs of any such change. On the night of August 14–15 Stalin entertained the Prime Minister at a banquet; the atmosphere was not altogether satisfactory, but on the following morning the Prime

---

[1] There can indeed be no reasonable doubt on this point. Mr. Churchill also took care during these discussions with Stalin not to commit himself to a cross-Channel invasion in 1943, but he laid up trouble (see below, Ch. XXXIV, Sections (i) and (ii)) by giving Stalin the impression that the invasion would certainly take place in that year. Mr. Churchill himself believed at this time (August 1942) that the operation could be carried out in 1943, and continued later to press for it, though the British (and American) General Staffs already thought it unlikely. See also J. R. M. Butler, *Grand Strategy*, III, Pt. 2 (H.M.S.O., 1964), 663.

Minister suggested that he might call on Stalin alone before he left Moscow.

Stalin was not available until 7 p.m. The Prime Minister then went to see him. This last meeting was much more cordial. The Prime Minister stayed to dinner with Stalin and continued a friendly conversation until 2.30 a.m. when he left to go to his aeroplane. Stalin said that Great Britain and the U.S.S.R. had no antagonistic interests. He seemed also to have come round again to a more favourable view of the North African plan.[1]

(iii)

Further Soviet propaganda for a second front: Mr. Eden's complaints to M. Maisky and protests to M. Molotov (August 20–September 30, 1942).

(a) In spite of the Prime Minister's warning at Moscow the Soviet press continued its reports of pressure on the British and American Governments. On August 20 Mr. Eden protested to M. Maisky against an article which had appeared in the *Soviet War News* on August 7—i.e. before Mr. Churchill had arrived in Moscow. This article referred in one sentence to the dishonour of Marshal Pétain, the existence of Major Quisling, and the capitulation of Tobruk. Mr. Eden told M. Maisky that we resented this association of Tobruk with Pétain and Quisling. M. Maisky appeared to agree that the passage ought not to have been printed. In general, however, the Foreign Office did not think it expedient to protest against Soviet propaganda about a second front. They had definite information of M. Maisky's efforts to persuade newspaper editors in London to exert pressure on the Government; M. Maisky was having little success, and as long as he was not doing much positive harm it seemed wiser to leave him alone.

(b) M. Maisky came to see Mr. Eden on September 4. He said that he wanted to review Anglo-Soviet relations. The results of the Prime Minister's visit had been good, as far as concerned his relations with Stalin and the understanding between the two Governments, although Mr. Churchill and Stalin had retained their respective views about a second front in 1942. M. Maisky had in mind, however, the relations between the British and Russian peoples. The Russian army and people had been led to expect a second front in 1942;

---

[1] In accordance with the Prime Minister's suggestion, the British and American Military Chiefs held two meetings with the Russians on August 15. The discussions dealt in more detail with the question of a second front and with the situation in the Caucasus.

(a) N4383/5/38. (b) N4590/5/38.

there would be widespread disappointment if these expectations were not fulfilled.

Mr. Eden answered that M. Maisky knew that we had not promised a second front. The communiqué about it had come from Washington. M. Maisky agreed, but maintained that, although the Soviet Government understood the position, there was a real danger of popular misunderstanding. It might be difficult to persuade the Russian people that operations in Africa were the equivalent of a second front in Europe. Mr. Eden pointed out that the Soviet Government could explain the significance of the African operations. M. Maisky replied that Africa was little more than a phrase to the average Russian. In any case what was our next plan? Did we propose a second front in Europe in 1943? Mr. Eden thought that this was looking very many moves ahead, and that a number of possibilities were open to us, but M. Maisky was not convinced that operations in Africa or Italy could ease the pressure on the Russian armies in the spring of 1943.

M. Maisky then made some suggestions: (i) Bombing of German cities. Stalin thought that our bombing was not only of military value but that it had a psychological effect in Russia. We should therefore keep this consideration in mind in our choice of targets. Some places, e.g. Nuremberg, Frankfurt, and especially Munich, meant much in Russia: other places, e.g. Saarbrücken or Karlsruhe, meant very little. It would be valuable if we sent photographs of 'blitzed' towns for reproduction in Russian papers. Mr. Maisky said that it had been suggested to him that we should send posters about British tanks supplied to Russia; he thought, however, that photographs of destruction in Germany would have more effect. (ii) Maintenance of supplies. M. Maisky hoped that the northern route would be kept open at all costs, and, if possible, used more fully, and that the southern traffic through Iran would be speeded up. When M. Maisky criticised the operation of the last northern convoy Mr. Eden showed his resentment at the emphasis on the one convoy that had suffered heavy losses, and said that no navy other than ours would have been able, as we had done for so long, to ensure safe deliveries. M. Maisky did not press the point. (iii) Red Cross. M. Maisky spoke of the excellent effect of Red Cross contributions to Russia during the previous winter. The contributions were now falling off: could we increase them?

Meanwhile in the United States M. Litvinov was speaking in (a) gloomy terms about Russian prospects and about the disappointment of the Russian people at the absence of a second front. Mr. Sumner

Welles regarded M. Litvinov's pessimism as a serious embarrassment, but his forecasts of disaster were confirmed at all events in certain particulars by a telegram of September 4 from Sir A. Clark Kerr.
(a) This telegram called attention to leading articles in Russian papers exhorting the troops to stand firm and threatening those who failed to do so. Sir A. Clark Kerr had heard for some time past rumours that in the earlier stages of the German southern offensive Russian morale had given way, with the result that Rostov and Novocherkask had fallen easily to the Germans. These rumours had now been confirmed from a trustworthy source who had also said that Stalin had visited the southern front just before the Prime Minister's arrival in Moscow, and that Russian losses in men and material had been very heavy. Equipment was difficult to replace owing to the interruption of communications, and the morale of the troops, after a long retreat, remained low. There had also been some disaffection among the Cossacks who had not yet forgiven the harshness of the deportations following the establishment of collective farms in their regions.

The Foreign Office asked Sir A. Clark Kerr whether in his opinion M. Litvinov was acting under instructions, and also whether it would be desirable to raise with M. Molotov the whole question of the attitude of the Soviet Government towards their Allies. Sir A.
(b) Clark Kerr considered that M. Litvinov would not have used such defeatist language if he had not been told to do so. On the other hand representations to M. Molotov would not produce any result. The Russian propaganda was directed as much to their own people as to Great Britain and America. The absence of a second front was a good cover for the Russian military failures and the Soviet Government could not refrain from using this explanation. A little later
(c) Sir A. Clark Kerr reported a conversation with a senior Russian officer who complained very bitterly of British and American inaction and spoke of suspicions in Russia that Great Britain was intriguing for a separate peace at Russian expense.

Mr. Eden still thought it better not to speak to M. Maisky about his propagandist activities until he went wholly beyond the limit which we could permit to an Ambassador. M. Maisky soon went
(d) so far beyond this limit that it became necessary to warn him. On September 18 Mr. Eden sent for him in order to tell him of our information that he had given a confidential talk to a number of American journalists whom he had invited to tea. Mr. Eden gave M. Maisky quotations from this talk. The quotations showed that M. Maisky had maintained that a second front in 1942 was not only necessary but 'entirely feasible'. Mr. Eden said that this phrase,

---

(a) N4566/30/38. (b) N4740/5/38. (c) N4788/5/38. (d) N4819, 4868/30/38.

which had been repeated more than once, could not be interpreted otherwise than as a criticism of the policy of His Majesty's Government. We resented such criticism from an Ambassador to foreign journalists.

M. Maisky gave a rather lame explanation of his words. He said that he had not been acting under instructions from Moscow. The interview had been 'off the record'; he had made it plain that the information was for the confidential guidance of the journalists and that he did not wish them to report what he had said, since it might do harm. Mr. Eden pointed out to him that our military decisions had been taken and would not be changed as a result of anything said by him or by Soviet newspapers and that there was nothing to be gained by criticising us. A week later the Foreign Office asked Sir A. Clark Kerr to raise the question of propaganda about a second (a) front with M. Molotov, not by way of a complaint but as a matter of importance to Anglo-Soviet relations. We did not expect the Soviet Government to stop all propaganda on the subject, but we thought that they were damaging their relations with us, and encouraging the Germans, by saying that we were breaking a pledge which we could fulfil without difficulty, and by supporting this charge of breach of faith with misrepresentations about German strength in Europe and North Africa.

Before he was able to carry out these instructions Sir A. Clark Kerr had a talk with Mr. Wendell Willkie during the latter's visit to (b) Russia. Mr. Willkie had thought at first that the Russians were trying to separate the British and the Americans. After more talk with M. Molotov, and an interview with Stalin, Mr. Willkie came (c) to the conclusion that this was not the case, although the Russians continually made distinctions between their Allies. Mr. Willkie thought that we might win over Stalin to our views, but that M. Molotov was unfriendly to us and was largely responsible for prodding Stalin into suspicion and hostility. Stalin had complained very strongly and bitterly that we were keeping a number of American Airacobra aeroplanes promised to him.[1]

Sir A. Clark Kerr attended a dinner given to Mr. Willkie on (d) September 26.[2] During a speech at the dinner Stalin spoke about the 'interception' of the Airacobras. Sir A. Clark Kerr replied with equal bluntness that Stalin seemed to have lost sight of the common cause in the interests of which the machines had been retained. Stalin was not

---

[1] These aeroplanes had been assigned to Great Britain and then promised by the British Government to Russia. On September 30 the Prime Minister informed Stalin that the machines had been unloaded in Great Britain at the urgent request of General Marshall.

[2] At this dinner, after M. Molotov had proposed a number of toasts without mention of Mr. Churchill, Mr. Willkie himself proposed a toast to Mr. Churchill.

(a) N4994/5/38. (b) N4911/5/38. (c) N4943/4943/38. (d) N4963/5/38.

offended at this reply, and three days later M. Molotov listened to
(a) Sir A. Clark Kerr's representations without showing irritation. He
tried to explain away the newspaper articles and denied that they
were doing harm to Anglo-Soviet relations or giving encouragement
to Hitler.

(iv)

*Exchanges with the Soviet Government concerning the treatment of war
criminals: British protests against an article in* Pravda *of October 19
(October 3–December 11, 1942).*

In the last fortnight of September there were fewer references in
the Russian press to the question of a second front. It was clear that
the British and American Governments were not to be diverted from
their plans by Russian propaganda. In any case, from the Russian
point of view, there was soon less need to continue an agitation on
the subject. The military situation began to improve in a remarkable
and unexpected way. The Germans had overreached themselves.
They had again captured large numbers of prisoners, but the main
Russian armies had escaped. In their advance beyond the Don the
German forces had come as far as the foothills of the Caucasus; they
had not cut off the oil supplies to Russia, and the Russians were now
in good fortified positions from which they could not easily be dis-
lodged. The Germans were also fighting in the outskirts of Stalingrad
by mid-September, but were meeting increasingly strong Russian
resistance. At the beginning of October there were signs not merely
that Hitler's boasts about the imminent fall of the city might be
mistaken, but that in his obstinacy he was committing the German
armies to disaster. As the weeks passed, and the winter came near,
the Russians began to see the possibilities of a great victory.

Nonetheless the Soviet leaders continued to be resentful and
unfriendly towards Great Britain and merely turned their irritation
and suspicion into other channels.[1] The most violent and, for that

---

[1] On October 5 Mr. Eden gave M. Maisky a detailed account of the latest convoy to
Russia. This convoy of forty ships had been escorted and protected by a very large number
of warships. Thirteen ships in the convoy were sunk by aircraft or U-boats. Mr. Eden then
said that he understood that M. Maisky had been criticising the operation. M. Maisky
denied that he had done so. Mr. Eden said that we regarded the operation of the convoy
as a great feat of arms and would deeply resent criticism on the subject. On October 8 the
Prime Minister warned Stalin that it would be impossible to send another convoy until
after the North African landings had taken place, but that ships would be sent independently during the moonless periods. The convoys would be resumed, if possible, in January
1943. At the same time the Prime Minister and the President told Stalin that they were
planning to send an Anglo-American strategic air force to serve under Russian strategic
command in the Caucasus.

(a) N5037/5/38.

matter, the most surprising expression of resentment took place in relation to British policy on the question of the punishment of war criminals.

This question had come into some prominence after a meeting of representatives of the Allied nations on January 13, 1942. The meeting adopted a resolution that war criminals should be dealt with by judicial procedure. After the meeting the Governments in exile from German-occupied countries began to press for action in (a) the matter. In July 1942 they made an official approach to the major Allies. Meanwhile during the Prime Minister's visit to the United States in June a proposal had been put forward for a United (b) Nations Commission which should collect evidence of war crimes. On August 6 the British Government communicated to the Soviet (c) and other Allied Governments certain preliminary ideas on the question. Public pressure also increased and a motion for discussion was tabled for October 7 in the House of Lords. On October 3 the (d) British Government informed the Soviet Government and other Governments concerned what they proposed to say on October 7 and invited their approval.

The Soviet Government did not answer the note of October 3; (e) all the other Governments (except the Chinese Government, whose reply was delayed) sent favourable replies. Hence on October 7 (f) Lord Simon made the proposed announcement in the House of Lords and Mr. Roosevelt issued a parallel statement in Washington. (g) On October 14, without prior consultation with the British Government or reference to earlier British communications on the subject, (h) the Soviet Government issued a declaration (in reply to the approach by the smaller Allies) setting out their views upon the question of the treatment of war criminals. In this declaration they advocated the immediate trial by an international tribunal of enemy war criminals already in Allied hands. The issue of this declaration was followed by a series of articles in the Soviet press criticising the attitude of His Majesty's Government with regard to the National Socialist leader Hess.

On October 15 Mr. Eden told M. Maisky that we did not like to (i) read in the newspapers even indirect replies to our official communications. Mr. Eden asked M. Maisky when we might expect the official reply and also instructed Sir A. Clark Kerr to do what he could to expedite matters. Mr. Eden added that there were strong technical arguments against the establishment of a special international tribunal and that Hess was not a good case on which to make a start, since he had been in England since May 10, 1941, and the

(a) C7398/61/18. (b) WP(42)277; C7182/61/18. (c) C7870, 7888/61/18. (d) C9477/61/18. (e) C9597/61/18. (f) C9700/61/18. (g) C9709/61/18. (h) C11012/61/18. (i) C9915, 9947/61/18.

worst atrocities, including all those in Russia, had been committed since that date.

On October 19 *Pravda* published an article on Hess.[1] This article (a) which, in Sir A. Clark Kerr's words, could be regarded only 'as an expression of official opinion', was 'most offensive'. The article (i) suggested that Great Britain might become a place of refuge for gangsters, (ii) dismissed the statements made in London and emphasised the wisdom of Mr. Roosevelt's declaration with the 'casuistical remark' that he said nothing about postponing trial until after the war, (iii) described the view that Hess was not liable for trial until after the war as an attempt to ignore his crimes and to regard him as an emissary of Hitler enjoying immunity in Great Britain.

Sir A. Clark Kerr thought that the article would poison the minds of the Russian people against us by giving official and pernicious colour to a myth which had already mystified and disturbed them. He considered, however, that the real purpose of the article and of the note of October 14 was to stir up public opinion in the United Kingdom against the British Government, and to play upon our fears that Russia might back out of the war or throw us over and stand alone. These possibilities were remote but could not be ignored.

Although the Foreign Office could find no special reason for this surprising attack, it was necessary to make some reply to it. Mr. Eden made a statement on October 21 in the House of Commons to the effect that (i) His Majesty's Government saw no reason for applying to Hess treatment other than that in process of elaboration by the United Nations for dealing with all war criminals, (ii) proposals for the establishment of a United Nations Commission for the investigation of war crimes had been submitted to and accepted by the United States Government and by all the Allied Governments in London; the reply of the Soviet Government was still awaited, (iii) Hess was being treated as a prisoner of war. There had not been and could not be any question of treating him as an envoy or giving him diplomatic or privileged status. Mr. Hull also stated in Washington that the United States Government did not support the Russian demand for the immediate trial of Hess.[2]

---

[1] The Tass agency issued free to the British press the full text of the article in *Pravda*. The article also appeared in *Red Star* on October 20.

[2] The Prime Minister wrote a minute to Mr. Eden on October 27 that 'it would be a great mistake to run after the Russians in their present mood; and still less to run around (b) with them chasing a chimera . . . I should treat the Russians coolly, not getting excited about the lies they tell, but going steadily on with our task. You must remember the Bolsheviks have undermined so many powerful Governments by lying, machine-made propaganda, and they probably think they make some impression on us by these methods.'

(a) C10029/61/18. (b) PMM 494/2.

On October 22 Mr. Eden told M. Maisky that he had read the (a)
Pravda article with astonishment and keen displeasure. The language
used about this country was intolerable between Allies. Mr. Eden
asked what the Russians would have said if we had shown one-tenth
such discourtesy. The War Cabinet decided on October 29 to
instruct Sir A. Clark Kerr to deliver a message personally to Stalin (b)
protesting against the *Pravda* article and reminding him that the
Soviet Government had not replied to the British communication of
October 3. Sir A. Clark Kerr was told to try to find out what were
the real Russian grievances. On the same day the British Government addressed a note to all the Governments concerned (including (c)
the Soviet Government) setting out their views on the functions and
constitution of the proposed United Nations Commission for the
investigation of war crimes.

The Soviet Government replied to this note and to the note of (d)
October 3 before Sir A. Clark Kerr had been able to see Stalin.
They claimed that the note of October 3 had not reached them
before October 6 and that they were unable to send a reply in time
for the parliamentary statement of October 7. They also repeated
their view that any leaders of Fascist Germany who might fall into
Allied hands during the war should be handed over at once for trial
by an international tribunal. For this reason the Soviet Government
regarded the British proposal as inadequate. They made no reference
to the obvious argument that their proposal for immediate trial
would certainly lead to the most savage reprisals by the Germans
against Allied prisoners of war.

Sir A. Clark Kerr delivered the British message to Stalin and
Molotov on November 5. The conversation lasted nearly two hours; (e)
M. Molotov's part in it was only to try to discredit the British case.
After a long bickering on the Russian side over the question of the
date on which the note of October 3 reached the Soviet Embassy,[1]
Sir A. Clark Kerr was able to introduce the subject of the *Pravda*
article. Stalin tried to divert the conversation by talking about the
delays which would result from the establishment of a United
Nations Commission. He then said that the *Pravda* article expressed
only the views of the newspaper, and not that of the Soviet Government. In any case the article was about Hess, and was not an attack
on Great Britain or on the British Government. Stalin appeared not
to know much about the article; Sir A. Clark Kerr noticed that when
he began to study it he 'dropped it like a hot potato'.

---

[1] The Foreign Office held a receipt to the effect that the note was delivered at the
Soviet Embassy at 2.53 p.m. on October 3.

(a) N5567/5272/38. (b) WM(42)147; N5566/5272/38. (c) C10375/61/18. (d) C10710,
12299/61/18. (e) C10718/61/18.

(a)   Sir A. Clark Kerr then read to Stalin a full statement about Hess which had been telegraphed to him by the Foreign Office. Stalin claimed that he had seen all the information in the press, but Sir A. Clark Kerr thought that he was in fact impressed by the statement and that he really had been afraid that the British Government might send Hess back to Germany. At all events Stalin concluded by saying that he wanted the British and Russian Governments to agree, and that Hess 'was not worth all this trouble'.

(b)   This was not the end of the matter. On November 12 the Soviet Government presented another memorandum repeating their previous charges, including the non-delivery of the note on October 3. The British Government replied to the note on December 11. The reply dealt only with the questions of principle relating to the trial of war criminals. Sir A. Cadogan dealt verbally with the other matters in the Soviet note when he gave the reply to M. Maisky. On the main subject the British note laid down at considerable length the views held at the time by the British Government, i.e. that the punishment of the chief enemy leaders should be decided, as a political question, jointly by the United Nations at the end of the war, and that the criminals of less importance should be tried in the domestic courts of the countries concerned.

(a) WP(42)502; C10635/61/18. (b) C12299/61/18.

CHAPTER XXVIII

The British attitude towards the Vichy Government from February, 1942, to the Allied landings in North Africa

(i)

The transport of supplies to Axis forces in Libya in French ships: proposed British note to Vichy: American demand for assurances from the Vichy Government (January–February 1942).

WITH the entry of the United States into the war the British Government had to assess the probable attitude of the Vichy Government to a new situation. Hitherto British policy towards Vichy had been concerned mainly with the immediate problem of limiting the amount of French assistance to the Axis Powers. This factor was still of great importance, but there might seem to be some chance now that the French would take encouragement from the unexpected German failure to break Russian resistance, and, above all, from the knowledge that the appeal which France had made in 1940 was at last being answered; there was now 'light at the end of the tunnel'[1] and the immense resources of the United States were available for the liberation of Europe.

The Prime Minister was inclined to look forward to a change of mind—and heart—at Vichy after the Allies had regained the initiative. He shared the general British view of the behaviour of Marshal Pétain and his Government since the armistice, but he was prepared to make a certain allowance, half-contemptuous, half-sympathetic for men in their situation who had committed a terrible blunder and could not easily extricate themselves from its consequences. Mr. Churchill was also by temperament a leader of resistance movements; he expected more pressure on Vichy at this stage from French opinion, especially in France and North Africa, than seemed likely to the Foreign Office, at all events from the information which they received. The Foreign Office did not look for anything good from any of the Vichy cliques. Marshal Pétain obstinately hoped that the Germans would allow the French to manoeuvre themselves, within the limits of the armistice, into a kind of neutrality. In view of Darlan's hatred of England, and concessions to Germany

---

[1] See Volume I, p. 258, note 1.

in 1941, the British Government could not trust his assurances about the French fleet. Darlan indeed had gone too far for most of his colleagues, or rivals, and the result of his policy had been to lose Syria for Vichy. On the other hand the Germans would not tolerate *attentisme* at Vichy; they held Laval in reserve, and would reinstate him in office if the Vichy Government showed signs of independent action. Admiral Leahy, at the end of 1941, thought that Darlan was beginning to have doubts about a complete German victory. Laval had no such doubts, or gave no sign of having them. At the least he expected the Germans to be able to negotiate a peace more favourable in the long run to themselves than to Great Britain; hence the permanent interests of France required not only submission but active collaboration with Germany. After the German attack on Russia Laval regarded a German victory as necessary to France, since the alternative would be the spread of Communism over Europe.

In these circumstances the Foreign Office found nothing to be gained by softness towards Vichy. Moreover from the autumn of 1941 French opinion generally was becoming more critical of the official policy of collaboration. The Germans had made few concessions to French opinion since the armistice. They had continued to use the French prisoners of war in their hands as a means of exercising pressure on the Vichy Government. Their financial treatment of France was harsh and, according to the terms of the Hague Convention of 1907, illegal.[1] Hitler had withdrawn, at least temporarily, his plans for large annexations of French territory,[2] but the Germans were already putting into effect administrative measures with the obvious intention of 'Germanising' as well as re-incorporating Alsace-Lorraine. Above all the Germans had reverted to type in the ferocity with which they were replying to sporadic acts of sabotage and attacks on individual members of their armed forces. Such attacks—as part of a deliberate plan of resistance—began after the volte-face of the French Communist party.[3] The German answer

---

[1] The scale and scope of payments exacted for the maintenance of the German army of occupation went far beyond the conditions laid down in the Convention. The Germans had also fixed the French rate of exchange at a figure which made it profitable for the army of occupation, and civilian officials, to buy consumption goods on a large scale and send them to Germany.

[2] Goebbels noted in his *Diary* on April 30, 1942, that 'if the French knew what the Führer intended to demand from them, their eyes would be opened wider', and that it was better for the time to keep silent about the German demands.

[3] Until the German attack on Russia, the French Communists had continued to denounce the 'imperialist' war and to recommend Franco-German collaboration on the analogy of the Russo-German treaty. After their change of policy the Communists were able to start organised resistance more quickly because they already had an underground organisation. Their change of attitude included an attempt, for propaganda purposes, to show themselves as the centre of resistance even before the Franco-German armistice. The Germans themselves, by asserting that the whole of the resistance movement was Communist, gave the Communist Party a kind of alibi for their former defeatism.

was to carry out (as elsewhere) savage reprisals against hostages on an increasingly large scale. The Vichy Government protested against these reprisals, but nonetheless continued their collaboration. Hence there was little left of the Marshal's pathetic claim to be standing between the French people and their conquerors. As French resistance increased the Vichy regime would become more isolated and discredited, and would be held responsible by Frenchmen not for saving them from the worst consequences of defeat but for connivance with German cruelty and oppression.

The British Government had no official relations with the Vichy Government; their only chance of exercising diplomatic pressures was through American action. In a sense, the British attitude towards France became something of a problem in Anglo-American relations, and particularly on the moral issue. The Americans had not suffered directly from the capitulation of France; they tended to make greater allowance for the circumstances in which this surrender had been made. They also set much more store than the Foreign Office on the possibility of obtaining some action by Vichy in their favour when they landed in North Africa and Metropolitan France. On the British view they had exaggerated, before their entry into the war, their own prestige and popularity with the French. They failed to see that the stubborn delusions of Marshal Pétain and the legalism by which the French High Command and most of the armed forces held to their allegiance to the Marshal as the Head of the French State would prevent any organised official resistance until it could have little more than a token value. Above all, the Americans, from the distance of Washington, did not understand—as the Darlan episode was to show—that an attempt to buy the last-minute support of collaborationists and quislings would offend not only French feeling, but the feeling of other European peoples who had suffered from German methods of warfare and occupation, and yet, unlike Vichy, had refused to come to profitable terms with them.[1]

As far as the treatment of Vichy was concerned, the difference between British and American policy in 1942 was mainly one of emphasis. On the need to prevent the Vichy Government from going beyond a strict interpretation of the armistice terms in their collaboration with the Germans, the United States Government felt as strongly as the British Government. Their language was rather milder, and they were always concerned to keep open their contacts with North Africa, but they left the French in no doubt of what the

---

[1] It is significant that Admiral Leahy, though he does not hide his contempt for the persistent intrigues at Vichy, gives no indication in his account (*I Was There*, Gollancz, 1950) of his mission to the Vichy Government that he realised why the British and other European Allies felt so deeply about the moral offence of French collaborationism.

(a) United States expected from them. The President telegraphed to Mr. Churchill on January 29, 1942, that nine days earlier he had sent to Admiral Leahy, United States Ambassador at Vichy, some notes for use in conversation with Marshal Pétain. The President wished to remind Marshal Pétain that the French Government and people must realise that he (the President) was about the best friend they had, and that in speaking of 'France' he included the French Colonial Empire. On the other hand any act by the French which gave the Germans and Italians 'aid and comfort' must harm the United States. The United States could not take such hostile action 'lying down'. The President said that the acquiescence of the Vichy Government in a German or Italian attack on unoccupied France or the French colonies would be playing the German game, while French resistance would seem to be 'normal and natural' and would have all possible American military and naval support.

Admiral Leahy spoke to Marshal Pétain on these lines, and in the presence of Admiral Darlan and M. Rochat.[1] Marshal Pétain said that the French would resist invasion by any one—Gaullist, German, British or American—and that there was no question of the use of the French fleet in a manner hostile to the United States, or of allowing Germany to use French bases in North Africa at the present time. Admiral Leahy's conclusion from the Marshal's remarks was that the Vichy Government would refuse to co-operate with the United States if the Germans attempted to move into French North Africa.

Nevertheless the question of Vichy 'aid and comfort' to the Axis arose at once in view of evidence reaching the British and United States Governments that French ships were being used to bring
(b) supplies from Metropolitan France to the Axis forces in Libya. The President telegraphed to the Prime Minister on February 10[2] that he had sent on that day a message through Admiral Leahy to Marshal Pétain that information to this effect had been received in the United States. The President once more made it clear that the United States Government realised the limitations set by the
(c) armistice upon the freedom of the Vichy Ministers. He then stated that if the French Government were to ship war materials or supplies to the Axis Powers and to render assistance to these Powers or to take any action which they were not bound to take under the terms of the armistice, they would place themselves in the category of governments directly assisting the declared enemies of the United States. Unless, therefore, the French Government gave formal assurances

---

[1] Secretary-General at the French Foreign Office. For the President's message and Admiral Leahy's interview, see *F.R.U.S.*, 1942, II, 123–6. For other Franco-American exchanges referred to in this section, see *F.R.U.S.*, *id.*, 126–147.
[2] The President's message was transmitted to the Prime Minister through the United States Embassy on February 12.

(a) T139/2, Churchill Papers/471; Z1066/175/17. (b) Z1332/175/17. (c) Z2309/28/17.

that no such aid would be given to Germany, Italy and Japan, and that French ships would not usefully help those countries in their acts of aggression, the United States Government would recall their Ambassador for consultation with regard to American policy towards France.

Lord Halifax reported on the night of February 14–15 that the (a) State Department were somewhat concerned at receiving no immediate reply from Marshal Pétain. They were afraid that the Vichy Government, when faced with the demand for a clear indication of their policy, might decide definitely to throw in their lot with Germany, and that they might be making arrangements for placing the French fleet at the disposal of the Germans. The Foreign Office, however, thought it more likely that the Vichy Government were merely taking time to consider their answer. In fact Marshal Pétain sent a reply in a note dated February 16. A paraphrase of this reply (b) was shown to Lord Halifax and was telegraphed by him to the Foreign Office on the night of February 19–20. Marshal Pétain spoke of his surprise at receiving the message after the very complete information which he and Admiral Darlan had given to the United States Ambassador on February 9. They had then said that in January French ships had carried only 1,029 tons of food supplies and 56 Italian lorries to Libya. Admiral Leahy had been assured that these shipments did not include war material or oil. Marshal Pétain considered that this information should have been sufficient to show that shipments were of negligible proportions and to put a stop to the campaign launched in London, on the basis of false reports, with the obvious intention of making the French Government a scapegoat for the British reverses in Libya. The United States Government should also remember that the French Government were bound to alleviate, where possible, the hardships imposed on France by the armistice and that they were obliged at times to accept certain adjustments in order to obtain equivalent advantages. France would maintain her neutrality in the war; it would be easier for the French Government if the United States Government would show some comprehension of the French position.

In telegraphing the text of the French note to Washington Admiral Leahy added his opinion that Marshal Pétain, and Frenchmen generally, were anxious to remain on good terms with the United States but that the note did not give the assurances for which the President had asked. The Foreign Office regarded the note—in which Darlan's hand was evident—as impertinent and evasive. Lord Halifax reported that the United States Government also considered it unsatisfactory; they were proposing to recall Admiral Leahy, and

---

(a) Z1331/28/17. (b) Z1513, 1517/28/17.

to instruct him to make it clear that, if the precise assurances required by the United States were not forthcoming before he left Vichy, American policy would be affected accordingly.

(a)   On February 21 Lord Halifax informed Mr. Eden that the President had instructed Admiral Leahy on February 19 to give an oral message to Marshal Pétain. In this message the President said that he did not lack understanding or sympathy for France in her present predicament. He noted with satisfaction that the French Government had maintained and would maintain the position of neutrality in which, subject to the terms of the armistice, France had been placed since June 1940. The President, however, had asked for official assurances that France would give no further military aid to Germany, Italy, or Japan. Marshal Pétain's reply contained no such assurances.

The President said that the United States had become engaged in a war in which thirty-seven nations were siding against the Axis. The United Nations would inevitably gain a final and complete victory. The President hoped that there need be no change in American policy towards France in her existing difficulties and tragic situation, but there must be a change if the French Government followed a policy of open assistance to the Axis beyond the terms of the armistice. Hence the President was asking Admiral Leahy to return for consultation (leaving a Chargé d'Affaires at Vichy). He looked for the assurances requested in his note of February 10 before Admiral Leahy left France.

(b)   Meanwhile, on February 16, the War Cabinet had approved a draft notification to the Vichy Government to the effect (i) that six named French ships, known to be carrying military supplies from French ports for the use of our enemies in the field, and any other French ships similarly employed would be attacked without further warning if met by British naval or air forces anywhere in the Mediterranean; (ii) that all shipping in waters off Tunisia was under suspicion, and that the responsibility would not be with His Majesty's Government if '*bona fide* French ships' were attacked in these waters by day or night.

The War Cabinet approved of this draft subject to the agreement

(c) of the United States. Lord Halifax discussed the draft with the State Department towards the end of February, but for the time being—owing to their own approach to Marshal Pétain—they delayed giving an answer. Meanwhile the Foreign Office had received reports that enemy submarines had refuelled at Martinique; these reports were transmitted to the United States with the suggestion that they should take strong action in the matter with Vichy.

(a) Z1546/28/17. (b) WM(42)21; WP(42)86; Z1504/880/17. (c) Z1768/28/17.

On the night of February 24–5 Lord Halifax reported that Admiral (a)
Leahy had delivered the President's message on the evening of
February 21 and that the Marshal would send a written reply.
Admiral Darlan had said to Admiral Leahy that French ships were
no longer carrying lorries to Tunisia. Admiral Leahy understood,
however, that shipments of food supplies had not been stopped. The
Marshal apparently gave an affirmative reply to the question whether
his written answer would contain the required assurance. Mr. Welles
had told Lord Halifax that if the United States Government received
these assurances, they would not recall Admiral Leahy, but on
February 24 Mr. Atherton seemed to doubt whether the Vichy
Government would offer assurances which the United States could
regard as satisfactory. The Foreign Office also considered that, if
Marshal Pétain gave the assurances, he would do so either because
Admiral Darlan had made arrangements to get round them or
because most of the material urgently needed by the Germans had
already been transported. It was possible that no more Italian lorries
were available for transport in French ships.

Admiral Leahy received Marshal Pétain's written reply on
February 24; Lord Halifax transmitted a summary of it from
Washington on the night of February 27–8. The French Government (b)
reaffirmed their intention, under the reserve of their armistice
obligations, to abstain from any action not in conformity with the
position of neutrality in which France had been placed since June
1940. They would not therefore give military assistance to any of the
belligerents in any theatre of operations, or allow the use of French
ships for war purposes; still less would they adopt a policy of open
assistance to the Axis Powers beyond the terms of the armistice. In
return for these assurances Marshal Pétain claimed the right to
expect from the American people a spirit of comprehension and
desire for agreement. In particular the French Government hoped
for the resumption of maritime traffic and of supplies to North Africa
(under the conditions originally stipulated); they also looked for a
satisfactory settlement of the St. Pierre–Miquelon incident and for
respect to the rights and interests of France in various parts of the
world. They hoped that the United States Government would put
a stop at once to the 'violent and tendentious' press and radio
campaign against the French Government.

The United States Embassy at Vichy had asked for a closer
definition of the assurances. They were told—as a personal opinion
of M. Rochat—that shipments of munitions would not be permitted;
that the shipment of lorries was doubtful, but that under international law a neutral was permitted to send supplies and foodstuffs

---

(a) Z1673/28/17. (b) Z1745/28/17.

to a belligerent. Mr. Welles said to Sir R. Campbell[1] that the United States Government would take the French assurances at their face value but would insist that all supplies to the Axis must cease, and that the question of the resumption of American supplies to North Africa must await the settlement of a number of other matters. Sir R. Campbell commented on the contradiction in the Marshal's note between the references to the terms of the armistice and to French neutrality; he asked whether the United States Government regarded France as a neutral or as in a state of suspended belligerency. Mr. Welles said that he considered Vichy as a belligerent under the armistice and as obliged to refuse to do anything outside the strict terms of this instrument. Mr. Welles said also that he wanted to gain time and to avoid a break with the Vichy Government, but that the United States Government were determined to hold them to the observance of the armistice terms.[2]

The Foreign Office considered Marshal Pétain's reply less bad-tempered and impertinent than the earlier message: they agreed

(a) also with Mr. Welles's handling of the matter. Lord Halifax reported on the night of February 28–March 1 that Mr. Welles thought our proposed note of warning to the Vichy Government most undesirable in view of the 'delicate' Franco-American negotiations. The Foreign Office regarded it as necessary to defer to Mr. Welles's opinion though they disagreed with it, and thought that our proposed action would in fact make matters easier for the United States; hence they proposed to raise the matter again later with Mr. Welles. The Admiralty took a similar view. The War Cabinet therefore decided

(b) on March 9 to hold up the note.

(ii)

Further negotiations between the United States Government and Vichy on the American terms for the resumption of supplies from the United States to French North Africa (March 5–April 14, 1942).

(c)   During the night of March 5–6 Lord Halifax reported that Admiral Leahy had been instructed to reply to Marshal Pétain on the lines indicated by Mr. Welles. The Foreign Office asked Lord Halifax to try to get from the State Department a full summary of their

---

[1] Minister in the British Embassy at Washington.

(d)   [2] On February 27 Mr. Welles summarised at a press conference the negotiations with the French and stated the desire of the United States Government for a further clarification of other important questions.

(a) Z1768/28/17. (b) WM(42) 32. (c) Z1745/28/17. (d) Z2309/28/17.

reply, and in particular, to find out whether the reply mentioned the questions awaiting settlement before the shipment of American supplies to North Africa were resumed. They suggested that the United States Government might ask the French to specify the articles of the armistice which they claimed to regard as covering the despatch of supplies for the Axis forces in Libya.

Lord Halifax replied on the night of March 12–13 that the (a) American reply had been shown to a member of his staff. The reply noted the assurances given by the French, and stated that in the American view the shipment of food, fuel, lorries and other supplies to the Axis forces in North Africa and other theatres of operations constituted 'military aid'. The United States Government therefore required further assurances on these matters before they discussed other questions with the French Government.

Lord Halifax pointed out that the reply did not mention the resumption of supplies to North Africa, but that the French Ambassador at Washington had been told that until the French Government had given satisfactory answers on the shipment of supplies to the Axis forces, the removal of the *Dunkerque*,[1] and the visit of a German submarine to Martinique, there could be no consideration of the resumption of shipments from the United States to North Africa. Lord Halifax also said that the State Department did not think that the Vichy Government maintained that they were obliged under the armistice to ship supplies to North Africa; their argument was that they were entitled to do so as neutrals.

In another telegram of the night of March 12–13 Lord Halifax (b) reported that Admiral Leahy had telegraphed on March 10 that in the temporary absence from Vichy of Marshal Pétain and Admiral

---

[1] On April 8, 1941, the Vichy Government had informed the United States Embassy at Vichy that they would delay the departure of the French battle-cruiser *Dunkerque* from Oran 'until the conclusion of an agreement in the subject' (see above, p. 63, n.1). M. Rochat gave his personal assurance that the plan for moving the *Dunkerque* had been given up for the time being. He promised that he would let the United States Embassy know of any change of intention. On February 19, 1942, in breach of this promise, the (c) *Dunkrque*, escorted by two destroyers and two submarines, sailed from Oran. Two days later an announcement was issued in Vichy that she had reached Toulon.

The United States Ambassador at Vichy was instructed to take the matter up with Admiral Darlan. On February 27, the latter told Admiral Leahy that the understanding had been conditional on the supply by the United States of foodstuffs to unoccupied France and North Africa, and on arrangements being made to prevent the British Navy from interfering with legitimate French shipping. The United States had not carried out their side of the bargain, and therefore he did not regard the understanding as binding on France. Admiral Darlan said that the *Dunkerque* would take approximately two years to repair at Toulon and would 'therefore be unavailable for the duration of the war'. If she had remained at Oran, she would have suffered progressive deterioration, and her value would have been permanently destroyed. British Admiralty experts, however, estimated that the ship would be ready for active service in about nine months from the date of her arrival in Toulon. See *F.R.U.S.*, 1942, II, 204–9.

(a) Z2159/28/17. (b) Z2161/28/17. (c) Z1584, 1894, 1967, 2587/21/17.

Darlan, the reply to the latest American note would be delayed. M. Rochat, however, had given the impression that the Vichy Government would not send any more shipments to the Axis forces in Libya. He said that some small shipments of a few tons of food and six or eight (*sic*) tankers were in course of delivery and could not be stopped. About 1,000 tons of the original 3,600 tons of oil had already been delivered; the French Government had approached the Italian Government with a view to preventing the shipment of the remaining 2,000 tons. They had argued that Italian insistence on delivery would endanger the future of the American economic programme to North Africa; they appeared also to have given the Italians to understand that, if the matter were settled quickly to the satisfaction of the United States Government, there was a possibility of a quick resumption of shipments from the United States to North Africa.

(a)   Admiral Leahy received two notes from Admiral Darlan on March 14 in reply to the American note requiring further assurances. The French Government gave the required assurances, but excepted from them the delivery of the remaining balance of food supplies and lorries still in transit. They repeated their demand for a contribution from the United States towards an understanding, and asked, in particular, for the resumption of supplies to North Africa, a settlement of the St. Pierre–Miquelon question, respect for the rights and interests of France throughout the world, and the cessation of the 'tendentious' press and radio campaign. Admiral Darlan's reply stated that the French Government had consulted the Germans, and had obtained their permission to give the assurances.

(b)   The second French note dealt in detail with the question of petrol. The note stated that certain deliveries of French petroleum products had been made to Libya as the result of requests from the Axis Governments at a time when the United States Government had suspended the execution of their programme of supplies to French North Africa. In March 1941 the Italians had demanded 5,000 tons of automobile petrol from Algeria; the French Government had refused the request on the ground that the United States was supplying North Africa with petrol. They had not now been able to use this argument. In view, however, of the receipt of an assurance from the United States Government regarding the resumption of supplies to North Africa, the French Government had appealed to the Axis Powers to be allowed to cancel the delivery of petrol beyond the exacted quantity of 3,600 tons. This appeal had been accepted, and the French were willing to make another approach with a view to

(a) Z2415/28/17. (b) Z2418/28/17.

the cancellation of the balance (about 1,580 tons) if they could say that American supplies of petrol were actually being resumed.[1]

On March 19, at the invitation of the State Department, Sir R. (a) Campbell and other members of the Embassy staff attended a meeting to discuss the question of supplies to North Africa. The American view was that the various assurances received from Vichy were sufficient to justify an experimental resumption of shipments to North Africa on a limited scale and that two French ships now at New York should be allowed to sail. Lord Halifax telegraphed on the night of March 21–2 that his staff had pointed out to the State (b) Department the contradiction between the assurances in the first French note that no further supplies other than those already in transit would be delivered to the Axis forces in Libya and the offer in the second note to try to get—on terms—the cancellation of the delivery of the balance of the original 3,600 tons. It was also pointed out that the reference to the receipt of assurances about the resumption of American supplies was premature and that there was a discrepancy between the figures given in the second note and those supplied by M. Rochat.

On March 23 President Roosevelt explained in a personal telegram (c) to the Prime Minister that he had been considering whether, as part of the United Nations effort, it might not be desirable to resume the programme of limited economic assistance to French North Africa, and also send more Red Cross aid to children in France. Mr. Roosevelt thought that the success of recent bombing operations, such as the attack on the Renault works,[2] must have brought home to the French people the fact that they were still in the war, and would thereby have weakened the case of the collaborationists. It would however be useful to supplement our own case by another method. At a time when the United Nations were preparing to forestall the enemy by force in various areas it seemed important to try to hold the Axis off from other areas by psychological and economic weapons. If the French went over to the Axis, we should also lose the Iberian Peninsula. The American observers in North Africa and the American Mission at Vichy were getting very important military and strategic information. If we wished to hold this remaining bridgehead to Europe as long as it served our purpose, we should reinforce our position by means of limited economic aid, and not just abandon the field to the Germans.

---

[1] See *F.R.U.S.*, *ib*, 148–50.
[2] The Renault factories, in the suburbs of Paris, were supplying war material to the Germans. They were bombed by the R.A.F. on the night of March 3–4.

(a) Z2411/68/17. (b) Z2453/28/17. (c) T448/2 No. 126 (Churchill Papers/187).

(a)   The Prime Minister suggested that we should tell the President that we did not object to the despatch of limited quantities of food to North Africa if the American observers retained their freedom of observation in the country. On the other hand nothing should be done to interfere with our Madagascar operation,[1] and the United States Government must not accept French assurances in such a way that the Vichy Government might be enabled to complain later of a breach of faith. Mr. Churchill also thought that we could now ask the President to allow us—when we landed at Madagascar—to drop leaflets explaining that the expedition was a joint Anglo-American, and not solely a British operation.

(b)   Mr. Eden agreed with the Prime Minister's view; he thought that we should insist on the condition that we received compensatory advantages in securing control of strategic materials at present going to Germany. He told the Prime Minister that he had been considering a scheme for sending milk concentrates to children in occupied territories generally. He could not yet begin to discuss this scheme with the Americans who would be asked to provide the milk, but he thought it better that supplies to unoccupied France should be brought within the general scheme, since children there were probably better off than in some other occupied territories. Mr. Eden suggested that, if the President gave economic help to the French, he should announce our agreement to it. Otherwise our enemies would say that the Americans sent milk, while we sent bombs.

(c)   After this exchange of views between the Prime Minister and Mr. Eden a meeting with representatives of the Admiralty and the Ministry of Economic Warfare was held on March 24 at the Foreign Office. These representatives agreed with the Foreign Office view that the State Department should insist upon applying to the French the requirements already laid down in the cases of Spain and Portugal, i.e. that deliveries from the Allies should depend on counter-deliveries of strategic materials to the United States or to Great Britain. They also wished to delay the resumption of supplies to North Africa until the Vichy Government had agreed to deal satisfactorily with the treatment of British subjects in French Morocco.

Lord Halifax was therefore instructed on March 25 that, if the United States could obtain complete satisfaction on the question of supplies to Libya, we should not object to the shipment of very limited quantities of 'navicerted' supplies to French North Africa on the condition that American observers could fulfil their duties in the country freely and that we secured compensatory advantages in the

---

[1] See below Chapter XXIX, section (ii).

(a) M106/2 (loc. cit.). (b) P.M.42/54 (loc. cit.) (c) Z2418/28/17.

form of control of strategic materials at present going to Germany. On the other hand the acceptance of the terms laid down by the Vichy Government would be dangerous to our war effort. We earnestly hoped that the United States Government would refuse them. Vichy was not entitled to suggest conditions under which shipments to North Africa should be resumed. The American and British Governments—not Vichy—were the givers, and were demanding that supplies to the Axis should cease before the resumption of American shipments was considered. We therefore wished to urge on the State Department that they should insist on a complete cessation of oil supplies to Libya—without regard to any alleged commitment to deliver a further 1,580 tons—before agreeing to allow the two Vichy ships now at New York to sail to North Africa.

In addition to the instructions to Lord Halifax the Prime Minister (a) sent a message to the President on March 27 in similar terms. He said that we did not mind 'your sending very limited quantities of supplies to French North Africa provided the American observers can penetrate the country freely, especially if you could get the compensatory advantages in securing the control of strategic materials now going to Germany'.

'We value your contacts with Vichy and it is well worth paying a price for them, but please nothing must interfere with Operation Ironclad [i.e. Madagascar] to which we are now committed, and no assurances by the French about defending their Empire like they did Indo-China should be accepted by the United States in such a way as to enable them to complain of a breach of faith.'[1]

The instructions to Lord Halifax crossed a telegram in which he (b) reported that Admiral Leahy had been instructed to reply to the French note of March 14. In the reply the United States Government noted with satisfaction the French assurances that their agreement not to provide military assistance to the Axis forces included the delivery and transport of supplies of any origin whatsoever; that no exception was contemplated to the agreement and that arrangements were being made to put a stop to any further delivery of petroleum products.

---

[1] The rest of the message was about Madagascar. Mr. Churchill asked whether we could drop leaflets referring to the expedition as Anglo-American. The President refused (c) this proposal on April 3. He said that his reason for refusal was that 'we [the United States] are the only nation that can intervene diplomatically with any hope of success with Vichy and it seems to me extremely important that we are able to do this without the complications which might arise by the dropping of leaflets or other informal methods in connection with your operation'. Mr. Churchill telegraphed his agreement on April 4. (d) See below, p. 327, note 1.

(a) T484/2, No. 59, Churchill Papers/265. (b) Z2528/28/17. (c) T530/2, Churchill Papers/265. (d) T532/2, Churchill Papers/265.

The note continued with a statement that the United States Government were confident that the assurances thus given represented the true feelings of the people of France; they were prepared to pursue the existing arrangements for the North African supply programme and to allow the two ships at New York to leave with cargoes under the same conditions as before; further sailings would depend on the settlement of the problems presented by the existence in North Africa of certain strategic raw materials such as cobalt and rubber.

With regard to the other questions raised in the French note the United States Government replied that their desire to maintain French sovereignty had been made clear many times. The United States Government fully respected French rights and interests; their announced intention to respect the sovereignty exercised by the French people (in the case of)[1] their various possessions should be clear evidence that the United States Government looked towards the restoration of the complete independence and sovereignty of the French people. The French people would appreciate that this declaration represented a recognition of their (? future)[2] rights and independence and that it conformed to the traditions of friendship and solidarity which bound the people of the two countries.

(a)   On March 24 Mr. Welles told Lord Halifax that the United States Government were now reasonably satisfied with the assurances received from Vichy concerning the western hemisphere, the French fleet, and supplies to the Axis. Mr. Welles said that in these circumstances the President had reached the decision recorded in the note to the French Government, and had decided also to go ahead with the economic programme for Spain.

(b)   Lord Halifax telegraphed that the State Department, 'spurred on no doubt by the White House', had acted more quickly than the British Embassy had expected. The Embassy had assumed, especially in view of the question of the treatment of British subjects in Morocco, that nothing would have been said to the French until the views of the British Government had been received. Mr. Welles, however, appeared to have refused to link the question of supplies with that of the treatment of British subjects, but was intending to send vigorous instructions to Admiral Leahy on the latter question.

The Foreign Office view was that the American reply, though not particularly good, might have been worse. There was no mention of

---

[1] These words were doubtful in the original text. *F.R.U.S.*, 1942, II, 152 gives 'over the various possessions of France'.

[2] These words were doubtful in the original text. *F.R.U.S.*, *ib*, confirms 'future'.

(a) Z2541/28/17. (b) Z2507/28/17.

St. Pierre and Miquelon among the counter-assurances for which Admiral Darlan had asked; the repeated mention of the French people would not be liked by Vichy and the declaration about American intentions referred to the future. On the other hand it was unfortunate that the United States Government had not tried to clear up the ambiguities about oil in the French notes.

The Foreign Office therefore instructed Lord Halifax on March 27 to ask whether the United States Government would insist on satisfaction over the oil question before allowing the two ships to sail from New York, and also whether they agreed with our view that they were not committed to accept all of Admiral Darlan's conditions. The enquiry was repeated to Lord Halifax on April 3. It (a) was pointed out to him that we must know exactly how far the Americans regarded themselves as committed to a policy of respecting French interests, territorial and otherwise, with all that such a policy might imply in the restriction of our own freedom of action.

Lord Halifax had reported on the night of April 1–2 that the (b) State Department had been considering our representations about the further shipments of oil. They also had information from Admiral Leahy that Marshal Pétain was resisting German pressure on him to restore Laval.[1] Mr. Welles therefore thought it unwise to compel the French to refer the oil question to the Armistice Commission; he wanted to strengthen the non-collaborationists by letting them have the two North African shipments quickly.

The Foreign Office also telegraphed on April 2 to Lord Halifax a (c) report which had reached them that the French battleships *Richelieu* and three cruisers (*Georges Leygues, Gloire* and *Montcalm*) were to leave Dakar for France on April 3. Since the United States Government had not insisted upon getting assurances about the *Dunkerque* before the resumption of supplies to North Africa, the Vichy leaders might assume that they could safely move the *Richelieu*. Lord Halifax was therefore instructed to inform the State Department of the very serious view which we should take of an attempt to move the *Richelieu* or the *Jean Bart* into the Mediterranean. We hoped that the State Department would ask for definite assurances that neither ship would be moved, and that they would not allow the two Vichy cargo ships to leave United States ports until such assurances had been received. Lord Halifax was also instructed to say that we could

---

[1] On March 27, on receiving information of a meeting between Marshal Pétain and Laval and of Laval's probable return to office, the United States Government warned Marshal Pétain that they would regard the return to power of Laval or ayone else 'so notoriously and completely identified with a policy of supine subservience to Germany' as a sign that the French Government could not carry out its assurances to the United States. *F.R.U.S., ib,* 160.

(a) Z2695/28/17. (b) Z2762/28/17. (c) Z2787/21/17.

not agree to allow Vichy to fulfil their alleged contract and to deliver a balance of 1,580 tons of oil to our enemies in the field. Nevertheless we would leave the decision in the matter to the State Department.

Meanwhile, in spite of their wish to avoid a complete break with Vichy, the United States Government held up the two ships for
(a) another reason. On March 28 Admiral Leahy addressed a note to the Vichy Ministry of Foreign Affairs stating that, if the State Department had known that the French in Africa were refuelling Axis aircraft, they would have hesitated to agree to the resumption of supplies to North Africa. They would, however, await further information on the facts before reconsidering their decision. The French authorities replied on April 2 that five Italian aeroplanes had landed on March 7 at the airfield of Algiers (Maison Blanche) and that, in order to get them away, they had been given about 2,200 gallons of fuel—the minimum necessary for their return flight to Italy. The French had protested to the Italian Armistice Commission at Turin about the incident.
(b)　　The State Department issued a public statement on April 7 to the effect that satisfactory assurances had been received from the Vichy Government and that the two French vessels in New York would now be allowed to sail with 'limited supplies' for North Africa. On the
(c) night of April 9–10 however, Lord Halifax reported that, according to Mr. Atherton, the United States Government had not agreed to Admiral Darlan's conditions or accepted any fresh commitments towards Vichy or in respect of French possessions overseas. The American attitude remained unchanged, i.e. while respecting French sovereignty they intended to deal on a *de facto* basis with the authorities —whoever they might be—actually exercising control in the different territories. They had shown this policy in their recent statement about French Equatorial Africa.[1] Mr. Atherton thought, however, that the Vichy Government were under increasingly severe pressure from Germany, and that, if they were to survive at all, they might soon be obliged to give way to a greater extent to this pressure. The State Department wanted to postpone such a surrender as long as possible but in his (Mr. Atherton's) opinion they were fighting a losing battle. They had already made their own relations with Vichy
(d) more difficult by appointing a Consul-General at Brazzaville in accordance with the policy (which they had announced at the end

---

[1] The United States Government had announced on April 4 their decision to set up a Consulate-General at Brazzaville. The announcement contained the sentence: 'As has been previously stated, this Government has treated with the French authorities in effective control of French territories in Africa, and will continue to treat with them on the basis of their actual administration of the territories involved.'

(a) Z3286/28/17. (b) Z2967/28/17. (c) Z3033/28/17. (d) Z1925/14/17; Z2855/2678/17.

of February in relation to French islands in the Pacific)[1] that they would deal with the Free French National Committee in matters affecting the defence of territories under the effective control of the Committee and of strategic importance to the United States.

This limited acceptance of the status of the Free French territories was very far from the comprehensive recognition for which General de Gaulle continued to ask. Nonetheless the Vichy Government protested against it. The State Department sent a stiff note of reply (a) to the French Ambassador at Washington. The note pointed out that France could be restored only by the complete defeat of Germany; a fact which must be known even to those who had 'sordidly and abjectly, under the guise of "collaboration", attempted to prostitute their country to the regime in Germany which is bent upon nothing less than the permanent enslavement of France'. The reason for the American action was that the Vichy Government were not in control of Equatorial Africa, and that such control was in the hands of Frenchmen who did not recognise the jurisdiction of Vichy but were fighting actively on the side of the forces of freedom. The French people could rest assured that the Government and people of the United States would 'continue to maintain unimpaired their full respect for the sovereign rights of the people of France', and that these rights would be restored intact to them by the victory of the United Nations.[2]

---

[1] This statement was as follows:—

'The policy of the Government of the United States as regards France and French territory has been based upon the maintenance of the integrity of France and of the French Empire and of the eventual restoration of complete independence of all French territories. Mindful of its traditional friendship for France, this Government deeply sympathises not only with the desire of the French people to maintain their territories intact, but with the efforts of the French people to continue to resist the forces of aggression. In its relations with local French authorities in French territories the United States has been and will continue to be governed by the manifest effectiveness with which those authorities endeavour to protect their territories from domination and control by the common enemy.

With the French authorities in effective control of French territories in the Pacific this Government has treated and will continue to treat on the basis of their actual administration of the territories involved. This Government recognises in particular that French island possessions in that area are under the effective control of the French National Committee established in London, and the United States authorities are co-operating for the defence of these islands with the authorities established by the French National Committee and with no other French authority. This Government appreciates the importance of New Caledonia in the defence of the Pacific area.'

[2] F.R.U.S., ib, 561–3.

(a) Z3171/2678/17.

(iii)

The return of Laval to power at Vichy: the attitude of the Foreign Office towards the Vichy Government: estimate of public morale in France (April–October 1942).

(a)   On April 14 Lord Halifax reported that the French had sent a lengthy note complaining that, in spite of the American agreement to allow the departure of the ships from New York, no progress had been made in deciding about their cargo. The details of the note mattered little, since the situation was now changed by the return of Laval to power. Admiral Darlan was dropped from the Council of Ministers, but was named as Marshal Pétain's successor[1] and head of the armed forces (and in this capacity entitled to attend Cabinet meetings). The American supplies were now suspended.[2] The War

(b)   Cabinet discussed on April 20 the probable policy of the reconstituted Vichy Government. Mr. Eden said that it was not yet possible to determine the significance of the return to power of Laval, but the reason might be German anxiety about the internal situation in France. The Germans might also be intending to make use of Laval and, through him, of French resources in connection with their spring campaigns. Meanwhile Field-Marshal Smuts wanted to ask the Vichy Minister in South Africa to leave the country. On the other hand the United States Government hoped that for the time being the Vichy representative in Canada would not be sent away, and that any request for him to leave should be timed to coincide with similar action in Washington. The War Cabinet considered that we should let the Canadian Government know that we should agree with a decision on their part to fall in with American wishes, but that there was no reason why Field-Marshal Smuts should not expel the Vichy representative from South Africa where his activities had been open to suspicion.[3]

If the Foreign Office had felt any doubt about Laval's attitude they soon had ample evidence. On the day of the discussion in the

---

[1] On the other hand Laval secured an alteration in the constitutional status of the Marshal (and any successor) as Chef de l'Etat Français by taking from him and attributing to the Head of the Government effective responsibility for policy.

[2] At the beginning of June the United States Chargé d'Affaires at Vichy was told by an official of the Vichy Ministry of Foreign Affairs that at recent meetings of the Armistice Commission the Germans had raised the question of the observers in North Africa, and the French had had great difficulty in making out a case for their retention in the absence of American shipments. Under pressure from the War Department, which was anxious to keep the observers, the State Department agreed to allow the ships to leave, in spite of the fact that the French had allowed more military lorries to be shipped for Axis use in North Africa. The question of further sailings was under discussion at the time of the North African landings, but no decision had been taken.

[3] The South African Government broke off diplomatic relations with Vichy on April 23.

(a) Z3180, 3282/28/17. (b) WM(42)50.

War Cabinet, Laval made a broadcast in which he attacked Great
Britain and said that no threats would prevent him from pursuing a
policy of agreement and reconciliation with Germany. On April 29 (a)
Mr. Matthews, United States Chargé d'Affaires in London, showed
Mr. Eden a report from Admiral Leahy of a conversation with Laval
on April 27 at which M. Rochat was present. Laval said that a
Russian and British victory over Germany would be followed by
bolshevism in Europe, and that he would rather see Germany win
the war. He thought it possible to arrive at an understanding with
Germany which would result in a lasting peace. Meanwhile he was
ready to defend France and the French Empire against all comers;
if the British or Americans should attempt to land in Metropolitan
France or in North Africa, he would resist them to the best of his
ability. He said that England had drawn France into the war and
was responsible for her present position, and that he would never
again make a friendly reference to the country. If he had the means
to do so, he would try to reconquer those parts of the French Empire
which General de Gaulle was occupying. In view of Laval's speech
the War Cabinet had already decided on April 24 to tell Mr. (b)
Mackenzie King that in our view the right course was for the
Canadian Government to break off diplomatic relations with Vichy.
The Canadian Government withdrew their Chargé d'Affaires from
Vichy, but did not break off diplomatic relations until the North
African landings. On April 17 the United States Government re-
called Admiral Leahy for consultation,[1] and did not send him back
or replace him by another Ambassador.

The course of events at Vichy had thus followed the lines expected
by the Foreign Office. A more favourable development in the near
future seemed unlikely. The Prime Minister, however, with his
mind turning to the North African invasion, was less inclined to
think a sudden change of attitude wholly out of the question. He was
also exasperated at General de Gaulle's intransigence and, in
the Prime Minister's words, absurd suspicions of British designs
on the French Colonial Empire.[2]

Mr. Churchill put his views in a memorandum which he circulated (c)
on June 5 to the War Cabinet. He wrote that, whatever our scorn
and distrust of the Vichy Government, we ought not to forget that
it was the only Government which might give us what we wanted
from France, i.e. the Toulon fleet and the entry into the French

---

[1] Owing to his wife's illness and death Admiral Leahy did not leave France until May 1.
A United States Chargé d'Affaires remained at Vichy. The British Government stated
publicly (in a speech by Mr. Eden at Edinburgh on May 8) their agreement with the
maintenance of Franco-American diplomatic contacts.

[2] For the difficulties with General de Gaulle at this time, see Chapter XXIX, section
(iii).

(a) Z3572/175/17. (b) WM(42)52. (c) WP(42)239.

North African provinces. The chances of getting these two things were not entirely negligible. The Vichy Government under Darlan, Laval, or perhaps Doriot, had to pay its way from week to week with its German masters. The alternative was the installation of a Gauleiter and complete occupation.

Mr. Churchill thought that the Vichy Government had not done more than was absolutely necessary to stave off this alternative. They had endured Oran, Dakar, Syria and Madagascar, the British blockade and British air-raids, with the least possible show of anger. This attitude had indeed been forced upon them by the anti-German feelings of the great majority of Frenchmen in occupied and un-occupied France and by the French conviction that they must not sever the future of France from the United States.

The real question not only for Vichy but for France was 'who will win the war?' At first the defeat of Germany seemed impossible, but the Russian campaign, the American entry into the war, the enormous staying power of Great Britain, and the evidence of our growing domination in the air had brought back hope to widening circles in France. The Germans were not even sure of the 'tools' tolerated by them at Vichy. They knew that it was in the interest even of such creatures to join the winning side once they were sure which side would win, and that they could also give the Allies a gift of inestimable value. Mr. Churchill had always been ready to act roughly towards Vichy, and had felt also that Vichy would put up with such treatment. He looked forward to a time in the war, which he could not fix but which might not be far off, when the great change of heart which had taken place in the French masses and the apparent certainty of an Allied victory would produce a sudden and decisive change in the action of the Vichy Government.

(a)   After reading the Prime Minister's views Mr. Eden sent him on June 11 an answer in the form of a draft memorandum for the War Cabinet. This draft summed up the previous behaviour of the leaders of the Vichy Government. Marshal Pétain had tried to keep within the armistice terms; his actions were based on the conviction that France was beaten, and must suffer, and that enough French blood had been shed. He regarded the complete military defeat of France as justifying the French desertion of Great Britain in 1940. We knew, however, that he and his fellow-collaborationists at Bordeaux had expected a British collapse within a very few weeks, and had deluded themselves that, if they accepted an armistice and thus accelerated a German victory, they would get better terms. Our most recent indication of Marshal Pétain's attitude was a speech to French officers at Chateauroux in which he had said: 'We must not be

_____

(a) Z5577/880/17.

aggressive, for that would be the ruin of our country. The country must know that we have been beaten. I spent three months after the Armistice telling this to all around me, and for the last two years I have been repeating it to myself every morning.' Marshal Pétain's defeatism was thus unlikely to change; his prestige in unoccupied France was very low, and in occupied France had disappeared.

Laval had never concealed his views. His conversation with Admiral Leahy on April 27 showed once again what we were to expect from him. He thought that a German victory, or possibly a negotiated peace would be preferable to a British or a Soviet victory. Laval was not merely paying his way with the Germans; he had staked his life on a German victory. Darlan's views were also well known. His statement about British action at Madagascar[1] had been more violent than that of any other Vichy leader. He had arranged for the transport by the French of supplies to the Axis in Libya and had tried to get Japanese help against us in Madagascar. The forces of resistance in France must regard with contempt the men who had made no public protest against the incorporation of Alsace-Lorraine into the Reich and the murder of innocent hostages by the Germans. It was very doubtful whether these forces would consent to be brought back actively into the war under the leadership of Marshal Pétain. The information received by the Foreign Office indeed showed that Pétain's age might not even save him from the fate which was awaiting Laval, Doriot, Déat, and perhaps Darlan. The weight of evidence was thus against any sudden decisive action by the Vichy Government in our favour.

The Prime Minister replied to this draft memorandum on June 14. He said that he had circulated his own paper because he thought that the Foreign Office were giving considerable currency to various French documents not of high authority, but tending to work up additional hatred against Vichy and to renew enthusiasm for General de Gaulle. The Prime Minister did not wish the Cabinet to be biased by a statement of the case on these lines. He had been a friend of France for thirty-five years, and had kept as closely as possible in touch with the French people. He therefore had 'a certain instinct' about them. It was easy to set out a case against Vichy, but allowance should be made for the 'unnatural conditions prevailing in a defeated country with a Government living on the sufferance of the enemy'. The Prime Minister still hoped that the French fleet might sail to Africa and that he might secure an invitation for British or American troops to enter French North Africa. In any event, for some time to come, Vichy alone could 'offer those good gifts'. At a

[1] See p. 364, note 1.

certain stage the lives as well as the interests of the Vichy leaders might depend on their making such offers. President Roosevelt shared the Prime Minister's view; so also (the Prime Minister believed) did the Chiefs of Staff. The position was 'so anomalous and monstrous that very clear-cut views' did not 'altogether cover it'.

The Prime Minister thought that the difference between his view and that of the Foreign Office was only one of 'emphasis'. He agreed that Mr. Eden should circulate his draft if he wanted a discussion in the War Cabinet, but he (the Prime Minister) would have to quote General de Gaulle's statements which would probably convince most people that the General should stay in England under our control and not be left to say what he pleased from Brazzaville.[1]

Mr. Eden replied on June 29 that he also thought that there was a substantial measure of agreement between the Prime Minister and himself. He therefore proposed to modify his draft. The Foreign
(a) Office prepared a new draft which was circulated to the War Cabinet on July 8. This memorandum referred to the information received from various quarters in France about the attitude of the forces of resistance. The general effect of the reports was to show the confusion of mind both in France and in North Africa. About 90 per cent of the people of occupied France, and perhaps 60 per cent in unoccupied France wanted an Allied victory, but we did not know their ideas about the future leadership of the country or the form of Government which they would wish to establish after the war. It was too early even to make a guess in the matter.

Hitherto our policy had been to encourage and co-operate with any Frenchmen who stood for resistance to the Germans and wished to work with us to this end. We had also said that it would be for the French people themselves to choose their own regime after the war without interference from us; many Frenchmen had understood us to mean—as indeed we meant—that we should not force General de Gaulle upon them against their will. We had recognised General de Gaulle as the leader of all Free Frenchmen who might rally to him in support of the Allied cause. General de Gaulle disliked the description 'La France Libre' and at his wish we had agreed to call his movement 'La France Combattante';[2] we had accepted this change of title mainly to show our appreciation of the 'symbolic value' of General de Gaulle in occupied France as the leader of French resistance. General de Gaulle was the only leader of French resistance to emerge since the collapse of France, but he could not substantiate a claim to be regarded as France or as the Head of the

---

[1] See Chapter XXIX, section (iii) for General de Gaulle's request for facilities to visit the Free French Colonial territories.
[2] See Chapter XXIX, section (iii).

(a) WP(42)285.

Government of France. There was in fact no French authority that could be regarded as generally representative of the French people.

General de Gaulle's failings were well known. His sudden actions could be dangerous. He was very suspicious, and, like all true Frenchmen, suffered deeply at the humiliation of his country. Many of his supporters found him as difficult to deal with as we had found him. Nevertheless the General had kept the flag of France flying by our side since June 1940. We had been largely responsible for 'building him up' in France; we could not drop him now. If we did so, most of his chief supporters would follow him. It was unlikely that we should find any other leader to take his place; his disappearance would also have a bad effect on the forces of resistance in France.

We had been unable to establish direct relations with the Vichy Government since the withdrawal of the French Embassy in London. We had made two attempts during the ensuing six months but the Germans had forbidden even the contact which the appointment of a British financial representative at Vichy would have provided. In any case Laval, who had announced his hope of a German victory, would not receive a British representative. We had stated publicly[1] on May 8, at Mr. Hull's request, our agreement with the policy of the United States in maintaining contact with the Vichy Government. We could not go beyond this statement, since any public support of the Vichy Government would weaken the resistance in France which we were pledged to assist and uphold. Marshal Pétain's policy was collaboration with the Axis within the terms of the armistice; his chief aim was to secure the unity of France and in his attempt to do so he had publicly declared his full confidence in Laval.

The Vichy Government hitherto had not surrendered the French fleet or North Africa to the Germans. They had also tried to keep the Germans to the terms of the armistice. They deserved some credit for this policy, though we should remember that French public opinion acted as a brake on the more ardent collaborationists. On the other hand we had no evidence for hoping that the present Vichy regime would be prepared to bring France actively into the war on our side. They might do so at a time when it was too late for their action to matter much, but they would take their decision on the facts of the military situation and not as a result of favours or gestures shown to them now. Some other leader, such as General Giraud,[2] might later obtain greater support in France than General de Gaulle; there was at present no sign of a rival to the latter. In spite of his collaborationist policy Marshal Pétain had kept the loyalty of the generals, including General Weygand, and even those known

---

[1] See p. 299, note 1.
[2] For General Giraud, see below, p. 359.

to be anti-German and well-disposed to us showed no sign of breaking away from Vichy.

In this confused situation the wisest policy for us must be (i) to continue our efforts to get France, and as much as possible of the French Empire, into the war again at our side, (ii) to support all the forces of French resistance without binding ourselves exclusively to any of them, (iii) to maintain our support of General de Gaulle, and to encourage him to strengthen his organisation by the enlistment of such representative Frenchmen as he could persuade to come over to join him.

(a)   At the beginning of October 1942, the Foreign Office drew up a memorandum[1] on French morale. They considered that opinion in France was anti-Axis, but not uniformly pro-British. Friendly feelings towards Great Britain had suffered severely under the shock of defeat and the effect of constant anti-British propaganda. Pro-American feeling had not been subject to these influences; hence, superficially at least, the Americans were more popular than the British, but the majority of Frenchmen looked for liberation to the United States and Great Britain jointly, and an outstanding military success, particularly on the territory of occupied France, would win general support. French morale, obviously, was very sensitive to the military fortunes of the United Nations. Until Laval's return to power, morale in occupied France was much higher than in the unoccupied territory; the people in both zones were anti-German, but in the unoccupied zone they were apathetic. Reports now indicated a rise of morale in this latter zone.

In the occupied zone anti-German feeling found expression in acts of violence carried out with disregard of personal risk. These acts, however, expressed in the main personal revolt against oppression and against the prevalent feeling of helplessness; they did not appear to be part of any centralised plan of campaign. Except within the Communist Party there was little evidence of widespread organisation of resistance. The small number of collaborationists in the occupied zone included industrialists who had long associations with German industry or who hoped to gain from German industrial predominance in the 'New Europe', financiers and middlemen who were making money out of their relations with the Germans, self-seeking politicians, and admirers of the Nazi system who hoped to lead a 'Nazi France'. On the whole the population of occupied France had reacted well to British air and other attacks directed

---

[1] The memorandum also represented the views of the three Service Departments and the Ministry of Economic Warfare.

(a) Z7673/81/17; JIC(42)381 (Final).

successfully against targets of importance to the enemy. There had been unfavourable local reactions to certain attacks which had caused high civilian losses.

Until Laval's return to power, and, more particularly, until his public statement that he hoped for a German victory, the people of the unoccupied zone, and especially the middle class, were only passively anti-German and concerned mainly with food and employment. Laval's pro-German declaration of June 22,[1] the campaign to send French workers to Germany, the deportation of Jews, the new compulsory labour decree, and increasing evidence of Gestapo activities had caused a considerable wave of resentment; labour in industrial areas had shown active resistance and restlessness. Peasant proprietors in most districts were better fed and less discontented than other classes; they were anti-Communist, and were probably influenced by fear of a complete Russian victory.

The army still appeared to retain hopes of revenge. At the outset of the regime it had limited itself to blind obedience to Marshal Pétain; the evidence now suggested that it would rally to the appeal of a non-political general with a nation-wide reputation even if this appeal were not backed by Marshal Pétain. The army would not follow General de Gaulle, and had a low opinion of the military capacity of Great Britain; it was not pro-British and had a certain tendency to xenophobia. On the other hand it was anti-German, and in Metropolitan France unlikely, as a whole, to fight against a powerful invading army of the United Nations. In the Vichy colonies the army would probably offer at least a token resistance against a superior invading force. The navy was in the main anti-British, but also anti-German and still more anti-Italian. The reaction of individual units could not be forecast. The results of favourable treatment after the armistice and of an undefeated record during the war had combined to maintain naval morale. The morale of the air force, though somewhat impaired by long inactivity, was favourable to the Allies; anti-British feeling was confined largely to senior officers, while anti-German feeling was general.

Among civilians, a majority of Frenchmen supported General de Gaulle as a symbol of resistance, but in the first instance the French would probably look for a leader within France; those who turned to General de Gaulle did so mainly *faute de mieux*, since other possible leaders, such as Pétain and Weygand, had lost much of their prestige. Although General de Gaulle's active followers were few, French morale would undoubtedly be depressed if we abandoned

---

[1] In this broadcast declaration Laval had said: 'I desire to re-establish normal and confident relations with both Germany and Italy. A new Europe will inevitably emerge from this war . . . one in which France must retain a place worthy of her. . . . I wish to see a German victory, since without it Bolshevism will tomorrow appear everywhere.' Laval also appealed for workers to go to Germany.

L

him. The Communist Party alone among the old political organisations had survived the collapse of France. Its structure and discipline were firmer than those of any other party. Its membership was said to be relatively large; it was said also to be ready to co-operate with other genuine resistance groups. There was no definite evidence of this willingness, but the Communist leaders might be afraid of betrayal if they confided in British or Gaullist agents. On the other hand fear of Communism was an important factor in determining the attitude of other sections of the population; fears of the political effects of a complete Russian victory, however, had recently diminished owing to the belief that such a victory was unlikely unless it were accompanied by Anglo-Saxon action in the west.

The Roman Catholic hierarchy had supported Marshal Pétain after the collapse, and had approved of his programme of a national revival based on religion and the family. Since the evident failure of this programme the clergy were becoming more conscious of the threat to the Church from totalitarianism. Some Catholic bishops had recently protested against Laval's anti-Jewish measures, and were perhaps afraid that, as in Germany, an anti-Catholic campaign would follow the anti-Jewish campaign. The country clergy, especially the younger priests, would certainly accept the lead of the bishops. The most important pro-Vichy and pro-German parties—the League of Ex-Servicemen (nominally under Pétain, but actually controlled by Laval), the Parti Populaire Français (under Doriot) and the Rassemblement National Populaire (under Déat)—were able to exercise an influence disproportionate to the amount of active support which they received, since they were not repressed like the resistance groups. On the other hand the Chantiers de Jeunesse established by Pétain, and providing training on military lines for 100,000 youth a year, were the most important influence at work on young Frenchmen. The Chantiers were organised by military officers, and were reported to be strongly anti-German, and of high morale.

Note to Section (iii). The French warships at Martinique and the radio station at Guadeloupe.

(a)   After the collapse of France the relations between the United States Government and the Vichy authorities in the French West Indies were governed by a semi-official agreement with Admiral Robert, the French High Commissioner. According to this agreement, Admiral Robert, in return for the continuance of a restricted trade between the United States and the French West Indies, undertook to allow no movement, without the permission of the United States, of the warships, aircraft or gold in his

(a) Z3555/3/17.

territory. This agreement was renewed after the entry of the United States into the war.

In February, 1942, Admiral Robert, without the knowledge of the United States authorities, allowed a German submarine to call at Martinique to land a wounded officer. The United States Government protested strongly about this incident, and asked for an assurance from the Vichy Government that Axis forces would never again be allowed to make use of French possessions in the Caribbean (including French Guiana). Unless this assurance were given the United States Government threatened to take over the French possessions. The Vichy Government replied that compliance with the American demand would be inconsistent with their claim to be regarded as neutral. They declared, however, that henceforward no warships or aircraft of a belligerent Power would be allowed to use their possessions in the West Indies. At the same time they asked for an undertaking that the United States Government would respect the neutral status of all French possessions in the western hemisphere (including St. Pierre and Miquelon) and, where necessary, re-establish Vichy sovereignty over them.

It appeared in fact that the Vichy Government intended to allow the United States Navy to continue its patrols around the French West Indies. The United States Government therefore took no further action except to reserve full liberty to do whatever might be necessary for the defence of the western hemisphere. They stated that they had 'no intention of altering basic French sovereignty whatever temporary measures might be required by the exigencies of developments of the war situation'.

About the middle of April, 1942, when Laval's return to office was already expected, Admiral Robert told Admiral Horne, of the United States Navy, that he had received instructions from Admiral Darlan not to obey any instructions except from him, and to keep to all assurances already given to the United States Government.

The Foreign Office, after Laval's return to office, suggested to the State Department that drastic steps should be taken to immobilise the French warships at Martinique (e.g. cutting off fuel supplies, removing breach blocks from guns). The United States Government, however, were unwilling to do anything further in the matter in view of Admiral (a) Robert's assurance. They had stationed heavy bombers within reach of Martinique, and could take immediate action if the Vichy assurances were not fulfilled.

On May 7 Lord Halifax reported, however, that the United States (b) were intending to send an ultimatum to Admiral Robert, and to sink the French ships if the terms were not accepted. The British Government also wished to put a stop to what the Prime Minister described as the 'spout of abuse' of the Allies broadcast from the French radio station at (c) Guadeloupe. The American negotiations with the Vichy authorities continued for a considerable time; the Foreign Office view was that the policy of the State Department was far too weak. In the end, however, the essential machinery of the warships was dismantled and the radio station closed down.

(a) Z3221/1720/17. (b) Z3800/1720/17. (c) Z3697/25/17.

Note on the French Squadron at Alexandria, June 1940–1943.

(a) The difficulties of dealing with the supporters of Vichy may be illustrated by the attitude of Admiral Godefroy who at the time of the collapse of France was in command of a French squadron of one battleship, four cruisers, two destroyers, and a submarine based at Alexandria under the supreme command of Admiral Cunningham. Admiral Godefroy and the great majority of his officers and men maintained allegiance to Marshal Pétain's Government, and refused to join General de Gaulle's movement, or to continue to take part in the war in company with the Royal Navy.

On July 4, 1940, Admiral Godefroy agreed to discharge all the oil fuel from his ships and to place them in a condition in which they could not fight. Three days later Admiral Cunningham reported that he had made an agreement with Admiral Godefroy for the immobilisation of the squadron. This agreement was a personal one between the two admirals. A new agreement would become necessary when Admiral Cunningham gave up his command. Admiral Cunningham was appointed to command the naval forces for the North African landings in 1942, and arranged to leave his command at Alexandria on April 1. He thought that, on balance, the best plan would be for his successor to renew the agreement without change. The agreement was satisfactory in that it rendered the French ships harmless; parts of all guns of the main armament had been removed, and torpedo warheads placed ashore.[1] The crews were reduced to one-third of their normal complement. The ships had been in harbour for two years, and their speed had thereby been affected; they were given a weekly ration of fuel sufficient only to work their auxiliary engines. Admiral Godefroy had observed all his undertakings, and the French squadron had caused no real trouble. Even during the Syrian episode, when we were engaging Vichy units off the Syrian coast, Admiral Godefroy's conduct was scrupulously loyal to the agreement. On our side we provided money to pay the French officers and men, and gave them supplies.

We had considered the seizure of the ships at the time of the Syrian expedition, and again later for the purpose of replacing our own cruiser losses. Admiral Cunningham had always opposed this step not only as a breach of faith, but for practical reasons; the French were believed to have prepared scuttling charges which could be fired easily and rapidly, so that we could not expect to get the ships intact. In any case, we could not use them for a long time, since they would have to be docked and would require considerable refitting; we would also have to make special arrangements for producing ammunition for their guns. The political repercussions at Vichy and Toulon of forcible action against the squadron needed no emphasis. Admiral Cunningham was indeed more anxious about the possibility of trouble with the main French fleet than with the squadron at Alexandria.

---

[1] It was, however, pointed out later that the secondary armament and A.A. guns remained in working order, and that parts for some of the main armament could be improvised to allow the firing of a few rounds.

(a) WP(42)137.

The War Cabinet considered Admiral Cunningham's view on March (a) 31. They thought that we ought to try to get an agreement more favourable to ourselves. We might, for example, offer to agree to the repatriation of the French crews (other than Gaullist sympathisers) and by starting propaganda about this offer, produce a state of things in which we could secure better terms; our ultimate objective was to obtain control of the ships.

It was therefore decided to renew the existing agreement temporarily, and to allow Admiral Harwood, who was leaving on May 5 or 6 to take up the command at Alexandria, to open new negotiations. The Admiralty continued to hold the view that the best policy was to renew the agree- (b) ment without much change. On the other hand Admiral Godefroy wanted a modification of the terms to allow reliefs to be sent for the personnel who had done long service abroad.

The War Cabinet accepted the Admiralty view that we could agree (c) without risk to Admiral Godefroy's request. Admiral Harwood therefore made the necessary arrangements. The position, however, became more difficult after the British defeat in Libya and the development of an Axis threat to Alexandria. Admiral Harwood discussed the new situation with (d) Admiral Godefroy. The latter said that his instructions were not to let his ships fall into any foreign hands. He would not agree to scuttle them before the Germans reached Alexandria, since there was a chance that they would allow the squadron to return to France. Admiral Harwood though that we might allow the ships to go to Bizerta if Admiral Godefroy would agree to certain conditions designed to secure that they did not fall into enemy hands.

The War Cabinet considered the question on June 29. They considered that if Admiral Godefroy refused to sail his ships from Alexandria if and when we were compelled to evacuate the port, he would be committing a hostile act and thus breaking the agreement. Action could not be delayed until the last moment, and a refusal to leave Alexandria in advance of our evacuation would also be a hostile act. Moreover the spirit of the agreement required that, if Admiral Godefroy left Alexandria, he should go to another port under British control. Admiral Harwood had advised, apparently on security grounds, against moving the ships through the Suez Canal, but the War Cabinet regarded this plan as the right course. If Admiral Godefroy refused to leave Alexandria on our orders when enemy occupation was imminent, we must destroy his ships. The War Cabinet thought that Admiral Harwood should give Admiral Godefroy a hint to this effect. Instructions in this sense were sent to the Commander-in-Chief, Mediterranean on June 30. On June 26 the Vichy Government had ordered Admiral Godefroy to try to reach a French port in the event of a British evacuation of Alexandria. Admiral Godefroy showed these instructions to Admiral Harwood. On July 2 Admiral Harwood reported that Admiral Godefroy had asked him to assure the British Government (e) that he would never let his ships fall into the hands of the Germans. On

---

(a) WM(42)32.2, C.A. (b) WP(42)185. (c) WM(42)63. (d) WM(42)83.2, C.A. (e) Z5493/21/17.

the following day Admiral Harwood was instructed not to take action until the fall of Alexandria was certain, but that the most drastic steps must be taken to see that none of the ships went back to French ports.

(a)   On July 9 Mr. Roosevelt telegraphed to the Prime Minister that the Vichy Government were insisting that the French ships must go to a French port, and not—as the United States Government had suggested— through the Suez Canal to a neutral port. The President was therefore proposing to suggest to Laval and Admiral Godefroy that the squadron should be promised a safe passage to Martinique (through the Suez Canal) where they would be immobilised for the duration of the war on the same basis as other French ships at the island. A similar suggestion had come from Mr. Casey. The War Cabinet thought that we should
(b) refuse to allow the squadron to go to Bizerta, and that we should support Mr. Roosevelt's suggestion irrespective of the military situation at Alexandria since in any case the ships would be in danger of air attack there. We should also point out that the squadron at Alexandria did not come within the scope of the armistice. The Prime Minister telegraphed on these lines to President Roosevelt.

After the immediate threat to Alexandria had lessened, the question ceased to be a matter of urgency. The Foreign Office, however, doubted whether Admiral Godefroy's attitude during the critical period had been in conformity with his agreement; they also felt disquiet at the fact that he was still in wireless communication with France.[1] The War
(c) Cabinet therefore asked Mr. Eden and the First Lord of the Admiralty
(d) to examine the whole question. They came to the conclusion that Admiral Godefroy so far had carried out the agreement and was unlikely to break it, even on orders from Vichy, unless the fall of Alexandria became imminent. He was unlikely, for practical reasons, to play us false while we retained firm control of the port, but we had to consider the possibility of a less scrupulous subordinate taking over control of the squadron. Admiral Godefroy's dominant motive was to save his ships for France; he would resist force from any quarter and the armament remaining in the ships was enough to ensure that their capture or forcible removal or even the destruction of their wireless could be carried out only after a major operation. Admiral Godefroy was unlikely to agree to the curtailment of the wireless facilities expressly reserved to him under the agreement. Even if we deprived him of them he could probably rig up a wireless set for use in emergency.

We therefore had to choose between allowing the agreement to remain in force, in the hope that Admiral Godefroy would agree to follow us before the Germans reached Alexandria rather than to see his ships destroyed, and contending that the recent refusal of the Admiral to agree, in the event of emergency, to sail his ships to some other port under Allied control had made the agreement invalid. In these circumstances we should apply pressure on Admiral Godefroy to accept a

---

[1] There was no evidence that Admiral Godefroy had used these facilities to our detriment.

(a) T975/2, No. 162, Churchill Papers/470. (b) WM(42)90.2, C.A. (c) WM(42)92.3, C.A. (d) WP(42)356.

revised agreement under the terms of which we could require the ships
to sail to another port. We could cut off all water and supplies from the
ships, and stop all shore leave unless the Admiral accepted our terms.
On the other hand he would probably be able to hold out for a considerable time, since he had ample provisions and could distil water on
board. In the last resort he would probably scuttle the ships.

The Admiralty, and Mr. Eden, favoured leaving the agreement
unchanged on the understanding that Admiral Harwood had clear
instructions to destroy the French squadron if the need should arise. The
War Cabinet accepted this view on August 13. The agreement thus (a)
remained in force, but once again the change in the military situation
brought the question to the front. On November 30 the War Cabinet (b)
were informed that, while some of Admiral Godefroy's officers wished to
resume fighting on the Allied side, others thought that this course would
mean breaking their oath to the Head of the State. In this situation
Admiral Godefroy had asked to be allowed to communicate with Marshal
Pétain or Admiral Abrial. The War Cabinet agreed to refuse this request,
and to wait for about a fortnight to see how matters developed.

On October 2, i.e. before the Allied landing in North Africa, Admiral (c)
Godefroy had expressed himself to the British Consul-General in the most
lamentable terms. He approved of the armistice, and indeed thought
that indirectly it had saved Great Britain. He asserted that French policy,
in the interests of France, must now be one of complete passivity; that
the Vichy Government had no moral right to endanger France by any
attempt at resistance and that no French sailor or soldier could in honour
fight against the Axis. He said it was impossible to tell who would win
the war, but he did not see how Germany could be beaten. The Prime
Minister hoped that the Allied landings in North Africa would have
brought a change in Admiral Godefroy's attitude in mid-December,
but the Admiral still refused to come over to the Allies. He told Admiral
Harwood that he could not give away his squadron without knowing (d)
that the legitimate Government of France agreed with this action.
He was willing to accept the orders of a stable Government in North
Africa as representing all Frenchmen outside France but would not
agree that Admiral Darlan was at the head of such a Government. He
also considered that, until they had taken Tunisia, the Allies could not
justify their claim to be able to liberate France. On the other hand the
Admiral said that he would not stand in the way of any officers and men
who wanted to join us.

On December 14 the War Cabinet decided—on Admiral Harwood's
recommendation—not to do anything for the time, on condition, however, that Admiral Godefroy carried out his undertaking not to prevent
officers and men under his command from joining the Fighting French.
The Prime Minister pointed out that Admiral Godefroy was drifting into
the position of an admiral in command of a fleet who did not recognise
allegiance to any Government. We were paying him and his officers and
were receiving nothing in return. We might allow the situation to

---

(a) WM(42)112. (b) WM(42)162. (c) Z7938/81/17. (d) WM(42)168.4, C.A.

continue until the end of the year, but would then have to take steps to put further pressure on him.

Admiral Godefroy was able to prolong this absurd position for another five months, and to show the lengths to which French legal pertinacity would go at a time when the interests of France obviously required full collaboration with the Allies. The assassination of Admiral Darlan had not made it easier for Admiral Godefroy to make up his mind to join the Allies, and by the time of the meeting between General de Gaulle and General Giraud at Casablanca his force was still idle at Alexandria, although there was a steady flow of individual sailors to the Fighting
(a) French. On January 26, 1943, therefore, the Prime Minister, who had gone to Cairo on his way to the Adana meeting with the Turkish Government, telegraphed to the War Cabinet that in view of the agreement between General de Gaulle and General Giraud it was time that the scandal of Admiral Godefroy's squadron was brought to a head. He proposed that the Admiral should now be invited to adhere to one or other general and that if he refused we should discontinue the £5,000 a week which we had been paying him since 1940. Unlike Admiral Harwood, the Prime Minister did not consider that Admiral Godefroy would scuttle his ships; if he did so, the Egyptian Government could probably take legal action against him for the damage to the harbour. Mr. Churchill did not favour a joint appeal to the Admiral from General de Gaulle and General Giraud; it would be difficult to organise because of the continuing rivalry between the two generals and their organisations, and General de Gaulle had gone back to London.
(b)   The War Cabinet considered this telegram, and a subsequent one from Mr. Casey setting out a detailed plan, on January 28 and 29. They thought it important from the point of view of French reactions in North and West Africa to work through the North African authorities, and that if possible Admiral Godefroy should be put in the position of disobeyng an order from General Giraud before we took action against him. They therefore proposed some modifications in Mr. Casey's suggested procedure.
(c)   Mr. Casey then arranged to see Admiral Godefroy on January 31 and to hand him an appeal from General Giraud. He reported that he would not produce the threat of cutting off the squadron's pay and supplies unless the Admiral rejected General Giraud's appeal out of hand. The
(d) appeal did not reach Cairo in time for the interview, but Mr. Casey told Admiral Godefroy that it was on the way, and urged him to consider it most carefully. If he was unwilling to join General Giraud, he might rally to the United Nations without specifying for the time being which elements he was joining. If he did not accept one or other of these alternatives, His Majesty's Government would not be able to go on providing pay and supplies for his squadron.

The War Cabinet did not like the suggestion that Admiral Godefroy should join the United Nations as distinct from the French. It would

---

(a) Tel. Stratagem 258, Churchill Papers/179; Z1592, 1594/39/17. (b) WM(43) 19.1, C.A.; WM(43)20, C.A.; Tel. Telescope 333 and 345 (Churchill Papers/179; Z1487/1266/69); Stratagem 283 (Churchill Papers/179; Z1593/39/17). (c) Z1596/39/17. (d) Z1598/39/17.

result in a situation as futile as the existing one, since his crews could only be made up from North Africa or by the Fighting French. Moreover they felt that the Admiral should realise that there was no middle course between joining his compatriots against the Axis or losing his means of support. Mr. Casey agreed not to take the initiative in urging Admiral (a) Godefroy to join the United Nations rather than either General Giraud or the Fighting French, but he asked for discretion to accept such an offer by the Admiral. He thought that some of the ships could be got away if their crews were combined, and the remainder could be manned later from North Africa.

Meanwhile on February 2 Admiral Godefroy had replied unfavourably (b) to General Giraud's appeal. He said that he remained faithful to the legitimate authority; but that if the time should come when he no longer felt it his duty to obey Marshal Pétain and respect the armistice— which was still in force—he would not fail to seize the occasion.

General Giraud had signified that he would be prepared to follow up (c) his appeal with a more peremptory message, perhaps carried by one of his officers. Mr. Casey therefore proposed that a senior French naval (d) officer should now come to Egypt with an order to Admiral Godefroy to recognise General Giraud's authority or resign his command. He also suggested that the officer should produce the documentary evidence of Marshal Pétain's communication to Admiral Darlan which was said to have been responsible for M. Boisson bringing over French West Africa. He thought this might provide Admiral Godefroy with the means he evidently needed of saving his face. Mr. Macmillan strongly opposed (e) this idea. He said it would be completely contrary to the policy we were pursuing in North Africa and that he could not agree to it without a direct order from the Prime Minister and the Cabinet. He pointed out later that the evidence of Marshal Pétain's order had in fact been shown to Admiral Godefroy in December at Darlan's instance and had had no (f) effect.

On February 4 Mr. Macmillan informed Mr. Casey that General (g) Giraud had decided not to intervene further in the matter for the time being. Mr. Macmillan thought that the General did not wish to court a further rebuff from Admiral Godefroy. Mr. Casey therefore told the (h) Prime Minister, who was now in North Africa, that if General Giraud would not go any further there was not much more that he (Mr. Casey) could say to Admiral Godefroy, since he understood that the War Cabinet had ruled out the original idea that the issue should be made one between the British Government and the Admiral.

From London the War Cabinet pointed out that they had only said (i) that 'if possible' Admiral Godefroy should be put in the position of disobeying an order before we took action against him. If General Giraud would not take further steps (Mr. Macmillan was told that he need not press General Giraud to send an emissary to Egypt), we should (j) have to base our action on the rejected appeal. The Prime Minister

---

(a) Z1618/764/17. (b) Z1601/39/17. (c) Z1597/39/17. (d) Z1601/39/17. (e) Z1617/764/17. (f) Z1937/39/17. (g) Z1668/764/17. (h) Z1949/39/17. (i) Z1949/39/17. (j) Z1668/764/17.

L*

(a) discussed the question with Mr. Macmillan in Algiers, and replied to Mr. Casey on February 6 that the essential thing was to cut off supplies. An order from Admiral Michelier[1] would help, but was of secondary importance. He wished to place it on record that he did not think that stopping supplies would lead to the scuttling of the ships or would upset

(b) Frenchmen elsewhere. It was arranged that Admiral Cunningham should ask Admiral Michelier to order Admiral Godefroy to put himself under his command. Admiral Michelier was also to be warned that we intended to stop the squadron's pay if Admiral Godefroy remained

(c) obdurate. Two days later Admiral Michelier told Admiral Cunningham that he and General Giraud would prefer to postpone any further *démarche* to Admiral Godefroy. They did not wish to force the pace and feared that another approach so soon after General Giraud's appeal would have no effect. Admiral Michelier also feared that British pressure would have an adverse effect on his own forces.

(d)   Mr. Casey had a long interview on February 10 with Admiral Godefroy, whom he found increasingly worried but still not to be moved from his 'completely intractable attitude' that he would not come in until the situation had so changed that 'his conscience, duty and honour' were satisfied; he was, however, unable to forecast the circumstances in which this might happen. He admitted that most of his officers wished to resume the fight when he himself found the right moment. Mr. Casey warned the Admiral most seriously of the consequences of his refusal to rally, but the Admiral declared himself ready to take all the consequences of his decision; he made several references to scuttling, or to seeking internment in a Turkish port. His only concrete proposal was to send a senior officer to Algiers to obtain information from Admiral Michelier so that he could 'more easily judge what he would do when the opportunity to resume the fight presents itself'. Mr. Casey also put to Admiral Godefroy the formal suggestion that he should join the Fighting French, but this was instantly rejected. Mr. Casey summed up the situation as follows: he believed that there was a real danger that Admiral Godefroy would scuttle his ships or attempt to leave Alexandria if we cut off his pay and supplies; his contacts confirmed the Admiral's claim that most of his officers were completely loyal to him and Mr. Casey concluded that they would obey the Admiral's orders. Admiral Harwood had taken steps to deal with the French squadron in harbour, though this would cause damage to other shipping there, but he did not have enough ships at hand to take action with the French force at sea. If we denounced the Harwood-Godefroy agreement the Admiral would be free to leave Alexandria unless we warned him that we should regard this as a hostile act. It would be simple to cut off pay and supplies after February 13, the next pay day, but if our object was to get the ships intact with their crews, Mr. Casey

---

[1] It was now thought that an order to Admiral Godefroy would come better from Admiral Michelier, Commander-in-Chief of the French naval forces in North Africa, than from General Giraud who as a soldier had no authority over Admiral Godefroy apart from his position as head of an administration which Admiral Godefroy did not recognise.

(a) Z1749/138/69. (b) Z1797/39/17. (c) Z1893/39/17. (d) Resmin Cairo tel. 290, Churchill Papers/179; Z2065/39/17.

reluctantly concluded that we should authorise Admiral Godefroy to send an officer to Algiers and should delay cutting off his pay and supplies. He did not rule out the possibility that with propaganda on our part the ships' captains might still impose a solution on the admiral.

The Prime Minister, however, was determined to act at once, and (a) telegraphed to Mr. Casey a message to be delivered to Admiral Godefroy on February 13. Mr. Churchill said that the British Government could not continue to pay £5,000 a week to Admiral Godefroy's fleet 'in order that they should remain in total inactivity while the world cause is being fought for by the peoples of so many lands'. He warned Admiral Godefroy that if he scuttled his ships he would not only be refusing to join those who were fighting the common enemy, but would even be obstructing them. Moreover the highest legal authorities advised him that 'an act of sabotage of this character' would render the Admiral and his men amenable to Egyptian law and that he would have to answer before the Egyptian courts. The Prime Minister told Mr. Casey that there was no objection to Admiral Godefroy sending an emissary to Algiers, but this must not delay our action, and Admiral Harwood was responsible for preventing the French ships from leaving harbour.

Mr. Casey, with Admiral Harwood, accordingly saw Admiral Godefroy (b) on February 13. He delivered the Prime Minister's message and a note stating that a revision of the agreement with Admiral Godefroy was called for in view of the fact that the Axis Powers had taken over and were using certain French warships. The British Government had decided to maintain the agreement in force for the present with the exception of their undertaking to provide pay after February 15. They regarded Admiral Godefroy's undertaking not to leave Alexandria without the Commander-in-Chief's consent as still binding, and warned him that any attempt to leave would be regarded as a hostile act, made with the intention of assisting the enemy. Admiral Godefroy showed no change in his attitude, but Mr. Casey now thought that he was not likely to scuttle the ships or to attempt to bolt in the immediate future. Meanwhile Mr. Casey still regarded a visit by a senior French naval officer from North Africa as essential.

Admiral Godefroy now asked the Egyptian Prime Minister to provide (c) his squadron's pay out of French money in Egypt, but Nahas Pasha reacted strongly to this suggestion and warned the Admiral that if he scuttled his ships he and his men could be punished under martial law for the damage done to an Egyptian port. The Egyptian Government would moreover have to reconsider their policy of hospitality towards French citizens and French interests in the country. Admiral Godefroy then wrote to Admiral Harwood saying that if the British decision to cut (d) off pay was only intended to remove the burden from the British taxpayer, he would have no objection to a modification of the agreement if he were allowed to obtain funds from France or elsewhere. If however the real intention was to put pressure on him, he would be obliged to consider

---

(a) Z2217/39/17. (b) MOS 61, T160/3, Churchill Papers/179; MOS 63, T161/3, Churchill Papers/179. (c) Z2312/39/17. (d) Z2417/39/17.

the agreement as broken. He admitted that if it could be irrefutably proved that the Axis had taken over French warships the letter of the agreement would be affected, but he contended that the intention had been to provide against the Vichy Government handing over their warships to the enemy, and not against the Germans seizing French ships after their occupation of Toulon and Bizerta as a result of the Allied landings in North Africa. The Vichy Government also attempted to

(a) transmit money for the squadron through the Swiss Government, but their request was refused.

(b) On February 20 Mr. Macmillan reported that General Giraud had now decided to send his Chief of Staff, Admiral Misoff, to Alexandria with a letter to Admiral Godefroy from himself and an order from

(c) Admiral Michelier. After he had seen Admiral Godefroy and many of his officers, Admiral Misoff told Mr. Casey that Admiral Godefroy had refused to accept Admiral Michelier's orders but finally had more or less promised to rally to General Giraud, though the nearest he would come to a date was 'probably after the liberation of Tunisia'. He still said that he would scuttle his ships if the British cut off his supplies and he had to send the men ashore. Mr. Casey thought that real progress had been made; he suggested that we should now hand over responsibility for the squadron to the North African authorities. If they were made responsible for supplies, they would gain practical control over the squadron before

(d) Admiral Godefroy actually came over. Mr. Macmillan endorsed this proposal but the Prime Minister thought it very unsatisfactory. He said that we were to be fobbed off with an indefinite delay, and suggested that as Admiral Godefroy had made no secret of his intention to scuttle his ships if further pressure were put on him, we might ask the Egyptian Government to put him under preventive arrest.

(e) On the same day that he wrote this minute, however, the Prime Minister received a message from General Giraud expressing the conviction that the squadron would rally as soon as the conquest of Tunisia was completed. General Giraud begged Mr. Churchill not to force a decision but to allow him to complete the negotiations. Mr. Churchill

(f) replied on March 11 that in deference to General Giraud's wishes he did not propose to take further coercive action against Admiral Godefroy for the time being, but he thought that the stoppage of pay should continue for a few weeks so that its resumption, including arrears which if necessary the British Government would pay, would operate from the date on which the Admiral accepted General Giraud's command. Mr. Casey was

(g) therefore informed that his plan was accepted, but that we must keep in our own hands the power to determine the movements of the French ships, the quantities of fuel delivered to them, and the date on which their armament was restored.

(h) By the end of March no officer from North Africa had arrived at Alexandria to deal with Admiral Godefroy, and Mr. Casey was reporting

---

(a) Z3074/39/17. (b) Z2447/39/17; Z2536/671/24. (c) Z2751, 2759/39/17. (d) Z2827/39/17; Z2297/348/17. (e) Z2966/39/17. (f) Z3344/39/17. (g) Z2297/348/17. (h) Z3652/39/17.

that although the British authorities in Egypt had recently been discouraging desertions from the French ships, on the ground that the
whole squadron was likely to come over soon and the men would be
needed, it was now likely that large-scale desertions to the Fighting
French would take place. He thought it essential that Admiral Michelier
should send an officer to discuss with Admiral Godefroy arrangements
for taking over responsibility for the supply and maintenance of the
ships. Mr. Macmillan was therefore instructed to urge the North African (a)
authorities to send an officer to Alexandria. He reported on April 7 that (b)
General Giraud did not propose to send an officer at the moment, but
wished to pay the squadron on a month-to-month basis in order to keep
a hold on Admiral Godefroy. It was thought certain that he would come
over when the Tunisian campaign was completed and the Sicilian
channel clear. General Giraud again asked that he should be allowed to
continue conducting the negotiations. The Prime Minister however was
adamant on the question of pay; he replied to Mr. Macmillan on April
12 that 'no pay of any kind should reach the recalcitrant squadron in
Alexandria harbour until they definitely come over to Giraud'.

On April 20 General Giraud told Mr. Macmillan that he was now (c)
sending an officer—Commandant Bataille—to Alexandria at once to
conduct all negotiations between the French squadron and the British
authorities. He thought that by accepting pay from North Africa Admiral
Godefroy was recognising his authority. He suggested that the recondi-
tioning of the ships should be started, and said that he would ask Admiral
Godefroy, as a symbolic act, to send a cruiser, or at least some destroyers,
to North Africa at once.

Eight days later Admiral Michelier informed Mr. Macmillan that a (d)
commissioner in charge of supply and Commandant Bataille were
leaving for Alexandria. He asked for authority for Commandant Bataille
to cash a cheque in Alexandria for £50,000 to cover pay for March and
April, and any other incidental expenses. Admiral Godefroy would be
asked, after Tunis and Bizerta had been captured, to consider himself
under General Giraud's orders; if he then refused to do so, no further
pay or supplies would be forthcoming. Mr. Macmillan hoped that this
plan would be accepted, particularly as Admiral Godefroy was reported (e)
to have told his officers that he had definitely decided to join General
Giraud and that the moment of doing so might be sooner than had been
expected. Nevertheless the Prime Minister telegraphed to Mr. Macmillan
on April 30 that the course proposed was exactly the opposite of what (f)
he had repeatedly prescribed; 'No payment should be made till they
come over and declare themselves under Giraud's orders. Then it would
be natural they should receive his pay. There is no objection to the
ships being docked meanwhile.'

Mr. Macmillan replied that he had understood that we had agreed (g)
to leave the handling of the question to General Giraud and had decided
not to take any further coercive measures. General Giraud had in fact

(a) Z4068/39/17. (b) Z4423/39/17. (c) Z4903/39/17. (d) Z5156/39/17. (e) Z5139/39/17.
(f) Z5156/39/17. (g) Z5372/39/17.

provided the squadron with £11,000 on April 7, before the Prime Minister's telegram of April 12.[1] General Giraud had made it clear on April 20 that he regarded Admiral Godefroy's force as to all intents and purposes under his command since they were accepting pay from North Africa. It would not be possible to prevent Commandant Bataille from cashing his cheque without special action by the Treasury or by putting pressure on General Giraud. Mr. Macmillan was very reluctant to do the latter, especially in the delicate state of negotiations between General Giraud and General de Gaulle. He did not believe that it was worth throwing away all that we had achieved with General Giraud and his administration by quarrelling with him over this comparatively minor point. Everyone at Algiers believed that Admiral Godefroy would rally within a month of the Germans being driven out of Tunisia.

The Admiralty and the Foreign Office agreed with Mr. Macmillan's arguments, and in addition the Foreign Office pointed out that if we insisted on holding up General Giraud's plan the North African authorities would certainly let it be known that we and not they were keeping back the pay, and this would not help our relations with the squadron when it did rally. They thought it was a pity that Mr. Macmillan had not reported earlier that General Giraud had paid out some money before the Prime Minister's message of April 12.

The final moves in the affair were made against the background of the rapid conclusion of the Tunisian campaign. The War Cabinet instructed Mr. Casey on May 11 that Commandant Bataille, who had arrived in Cairo a week earlier, should be asked not to make any payments if

(a) Admiral Godefroy had not yet rallied. He replied that no issue of pay would be made from British sources. Commandant Bataille was returning to Algiers with a letter from Admiral Godefroy asking certain political questions. It was expected that the answers would be favourable, and if so Admiral Godefroy would probably come over in about a week's time.

(b) Mr. Macmillan said he would certainly urge General Giraud to adopt the formula 'No rallying, no pay' but he repeated that payment on Commandant Bataille's cheque could be stopped only from London. The Treasury informed the Foreign Office, however, that we could not interfere with the North African authorities' disposal of their own sterling; the Foreign Office therefore considered that the only way of stopping the payment of the money was to put pressure on General Giraud and to ask Commandant Bataille not to issue any pay pending instructions from Algiers. Instructions to this effect were therefore sent to Mr. Casey and Mr. Macmillan on May 14. Mr. Macmillan was instructed to tell General Giraud that the Prime Minister saw the gravest objections to further payments to Admiral Godefroy before he had definitely come over to the Allied side. We therefore asked him to instruct Commandant Bataille not to pay out the money. The Prime

(c) Minister himself sent Mr. Macmillan a telegram reinforcing these

---

(d)   [1] On April 27, Mr. Casey had reported that there was no evidence that Admiral Godefroy was receiving any money. He had recently cashed the fleet reserve.

(a) Z5633/72/17. (b) Z5614/39/17. (c) Z5614/39/17. (d) Z5158, 5159/39/17.

instructions. He said there was now no reason why the Alexandria squadron should not announce their adherence to General Giraud.

Commandant Bataille had by now returned to Algiers; before leaving (a) he told Admiral Leatham[1] that he did not propose to make any more payments before the end of May, but, as the Foreign Office had expected, (b) he had already issued the squadron's pay for March and April. General Giraud told Mr. Macmillan that no more pay would be authorised until Admiral Godefroy reported a definite decision to send his ships to join the French navy in North Africa.

Admiral Godefroy's decision to join General Giraud was finally taken (c) on May 17, four days after the end of fighting in Tunisia. He informed Admiral Leatham that he had asked Admiral Michelier to send additional crews as soon as possible. He said that he wished to be the first to inform Vichy, but would only do so at a moment chosen by the Commander-in-Chief. In reporting Admiral Godefroy's letter to the Admiralty, Admiral Leatham pointed out that we could not prevent Admiral Godefroy from communicating with Vichy by wireless, and that the Axis were likely to learn of his decision from the arrival of the crews and the docking of the ships. The best solution would therefore be to delay the message until shortly before the first ship sailed. The Admiralty thought that there was no reason why the enemy should be gratuitously informed of Admiral Godefroy's intention, and instructed Admiral Cunningham to suggest to Admiral Michelier that as Admiral Godefroy now presumably acknowledged his authority he should forbid communication with Vichy on the grounds of operational security. Admiral Cunningham himself sent a message to Admiral Godefroy on May 22 (d) asking him not to communicate with Vichy. The message was too late. On the previous day Admiral Godefroy had told Admiral Leatham that (e) he was going to inform Vichy that night; Admiral Leatham appealed to him not to send a message pending the outcome of discussions with the Admiralty and Admiral Cunningham, but later in the day Admiral Godefroy said that he had sent his message; it was too serious to be delayed any longer. Next day he told Admiral Leatham that Vichy's reply had been to order him to scuttle his ships, and that he had refused to obey these orders. He now promised not to send any more cypher messages.

The battleship *Lorraine* and the four cruisers finally left Alexandria on June 22 for Dakar via the Suez Canal. The destroyers and the submarine went to North Africa through the Mediterranean.

---

[1] Acting Commander-in-Chief, Levant.

(a) Z5729/39/17. (b) Z5802/39/17. (c) Z5803/39/17. (d) Z6167/39/17. (e) Hist. (G)2, No. 374.

CHAPTER XXIX

British relations with General de Gaulle from February, 1942, to the Allied landings in North Africa

(i)

General de Gaulle and his Movement: the dispute with Admiral Muselier (February–April 1942).

THE British and United States Governments were closer in their treatment of the Vichy Government in 1942 than in their respective attitudes toward General de Gaulle and the Free French Movement. The official American view was that the existence of the Free French Movement was an obstacle to the efforts of the United States in keeping Vichy from complete subservience to the Germans. Mr. Hull, in particular, treated the Free French as though they were only a nuisance to the Allies. The President accepted Mr. Hull's view, and seems to have been influenced by Admiral Leahy.[1] Although Admiral Leahy in fact knew little of France—or of the French language—it is remarkable that he failed entirely to understand General de Gaulle's position. The President's lack of imaginative sympathy is even stranger.

General de Gaulle himself was at this time in a difficult position. He had not secured the support for which he had hoped among leading Frenchmen in France or in the Empire. He could not yet produce convincing proof of the importance of his Movement (and of his own name) as a rallying point for resistance in France. He had to make it clear to French opinion that he was neither, as the Germans called him, a British mercenary nor, as Marshal Pétain regarded him, a traitor and a renegade officer. The Americans paid no attention to his insistence upon the point of honour and his deep conviction that France would lose more in the long run by Vichy *attentisme* than she had lost by military defeat. The British military authorities might have treated him with more cordiality and have made more

---

[1] After his return to the United States from Vichy, Admiral Leahy became, on July 20, Chief of Staff to the President in his capacity of Commander-in-Chief of the Armed Forces of the United States. While at Vichy he had written to the President unfavourably about the Gaullist movement. In his book *I Was There* he is continuously hostile to General de Gaulle, in spite of the fact that M. Herriot told him—during his last week at Vichy—that he (M. Herriot) 'and his followers did not believe that de Gaulle or his movement had committed any offence against France, but, on the contrary, were fighting for French survival and French ideals' (p. 113).

use of his remarkable military talent. In Great Britain and abroad (except in Equatorial Africa) General de Gaulle was not specially fortunate either on the French or the British side in the liaison between the Free French and His Majesty's Government.

On the other hand, as time passed, General de Gaulle did not become a more sympathetic or understanding partner. He failed to understand the Prime Minister's generosity of mind and deep sympathy for France. He never learned to distinguish between essentials and non-essentials in his perpetual and over-wrought efforts to assert the independence of France. He was unreasonably suspicious of British motives. It was almost impossible to convince him that Great Britain had no designs on the French Empire; he was unwilling to take into account adequately the manifold responsibilities resting on the British Ministers and Chiefs of Staff. He never realised or, at all events, rarely showed that he appreciated the extent to which they and the Foreign Office were advocating his claims in the United States; still less did he show—except very occasionally—any comprehension of the difficulties which he was causing in the actual prosecution of the war by his exaggerated concern for the dignity and honour of France. There were times indeed when in his preoccupation with the restoration of an integral France after the war he seemed to forget that British lives were being expended to make victory possible.

At the beginning of the year 1942 General de Gaulle had caused the Prime Minister great trouble by his action over the small affair of St. Pierre and Miquelon.[1] This business was hardly settled when a crisis arose within the Free French Movement over the relations between General de Gaulle and Admiral Muselier, the Commander of the Free French Navy. Later in the spring General de Gaulle's suspicions over British action in Madagascar, and continuous friction with him over Syria,[2] were especially serious because he pushed forward his grievances unreasonably at a very dangerous period in the war.

Nonetheless the Foreign Office, who made more allowance for General de Gaulle's susceptibilities than he ever made for any British Minister, soldier or official, did their best not only in London but in Washington to help the Free French Movement at a time when the Prime Minister—with considerable excuse—had almost lost patience with General de Gaulle and had come to regard him more as a liability than as an asset to the Allies. Finally, in the latter part of September 1942, when the General's attitude over Syria had become intolerable from the British point of view, relations with

---

[1] See Chapter XXI, Section (iv).
[2] See Volume IV, Chapter LIII.

him nearly reached breaking-point. It is hardly possible to avoid putting the greater part of the blame for this tragic and absurd position on the General himself. The tension relaxed largely through the influence of the Foreign Office with the less excitable members of General de Gaulle's own staff, and for the time at least British collaboration with the Movement continued—uneasily, but without an irreparable breach.

Although the events following the invasion of North Africa belong to a different period of the war, and a different set of circumstances, there was little change in the general picture. On the one side the Americans—in the Foreign Office view—still overlooked, especially, the moral importance of General de Gaulle's Movement. The Prime Minister inclined to lose patience with the General's irritating incapacity to distinguish the wood from the trees, while the Foreign Office took on the whole a more conciliatory and mediating attitude, and made more allowances for General de Gaulle's peculiar temperament and position.

At the beginning of 1942, after a long period of friction which reached its worst in the St. Pierre–Miquelon incident, the Foreign
(a) Office considered that one of the causes of trouble with General de Gaulle was the one-sided nature of his agreement of August 7, 1940,[1] with His Majesty's Government. This agreement pledged British support, not to a Free French Movement, but to an individual— General de Gaulle—upon whom the Movement was made to depend; on the other hand General de Gaulle was not committed in writing to any counter-obligations to the British Government. This position was unfortunate from the point of the Free French, since General de Gaulle had too much power within the Movement, and Frenchmen hesitated to leave France at great risk to themselves and their families only to put themselves under the dictatorial authority of one man.

The desirable course therefore was to give real powers of decision and execution to the French National Committee, in other words, to insist on our decision of September 25, 1941,[2] that we should deal only with the Committee on matters of policy, while leaving General de Gaulle to act as Free French Commander-in-Chief. On the other hand the Committee consisted solely of General de Gaulle's nominees and was purely advisory, so that, in dealing with it, we should actually be dealing, as before, with General de Gaulle himself. At his meeting of September 12, 1941, with General de Gaulle, the Prime Minister had suggested the formation of a Free French Council

---

[1] See Volume I, pp. 407–8.
[2] See above, pp. 81–2.

(a) Z255/90/17.

with an effective voice in shaping the policy of the movement. General de Gaulle, however, had avoided anything which would lessen his own powers. Hence we should have to tell the General that we intended to carry out the decision of September 1941 to deal on matters of policy with the National Committee, and to secure that the Committee had the necessary executive authority. The Prime Minister was inclined to think that this question should be raised and settled before we began to carry out our plans for North Africa. Unfortunately there were obvious difficulties. Apart from the objections which General de Gaulle would make to an alteration in the relations between himself and the Committee there were no outstanding figures who could be brought into the Committee in order to strengthen it against the excessive personal domination of the General himself; even if such persons could be found, the result might be only to make the Committee a battleground of factions. The alternative, therefore, was to insist that General de Gaulle should co-operate on our terms and conform with the broad lines of our strategy and foreign policy. In other words, we could not avoid the troubles caused by General de Gaulle's temperamental methods and exaggerated views of his position as leader of French resistance. We could only do our best to mitigate the difficulties by a common-sense admixture of firmness and tact.

The desirability of limiting General de Gaulle's personal authority was shown at once when the General provoked a serious crisis in his own Movement over the relations between himself and Admiral Muselier. There had been disputes between General de Gaulle and (a) Admiral Muselier for many months; an open breach between them had been averted in September 1941, through the intervention of Mr. Eden and Mr. A. V. Alexander. After Admiral Muselier's return from St. Pierre at the end of February, General de Gaulle alleged that he had been intriguing against him. Admiral Muselier therefore resigned from the French National Committee; General de Gaulle retorted by relieving him of the post of Commander-in-Chief of the Free French Naval Forces and appointing Captain Auboyneau as his successor.

The Admiralty considered that the removal of Admiral Muselier would have a very bad effect on the efficiency of the Free French Navy. Mr. Eden had a long and somewhat difficult interview with (b) General de Gaulle on March 5, but was unable to persuade him to change his decision. The War Cabinet examined the question from (c) the naval point of view and decided to inform General de Gaulle that, while we would not insist upon Admiral Muselier remaining

---

(a) Z2264/97/17; Z1051/28/17. (b) Z1956/97/17. (c) WM(42)29.

a member of the French National Committee, we could not allow him to be deprived of his post as Commander-in-Chief of the Free French Navy. If General de Gaulle would not agree, we should have to take the necessary steps to ensure that our wishes were carried out.

(a)　General de Gaulle refused to allow the Admiral to keep his command and ordered him to take immediate leave of absence. On

(b)　March 8 General de Gaulle wrote to Mr. Eden explaining the reasons why he felt unable to allow us to interfere with his decision. He said that his Movement had been built up on the basis of fidelity to the alliance with Great Britain for the common victory; he knew that the Movement could not even continue in its present form without British support. On the other hand he could not maintain his own leadership and responsibility if the attitude of His Majesty's Government towards the Free French were inconsistent with measures taken by him and by the French National Committee. In such a situation their task would be impossible. They thought it essential to remain faithful to their aims of restoring France and reconstituting national unity in the war at the side of the Allies, but they could not sacrifice anything of the independence and sovereignty of France.

(c)　The War Cabinet on March 9 asked Mr. Eden to tell General de Gaulle that we maintained our view that Admiral Muselier should continue to hold his post as Commander-in-Chief of the Free French Navy. We made our request in the matter 'speaking as one Ally to another', but if General de Gaulle refused the request we should have to review our agreement with him as leader of the Free French Movement. Mr. Eden saw General de Gaulle on March 10. After a heated discussion the General agreed not to make a public statement to the effect that Admiral Muselier was no longer in command of the Free French Navy. The position would be that the Admiral was on leave, and at his (General de Gaulle's) disposal. If Admiral Muselier obeyed the instructions to go on leave, General de Gaulle would be willing to discuss with Mr. Eden, the First Lord of the Admiralty and the First Sea Lord, matters relating to the future collaboration of the Free French naval forces with His Majesty's Navy.

The situation became even more difficult because Admiral Muselier, instead of going on leave, appeared at his headquarters

(d)　when General de Gaulle went there to address the naval staff. The General regarded this incident as an act of insubordination on the Admiral's part, sentenced him to thirty days fortress arrest, and asked the British authorities to carry out the sentence. The Foreign

(a) Z2065/97/17.　(b) WP(42)117; Z2151/97/17.　(c) WM(42)32; Z2119/97/17.
(d) Z2120, 2122/97/17.

Office considered that General de Gaulle was within his legal rights in imposing this sentence and in asking us to carry it out, but there were obvious political objections against such action. The British authorities therefore took no steps to carry out the sentence; General de Gaulle then threatened to retire to the country, and announced that he would not come back until the sentence had been executed. On British advice Admiral Muselier also left London for the country.

The Prime Minister's view—before Mr. Eden's interview with (a) General de Gaulle on March 5—was that General de Gaulle and Admiral Muselier should sink their differences and work together. There could be no question of resignation or dismissal, or of the Free French Fleet leaving the Free French Movement and passing wholly under the orders of the British Admiralty. Admiral Dickens[1] (b) saw General de Gaulle on the evening of March 16 but was unable to persuade him to change his attitude. Earlier in the day Mr. Alexander had told the War Cabinet that the dispute between (c) General de Gaulle and Admiral Muselier might split the Free French Movement. Mr. Eden thought that we should have to choose between insisting that Admiral Muselier retained his post and negotiating a new agreement with General de Gaulle. Admiral Muselier had now put himself in the wrong, and General de Gaulle would not give way. Two days later the War Cabinet again dis- (d) cussed the matter. They thought that they would have to support General de Gaulle, but that there would be great trouble with the Free French Navy if Admiral Muselier did not retain the post of Commander-in-Chief. They also considered it desirable to revise the agreement with General de Gaulle, particularly in relation to the Free French Navy.

The Foreign Office had suggested a solution on the lines that Admiral Muselier should stay away in the country on sick leave for four weeks and that the post of Commander-in-Chief should remain in abeyance until Captain Auboyneau's return.[2] Admiral Muselier should recommend Captain Auboyneau for promotion to the rank of Admiral, and General de Gaulle should rescind his decree declaring Admiral Muselier to be unattached. We would conclude a revised agreement with General de Gaulle, and the General would under-take to offer Admiral Muselier either the post of Inspector-General or some other important command on the termination of his sick leave. The War Cabinet accepted these proposals. General de Gaulle, after another stormy interview, also accepted them. Admiral

---

[1] Principal Naval Liaison Officer with the Allied Navies.
[2] Captain Auboyneau was in command of the Free French Naval units in the Pacific.

(a) Z2007/97/17. (b) Z2362/97/17. (c) WM(42)34. (d) WM(42)35.

Muselier, however, refused the post of Inspector-General and would take nothing except the Command-in-Chief of the Free French Navy. On May 15 he resigned from the Free French Movement.[1]

(ii)

The British expedition to Madagascar: the reactions of General de Gaulle: failure of attempts to reach an arrangement with the Vichy French in Madagascar (April–August 1942).

The next important crisis with General de Gaulle came over the question of Madagascar. Before Laval had returned to power the British Government, with the co-operation of Field-Marshal Smuts in South Africa, had decided to send an expedition to occupy Madagascar. This plan had been under consideration since December 1941. The purpose of the expedition was to prevent an occupation of the island by the Japanese with or even without the connivance of the Vichy Government. Madagascar was of great strategic importance for control of the Mozambique channel and the sea route round the Cape to East Africa, India and the Middle East. The French authorities in the island had accepted the Vichy Government, and could not be trusted to resist Japanese demands on them.[2] We had not sufficient forces available to hold the island against a very strong Japanese force, but in view of the distances involved the Japanese might well hesitate to commit a large force to an attack.

(a)   The War Cabinet considered on April 24 whether the change of Government at Vichy made it desirable to postpone the plan in case Laval might retaliate by further concessions to the Germans. The transports from Great Britain had already turned the Cape, and arrangements had been made to carry out the operation early in May with two or three brigades. It was hoped that these troops would be supported by an air force from South Africa. The Foreign Office did not regard postponement as necessary. The United States Government approved of the operation. In view of their desire to avoid a complete breach with Vichy, they had wished not to be associated openly with it, but, after appeals from the Prime Minister

---

[1] Admiral Muselier returned to the Movement after the agreement between the National Committee and General Giraud in 1943.

[2] They were also suspected of allowing Japanese submarines to use the port of Diego Suarez.

(a) WM(42)52.1, C.A.

on April 24 and 28,[1] President Roosevelt agreed to tell the Vichy (a)
Government of his approval, and also to make a public announcement to this effect. Meanwhile the War Cabinet decided to go
forward with the plan, subject to a change of decision if circum- (b)
stances should require it. They considered the matter again on
April 29. They understood that the consequences might be serious if
the French naval forces at Dakar attempted to prevent us from using
Freetown, but the Prime Minister and Mr. Eden thought that the
risk of hostile action from Vichy must be taken. The first landings
were carried out in the early morning of May 5. The British force
took Diego Suarez on May 8; the French authorities opposed the
landing, and were ordered by Vichy to continue their resistance
elsewhere in the island.

After the surrender of Diego Suarez, Admiral Syfret, the British (c)
Commander-in-Chief of the combined operation, informed the
Governor-General of the island[2] that, if the French administrative
staff would co-operate with the United Nations, they would remain
in office, and would not be required to take part in the war side by
side with those parts of the Empire which were still fighting. The
Governor refused this offer.

Admiral Syfret reported that there was 'universal hatred' of the
Free French in Diego Suarez, and that it would be most unwise to
introduce them into the administration of the island. This report was

---

[1] On April 24 the Prime Minister had asked the President whether, in view of the
changed circumstances—i.e. the return of Laval to office and the withdrawal of Admiral
Leahy—since his message of April 3 (see above, p. 293, note 1), he would now allow the
dropping of leaflets in Madagascar and France which would give the impression that
America was associated with the expedition*, and that, conjointly with Britain, she
guaranteed the return of Madagascar to France after the war.

On April 28 the Prime Minister sent another message asking that, if possible, a token
United States detachment should join the occupying forces and that, in any case, the
United States Government should inform the Vichy Government and announce publicly
that the expedition had American support.

The President replied on April 29 that he was making a speech on that evening in
which he would explain American policy towards France and American concern over
the return of Laval to power. The President proposed to say that 'the United Nations will
take measures if necessary to prevent the use of French territory in any part of the world
for military purposes by the Axis Powers'. Mr. Roosevelt also agreed to Mr. Churchill's
proposal that he should announce American approval of the Madagascar operation. He
proposed also to tell the French Ambassador in Washington that, if necessary, American
troops and ships would 'use [Madagascar] in the common cause of the civilised peoples'.

The President's message to the Vichy Government was sent on May 4, and released to
the press on the same day. See *F.R.U.S.*, 1942, II, 698–9. Laval made a very strong
protest to the United States Government about the message.

* Mr. Churchill and Mr. Roosevelt used throughout the code word 'Ironclad' for the
expedition.

[2] M. Annet. He had been appointed Governor of the French Cameroons by the Pétain
Government in 1940, but the territory had rallied to the Free French before he could get
to it.

(a) T613/2, No. 75, April 24; T648/2, No. 81, April 28; T650/2, No. 142, April 29
(Churchill Papers/265). (b) WM(42)54, C.A. (c) Z3923, 5006/23/17.

exaggerated, but the remoteness of Madagascar, the effect of German propaganda and of German and Japanese victories, and the complete subservience of the Governor to Vichy had produced a situation of indifference to the Allies among the 'average' Frenchmen

(a) in the island. On the other hand General de Gaulle had already suggested—before he knew of the British expedition—that the Free French should occupy Madagascar; he was certain to object very strongly to an accommodation with the Vichy authorities or indeed to an arrangement which did not add Madagascar to the territories

(b) controlled by the Free French Movement. The War Cabinet had agreed on May 5 that at some stage the Free French should be given a share in the administration of the island, but that as yet no decision could be taken.

General de Gaulle indeed was both dismayed and angry at the fact that the expedition had been planned and carried out without the knowledge and participation of the Free French. He was not less

(c) indignant at a communiqué issued by the United States Government on May 4 stating that the island would be restored to France (i.e. to the Vichy Government) if its occupation were no longer essential

(d) to the common cause of the United Nations. On May 9 M. Eboué,[1] Governor-General of French Equatorial Africa, transmitted a note of protest from the French National Committee to Mr. Mallon, United States Consul at Brazzaville. M. Eboué had been instructed to give the note also to Mr. Parr, the British Consul-General. After seeing Mr. Parr, M. Eboué thought that a formal communication was unnecessary, and therefore merely gave him a copy of the note.

(e) On May 11 General de Gaulle—after an earlier refusal to do so—came to see Mr. Eden. Mr. Eden explained that we had not invited the Free French to join in the expedition because we had thought it undesirable for Frenchmen to fight against Frenchmen. We had realised that our decision might be embarrassing to the Free French Movement but Frenchmen generally seemed to have appreciated our reasons.

General de Gaulle said that he understood the military reasons for our undertaking the operation alone. Soldiers had a right to settle these things; he might himself one day undertake an operation without consulting any one. He objected, however, very strongly to our offer to the Governor, and protested against what he called our procedure in disposing of French territory without reference to himself.

---

[1] M. Eboué, whom General de Gaulle had appointed Governor of French Equatorial Africa, was one of the most remarkable figures among the General's supporters. M. Eboué was born in French Guiana, but was of African descent.

(a) Z1435/23/17; Z3356/210/17.   (b) WM(42)57.   (c) Z3733/23/17.   (d) Z4600/23/17.
(e) WM(42)61; Z3955/23/17.

Mr. Eden replied that he had in fact asked General de Gaulle to come to see him earlier and that, if the General had been willing to do so, it would have been possible to issue a statement that he approved of the reasons for our action. General de Gaulle repeated his unwillingness to approve of any British operation on French territory conducted without reference to the Free French Movement. Mr. Eden said that he could not understand the General's attitude; he assumed that General de Gaulle would rather have the British than the Japanese in Diego Suarez. Mr. Eden then said again that he was willing to discuss the future administration of the territory. General de Gaulle replied that in due course, after we had completed our occupation, he would be ready to take part in a discussion, but that any proposals must come from our side. He suggested, however, that General Legentilhomme, a member of the French National Committee and Commissioner for War, knew Madagascar, and would be a good choice if any one were sent from London.[1]

Meanwhile the War Cabinet had to decide whether they would continue military operations in Madagascar. There were obvious (a) advantages in securing control of the whole island. We could establish naval and air bases for patrolling the Mozambique Channel, and could save shipping by obtaining from Madagascar some supplies which otherwise we had to send to India and the Middle East via the Cape. The United States urgently needed supplies of mica and graphite from Madagascar and, if we did not act at once, might come to an arrangement with Vichy which would tie our hands. In a telegram of May 15 to Admiral Syfret, commanding the British naval force, the Prime Minister had pointed out that the naval position in the Indian Ocean had improved[2] since the Madagascar operation had been planned, and that the British fleet in eastern waters would be strengthened early in July. The Prime Minister thought it unlikely that the Japanese would now risk the 10,000 men and naval escorts which would be necessary to take Diego Suarez. On the other hand we could not lock up a force of any size in Madagascar; if, therefore, it was not possible to take Tamatave and Majunga within a few days, we might find it better to try to come to some arrangement with the French authorities. We had had to indicate that the Free French would be associated with the administration of the island, but we had done so for the sake of

---

[1] On May 13 a statement was issued, in agreement with General de Gaulle, that the purpose of the occupation of Diego Suarez was to deny the use of the place to the enemy, and that the British Government intended that the French National Committee should play its 'due part in the administration of the liberated French territory', since the Committee were 'co-operating with the United Nations as the representative of Fighting France'. (For the title 'Fighting France', see below, section (iv) of this chapter.)

[2] i.e. with the American victory in the battle of the Coral Sea.

(a) WP(42)242.

maintaining the Free French Movement; the Free French representatives—if they came at all—could not arrive for several months.
In any case we should not upset the local situation in their
interest.

During the next few weeks 'unofficial' local negotiations were
opened with some of the French authorities through the agency of a
British subject resident in the island. The French Governor took no
part in these unofficial exchanges, though it appeared likely that he
knew of them. At the beginning of June, however, it was clear that
the Governor would not disobey instructions which he might receive
from Vichy, and that the negotiations were unlikely to succeed.

(a)   The War Cabinet discussed the situation on June 8. A second
American victory—the battle of Midway Island (June 4–7)—had
caused even heavier losses to the Japanese fleet, and indeed—although
the fact was not at once realised in Great Britain—put an end to
Japanese initiative in the Pacific as well as any chance of a break-out
on a large scale into the Indian Ocean. There were now stronger
arguments against locking up in Madagascar troops urgently
needed elsewhere. The War Cabinet, at the suggestion of the Prime
Minister, decided to find out more about the local situation and to

(b) consult Field-Marshal Smuts again before taking further steps. The
position was explained to General de Gaulle by the Prime Minister
on June 10[1] and more fully by Mr. Eden on June 29.[2] Mr. Eden said
that we were trying to obtain control of Madagascar by negotiation
and, although we would do nothing which might exclude eventual
Free French participation in the administration, we could not
associate them at once. General de Gaulle's attitude in the matter was
for the time more friendly, though he said that he expected no result
from our efforts at negotiation.

There was, in fact, no result. The deadlock remained unbroken

(c) throughout the months of June and July. On July 25 the Chiefs of
Staff reported to the Prime Minister that no progress had been made
in the negotiations with the Vichy authorities, and that we were
unlikely to reach a satisfactory *modus vivendi* in the island without
undertaking military operations against Tamatave and Majunga.
The Vichy Governor was playing for time, but might capitulate if
confronted with force. The Chiefs of Staff therefore recommended

(d) that the operations should be carried out. They reported on August 6
that the troops and shipping available locally were sufficient for the
work.

---

[1] For this conversation, see also below pp. 336 and 340.
[2] See also below pp. 339–40.

(a) WM(42)72. (b) Z5123/4949/17; Z5382/23/17. (c) COS(42)213(o). (d) COS(42)
221(o); WP(42)345.

The War Cabinet discussed these reports on August 7. Mr. Eden (a) said that the political considerations involved were evenly balanced. We should consider the possible effect on opinion in France, and on our proposed expedition to North Africa. The Americans were anxious to placate the Vichy Government, and might regard further action at Madagascar as undesirable for the time. The War Cabinet therefore decided to postpone decision for a week, and Mr. Eden proposed to submit a memorandum on the political implications of the plan.

In this memorandum (submitted on August 10) Mr. Eden took (b) the view that there were no political reasons why we should not carry out the operation. He considered that the Vichy Government probably expected to lose the whole of the island, and that their reaction to the loss would not be more vigorous than at the time of our occupation of Diego Suarez. Laval might use the opportunity to make more concessions to the Germans, but he could always find a pretext for doing so.

We had undertaken to give the Fighting French their due share in the administration, and should do so as soon as possible after the Vichy authorities had surrendered. We should also tell the French National Committee—in General de Gaulle's absence[1]—of the operation a few hours before it was carried out. Finally, we should not include in the terms of surrender a promise of unconditional repatriation of the French troops in the island. We needed them as a lever to get back our own men held by Vichy.

The War Cabinet agreed on August 11 that the operation should (c) be carried out. On September 10 the 29th British Infantry Brigade captured Majunga against slight opposition. The brigade was then re-embarked, and taken to the east coast, where Tamatave was taken on September 18. Five days later the capital of the island fell, and the Governor-General, with some of his staff, retreated to the south. On November 5, after another successful British action against the French forces some three weeks earlier, the Governor-General surrendered.

The long delay in completing the military operation turned out to be advantageous from the political point of view. Owing to the disputes with General de Gaulle over Syria,[2] the question of Free French participation in the administration of Madagascar was for a time in suspense. Only in mid-October, after a settlement of the Syrian dispute, was an arrangement over Madagascar practicable. The actual appointment of General Legentilhomme as Governor-General was not announced until November 11 and the General did

---

[1] General de Gaulle was in the Middle East.
[2] See Volume IV, Chapter LII, section (iii) and (iv).

(a) WM(42)107. (b) WP(42)350; Z6366/23/17. (c) WM(42)110.1, C.A.

not reach Madagascar before January 1943. The delay and the course of events in North Africa thus allowed the French officials in the island time to change their views without loss of face.

(iii)

General de Gaulle's messages to General Catroux and to the Free French authorities in Equatorial Africa: correspondence with the United States on behalf of the Free French Movement: General de Gaulle's adoption of the title 'La France Combattante' for his Movement (May–July 1942).

At the end of June 1942, General de Gaulle was inclined at least temporarily to give up his suspicions of His Majesty's Government since he had new evidence of British goodwill in regard to a request which he made for a change in the name and general designation of the Free French Movement; he also realised the efforts made by His Majesty's Government to improve the relations between the Free French and the United States.

This period of relative calm, however, had followed another short
(a) crisis. At his interview[1] with Mr. Eden on May 11, 1942, General de Gaulle said that the position of his Movement was becoming increasingly difficult. If the other Allies did not treat the Free French as full Allies, the Movement would break up. Mr. Eden pointed out that most of the difficulties which the General had in mind seemed to have arisen among the Free French themselves. General de Gaulle admitted that a small number (who were 'cultivated' by the British and American authorities) were causing trouble; on the other hand Allied policy had been responsible for a series of incidents—Syria, the Muselier affair, Madagascar and New Caledonia[2]—which were disintegrating the Movement. The General made a bitter attack on the United States Government from whom the Free French, who were fighting Allies, received nothing but cold disregard while the Vichy Embassy at Washington was treated with every consideration. Frenchmen might well ask why they should be more resolute than the United States Government who were apparently content that the French should be neutral. The fundamental point was that the Allies should adopt the right moral attitude towards the Free French Movement. 'His Majesty's Government sometimes did so; the Americans never.'

---

[1] See above, pp. 328–9.
[2] Admiral d'Argenlieu, Free French High Commissioner in the Pacific, complained that the American and Australian military authorities made arrangements affecting New Caledonia without consulting him.

(a) Z3955/23/17.

During this time General de Gaulle's suspicions were increased by the unwillingness of the British Government to allow him to leave England. The return of Laval to power, and the evidence of closer collaboration between the Vichy Government and the Germans had forced General de Gaulle more and more into a defensive position with regard to the French Empire. Hence he felt that it was his duty to visit the French overseas territories for which he was trustee. He (a) asked the British Government in April 1942 to give him an air passage to Cairo. Mr. Eden thought that, as long as General de (b) Gaulle was recognised as the leader of Free Frenchmen and President of the Free French National Committee, we could not logically—or even constitutionally—prevent him from visiting territories administered by the Committee. On the other hand his visit to the Middle East in 1941 had caused much trouble. He had recently delivered a violent attack on the United States Government over their attitude to the Free French Movement. He might make another attack on them or on the British Government from Radio Brazzaville. The situation in Syria and the Lebanon was also sufficiently difficult without the complication of a visit by General de Gaulle. Nevertheless Mr. Eden thought it better to let him go unless we were prepared to withdraw British recognition from him.

The Prime Minister, however, considered that it would be most dangerous to allow the General to renew a campaign of anglophobia. On April 16, after bringing the matter before the War Cabinet, the Prime Minister ruled that he must not be allowed to go. A week later Mr. Eden asked General de Gaulle to defer his visit in order to be (c) on hand for consultation, especially in view of the situation in France. The General agreed with comparative readiness. On May 27 Mr. Eden raised the matter again with the Prime Minister. Once more (d) the Prime Minister refused to agree; he noted that 'There is nothing hostile to England this man may not do once he gets off the chain'.

Mr. Eden brought the question before the War Cabinet on June 2. (e) He said that he was willing to try to persuade the General to postpone his visit again, but that, if he failed to do so, he would not think it wise to forbid General de Gaulle to go abroad. The Prime Minister repeated his view that there were grave risks in allowing General de Gaulle to go to West Africa where he might make statements very unfavourable to Great Britain. It would be much better for the General to stay in England until a proper Free French Council had been formed.[1]

---

[1] See also the Prime Minister's memorandum summarised above, pp. 299–300.

(a) Z3399/81/17. (b) Z3443/608/17. (c) Z4226/298/17. (d) PMM42/115; Z4818/298/17. (e) WM(42)71.1, C.A.

(a)   On June 8 M. Eboué and General Leclerc, commander of all forces in Free French Africa, addressed jointly a note to Mr. Parr. The note began by pointing out that the only objects of the Free French Movement were the restoration 'dans son intégrité' of France and the Empire; although the Movement did not exercise authority over more than a limited area, it was approved by the great majority of Frenchmen, and in 1940 the Prime Minister's attitude towards General de Gaulle and his supporters had given the Movement positive encouragement. The note then went on to declare that, in the event of some entirely unexpected change in the policy of Great Britain or of her Allies, the population and the civil and military authorities of Free French Africa would carry out whatever orders they might receive from General de Gaulle whom they regarded as their sole leader until the French people had recovered their independence.

Mr. Parr told M. Eboué and General Leclerc that he could give the fullest assurances that His Majesty's Government would never even think of profiting by the tragic situation of France to advance British interests at French expense. In his telegrams to the Foreign Office reporting the note he explained that M. Eboué and General Leclerc felt that they had undertaken two responsibilities in joining the Free French Movement; they were pledged to continue the war and to restore their country. The second pledge could not be fulfilled if they allowed any diminution of the status of France before the world. If General de Gaulle should consider that our attitude prevented him from carrying out this pledge, and should withdraw from collaboration, they would respect his decision not merely out of loyalty to their chief but with full endorsement of the reasons which had led to his decision.

General Leclerc said to Mr. Parr that he could understand why reasons of military necessity might preclude the use of a mixed force—British and Free French—in any given operation, but that if we excluded the Free French from our plans dealing with the status and administration of French territories, we should be depriving the Free French Movement of all meaning and proclaiming to the French people that General de Gaulle and his followers would have been wiser not to have remained faithful to the engagements of France, but to have adopted the 'attentisme' which our attitude in the cases of Madagascar and the French West Indies seemed about to justify.

Mr. Parr's first telegram reporting this note was received in the Foreign Office on June 9. On June 10 he telegraphed, after seeing M. Eboué and General Leclerc, that they had sent their note after

---

(a) Z4881, 4894, 4942, 4943, 5391/298/17.

getting a message from General de Gaulle on June 6, and that they had not previously told him that in this message General de Gaulle represented himself as not being allowed to leave the United Kingdom and attributed our unwillingness to let him come out to Africa as due to reasons connected with Madagascar and probably with Dakar. In a later despatch—received on June 30—Mr. Parr explained at greater length the views of the two Free French representatives. General Leclerc said that he felt that the exclusion of General de Gaulle and the Free French Movement from action taken by us affecting French territories and French interests must imply a decision to dispense with the assistance of the Free French as Allies. M. Eboué spoke in similar terms. They were extremely pleased and clearly relieved by a telegram from General de Gaulle giving an account of his conversations[1] with the Prime Minister and Mr. Eden, but they remained uneasy with regard to the United States.

Mr. Parr thought it most disquieting that two men of such high character and achievements should have felt bound to make a communication of this kind. He did not think that they really doubted either the good faith of His Majesty's Government or the goodwill of the British public. He considered that the reason lay in the nature of the Free French Movement. This Movement was a crusade by men who felt bitterly the dishonour and humiliation as well as the defeat of their country. They could not achieve the moral purpose of this crusade merely with the victory of the Allies; they knew that their own material contribution to this victory, however high their feats of arms, would not be commensurate with the former status of France. General de Gaulle was not only their military leader; he was the living symbol of a mission which made them more than a fighting force. Their self-imposed discipline, which should not be confused with any leanings towards fascism, meant complete loyalty to General de Gaulle because they were convinced that his conception of their task corresponded with the circumstances of their tragedy, and that his failure would be the end of their hopes for the restoration of France.

For these reasons they felt bound to insist that they had a right to be consulted on every question affecting French territory and French interests. They would admit that acquiescence in a decision to exclude them on grounds of expediency might constitute a passive contribution to the conduct of the war, but it would leave them ultimately in the position of clients whose material goods were restored to them at the price of their spiritual liberty.

---

[1] See below, pp. 336-7.

The Prime Minister did not know of the contents of General de
(a) Gaulle's message to Brazzaville when he saw him on June 10.[1] The
conversation had been friendly. The Prime Minister had congratulated the General on the fine behaviour of the Free French at
Bir Hacheim, and had explained that we had not asked the Free
French to join in the expedition to Madagascar because, rightly or
wrongly, we had thought that we should meet with less resistance
if we acted alone; we had also to consider American views. General
de Gaulle hinted at British and American plans for expeditions to
Dakar or the bend of the Niger and for coming to terms in these
areas with the Vichy authorities. Mr. Churchill assured General de
Gaulle once again that we had no designs on the French Empire.
General de Gaulle accepted these assurances, and agreed that, in
general, British policy was well disposed to the Free French. He
complained of the attitude of the United States towards his Movement and said that on the celebration of Memorial Day the United
States Government had invited the Vichy Military Attachés but not
the Free French.

In spite of his friendly attitude to the Prime Minister, General de
Gaulle was still in a state of excitement and suspicion over British
and American plans and highly indignant at the postponement of his
visit to the Free French territories. In addition to the message which
(b) he had sent to M. Eboué and General Leclerc, General de Gaulle
also sent instructions to General Catroux[2] expressing the fear that
His Majesty's Goverment had designs on Madagascar and might
never return the island fully to France, and that they might also be
planning action with the Americans at Dakar from which the Free
French would be excluded. General de Gaulle had apparently said
that, if the two Governments showed such lack of confidence in the
Free French, he would have to separate himself and his Movement
from us. He had also complained often to General Catroux
that British policy aimed at the elimination of France from the
Levant.

Mr. Eden felt bound to ask for an explanation from General de
Gaulle about these messages, especially in view of his more friendly
attitude in the interview of June 10 with the Prime Minister. Mr.
(c) Eden therefore invited him to the Foreign Office on June 13. General
de Gaulle said that he had received reports from General Catroux
about his relations with General Spears and from Brazzaville about
a possible 'threat' in the region of the bend of the Niger; he had also

---

(d)   [1] Mr. Parr's telegram about the message was not received in the Foreign Office until
9.20 p.m. on June 10.
       [2] General Catroux informed Mr. Casey of these instructions.

(a) Z5123/4949/17. (b) Z4697/95/17. (c) Z5014/90/17. (d) Z4943/298/17.

heard from America about another 'threat' to Dakar. The cumulative effect of these reports had been to cause him and his representatives abroad the greatest anxiety. He had spoken about these matters to Mr. Peake,[1] but had received no reassurances from him. He remembered that when he had last intended to go abroad Mr. Eden had dissuaded him from doing so, and we had then attacked Madagascar without warning. It was therefore natural that he should consider it at least possible that we had some similar plan in our minds again, and that once more we or the Americans or both of us were going to undertake operations against French territory without Free French co-operation or regard to French sovereignty.

Mr. Eden replied that, even if these suspicions were justified—and they were not justified—General de Gaulle ought not to have sent such disquieting telegrams to his representatives abroad, without first consulting the Foreign Office. General de Gaulle said that he had felt it right to warn his people of what might happen. After seeing the Prime Minister he had sent another telegram of a more (a) reassuring character and was willing to telegraph again. Mr. Eden tried to make General de Gaulle see the effect of these continued suspicions in his relations with the British Government. General de Gaulle then repeated that he had very little suspicion of us, but that he deeply suspected the Americans. He asked whether Mr. Eden was sure that the Americans were not planning something against Dakar. The Americans did not even regard the Free French as belligerents; their policy was to disintegrate the French Empire and to neutralise France, while his policy was to bring France into the war on our side. Mr. Eden suggested that General de Gaulle was treating the State Department in the wrong way, but the General maintained that the faults were on the American side.

Meanwhile the British and United States Governments had been discussing the question of their relations with General de Gaulle. The United States Government were themselves considering the question of relations with the Free French, especially in view of the deterioration in their relations with Vichy after Laval's return to power. The British view was that General de Gaulle's sense of grievance against the United States was 'not unfounded'; that the United States Government should give to the French National Committee a similar recognition to that given by the British Government, and that the return of Laval to power and the increasing disrepute into which Marshal Pétain had fallen should make it easier

---

[1] His Majesty's Representative with the Free French National Committee.

(a) Z5072, 5275/90/17.

M

for the United States to be more forthcoming in their attitude to the
Free French.

(a)   Mr. Welles told Lord Halifax on May 8 that in his opinion the
United States Government ought not to recognise any refugee group
as a French Government, and that General de Gaulle lacked the
personal qualities necessary for a recognised head of a French
resistance movement and was very badly advised by his entourage.
Mr. Welles had suggested that the two Governments should organise
a strong French National Committee, preferably by reinforcing the
existing committee. The functions of the new Committee would be
consultative with regard to the British and American Governments,
and administrative with regard to the Free French territories.
General de Gaulle would be a member of the Committee, charged
with certain military responsibilities.[1]

Mr. Eden telegraphed to Lord Halifax on May 13 that we agreed
that it would be a mistake for the United States to recognise the
French National Committee as a Government or indeed to go
further than ourselves in the degree of recognition accorded to
General de Gaulle. On the other hand, in spite of his defects and his
extravagant conception of his mission, there was in our opinion no
alternative to General de Gaulle. The chances of men like MM.
Herriot or Jeanneney leaving France were very slight; nothing
was to be expected from the attempts made by certain Frenchmen—
e.g. M. Chautemps—in America to form a 'middle movement'
composed of time-servers who did not approve of General de Gaulle
and thought that Marshal Pétain was 'doing his best'. We hoped
that the United States Government would give these attempts no
encouragement; M. Chautemps was the worst type of French
politician and held a large responsibility for the surrender at
Bordeaux in 1940.

We wanted to encourage French resistance in every way open to
us, and to bring back into the war as much of the French Empire as
possible in the hope that a Fighting France might take her place at
the peace conference as one of the United Nations. For this reason
we ought to develop the closest contact with the French people. If
the United States Government agreed with our aims, we hoped that
they would also agree on the means of achieving them. Our solution
of the difficulties with General de Gaulle was not to displace him
but to reinforce his Committee as best we could with a few more
independent members who would not merely obey him blindly. We

---

[1] For the American account of this conversation, see F.R.U.S., 1942, II, 511–13. In this
account Mr. Welles did not use the word 'refugee'. He said that the Free French movement 'as represented by General de Gaulle and his associates was rapidly falling to pieces'.

(a) Z3922, 3953/115/17.

were trying to bring over from France some left-wing leaders of the
Liberation Movement who could speak with authority on opinion
in France and, if necessary, stand up to General de Gaulle.

In view of its governmental responsibilities in respect of Free
French territories the Committee must have executive and not solely
consultative functions. Moreover General de Gaulle's increasing
contacts in France required that the Committee should have a
political 'flavour'. The time might also come for the General to
launch a programme of wider appeal under which he might attract
many Frenchmen outside France who had hitherto refused to join
him.

Lord Halifax put these arguments to Mr. Welles on May 14 in the (a)
form of an *aide-mémoire*[1] in which he included the considerations
which Mr. Parr had set out in a telegram of May 11 from Brazzaville.[2] Mr. Welles accepted Mr. Eden's view that General de Gaulle
should remain Chairman of the Committee; he was attracted by
the idea of bringing over a few Frenchmen from France who would
not be subservient to General de Gaulle. After further discussion
Mr. Hull gave Lord Halifax an *aide-mémoire* on June 11 setting out (b)
the terms upon which the United States Government proposed to
give official recognition to General de Gaulle and the French
National Committee. Mr. Eden suggested some changes in the text
which they thought would make it more satisfactory to General de
Gaulle. Mr. Hull asked that Mr. Eden should communicate the
text to General de Gaulle under pledge of secrecy.

Mr. Eden made this communication on June 29. The text stated (c)
that the United States Government were subordinating all questions
to the one purpose of winning the war. The French National Committee had the same objective, and was undertaking active military
measures for the preservation of French territory for the French
people. The United States Government recognised the contribution
of General de Gaulle and of the National Committee to the common
cause and wished to lend all possible military assistance and support
to the Committee as a symbol of French resistance in general to the
Axis Powers. The United States Government agreed with the view
held by the British Government and also, as they understood, by the

---

[1] For the text, see *F.R.U.S.*, *ib.*, 517–20.
[2] In this telegram Mr. Parr reported the disquiet felt in French Equatorial Africa over
the policy of the United States towards the French Empire, and the tendency to hold   (d)
Great Britain responsible for this policy. General Leclerc had said to Mr. Parr that the
Americans apparently failed to realise that 'not merely in colonies that had rallied to the
[Free French] Movement, but in Occupied France and among a great proportion of
Frenchmen elsewhere, the presence of the invader and the existence of de Gaulle were the
only two things which counted'. Mr. Parr thought that if General de Gaulle withdrew,
there was no chance of the French territories continuing to support the Movement.

(a) Z4035/115/17. (b) Z4947/115/17. (c) Z5383/115/17. (d) Z3954/18/17.

French National Committee, that the destiny and political organisation of France must be determined, in the last analysis, by the
French people under conditions giving them freedom to express their
desire unswayed by any form of coercion. In pursuing their common
war objective the United States would continue to deal with the
local free French officials in their respective territories, and would
appoint representatives in London for consultation with the French
National Committee.

After some discussion on the detailed phrasing of the statement,
General de Gaulle accepted it, apparently with considerable satis-
(a) faction. On July 9 the State Department therefore issued to the
press the memorandum sent to the Free French, together with a
statement that Admiral Stark and Brigadier-General Charles L.
Bolte had been appointed as representatives of the United States to
consult with the French National Committee in London, and that
General de Gaulle had welcomed these appointments.[1]

While these discussions were taking place between the British and
United States Governments, General de Gaulle had raised the
(b) question of a change in the designation of the Free French Movement. General de Gaulle had been using the term 'Fighting France'
—'La France Combattante'—as a description of the Movement
before his conversation with Mr. Churchill on June 10. He appears
(c) on this occasion to have asked the Prime Minister's consent to the
change of name.[2] General de Gaulle's reason for wanting the change
seems to have been that the term 'Free France' did not recognise
that he had anything to do with the forces of resistance in Metropolitan France who were not 'free'. He also considered that the term
was now misleading as a description of his own Movement since
other self-styled 'Free Movements' had been established by nationals
of enemy countries.

Mr. Eden thought that General de Gaulle must be allowed to be
the best judge of his own interest in the matter, though the Foreign
Office pointed out that the Vichy Government were careful to avoid
using the term 'Free Frenchmen', since it was impossible for them
to bring Frenchmen to trial merely because they called themselves
'Free'. The Vichy Government indeed appeared to have asked the
State Department not to use the term; the latter always referred to

---

[1] On July 25 General Marshall called on General de Gaulle and thereby implied that
the Americans were treating him as an ally.

[2] According to the French record of this conversation, Mr. Churchill said to General de
(d) Gaulle that he had intentionally used the term 'Fighting French' in a speech in the House
of Commons. He thought that the term 'La France Combattante' was better than 'La
France Libre', and advised General de Gaulle to discuss with the Foreign Office the
possibility of adopting it.

(a) Z5813/115/17. (b) Z4949/4949/17. (c) Z5555/4949/17. (d) Z5123/4949/17.

the 'French' National Committee. Vichy had adopted the words 'Gaulliste' and 'Gaullisme', and incidentally had done General de Gaulle a considerable service by associating his name with French resistance.

General de Gaulle's proposal for a change of terminology also involved a new definition of the French National Committee. M. Dejean[1] suggested a formula describing the Committee as the 'organe directeur de la France Combattante, ayant seul qualité pour organiser la participation française à la guerre, et représenter auprès des Alliés les intérêts français, notamment dans la mesure où ceux-ci sont affectés par la poursuite de la guerre'. The Foreign Office regarded this claim to 'sole competence' in representing all French interests as too wide since it would be tantamount to implying that we regarded the Committee as the Government of France. After discussion with the Free French representatives, a formula was agreed in the following terms:

'(a) La France Combattante.

Ensemble des ressortissants français, où qu'ils soient, et des territoires français qui s'unissent pour collaborer avec les Nations Unies dans la guerre contre les ennemis communs; et symbole de la résistance à l'Axe de tous les ressortissants français qui n'acceptent pas la capitulation et qui, par les moyens à leur disposition, contribuent, où qu'ils se trouvent, à la libération de la France par la victoire commune des Nations Unies.

(b) Comité National Français.

Organe directeur de la France Combattante. Organise la participation à la guerre des ressortissants et des territoires français qui s'unissent pour collaborer avec les Nations Unies dans la guerre contre les ennemis communs, et représente leurs intérêts auprès du Gouvernement du Royaume-Uni.'

The first part of definition (a) thus took the place of the earlier definition of Free Frenchmen as those who rallied to General de Gaulle in support of the Allied cause. General de Gaulle's own name no longer appeared, and the new definition made it clear that the persons and territories constituting 'La France Combattante' formed a unity for the purpose of continuing the war. The second part of definition (a) marked a new step since it recognised General de Gaulle's Movement for the first time as a symbol of French resistance in general, whether in France or elsewhere. In definition (b) the National Committee was recognised as representing the unity of 'La France Combattante'. On the other hand the Committee

---

[1] National Commissioner for Foreign Affairs.

was not defined as competent to represent internationally Frenchmen who did not form part of the organised body of 'La France Combattante'.

Mr. Eden informed the United States Government about these proposed definitions in view, particularly, of the negotiations which Mr. Hull was carrying out with regard to a statement about the relations between the United States Government and the French National Committee. Mr. Hull raised no objection to the change but suggested that we should not announce it until after the American statement had been made.

(a)   The announcement was made on July 14. The Free French (now referred to officially as the 'Fighting French') went considerably beyond the interpretation authorised on the British side for the new terminology, but Mr. Eden did not think it necessary at the time to insist on our interpretation in documents circulated by them solely among their own supporters. On the other hand the Foreign Office found it convenient to use certain definitions agreed by the French National Committee, e.g. the liberated French territories overseas, such as Free French Africa, and the Free French forces retained their former appellation.

(iv)

The question of associating General de Gaulle with the planning of operations for a landing in Metropolitan France: further controversies over Syria and Madagascar: the Prime Minister's interview of September 30 with General de Gaulle (July–September 1942).

The improvement in the relations with General de Gaulle at the end of June and in early July did not altogether remove the Prime Minister's doubts about the General's attitude towards Great

(b)   Britain. The Prime Minister was thus unwilling to accept without reservation the Foreign Office view that General de Gaulle was not fundamentally anti-British, and that he seemed to show an anti-British bias mainly because as a very patriotic Frenchman he felt a sense of frustration owing to his limited powers of action, and because he had to protect himself against propaganda from Vichy and the Germans that he was nothing but a British mercenary. During the next two months General de Gaulle's intransigence seemed at least on the surface to support the Prime Minister's opinion.

(a) Z6221/4949/17. (b) Z5974/608/17.

General de Gaulle left England at the end of July for his postponed visit to the Free French territories. He had a friendly conversation (a) with the Prime Minister on July 29, and, on the previous day, with Mr. Eden. General de Gaulle had written to the Prime Minister on (b) July 25 urging the concentration in Great Britain of all available Free French forces for participation in operations in the west, and the association of the Free French High Command, as part of the inter-Allied High Command, with the plans and decisions regarding such operations. General de Gaulle referred to these questions generally in his talks with the Prime Minister and Mr. Eden, but their treatment required detailed consideration by the Chiefs of Staff and the War Cabinet. The Chiefs of Staff, on July 28, came to the conclusion that it would be undesirable either to bring back the Free French forces from the Middle East and Africa or—for reasons of security—to associate the Free French High Command at an early stage with the planning of major operations. Mr. Eden, however, thought that a number of important political considerations were involved in General de Gaulle's requests and that the War Cabinet ought to examine the general question of our collaboration with General de Gaulle in matters connected with the preparation of possible operations in Metropolitan France. The Foreign Office therefore drew up a memorandum which Mr. Eden circulated (c) to the War Cabinet on August 8.

The memorandum dealt with three aspects of the general question. Should General de Gaulle participate in major operations in metropolitan France, and, if so, at what stage should he be brought into consultation with regard to them? How far should General de Gaulle control the organisation of action in France preparatory to such operations, the conduct of subversive operations, and the collection of intelligence? To what extent should the General be consulted in advance about the administrative problems likely to arise in French territory liberated by the Allies?

By the agreement of August 7, 1940, General de Gaulle was authorised to raise a French force of volunteers to be used against our common enemies. Hence, if we did not allow the Fighting French to take part in major operations in Metropolitan France we should be reversing our policy towards General de Gaulle. We had recently recognised 'La France Combattante' as a symbol of the resistance to the Axis of all French nationals who refused to accept the capitulation, and who, by the means at their disposal, wherever they might be, contributed to the liberation of France by the common victory of the United Nations. The chief organisations of resistance in France seemed to be looking to General de Gaulle as

---

(a) Z6442/90/17; Z6134/23/17; Z6133/608/17. (b) COS(42)212(o). (c) WP(42)349.

their leader. At his request we had brought over from France representatives of these organisations to join the French National Committee; our policy had been to encourage collaboration between the General and the resistance movements. It was also part of our military plan to use the resistance organisations for sabotage and for promoting a rising in France at the right time in support of our invasion.

The spirit of resistance was higher in occupied France—with a population of 28 million—than among the 12 million people of unoccupied France. We had reason to think that the people of occupied France would expect General de Gaulle to play a part in our operations and would not understand it if British or American forces arrived without their Fighting French Allies. It might be argued that General de Gaulle's appearance in France would destroy any chance of bringing the Vichy Government over to our side, but there were great doubts whether Vichy would be acceptable to the forces of resistance in France as the Government under which the country would come back into the war. No one indeed could foresee what would happen in France when we arrived, but the resistance movements were likely to put General de Gaulle forward as the predominant French authority in Metropolitan France, perhaps as President of an interim Administration. Thus there were strong political grounds for allowing General de Gaulle to participate in major operations undertaken in Metropolitan France. If, for security reasons, we could not associate him at an early stage with the planning of such operations, we might discuss with him these military problems on a hypothetical basis. He was justified in expecting to be consulted, and his advice would be of value. We should then bring him into detailed consultation as soon as security considerations allowed.

(a)   General de Gaulle had sent to the Foreign Office on August 4 a memorandum asking that the co-ordination of preparatory action in France with the Allied plans should be transferred to the Allied High Command in charge of the operations, and that under their general strategic direction, he should be in supreme command of the internal French front. Hitherto the view of the British authorities concerned had been that they must maintain their own organisation and that they could not allow the establishment of a Free French organisation working without their knowledge. The Foreign Office thought that, in view of the increasing intimacy between General de Gaulle's headquarters in London and the French resistance movements, our policy should be re-examined. The Chiefs of Staff had also ruled that for the time being there should be no consultation

(a) Z6363/6280/17.

with General de Gaulle on the problem of the maintenance of law and order in the liberated territories. The Foreign Office regarded it as desirable that the General should be brought into a discussion of administrative questions since he would be invited by the resistance organisations to take part in the administration of these territories.

In introducing the Foreign Office recommendations to the War (a) Cabinet on August 20, Mr. Eden said that it had already been agreed that the Fighting French should be associated with the administration of Madagascar. He accepted the view that we could not use them in the North African expedition (though he was in fact disturbed at the amount which they seemed to know about the plan for such an expedition); on the other hand, the more we could associate them with our preparations for operations in France, the less trouble we should have about leaving them out of our plans for North Africa. Mr. Eden added that he was less hopeful than the Chiefs of Staff with regard to the response likely to be obtained from the Vichy army.

The Chiefs of Staff considered it impossible to accept the Foreign Office suggestion to discuss operations in France on a hypothetical basis with General de Gaulle. The General would certainly ask for more details, and we could not ensure that these details would be kept secret. The War Cabinet acquiesced in the view of the Chiefs of Staff and decided that for the time no steps should be taken to associate General de Gaulle with the planning of major operations in Metropolitan France.

On the other hand the War Cabinet thought that we should try to get closer collaboration with General de Gaulle in regard to organising secret preparatory action in France, but that we should not hand to him the control of such organisation. We should also discuss with him, on a somewhat hypothetical basis, and after we had obtained American consent, the administrative problems which we were likely to meet in liberated French territory.

In view of the difficulties raised by General de Gaulle in Syria[1] (b) Mr Eden suggested that no reply should be sent to the General's letter of July 25 until after he had returned to England. For similar reasons the Foreign Office considered it undesirable to risk further trouble of the kind experienced in Syria by handing over the administration of Madagascar to the Fighting French. This question had become of immediate importance owing to the decision to

---

[1] See Volume IV, Chapter LII.

(a) WM(42)114.2, C.A. (b) Z6662/3507/17.

M*

(a) occupy the whole island.[1] On September 9 Mr. Eden told M. Pleven[2] and M. Dejean that we were about to undertake further operations in Madagascar. We should not make a public announcement until the operations had reached a certain stage. It was therefore important that neither General de Gaulle nor the French National Committee should make any statement about the operation in advance of our official announcement. Mr. Eden then said that we had intended to ask the National Committee to take over the administration of the territory occupied as a result of our operations; we had also thought of suggesting that General Legentilhomme, whom General de Gaulle had once mentioned[3] as qualified for the post, should go to Madagascar in order to be ready to take over the territory without delay. In view of General de Gaulle's attitude over the Levant States, and his unjustified suspicions of the good faith of His Majesty's Government, we could not at present proceed on these lines. If, however, General de Gaulle would come to London at once—as the Prime Minister had invited him to do—for a discussion of the Levant question, we could also discuss the possibility of carrying out our original intention with regard to Madagascar. Otherwise we should have to make our own arrangements for the island. We did not want the responsibility of administering Madagascar, but would be compelled to do so, and would probably organise some kind of military government.

M. Pleven said that he was surprised that we should have placed the National Committee in this dilemma. He saw no reason why events in Syria should affect our policy in Madagascar. The French National Committee would not suggest that owing to their troubles with us in Syria, they should call off the Free French fighter squadrons collaborating with the Royal Air Force over French territory. We were in fact offering to let the Fighting French into Madagascar at the price of turning them out of Syria. M. Pleven urged that we should offer unconditionally to fulfil our public undertaking to entrust the administration of Madagascar to the Fighting French, and then ask General de Gaulle to come to London for a discussion of ways and means.

Mr. Eden said that he must protest very strongly against M. Pleven's statement about our intentions in Syria. Did he and General de Gaulle really think that we wanted to displace the French in Syria? It was essential that General de Gaulle should return to London in order to get the matter clear. The General's talk to all and sundry in Syria, and particularly to the Americans, was doing

---

[1] See above, p. 331.
[2] National Commissioner for the Colonies. In October, 1942, M. Pleven succeeded M. Dejean as National Commissioner for Foreign Affairs.
[3] See above, p. 329.

(a) Z6976/23/17.

him great harm in London and Washington. What he said to the Americans came back to us at once through the State Department, and the telegrams reporting it were circulated to the Cabinet. Even the General's best friends were wondering what his intentions were. Mr. Eden could not propose to his colleagues in these circumstances that the administration of Madagascar should be handed over to General de Gaulle. In the General's present mood there was the risk of some ill-considered act such as his proposal to assume the military command in the Levant States at a given date.

Mr. Eden said that he had done his best for General de Gaulle, and had secured agreement by all concerned to an early transfer of the administration of Madagascar to the Free French but that, owing to the General's fault, it was now necessary to make a fresh start. As past experience had shown, General de Gaulle would gain more from us by talking things over quietly and reasonably than by starting a campaign against us. M. Dejean thought that Mr. Eden had suggested a good way out of the deadlock between General de Gaulle and ourselves, and that it would be well worth while for the General to come back to London. M. Pleven was not satisfied, but admitted finally that a bad solution of our difficulties might be better than no solution. On the following day the French National Committee agreed that M. Pleven should telegraph to General de Gaulle on behalf of the Committee, and that M. Dejean should send a personal telegram advising his return, and mentioning the importance of the Madagascar question.

General de Gaulle, in fact, agreed to come back to London on or (a) about September 23. On the other hand Mr. Winant was afraid (b) that, if we allowed a Fighting French administration into Madagascar, the result might be to stiffen French resistance in North Africa. Mr. Winant asked whether we could not spin out our negotiations until after the Allied landing in North Africa. Mr. Eden did not regard this plan as practicable. In a memorandum of September 22 (c) for the use of the Prime Minister he considered it necessary to have an immediate discussion with General de Gaulle, and to make it clear that we could not continue our relations with him unless he changed his general attitude towards us. On the Syrian question it was essential that General de Gaulle should give up his suspicions that we wished to drive the French out of the Levant, and should recognise that we had an overriding military interest at least as long as the war lasted in the fulfilment of the French promises to the Levant States, and that we could not separate questions affecting these States from questions affecting the whole Middle East area, or accept the view that 'France' alone—for whom General de Gaulle

---

was not yet in a position to speak—had given independence to the Levant. Our good faith was as much engaged as that of General de Gaulle in the promise of independence, and we were entitled to insist that this promise should be carried out. The most satisfactory step which the French could take would be to announce the holding of elections within a specified time. Until we reached agreement on the Syrian question, we could not discuss with the General other matters such as Madagascar.

We ought to warn General de Gaulle about his behaviour to us. The series of crises into which he brought us on the slightest pretext caused us more trouble than our negotiations with all the other Allied Governments in London. General de Gaulle seemed to care more for points of prestige than for winning the war. Unless he changed his attitude and took wiser advice he would damage irretrievably his relations with the United Nations. We had implied, however, that, if General de Gaulle would meet us on the Syrian question, we should let the Fighting French into Madagascar. The Chiefs of Staff had suggested that the Fighting French should not take over the administration of Madagascar until we had landed in North Africa; but we could hardly keep silence about the matter for another ten weeks. In any case we had to make some arrangements for the island; if we did not hand it over to General de Gaulle we should precipitate a crisis with him.

The Chiefs of Staff shared Mr. Winant's fears that the transfer of the administration of Madagascar to the Fighting French might stiffen French resistance in North Africa. The Foreign Office, however, considered that the knowledge that the Fighting French were successfully administering Madagascar might well have the opposite effect, i.e. General Noguès and Admiral Esteva might come to terms more quickly if they realised that the Americans were not dependent on them for the maintenance of a French administration in North Africa. Finally, any step which looked like the abandonment of a promise to General de Gaulle would have a bad effect on opinion in France even among those Frenchmen who did not support him. The Foreign Office therefore suggested that, if we could reach a satisfactory agreement with General de Gaulle about the Levant States, we should inform him that we proposed to associate the Fighting French in the administration of Madagascar on conditions to be agreed between us. We should negotiate this agreement at once.

We had already settled with the Americans that General de Gaulle should not take part in the North African expedition, and should have no share in the administration of the territory.[1] This decision

---

[1] See, however, below, p. 355.

would mean another crisis with General de Gaulle, but the success of the North African plan would transform the whole situation. If the French in North Africa resumed the war against the Axis, the importance of General de Gaulle would diminish: he might indeed coalesce with the larger body of anti-Vichy Frenchmen in North Africa.

The memorandum of September 22 brought out clearly the differences of view between the Prime Minister and the Chiefs of Staff and the Foreign Office. The latter had now been defending General de Gaulle, in spite of the burden which his intransigence laid on them, for a good many months. Unfortunately General de Gaulle himself continued to be the greatest obstacle to the improvement of relations. The Prime Minister and Mr. Eden saw the General (a) and M. Pleven on September 30. They discussed Syria[1] and Madagascar, and once again went over the old question of General de Gaulle's position in relation both to France and Great Britain. The meeting ended in something very near to a complete break. General de Gaulle would not yield over the Levant States, and insisted nevertheless that we should give Madagascar to the Fighting French. General de Gaulle claimed that he spoke for 'France'; the Prime Minister replied that he recognised the General as a very honourable part of France, but not as 'France'. General de Gaulle said that he could not accept a diminution of the position of France anywhere, or the neutralisation of France by the British and their Allies. He knew that his responsibilities were greater than the means at his disposal. The Prime Minister told General de Gaulle plainly that the great difficulty lay in working with him; wherever he went there was trouble. The Prime Minister said that General de Gaulle, instead of waging war with Germany, had waged war with England. He had not shown the least wish to assist us, and had himself been the greatest obstacle to effective collaboration with the Americans and ourselves. General de Gaulle said that he would take the consequences of this breach of collaboration ('Je tiendrai les conséquences'). The conversation then closed.

Neither the Prime Minister nor General de Gaulle interpreted this unprofitable discussion as a final break, and discussions over Syria were in fact resumed early in October with the French National Committee. The Foreign Office also heard that General de Gaulle had sent a communication to the United States Government on the lines of his letter of July 25 to the Prime Minister, and that General

---

[1] For a fuller account of the discussion about Syria, see Volume IV, Chapter LII, section (iv).

(a) Z7530/90/17.

Eisenhower had been asked to reply after consulting the British authorities. General Eisenhower's view was that we should associate General de Gaulle in some measure with the planning of operations in Europe. For the time, however, the question of the relations with General de Gaulle over the North African landing were of more immediate importance. After the landing had taken place, the decision about a reply to General de Gaulle's requests of July 25 was again postponed, and the whole matter was merged in the wider subject of Anglo-American relations with the Fighting French.

CHAPTER XXX

The Allied landings in North Africa: the Darlan affair: appointment of General Giraud as High Commissioner

(i)

The preliminaries of the North African landings: Anglo-American exchanges of view on political and administrative questions: Foreign Office memorandum of August 20, 1942: decision not to invite the Fighting French to participate in the landings: American negotiations with General Giraud (August–October, 1942).

THE joint Anglo-American military planning of the North African expedition began in August 1942, but on the British side—where the enterprise had been looked on more favourably—considerable thought had already been given to all aspects of the operation including the administrative and other 'non-operational' problems which would require urgent solution. Soon after the appointment of General Eisenhower as Allied Commander-in-Chief, a short preliminary directive for the Commander-in-Chief was (a) drawn up in London and sent for approval to Washington. A larger appreciation, including a brief statement of the political background, had also been prepared and was ready for communication to General Eisenhower. An outline plan of operations was also in preparation; most of the work on it was being done by the British planning staff.

On the political and economic side the proposed expedition raised a number of complicated questions upon which it was necessary to try to reach general agreement with the Americans before the landing had taken place. The first and most important question was the form and character of the French administration. The Foreign Office assumed that many—perhaps a majority—of the French officials would remain at their posts and that for the most part existing administrative machinery would continue to function. There was indeed no satisfactory alternative. The administration of these large French African territories was vast and complex; inexperienced officials or even experienced officials without local knowledge might

(a) Z8328/8325/17.

cause administrative confusion and even serious disturbances. In any case the Americans would not consider handing over the administration to the Fighting French. It would therefore be necessary to issue a general declaration of policy both to the French authorities and population and to the native rulers. The declaration of policy would also have to deal with the question of annulling Vichy legislation and administrative measures of an objectionable and discriminatory kind—e.g. anti-Jewish laws—and with the protection of all persons who had been imprisoned or suffered damage owing to their loyalty to the Allied cause.

On the economic side the problems were equally complicated. We should have to deal with the surplus production which, after meeting the needs of the population of the territories, had been sent to France or elsewhere. For this purpose we should require an Allied or joint Allied and French Commission for each territory, and arrangements for the allocation of supplies and eventually for concluding an economic agreement.

(a)   The Chiefs of Staff discussed with General Eisenhower on August 3 the provision of a Political Officer who would be able to give advice on political and other non-military matters in connexion with the planning of the North African campaign. General Eisenhower wanted the adviser to be British, and suggested that his duties in co-ordinating the various interests concerned should cover the political section, under Colonel Donovan[1] who was already attached to the Commander-in-Chief's staff, as well as the British non-military or quasi-military services. It was suggested that Colonel

(b)   Oliver Stanley might take the post, but he was unable to do so. The appointment was then given to Mr. W. H. B. Mack, of the Foreign Office. For obvious reasons Mr. Mack's duties were kept secret; he was officially entitled Political Liaison Officer with the United States Forces in the United Kingdom, with the duty of maintaining contact on non-military matters between the United States Commander and the War Cabinet Office and British Government Departments.

The Foreign Office were also preparing a plan for joint Anglo-American action in relation to the Governments and territories concerned. This plan covered the pre-operational, operational, and post-operational periods. The Foreign Office considered that these matters might be dealt with in a preliminary way by Lord Halifax and that detailed discussions could follow in Washington or London.

(c)   A memorandum was therefore given to Lord Halifax[2] on August 20 for submission to the State Department. The memorandum,

---

[1] See Volume I, pp. 528–9.
[2] Lord Halifax was at this time in London.

(a) Z8326/8325/17. (b) Z8330/8325/17. (c) Z8332/8325/17.

which had been seen by the Chiefs of Staff, and embodied their suggestions, made the following recommendations for the pre-operational period: (i) There should be no sudden change in our policy towards French North Africa likely to arouse French suspicions. We should therefore continue the existing arrangements for the shipment of oil and other supplies. Admiral Leahy considered that the American observers in North Africa had been able to (a) ensure that, with minor exceptions, articles sent to the French had not been passed on to the Germans or Italians. Even if the oil shipped to North Africa reached the enemy, the military disadvantages of a change of policy would outweigh the advantages of cutting off the supplies. We should also aim at keeping the observers in North Africa and at predisposing opinion there in favour of the United Nations. (ii) We had already agreed to American proposals for (b) sending limited supplies to French West Africa in return for the posting of observers. We regarded it as important to take West Africa into account since we might hope to bring it over peacefully to our side if we were successful in North Africa. (iii) The British and American Governments should maintain their normal 'friction' with the Vichy Government, but should avoid a clash with French naval forces, and should leave the question of the French warships at Alexandria in suspense for the time.[1] We had also agreed to American proposals for sending milk, etc. to unoccupied France. (iv) The best course with regard to Spain would be to continue the existing policy of keeping supplies to a minimum necessary for maintaining the Spanish economy. Any curtailment might have undesirable political effects; we might even extend unobtrusively our economic aid in supplies of no direct military use. We should maintain our present cautious contacts with possible dissident and anti-Axis elements but, on balance, it would not be to our advantage to try to bring a change of government in Spain during the pre-operational period. Our policy would thus continue to aim at discouraging either the grant of facilities by Spain to the Axis Powers or a Spanish move into French Morocco, and at encouraging Spanish resistance to a German invasion and the formation—if the Germans invaded Spain—of an anti-German Spanish Government outside the country.[2]

The memorandum then summed up the general lines of policy which might be adopted during the operational and post-operational periods. We expected resistance to our invasion, but hoped that the French armed forces and civil administration might soon collaborate

---

[1] See Chapter XXVIII, Note to section (iii).
[2] See also Volume IV, Chapter XLVII, section (ii).

(a) Z8327/8325/17. (b) Z8332/8325/17.

with us in spite of orders to the contrary from Vichy. This collaboration would probably be limited to the defence of North Africa, and our occupation of part of the French territories—e.g. Algeria—would probably not bring over other parts, e.g., Morocco or Tunisia. The United States Government would doubtless put out an explanation and appeal to all parts of French North Africa as soon as our operations had begun. We ought also to make a joint study of the arrangements for the administration of the territory which we should occupy. The British Government would hope to reappoint consular officers as soon as possible in French North Africa.

In West Africa the French would probably await developments; here also we assumed that the United States Government would try to bring the authorities over to the side of the Allies.

The Vichy Government would probably come under pressure in one direction from the French public, who would be encouraged by American action on French territory, and from another direction by the Germans. The Germans were likely to compel the Vichy Government to order resistance in Africa and might turn them out to give place to an even more actively collaborationist Government under Doriot. The Germans would also extend their control over the unoccupied zone of France and might occupy it.

The United States Government were in a better position than the British Government to decide upon a policy towards Vichy; the British view was that, after the operation had begun, an approach should be made to Marshal Pétain and to Admiral Darlan as Commander-in-Chief of all the French forces. We should give the necessary assurances about the future of the territories concerned and ask that the French Forces in North Africa should be told not to resist us, and that they should be left free to collaborate with the United Nations and thus hasten the liberation of France. We could hardly expect Marshal Pétain to give a satisfactory answer, or to leave France in order to establish a new Government in North Africa; on the other hand he might be persuaded to allow others to leave for this purpose. We should try to establish contact with Generals Weygand and Giraud.

The Spanish reaction would depend on the degree of pressure which the Germans could exercise at Madrid, and on the knowledge of the economic consequences of losing the supplies which Spain was receiving from the United Nations. If the Germans invaded Spain before our operation was succeeding, the Spanish Government would probably not resist them. No organised opposition could be counted on in Spain itself, though the population would be hostile. Our increased use of Gibraltar for air operations would not be likely to bring Spain into the war against us; if there were no German invasion the Spanish Government would probably continue their policy of keeping out of the war, though they might take the opportunity of invading French Morocco to enforce their claims if the French moved troops from Morocco to resist the Allies. We thought it desirable to continue economic aid to Spain during as well as before the operational period. Once we were firmly established in North Africa, we should be in a better position to decide on our future policy towards Spain.

After references to Portugal, where public opinion was likely to welcome an Allied success, the memorandum dealt with the difficult problem of the part which the Fighting French should take in the operation. If we did not allow General de Gaulle to take any part in it, we should have to face a major crisis with him, particularly if, in order to avoid risks of leakage, we had not given him advance information of our plans. The arguments against bringing him in were that he seemed to have no large following in North Africa, and that the association of his forces with the Anglo-American expedition might stiffen French resistance. General de Gaulle had not the personnel necessary for the administration of occupied territory and would probably not secure the services of the existing civil or military officers. On the other hand if he were entirely excluded from North Africa, his prestige would suffer in Metropolitan France and there would be a difficult situation in the Fighting French colonies.

The British view was that, since we were unable to associate his forces with the operation, we should inform General de Gaulle of our plan only a few hours in advance and invite him to appoint a military mission to represent him with the Allied Commander-in-Chief. We should explain why we had been unable to invite the participation of the Free French forces, and say that in these circumstances it would have been an embarrassment to all concerned if we had told him earlier of our plans. We fully recognised the significance (a) of Fighting France; our suggestion of a military liaison mission was intended to mark this recognition. We realised also General de Gaulle's interest in the future administration of the territory, but could come to no decisions until we had seen the attitude of the French armed forces and administration and of the population generally. Our object was to promote the collaboration of all Frenchmen with the Anglo-American effort to restore the greatness and independence of France. We should ask General de Gaulle to send the necessary explanations to the Fighting French colonial administrations and we should hope that he would see the advantage of giving public approval to our operation. If, as was hoped, the French forces of resistance grouped themselves in North Africa in opposition to the Axis, the relations between them and the French

---

(a) Z8332, 8413/8325/17.

National Committee would be for the two groups to settle among themselves.

There was some delay before Lord Halifax was able to discuss the
(a) British memorandum with Mr. Roosevelt. On September 10, however, Mr. Roosevelt gave Lord Halifax his views on the political side of the North African operation. He had read the British memorandum, but thought that most of the matters with which it dealt could be taken up at a later date. He made no comment on the proposals with regard to General de Gaulle. He hoped that it would be possible to give the operation an American appearance during the initial period. He repeated his view that the United States should deal with North and West African questions, and Great Britain matters concerning Spain and Portugal. Lord Halifax thought that for the time Mr. Roosevelt would not be more definite and that he did not want the State Department to handle the political aspects of the operation. Lord Halifax's conclusion was that the best plan would be for us to negotiate directly with General Eisenhower.

The Foreign Office agreed with this suggestion, and thought that Mr. Mack's appointment provided a good means of communication. We also recognised that the operation in its initial stages should be given a predominantly American appearance, but we were taking part in it, and would have a close interest in what was done in the territory after the expedition had succeeded. We therefore assumed that the United States Government would work in close concert with us.

Lord Halifax was also instructed to raise with the President the question of the American and British communications to General Franco. After consultation with Sir S. Hoare Mr. Eden suggested that these communications should take the line that the Allied action did not threaten Spanish territory or interests, and that it would indeed facilitate trade between Spain and the United States and Great Britain. Mr. Eden agreed with Sir S. Hoare that it would be unwise to hint at sanctions if General Franco's reactions were hostile.

On October 12 Mr. Eden put forward, in the first place to other Government departments, the Foreign Office proposals for dealing with General de Gaulle. The proposals did not include the suggestion of a military liaison mission since the Foreign Office understood that the Americans would not be in favour of it. The Chiefs of Staff, however, on October 16, said that, in case of a last-minute postponement of the operation owing to weather conditions, they did not want General de Gaulle to be told of it before the landings had begun. The Prime Minister then decided that he would himself see General de Gaulle, and inform him of the operation, as soon as the hour of assault had been definitely fixed. (This would be about 10 p.m. on November 7.) The Prime Minister let the President know of this (a) suggestion on November 5. President Roosevelt replied on the same day that he thought it undesirable to say anything to General de (b) Gaulle until after the landings had begun. The Prime Minister (c) replied on November 6 accepting this view.[1]

Although the British Government had acquiesced in giving the operation in its initial stages an exclusively American appearance, it would be necessary at some stage to refer to British participation, if only to prepare the way for the advance of British forces. Mr. Eden (d) thought that at least President Roosevelt's public statement, if not also his messages to Marshal Pétain and the French and Moroccan authorities, should contain some indications that His Majesty's Government was supporting and collaborating in the operations and that a British statement might be issued proclaiming our solidarity with the Americans. The best plan would be for the President (as General Eisenhower had suggested) to make his proclamation in the name of the United Nations, and for us to associate ourselves with the operation on lines similar to the American statement of support of our action in Madagascar.

In fact the first American text of the messages as received from (e) Washington contained only one reference to the Allies and spoke otherwise only of American forces. Lord Halifax was instructed to (f) explain why the British Government thought that a definite reference to British participation was necessary. The President agreed to insert it, though not in the form suggested by the Foreign Office. The President's message also included a friendly mention of Marshal Pétain, but General Eisenhower recommended that this reference should be taken out, especially in view of the report that Marshal Pétain intended shortly to broadcast in favour of sending French workers to Germany.[2]

On October 27 Mr. Roosevelt sent to the Prime Minister the (g) draft of a proposed statement to be issued to the American press immediately after the landings. The statement mentioned that the British Navy and Air Force were assisting in the landing and that the American army would very soon be reinforced by a considerable number of British divisions. The expedition was described as a move to prevent the occupation of North or West Africa by the Axis

---

[1] See also below, section (v).
[2] The text as finally agreed was recorded by Mr. Roosevelt and actually transmitted from London.

(a) T1435/2, No. 185, Churchill Papers/439. (b) T1440/2, No. 207, Churchill Papers/439. (c) T1445/2, No. 186, Churchill Papers/470. (d) Z8360/8325/17. (e) Z8397/8325/17. (f) Z8387/8325/17. (g) T1376/2, No. 199 (Churchill Papers/470; Z8404/8325/17).

Powers and 'to deny to the aggressor nations a starting point from which to launch an attack against the Atlantic coast of the Americas. In addition it provides an effective Second Front assistance to our heroic Allies in Russia.'

Some opinion in the Foreign Office had doubts about the reference to a second front in view of the previous agreement that the expedition was to be described not as a second front but as an operation of the first importance which opened up possibilities for future action against the Axis in Europe. This description had been accepted because it maintained the 'war of nerves' and gave the impression that the Allies might attempt at any time a landing on the western Atlantic sea coast. On the other hand the statement was an American affair, and need not prevent us from continuing our propaganda on the lines previously agreed. In any case the reference to the second front would cut the ground from the Russian propaganda that the Americans had wished for a second front in Europe and that we had opposed the plan.

(a) The Prime Minister and Mr. Eden, however, and Sir A. Cadogan were strongly in favour of allowing the American text to stand. Mr. Churchill pointed out to Mr. Eden that 'it was the American communiqué [about a second front] that got us into trouble during M. Molotov's visit and that they should get out of it is all to the good'. Furthermore the operation was 'our major contribution at the present time', and the Prime Minister himself intended to speak of it as a 'full discharge of our obligations as Allies to Russia'. Any propaganda in contradiction to this point should be 'dimmed'. The

(b) Prime Minister also proposed in due course—probably about the middle of November—to make it clear that we were mounting a great attack in England. He regarded 'the holding front we maintain here and the overseas flanking move by the south as part of one integral operation'.

(c) The Foreign Office also received a copy of the message which President Roosevelt proposed to send to Marshal Pétain. The Prime Minister thought that the terms of this message—in which the President referred to the Marshal as his 'dear old friend'—would do great harm in turning a number of Frenchmen in France against the United States, and that it would have a very bad effect indeed on General de Gaulle's supporters. Mr. Eden agreed with this view, and the Prime Minister telegraphed accordingly to Mr. Roosevelt. Mr. Roosevelt rewrote the message in a form less likely to cause offence.

One further matter of the highest importance had been left in American hands. The President and his advisers had felt even more

---

(a) PMM 512/2. (b) Z8404/8325/17. (c) Z8408/8325/17.

strongly than the Prime Minister and Mr. Eden that the chances of getting French collaboration would be lessened if General de Gaulle were associated with the landings. The Americans believed, however, that they could use another French high officer, General Giraud, with more hope of success. General Giraud had escaped from prison in Germany in April 1942. He had been captured at Sedan in May 1940, and was not associated with the defeatist acts of Marshal Pétain's Government. He was also wholly outside the Gaullist movement. In the months after his escape General Giraud had been living on the Riviera in unoccupied France. Here he was in somewhat vague contact with a group of officers in North Africa who were planning a military revolt there and in southern France to coincide with the expected Allied invasion of northern France. This group wanted to get American help and had approached Mr. Murphy, the American Consul-General at Algiers.[1]

The American negotiations with General Giraud began in mid-October.[2] They resulted—almost inevitably—in a good deal of misunderstanding. For security reasons it was impossible to tell General Giraud all the facts. The General himself was neither quick-minded nor forthcoming. In particular he wanted to be in command of the whole enterprise (of which he still knew very little); he also thought that he had an American promise that the command would be transferred to him as soon as the landings were secure. The American answers to his questions were not, from his point of view, satisfactory, but he agreed to come to Gibraltar on November 4–5. Owing to bad weather he was delayed, and did not arrive until the late afternoon of November 7, i.e. less than twelve hours before the landings were due to begin. To the exasperation of the Americans he still insisted that he should be given the supreme command. He maintained this claim until the following morning. He did not fly to Algiers until November 9. He and his American sponsors then had to deal with a situation entirely different from anything which they had expected.

---

[1] As the senior United States diplomatic representative in North Africa Mr. Murphy had been in charge of the American 'observers'. In September 1942, he was appointed President Roosevelt's special representative in North Africa. After the Allied landings he became head of the Civil Affairs section at General Eisenhower's headquarters. See also below, p. 383.

[2] I have not dealt in detail with these negotiations since they were conducted by the Americans, though the British authorities were informed of them. Mr. Mack was present at the interviews with General Giraud on his arrival at Gibraltar.

(ii)

The Allied landings in North Africa: General Eisenhower's negotiations with Admiral Darlan: British disquiet at the situation (November 8–16, 1942).

The Allied landings in North Africa were made on November 8. The great Anglo-American convoys had sailed under British naval protection from British ports between October 22 and 26; large reinforcements were also on their way from the United States. The secret of their destination was well kept, and the general military situation was more favourable than at any time during the past twelve months. Except at the port of Algiers the landings met with little resistance in Algeria; the Americans were opposed more strongly than had been expected at Oran and Casablanca, but the French ceased fighting on November 12. The Allied forces moved forward as quickly as possible to Tunisia in the hope of seizing the ports before the enemy could send reinforcements across the Mediterranean. They might have succeeded, in spite of bad weather conditions and supply difficulties, if, instead of allowing German landings by sea and air at Bizerta and Tunis, the French in the area had resisted the Germans as they had resisted the Allies in Morocco; even so, a small British force nearly reached the ports, but was held up near Mejez-el-Bab. Here, or rather in this area, the Allies remained until the spring when the attack was resumed in full force.

The first and most imperative need after the landings and during the rapid eastward move was to secure the safety of the Allied communications and the passive or, if possible, the active co-operation of the French. General Eisenhower found the attitude of the French much less favourable than he had been led to expect from American forecasts and intelligence reports. Neither the American nor the British Government had realised the extent to which French opinion would hold fast to the Vichy regime as the one rallying point left in the humiliation and confusion of defeat; the authority of Marshal Pétain had a psychological basis which went beyond official habits of obedience to a legitimate central authority and included more than a desire not to risk the loss of office and income. General Béthouart— a strong friend of the Allies—summed up the matter in the words: 'la mystique de Pétain est épouvantable'.

The attitude of official opinion was the more important because, outside a small and active Gaullist minority, the population was for the most part politically indifferent or at all events unwilling to run any risks for a political cause. Even in Algeria, which was legally part of Metropolitan France, the European population was only 980,000, of whom at least one-eighth were of Italian or Spanish descent; the Jewish population was 100,000 and there were over 6,000,000 Arabs. French Morocco had some 210,000 Europeans (174,000 of French descent), 150,000 Jews and a Moslem population of about 6,000,000; there were about as many Europeans in Tunisia (a) as in Morocco, but not very far short of half of them were of Italian descent. Most of the French were agriculturalists—peasants or large proprietors; they had suffered comparatively little from the war. Their export trade had continued without serious interruption, and the prices received for their goods had been adequate; they had also obtained—partly owing to American policy preparatory to the Allied landings—at least their minimum import requirements. It was therefore unlikely that in the mass they would exercise an important influence on the civil administration—still less on the army—or that public opinion would compel the authorities to take up an enthusiastic attitude about the Allied war against the Axis.

The fact that the majority of Frenchmen in civil or military authority in North Africa regarded Marshal Pétain not as a 'quisling', but as the representative of the 'pouvoir légitime', and as the shield of their consciences, involved General Eisenhower in grave political difficulty before his forces had completed their landing. The Americans found that—contrary to expectation—General Giraud did not get much support, or even make much effort to secure it. Mr. Murphy had also hoped for the collaboration of General Juin, French military commander in North Africa; he could not be sure of it, and had not thought it safe to tell General Juin about the pro-jected landings.[1] In any case the Americans—and General Juin—had to deal with an unforeseen situation. Admiral Darlan, who had just completed a tour of inspection in North Africa, was called back suddenly to Algiers on November 5 because his son had been taken ill there with an attack of infantile paralysis. The Admiral was still at Algiers at the time of the Allied landings.[2] His presence was most awkward for General Juin; there was indeed very little chance that the French military and civil authorities would accept his

---

[1] General Juin told Mr. Murphy on November 5 that he had orders to defend North Africa against all invaders. He hoped that the 'provocation' would come from the Germans. He would then ask for American aid. If, however, the Americans attacked first, he would be bound to resist them. *F.R.U.S.*, 1942, II, 425.

[2] Admiral Darlan appears to have made contact with Mr. Murphy through Admiral Fenard (see Volume III, Chapter XXXVI, section (v)) in May, 1942. Later, in October, 1942, Admiral Darlan warned Mr. Murphy of possible German action against French North Africa owing to suspicions of an American move. Admiral Darlan suggested that he might bring the French fleet to North Africa, if he could be sure of American military (b) and economic help. Mr. Murphy did not reject this suggestion, but General Mast, General Giraud's representative in Algiers, thought (not without reason) that Darlan could not be trusted and that anyhow his cooperation was not necessary. (Murphy, *Diplomat among the Warriors* (Collins, 1964), 118.

(a) Z4602/52/17 (1943). (b) S.I.C./E/North Africa/3(A), Pt. II.

(General Juin's) orders against the overriding authority of Admiral Darlan, and General Juin himself recognised this fact.

Admiral Darlan himself at first ordered that the landings should be resisted. He later gave way to the extent of sending a telegram to Marshal Pétain explaining the situation. At 11.30 a.m. on November 8 he sent a second telegram that Algiers would probably be taken during the evening. At 5 p.m. he told Marshal Pétain that he had agreed to negotiate the surrender of the city of Algiers. Later in the evening he sent a message to General Eisenhower's headquarters asking for the opening of negotiations. On the morning of November 9 General Giraud, and a few hours afterwards (owing to bad weather) General Mark Clark, General Eisenhower's deputy, left Gibraltar for Algiers to see the Admiral. The first meeting with Admiral Darlan, on the evening of November 9, had no result except to confirm the impression that, without any 'legitimate' French backing, General Giraud would not bring any waverers over to the Allied side. On the following morning General Clark had another interview with Admiral Darlan. He came to the conclusion, which was actively shared by Mr. Murphy, that he would save time—and a saving in time meant a saving in lives—if he came to an arrangement with the Admiral. Admiral Darlan himself was now able to see that the Allied landings were in great force, and that they were succeeding. He also realised that the Germans were beginning to take counter-measures, which would include the occupation of hitherto un-occupied France and, therefore, the control of the Toulon fleet.

General Clark did not wait for consultations between Washington and London. He informed General Eisenhower that he could make a settlement with Admiral Darlan; he gave the Admiral half an hour in which to accept his terms. These terms were that Admiral Darlan should order a general cessation of French resistance to the Allies; that he should assume authority in the name of Marshal Pétain over all French North African territories, and instruct all officials to continue at their posts; and that he should order the Toulon fleet to put to sea if there were any danger that the Germans might attempt to seize it.

Admiral Darlan accepted these conditions. The Germans, however, intercepted his message to this effect to Marshal Pétain; they also showed it to Laval.[1] Laval insisted by telephone that Marshal Pétain should disavow the Admiral's action. Since it seemed for a time that the Admiral was willing to withdraw his orders, General Clark put him under arrest. A further secret message from Marshal Pétain approving Darlan's orders, and the German announcement that they were entering the unoccupied zone completed Admiral

---

[1] Laval had gone to Munich on November 9 to see Hitler.

Darlan's change-round. On November 11 he gave definite orders that the French fleet should leave Toulon, and that Admiral Esteva, the Resident-General of Tunisia, should join the Allies.[1] On November 13 General Eisenhower went to Algiers and accepted the agreement which General Clark had made with Admiral Darlan.

These Franco-American negotiations took place without any reference to the British Government. The British authorities in London indeed had very little information of what was happening; a message on November 10 mentioned, first, that Admiral Darlan (a) had been taken into protective custody, and that General Clark had conferred with him and also with General Giraud on the previous night, but that the situation was very confused and the conferences were being resumed. A later telegram of November 10 reported that, as a result of an interview with General Eisenhower's representative (b) (General Clark), Admiral Darlan had ordered all French sea, land and air forces in North Africa, including Tunisia, to cease operations. On November 11 there were two more telegrams containing a mention of Admiral Darlan. The first telegram referred to confer- (c) ences between the latter and Generals Clark and Giraud; the second —a telegram of 7 p.m. from General Eisenhower to General Marshall —reported the former's hope that General Clark could use Admiral Darlan to bring the French forces in Tunisia over to the Allied side. General Eisenhower also hoped that, if Admiral Darlan had any influence with the French fleet, there might be some chance of getting it out of Toulon and over to our side.[2]

---

[1] These orders were not obeyed. The admiral commanding the Toulon fleet refused to put to sea. On November 27, when the Germans attempted to seize the fleet, he scuttled over forty warships which a few days earlier he might have saved. Laval not only ordered Admiral Esteva to assist the Germans, but sent Admiral Platon, an extreme collaborationist, to Tunis to ensure that his orders were carried out. Admiral Esteva and Admiral Derrien, who was in command of the naval forces, allowed the Germans to occupy an important airfield and to land troops. General Barré, in command of the land forces, moved his troops inland, put them under the authority of General Giraud and defended a position in the hills, but the opportunity of holding the ports for a few days until the Allies arrived had been lost.

[2] On November 11 the Prime Minister telegraphed to the President that the British Government was 'under quite definite and solemn obligations to de Gaulle and his Movement', and must 'see they have a fair deal'. Mr. Churchill wanted 'to avoid at all (d) costs the creation of rival French *émigré* governments, each favoured by one of us'. He did not mention the name of Admiral Darlan, and does not seem to have had in mind the possibility that the Admiral would be maintained in a position of authority.

The context of Mr. Churchill's telegram was General de Gaulle's request to be allowed to send a mission to North Africa (see below, p. 391). Mr. Roosevelt replied to Mr. Churchill that 'in regard to de Gaulle, I have hitherto enjoyed a quiet satisfaction in leaving him in your hands. Apparently I have now acquired a similar problem in brother Giraud. I wholly agree that we must prevent rivalry between the French *émigré* factions, and I have no objection to a de Gaulle emissary visiting Giraud in Algiers. We must remember that there is also a cat-fight in progress between Giraud and Darlan . . . The principal thought to be driven home to all three of these prima donnas is that the situation is today solely in the military field, and that any decision by any one of them, or by all of them, is subject to review and approval by Eisenhower.' Churchill, IV, 566.

(a) Hist. (G)1, No. 34. (b) Hist. (G)1, No. 38. (c) Hist. (G)1, Nos. 43 and 45. (d) T1480/2, No. 188, Churchill Papers/470.

(a)   On November 12 General Eisenhower reported that General
Giraud and Admiral Darlan had reached a tentative agreement
whereby the former would be the military and the latter the political
head of the French 'organisation' in North Africa. Admiral Darlan
had sent a message to the French fleet, but General Eisenhower
thought that he had delayed too long, and that the message would
not be obeyed. Meanwhile one incidental result of the German
breach of the armistice terms in entering unoccupied France was
to increase the prestige of Admiral Darlan as the representative of
Marshal Pétain and of duly constituted French authority. Marshal
Pétain could no longer be regarded as a free agent, even by the
supporters of Vichy; Admiral Darlan could claim that legal power
to give orders was vested in himself.

These fragmentary messages placed the British Government in a
very difficult position. The responsibility for decisions in North
Africa was American; in any case, even if more information had
reached London about the course of events, it was impracticable
during the first dangerous days following the landings to interfere
with the actions of the Commander-in-Chief. On the other hand
the decision to accept the support of one of the most important
French 'quislings', and to maintain him in authority, was repugnant
to British feeling and certain to have very serious political consequences.[1] Public opinion in Great Britain did not realise the extent
to which the American decision had been taken without reference to
the War Cabinet or the Foreign Office; a full public explanation
would have meant a breach of confidence in regard to the United
States Government.

Until they had more information (and even as late as November 28
(b) the Foreign Office complained of the inadequacy of the reports sent
to them)[2] the British Government could only state their views in
(c) general terms. After consultations with the Prime Minister Mr. Eden
telegraphed to Mr. Mack on the night of November 12–13 to ask

---

[1] As recently as May, 1942, Admiral Darlan had given public evidence that his attitude
towards Great Britain remained bitterly hostile. On May 6, 1942, he had sent the following
message to the Vichy forces in Madagascar:

'Once again the British, instead of fighting their enemies, seek the easiest path of
attacking a French colony far from the metropolis. Marshal Pétain has asked you to defend
Madagascar, and I know that you have responded patriotically to his appeal. Firmly defend
the honour of our flag. Fight to the limit of your possibilities and make the British pay
dearly for their act of highway robbery.

The whole of France and its Empire are with you at heart. Do not forget that the
British betrayed us in Flanders, that they attacked us treacherously at Mers-el-Kebir,
Dakar, and in Syria, that they are murdering civilians in the metropolitan territories, and
that they tried to make the women and children of Jibuti die of hunger. Defend yourselves.
You are defending the honour of France. The day will come when England will pay.
Long live France.'

[2] See also p. 377, note 1.

(a) Hist.(G)1, No. 49. (b) Z9602/8325/17. (c) Z8757/8325/17.

whether there was any question of accepting Admiral Darlan as head or member of a French administration set up in North Africa. The Prime Minister considered that, if Admiral Darlan could bring the French fleet out of Toulon or give decisive help in securing Tunis, he would have established a claim to a 'seat on the band-wagon'. Otherwise his inclusion in a French administration in North Africa, even with General Giraud's consent, would cause more trouble than it would be worth.[1] Mr. Mack was also told to say that we could not accept General Giraud as Commander-in-Chief of all French forces, both in North Africa and in the French Empire. We had agreed to his appointment in North Africa but we could not allow him authority over the many important colonies which owed allegiance to General de Gaulle and had been with us 'through all the dark days'.

On November 13 Lord Halifax was instructed to tell the President or Mr. Hull that the inclusion of Admiral Darlan in a French administration would be most unpopular in Great Britain unless he had brought over the French navy, and that all hopes of unifying the French Empire in the war against the Axis would be frustrated since neither General de Gaulle nor anyone else in the Fighting French Movement would collaborate with the Admiral.

Mr. Mack reported at 6.15 p.m. on November 13 that he was sure (a) that General Eisenhower accepted the British view that there should be no question of including Admiral Darlan in the administration unless he had brought over the fleet. General Eisenhower—accompanied by Admiral Cunningham—had gone to Algiers (from his headquarters at Gibraltar) with the intention of telling the French leaders that they must agree immediately about their policy. If they did not at once choose a leader, he would make his own choice and take over complete control. General Clark considered an agreement between General Giraud and Admiral Darlan as likely.

In the afternoon of November 14 a message from General Eisen- (b) hower to the Combined Chiefs of Staff was received in London. General Eisenhower explained that the state of opinion in North Africa was in many respects entirely different from the expectation of the Allies. The main facts were the supreme importance of Marshal Pétain and the view of the French military, naval and civilian authorities that Admiral Darlan alone had a right to 'assume the Marshal's mantle'. General Giraud himself had come to recognise these facts and to see that there was no support for him in isolation.

---

[1] In the original draft the Foreign Office had gone further than the Prime Minister, and opposed Admiral Darlan's inclusion in the administration, even if he had brought over the fleet and facilitated a rapid advance into Tunisia.

(a) Z8767/8325/17. (b) Z8884/8325/17.

The initial French resistance was offered in the belief that the Marshal wished it; for this reason General Giraud was assumed to have acted at least with a touch of treachery in ordering no resistance to be made. The fighting in Morocco was stopped by Admiral Darlan's order,[1] and in Tunis Admiral Esteva would not obey anyone else.

General Eisenhower said that the gist of his agreement with the French was that they would at once do what they could to assist in securing Tunisia and would organise French North Africa for effective co-operation in the war. General Giraud was an 'enthusiastic supporter' of the agreement and had accepted the post of military chief under Admiral Darlan because he realised that, otherwise, even with the moral and military support of the Allies, he could do nothing.

If therefore the Allied Governments were to repudiate the agreement which General Eisenhower had made, they would lose all hope of obtaining organised French co-operation in North Africa and of securing the French fleet. The French armed forces would resist, actively or passively; the Allies would need more troops, and would also be losing time.

General Eisenhower recognised that the British and American Governments had commitments to 'certain elements' of the French people throughout the world; he was not attempting to extend the agreement with Admiral Darlan beyond the areas in which it was necessary for it to operate. He proposed that if, on receiving his explanation, the two Governments were still dissatisfied, they should send a joint mission, including, if desired, Fighting French representatives, to his headquarters, where he felt certain that he could convince them of the rightness of his policy.

(a)   Admiral Cunningham also telegraphed to the Admiralty on November 14 that, unless we accepted Admiral Darlan, we should have to proceed with a military occupation of the whole of North Africa, and probably to face a renewal of hostilities with the French. If we rejected Admiral Darlan, we should lose Admiral Esteva and all chance of a rapid occupation of Tunisia. General Giraud had practically no influence with the French, and had realised the fact and therefore agreed to work with Admiral Darlan. Admiral Cunningham believed that Darlan had honestly tried to bring over the Toulon fleet, and that he might succeed. No one liked him, but he was the only man with the necessary following, especially among the French officials. Admiral Cunningham suspected that Darlan

---

[1] The Foreign Office had information that in any case General Noguès in Morocco had supplies enough to last only for one more day's fighting.

(a) Hist. (G)1, No. 57.

had foreseen 'something of this sort', since he had all his family in Algiers.[1]

The Prime Minister decided, after consulting Mr. Eden and (a) Field-Marshal Smuts, to send a message to President Roosevelt about General Eisenhower's action. He said that he could not regard the arrangement as 'permanent or healthy', but that, since General Eisenhower's decision was endorsed by our own commanders on the spot, we had no choice but to accept it as necessary 'for maintaining local and interim equilibrium and for securing the vital position in Tunis'. The Prime Minister added: 'we feel sure you will consult us on the long-term steps pursuing always the aim of uniting all Frenchmen who will fight Hitler'.

General Eisenhower also telegraphed on November 14 a draft (b) of a proposed press release on the agreement with Admiral Darlan. The draft contained a sentence to the effect that the Allied Commander-in-Chief had been assured that all important elements in French North Africa concurred in the action taken and would co-operate in a provisional Government headed by Darlan. The Prime Minister telegraphed to President Roosevelt his hope that (c) neither this draft nor 'anything like it' would be published. A new text was therefore drawn up, and issued on November 16.

On the evening of November 15 Admiral Darlan announced over (d) the wireless in French North Africa the appointment of General Giraud as Commander-in-Chief of the land and air forces, and Admiral Michelier as head of the naval forces in North Africa. Admiral Darlan had wished to include in his announcement a statement that neither General de Gaulle nor any of his committee would be recognised in French North Africa, but General Eisenhower had told the Admiral of his strong disapproval of any such reference. No mention of General de Gaulle was therefore made in the broadcast.

On the other hand, Admiral Darlan's broadcast contained a definite reference to Marshal Pétain as the source of his own authority. (e) He said that owing to the German entry into unoccupied France Marshal Pétain was no longer able to let the French people know his real thoughts, but that on November 9 the Marshal had sent him a telegram that he was satisfied with his presence in Africa. On November 11, in view of the fact that he (Admiral Darlan) was 'deprived of his freedom', Marshal Pétain had appointed General

---

[1] There is no evidence on this question in the Foreign Office archives, but records of later conversations with French military authorities appear to confirm the view that Admiral Darlan's presence in Algiers on November 8 was due solely to his son's illness.

(a) T1506/2 (Churchill Papers/442; Z8884/8325/17). (b) Z9012/8325/17. (c) T1506/2 (Churchill Papers/442; Z8884/8325/17). (d) Hist. (G)1, Nos. 62 and 64. (e) Z391/5/69(1943).

Noguès as his deputy. Two days later General Noguès, on seeing that Admiral Darlan was 'in full possession' of his 'liberty of action', returned to him, with the full approval of the Marshal, the powers which he (General Noguès) had been given. Admiral Darlan therefore declared that all military and civil officials who had given an oath of allegiance to Marshal Pétain should consider themselves faithful to the Marshal by carrying out his (Admiral Darlan's) orders.

(a)   General Eisenhower telegraphed on November 16 that, although he understood the reasons why the Prime Minister had asked for delay, he regarded it as essential for military reasons to issue locally a short statement announcing that the Allies would deal with the provisional North African Government set up by Admiral Darlan in all matters affecting the Allied forces in North Africa and their relations with the local population. General Giraud and Admiral Michelier would be mentioned in this statement. General Eisenhower also said that, if it were necessary to enter into a formal agreement with Darlan and his associates extending beyond the scope of immediate military operations and objectives in North Africa, he would submit the draft to the United States and British Governments.

(iii)

President Roosevelt's statement of November 17: General Eisenhower's formal agreement with Admiral Darlan: unsatisfactory position in French West Africa (November 17–25, 1942).

(b)   On November 17 Mr. Roosevelt issued a statement of policy in order to explain the American position. He said that he had accepted the political arrangement made in North Africa as a temporary expedient, justified solely by the stress of battle and applying only to the immediate local situation. No permanent arrangement would be made with Admiral Darlan, and the United States command in North Africa had no authority to discuss the future government of France or of the French Empire. The President recognised that public opinion in the United Nations would never understand the recognition or reconstitution of the Vichy Government in France or in any French territory. The United States Government were opposed to Frenchmen who supported Hitler and the Axis and the President had asked for the liberation of all persons in North Africa imprisoned for their

---

(a) Hist. (G)1, No. 64. (b) Z391/5/69(1943); Z9897/8325/17.

opposition to the Axis and also for the abrogation of all laws and decrees inspired by Nazi Governments or ideology.[1]

The British Government had no option but to accept this statement and to try to secure that the policy laid down in it was carried out. A Foreign Office minute of November 17 summed up the matter:

'The questions (i) how to apply this policy so long as Darlan is in authority, and (ii) at what point and by what methods Darlan is to be eliminated must be governed by military considerations. But as soon as the military situation permits it would be desirable to get rid of Darlan, and policy meanwhile should be shaped, so far as possible, with this object in view.'

Thus we should insist upon the abrogation of 'obnoxious legislation', and make the maximum demands upon the Admiral to introduce democratic measures in Algeria and in the Moroccan and Tunisian protectorates. We might hope that 'strong doses of this medicine might, before long, make him uncomfortable, and make it easier to unseat him when the time comes'.

Mr. Eden instructed Lord Halifax to insist to the United States (a) Government that all British and Allied internees should be released forthwith, and that Free French sympathisers and our other friends in North Africa should no longer be victimised. The Prime Minister also sent a personal message to Mr. Roosevelt on the night of (b) November 17–18 emphasising the deep currents of feeling stirred up by the arrangement with Admiral Darlan and urging that this arrangement could be only a temporary expedient. The Prime Minister said that 'we must not overlook the serious political injury which may be done to our cause, not only in France, but throughout Europe by the feeling that we are ready to make terms with the local Quisling'. Mr. Roosevelt replied on the morning of November (c)

---

[1] On November 13 Mr. Welles, at the President's request, sent to General Marshall for his comments the draft of a telegram instructing Mr. Murphy (i) not to include among Vichy officials retained in the North African administration 'those to whom well-founded objection might be taken'; (ii) to obtain the release from prison of 'any elements whose sole crime' was to have aided the cause of the United Nations or to have violated a law whose purpose was to impose restrictions on aid to the United Nations; (iii) to secure the removal of 'anti-Jewish measures imposed as a result of Vichy's surrender to German pressure'. General Marshall replied on November 16 that he thought it advisable to suggest to General Eisenhower that the President's wishes should be carried out only when he (General Eisenhower) thought such measures practicable. General Marshall said that the first measure appeared to be directed against Admiral Darlan and that the measures to alleviate the conditions of the Free French and the Jews might involve 'the immobilisation of large numbers of American troops desperately needed elsewhere', since the release of 'a large number of individuals' would 'undoubtedly constitute a disturbing element in a most difficult situation'. The President agreed with General Marshall's proposal. *F.R.U.S.*, 1942, II, 437 and 442–3.

(a) Z8853/8325/17. (b) WM(42)154; T15192/2, No. 193, Churchill Papers/422. (c) T1522/2, No. 213, Churchill Papers/442.

N

18 that he too had 'encountered deep currents of feeling about Darlan' and had therefore issued his statement on the matter.

(a)   Mr. Eden also sent Lord Halifax on November 17 a statement of the British view. The statement accepted the military reasons for collaborating temporarily with Admiral Darlan. We could not, however, have 'any confidence in him as the permanent head of a North African administration'. Admiral Darlan was 'universally distrusted and despised in France and throughout occupied Europe'. General de Gaulle had already[1] made it plain that he could not work with him. General de Gaulle's standing in the United States was not what it was in Great Britain, but we were pledged to him, and our public opinion would not tolerate anything which had 'the appearance of throwing him over in favour of Darlan'. An even more serious consideration would be the 'disturbing and disillusioning effect' which a permanent arrangement with Admiral Darlan would have upon 'the great body of men and women in France who are our friends'. The feeling would also grow in other occupied countries that in the last resort we should also make terms with their 'Quislings'. The Soviet Government would also object, and the recent improvement—'so painfully achieved'—in our relations with them might receive a set-back.[2] Above all there was our own moral position. 'We are fighting for international decency, and Darlan is the antithesis of this.'

Hence we ought not to commit ourselves to Admiral Darlan as permanent head of an administration in North Africa. We intended to raise a French army in North Africa, but we could not be sure of the use to which Admiral Darlan would put it. We did not know the long-term plans of the United States Government: presumably they would wish, after the Allies were firmly established in Tunisia, to put men who had their confidence into the key positions in North Africa. These measures would require the elimination of Admiral Darlan. It should be possible to find men who, even if they had not come out openly on our side in the past, were not 'contaminated by Vichy' and had not actively co-operated with the enemy. These men could form, not a Government, but a Provisional Administration under which we should hope to unite all 'resisting Frenchmen', including those who had joined Fighting France.

(b)   Mr. Roosevelt telegraphed to Mr. Churchill on November 20 that he had told the press in confidence of the 'old Orthodox Church proverb used in the Balkans that appears applicable to our present Darlan–de Gaulle problem: "My children, it is permitted you in

---

[1] See below, section (v) of this Chapter.
[2] For the Soviet attitude, see Note to section (iv) below.

(a) Z8852/8325/17. (b) T1545/2, No. 219 (Churchill Papers/442; Z9550/8325/17).

time of grave danger to walk with the devil until you have crossed the bridge" '.

Mr. Roosevelt went on to suggest in his message that he and Mr. Churchill might consider the appointment in North Africa of one British and one American representative with authority 'not to administer civil functions but to hold a veto power over French civil administrators, and to direct them in rare instances to follow out certain policies'. Thus, if Darlan failed to carry out Mr. Roosevelt's instructions for the release of all political prisoners in North and West Africa, General Eisenhower would have to exercise his authority as Supreme Commander and to take independent action in the matter.

The Foreign Office agreed with the President's suggestion, though they wished to be sure that the representatives would not be accredited to Admiral Darlan or to the French administration, but would act as the political agents of their respective Governments on civilian matters and concert their action with the Allied Commander- (a) in-Chief. Mr. Churchill telegraphed in this sense to Mr. Roosevelt on November 24.

On the night of November 19–20 General Eisenhower sent to (b) London a copy of a draft protocol recording the arrangement between himself and Admiral Darlan. He explained that the preamble which referred to the appointment of Admiral Darlan as High Commissioner in French North Africa did not imply any obligations on the Allied side to perpetuate Darlan in any position or to support him there. The agreement was merely one between a commander in the field and a commission exercising ordinary civil and military functions in the theatre in which he was operating; the terms of the agreement were intended only to facilitate the operations of the Allied forces in North Africa.

General Eisenhower repeated in another telegram on the night of (c) November 19–20 that if his arrangement with Admiral Darlan were set aside before the army had attained its military objectives the results would be disastrous. General Eisenhower had tried to force General Giraud upon the existing French administration, but General Giraud had 'collapsed under him', and had finally admitted that he could not control the situation without military support on a scale which General Eisenhower was unable to provide. Field- (d) Marshal Smuts, who saw General Eisenhower and Admiral Cunningham on the morning of November 20, telegraphed to the Prime Minister that in his view it would be a great mistake to create the impression that Admiral Darlan would be discarded at an early date.

(a) T1590/2, No. 212, Churchill Papers/442. (b) WP(42)537. (c) Z9800/9280/17. (d) WP(42)537.

The statements already published about Darlan had had an un-
settling effect on the French leaders in North Africa; for example,
General Noguès had threatened to resign. From the point of view,
therefore, of securing French co-operation nothing could be worse
than to spread the idea that we were merely using Darlan and his
friends and that we would get rid of them as soon as they had served
our purpose. Admiral Darlan was not General Eisenhower's choice;
he had been chosen by the other French leaders—some of whom
were his enemies and our strong supporters—because they considered that they could not do without him.[1]

(a)   The War Cabinet discussed the text of the draft protocol on
November 21. Mr. Roosevelt had already telegraphed to General
Eisenhower[2] that he was prepared to approve the draft, but that he
wanted to keep the arrangement on a military and not on a political
basis, and to avoid the signature of any form of diplomatic document.
He would prefer the agreement to take the form of an announcement
by General Eisenhower and a statement of Admiral Darlan's
concurrence. The President did not want to elevate Darlan to the
position of a national plenipotentiary. Mr. Eden pointed out that the
terms of the agreement were unnecessarily favourable to Admiral
Darlan, but the Prime Minister considered that at a critical moment
in the conduct of the campaign General Eisenhower ought not to be
worried with detailed amendments to the draft. The Prime Minister
thought that, in view of the President's intention, we could regard
the agreement as a transaction in the field rather than as a diplomatic
document. The document stated that by common agreement among
leading French officials in North Africa a High Commissioner in
French North Africa had been established in the person of Admiral
Darlan. This statement was a recital of facts and did not commit us
to Admiral Darlan as High Commissioner in perpetuity. There
would be nothing to prevent General Eisenhower from broadening
the basis of government in French North Africa at a later date, if
circumstances should make this course desirable. General Eisenhower indeed had expressed this view in his comments on the draft.

The War Cabinet accepted the Prime Minister's opinion, and
General Eisenhower took steps to safeguard the character of the
(b) agreement by excising the word 'protocol' from it. He described it
as a mere statement of the method by which the Commission set up

---

(c) [1] Admiral Cunningham had telegraphed on November 18 that he feared the local
repercussions of the President's statement of November 17. No one liked working with
Darlan, but with the Allied forces strung out in the race for Tunisia, we could not afford
a renewal of hostilities with the French. Whatever his underlying motives might be,
Darlan was genuinely co-operating with the Allies.
[2] A copy of this telegram was given to the Prime Minister.

(a) WM(42)156; Z9079, 9080, 9338/8325/17. (b) Z9338/8325/17. (c) Hist.(G)1,
No. 70.

by the French authorities in North Africa would assist and co-operate with the Allied Commander-in-Chief.

The need to keep Admiral Darlan in check was shown at this time by a message which he asked the Allied authorities to transmit (a) to all French Ambassadors or Ministers at Allied and neutral capitals where diplomatic missions were still open. The message explained that Marshal Pétain had lost the power to express his true thoughts but that he remained the symbol of France. Admiral Darlan was therefore assuming in his name the defence and administration of the French Empire until he could return this sacred trust into the Marshal's hands.[1]

Lord Halifax was instructed to inform the State Department that we were not disseminating the message since it appeared to be in conflict with the President's intention that the arrangement with Admiral Darlan should be only temporary and local. The President agreed (b) that the message should not be sent through American official channels since the United States did not recognise 'any Government of France at the present time'. The President did not, however, object to the transmission of the message by Admiral Darlan through ordinary commercial channels in Algiers.[2]

On November 23 Admiral Darlan informed General Eisenhower (c) that, after negotiations at Algiers with French representatives from Dakar, M. Boisson, the Governor of French West Africa, and the French forces of Dakar, wished to join him (Admiral Darlan) in fighting the Axis. This news seems to have brought an improvement in the positive attitude of the French authorities in North Africa, (d) since General Eisenhower reported on November 25 that they had agreed to intern all pro-Axis partisans in the Constantine area and to place guards in vulnerable points. On the other hand the behaviour of the French authorities in West Africa showed the complexities of the situation and the stubborn attitude still taken by the 'rallied' or 'rallying' Vichy supporters. M. Boisson, in a broadcast announcing his decision to accept the orders of Admiral Darlan, (e)

---

[1] On November 20 Admiral Darlan broadcast a statement in reply to Marshal Pétain's announcement depriving him of his offices. Admiral Darlan maintained that the Marshal (f) was not a free agent. He went on, however, to affirm his view of Marshal Pétain as the 'living embodiment of France', and to praise the policy which the Marshal had followed since the armistice. Admiral Darlan himself had been a loyal collaborator of the Marshal; he now repeated, with the certainty of being the real interpreter of his (Marshal Pétain's) wishes, the order to fight at the side of the American and Allied forces.

[2] In spite of the President's ruling, the message was transmitted not by Admiral Darlan but by the American authorities in London. In order to avoid a false impression that the two Governments approved the contents and implications of the message, Mr. Eden sent a circular telegram to His Majesty's Missions explaining the facts, and making it (g) clear that His Majesty's Government was not a party to the despatch of the telegrams and did not recognise Admiral Darlan's administration as a French Government.

(a) Z9131/8325/17. (b) Z9132/8325/17. (c) Hist.(G)1. No. 93. (d) Hist.(G)1, No. 103. (e) Z391/5/69(1943). (f) Z391/5/69 (1943). (g) Z9131, 9132/8325/17.

said that he would not have done so if he had not been certain that, in taking such a step, he was remaining faithful to his oath to Marshal Pétain. On November 24 the French were still protecting their frontiers against a possible advance by British or Free French troops and as late as November 27 a Royal Air Force reconnaissance over Dakar was met with heavy and accurate anti-aircraft fire. Even

(a) on December 2 M. Boisson was unwilling to release all prisoners—including British internees—in West Africa without a promise of release of prisoners held by the Fighting French in French Equatorial

(b) Africa. The British authorities telegraphed a message to Washington on December 4 that M. Boisson should be required immediately to release British and other non-French Allied internees. We would allow M. Boisson to bargain the release of any Fighting French against the interned Vichy French, but we could not allow him to continue to hold British subjects on account of a disagreement between Frenchmen.[1]

(iv)

Further British representations to the United States Government on their employment of Admiral Darlan and the political situation in North Africa: decision to appoint Mr. Macmillan as British Minister Resident at General Eisenhower's headquarters: assassination of Admiral Darlan: appointment of General Giraud as High Commissioner (November 26–December 27, 1942).

(c)   On November 26 Mr. Eden wrote a minute to the Prime Minister in which he pointed out that the French authorities in North Africa were not following the lines laid down in the President's statement. Admiral Darlan, in a letter of November 21 to General Clark, had made it clear that he interpreted the term 'temporary', in relation to his own appointment, as meaning 'until the liberation of France'. We could be sure that the Admiral would use all his skill to fortify himself in his present position. He had also made it clear that he regarded himself as holding his authority from Marshal Pétain, and, if we were to judge from statements put out by the North African wireless stations, allegiance to the Marshal still remained 'an article of faith among those who are in authority in North Africa'.

Mr. Eden realised that the immediate situation was governed by military considerations, but he felt that there were grave military

---

[1] The general terms on which French West Africa and Togoland joined the Allies were signed on December 7.

(a) Hist.(G)1, No. 150. (b) Hist.(G)1, No. 156. (c) Z9897/8325/17.

risks in continuing to deal with Darlan and his associates. Mr. Eden considered that 'no one who maintains his allegiance to the Marshal can be trusted to be wholeheartedly on the side of the United Nations. We are dealing with turncoats and blackmailers and until the French administration and armed forces are in better hands it would not be safe to arm them with modern weapons.'

Above all, there was the moral aspect to the matter. Our propaganda to France was almost at a standstill because we had made terms with men whom we had proclaimed in the past to be—as they had been—the betrayers of France and the servants of the enemy. The resistance of the French people had been steadily stiffening, but our appeal to them was now stultified. We could not speak to them 'with a clear voice' until the Vichy element had been eliminated from the French administration in North Africa. In Europe as a whole, 'the filthy race of quislings', as the Prime Minister had described them, 'will take heart since they now have reason to think that, if only they happen to be in authority when the forces of the United Nations arrive', they will be treated as the governments of their respective countries.

Mr. Eden again urged that, if we did not eliminate Darlan as soon as the military situation allowed, we should be committing a political error which might have grave consequences not only for our own good name in Europe, but for the resistance of the oppressed people for whose liberation we were fighting. He suggested that the time had come for a discussion with the United States on the means of giving effect to the President's statement. For this purpose the Foreign Office had drawn up a draft telegram to Lord Halifax.

The Prime Minister thought that it would be better to wait for a time before making another approach to the United States. On (a) December 4, however, Mr. Eden repeated his suggestion for a discussion with the United States. He called the attention of the Prime Minister to a statement by General Eisenhower which was open to misrepresentation and had in fact deeply offended the Fighting French.[1] Mr. Eden thought that the United States Government should assist General Eisenhower on the political side by providing him with a special political adviser.

The Prime Minister now accepted Mr. Eden's view. A telegram was therefore sent on December 5 to Lord Halifax instructing him to explain the anxiety felt by the British Government that, in spite of the President's statement of November 17, Admiral Darlan appeared

---

[1] In a broadcast of December 3 General Eisenhower congratulated the people of North Africa, Admiral Darlan, General Giraud, and the French armed forces on the manner in which they had rallied to the United Nations. General Eisenhower said that 'all Frenchmen worthy of their country's great past' had 'forgotten their small differences of ideas' and were 'ready to fight hand in hand to vanquish the Axis'.

(a) Z9714/8325/17.

to be 'digging himself in more and more firmly'. He had assumed in his latest proclamation the office of Chief of State and the rights and responsibilities of the Government of France in the French Empire,[1] and still regarded himself as holding his authority from Marshal Pétain. His administration was in fact a Vichy régime and some of our best friends—such as Generals Béthouart and Mast—were still without active employment.

We understood the operational advantages of the arrangement with Darlan during the present critical period, but we regarded it as essential, as a first step, that early effect should be given to the President's statement in the internal political sphere. We should insist on the rescinding of anti-democratic legislation, the restoration of the right of free association for Trade Unions, the suppression of Fascist organisations, and the release of British and Allied internees and French and other sympathisers with the Allies. A start should be made with the dismissal of pro-Axis officials, and we should have ready a list of those whom we would wish to see in key positions in a new administration.

We therefore thought it urgent to carry out the President's suggestion that we and the United States should send to Algiers political representatives of high authority to deal with these questions. We could not expect General Eisenhower to be conscious of the far-reaching effects elsewhere of developments in North Africa. His recent message to the population of North Africa, with its implication that all Frenchmen supported Admiral Darlan, or ought to do so, was not happily conceived; in any case a commander in the field should not be called upon to make political pronouncements.

The American and British civilian representatives should also try to bring about an agreement between General de Gaulle and a

---

[1] During the night of December 4–5 Mr. Mack telegraphed that these claims were not put forward in an official statement; they had appeared only in a 'commentary'. The facts (according to a Foreign Office minute of December 8) appear to have been that (a) Radio Maroc announced on December 1 that 'the High Commissioner, representing French sovereignty and assisted by the services of the High Commissariat, exercises the functions and prerogatives of the Chief of State. The High Commissariat will assume the rights and duties of a Government in every country concerned. . . . At the side of the High Commissioner . . . the Imperial Council will, from now on, represent the various territories of the Empire.' An American commentator broadcasting from Algiers on December 2 referred to 'Darlan's decree published today' and on December 3 Algiers radio repeated the announcement that Admiral Darlan had assumed the title of 'Head of State'. Radio Maroc quoted a statement of December 2 in Admiral Darlan's official gazette (*Journal d'Alger*) to the effect that the Admiral had assumed leadership *de jure* and *de facto* of the French Colonial Empire.

It was therefore not surprising that the inference drawn from these announcements was that Admiral Darlan had issued some form of proclamation claiming these powers for himself. The British press drew this conclusion; so also did the Fighting French, and Mr. Hull had found it necessary to make a statement on the subject. In any case it was significant that Admiral Darlan had allowed all his publicity services to broadcast commentaries as though he had issued a proclamation.

(a) Z9796/8325/17.

North African administration, and thus unite the French Empire once again in the war. No united effort would be possible under Admiral Darlan, but an agreement might well be made with a regime which had broken with Vichy and was pledged to administer the laws of France as they stood before the armistice until the people of France could elect a constitutional Government.

On December 5 General Eisenhower sent a personal message to (a) the Prime Minister.[1] He said that the Chiefs of Staff did not appear to have received certain messages despatched from his Headquarters, and that he wanted to give the Prime Minister a personal account which would bring him reasonably up to date on the situation. He began with a summary of the military position. He explained that, according to plans agreed in London, he had taken every risk in an attempt to get into Tunisia before the Axis Powers reached the area. He had thus sent troops forward before he was sure of the attitude of the French. In this forward rush the troops had outrun the existing possibilities of supply and immediate reinforcement and even of reasonable air support. They had failed to get into the critical points ahead of the Axis largely owing to the 'senselessness' of the local French officials who had supported Vichy instead of Admiral Darlan. If French forces in the area had resisted even feebly during the critical period from November 9 to 15, the gamble would have been won.

After giving further military details General Eisenhower said that in the political field there had been a failure in transmitting information, and that owing to difficulties of organising an adequate censorship, stories had been allowed to circulate which had no foundation in fact. It was alleged, for example, that the United States military authorities were dealing with Admiral Darlan on matters not concerned with the military situation, and that they were supporting him in his claims to a permanent authority rather than as the temporary head of the local Government.

General Eisenhower said that these rumours were entirely untrue. He told Admiral Darlan at every meeting that, as far as the United States headquarters were concerned, he was the head of a local *de facto* organisation through which the Allies were enabled to secure the military and civil co-operation necessary for the campaign. Admiral Darlan knew that General Eisenhower had no power to go beyond this arrangement. The Admiral's co-operation was, however,

---

[1] The message was sent from General Eisenhower's Headquarters to the Chiefs of Staff in London for transmission to the Prime Minister. The Prime Minister does not appear to have sent a copy of it to the Foreign Office. The Chiefs of Staff had sent a message to General Eisenhower on December 4 asking for more information and stating (b) that they had found much difficulty in following accurately the course of operations.

(a) Hist.(G)1, No. 171. (b) Hist.(G)1, No. 162.

N*

necessary, since he alone was the source of all the practical help which the Allies had received. The line of communications ran for 500 miles through mountainous country to Tunisia, and the French could do sufficient damage—without fear of detection—to compel the Allies to retreat hastily to the ports. General Giraud had quickly given up trying to help; and it was solely owing to Admiral Darlan that we were fighting in Tunisia and not in the neighbourhood of Bône or to the west of it.

(a) The Prime Minister sent a friendly reply on December 7 congratulating General Eisenhower on the Allied advance, and fully endorsing his decision to take risks. The Prime Minister said that he was sorry that General Eisenhower had been bothered in the midst of an exciting battle by the 'Darlan business'. The Prime Minister would cover all 'necessary action' to the best of his ability; he felt sure that General Eisenhower would avoid formal long-term commitments with Darlan.

(b) Lord Halifax replied on December 6 to his instructions of the previous day that he would try at once to see the President, or Mr. Hull, or both of them in order to give them our views. He pointed out that Mr. Hull was very sensitive to criticism about his policy with regard to Vichy, and had already condemned anxieties and protests about Darlan at a time when our main purpose should be to win the war. Lord Halifax hoped that it would be possible to meet critics of the situation by emphasising that neither we nor the Americans were responsible for Admiral Darlan's unilateral assumption of power outside the arrangements made by General Eisenhower on the basis of the President's statement.

(c) Before seeing the President on December 8 Lord Halifax had a talk with Admiral Leahy. Admiral Leahy distrusted Darlan, and thought that he might turn against us if the military situation went wrong. On the other hand he did not think that we should be able to get rid of him quickly. He (Darlan) had said to General Eisenhower that he would be ready to retire when the position was stabilised in North Africa, but Admiral Leahy doubted his sincerity, and recognised the extent to which he was 'digging himself in'.

(d) Lord Halifax's interview with the President was not satisfactory. The President said that he had given General Eisenhower instructions to present all arrangements with Admiral Darlan as on the unilateral basis of his (General Eisenhower's) military authority. He thought that General Eisenhower should work for the restoration of civil rights and the revocation of all discriminating measures, but that he would have to go slowly. He agreed with the idea of sending qualified political representatives—subject always to the final

---

(a) Hist.(G)1, No. 178. (b) Z9765/8325/17. (c) Z9860/8325/17. (d) Z9886/8325/17.

authority of General Eisenhower—and did not know why more progress had not been made with the proposal. He suggested that Mr. Murphy, who was already serving as Civil Affairs Officer on General Eisenhower's Staff, or Mr. Matthews of the United States Embassy in London, might be the American representative.

Lord Halifax thought that the President did not contemplate early action to get rid of Admiral Darlan, and that he had in mind the establishment of some kind of joint Anglo-Franco-American Commission upon which Darlan would serve with a reduced status. Lord Halifax said to the President that public opinion in Great Britain, France, and elsewhere would not be satisfied with this arrangement. Mr. Roosevelt's reply was that doubtless the Czechs would now ask him whether he intended, when we were liberating Czechoslovakia, to make terms with Czechoslovak 'quislings'; he would say, 'not necessarily: everything will depend on circumstances, and whatever we have to do for military reasons during the war will not prejudice your freedom of choice later'. On the following day Mr. Hull spoke to Lord Halifax in similar terms that the operations in North Africa (a) were at a critical stage, and that, with their long line of military communications, the United States could not afford to risk upsetting the arrangements with Admiral Darlan.

Mr. Eden was particularly concerned over the President's apparent change of view on the question of civilian representatives. The plan (b) as put forward had been for representatives of the standing of a High Commissioner or Minister Resident. In suggesting that the political representative should be subject to General Eisenhower's authority, and in proposing Mr. Murphy for the post, the President was clearly doing no more than maintain existing arrangements. It seemed to the Foreign Office that the War Department must have intervened in the matter. Mr. Eden regarded Mr. Murphy as an unsuitable candidate, since he had been a leading advocate of the arrangement with Admiral Darlan and was strongly anti-Gaullist— he had described the Gaullists as 'subversive elements'.

Mr. Eden also thought that Lord Halifax had not understood what we wanted and that we should now try to force the hand of the United States Government by putting our own nominee, and saying that we proposed to send him out at an early date. In view of Mr. Hull's complaints, Mr. Eden instructed Lord Halifax on December (c) 10 to point out to the United States Government that we had been taking care not to throw a disproportionate share of the blame for the Darlan situation on the United States. We made a point of speaking of the 'Allied' and not the 'American' Commander-in-Chief and Headquarters. We had also been trying to persuade the Fighting

---

(a) Z8946/8325/17. (b) Z9886/8325/17. (c) Z9765/8325/17.

French that violent language on their part would hamper she conduct of military operations.

(a)   Meanwhile reports of a disquieting kind about the political and administrative situation in North Africa continued to reach the Foreign Office. Mr. Gascoigne, His Majesty's Consul-General at Tangier, for example, had reported on December 7 in serious terms about the position in French Morocco, and had said that his American colleague in Tangier was equally disturbed at the lack of civil control by the United States military authorities. The United States Chargé d'Affaires mentioned a number of notorious pro-German sympathisers who 'ought to be in gaol'. The civil administration was being carried on by Vichy officials without American supervision; their actions were causing much adverse criticism of the Americans and ourselves.

At the suggestion of the Prime Minister the Foreign Office drafted for him a personal telegram to Mr. Roosevelt calling attention to the facts and pointing out that, if we had any serious military set-backs in Tunisia, we might get into grave difficulties from the hostile elements within the French administration. The situation therefore reinforced the need of immediate political and administrative help for General Eisenhower.[1]

(b)   This message from the Prime Minister was despatched on the
(c) night of December 9–10. On December 10 a member of the British Embassy staff in Washington was shown the text of a telegram[2] sent by the State Department to General Eisenhower with instructions that it should be communicated to Admiral Darlan. This telegram recognised the contribution which Admiral Darlan was making in the campaign which had begun in Africa as a prelude to the liberation of all French people from Axis rule. Until the aims of the Atlantic Charter were fulfilled and all peoples were free to decide their own future, other questions had to remain in suspense. As long, therefore as Admiral Darlan continued to direct his efforts to the specific end of resistance to the Axis, he had a definite and positive contribution to make to the policy of the United States. This would not be so if he devoted himself to building up an organisation not directly concerned with the military effort, since there were other Frenchmen with different political aims who were also making important contributions in the military field.

---

[1] At the time of the Christmas parliamentary recess (and before Admiral Darlan's assassination) the Prime Minister had reason to expect strong criticism, after the re-assembly of Parliament, about the political situation in North Africa.
[2] The United States Ambassador in London gave a copy of this telegram to the Prime Minister on December 11.

(a) T9822/25/17.   (b) T1693/2, No. 227 (Churchill Papers/442; Z9822/25/17).
(c) Z9947/8235/17.

Mr. Eden, however, was not at all satisfied with these instructions; he criticised, in particular, the laudatory reference to Darlan's contribution to American policy, and considered that this reference would have a bad effect in Moscow. Similarly the Foreign Office wished to alter the text of a public statement which the President (a) had asked Admiral Darlan to make. In this statement the Admiral was to refer to the 'amnesty' already granted to those against whom action had been taken on account of their pro-Allied sympathies. The Foreign Office pointed out that 'amnesty' was hardly the word to use in respect of those whose only 'crime' had been to support the Allied cause. The statement also contained a phrase that in leading North and West Africa against Germany and Italy and into the ranks of the United Nations Admiral Darlan had no personal ambitions. In spite of this disclaimer, the phrase would be open to the criticism that the United States Government were recognising Admiral Darlan who had been collaborating with the enemy for two and a half years, while they still refused to recognise as one of the United Nations the Fighting French who had been fighting the Axis for this same period. Finally the statement seemed to imply that Admiral Darlan would be maintained in his position until France had been freed. The British view was that it would be a mistake to sponsor any statement by Darlan which was open to this interpretation. The statement, which was bitterly criticised by the Fighting French, was in fact issued on December 16 without giving time for any British comments to reach the American authorities in Washington or General Eisenhower.

Meanwhile the United States authorities put to General Eisen- (b) hower the complaints in Mr. Churchill's telegram of the night of December 9–10. They referred particularly to allegations that (i) Fascist organisations were continuing their activities and were vicitimising our former French sympathisers, many of whom had not yet been released from prison; (ii) well-known German sympathisers who had been ousted had now been reinstated in their offices; (iii) as a result of an almost complete absence of control on the frontier between the French and Spanish zones of Morocco, Axis agents and other 'undesirables' were crossing the frontier in both directions; (iv) there was no Allied control of censorship, and nothing to prevent enemy agents from communicating with Europe; Germanophil Spanish Consuls were also sending full reports about the military situation; (v) there was veiled anti-Allied propaganda in the press and radio, and positive enemy propaganda was increasing.

General Eisenhower had reported on December 13 that he had (c) spoken frankly to Admiral Darlan on the lines of the instructions

---

(a) Z10467/8325/17. (b) Z10139/8325/17. (c) Z10168/8325/17.

sent to him on December 10 and warned him that anything which could be interpreted as political manoeuvring on his part to extend the scope of his influence outside French North and West Africa would react definitely against him in his contacts with the American army and Government. Admiral Darlan's reply was that he had no intention of trying to extend his political influence to other countries, and that henceforward he would present to General Eisenhower's headquarters, for despatch to Washington, any message intended for former French official personnel outside French North or West Africa. The United States Government could thus determine whether the message conformed to their policy. Admiral Darlan repeated his promise of complete co-operation in the local military effort and in all other ways deemed appropriate by the United States. He also said again that only a free French people could select their future rulers.

(a)   On December 14 General Eisenhower replied to the list of complaints sent by Mr. Churchill. He said that he knew of these reports, and that he had been dealing with them, and would continue to do so. Some of the reports came from Axis sympathisers or even from enemy agents wishing to create trouble. Others came from disappointed office-seekers. The de Gaulle element was also dissatisfied, and was stimulated from outside, though they were few in numbers, and there was a definite anti-Gaullist feeling among officers in the army and navy. General Eisenhower said that the activities of Fascist organisations were being discontinued or kept under close observation, and that he could find no cases in which well-known German sympathisers had been reinstated. All officers and men imprisoned for aiding our landing had been released and reinstated. The frontier control and the censorship arrangements were being taken in hand; the reason why privileges enjoyed by the Spanish consuls had not been withdrawn was the obvious need of avoiding friction with Madrid.

Mr. Eden considered that General Eisenhower's answer was too optimistic, and that the facts in our possession showed, for example, that the reinstatement of German sympathisers and the victimisation of our friends continued. On the other hand we should not 'snipe at' the Americans. They had extremely difficult problems. It was impossible to change the whole basis of French administration within a few weeks, or to transform a pro-Vichy régime without a long process of 'disinfection and re-education'. The trouble was that with Darlan at the head of affairs, the process would not operate effectively.[1]

---

[1] The Foreign Office noted on December 17 that General Eisenhower, in accordance
(b) with Mr. Roosevelt's instruction, was taking care to secure that any arrangements made with the French administration, e.g. the agreement between Admiral Darlan and M. Boisson, were announced by himself in a unilateral declaratory form, and not in the form of bilateral agreements with Admiral Darlan.

(a) Z10218/8325/17. (b) Z9478/8325/17.

Mr. Eden decided to draw up a memorandum, for submission to General Eisenhower, pointing out that the situation showed how great was the need for immediate political and administrative assistance in North Africa. We should offer to give all assistance in our power, and from our previous experience, we were likely to find that our offer would be accepted.[1]

Although the United States Government had taken action on the British complaints with regard to the pro-Vichy activities of the French local authorities, they did not respond as quickly to the British insistence upon the appointment of senior political advisers to General Eisenhower. Field-Marshal Dill reported from Washing- (a) ton on December 12 that he had had some private conversations on the subject with his American service colleagues. Admiral Leahy had said that no decision had been taken on the American side, but that it was definitely regarded as impracticable for the time to impose a joint American-British political authority upon Admiral Darlan. The American view was that Mr. Murphy was fully qualified to give political advice to General Eisenhower, though Admiral Leahy thought that it would be wise to promote him (Mr. Murphy) in order to increase his authority. If the British Government thought some more senior British representative to be necessary—e.g. a senior Ambassador—there was, in Admiral Leahy's view, no reason why they should not act unilaterally in the matter, subject to General Eisenhower's agreement. Field-Marshal Dill reported that Admiral Leahy clearly felt that we should have Darlan with us for a very long time, but that, unless we had a severe defeat, he would not attempt any 'double-crossing'.

On December 15 President Roosevelt formally appointed Mr. (b) Murphy as his personal representative in North Africa with the rank of Minister. Mr. Murphy would continue on General Eisenhower's staff in his capacity of Civil Affairs Officer until the War Department suggested a change. The British Government had now to decide whether they would have to agree to a similar subordinate position for their own representative, or whether they would carry out their plan of appointing a representative of ministerial status with a more independent position.

The War Cabinet discussed the matter on December 21, without (c) reaching a decision. On December 23 the Prime Minister told the (d) War Cabinet that, after discussion with some of his colleagues, he had sent a telegram to the President explaining that the differences between our systems of Government made it impossible to secure exact

---

[1] A memorandum on these lines was drawn up but the text was not agreed before the (e) situation was changed by the assassination of Admiral Darlan.

(a) Hist.(G)1, No. 210. (b) Hist.(G)1, No. 255. (c) WM(42)171. (d) WM(42)172; T1748/2, No. 239, Churchill Papers/442. (e) Z10679/8325/17.

similarity,[1] but that we proposed to send a junior Minister to North Africa with the title of 'His Majesty's Government's Political Representative at General Eisenhower's headquarters'. The Minister would report directly to the Prime Minister, and would be equal in rank with Mr. Murphy.

The Prime Minister explained to the War Cabinet that it was important for our representative to retain his ministerial status, and that for this purpose he might be seconded from his existing office. The essential point was that, while working in consultation with the United States authorities and relieving General Eisenhower of part of his political burdens, our representative should be free to report to his own Government.

(a) Mr. Roosevelt suggested that the appointment should be postponed until the situation was more clear, but the Prime Minister, with the approval of the War Cabinet, considered that there should
(b) be no further delay. On December 30 the Prime Minister, who had sent two further messages to the President, was able to tell the War Cabinet that Mr. Roosevelt had agreed to our proposal, and that our representative would have the title of 'Minister Resident at Allied Headquarters in French North Africa'.

The War Cabinet appointed Mr. H. Macmillan, M.P., to this
(c) post.[2] Mr. Macmillan's primary functions were described in a directive as those of reporting on the political situation in French North Africa and future plans for the territory, and of representing to the Commander-in-Chief the views of His Majesty's Government on political questions. Mr. Macmillan would thus report to the Prime Minister. He was not accredited to any French authority, and in view of the fact that the French administration was being treated as a temporary *de facto* local administration, his relations with the French authorities would be of an informal character.

On December 24 Admiral Darlan was assassinated by a young Frenchman.[3] The situation was thus radically changed. It was

---

[1] Mr. Churchill continued: 'For example, by "minister" I meant "political minister", and you think "diplomatic minister".'

[2] Mr. Macmillan was Parliamentary Under-Secretary of State for the Colonies. Mr. R. M. Makins, of the Foreign Office, accompanied Mr. Macmillan as an assistant. Mr. Mack continued to hold the post of British Civil Liaison Officer on General Eisenhower's staff.

[3] The assassination was apparently organised by a small French group in North Africa
(d) (some of whom were in positions of authority). This group had tried to use the Allied landing as a means of establishing in North Africa an authoritarian régime under the Comte de Paris (the French royalist 'pretender'), with the ultimate object of setting up a régime of this kind in France. The assumption of power by Admiral Darlan had upset the plans, but they hoped that, if he were out of the way, the Allies might turn to the Comte de Paris. They also hoped for support from General Giraud. When these hopes were disappointed they put forward charges against the Gaullists of complicity in the assasssination.

(a) T1756/2, No. 245, Churchill Papers/442; WM(42)174. (b) T1759/2, No. 242; T1769/2, No. 246; T1770/2, No. 247 (Churchill Papers/442). (c) Z2624/5/69 (1943). (d) Z24/24/69 (1943).

necessary to find at once a new head of the French administration. The Foreign Office view was that General Giraud was the only man (a) likely to rally all sections of French opinion inside and outside North Africa, and that his appointment would make also possible a joint Anglo-American policy. General Eisenhower also agreed that (b) General Giraud would be the best successor. General Giraud was thus appointed High Commissioner. He announced his appointment (c) in a short broadcast statement on December 27 appealing for all Frenchmen to stand in unity behind him, in order to assure, with the help of the Allies, the success of their armies.

Note to Section (iv). Enquiries from the Soviet Government with regard to the political situation in North Africa (November 16, 1942–January 1, 1943).

As the Prime Minister had expected the British successes in Libya and the invasion of French North Africa, together with the continued improvement in the Russian military position, greatly eased the strain in Anglo-Soviet relations. Stalin had made a statement on October 3 to a repre- (d) sentative of the United Press in the U.S.S.R. to the effect that Allied aid had been of little value to the U.S.S.R. in drawing off German forces. In another statement on November 14 Stalin commented favourably on the North African landings as producing a 'certain relaxation in the pressure on the U.S.S.R.' and as giving the initiative to the Allies. On November 16 M. Maisky, in congratulating Mr. Eden on the African (e) victories, said that he thought that the worst period for Anglo-Soviet relations was now past. The Soviet Government were, however, anxious about Admiral Darlan's position, and M. Maisky asked Mr. Eden for an explanation of the matter.

Mr. Eden said that the arrangement was an interim one and had been arrived at for military reasons. We had to reach Tunis as rapidly as possible and it appeared that the positions of Marshal Pétain and Admiral Darlan, as the Marshal's lieutenant, were much more powerful than we had supposed. General Giraud had practically no following in North Africa. Hence General Eisenhower had thought it necessary to make use of Admiral Darlan to facilitate his advance.

M. Maisky said that he fully understood the reasons, but supposed that as soon as North Africa was in our hands we should have no further need for Admiral Darlan. He clearly thought that the permanent installation of the Admiral as the head of a Government in North Africa would be very difficult to explain to occupied countries. On November 20 (f) M. Maisky asked to see Mr. Eden in order to put a question to which the Soviet Government desired a reply. They had heard from various sources that His Majesty's Government and the United States Government were considering the establishment of some form of French Government in North Africa. Was this true, and, if it were true, why had they

(a) Z10616/8325/17. (b) Z10772/8325/17. (c) Z3871/5/69 (1943). (d) N5089/30/38. (e) Z8947/8325/17. (f) Z9477/8325/17.

not been informed and consulted? As His Majesty's Government were aware, the Soviet Government were greatly interested in the future of France.[1]

Mr. Eden answered that there was no mystery in the matter and that the Soviet Government had been fully informed, and that he had himself described the position to M. Maisky. Mr. Roosevelt's statement of November 17[2] had clearly set out the attitude of the two Governments. A temporary arrangement had been made with Admiral Darlan in order to facilitate our military operations. There was no commitment about the future. Mr. Eden asked M. Maisky why the Soviet Government had put the question 'in this somewhat abrupt official form'. M. Maisky, speaking 'off the record', thought that the Soviet Government were afraid that a permanent arrangement might be made with Admiral Darlan and also with other French politicians such as Flandin and Pucheu who were said to be in North Africa. An arrangement of this kind would do incalculable harm; the effect of our coming to terms with Admiral Darlan were already bad.

Mr. Eden said that we had no reason to hold a brief for Admiral Darlan, whose treachery towards us had been consistent. On the other hand it was of the first importance to gain the whole North African shore at the earliest possible date. Furthermore the quicker we realised our objectives, the less chance was there of trouble with Spain. Mr. Eden thought that the Soviet Government wished to warn us that a Government of men such as Admiral Darlan, Flandin and Pucheu, who had been notoriously anti-Russian, would seriously injure Anglo-American relations with the Soviet Government.

(a) On November 24 Sir A. Clark Kerr had a long talk with M. Molotov. He found that M. Molotov was more interested in the political than in the military side of the North African operations; he was anxious about the position of Admiral Darlan and hoped that the Soviet Government would be consulted about the establishment of a Government in North Africa. Sir A. Clark Kerr's telegram crossed a message of thanks from the

(b) Prime Minister for congratulations sent by Stalin on the successes in North Africa. The Prime Minister made a reference to the political situation in the words:— 'Do not be disturbed about the rogue Darlan'.

(c) Stalin replied on November 27 in terms which did not suggest that he was in fact disturbed by the use made of Admiral Darlan. Stalin hoped that a reference in the Prime Minister's message to 'pinning down the Germans in the Pas de Calais' did not mean that the promise of a second front in 1943 would not be fulfilled.

(d) On December 3 the Prime Minister sent another message to Stalin informing him that Mr. Roosevelt had suggested a meeting in North

---

[1] The United States Government, with whom the Soviet Government also raised the point about consultation, thought that the Russians were asking for assurances 'in order to bind our hands as to whom we intend to deal with when the time comes on the Continent, and not North Africa alone'. *F.R.U.S.*, 1942, II, 469.

[2] See above, p. 368.

(a) Z9478/8325/17. (b) T1584/2, Churchill Papers/393. (c) T1608/2, Churchill Papers/393. (d) Argus 370, T1648/2, Churchill Papers/420.

Africa. The Prime Minister hoped that Stalin would be able to come to the meeting, since it was necessary to decide upon the best means of attacking Germany in Europe with all possible force in 1943. This question could be decided only 'between the Heads of Governments'. Stalin (a) replied on December 6 that, although he welcomed the proposal for a meeting of the three Heads of Governments to fix a common line of strategy, he could not leave Moscow. He also repeated his view about the urgency of a second front, but made no reference to Admiral Darlan. Mr. Churchill answered on December 12 that he could give no reply (b) about a second front without consulting Mr. Roosevelt, and that for this reason he wanted the proposed meeting. On December 29 Mr. Churchill (c) told Stalin that he was going alone to meet Mr. Roosevelt.

The Foreign Office considered it essential that the United States Government should discuss the political situation in North Africa directly with the Russian Government. They therefore asked Lord (d) Halifax whether the Russians had expressed any views on the matter in Washington. Lord Halifax replied on December 10 that M. Litvinov (e) was not much interested in Admiral Darlan, but that the American Chargé d'Affaires at Moscow had been questioned on the subject more than once and that M. Molotov had spoken to him on the lines of his conversation with Sir A. Clark Kerr.

On December 17 Lord Halifax telegraphed that the State Department (f) had been asked by the Soviet Government about the position in North Africa and the intentions of the United States Government. They had instructed their Chargé d'Affaires to give an explanation to M. Molotov. The explanation had been accepted, and M. Molotov had repeated the expressions of satisfaction which Stalin had used to the Prime Minister.

On December 17 Mr. Baggallay[1] was sent a reply to Sir A. Clark (g) Kerr's telegram reporting his interview of November 24 with M. Molotov. He was instructed that there was no intention of setting up a French Government in North Africa. The statement issued by the United States Government was clear on this point and General Eisenhower had said that he would deal with Admiral Darlan merely as the *de facto* head of the local administration. In order to emphasise the position the arrangements had been announced in a unilateral form by General Eisenhower as Commander-in-Chief and not in the form of a bilateral agreement with Admiral Darlan. Mr. Roosevelt had said that no one in the United States army had authority to discuss the future Government of France or of the French Empire. This future Government of France would be established by the French themselves after their liberation.

The British Government had not entered into formal relations with Admiral Darlan and as yet had no political representation with the French at Algiers. The Consulates at Algiers and Casablanca had been re-opened, and those at Rabat and Dakar would be re-opened, on a *de*

---

[1] Sir A. Clark Kerr was on leave.

(a) T1677/2, Churchill Papers/420. (b) Argus 390, T1706/2, Churchill Papers/402. (c) T1771/2, Churchill Papers/402. (d) Z9478/8325/17. (e) Z10002/8325/17. (f) Z10333/8325/17. (g) Z9478/8325/17.

facto basis. We had no responsibility for the original arrangement with Admiral Darlan, but we had acquiesced in it for military reasons. The United States Government were responsible for political and military affairs in North Africa. With regard to the future we had already told the United States Government our misgivings that the present régime in North Africa might establish itself beyond the period required by the military situation. We thought that plans should be made for a regime which would rally the whole of the French Empire and the forces of resistance in France. Hence we had welcomed an American proposal for the appointment of civilian representatives who would relieve the Commander-in-Chief of political responsibility. These representatives would not be accredited to the French. Finally, we would try to 'keep in step' with the Soviet Government, although the latter would doubtless wish to discuss North African affairs primarily with the United States Government. Mr. Baggallay carried out his instructions on December 18. M. Molotov expressed himself satisfied, but asked that he should continue to be kept informed about the situation.[1]

(v)

General de Gaulle and the Allied landings in North Africa: the attitude of General de Gaulle and the French National Committee to the policy of collaboration with Admiral Darlan.

(a)   The final arrangements between the Prime Minister and the President with regard to telling General de Gaulle about the North African landings were that nothing should be said to him until after the assault had begun.[2] The result of this arrangement was that, in fact, General de Gaulle first heard of the operation over the wireless and in the press. The Prime Minister and Mr. Eden, however, had taken such steps as were open to them to lessen any resentment which the General might feel. The negotiations over Syria[3] were being conducted in a better atmosphere, and General de Gaulle was anxious not to lose the chance of securing the administration of Madagascar. The Prime Minister, in a characteristic gesture, had tried to restore the personal relationship between General de Gaulle and himself after their strained interview of September 30. On

(b)   October 29 he asked Major Morton to see General de Gaulle and to give him a personal message of congratulation on the enterprise

---

[1] In view of this request a further telegram of information was sent to Moscow for communication to M. Molotov.
[2] See above, p. 357.
[3] See Volume IV, Chapter LIII, section (v).

(a) Z8413/8325/17. (b) Z8501/90/17.

of the Fighting French submarine *Junon*[1] and of regret that the French force fighting in Egypt had recently suffered relatively heavy casualties. The Prime Minister also asked Major Morton to say that, in spite of the difficulties which had arisen between His Majesty's Government and Fighting France, in which he (the Prime Minister) felt that General de Gaulle might have been more accommodating, he did not forget the part played by General de Gaulle after the defeat of France and subsequently by his Movement.[2]

Major Morton delivered this message on October 30. General de Gaulle's response was of a friendly kind. He recognised the immense burden which the Prime Minister had to carry. He added that he too had great burdens. He felt that he represented France, and that to do so it was essential for him to 'make himself difficult'.

The Prime Minister and Mr. Eden thought that the exclusion of the Fighting French from the North African landings would seem less marked if General de Gaulle were able to announce that the French National Committee were taking over the administration of Madagascar.[3] We might indeed be involving ourselves in trouble about local matters in Madagascar, but the wider consideration was of (a) more importance. Hence Mr. Eden told General de Gaulle on November 6 that His Majesty's Government were willing to resume negotiations about Madagascar and, if General de Gaulle wished, to issue immediately a public statement that the negotiations were taking place, and that General Legentilhomme had been nominated by the French as High Commissioner and would shortly go to Madagascar. General de Gaulle said at first that he would rather defer a public statement until the negotiations were complete.

The Prime Minister and Mr. Eden saw General de Gaulle at (b) 1 p.m. on November 8. The Prime Minister explained that the operations in French North Africa were an American enterprise, and that British forces were taking part in them under the supreme command of General Eisenhower. Mr. Churchill had wanted to let General de Gaulle know what was happening but, in view of the fact that 250,000 American soldiers were on the seas, President Roosevelt had strongly urged that nothing should be said until the

---

[1] The *Junon* had sunk a large German supply ship in a Norwegian fjord and had driven another German ship aground.

[2] The Prime Minister did not consult Mr. Eden before sending this message. On hearing of the message Mr. Eden told the Prime Minister that the Foreign Office were continuing to take a stiff attitude towards General de Gaulle, and that he was afraid that Mr. Churchill's 'olive branch' might give the impression of a difference between the policy of the Prime Minister and that of the Foreign Office. M. Pleven, however, reported to the Foreign Office that the message had been well-timed, and that the General was now anxious to co-operate.

[3] The final surrender of the Vichy forces in Madagascar took place on November 5. See above, p. 331.

(a) Z8539/23/17; Z8413/8325/17. (b) Z8613/8325/17.

expedition had landed. Since we had agreed to American command in policy as well as in strategy, Mr. Churchill had felt bound to conform to the President's wish.

Mr. Churchill told General de Gaulle of the arrangements to get General Giraud out of France and of the visit of an American general to North Africa two or three weeks earlier to consult with French officers about the landing. Finally Mr. Churchill urged General de Gaulle to speak his mind freely on the situation and assured him that our support of him and of Fighting France remained a basic element in our policy. With this fact in mind General de Gaulle should be able to arrange matters with General Giraud to the satisfaction of all parties.

General de Gaulle reminded the Prime Minister that he had always hoped that by reuniting the French Empire he could lead France back to fight with the British against the Axis. Treason had prevented him from carrying out this plan, and it had proved necessary to rally the French Empire piecemeal. He was entirely of opinion that the pieces must be put together to form a single centre of resistance. There must not be a 'Giraud party of resistance' and a 'de Gaulle party'. The French people—who alone mattered— would be confused by a multiplicity of leaders, and only the Communists would gain.

General de Gaulle thought that for the operation in North Africa the choice of General Giraud was excellent. General Giraud had not signed the armistice with the Germans; he had escaped from Germany and was 'without reproach'. General de Gaulle considered that the Americans were right to go to North Africa, but that they would be mistaken if they fostered any division between the various elements ready to fight the Axis. He was sure that, if the Prime Minister and the President agreed together, they could jointly put pressure upon Frenchmen to create and follow a single centre of resistance.

The Prime Minister said that in a few days' time he would broadcast to Frenchmen and make clear to them what General de Gaulle had done to keep the flame of resistance alive. General de Gaulle said that he himself did not matter; he was ready to put himself under any other Chief who carried with him the mass of the French people.

The Prime Minister pointed out that the sole object of the Americans was to disembark in North Africa. They had believed that they could do so more easily if in the initial stages they did not mention Fighting France or draw attention to British co-operation. The Prime Minister warned General de Gaulle not to take the American attitude amiss and above all not to quarrel with the Americans; His Majesty's Government had fully concurred in the

American plan. Finally he urged the General to announce the appointment of General Legentilhomme as High Commissioner in Madagascar, since this appointment would show that the British were not abandoning Fighting France. General de Gaulle agreed that it would be a good plan to make the announcement at this time.[1] He also proposed to broadcast during the evening (November 8) and would send the text of his speech to Mr. Eden for his concurrence.

General de Gaulle asked the Prime Minister formally in the (a) afternoon of November 10 for his good offices in favour of sending a mission to North Africa. The mission, which would be headed by M. Pleven, would confer with General Giraud on the best way of securing the unity of French resistance in North Africa. Mr. Eden thought that the plan was reasonable, and mentioned it to the American Ambassador.[2] The Ambassador consulted the United States Government, and heard from Mr. Hopkins on November 12 that the President had no objection to the despatch of a Fighting French Mission on the condition that it did not interfere with General Eisenhower's military control. General Eisenhower, on the other hand, thought it desirable that the Mission should be post- (b) poned for a time. If the Mission came too soon, it might disturb the 'delicate arrangements' with the French leaders and weaken the position of General Giraud, while if it were to arrive and be rebuffed a subsequent reconciliation would be more difficult. In view, however, of the position assigned to Admiral Darlan, the French National Committee decided on November 14 to postpone sending a mission in case it might appear to be going with the purpose of conferring with Admiral Darlan.

In spite of his favourable remarks to the Prime Minister about (c) General Giraud, General de Gaulle spoke to Admiral Stark in strong terms criticising General Eisenhower's appointment of General Giraud and claiming that the latter had destroyed his chances or representing French opinion (i) by writing to Marshal Pétain earlier in 1942 that he agreed to accept the Marshal's guidance,[3] (ii) by refusing to establish contact with the Fighting French, and (iii) by accepting from the American authorities an appointment to command French troops in action to assure the liberation of France. General de Gaulle's view was that he was himself concerned with recreating French unity in order to assure effective French participation in the war of liberation, and that he could not agree to the

---

[1] A communiqué on Madagascar was issued on November 11. General de Gaulle did not mention Madagascar in his broadcast of November 8.
[2] The Prime Minister was not available at the time for consultation, but later agreed with Mr. Eden's action.
[3] See below, pp. 392–3.

(a) Z8756/8325/17. (b) Z9114/8878/17. (c) Z8885/8325/17.

assumption of responsibility by other Governments on matters of exclusively French concern. The Prime Minister considered that General de Gaulle was most unwise to antagonise General Eisenhower and the United States Government who could 'brush him aside quite roughly without trouble to themselves'.

If General de Gaulle regarded the appointment of General Giraud as a mistake, he could not find words strong enough to express his complete disgust at the willingness of General Eisenhower to come to
(a) terms with Darlan. On November 14 he wanted to publish a communiqué dissociating himself and the French National Committee from the American action in recognising Admiral Darlan. In view of the wishes of the Prime Minister and Mr. Eden, General de Gaulle postponed the issue of this communiqué. On November 15 he wrote to the Prime Minister asking to be allowed to speak to the French people over the British wireless. He also hoped that the British Government would make it clear that they were not in agreement with American policy with regard to Admiral Darlan.
(b)   On November 16 the Prime Minister and Mr. Eden saw General de Gaulle. The General said that he would not be a party to any arrangement, however temporary, which gave authority to Admiral Darlan. He maintained that no immediate military advantages could justify dealings with a traitor. He said also that he must state publicly his own position and at least dissociate himself from the negotiations in North Africa. The Prime Minister tried to persuade General de Gaulle not to issue his communiqué at once; he did not feel able to insist on further delay when the General said that he had already postponed it for forty-eight hours, and could not wait any longer. The communiqué was therefore issued on the afternoon of November 16. In it General de Gaulle announced that he and the French National Committee were taking no part in, and assumed no responsibility for the negotiations in North Africa with the representatives of Vichy. If the negotiations resulted in confirming the Vichy régime in North Africa, such a decision obviously could not be accepted by Fighting France. The union of all French territory overseas in the struggle for liberation should be achieved under conditions consonant with the will and dignity of the French people.
(c)   Three days later General de Gaulle and M. Pleven saw Mr. Eden at the Foreign Office. They brought with them messages showing the grave effect upon the resistance movement in France of the American handling of the political situation in North Africa. They also showed Mr. Eden a letter of May 4, 1942, from General Giraud to Marshal Pétain in which the former gave to the latter his word of honour that he would do nothing to disturb the relations of the

Vichy Government with Germany or to hamper the policy which the Marshal had asked Admiral Darlan and Laval to carry out. General de Gaulle argued that this letter had completely destroyed General Giraud's credit with the resistance organisations. The General then repeated his views about the situation. He said that he wanted to broadcast to the French people on November 20; Mr. Eden agreed that he should do so if, as was usual, he submitted the text to the Foreign Office before the broadcast was delivered.

General de Gaulle, however, did not broadcast on November 20. (a) He told Mr. Peake on this day that, in view of Admiral Darlan's broadcast,[1] he had to reconsider his position. He now wished to broadcast on November 21, and to explain to the French people what Darlan was doing in North Africa and 'what Darlan meant'. If he (General de Gaulle) were not allowed to state his views in this way, he could no longer maintain the moral authority for which the name of his Movement[2] stood in Metropolitan France; it would be better that the Movement should be dissolved rather than that Frenchmen who were enduring so much should see him as their betrayer. General de Gaulle also complained of the interpretation given by an American radio broadcast in French to the President's definition of the arrangement with Admiral Darlan as 'temporary'.

The Foreign Office inclined to agree with General de Gaulle's complaint about the American radio comments implying that 'temporary' meant 'until the end of the war', but they did not want General de Gaulle to aggravate matters by a polemical broadcast. The Prime Minister refused to allow the broadcast. He explained to General de Gaulle on November 24 that he wished to avoid anything (b) which might make the task of the British and American troops in North Africa more difficult or lead to unnecessary loss of life. The Prime Minister had also felt that, as the expedition to North Africa was under American command, President Roosevelt should see the proposed broadcast before it was given. He had telegraphed the text to the President saying that he did not think it advantageous. The President had not replied, and the Prime Minister doubted whether he would do so.

Meanwhile on November 19 General de Gaulle had said to (c) Admiral Stark that since the Allies refused to consult him about their military plans in North Africa he intended to act without consulting them in Free French Africa. He had therefore instructed the military authorities in Free French Africa to do all in their power to bring over as much French territory as possible to Fighting France. He

---

[1] See above, p. 373, note 1.
[2] It is possible that the text of Mr. Peake's report should read: 'his name and his Movement'.

(a) Z9034/90/17. (b) Z9382/90/17. (c) Z9153/8325/17.

hinted that General Leclerc would be undertaking operations at once from the Lake Chad region against neighbouring Vichy territory.

(a)   At his interview with the Prime Minister on November 24 General de Gaulle said that President Roosevelt had invited him to visit Washington some time before December 15 and that he could not refuse the invitation.[1] He spoke of a conversation between the President and M. André Philip, the Fighting French representative at Washington. The President had told M. Philip that he would employ any means to win the war—e.g. he would even make use of Laval. As Commander-in-Chief of the United States forces he exercised supreme authority in territory occupied by the American army; he could thus give orders to Darlan, and the latter would have to obey. He would deal similarly with the local authorities if American forces were operating in Metropolitan France.

(b)   From this time, however, although he still refused to consider an agreement between the French National Committee and Admiral Darlan or to recognise in any way the legality of the Vichy Government, General de Gaulle seemed not unwilling to come to an agreement with General Giraud, and did not exclude General Noguès, in spite of his views of the latter's 'time-serving' character.

(c)   On December 2 General de Gaulle asked that he should be allowed to send General d'Astier de la Vigerie (who had formerly commanded the French air forces in north-eastern France) with a small delegation to study the situation in North Africa. Mr. Eden supported this plan, and obtained American consent to it.[2]

In view of Admiral Darlan's broadcasts and, more particularly, of
(d)   General Eisenhower's statement of December 3, General de Gaulle arranged for a full statement of the attitude of Fighting France to be broadcast on December 6 from Radio Brazzaville. After speaking of the continuance of French resistance, in spite of the acts of the Vichy 'usurpation', General de Gaulle used these words of the French

---

[1] The President had raised the question of a visit by General de Gaulle to the United States in his conversation of September 10 with Lord Halifax (see above, p. 356). The
(e)   Foreign Office thought that the President's object was to keep relations between the United States and General de Gaulle steady during the preparation and execution of the North African operation.
(f)   Mr. Eden had not wished the General to go to Washington in September, since he wanted to reach agreement with him about the Levant States and Madagascar, and discussion of those questions was bound to take some time. The proposal for the American visit had accordingly been deferred.
(g)   On November 25 Admiral Leahy sent word from Washington to Commander Kittredge, Admiral Stark's assistant, that General de Gaulle had not been invited to visit the United States. The President would willingly receive the General, but the visit must be on the General's own initiative. The Foreign Office thought it equally desirable for General de Gaulle to go to Washington whether by invitation or on his own initiative.
[2] See below, p. 401, note 1 for this visit.

(a) Z9382/90/17. (b) Z9659/8325/17. (c) Z9797, 9952/8878/17. (d) Z391/5/69(1943).
(e) Z6998/608/17. (f) Z9212/608/17. (g) Z9279/115/17.

National Committee which drew its authority from the 'consentement spontané des Français':

'. . . Nous somme prêts, dès à présent, à faire en sorte que soient liées entre elles, afin de frapper l'ennemi, les actions de toutes les forces françaises organisées où que ce soit. Nous sommes certains que le fait seul de nous unir tous dans la guerre aura tôt fait de nous unir aussi sur tout ce qui est essential au salut et à la grandeur de la France.' The union and common action of Frenchmen must recognise, however, certain facts. 'La nation n'admet pas qu'un quarteron d'hommes qui symbolisent la capitulation, la collaboration, l'usurpation, et qui ont usé et abusé contre les libérateurs de la discipline des autres, en usent et abusent maintenant pour singer l'honneur et le devoir. La nation n'admet pas que ces hommes, ayant failli dans la guerre étrangère et se sentant condamnés, puissent ménager leur destinée en créant les conditions d'où sortirait la guerre civile. La nation n'admet pas leur pouvoir, tiré d'une parodie grotesque de droit divin. . . . M. Hitler voulait, a-t-il dit, "pourrir notre guerre". La nation ne veut pas, elle, qu'on pourrisse notre libération.'

On December 8 Mr. Eden had a talk with General de Gaulle and (a) General Catroux.[1] General Catroux said that the Fighting French realised that the Darlan arrangement had been decided by military considerations, but that nonetheless it was dangerous to leave a man like Darlan, who could not be trusted, in a position enabling him to sever the long line of Allied communications. General de Gaulle considered that any military advantages in the arrangement were outweighed by the political disadvantages. The Americans had leagued themselves with the forces of capitulation. General de Gaulle recalled an interview between M. Reynaud and Mr. Bullitt when the French Government had been about to leave Paris. Mr. Bullitt had said that he would remain in Paris. This attitude had greatly disquieted M. Reynaud, since it seemed to show that, in Mr. Bullitt's view, France was already lost, and that the Americans had come down on the side of capitulation.

General de Gaulle held that the Americans were making a great mistake in ignoring the fact that modern war was an affair of peoples, and not merely of armies. President Roosevelt had paid too much attention to the group of men who had taken power at Vichy and too little to the French people about whose views the United States Embassy at Vichy seemed to know nothing. In these circumstances it was wrong to put into the hands of General Eisenhower the policy of the United States and Great Britain towards France.

---

[1] General de Gaulle had asked General Catroux to come to London from Syria for consultation.

(a) Z9953/8325/17.

General de Gaulle trusted the President's good faith, but regarded him as badly advised at Algiers, especially by Mr. Murphy. No one of the Americans at Algiers seemed to have any idea of the wider political implications of what they were doing.

General de Gaulle said that no political regime had substance or stability unless it were based on some political or moral idea or had a 'mystique'. There were three movements in France which had some reality, since all of them possessed a 'mystique'. The Vichy regime, much as General de Gaulle detested it, had some foundation since it was based upon the myth of Marshal Pétain. The Communists obviously had a philosophical basis for their action; so had the Gaullists. The dealings of the American and British Governments with these movements were obviously of the greatest importance for the future. Neither the Communists nor the Vichy movement, which the United States Government were supporting and perpetuating in North Africa, could be pro-British. The Gaullists alone comprised those elements in France which had always been most firmly attached to the British connexion. If, owing to the Americans, the Vichy régime were firmly established in the France of the future the blame would fall largely on the British Government. The Americans would retreat from Europe, and, in any case, the French people realised American ignorance of European problems, but the judgment of France would be that Great Britain ought to have known better.

General de Gaulle also pointed out that the Soviet support of his Movement was purely tactical. M. Molotov had told him frankly that the Soviet Government would support Fighting France as long as it was successful, but if the Movement should wane, full Soviet support would be given to the Communists. The General said that he had remarked a few days earlier to the Prime Minister that President Roosevelt was losing the moral leadership of Europe and that the Prime Minister ought to take it upon his own shoulders. In any event British policy should be stated clearly even if the statement disclosed a difference between London and Washington.

In answer to a question from Mr. Eden, General de Gaulle said that he thought that he could come to an agreement with the French authorities in North Africa to unite the French Empire in the war if Admiral Darlan were removed from office; the solution would be to establish an enlarged National Committee at Algiers, with General Catroux as High Commissioner or Delegate-General and General Giraud in charge of military affairs. General de Gaulle appeared to agree with a remark of General Béthouard (reported by Mr. Mack) that any change would have to be effected by Frenchmen and not by foreigners, but he had no practical suggestion about the steps whereby the change could be carried out. He said that one point on which he was in agreement with Admiral Darlan was on the need of absolute respect for French sovereignty. Mr. Eden once more explained the complexities of the position. He said that one of the troubles was 'the Lafayette tradition', i.e. the American view that they knew better than the English how to handle French affairs.

President Roosevelt found it necessary to postpone General de Gaulle's visit until early in January. The General did not seem to object to this postponement: he arranged to leave England on December 25 and to travel via Accra, and to bring General Catroux with him. He discussed in a friendly way with Admiral Stark on (a) December 17 his general view of the situation, and his wish to explain the *raison d'être* of his own Movement to the President and to show why he was bound to refuse any association with Admiral Darlan. On the other hand a day later General de Gaulle asked Mr. Peake (b) to enquire what would be the attitude of the British Government to those parts of the French Empire which had joined Fighting France if he and the National Committee should decide that they could make no further contribution to the Allied cause, and must dissolve their Movement. General de Gaulle said that he was putting this question after giving the North African situation the most careful thought. He had accepted the decision to deal with Admiral Darlan on a temporary basis in order to effect a rapid lodgment in North Africa and to establish military communications, but it had become clear, as the weeks passed, that Darlan represented a method of winning the war and was not being utilised merely for military expediency.[1] He was the symbol of a view of the future of France incompatible with the stand which General de Gaulle and the National Committee had taken, and with the policies to which they were committed.

General de Gaulle said that since the *débâcle* of June 1940, there were only two roads of salvation for France: the French Empire must be brought back into the most active and complete participation with the United Nations in the war, and Frenchmen in France and elsewhere must be led to offer the maximum resistance to the forces of the Axis. If these two purposes were achieved France might regain her place in the concert of nations. General de Gaulle was entirely convinced that France must achieve her own salvation by her own efforts. No Ally, however sincere and well-meaning, could give her back her soul, and indeed the greater the efforts made on her behalf, if she did not fully share in them, the greater would be her sense of impotence and inferiority when the war was won.

---

[1] General de Gaulle pointed out that President Roosevelt's statement of November 17 with regard to the temporary and provisional nature of the arrangements with Admiral Darlan had not been published in any North African newspaper or broadcast from any North African station.

(a) Z10550/8325/17. (b) Z10571/90/17.

General de Gaulle could not escape the conclusion that the United States did not hold this view. All their acts—and their failures to act—since the arrival of the American forces in North Africa pointed to a belief that they could win the war in their own way and by their own methods; that this or that Frenchman could be used and cast aside, and that at the end of the war a hopeless and helpless France could be told that, although Darlan might be the master of North Africa and of the considerable military resources of which he would then dispose, the French people were free to reject him if they did not like him.

It had seemed, in the first stage of the North African operations, that the chief obstacle to French unity was likely to be the personality and past record of Admiral Darlan. General de Gaulle now felt that his own personality and the ideas for which he stood were in danger of impeding the unity of the Allies. He would not ask how this change had come about, but he must face facts, and accept the position if it became clear to him that the French National Committee was running counter to the real purposes of the United Nations, whatever their declared principles might be. His conscience would not allow him to acquiesce in what was happening; he would therefore have to withdraw and to leave the United Nations free to convince the French people that the road of Darlan and expediency was the road which they had to follow.

General de Gaulle said that he was not criticising the British Government. He and they had stood by each other in dark days; there was not much difference between their views, but the United States were materially far the most powerful of the Allies, and if they meant to carry through their present policy, and possibly to employ Laval in France, Degrelle in Belgium, Quisling in Norway, and similar instruments elsewhere, the British Government might be unable to prevent them.

Mr. Peake did not send an account of this conversation to the Foreign Office until December 22. Within two days, the assassination of Admiral Darlan had made it unnecessary for an answer to be given to General de Gaulle's question, or for the General to go at once to put his case to President Roosevelt.[1]

---

[1] General Catroux, however, went to Washington (from Beirut) on December 25.

CHAPTER XXXI

British relations with General de Gaulle in 1943: establishment of the French Committee of National Liberation: British recognition of the Committee, August 27, 1943

(i)

Relations between General de Gaulle and General Giraud: further statements to the United States Government of British views on the policy of the Allies towards the French Empire: Mr. Hull's complaints about British policy (December 27, 1942–January 15, 1943).

T HE Prime Minister on December 27 and Mr. Eden on December (a) 28 discussed with General de Gaulle the situation arising out of the assassination of Admiral Darlan. General de Gaulle developed once again his view of the need for a single French authority rather than (as the Americans seemed to favour) a federation of which the Fighting French would form part. He repeated his willingness to work with General Giraud, but regarded him as qualified for a military rather than a political rôle. General de Gaulle was also willing to work with General Noguès; he was less ready to co-operate with M. Boisson,[1] though the Prime Minister thought that he might be persuaded to do so.

General de Gaulle had suggested an early meeting with General Giraud on French territory, either in Algeria or in the Chad region, with a view to establishing a central provisional French Government. General de Gaulle sent his message to General Giraud on December (b) 25 for transmission to North Africa through the American Embassy. The Embassy appears not to have regarded the message as urgent, and did not despatch it until the late afternoon of December 26, or send a copy to President Roosevelt until (on December 27) Mr. Eden asked them to do so. The message was delivered to General (c) Giraud on December 28. According to General Eisenhower, General Giraud's immediate reaction was favourable, but he wanted time for reflection before replying to the message. He thought that hasty

---

[1] For M. Boisson's attitude from 1940 to 1942 and at the time of the Allied landings, see Volume III, ch. XXXVI.

(a) Z151/5/69(1943); Z10868/8325/17. (b) Z152/30/69. (c) Z10771/90/17; Z10819/8325/17.

399

action would be unwise, and that it might be better, in view of the bitter personal attacks exchanged between the opposing French groups, to arrange a preliminary meeting at which their respective representatives could prepare the way for a later meeting between General de Gaulle and himself. He was hopeful that a little time and proper direction would lessen the hostility to General de Gaulle which many French army officers seemed to feel.

(a)   The delay in the transmission of General de Gaulle's message caused suspicion at the French National Headquarters, especially since General de Gaulle had received a message from Mr. Roosevelt again postponing his visit to the United States but giving no reason for this action, while at this same time representatives of General Giraud were conferring at Washington with the State Department. M. Pleven said to Mr. Strang on December 28 that he considered the United States Embassy and military headquarters in London to be strongly anti-Gaullist, and that he doubted whether the Americans really wanted General de Gaulle and General Giraud to join forces. M. Pleven suspected that the Americans wished to run French affairs in North Africa, and that they knew very well that General de Gaulle, who had always taken an independent line with the British Government, would insist on due respect for French authority. General de Gaulle himself spoke on similar lines to Mr. Peake. He regarded as a first objective the establishment of a French army in North Africa which would fight quickly and effectively against the Axis. The army could serve under a British or an American general, but must be responsible to a French political authority which had placed it at the disposal of the Allies. General de Gaulle thought that General Giraud had not yet realised that such an army could not be raised by an American authority.

(b)   General Giraud sent his reply to General de Gaulle on December 29: the reply was given to General de Gaulle by the American Embassy in London in the afternoon of December 31. Although General Giraud agreed on the need for a union of all French people in the war for the liberation of France, he considered that, owing to the excitement resulting from Admiral Darlan's assassination, the moment was not suitable for a meeting between himself and General de Gaulle. He suggested that, in view of the rapid military developments, General de Gaulle should send a representative to arrange for the co-operation of the French forces now engaged in battle against the common enemy.

This message said nothing about the formation of a central French authority. On December 31 the French National Committee issued a statement of their attitude. They pointed out that the establishment

---

(a) Z10770/90/17. (b) Z30/30/69.

of a provisional central government of some kind was an essential pre-condition to military co-operation; otherwise there would be Frenchmen fighting on the Allied side, but no political representation of French interests either during the war or at the end of it. The Provisional Government would take a place as a fifth unit among the United Nations. The Foreign Office considered that General de Gaulle's arguments were not unreasonable, though they tried to dissuade him from issuing any statement which might prejudice discussion.

General de Gaulle replied to General Giraud on January 1, 1943; (a) he proposed a meeting at Fort Lamy, Brazzaville or Beirut if the situation in Algeria made it undesirable to hold a meeting there. He repeated his view that a provisional central French authority was necessary. General Giraud answered on January 5 that he had (b) no free time before the end of the month; he suggested a meeting at that date with General de Gaulle at Algiers. He again gave his view that the military representatives of the two parties should meet at once. General de Gaulle continued this exchange of messages by (c) a somewhat abrupt answer to General Giraud on January 7. He was as unwilling as General Giraud to give up his position. He said that the meeting should take place before the end of January and that delay would do harm. He agreed, however, to send an officer to Algiers in spite of the fact that his previous emissary, General d'Astier de la Vigerie, had been asked to leave Algiers almost at once.[1] Finally General de Gaulle thought it unsuitable that he and General Giraud should communicate 'by means of texts handed to foreign organisations'; he was therefore prepared to give General Giraud a code in order that they could keep in contact by cypher between London, Algiers and Brazzaville.[2]

During this period of exchanges between the two French leaders, Mr. Eden also had a direct statement on December 31 of General Giraud's views through Mr. J. E. M. Carvell, His Majesty's Consul-General at Algiers. General Giraud, who had asked the Consul- (d) General to call on him, was most friendly and frank in his

---

[1] General d'Astier had arrived in Algiers on December 19, and had held conversations with General Eisenhower, Mr. Murphy and General Giraud. He had also seen Admiral Darlan. The visit was on the whole a success, and General Eisenhower reported on December 21 that it might have improved slightly the internal situation. It confirmed (e) the impression that, although the Fighting French would have nothing to do with Darlan or General Noguès, an agreement with General Giraud would not be a very difficult matter. General d'Astier, however, alarmed the French officials because he represented himself as being on an official mission; he seemed to have the intention of making an extensive survey of the country. General Giraud recommended that the visit should not be prolonged, since it might be a disturbing element at a critical time. General Eisenhower then decided to ask General d'Astier to return to London.

[2] General Giraud accepted this proposal.

(a) Z288/30/69. (b) Z289/30/69. (c) Z326/30/69. (d) Z5/5/69. (e) Z10628/8325/17.

O

conversation. He said that the political situation in Algeria must take second place to military considerations, and could wait, but that it was all-important to bring about French unity, and with it Franco-Allied unity. He wanted to send emissaries to London—perhaps a Consul-General—who could explain to the Prime Minister the political situation in North Africa and carry on conversations with General de Gaulle. He also wanted to send a representative to deal with financial and economic questions.

Mr. Eden was disposed to accept, not a Consul-General, but some representative of General Giraud, especially in view of the possibility (a) of discussions with General de Gaulle. On the other hand General Giraud gave a bad impression after Admiral Darlan's assassination by allowing the arrest of a number of Allied supporters on an allegation that they were concerned with a plot for the murder of the general himself and Mr. Murphy as well as of Admiral Darlan. In spite of British and American protests, General Giraud insisted upon keeping the arrested persons in custody; he maintained that there really was a plot, and that his own life was threatened. In these circumstances General Eisenhower felt bound to await the result of a judicial enquiry, but the view of the British authorities was that General Giraud had been given bad advice, and that immediate changes were required in his administration.[1] For this reason, and until the arrested men were released, the Foreign Office were un-willing to make a public statement favourable to General Giraud's (b) administration. On January 4, however, Mr. Macmillan was author-ised to tell the general that we should be glad to see his emissaries but that they should come, in the first instance, only for a short visit in order to establish contact and exchange information. It would be useful for them to make contact with the French National Committee in London, though this was a matter for the emissaries themselves to arrange.

General Catroux came, at his own request, to see Mr. Eden on (c) January 12. Mr. Eden said that the British Government hoped for an agreement between General de Gaulle and General Giraud, and were concerned at the slowness with which the negotiations were developing. Mr. Eden suggested that General de Gaulle might respond to the proposal for preliminary conversations to prepare the way for a meeting and that General Catroux might himself go to see General Giraud.

---

[1] Mr. Mack considered, at the end of December, that about four-fifths of the French (d) population of Algeria were 'neutral' in sympathy; about 12–15 per cent were pro-Ally, and about 5 per cent pro-Axis.

(a) Z10908, 10909, 10916/8325/17; Z212, 264/5/69.   (b) Z5/5/69.   (c) Z676/30/69. (d) Z397/5/69.

General Catroux agreed with this suggestion, and said that he had made it to General de Gaulle, but the latter seemed nervous about the consequences of a visit, and thought it better for General Catroux to see General Giraud outside North Africa—possibly at Gibraltar. Within a few days, however, a new development made it impossible for General de Gaulle to avoid a decision. The Prime Minister and the President, at their meeting with the Combined Chiefs of Staff at Casablanca, agreed to try to bring Generals de Gaulle and Giraud together in the hope of getting thereby an agreement between the two French parties.

Meanwhile, in view of Mr. Macmillan's appointment, and of the proposals for a *rapprochement* between Generals de Gaulle and Giraud, Mr. Eden had considered it even more urgent to secure Anglo-American agreement on a common policy towards the French Empire. As a first step towards clearing up the position he decided to put before the United States Government a statement of the British view. Lord Halifax was therefore sent a telegram of instruc- (a) tions on January 2, 1943. The telegram was not submitted to the War Cabinet or shown to the Prime Minister before despatch because it merely summarised the policy which we had hitherto been trying to carry out.[1] The statement began with the assumption that the United States Government agreed with us in wishing to see the French Empire united as soon as possible under a single authority, and making its maximum contribution to the war effort. Although this result could be achieved only by an agreement reached by Frenchmen with Frenchmen, the British and American Governments would do everything in their power to promote it. Our own experience in dealing with the Free French authorities since June 1940 led us to suggest, as the best solution, the establishment in Algeria, that is to say, on the soil of a department of France, of a single authority in place of the French National Committee in London and General Giraud's administration in Algiers. Our two Governments, and doubtless other Governments, would recognise such an authority merely as a *de facto* administration provisionally exercising French sovereignty over certain departments of France and over the whole French Empire (except Indo-China), until the establishment of a Government chosen by the French people themselves. This *de facto* administration would not be recognised as the Government, or even as the Provisional Government of France, but it would maintain relations with foreign Governments by an informal exchange of representatives. It would be treated as an

---

[1] The Prime Minister read the telegram on January 4, and considered it a very able statement of policy.

(a) Z117/117/69.

Allied Power and be admitted formally to the number of the United Nations. Agreements relating to the various parts of the French Empire would be made normally with the central authority and not with the local colonial administration. Economic agreements might be made on a tripartite basis like the agreements in respect of French Equatorial Africa and the Cameroons at present under negotiation between the British and American Governments and the French National Committee.

The special powers of the Allied Commander-in-Chief exercised in French North Africa in virtue of his command of military operations would be redefined in a formal agreement between the United States Government and the central French authority, possibly on the lines of the agreement about Madagascar recently concluded between the British Government and the French National Committee. This agreement recognised the provisional exercise of sovereignty by the National Committee, and the Committee conferred upon the Commander-in-Chief the powers exercised by him. General Giraud had recently raised with General Eisenhower the question of respect for French authority; we could regard it as certain that the Fighting French element in any new North African administration would not be less sensitive on the point. French North Africa would therefore be regarded as Allied territory in which the Allied Commander-in-Chief was vested with extensive powers rather than as 'quasi-occupied' territory where he possessed administrative authority. As a counterpart, we should require that the central French authority should conduct itself in all respects, internally and externally, as an Allied administration. All links with Vichy must therefore be broken, or, at all events, there must be no revival of the claims to unbroken succession through Darlan from Pétain. We should also require a return to the laws of the Republic.

Finally, Lord Halifax's instructions referred to the statement of policy issued on December 31 by the Fighting French headquarters in London, and especially to the point made in this statement that the unification of the military effort of the French Empire must result from the creation of a central political and administrative authority, and not *vice versa*.

Anglo-American agreement was indeed necessary not only for urgent military and political reasons in North Africa but in order to put an end to a potentially dangerous source of friction between the British and American Governments. In spite of many previous (a) explanations sent by the Foreign Office, Mr. Hull continued to complain about British attacks on the French policy of the State

---

(a) Z47, 102/47/17; Z474, 478/117/69.

Department, and about the support which the British Government were giving to General de Gaulle. Mr. Hull's view—in reply to the British plan for creating a central French authority—was that any such civil authority would consider itself the constituted Government of France after the liberation of the country. Mr. Hull suggested that an attempt to establish a united civil administration would lead to unrest to the detriment of the military effort, and that it was better to concentrate on military necessities and to do nothing which might encourage 'political jockeyings, etc'. On January 8 Mr. Matthews, the United States Chargé d'Affaires, spoke to Mr. Eden about Mr. Hull's complaints.[1] He reported Mr. Hull's comments to Lord Halifax and Sir R. I. Campbell that, while the United States Government had tried to defend the British Government from attacks in the United States, especially as regards India, the British Government were creating the impression of assisting Fighting French propaganda which was continually attacking the United States. Mr. Eden replied that no official assistance was being given to Gaullist propaganda; that we were in fact trying to restrain it and would certainly not encourage any propaganda aimed at arousing bitterness against the United States Government. Mr. Matthews also stated that, in Mr. Hull's view, the American people felt General de Gaulle to be more interested in his own political supremacy in the French Empire than in the battle in North Africa; that the entire British radio and press and many British leaders had shouted approval of a broadcast by General de Gaulle on January 2[2] to which Mr. Hull objected, and that this support of de Gaulle would soon give rise to differences between the United Kingdom and the United States.

Mr. Matthews said that these reports about publicity did not come from him; he admitted that in fact no political leader in Great Britain had referred to General de Gaulle's statement. After this interview the Foreign Office investigated the complaints against the B.B.C. and found them groundless. The representatives in London of the American Office of War Information had been fully satisfied with the B.B.C.'s broadcasts. The Foreign Office suggested that Mr. Hull might have been thinking of the broadcasts from London of American commentators who had a free hand subject to the

---

[1] A telegram of January 6 to Washington had instructed Lord Halifax to point out once again that there was a very strong feeling in Great Britain against the connexion with Darlan and Vichy. We could not suppress all comments on the subject and the remedy was to agree on an Anglo-American policy. (a)

[2] The reference appears to be to a statement issued by General de Gaulle on January 2 alleging, *inter alia*, that there was increasing confusion in French North and West Africa, and that the French people were 'amazed at the strange fate of that part of the Empire most recently liberated'.

(a) Z102/47/17.

censorship of news. Such commentators had been 'aggressive' in their criticism, but similar or even stronger views had been expressed by American radio commentators from North Africa.

Although Mr. Hull's complaints were ill-founded, the Foreign Office thought it desirable once again to state clearly the British view of General de Gaulle and the Fighting French Movement and to point out that the matter had wide implications and ought not to be considered solely in regard to military operations in Tunisia. A
(a) full statement was therefore telegraphed to Lord Halifax on January 15 for transmission to the State Department. Lord Halifax was instructed that we did not, and would not recognise or support General de Gaulle or the French National Committee as the Government or as the provisional or prospective Government of France. We regarded them as a *de facto* administration, provisionally exercising French sovereignty in certain parts of the French Empire pending the establishment of a Government chosen by the French people themselves. We thus treated them as an ally in the war against the Axis.

General de Gaulle had well deserved this measure of support. He had placed himself at the head of French resistance at the time of the capitulation of France, and had stood faithfully by us, and brought over valuable territories to us in 1940. Although he depended in part on us for his finances, General de Gaulle had never been subservient to us. He was of autocratic and uncompromising temper —his personality was a grave impediment to his cause—and was proudly tenacious of French interests as he saw them. He had little use for the normal processes of international intercourse, and had more than once brought our relations with him near to breaking-point. Nevertheless, we had always been patient with him, partly for the sake of France, whose resistance he worthily represented, partly also because—whether or not he was anglophobe—he sincerely believed that Germany was the enemy and that the future of France lay with the Anglo-Saxon Powers and Russia. For this reason, although he was a man of the Right, he was supported by people of all shades of opinion—especially Left opinion—in France.

In this latter respect General de Gaulle differed fundamentally from the 'architects of the capitulation and of the policy of collaboration' who either believed actively or concluded with reluctance that France had no future except in association with Germany. Herein lay General de Gaulle's main quarrel with the men who had imposed themselves on France as the Vichy Government and were still

---

(a) Z474/117/69.

strongly represented in North Africa. These elements, according to General de Gaulle, gave a wrong impression of the French people, whose resistance to the invader had been steadfast and heroic.

On these grounds we had thought it right to facilitate General de Gaulle's assumption of the provisional administration of those parts of the French Empire liberated by us from the rule of a Government which was collaborating with our enemies and the enemies of France,—e.g. Syria, Madagascar, and, latterly, Jibuti. We had preferred to instal a French administration which we could trust to be genuinely anti-Axis rather than to take the risks of compounding with a régime of doubtful loyalty. In Madagascar—once the military resistance had been overcome—and in Jibuti, it was sufficient to remove a few Vichy recalcitrants for the population to rally willingly to Fighting France. General Legentilhomme had just had a most enthusiastic popular reception on his arrival in Madagascar.

We were not backing General de Gaulle for first place in North Africa; he and General Giraud should try to come to terms. We had welcomed the appointment of the latter and would gladly collaborate with him. General de Gaulle had no quarrel with him, and we should do our best to promote an agreement which would unite the French Empire in the war. We had already suggested to the United States Government the lines of such an agreement.[1] It was alleged that General de Gaulle wanted to control civil affairs and to leave military affairs to General Giraud. General de Gaulle had never made this claim to us—indeed it would have been out of character for him to discuss such matters with us. We had told him that in our view he would be wise to establish contact first on a lower level. We also thought that in his own present and future interests, he would do best to take an active military rôle rather than a political rôle in North Africa, but even if we offered advice on this question, General de Gaulle would not accept it.

General de Gaulle might well have political ambitions in North Africa. Frenchmen alone must decide whether he achieved them; our policy was certainly not to impose them. We had inclined to think that after the Allied invasion of North Africa, General de Gaulle's position might decline. Matters had turned out otherwise, and the Darlan episode had increased the General's prestige. In any event General de Gaulle could bring to the common fund a valuable contribution, namely, a substantial part of the French Empire, and a great and resounding name in France. We therefore hoped that the United States Government would come to look upon him in time with more understanding and sympathy.

---

[1] See above, pp. 403–4.

Before this telegram reached Lord Halifax some progress had been made in North Africa towards clearing up matters. Mr. Macmillan arrived at Algiers on January 2, 1943. He discussed the political situation with the American authorities, and the latter also
(a) received from Washington on January 10 a full summary of the British views sent to Lord Halifax on January 2. By January 14 General Eisenhower, Mr. Murphy and Mr. Macmillan had reached agreement on certain general lines of policy.

(b)   (i) The overriding consideration was that nothing should be done which would cause a state of unrest in North Africa.

(ii) On the other hand, some action was necessary in order to prevent trouble breaking out. There was widespread dissatisfaction with the existing political arrangements and danger of further acts of violence or outbreaks of strikes. In any case the dissatisfaction was having a bad effect on the local French war effort as well as upon opinion generally. It was therefore essential to show that the Allies really intended to put into practice the principles of freedom and justice about which they had spoken so much in their declarations of policy.

(iii) The main subjects of dissatisfaction were that the wrong men were in office; that many high positions were held by soldiers and officials who had collaborated with Vichy; that many of the supporters of the Allies were still being badly treated, and that many measures introduced during the Vichy régime were still in force— e.g. the anti-Jewish decrees,[1] and the Fascist Youth Organisations.

(iv) The first step must therefore be to purge the administration, firstly in Algeria and then in Morocco. Owing to the touchiness of the French in matters affecting French sovereignty it was necessary to go cautiously and to begin with the replacement of a few key men. We should continue to do our best for our friends who were still being victimised, and to press for the abolition of Vichy legislation, but we could not get full results until the right men were in high office.

(v) An essential feature of this programme was an early meeting and agreement between Generals Giraud and de Gaulle. General Eisenhower welcomed the suggestions made through Lord Halifax at Washington, and hoped that the two French leaders would reach an understanding which would allow the constitution of a unified

---

[1] The severe anti-Jewish measures enforced in North Africa by the Vichy Government included the abrogation of the so-called 'décret Crémieux' of October 1870 which had given French citizenship to all native Jews in Algeria. The abrogation of this decree was not unpopular with the Moslem population. General Giraud continued to argue that an immediate return to the provisions of the decree would provoke dangerous Moslem reaction.

(a) Hist.(G)2, No. 54; Z523/5/69. (b) Z1647/5/69.

French Administration throughout the French colonial Empire. Although, as the Foreign Office had suggested, such an administration would be purely provisional, and not even a 'provisional Government'—though it might be recognised as one of the United Nations—there was little doubt that in practise the post-war regime in France would take on much of the character of this provisional administration. For this reason it was especially necessary to maintain the liberal character of the administration. Even with a 'purge' of the Giraud Administration and the introduction of new men from the French National Committee such a task would not be easy; many of our own friends, out of disgust at the condition of French politics before 1940, looked to quasi-authoritarian solutions, and would not support the liberalism which we desired as the basis of the provisional administration. We should therefore have to try to find new men—civilians—upon whom we could rely to prevent the establishment of a quasi-fascist regime.

On January 14 Mr. Macmillan left Algiers for Casablanca to (a) meet the Prime Minister and President Roosevelt at their conference with the Combined Chiefs of Staff.[1] The purpose of this conference was to decide upon Allied strategy in 1943. The President (who did not want to bring Mr. Hull) had sent a message to Mr. Churchill on December 14 that only the Service chiefs and their advisers should attend, and that they would need 'no Foreign Affairs people with them', since their work would be 'essentially military'. Mr. Churchill accepted the President's suggestion. Hence neither Mr. Eden nor Sir A. Cadogan went with him to the conference. Mr. Hopkins accompanied the President, and Mr. Murphy and Mr. Macmillan were also present. The President's wish to exclude 'Foreign Affairs people' was not altogether fortunate. Allied military strategy could not be decided without taking account of political considerations. It is probable that, if the Foreign Office and the State Department had been represented, a public statement about 'unconditional surrender' would have been made, if at all, in clearer terms.[2] In any case, when Mr. Macmillan arrived at Casablanca he found that the Prime Minister and the President had already decided to invite Generals Giraud and de Gaulle to Casablanca, and that they had (b) also contemplated an agreement on less ambitious lines than that proposed by the Foreign Office. The Prime Minister, who seems to have taken the lead in drawing up the actual plan, did not propose an immediate 'fusion' between the French National Committee and General Giraud's administration but, at the President's suggestion,

---

[1] See below, p. 546. The conference was held at Anfa camp near Casablanca.
[2] See Volume I, Introduction, pp. liv–v, and Volume V, Chapter LXI, section (ii).

(a) Z1647/5/69. (b) Z1364/30/69; Z1366, 1647/5/69; Z1487/1266/69.
O*

merely a reconstitution of each of the two bodies to include representatives of both parties. A 'fusion', resulting in the establishment of a central organisation, would take place at some later date. The President agreed with this view, and wished to avoid commitments about the French possessions in the Pacific; he therefore wanted an agreement between the two French leaders to be confined to French African territories. The Prime Minister's proposal allowed for the appointment of British and American advisers to the reconstituted French North African administration and the National Committee.[1] The Prime Minister and the President also drew up a draft statement which might be made by the two generals.[2]

(a) Mr. Eden was asked for an opinion on these proposals, and on the probable attitude of General de Gaulle towards them. Mr. Eden replied on January 22 that General de Gaulle would regard as incomplete any arrangements which did not establish in North Africa a central authority, of which he would be chairman and General Giraud commander-in-chief, for the whole of the French Empire. He would also object to the participation of British and American political representatives in the proposed organisation for North Africa. Mr. Eden himself thought that it would be enough to arrange for an Anglo-American liaison with the French organisation. Otherwise he accepted the Prime Minister's proposals as a temporary measure.

(ii)

General de Gaulle's meeting with General Giraud at the Casablanca Conference, January, 1943.

(b) On January 16 the Prime Minister sent General de Gaulle through Mr. Eden an invitation to Casablanca for discussions with General Giraud. Mr. Eden telegraphed that he was seeing General de Gaulle on the morning of January 17, and would give him the invitation. General Eisenhower conveyed a similar invitation to General Giraud at Algiers. General Giraud accepted the invitation and arrived at Anfa camp on January 17.

---

[1] The two political representatives of the United States and Great Britain—Mr. Murphy and Mr. Macmillan—would 'sit in as advisers' to the French African commission; the National Committee would be 'advised through the existing channels by the appropriate British and American advisers'.
[2] This statement included a reference to the organisation and equipment (principally from American and British resources) in Africa of a French army of 250,000.

(a) Z1274/1266/69. (b) Z1364/30/69; Z1647, 1648/5/69; Z1268, 1487/1266/69.

General de Gaulle, however, would not agree to a meeting at Casablanca. He said that he did not wish to meet General Giraud under the auspices of the Allies who might press him to accept a compromise. In answer to Mr. Eden's argument that the Prime Minister had obviously been at pains to arrange a meeting, and that such a meeting was in the interest of all concerned, General de Gaulle replied that our interests and his might not be the same. We had never understood that the Fighting French Movement was the real force in France. There were only two alternatives: Fighting France and Vichy. General Giraud, who had tried to balance between them, was no force at all. General de Gaulle said that we had made a mistake in going into North Africa without him, and that we were now in difficulties, and asking him to help. He was willing to meet General Giraud alone at Fort Lamy in the following week, and hoped that the Prime Minister would press this proposal. The right course would be for General Giraud to rally to the Fighting French: he could then become a member of the National Committee and be appointed to the command of the French forces.

General de Gaulle argued that he would be doing a disservice to France by compromising at the behest of the Allies with General Giraud and the Vichy men surrounding him. Mr. Eden and Sir A. Cadogan, who was present at the interview, pointed out that the message proposed direct talks between the two Frenchmen, and that General de Gaulle would also have an opportunity of explaining his position to the President. General de Gaulle said that this latter consideration was a different matter, and that, if the President wished to see him, he could ask him to America. Mr. Eden continued to say how much he would regret a refusal by General de Gaulle to co-operate with the Allies in bringing the war to a successful conclusion. General de Gaulle replied that, if victory were won for the Vichy elements, France would not have won much. Finally, General de Gaulle was persuaded to think over the matter, and to return in the afternoon.

General de Gaulle came back to the Foreign Office at 5 p.m. with a message of refusal for the Prime Minister. The message repeated the General's main arguments that he wanted 'simple and direct talks between French leaders', and not conversations conducted in 'the atmosphere of an exalted Allied Forum'. He also complained of the suddenness with which the proposal had been made to him. He was telegraphing again to General Giraud his suggestion for a private meeting between them. Mr. Eden pointed out once again that the Prime Minister had in fact offered 'simple and direct talks between French leaders' and that the consequences of a refusal to take the opportunity would be deplorable, but General de Gaulle would not be moved. On January 18 the Prime Minister sent

(a)   another message to General de Gaulle pointing out that the invitation
to him came also from President Roosevelt,[1] and that a refusal must
have very serious consequences. General de Gaulle could not expect
an invitation to visit the United States in the near future if he rejected
the chance of coming to Casablanca. Mr. Churchill had attempted
to bridge the difficulties which had existed between the Fighting
French movement and the United States; he could do no more in
the matter, and His Majesty's Government would have to review the
position with regard to the Movement while General de Gaulle
remained at the head of it. Mr. Churchill, in a covering message to
Mr. Eden, regretted that, owing to reasons of secrecy (about the
Casablanca Conference) it was impossible to appeal directly to the
French National Committee. Mr. Churchill thought General de
Gaulle's refusal entirely deplorable, and felt that, if he persisted in it,
his removal from the headship of the French Movement would be
necessary.

General de Gaulle did not answer on January 19; meanwhile
General Giraud waited at Anfa. Mr. Eden replied during the night
of January 19–20 that General de Gaulle had made a pretext in order
to avoid seeing him and that he had therefore delivered the Prime
Minister's second message to him in writing. At midnight on
January 20–1 Mr. Eden telegraphed that General de Gaulle had at
last decided to accept the invitation and that he would be leaving
England forthwith. Owing to bad weather, however, the General's
flight was postponed, and he was not able to reach Casablanca until
midday on January 22.[2]

The consequences of General de Gaulle's action were disastrous.
He had put the Prime Minister, who had been arguing on his behalf,
into an embarrassing and indeed absurd position.[3] He had given a
strong argument to those Americans who had always regarded him
as an obstacle to French unity and to the successful prosecution of the
war. In particular his negative attitude seemed to justify what he

---

[1] In the first message delivered through Mr. Eden no mention was made of the President.
Mr. Eden asked that he should be free to say that the President was at Casablanca, since
otherwise General de Gaulle might resent the fact that he had not been told. Mr. Eden,
apparently did not say to General de Gaulle that the invitation was also from the President,
though General Eisenhower may have done so.

[2] Mr. Macmillan suggested on January 18 and again on January 20 that General
Giraud, who was willing to do so, should invite General de Gaulle to come to Anfa Camp
in reply to his (General de Gaulle's) proposal for a meeting. Mr. Macmillan thought that
General de Gaulle's rejection of an Anglo-American invitation was due to reasons of
national pride and that he might accept an invitation from General Giraud. The Foreign
office considered subsequently that it was unfortunate that the Prime Minister and the
President had been unwilling to act on Mr. Macmillan's suggestion.

[3] On hearing of General de Gaulle's refusal to accept the invitation sent to him,
President Roosevelt merely laughed.

(a) Z1269/1266/69.

had described as the American policy of compounding with the *de facto* holders of power in French North Africa, whatever their antecedents and their relations with Vichy. From his own point of view General de Gaulle also missed a chance of meeting on an informal basis the British and American Chiefs of Staff, and of taking part in the general discussions outside the meetings of the conference.

Even so, although he did not arrive until the Conference was coming to an end, General de Gaulle might still have done something to repair the blunder of his earlier refusal to attend. At first, however, he made matters worse by taking a tactless and intransigent line, and by failing to respond to the evident goodwill of the Prime Minister and the President. He began by a luncheon with General Giraud in which he abused Darlan and others without making any practical proposals. He told Mr. Macmillan later in the afternoon that the Conference was in a 'curious setting'—a meeting on French soil with only American troops in sight.[1] On the other hand it was clear that he wanted to make an agreement with General Giraud; the difficulty remained that neither general would allow a superior position to the other.

The Prime Minister and the President had conversations with General de Gaulle on January 22. The French were then left to discussions among themselves. They had not reached agreement by the afternoon of January 23. General Giraud had put forward a plan under which he would be Commander-in-Chief, and would be assisted by two delegates, one for French North and West Africa, the other for the territories administered by General de Gaulle. The Commander-in-Chief and the two delegates would together constitute a Comité de Guerre charged with the government of the territories as a whole. The Comité de Guerre would be assisted by various other French personalities, and would thus constitute a Directory. The Directory would be advised by a Federal Council and the machinery of government would be maintained through a number of Secretaries of State.

General de Gaulle refused to accept this plan. He considered that Fighting France had alone maintained 'l'idée française' and that the last-comers could not enjoy the same rights as those who had been fighting from the beginning. General de Gaulle did not consider himself free in the matter; his troops would not understand why he should be put in the second place in relation to some one whom he regarded as a man of Vichy. There was thus only one solution. General Giraud must rally purely and simply to Fighting France;

---

[1] General de Gaulle recurred later to the point of principle involved in the matter. He told Mr. Macmillan on January 24 that he regretted that military questions should have been settled at the conference without reference to France. He said that he would have come immediately if he had been invited to take part in the military conference.

he would be given the military command, while General de Gaulle would take the civil authority. The relations between the two generals would thus resemble those between Foch and Clemenceau. After more discussion General de Gaulle held to his point of view, although he admitted that he might thereby lose all American support. He considered that, even so, 'l'idée française' could be maintained by Fighting France. He added that in his view General Giraud was the 'man of the Americans', while he—General de Gaulle—remained entirely French.

General Giraud in turn refused to accept General de Gaulle's plan on the grounds that it would not be approved either in North Africa or in France. It was thus obvious that no agreement would be reached without strong Anglo-American pressure. There were also signs that the President, with the support of Mr. Murphy, was inclined to break with General de Gaulle, on the view that he was not ready to co-operate with the Allies in carrying on the war. Mr. Macmillan, however, and, on the American side, Mr. Hopkins, worked to bridge the gap between the French leaders. Mr. Mack put to General de Gaulle's representatives a plan which the Prime Minister suggested to the President on the previous evening and which recognised the 'deux grands chefs' as co-equal leaders.[1] General de Gaulle's representatives thought that their chief would accept a plan of this kind.

At 9 p.m. on January 23 Mr. Macmillan and Mr. Murphy had a conversation, lasting an hour and a quarter, with General de Gaulle. Although General de Gaulle continued to hold that General Giraud should rally to Fighting France, he was willing to accept the plan of co-equality, i.e. a fusion between the two organisations by means of a Conseil de Guerre of which he and General Giraud would be alternate Chairmen. He would insist on various conditions such as the exclusion of persons connected with the Vichy régime and a declaration severing all connexions with Marshal Pétain. If 'fusion' on these lines were not possible, General de Gaulle thought that the two organisations should be left intact, and that they should merely establish liaison and agree to abstain from propaganda against one another.

During the night of January 23–4 the Prime Minister and the President discussed with Mr. Macmillan, Mr. Murphy and Mr. Hopkins the possibility of getting an agreement. The President and Mr. Murphy continued to regard as useless any further negotiation with General de Gaulle; Mr. Macmillan, with the support of the Prime Minister and Mr. Hopkins, felt that another attempt might

---

[1] This plan had already been put to General Giraud's representatives, but they (and Mr. Murphy) had not regarded it as practicable.

be made to discover a formula acceptable to both sides which would provide the machinery for ultimate fusion between them. After considerable discussion, and extensive amendments, a draft text was drawn up of a joint declaration which the two generals would be invited to make. The effect of this declaration would be to commit them to achieve union as quickly as possible, and to enter into a solemn pact to maintain the closest liaison. The declaration also provided for the establishment of a 'representative committee' of which the generals would be joint chairmen.

On the morning of January 24 the draft declaration was presented to the generals. General Giraud accepted the draft in principle, though he disliked the term 'solemn pact' and was opposed to the idea of joint chairmen. General de Gaulle would not subscribe to a joint declaration, but wished to issue a separate communiqué; he said that his communiqué would be somewhat on the lines of the draft. He was also unwilling to agree to the formation of a representative committee and, like General Giraud, objected to the reference to a 'solemn pact'. Conversations then took place between the staffs of the two generals with a view to finding a formula acceptable to General de Gaulle. The latter now gave way on the question of a joint declaration; he still refused to accept a representative committee, and would not go beyond a provision for liaison.

General Giraud then prepared another text omitting any reference to a representative committee and speaking only of a 'Comité de Liaison'. Mr. Macmillan took General Giraud to see the Prime Minister in order to discuss the text and also to take leave of the Prime Minister.[1] The Prime Minister suggested some amendments to the text in order to bring out the common intention of the Generals to achieve the defeat of the enemy and the liberation of France by all the means in their power. General Giraud agreed to amend the draft accordingly.

Before the end of the interview Mr. Macmillan left to bring General de Gaulle and his staff (including General Catroux) to take leave of the President. General de Gaulle told the President that he could not accept General Giraud's revised draft.[2] At this point the Prime Minister entered the President's room. On finding that General de Gaulle had refused to accept the draft, Mr. Churchill suggested that General Giraud, who was on his way back to his own

---

[1] The Prime Minister and the President had arranged to leave Anfa Camp shortly after 1 p.m. It would appear (from one of the two accounts in the Foreign Office archives of the sequence of events on January 24) that, before seeing General Giraud to discuss the amended text, the Prime Minister had seen General de Gaulle—also for a farewell call—and had told him in strong terms that he must agree to some joint statement with General Giraud.

[2] i.e. the draft which General Giraud had shown to Mr. Churchill.

villa, should be brought into the room in order to see whether the two French generals could not agree at least upon some formula which might be announced to the world.

Mr. Macmillan therefore caught up with General Giraud, and brought him to the President's room.[1] General Giraud once more said that he was ready to be associated with General de Gaulle in some form of public declaration. The Prime Minister and the President strongly urged General de Gaulle to agree. After a short discussion General de Gaulle consented. It was then arranged that a new formula should be drawn up during the afternoon by agreement with the two parties. The two generals, with the Prime Minister and the President, then walked into the garden of the President's villa, where they were photographed in the act of shaking hands and with the two statesmen standing by them.[2]

After the Prime Minister and the President had left Anfa the staffs of the two Generals reached agreement on the terms of a brief communiqué:

> 'A l'issue de leurs premiers entretiens en Afrique du Nord Française, le général de Gaulle et le général Giraud font en commun la déclaration suivante: "Nous nous sommes vus. Nous avons causé. Nous avons constaté notre accord complet sur le but à atteindre qui est la libération de la France et le triomphe des libertés humaines[3] par la défaite totale de l'ennemi.
> Ce but sera atteint par l'union dans la guerre de tous les Français luttant côte à côte avec tous leurs alliés." '

It was also agreed that, in addition to the joint declaration, each general would issue a communiqué of his own—the one from London, and the other from Algiers—and that, before publication, the text of each communiqué would be shown to the other party.

---

[1] According to his own notes, Mr. Hopkins fetched General Giraud (R. E. Sherwood, *Roosevelt and Hopkins* (New York, 1950), 693; *The White House Papers of Harry L. Hopkins*, II, 690). It seems likely that Mr. Macmillan and Mr. Hopkins went together on the errand.

[2] The newspaper correspondents and camera men had flown from Algiers to Anfa on the previous day. The President had arranged for a press conference with them at 12 noon without reference to Generals de Gaulle or Giraud.

[3] On his return to England General de Gaulle told Mr. Peake that he had tried to insert in the joint communiqué a phrase about the defence of democracy and democratic
(a) institutions, but that General Giraud had struck out the words, and had substituted 'libertés humaines'. General de Gaulle said that he and General Giraud were divided on these questions of principle, and that he was pessimistic about their future relations because he did not see how the gulf between them could be bridged.

(a) Z1467/5/69.

(iii)

British representations with regard to the agreement at Casablanca between the United States Government and General Giraud (January 27–May 28, 1943).

If the Casablanca Conference had not brought a satisfactory arrangement between Generals de Gaulle and Giraud, it had produced a tiresome misunderstanding on the question of the relations between the Allies and General Giraud. On January 27 Mr. Murphy (a) gave Mr. Macmillan copies of two documents.[1] The first of these documents was entitled a 'résumé of arrangements in principle resulting from the conversations at Anfa'. Mr. Murphy said that it was a French document read over and approved by the President with certain amendments. The second document was apparently also French, and was also approved and signed by the President. (b) The first document dealt with the re-equipment by the United (c) States of the French forces in North Africa, and with the fixing of the rate of exchange between the franc and the dollar. The document also laid down that propaganda in French for France should be carried out from African territory by the French authorities. The document stated that the President and the Prime Minister and General Giraud had agreed that it was to their common interest for all the French fighting against Germany to be reunited under one authority, and that General Giraud should receive every facility for bringing about this union. The second document was a political statement containing the following sentences:

'In the interests of the French people . . . the Governments of the United States and Great Britain recognise in the Commander-in-Chief [i.e. General Giraud] with his headquarters at Algiers, the right and duty of preserving all French interests. . . . They bind themselves to aid him by all means in their power until . . . the French people and the French nation shall be able to designate their regular Government.

'General Eisenhower and Minister Murphy will work out with [General Giraud] the details of the present understanding. In so doing they will be governed by conversations exchanged in Washington between December 28th and January 2nd by representatives of General Giraud and the State Department, and decisions which have been made by President Roosevelt, Mr. Churchill and General Giraud at interviews at Casablanca between January 17th and January 24th.'

---

[1] For the origin of these documents, see a Note by A. L. Funk in the (U.S.) *Journal of Modern History*, vol. XXVI (1954), pt. 3, 246–54.

(a) Z1336/5/69. (b) Z1337/5/69. (c) Z1338/65/69.

(a)   Mr. Macmillan thought that President Roosevelt had not actually seen the documents until the morning of January 24, and that in the pressure of business he had not realised their significance. The President could not have intended to endorse the idea of a sole trusteeship for General Giraud; any such endorsement would have been contrary to the American policy of refusing commitments which might invest General Giraud with authority to speak for the French people. His Majesty's Government would also wish to express a view on the question of control of propaganda. Mr. Macmillan proposed to raise the latter question at Algiers, but he felt the difficulty of challenging or changing a document signed by the President and in the possession of General Giraud.

Mr. Eden replied to Mr. Macmillan on January 29 that no publicity should be given to the two documents and that they should be regarded as in suspense until His Majesty's Government had been given a chance of considering them. We could not agree that General Giraud should be the sole trustee of all French interests not under Axis control and we should want to consider most carefully the proposal that the French authorities in North Africa should control propaganda to Metropolitan France. The form of the documents was also disturbing. They committed us to a certain attitude towards General Giraud; the elaboration of the details was left to General Eisenhower and Mr. Murphy, apparently without reference to His Majesty's Government, and on the basis of Franco-American conversations in Washington about which we had no knowledge and of decisions at Casablanca of which we had no record.

Mr. Eden consulted the Prime Minister (who was still in North Africa)[1] on the documents. The Prime Minister replied that he had
(b)   not seen either of them and that the President had not consulted him about them. He thought that the clause about propaganda referred only to propaganda from North Africa, but that in any case, our opinion should have been asked. The Prime Minister said that he would make enquiries on the matter in Algiers.

(c)   On February 3 the Prime Minister telegraphed to Mr. Eden for his views on the amendments required in the two documents. Mr. Eden replied on February 4 that there were three possible courses: the documents could be regarded as binding only on the United States Government, and be signed only by the President, or as binding on the United States and British Governments; in this case

---

[1] After the Casablanca Conference Mr. Churchill went to Marrakesh for three days. He left for Cairo on January 26, and went thence to Adana, Cyprus, and back to Cairo. He spent two days in Tripoli, returned to Algiers on February 5 and London on February 7.

(a) Z1339, 1340/5/69. (b) Z1487/1266/69. See also C.P. 442/5, for the exchange of telegrams with Mr. Churchill. (c) Z1619/5/69.

the Prime Minister as well as the President should sign them, or the documents should be annulled or wholly recast. The third course seemed best to Mr. Eden, but if it were necessary to adopt the first course, the references to His Majesty's Government and, in one case, to the Prime Minister should be omitted. Mr. Eden pointed out other references or statements (including those mentioned earlier to Mr. Macmillan) in the documents which required attention—e.g. the North African expedition was not the first act of liberation of territory held by the Axis Powers. Apart from the obvious case of Abyssinia, we could claim to have liberated Syria and Madagascar, and General de Gaulle could claim to have liberated Equatorial Africa. Or, again, the text of the second document implied that the relations between France and 'foreign Powers' other than the United States could be regulated by a letter exchanged between an American Consul and a French General.[1]

The Prime Minister thought it desirable that the documents should carry the joint endorsement of the United States and Great Britain. He therefore saw Mr. Murphy at Algiers, and agreed (a) provisionally with him on a revised text following the lines suggested by the Foreign Office.[2] The new text was telegraphed by Mr. Murphy to President Roosevelt; Mr. Murphy also showed it to General Giraud who agreed with the changes.

There was a long delay before the text of the documents was finally settled. Lord Halifax asked Mr. Welles on March 12 whether he could give any information on the subject. Mr. Welles said that (b) he had asked the President every time he had seen him during the last fortnight, but without success. Admiral Leahy, in whose hands he had now put the matter, had not been more successful. On March 18 however, Mr. Murphy gave Mr. Makins a copy of a letter which (c) he (Murphy) had written to General Giraud and which followed more or less the lines of the British redraft.

On the night of April 5–6 Lord Halifax reported that Mr. Welles (d) had telephoned that, subject to amendments (with which, in the main, Mr. Eden agreed), President Roosevelt accepted the revised texts. Mr. Eden suggested to the Prime Minister that Mr. Macmillan and Mr. Murphy should be instructed to address identical letters

---

[1] The text of paragraph 2 of the second document ran: 'The form of relations between France and foreign Powers temporarily occupying part of French territory . . . [has] been defined in a letter exchanged between Consul Mr. Murphy in the name of President Roosevelt and General Giraud before the landing'.

[2] Mr. Murphy said to the Prime Minister that the document had no validity without his (the Prime Minister's) signature, but did not explain why in this case he had returned it, with the President's marginal notes and approval, to General Giraud. General Giraud expressed surprise when the Prime Minister told him that he had not seen the documents before they were given to him (General Giraud).

(a) Z1756/5/69. (b) Z3383/5/69. (c) Z4272/5/69. (d) Z4278/5/69.

to General Giraud covering the documents and stating that they had the approval of their respective Governments. The Prime Minister agreed with this plan, and after further delay the revised texts were (a) communicated to General Giraud jointly by Mr. Macmillan and Mr. Murphy on May 28, 1943. The 'political' clauses read, in their final form, as follows:

(b)   'The French nation and the French people are the only ones[1] who may fix their representation and designate their Government. Because it is impossible for the French motherland to exercise freely her will, France does not possess a recognisable Government and the question of the future government of France is not capable now of final solution.

In the interests of the French people, in order to safeguard France's past, her present and her future, the President of the United States and the British Prime Minister attribute to the French Commander-in-Chief, with his headquarters at Algiers, the right and duty of acting as a trustee for French interests, military, economic and financial, in French territories which are associated or which hereafter become associated with the movement of liberation now established in French North and West Africa. They bind themselves to aid him in this task by all the means in their power.

On the political plane it was agreed between the President of the United States, the Prime Minister of Great Britain and General Giraud that it was to their common interest for all French fighting against Germany to be reunited under one authority, and that every facility would be given to General Giraud and to the French National Committee under General de Gaulle in order to bring about this union.'[2]

(iv)

Relations between General de Gaulle and General Giraud after the Casablanca Conference: proposals of the French National Committee: General Giraud's speech of March 14, 1943.

(c)   After the conversations at Casablanca General Giraud told Mr. Macmillan and Mr. Murphy that he was proposing to release all the political prisoners arrested since the landings, and, particularly,

---

[1] *sic:* the documents were first drawn up in French, and the American authorities do not appear to have provided an adequate translation.
[2] This last paragraph was taken unchanged from the original memorandum.

(a) Z6543/5/69. (b) Z4278/5/69. (c) Z1517, 1544/5/69.

since the assassination of Admiral Darlan, and to drop the proceedings outstanding with regard to an alleged plot. He proposed to restore the property of Jews which had been confiscated under Vichy legislation and to abrogate other anti-Jewish measures. He thought that these and other administrative changes and the employment of new men in civil and military posts would make it easier to obtain the co-operation of General de Gaulle. Mr. Macmillan was more guarded in his view of General Giraud's promises than Mr. Murphy; nevertheless he hoped that the General would carry out these undertakings, especially if he were kept continually under pressure to do so.[1]

On General de Gaulle's side the presence of M. Massigli[2] and of General Catroux on the French National Committee tended towards (a) smoother relations with the British Government. The Foreign Office welcomed the appointment by General de Gaulle of General (b) Catroux as head of a Fighting French mission to General Giraud. They also hoped that M. Massigli would be able to restrain the Fighting French from making in their own journals and in conversation with American and British journalists bitter attacks on American policy. Mr. Hull continued to complain in strong terms of these attacks, and to assume that the Foreign Office had some responsibility for them, or at all events could do more than they were doing to stop them. The Foreign Office regarded Mr. Hull's complaints as unreasonable. We also suffered from the lack of moderation on the Gaullist side. We had already explained that we did not allow French wireless propaganda from London to criticise American

---

[1] The difficulty of making progress in administrative reform as well as in controversial political questions in North Africa was increased by the unexpected prolongation of the military campaign. The Allies incurred a serious reverse between February 14 and 20. The enemy broke through the Kasserine Pass and inflicted heavy losses in men and material on the American forces. The position was for a short time dangerous; the German and Italian forces in Tunisia had been joined by Rommel's army, and owing to difficulties of supply, General Montgomery had not yet been able to resume full pressure on the enemy, and indeed had only two divisions facing the so-called Mareth line in Tunisia. Fortunately a third division had reached the line before Rommel turned his armour to attack the Eighth Army. Meanwhile the enemy attack on the Tunisian-Algerian border was defeated, and General Alexander had time to reorganise the defence in the Kasserine-Tebessa area. The Kasserine Pass was recaptured on February 25 without much opposition. On the night of March 20-1 the Eighth Army attacked the Mareth line, and ultimately outflanked it. Rommel's main force then withdrew to the next defensive line on the Wadi Akarit, but was driven out of it on April 6. On the following day American troops from the western area of Tunisia joined up with patrols of the Eighth Army.

Henceforward the fall of Tunisia was only a matter of time. After heavy fighting the Allies closed in on the Bizerta–Mejez–Enfidaville area. The Germans, who were now greatly outnumbered in tanks and in the air, had no means of escape. The last phase of the attack opened on the night of May 5-6. On May 7 the British entered Tunis, and the Americans Bizerta. Six days later General Alexander reported that enemy resistance had ceased and that the Tunisian campaign was over.

[2] M. Massigli had recently arrived from France to join the French National Committee. He was appointed Commissioner for Foreign Affairs on February 5.

(a) Z1389/1388/17. (b) Z1695/117/69; Z1760/5/69.

policy, or to 'boost' General de Gaulle at the expense of General Giraud, but we had less influence over the Fighting French press, and could not prevent the Fighting French from talking to British and American press correspondents in London. On February 22
(a) the United States Chargé d'Affaires brought to Mr. Eden another complaint from Mr. Hull about remarks made by General de Gaulle. Mr. Hull had said that, since the British Government were supplying General de Gaulle with funds, it seemed difficult to reconcile such a state of affairs with the comments made by the General. Mr. Eden replied that we also had had considerable experience of similar provocative remarks directed against ourselves; he asked whether Mr. Hull really suggested that we should cut off General de Gaulle's funds.

In the last week of February there semed more hope of a definite agreement between General de Gaulle and General Giraud. The
(b) French National Committee had accepted the draft of a document which they proposed to present to General Giraud. Their proposals were for fusion between the two French movements on the conditions that the armistice should be repudiated; that the connexion with Vichy should also be repudiated, and the laws instituted by Vichy repealed as far as conditions allowed; that no attempt should be made for the present to set up a French Government, but that all acts carried out by French authorities should be liable to review by a Constituent Assembly after the liberation of France.

If General Giraud accepted these conditions the French National Committee proposed the immediate co-ordination of military forces, co-operation in economic matters and the establishment of diplomatic union so that the two sections of French opinion should speak with one voice abroad. There was, however, still the personal difficulty between General de Gaulle and General Giraud. On February 24—the day after M. Massigli had told Mr. Eden of the
(c) French proposals—General de Gaulle spoke to Mr. Peake about the deterioration in General Giraud's position; he said that no agreement could be reached until General Giraud had separated himself from advisers who were still trying to reinsure themselves with our enemies.

The impression of the Foreign Office was that General de Gaulle
(d) was not eager to start negotiations because he thought that time was on his side and that North African opinion was developing in his favour. General de Gaulle had asked the British Government for facilities for a tour of Fighting French territories; the Foreign Office

---

(a) Z2576/2/17. (b) Z2594/30/69. (c) Z2610/30/69. (d) Z3373/5/69.

suspected that the tour would be made an excuse for delaying the negotiations at Algiers. General de Gaulle was therefore told that his request could not be granted until progress had been made in the negotiations. On the other side General Giraud's attitude was not helpful. Although he appeared to want an agreement, he was taking an uncompromising line in order to convince himself and others of the strength of his position and to show General de Gaulle that he intended to be master in his own house.

So matters stood until the middle of March when a sudden change took place. The French National Committee sent their proposals to Algiers for comment by General Catroux. The text finally accepted by the French National Committee was less uncompromising than (a) the Foreign Office had expected. The Committee laid down four conditions for union—the repudiation of the armistice, the restoration of the fundamental 'libertés humaines' (General Giraud's own phrase in his communiqué after the Casablanca meeting), the re-establishment of republican forms of Government, and an assurance that nothing would be done to prejudice the decision eventually to be taken by the French people about the constitution of France.

The suggestion that General Giraud and his Administration should join an enlarged French National Committee was put forward as the best solution, but not as essential to an agreement. The National Committee were in fact ready to accept military, economic and diplomatic co-operation in advance of a general agreement. There were a few sentences to which General Giraud might have taken exception. Otherwise the document seemed likely to increase the chances of a settlement.

The proposals were submitted to General Giraud by one of General de Gaulle's representatives, apparently in error, before General Catroux (who was still in Syria) had seen them. General Giraud's first reaction was unfavourable. On March 14, however— (b) when the French National Committee published the proposals—he made a speech to a meeting of Alsatians and Lorrainers in Algiers. The speech, which was broadcast, accepted the main points of the French proposals without actually referring to them. General Giraud repudiated the legality of all French legislation subsequent to June 22, 1940, on the ground that the free expression of French sovereignty had been interrupted since that date. He said it was necessary to draw certain conclusions from the situation as regards measures and as regards men. It was not practicable to undo everything at once, but much had been remedied, and steps would be taken to re-establish French traditions—e.g. by the recall of the municipal assemblies and Conseils Généraux and the abrogation of

---

(a) Z3204, 3467/30/69. (b) Z3422/30/69; Z3871/5/69.

all laws of racial discrimination. General Giraud spoke of the importance of the union of all Frenchmen outside France, and offered
co-operation with all those who accepted the fundamental principles
of which he had spoken and were willing to join in the solemn pledge
which he was giving to the French people that their right to choose
a provisional Government would be respected. General Giraud
followed this speech by an invitation to General de Gaulle to come
to Algiers.

At a meeting on March 15 the War Cabinet regarded General
(a) Giraud's speech as providing a basis of agreement between the two
French parties. They considered that, as an encouragement to
General de Gaulle, an Anglo-American statement might be made
welcoming the declaration and suggesting that in the view of the
British and American Governments there was now no difference of
principle between the aims of General Giraud and the French
(b) National Committee. Mr. Hull, in fact, issued a statement on March
(c) 15 supporting the declaration; he thought that the best plan would be
for the Prime Minister to make a similar statement and for the
United States Government to endorse it. The Prime Minister,
therefore, in answer to a parliamentary question on March 17, spoke
(d) on the lines suggested by the War Cabinet, and on the same day
Mr. Hull announced his agreement with the Prime Minister's
statement.

(v)

Further exchanges between General de Gaulle and General Giraud: General
de Gaulle's departure to Algiers, May 28, 1943.

In spite of the Anglo-American view that General Giraud's
declaration had provided the basis of an agreement between the
French leaders, the problem of French union was not yet solved.
(e) Apart from the personal differences between General de Gaulle and
General Giraud, there was a real difference between their ideas on the
future of France. Moreover as the military situation improved, and
the political problems connected with the liberation of Metropolitan
France began to require practical decisions, the divergencies between
the British attitude and that of the United States became more
obvious, or at all events of more practical significance.

(a) WM(43)40. (b) Z3473/5/69. (c) Z3432/5/69. (d) Z3871/5/69. (e) Z4105/77/17.

On March 19 Mr. Strang, who had accompanied Mr. Eden on a visit to the United States,[1] discussed the problem with Mr. Atherton.[2] Mr. Atherton's view was that, whether France was liberated by a withdrawal of the German forces or by their ejection by an Allied landing, care should be taken not to allow the assumption of authority either by a French army or by the administration set up to govern the French Empire since in either event there would be civil war in France. No French general could represent the French people, and no civilian authority which might emerge in Algiers could have a claim to exercise governmental authority in France. Any French force participating in the liberation of France must be integrated as part of the army of the United Nations; the latter must give the people of France breathing-space so that they could evolve their own administration and form their own Government. Mr. Strang asked whether Mr. Atherton meant that the United Nations should occupy French territory. Mr. Atherton thought that an occupation would hardly be necessary, but that certain key points would have to be in Allied hands. Mr. Strang told Mr. Atherton that the French would not accept the policy which he had suggested.

The Foreign Office thought that Mr. Roosevelt believed more strongly than the State Department that for some time to come it would be necessary to extend the holding of key points to outlying parts of the French Empire. The Foreign Office considered that Mr. Roosevelt might have two reasons for this wish to maintain Allied and, in the last resort, American influence over a French Government. In the first place France would be weak and impoverished and therefore unable to sustain the burden of armaments necessary for defence. Mr. Roosevelt might also be afraid that the section of French opinion which favoured Franco-German collaboration might become predominant again at some time and might put the French Empire at the disposal of a Germany which had recovered her military strength.

Although the Foreign Office did not accept this forecast, they felt that it could not be dismissed out of hand. It could be argued that France had suffered exhausting losses in the first World War owing to the slowness with which Allied assistance had reached her. After

---

[1] See also Volume V, Chapt. LXI, section (iii).

[2] Mr. R. Atherton was acting Chief of the Division of European Affairs in the Department of State.

Mr. Eden and Mr. Hull, in a conversation of March 22, also touched generally on the position of the French National Committee. Mr. Hull repeated his complaint that the British Government did not support the United States Government against what he regarded as General de Gaulle's misrepresentations of American policy. Mr. Eden tried to convince Mr. Hull that General de Gaulle did not want to set up a provisional government but merely to establish some kind of unified French authority which could deal with French questions everywhere. Mr. Hull said that it was essential to avoid repeating the situation already presented by some refugee governments which were working to establish themselves in their respective countries after the war. *F.R.U.S.*, 1943, II, 77–81.

the war these Allies had thwarted the attempts of the French to safeguard themselves against a renewed German attack. France was overwhelmed again in 1940 before Great Britain could give adequate support and before the United States entered the war. The defeatists and collaborationists thus had a case for urging that the country could not afford to risk war with Germany again, and that it would be better for France to collaborate with the Germans in the organisation of Europe (in which French intelligence and skill would come to play a leading part) rather than ally herself once more with Great Britain and the United States whose assistance never reached her in time.

Whatever the validity of their long-range assumptions, the President and the State Department were affected too much in their view by an antipathy to General de Gaulle and his Movement. In the case of Mr. Hull and Admiral Leahy there was almost an element of personal animosity; the President's attitude was one of slightly contemptuous tolerance, and the State Department had always tended to underrate the support which Gaullism had in France. This miscalculation was due largely to the fact that the United States Embassy in Vichy had given wrong estimates of the situation, but these estimates had been repeated so often that they had come to be accepted in Washington as accurate.

Furthermore, although the Gaullist proposals to General Giraud had not insisted that his organisation should be incorporated into the French National Committee, there was no doubt that the latter would require some form of central organisation and authority. (a) From the British point of view this demand appeared reasonable, since many questions of an administrative kind were beginning to arise in regard to future Allied operations in France and consultation with the French upon such questions was necessary. Similar questions were being discussed with the Allied Governments in London. The British Government wished to deal with a single French authority in order to ensure that Frenchmen outside the area of German occupation were at least in agreement about matters such as the appointment and dismissal of officials—prefects, mayors, etc.—or the selection of liaison officers to be attached to the Expeditionary Force.

The immediate difficulty, however, lay in finding a compromise over the claims of each of the two French generals to assume the leading rôle in the new organisation, whatever form it might take. The matter, as the British Government always recognised, was one for Frenchmen to decide among themselves, but owing to the French failure to reach a decision, the British Government could not avoid

(a) Z3618/30/69.

being drawn into disputes which they regarded as short-sighted and exasperating. Thus when General de Gaulle wished to go to Algiers (a) at once, and, on the other hand, General Catroux, who had begun discussions with General Giraud, considered it advisable that there should be time for these discussions to clear the situation before General de Gaulle's arrival, the British Government could not stand aside, since they would have to provide the transport or acquiesce in the use of a Fighting French ship. They also had to consider the possible effect of General de Gaulle's arrival at Algiers—and the consequent demonstrations or counter-demonstrations—at a time when the Tunisian campaign was in full operation.

The question of General de Gaulle's visit indeed brought about another crisis. On April 2 the Prime Minister saw General de Gaulle and M. Massigli. The Prime Minister referred to General de Gaulle's (b) request for facilities to take him to Algiers. He pointed out that General Eisenhower must be consulted because North Africa was in his sphere of command. The Prime Minister then said that he assumed that General Catroux would come to London to report. General de Gaulle answered that that was not his idea, and repeated that he wished to go at once to Algiers.

The Prime Minister reminded General de Gaulle that the situation had turned to his disadvantage owing to his refusal to come to Casablanca. The Prime Minister mentioned recent Gaullist demonstrations in North Africa. Further troubles of this kind would be deplorable and the risk of them showed how necessary it was to reach an agreement, and to avoid disorders which would only increase American antagonism. General de Gaulle said that he was ready to agree with the respectable elements in North Africa; he did not wish to stir up trouble, but people were sometimes impelled by their sentiments to make some demonstration.

The Prime Minister said that he would do everything possible to help towards an agreement. He was convinced of the necessity of a strong France after the war, and could not contemplate a Europe without France as a great Power. For this reason he was working as hard as General de Gaulle and as General Giraud for the union of Frenchmen now. General de Gaulle said that the Fighting French had remained in the war because they had believed in the Prime Minister's goodwill and that of Great Britain.

M. Massigli asked the Prime Minister whether it would be possible—after French union had been achieved—for the United Nations to recognise in some way the organisation representing all Frenchmen outside France even though full recognition as a Government might not be practicable. The Prime Minister said that it did

---

(a) Z4158, 4159/1868/69. (b) Z4271/1868/69.

not rest with him to resolve a question of this kind, but that a favourable answer was not improbable on the understanding that the people of France must be free to decide their own future.

(a)   General Eisenhower replied to General de Gaulle's proposal for an immediate visit to Algiers that, while he did not wish to put any obstacle in the way of the visit, he would be grateful for postponement until General de Gaulle felt that the ground had been sufficiently prepared for a rapid settlement. General Eisenhower felt that, in view of the approaching crisis in the Tunisian operations, it would be most undesirable to have at the same time a protracted political crisis. The Prime Minister sent a message to General de Gaulle on April 4 that he was sure that as a soldier he would appreciate the force of General Eisenhower's reasons for postponement. General de Gaulle, however, issued a statement on April 5—without consulting the British authorities—to the effect that his departure for Algiers had been postponed in accordance with General Eisenhower's request. He (General de Gaulle) regretted the delay which could not be prolonged without serious consequences. He and several members of the Committee had been ready for some days to leave for Algiers in order to re-establish the unity of the French Empire 'which was necessitated by the national interest and demanded by French opinion at home and overseas'.

The Foreign Office regarded this communiqué as unfair to General Eisenhower, and likely to have a harmful effect upon the negotiations with General Giraud, but they could secure only that the B.B.C. did not broadcast it in any of their services. General de
(b)   Gaulle also asked Admiral Stark to send a message to General Eisenhower. The Foreign Office considered the terms of this message to be tactless, and requested that it should not be transmitted until the Secretary of State had had time to consider it.[1] On the morning of April 7 a communiqué was issued from No. 10 Downing Street, that the Prime Minister wished it to be known that he was in full agreement with General Eisenhower in deprecating a visit by General de Gaulle to Algiers during the battle crisis in Tunisia which required the undivided attention of the Allied High Command.

On April 8 General Catroux left Algiers for London. General
(c)   Catroux had been in favour of the postponement of General de Gaulle's visit; he thought that the General underrated the difficulties

---

[1] Mr. Eden told General de Gaulle his opinion of the message and arranged for him to
(d) see the United States Ambassador. After an interview with Mr. Winant, General de Gaulle undertook to draft a more friendly message. General de Gaulle decided finally not to send a message but to leave the Foreign Office to explain to General Eisenhower why he was so much disappointed over the delay.

(a) Z4188/30/69. (b) Z4319/1868/69. (c) Z4161/30/69; Z4370/1868/69. (d) Z4417, 4454/1868/69.

of agreement and wanted to come to Algiers not so much to negotiate as to create a movement of popular opinion in his favour. In fact there would be opposition as well as support, and serious disturbances might result. General Catroux thought that General de Gaulle (a) would not get an agreement unless he consented to take second place to General Giraud.

General Catroux's visit to London brought some progress. The (b) French National Committee—after long discussions—agreed to put forward the suggestion that General Giraud and General de Gaulle should be co-Presidents of a united organisation: the former would be 'President No. 1', but would give up his command of the army. This command would go to a third person—possibly to General Juin. General Giraud, however, had been insisting that he should keep for himself the military, as well as the civil presidency. The National Committee considered that, in accordance with French Republican tradition, the civilian authority should be supreme and that the Commander-in-Chief should therefore have no part in the civilian administration. Hence if General Giraud wished to retain the military command, he could not also be a co-President of the administration. General de Gaulle reported these views to Mr. Eden (c) on April 16. Mr. Eden said that he had spoken to the Prime Minister, and was authorised to tell General de Gaulle that, if he and General Giraud were willing to come to an agreement on a basis allowing for the acceptance of two equal chiefs, i.e. General Giraud and himself, we should be willing to recognise the agreement, and would do our best to get it supported by others.

General Catroux returned to Algiers in order to put the proposals to General Giraud. General Giraud was at first unwilling to make concessions; after a discussion with Mr. Macmillan he produced a (d) document which went a considerable way towards meeting the views of the National Committee. He suggested a Council, on the lines of a Cabinet, with full collective responsibility. Within this Council there should be a small executive committee. He and General de Gaulle would preside in turn over the Council and the Committee. This arrangement would not constitute a 'duumvirate', since the responsibilities of the two bodies—Council and Committee—would be collective. On the other hand, although he accepted the doctrine of ultimate civilian responsibility, General Giraud regarded it as essential, in the circumstances of the war, that the Commander-in-Chief should be a member of the administrative body. He did not actually claim for himself the post of Commander-in-Chief; Mr. Macmillan indeed thought that he would agree to some compromise in the matter. At all events General Giraud invited General de

(a) Z4494/30/69. (b) Z4644, 4844/30/69. (c) Z4791/30/69. (d) Z5090, 5096, 5188, 5189, 5194, 5235/30/69.

Gaulle and, at most, two or three other representatives of the National Committee to meet him as soon as possible after May 5 at Marrakesh or Biskra. After they had reached agreement on the main points of their union, the two Generals would go together to Algiers.

The Prime Minister saw General de Gaulle on April 30. General
(a) de Gaulle still refused to agree that General Giraud should combine supreme military and political authority. He also said that he wished to meet General Giraud at Algiers, and not elsewhere. The Foreign Office considered that General de Gaulle would be making a grave mistake to refuse General Giraud's invitation or to regard his memorandum as a final word. They agreed with Mr. Macmillan that, if the negotiations broke down over General de Gaulle's obstinacy, the Americans would certainly support General Giraud: on the other hand, if General de Gaulle met General Giraud, and if an arrangement were made between them, the position of the former would become increasingly strong in the new organisation. General Giraud was losing influence owing to the ineffectiveness with which he was carrying out his promises in the political sphere. General de Gaulle's own personality, and the strength of his advisers—especially M. Massigli and General Catroux—would certainly tell in his favour. Finally, a meeting at Biskra would be to General de Gaulle's advantage since it would be held at a place outside British and American influence.

The British view was put in the strongest terms to General de Gaulle: the General's reply was to make a provocative speech at a
(b) meeting on May 5 of his supporters in London. This speech, which was broadcast in the Fighting French radio programme,[1] attacked the administration in North Africa and reaffirmed General de Gaulle's statement that he wanted the meeting with General Giraud to take place at Algiers. The speech caused great offence to General Giraud, and almost brought General Catroux to resign.

In view of this situation, M. Massigli was asked to come to the Foreign Office and was told to inform General de Gaulle of the dangerous consequences of his attitude. We had done our best to help him, and could do no more. The broad position was that while French soldiers were fighting in Tunisia General de Gaulle was haggling in London over the question whether he should meet General Giraud in one town in North Africa rather than another, and was also making speeches which only did harm to the cause of French union.

---

[1] The Foreign Office gave instructions to the B.B.C. that in future no public statements by General de Gaulle were to be broadcast in the B.B.C. foreign programmes without their permission. General de Gaulle's own broadcasts were already subject to this condition.

(a) Z5431/30/69. (b) Z5370/30/69.

M. Massigli was also told to put to General de Gaulle the fact that his speech and the line taken by the Fighting French press in London and abroad were damaging Anglo-American relations, and that as we were supplying the National Committee with funds, the United States Government considered that we had a certain responsibility for the anti-American attitude of their press. M. Massigli himself agreed with the British view of the follies of the Fighting French press. He also agreed that General de Gaulle ought to accept General Giraud's invitation. He sent a message on May 6 to General Catroux telling him that he hoped for a settlement.

Meanwhile Mr. Macmillan was trying to smooth matters out with General Giraud and to suggest an arrangement whereby (a) General Giraud would accept Algiers as a meeting place if General de Gaulle accepted the main principles of the proposals sent to the National Committee. On May 7 there appeared to be a turn for the better. General de Gaulle seemed to be influenced by reports of irritation among the Fighting French troops and his civilian supporters in North Africa over the bickering about a meeting-place. At all events he issued a communiqué to the effect that there were no important divergencies of view between the two parties, and (b) that in order to secure a calm atmosphere the National Committee had instructed their supporters in North Africa to abstain from any demonstration ('toute manifestation intempestive') on the occasion of General de Gaulle's arrival in Algiers. A week passed, however, without any further move of importance. General de Gaulle continued to insist upon Algiers as a meeting place, and, on May 15, the Fighting French press service in London reported a message (c) from the Council of French Resistance[1] (in France) to General de Gaulle demanding that the meeting should take place at Algiers and that General de Gaulle should be recognised as President of a provisional Government with General Giraud as military commander.

Sir A. Cadogan spoke to M. Massigli about the harm which this (d) announcement would cause. M. Massigli said that General de Gaulle had sent a telegram to General Giraud that the message would not affect his policy. M. Massigli raised the point (which General de Gaulle had already used in argument) that a meeting in Algiers was desirable on practicable grounds in order to allow consultation

---

[1] The Conseil National de la Résistance was formed in May 1943 to co-ordinate the activities of the various Resistance groups (including the Communists). A committee of five members representing different groups had met at Lyons in the previous November. The early co-ordination of these groups was largely the work of M. Jean Moulin, a supporter of the Free French, who was dropped by parachute in France in January 1942. After the Germans had arrested and killed M. Moulin in June 1943, M. Bidault became President of the Conseil National de la Résistance.

(a) Z5403/30/69. (b) Z5467/30/69. (c) Z5728/30/69. (d) Z5818/30/69.

with other French supporters of General de Gaulle. The Foreign Office thought that this requirement might be used as a means to secure a compromise, i.e. General Giraud might suggest somewhere near Algiers but not in the city. M. Massigli also thought that a face-saving arrangement could be reached by the proposal of a place not hitherto mentioned.

Mr. Macmillan was therefore instructed on the night of May 15–16 to suggest, if he thought it desirable, to General Giraud that he should invite General de Gaulle to a place near Algiers where he could easily obtain the contacts which he might wish to make. Fortunately there was no need for further discussion about the place of meeting. General de Gaulle's reply to General Giraud's proposal had reached the latter on May 13.[1] The reply maintained General

(a) de Gaulle's view that the meeting should take place at Algiers in order to allow contact with the National Committee (General de Gaulle made a bitter reference to his 'isolation' at Anfa). The National Committee also reaffirmed their objection to the proposal that General Giraud should retain the post of Commander-in-Chief and at the same time be a member of the Council. Finally the National Committee had different ideas from those of General Giraud on the mode in which a legal Government would be re-established in France. The National Committee wanted the establishment of a consultative National Council, including delegates of the Resistance Movement in France; this Council would hold elections or a plebiscite in France as soon as possible after the liberation of the country, and then hand over authority to a Government formed as a result of the elections. General Giraud, on the other hand, proposed that the Conseils Généraux in the French Departments should choose representatives who would form a National Assembly. The Assembly would appoint a provisional Government, and fix the date of the elections—probably about a year after the liberation. The delay would give time for passions to cool in France, and the use of the Conseils Généraux, which contained few Communists, would avoid the risk of civil war in France.

(b)   General Catroux came to London on May 21 with General Giraud's answer. This answer made no reference to the problem of the Commander-in-Chief but accepted the idea of a meeting at Algiers if General de Gaulle would agree to two principles, the collective character of Cabinet decisions, and the election of a provisional Government in France in accordance with the requirements of French constitutional law. General de Gaulle did not specifically

(c) refer to the two conditions, but replied that he found General

---

[1] The reply was dated May 10. There appears to have been some confusion on the French side about the despatch or delivery of the reply.

(a) Z5817/30/69. (b) Z5800/30/69. (c) Z6083, 6084/30/69.

Giraud's letter acceptable. General Giraud accepted this reply. On May 28 General de Gaulle left London for Algiers. (a)

This turn for the better in the controversy between the French generals was opportune, since Mr. Churchill was now in Washington, and susceptible to strong American pressure on the subject of General de Gaulle. On May 8 Mr. Roosevelt had drawn up a memorandum of complaints against the General which he proposed to take up with Mr. Churchill.[1] It is uncertain whether the President actually 'took up' the memorandum, but Mr. Churchill records that 'almost every day he [the President] handed me one or more accusing documents against de Gaulle'. Mr. Churchill adds that he was 'at this time most indignant with de Gaulle. . . . It hung in the balance whether we should not break finally with this most difficult man.'[2] Mr. Churchill, in fact, telegraphed to Mr. Eden on May 21 suggesting that the War Cabinet should consider a definite break with General de Gaulle. The War Cabinet did not agree with this proposal. Mr. Attlee and Mr. Eden replied on May 23 to Mr. Churchill that the negotiations between the two French generals were now nearer to success than at any previous time, and that, since the British and United States Government had been trying for the past four months to bring the generals together, it would be a mistake to abandon this policy just when it appeared to be succeeding. If we removed General de Gaulle, the French National Committee would probably break up since there was no alternative to him. We should risk making him a national martyr and find ourselves accused by Gaullists and non-Gaullists of interfering in French internal affairs.[3]

(vi)

The establishment of the new French Committee of National Liberation, May 30–June 3: further disputes over the question of the French army command: resignation of General de Gaulle, June 10; settlement of the question of the army command, June 11–22, 1943.

With the arrival of General de Gaulle in Algiers on May 30, the union of the two French groups seemed at last to have been secured.

---

[1] The memorandum described General de Gaulle's 'course and attitude' as 'well nigh intolerable', and pointed out that the Gaullist propaganda which was causing trouble in Algiers was being 'financed in whole or in part by British Government funds'. Mr. (b) Roosevelt was inclined to think that 'when we get into France itself we will have to regard it as a military occupation run by British and American generals'. *F.R.U.S.*, 1943, II, 110–2.

[2] See Churchill, IV, 716.

[3] The telegram added that 'we suspect that Murphy is becoming impressed by the evidence of rising Gaullism in North Africa . . . and prefers to ascribe this to Gaullist propaganda rather than admit that he was wrong about Gaullist strength in North Africa (c) as he was about anti-British feeling there'.

(a) Z6145/30/69. (b) See also P.M. 402/32(A), vol. I. (c) WM(43)75, C.A.

P

Nevertheless the plan nearly broke down in its final stages. Neither of the protagonists was without responsibility for this crisis, but General de Gaulle, in the British view, caused most of the trouble.

(a) The two generals, each with two representatives,[1] met on the morning of May 31 in order to constitute the new Committee. General Catroux was also present; both parties agreed that he should be co-opted to the Committee. Unfortunately the meeting had no agenda, and no secretary. No motion was put forward; General Giraud opened the proceedings by asking whether anyone had anything to say. General de Gaulle and General Georges then spoke at length, and the debate continued, without reaching a conclusion, on the question whether certain individuals—in particular, M. Peyrouton,[2] General Noguès and M. Boisson—should be dismissed; General de Gaulle insisted on these dismissals before the Committee was formed. General Giraud would not accept this prior condition. Later in the day the two generals had an unsuccessful private meeting, at which General de Gaulle seems to have spoken strongly against British and American influence, and to have refused even to call upon General Eisenhower.

On the morning of June 1 Mr. Macmillan and Mr. Murphy saw General de Gaulle. The General put his views strongly, but did not appear to think that the negotiations would break down. He also asked Mr. Murphy to arrange for him to pay a call on General Eisenhower; Mr. Macmillan arranged similar visits to General Alexander and Air Chief Marshal Tedder. In the evening of June 1 Mr. Macmillan urged on M. Monnet the importance of holding another meeting of the two generals, their four representatives and General Catroux, and of bringing forward at this meeting a formal resolution for the establishment of an Executive Committee, and, as succeeding items on the agenda, the reappointment or otherwise of Governors-General and Residents-General in the French Empire, and certain immediate changes in the Army Command.

Mr. Macmillan also saw General Catroux. General Catroux said that General Giraud was prepared to go on with the formation of the Committee, but that General de Gaulle had refused to come to a decision until the following day (June 2). General Catroux said that he and M. Massigli intended—even if General de Gaulle objected— to write on June 2 to General Giraud asking for an early meeting so that the Committee could be set up.

Unfortunately a new incident during the night of June 1-2 brought almost a complete break between the two protagonists.

---

[1] General de Gaulle's representatives were MM. Massigli and Philip; General Giraud had chosen M. Monnet and (at the last moment) General Georges.

[2] See below, p. 435, note 1.

(a) Z7144/30/69; Z7016/5/69.

About 9 p.m. General de Gaulle received a letter from M. Peyrouton[1] offering his resignation. The offer was made to General de Gaulle in the latter's capacity as President of the Executive Committee. At 1 a.m. General Giraud received from M. Peyrouton a letter (written some time after 11.30 p.m.) in similar though not identical terms.[2]

Each of the two generals replied to M. Peyrouton. General de Gaulle accepted his resignation, without consulting General Giraud, gave instructions that the Secretary-General should carry on the government of Algeria, and promised M. Peyrouton an appointment in the French Army of the Levant. At 11 p.m. General de Gaulle's press officer gave the correspondence to the press. General de Gaulle then wrote to tell General Giraud what he had done. This letter was delivered about 1 a.m.

General Giraud, on receiving M. Peyrouton's letter of resignation, sent a reply accepting it and offering M. Peyrouton an appointment in the army.[3] This correspondence was also given to the press. Meanwhile General Giraud wrote two letters to General de Gaulle. In the first letter he expressed his astonishment at General de Gaulle's action, and proposed a meeting at 10 a.m. on June 2. In the second letter (written, apparently, without consulting his advisers) General Giraud made wild accusations against General de Gaulle to the effect that he wished to introduce into France a political system on the Nazi model; General Giraud demanded a public disavowal of such intentions before any further discussions took place.

---

[1] The appointment of M. Peyrouton as Governor-General of Algeria had been announced on January 20, 1943. M. Peyrouton was an able and experienced administrator and had been Resident-General in Tunis: he was anti-German, but had served (a) as Secretary-General of the Police administration and as Minister of the Interior in the Vichy Government from shortly after the armistice until December 1940. If he could claim credit for the arrest of M. Laval, he was equally responsible for the arrest of MM. Reynaud and Mandel, and for the internment of some 15,000 Frenchmen.

M. Peyrouton had been sent as Ambassador to Buenos Aires by Admiral Darlan; he remained in Buenos Aires after M. Laval had dismissed him from his post. Admiral Darlan had suggested to Mr. Murphy his appointment as Governor-General of Algeria. Mr. Murphy had accepted the suggestion, and had passed it to the State Department. M. Peyrouton was given facilities to come to Algiers where he arrived on January 16.

Although the Foreign Office were not officially consulted about M. Peyrouton's appointment, they had acquiesced in it not because they regarded him with favour, but for the reasons that he was at least better than some of the members of the French administration in North Africa and that—since a Gaullist appointment to the Governor-Generalship of Algeria would have met with strong local opposition—it was impossible to find anyone else of comparable ability or experience. Later, however, on considering further M. Peyrouton's record, the Foreign Office regarded their acquiescence as a mistake. General de Gaulle was, for obvious reasons, strongly opposed to the appointment.

[2] M. Peyrouton's motives in writing the two letters remain uncertain, as far as evidence from the British side is concerned. M. Peyrouton's own explanation was that he had made a mistake. The British authorities thought that General de Gaulle's action in the matter was deliberate and that he wanted to avoid the establishment of a committee with collective responsibility—on which he would be outvoted.

[3] M. Peyrouton had asked for an appointment as captain in the French forces.

(a) Z1270, 1277/1266/69.

General Giraud seems at this time to have lost his nerve, and to have believed that General de Gaulle was preparing a *coup* against his authority, and that some 3,000 Fighting French troops had been brought to Algiers, ostensibly on leave, in order to support this *coup*. General Giraud therefore appointed Admiral Muselier as a member of his Cabinet to keep order in Algiers, and called up a number of French colonial troops.

There was no foundation for these suspicions. General de Gaulle had no intention of attempting a *coup*, and, indeed, told Mr. Macmillan with amusement of the precautions taken against him. On the other hand General de Gaulle's own supporters thought that his letter to M. Peyrouton was a grave error; General Catroux and M. Massigli spoke strongly to General de Gaulle on the morning of June 2. Mr. Macmillan and Mr. Murphy, however, with their respective staffs, tried to reconcile all parties; Mr. Macmillan appealed to General de Gaulle to be patient, and to take an opportunity which would allow him to obtain for himself and his supporters an influence extending beyond the war to the reconstruction of France. If he missed this chance of unity, General de Gaulle might well be condemning France to further divisions now and to the prospect of civil war after her liberation.

These efforts at peace-making, and the advice of their own moderate supporters, finally persuaded the two generals to come to an agreement. They met again on the morning of June 3, and by 2 p.m. had settled the constitution of a Committee of National Liberation. The Committee would consist of Generals Giraud and de Gaulle as Presidents, and Generals Catroux and Georges, and MM. Massigli, Monnet and Philip as members. It was described as the French central authority, exercising its powers over the territory and forces hitherto under the authority of the French National Committee or under the civilian and military Commander-in-Chief (i.e. General Giraud). The Committee proposed at once to take all measures necessary for the fusion of the administrations of the two organisations. It pledged itself to re-establishing the laws of the Republic and the republican régime, and to the surrender of its own powers to a provisional government which would be constituted in conformity with the laws of the Third Republic as soon as the liberation of the Metropolitan territory of France made this transfer possible, and, at the latest, on the total liberation of France.

M. Massigli explained to Mr. Macmillan on June 3 that the Missions of the two Generals would present official notes in London and Washington announcing the formation of the new Committee and asking that the British and United States Governments should recognise it. The Committee, in fact, had an immediate welcome from the Prime Minister. Mr. Churchill had come to Algiers with

Field-Marshal Dill and General Marshall on May 28 in order to discuss strategic plans. Mr. Churchill asked Mr. Eden to join him in view of the importance of the French discussions.[1] On June 4 Admiral Cunningham gave a luncheon to the British Ministers and the members of the new Committee.

Even after these solemn affirmations of French unity, the trouble was not over. The problem of the French military command had not been decided; the question of the dismissals also remained to be discussed. Above all, neither General de Gaulle nor General Giraud had been reconciled to the other's point of view or had shown willingness to accept a compromise. Outside these disputes between Frenchmen there remained also the differences between the British and American views of the future of France, and the methods of re-establishing constitutional government in the country after the war. The attitude of General de Gaulle throughout the negotiations had increased the antipathy felt by the State Department towards the Gaullist movement, and had made it harder for the Foreign Office to convince either the President or his advisers that their view of French opinion was mistaken and that persistence in this view might lead to grave risk of civil war in France. The problem was still more delicate, from the Foreign Office point of view, because the Prime Minister had lost patience with General de Gaulle and inclined to accept the American view that he was a danger as well as an embarrassment.

On June 8 the new Committee of National Liberation announced their decision to form an inner Cabinet responsible for the general (a) conduct of the war and a Commissariat for the discharge of public business. The Commissariat included M. Massigli (Foreign Affairs), M. Philip (Interior), M. Pleven (Colonies) and General Catroux (Co-ordination of Moslem affairs). M. Puaux was appointed Resident-General in Morocco in place of General Noguès, and M. Helleu as High Commissioner in Syria and Lebanon in place of General Catroux. Mr. Macmillan thought at this time that matters were (b) going fairly smoothly; he was encouraging Mr. Murphy to keep in close touch with General de Gaulle in order to avoid the impression that the Americans were 'running' General Giraud and the British General de Gaulle.

---

[1] The Prime Minister telegraphed to the War Cabinet on May 29 suggesting Mr. Eden's visit in the following terms: 'It seems to me important that Eden should come here for a few days. He is much better fitted than I am to be best man at the Giraud-de Gaulle wedding. He ought to be conscious of the atmosphere and in touch with the actors in what may easily be a serious drama. General Georges has just visited me. He is in great form, and working closely with Giraud.'

(a) Z6613/5/69. (b) Z6722/4573/69.

(a)　　On June 5 Mr. Macmillan forwarded to the Prime Minister[1] a copy of a telegram which he had received from President Roosevelt for the Prime Minister. The President put in a strong plea for the retention of M. Boisson as Governor-General of French West Africa, and also reminded the Prime Minister that in the last analysis North Africa was under British-American military rule. The President also thought that the news coming from Algiers had a strong Gaullist bias.

The Foreign Office considered it unfortunate that the President should continue to reason on these lines, and that there was no one in Algiers with sufficient authority to give him a true picture and to explain that—as General Eisenhower well knew—North Africa was not 'under British-American military rule' and that the French would not accept foreign coercion in matters which were primarily their own concern. The Foreign Office also had a very adverse report on M. Boisson from Mr. Meiklereid, His Majesty's Consul-General at Dakar.

On the other hand the Prime Minister (with Mr. Eden's concurrence) instructed Mr. Macmillan to associate himself with the
(b) President's views about M. Boisson;[2] he also asked whether anything could be done about the presentation of news from Algiers. Mr. Macmillan told General de Gaulle the British and American view
(c) on June 7: the general said that a decision about M. Boisson would not be taken at once. He also agreed that the Committee as a whole would have to settle the matter.

General de Gaulle explained to Mr. Macmillan his ideas about the military command. He did not object to the retention by General Giraud of the title of Commander-in-Chief, but could not allow him actual control since he regarded him as incapable either of reorganising the French defence forces or of commanding an army in the field. A complete reorganisation of the defence forces was, in General
(d) de Gaulle's view, essential. Two days later Mr. Macmillan reported that General de Gaulle had asked for the post of Commissioner for National Defence, and that General Giraud had refused his proposals and was talking of resignation.
(e)　　On June 10 General de Gaulle himself offered his resignation from the joint presidency and membership of the Committee. His alleged reasons were the atmosphere of distrust in which he found himself, and the inability of the Committee to take rapid and clear

---

[1] The Prime Minister had returned to London.

[2] In his telegram of June 6 to the President the Prime Minister said that he would be
(f) 'strongly opposed to Boisson being dismissed from his post'.

(a) Z6634/30/69. (b) T741/3 (Churchill Papers/181; Z6634/30/69). (c) Z6635, 7033/30/69. (d) Z6649/30/69. (e) Z6678, 6709/30/69. (f) T740/3, No. 300 (Churchill Papers/181; Z6634/30/69).

decisions. General Eisenhower considered that the real reason was
the difference of view over the command of the French forces.

Mr. Macmillan reported on the night of June 11–12 that it was (a)
unnecessary to regard General de Gaulle's resignation as final. He
thought that on the military question the majority of the Committee
was on General de Gaulle's side. The dispute was an old one, and
General de Gaulle felt that he was dealing with the same type of
opposition, especially in the case of General Georges, which had
opposed or at least failed to secure the modernisation of the French
army before 1939. Mr. Macmillan said that the 'moderates',
including General Catroux, M. Massigli, M. Monnet, and M. Philip,
were proposing an arrangement which would distinguish between
the 'preparation' of the armed forces and their use in war. General
de Gaulle, as Commissioner of National Defence, would deal with the
modernisation and reform of the forces, and the removal of incom-
petent or politically unsound personnel. General Giraud would
retain the strategic command, and take charge of all arrangements
with the Combined Chiefs of Staff.

The Prime Minister regarded this proposed compromise as unsatisfactory. He had already sent to Mr. Macmillan on June 11 a (b)
copy of a telegram from President Roosevelt to General Eisenhower.
In this telegram the President insisted that M. Boisson should be kept
at his post, since it would be unsafe to give General de Gaulle control
of Dakar. The President also said that he would feel uneasy if
General Giraud did not have complete control of the French army
in North Africa. The Prime Minister agreed with the President's
views and instructed Mr. Macmillan to support them, and to make
it clear to General de Gaulle that, if he resigned from the Committee,
and thus marred the unity of Frenchmen, he would not be allowed
to return to Great Britain; the Prime Minister would have to make
statements to the public at home and to the French people explaining
why General de Gaulle had completely forfeited the confidence and
goodwill of His Majesty's Government.

On June 12 the Prime Minister replied to Mr. Macmillan's
telegram reporting the compromise proposals. He disagreed with the
proposals on the ground that General de Gaulle would use his power
of 'purging' the army in a bitter and vindictive way. The Prime
Minister hoped that Mr. Macmillan would bear in mind the fact
that, if General de Gaulle should obtain control of the new Committee, a situation of great difficulty would arise between him and the
United States Government. In such case the Prime Minister would
support the President. The Prime Minister also stated that he
regarded General Georges with approval.

(a) Z6718/30/69. (b) Z7065/30/69.

(a)   The Foreign Office did not share the Prime Minister's favourable view of General Georges; they regarded him as more reactionary in his views than General Giraud. Moreover, although they deplored General de Gaulle's tactics, and considered that he was trying to dominate the Committee by dictatorial methods, they were also aware that his resignation would be a serious matter. Generals Giraud and Georges would then have a free hand; they would continue their reactionary methods with the certain result that, in spite of American support, the French people would have nothing to do with them after the Liberation.

(b)   Meanwhile General Giraud himself rejected the compromise proposal. In order to break the deadlock Mr. Macmillan and Mr. Murphy thought that General Eisenhower should be advised to see Generals de Gaulle and Giraud and to explain to them the attitude and military requirements of the British and American Governments with regard to the command and organisation of the French army since the Gaullists in particular were in doubt about the actual position. General Eisenhower was at this time away from Algiers but agreed to see the generals on June 19.

        Before the meeting took place the affair was further complicated
(c)   by the attitude of President Roosevelt. The President sent a message to Mr. Churchill in very strong terms on June 17 that the time had come to break with General de Gaulle.[1] The President regarded General de Gaulle as unreliable, unco-operative and disloyal. In any case we could not allow General Eisenhower to spend more time over the local political situation which General de Gaulle had done so much to aggravate. We had pledged ourselves, and could renew our pledge to liberate the French, but we could not have our military operations endangered by General de Gaulle. We ought therefore to encourage the creation of a new Committee of Frenchmen who really wanted to fight the war and were not always thinking about politics; meanwhile we could deal with the French military authorities whom we had already recognised. The first step would be to defer a further meeting of the Algiers Committee. The President had informed General Eisenhower that the United States

---

[1] The reason for this sudden outburst by the President seems to have been a misunderstanding about the measures taken by the Committee on June 8 (see above, p. 437). These measures included doubling the numbers of the Committee. Neither Mr. Macmillan nor Mr. Murphy reported this fact until about June 16, though it was mentioned at the time in the press, and the announcement of the formation of the Committee on June 3, after stating the names of the seven members, had said that it would later be completed by the addition of other members. The President—and the Prime Minister—took the view that General de Gaulle's intention in increasing the numbers of the Committee was that he wanted to 'pack' it with his own supporters. In a further message to the President Mr. Churchill said that he did not agree that the time had come to break with General de Gaulle, though it might be necessary to do so on the question of the control of the army.

(a) Z7245/30/69. (b) Z6900/30/69. (c) T839/2, No. 288, Churchill Papers/181.

Government would not allow the control of the French Army in North Africa by any agency not subject to his (General Eisenhower's) direction, and would not permit General de Gaulle to direct personally or control through a Committee the French African army either in the field of supplies, training or operations.

The Prime Minister replied to the President on June 18 that he (a) agreed upon the urgent necessity of keeping the French Army command in North Africa in loyal and trustworthy hands. He also agreed that no confidence could be placed in General de Gaulle's friendship for the Allies and that the President was right in his instructions to General Eisenhower. On the other hand, Mr. Churchill was not in favour of breaking up the Committee or forbidding it to meet. He thought that, if the Committee were faced with the choice between acceptance of General Eisenhower's instructions or 'placing themselves in definite opposition to the two rescuing Powers', they would accept the Allied wishes by a majority. General de Gaulle would then have to decide between submission and resignation. If he resigned, he would put himself in the wrong with public opinion, and we could take the necessary measures to prevent him from creating a disturbance. If he submitted, we should probably have further trouble in the future, but this would be better than sweeping away a committee upon which many hopes were founded among the United Nations as well as in France.

The Prime Minister informed Mr. Macmillan of the President's (b) message and instructions to General Eisenhower, and of his own agreement that General de Gaulle should not be allowed control of the army. The Prime Minister thought that General Georges or some other officer enjoying the confidence of the 'rescuing Powers' should be appointed Minister[1] of Defence.

General Eisenhower, like Mr. Macmillan, took the view that he could settle the matter by discussion, and telegraphed accordingly to President Roosevelt. At his meeting with the two French Generals (c) he made it clear that in view of his responsibilities, and of impending military operations, he must insist upon leaving the effective control of the French forces in the hands of General Giraud with whom he had worked during recent months. He did not wish to interfere with any internal organisation upon which the Committee might decide, but he must be satisfied that there was a Commander-in-Chief and that General Giraud held this office with real powers of control. After a discussion lasting for three-quarters of an hour General de Gaulle left the conference in great anger saying that he could not be a party to the breach of French sovereignty implied in General

---

[1] The correct term would have been 'Commissioner'.

(a) T842/3, No. 316, Churchill Papers/181. (b) Z7110/30/69. (c) Z7056/30/69.
P*

Eisenhower's request. A written statement of General Eisenhower's view was given to the Committee on June 20; Mr. Macmillan thought that they would accept it.

(a)   Two days later M. Massigli gave to Mr. Macmillan and Mr. Murphy the text of a French decree concerning the command and reorganisation of the French fighting services. Although M. Massigli said that the Committee were not replying formally to General Eisenhower's communication, the decree in effect met the Allied requirements. The decree laid down that the Committee of National Liberation would be responsible for the general direction of the French war effort and would control all the French forces. A permanent military committee consisting of Generals Giraud and de Gaulle and the French Chiefs of Staff would be constituted with responsibility for the unification, organisation and training of these forces. M. Massigli said that the Committee had also approved two other decrees fixing the areas of the respective commands of Generals de Gaulle and Giraud and appointing their Chiefs of Army Staff. General Giraud would be Commander-in-Chief in North and West Africa and General de Gaulle in other parts of the French Empire.

(b)   Mr. Macmillan thought the new arrangement not unsatisfactory.

(c)   The Prime Minister also recommended its acceptance to President Roosevelt; he doubted whether it would last, but saw no reason for interfering with it since it safeguarded the military security of the Allied forces.

(vii)

British proposals for the recognition of the French Committee of National Liberation: differences of view between the Prime Minister and the Foreign Office: American opposition to recognition: discussions at the Quebec Conference: British recognition of the Committee (July 2–August 27, 1943).

On June 7, 1943, Mr. Eden received from the French Committee a note asking for official British recognition as 'the body qualified to ensure the conduct of the French effort in the war within the framework of inter-Allied co-operation as well as the administration and defence of all French interests'. From the Prime Minister's point of view one of the advantages of the new arrangement was that the Committee would take the place of General de Gaulle. The Prime

(d)   Minister had telegraphed to Mr. Roosevelt on June 6 that he

(a) Z7075/5/69. (b) Z7145/30/69. (c) T880/3, No. 327 (Churchill Papers/181; Z7145/30/69). (d) T740/3, No. 300 (Churchill Papers/181; Z6634/30/69).

regarded the formation of the Committee as bringing to an end his official connexion with General de Gaulle as leader of the Fighting French, and that he proposed to transfer the relationship to the new Committee as a body.

Mr. Churchill made a formal statement to this effect in the House (a) of Commons on June 8. He said that the formation of the Committee, 'with its collective responsibility, supersedes the situation created by the correspondence between General de Gaulle and myself in 1940. Our dealings, financial and otherwise, will henceforward be with the Committee as a whole.' The 'further and larger question' of the 'degree of recognition' of the Committee as 'representative of France' required consideration by the British and United States Govern- ments. The Prime Minister hoped that, if things went well, a solution satisfactory to all parties might 'shortly be reached'.

The circumstances of General de Gaulle's resignation seemed to show that things were not going well. Mr. Eden telegraphed to Lord Halifax that he had been on the point of instructing him to (b) discuss with the United States Government the question of recog- nition. He now hoped that the United States Government would agree to delay while the Committee was engaged in internal disputes. Lord Halifax reported on June 13 that on June 10 Mr. Welles had (c) again complained to him that the British Government were paying the French National Committee. Mr. Welles suggested that we should now transfer these payments to the new Committee of National Liberation. Lord Halifax thought the Americans were obsessed by this financial question, but that it would be an advantage if we could make the transfer; the fact that we could do so only after the recognition of the new Committee was an argument in favour of recognising it at once. The Prime Minister proposed, in a draft reply, to say that we should begin by recognising the Committee—acting through a majority—as the recipient of money and arms. We were therefore proposing to make no further payments to General de Gaulle after June 11, and would raise the question of the scale of payments hitherto made to the French National Committee in view of the considerable revenues available to the new Committee in Algiers.[1] We should do our utmost to strengthen the new Committee, irrespective of the question whether General de Gaulle was a mem-

---

[1] On June 11 the Foreign Office had informed Mr. Macmillan that the Treasury had made the usual monthly payment to General de Gaulle's account, but that he should (d) inform M. Massigli that were we not making any more payments to the Fighting French, and that any future payments would be made to the new Committee in its collective capacity. We expected the new Committee in due course to become self-supporting, apart from Lend-Lease and similar military supplies from ourselves and the Americans. Mr. Macmillan carried out these instructions, and Lord Halifax told Mr. Hull of them on June 17.

(a) *Parl. Deb. 5th Ser., H. of C.*, Vol. 390, cols. 568–9. (b) Z6678/30/69. (c) Z6775/6504/69. (d) Z6842/68/17.

ber of it, and, if he were a member, as long as he did not obtain mastery over it. The second stage of recognition raised the wider question of how far the Committee could be said to represent France. Mr. Churchill thought that we should require proof of the trustworthiness of the Committee over a definite period.

There was now a certain confusion about the American attitude.

(a) On June 15 Lord Halifax reported that Mr. Atherton had told a member of the Embassy staff that we had better wait until the situation had cleared at Algiers, and until we were sure of the value of the Committee as a body with which we could collaborate in the prosecution of the war, but that when the situation was clear, early

(b) action would be desirable.[1] Two days later Mr. Macmillan telegraphed that the State Department were considering the question of recognition. Mr. Macmillan thought that we should not hold back

(c) from discussing the matter with the United States Government.[2] On June 19 Lord Halifax reported that the State Department had telegraphed to General Eisenhower, for his comments, the text of instructions to be given to Mr. Winant for discussing the question

(d) of recognition with Mr. Eden. On this same day Mr. Eden sent to the Prime Minister a minute on the latter's draft instructions to Lord Halifax. Mr. Eden agreed in general with the Prime Minister's view, but thought it better to wait a little before asking Lord Halifax to make any statement to the United States Government. He suggested that when we recognised the new Committee as a proper recipient of money and arms we should also recognise it as administering those parts of the French Empire which were collaborating in the war against the Axis. The next step would be more difficult, but the Committee had not asked to be recognised as 'representing France'. Mr. Eden agreed that we could not give them a limited recognition until we had definite proof that they deserved it; even so we should have to take care that we did not invest the Committee with attributes belonging only to the fully recognised Governments of sovereign States.

(e) On June 23 the Prime Minister telegraphed to the President that it would be 'most unwise to commit ourselves' to any recognition of the Committee, 'which they will certainly demand, as representative of France in some degree or other', until we knew more clearly 'how

(f) they are going to behave'.[3] On June 24 the British Embassy at

---

[1] Mr. Churchill minuted on this last point to Mr. Eden: 'Surely we agree on this.' Mr. Eden answered 'Yes'.

[2] Mr. Churchill minuted on this telegram (June 18): 'Better wait now'.

[3] This message, which dealt also with the composition of the Committee, was sent when the Prime Minister and the President were still under the impression that the enlargement of the Committee was a manoeuvre by General de Gaulle.

(a) Z6880/6504/69. (b) Z6881/6504/69. (c) Z6988/5571/69. (d) Z6775/6504/69. (e) T873/3, No. 325 (Churchill Papers/181; Z7164/6504/69). (f) Z7274/6504/69.

Washington sent to the Foreign Office the text of the draft instructions to Mr. Winant. These instructions, which had been approved by General Eisenhower, had been given to the Embassy unofficially through the Joint Staff Mission. Mr. Winant himself does not appear to have taken up the subject with the Foreign Office and on (a) June 25 Lord Halifax reported that, in answer to a question, Mr. Atherton had implied that the State Department had not given the matter any serious thought, and, at the moment, had no intention of raising it.

The War Cabinet decided on June 28 that we should try to build (b) up the authority of the civilian members of the Committee, but that, in view of the American attitude, it would probably be undesirable for the time to accord the Committee full recognition. On July 2, however, Mr. Eden circulated to the War Cabinet a memorandum (c) on the question of recognition. He explained that he had been on the point of instructing Lord Halifax to make proposals to the United States Government for the recognition of the Committee when the dispute had broken out between General de Gaulle and General Giraud over the command and control of the French fighting forces. This dispute had now been settled, and the Committee under the influence of its civilian members was now trying to get down to departmental work. The most effective means of carrying out the policy of building up the authority of the Committee must be to give it some form of recognition. Otherwise we could not easily persuade the press and public opinion that our policy was to support the Committee on a basis of collective responsibility, and not to back one or another French General. The Soviet Government wanted to recognise the Committee, and had delayed doing so only at our request. We should find it difficult to persuade them to delay much longer. Mr. Eden therefore asked the War Cabinet to allow him to take up the question of recognition with the United States and Soviet Governments. He proposed the following formula:

'His Majesty's Government are happy to recognise the French Committee of National Liberation as administering those parts of the French overseas empire[1] which acknowledge their authority, and as having assumed the functions of the former French National Committee in respect of territories in the Levant. They also recognise

---

[1] On the night of July 25–6 the Foreign Office telegraphed to Washington and Moscow (d) certain amendments to their draft. The revised text here read: 'those French overseas territories which acknowledge its authority'. The reason for this change was to include Algeria, which was part of Metropolitan France.

(a) Z7266/5/69. (b) WM(43)89. (c) WP(43)391; Z7589/5/69. (d) Z8333/6504/69.

it as the body qualified to ensure the conduct of the French effort in the war within the framework of inter-Allied co-operation as well as, in principle, the administration and defence of French interests.[1] The practical application of this principle to the different categories of French interests must be reserved for consideration in each case as it arises.

'His Majesty's Government have taken note of the Committee's determination to continue the common struggle, in close co-operation with all the Allies, until French and Allied territories are completely liberated and until victory is complete over all the enemy Powers. They count on the Committee to afford such facilities in the military and economic sphere in the territories under their administration as may be required by the Governments of the United Nations for the prosecution of the war. In respect of certain of these territories agreements already exist between the French authorities and the British or United States authorities. The creation of the French Committee of National Liberation may make it necessary to revise these agreements,[2] and pending their revision all such agreements concluded since June 1940, except in so far as these have been automatically made inapplicable by the formation of the French Committee of National Liberation, will remain in force.'[3]

The Prime Minister sent a minute to Mr. Eden on July 5 that he did not know that he (Mr. Eden) was intending to bring the question of recognition formally before the War Cabinet. The Prime Minister thought that Mr. Eden's proposal was 'altogether premature', and that we ought to know more about the disposition of the Committee towards ourselves, and see more of its actions before we recognised it. Furthermore, the desire to obtain recognition was 'our most potent lever to ensure the good behaviour of the Committee'. The Prime Minister hoped that Mr. Eden would not press for a decision on the matter.

Mr. Eden at first drew up a reply to the Prime Minister that he had already decided to withdraw his paper because he thought that some delay was desirable. He had heard that M. Massigili was coming to London. Mr. Eden wanted to discuss the whole question with him. At the same time Mr. Eden thought that in our own

---

[1] In the revised draft this sentence ended at 'co-operation' and the remainder of the paragraph was altered to read: 'His Majesty's Government take note with sympathy of the desire of the Committee to be recognised as the body qualified to ensure the administration and defence of all French interests. The question of the extent to which it may be possible to give effect to this request in respect of the different categories of such interests must however be reserved for consideration in each case as it arises.' This change was made in order to avoid giving the impression that we had in effect recognised the claim of the Committee to administer and defend all French interests; a claim of this kind would be the prerogative of a legally constituted Government.

[2] In the revised text the words 'His Majesty's Government assume that' were inserted.

[3] In the revised text the words 'as between His Majesty's Government in the United Kingdom and the French Committee of National Liberation' were inserted.

interest we ought to recognise the Committee without too much delay. Our proposed formula did not in fact give much more in the way of recognition than we had given to the former Fighting French National Committee with whom—apart from General de Gaulle's temperamental reactions—our relations had been harmonious and constructive. We ought to act in agreement with the United States Government, but General Giraud, who was visiting Washington, would probably raise the question of recognition with President Roosevelt.

Mr. Eden decided not to send this minute, since the Prime (a) Minister, after hearing from Mr. Macmillan on July 6 that General Eisenhower and Mr. Murphy were proposing immediate recognition (b) of the Committee, agreed to telegraph to the President for his opinion, and to give him the text of Mr. Eden's proposed formula.

Mr. Eden now asked Mr. Strang to draw up a memorandum on (c) American policy towards France and the French Empire for cirula-tion to the War Cabinet if the Prime Minister agreed with its terms. The memorandum stated that the policy of the United States Government appeared to be that they did not wish to see a strong central administration for the French Empire built up in Algiers. They would prefer, if possible, to deal separately with each part of the French Empire. They disliked the growth of an independent spirit in any French administration and considered that any French authority with whom they might deal should accept their demands without question. The fusion of the administrations of General Giraud and General de Gaulle had been unwelcome to them; they would have liked to break up the Committee of Liberation, turn out the Gaullist members, and set up a puppet committee subservient to the Allied Powers and to General Giraud with whom alone they would continue to deal on a purely military basis.

The United States Government had stated officially that they favoured the integral restoration of the French Empire, but the President had suggested privately to us[1] that Indo-China[2] and certain French islands in the Pacific should be placed under United Nations trusteeship and that Dakar and Bizerta should be held as bases by the United States and British Governments respectively. The President had also spoken of detaching an area in north-east France, including Alsace-Lorraine, and incorporating it in a new buffer state to be called Wallonia. There were grounds for believing

---

[1] The text of the memorandum reads 'us'. The suggestion seems to have been made to Lord Halifax and to the Pacific Council in Washington.
[2] See also Volume IV, Chapter LX, note to section (ii).

(a) Algiers tel. 1143, T963/3; Algiers tel. 1146, T968/3 (Churchill Papers/181).
(b) T979–80/3, Nos. 348–9, Churchill Papers/181. (c) Z8225, 8226/6504/69.

that some at least of the governing authorities in Washington had little belief in the future of France, and perhaps did not wish to see her restoration as a great Imperial Power. Dr. Beneš, since his visit to Washington, had said to Mr. Eden that the Americans were not so much anti-Gaullist as anti-French, and that, after backing Marshal Pétain and being 'let down' by him, they felt resentful in all their dealings with France, and regarded her as a Latin Power, like Spain and Italy, with no great future in Europe.

Our own views were very different. We had declared our intention to restore the greatness and independence of France. We had no designs on French territory, and could have no sympathy with policies aiming at the disintegration of colonial empires. In his speech at the Guildhall on June 30, 1943, the Prime Minister had mentioned France, together with the three other Great Powers allied to us in the war, and had said that we hoped for a revival of French unity and true greatness. Our manifest interests were in this direction. Our main problem after the war would be to contain Germany. The Anglo-Soviet treaty was designed to secure Soviet collaboration for this purpose on the eastern flank of Germany; we needed to balance this treaty by an understanding with a powerful France in the west. These arrangements would be indispensable for our security, whether or not the United States collaborated in the maintenance of peace on this side of the Atlantic.

These considerations should govern our policy towards France. France had stood twice between us and the assault of the German aggressor. In all our dealings with the French we should have regard to their susceptibilities in matters of prestige and sovereignty. We should do everything to raise French morale and promote French self-confidence. We should be patient with manifestations of French sensitiveness and with an excited and suspicious French nationalism which was natural in the circumstances. In dealing with European problems in the future, we were likely to have to work even more closely with France than with the United States and, while we should concert our French policy with the Americans, there were limits beyond which we ought not to allow British policy to be governed by American policy. The other Allied Governments were watching events in Algiers; what was done by the Americans and ourselves would affect opinion not only in France but in occupied Europe as a whole. There was evidence that feeling against the Americans was growing not only in North Africa but in Metropolitan France as a result of their repeated affronts to French susceptibilities, their protection of doubtful personalities, and their open hostility to the Gaullists. It was not to our interest that this feeling should become directed against ourselves or that we should lose the moral authority which we had acquired in Europe.

Europe expected us to have a European policy of our own, and to state it. Such a policy must aim at the restoration of the independence of the smaller European Allies and of the greatness of France. In the pursuit of this policy we must support and encourage by every means in our power those elements in all countries which were steadfastly resisting the enemy at grave peril to themselves. We ought therefore to build up the French Committee as a living symbol to the people of occupied France, and to strengthen it in its collective capacity, though we should not recognise it as the government or even the provisional government of France. Its members were at one with the French resistance movements in believing that the future of France lay with the Anglo-Saxon Powers and Russia and in repudiating those Frenchmen who had thought it right or expedient or profitable to collaborate, even temporarily, with the Germans. Rightly or wrongly, the United States Government were suspected in Europe of a tenderness towards non-resisting and collaborationist elements in France. We had reason to think that they were still in touch with Marshal Pétain. They were deeply hostile to General de Gaulle and seemed to have little sympathy—in spite of our efforts to persuade them—with the more active of the resistance movements.

We had had no reply to the Prime Minister's message to the President giving our proposed formula of recognition; there was no sign that the United States Government were prepared to deal formally with the Committee of Liberation. We, on the other hand, had intimate dealings with the French in Syria and Madagascar, and there were French forces stationed in Great Britain. It was thus inconvenient from the political and legal point of view not to have formal relations with the authority whom in fact we regarded as responsible for all the French territories and armed forces collaborating with us in the war. Mr. Eden was proposing to speak to the United States Ambassador, and to ask whether the United States Government had any comments to make on our proposed formula of limited recognition.[1]

Mr. Eden sent a draft note based on this paper[2] to the Prime (a) Minister on July 13. The Prime Minister himself wrote on July 13 a note, for circulation to the War Cabinet, on the policy of the (b) United States towards France.[3] In this paper Mr. Churchill empha-

---

[1] The memorandum also referred to a telegram of July 14 from Mr. Macmillan urging prompt recognition. Mr. Macmillan pointed out that, whether we recognised it or not, the Committee was likely to continue, and that, if it broke up, it could give place only to (c) a purely de Gaulle administration. A long delay in recognition would cause general French ill-feeling against us.

[2] The copy summarised above was a slightly revised version of the memorandum but without substantial changes in the text.

[3] The Prime Minister stated that he had seen the Foreign Office paper only after dictating his own note. The note was not, in fact, circulated by the Prime Minister to the War Cabinet.

(a) Z8226/6504/69. (b) Churchill Papers/181/8. (c) Z7839/6504/69.

sised the President's dislike and distrust of General de Gaulle, and agreed that we were unlikely by an exchange of despatches between the Foreign Office and the State Department to alter the policy of the United States. Time and events alone could change this policy. What then were we to do? Mr. Churchill gave his own view of General de Gaulle. At the time of the General's visit to Brazzaville in 1941[1] Mr. Churchill had formed the opinion that he was thoroughly anti-British. This opinion had been confirmed by every British officer or official abroad who had had dealings with him. For some time past, therefore, Mr. Churchill had regarded him as 'a personage whose arrival at the summit of French affairs would be contrary to the interests of Great Britain'.

Mr. Churchill thought that General de Gaulle's personality was also detrimental to the main interests of France. He was too much of a dictator, and too ambitious for himself. He was inclined to set himself up as the supreme judge of the conduct of all Frenchmen at the time of, and since, the collapse of France, and to appropriate to himself and his followers 'the title deeds of France'. Mr. Churchill had no doubt that he would cause a civil war in France; according to General Giraud he had already spoken of the need for a 'révolution sanglante'. He would make anti-British alliances and combinations 'with gusto' if he thought it in his interest to do so.

Mr. Churchill therefore was convinced that we ought not to quarrel with the United States over General de Gaulle; above all, we could not allow him or his followers 'to cloud or mar those personal relations of partnership and friendship which I have laboured for nearly four years to develop between me and President Roosevelt by which, I venture to think, the course of our affairs has been most notably assisted'. Mr. Churchill said that his colleagues must 'face this position squarely', since it was 'fundamental' as far as he was concerned. He thought that if he explained it to Parliament or by broadcast to the nation, he would receive a full measure of support. 'Whether this be so or not would make no difference to what I believe to be my duty.'

Mr. Churchill realised that we had ourselves built up Gaullism in France and also that many Frenchmen who had acquiesced in the Bordeaux Armistice were now anxious to rally to the side of victory. General de Gaulle's following, however, would be greatly diminished when it was realised that he stood between France and the goodwill of the 'Rescuing Powers' and, particularly, of the United States. On the other hand we did not wish to dishearten the French people by a sudden shock. Hence we had tried for a good many months to bring about a union between the French whom the Americans supported

---

[1] See above, pp. 79–80.

in North Africa and the French National Committee in London, and especially between Generals Giraud and de Gaulle. Mr. Churchill considered that he had been prevented from arranging a settlement at Casablanca only by the 'preposterous conduct' of General de Gaulle. Since that time the President had armed General Giraud's troops in North Africa, and was now 'much concerned over the demeanour and control' of this French army. Meanwhile the Gaullist organs in London and at Brazzaville, with their supporters in the British and American press, had 'ceaselessly criticised American policy' and had bitterly antagonised the President as well as Mr. Hull.

'For all these reasons we had hoped that the personality of General de Gaulle should be merged first in the National Committee in London', and now in the Committee of National Liberation. This latter Committee, under civilian influence, was acquiring a collective character. We should allow those healthy tendencies to develop and, if in the next few months it became clear that General de Gaulle and his 'faction' were not in control of the Committee, we might secure from the President the kind of recognition proposed in the British formula. Meanwhile we should continue to deal with the Committee on a *de facto* basis and transfer to it in its collective capacity the engagements previously made with General de Gaulle. We should thereby be according some recognition to the Committee, but we should be making unnecessary trouble with the United States if we emphasised the point or did anything of a *de jure* character at the present stage. A formal recognition would cause the greatest offence in Washington and draw upon the Administration the hostile criticism of the President's political opponents.

Mr. Churchill wrote that he had repeatedly stated that it was a major British interest that France should be strong after the war. He was afraid, however, that the anti-Gaullism of the United States Government might 'harden into a definite anti-French feeling'. We could prevent any such dangerous tendency if General de Gaulle were gradually absorbed into the Committee. We might by this time have secured for France and the French Empire a recognised place in the Councils of the Allies. General de Gaulle's 'follies and misbehaviour' had prevented us from so doing, but we might yet succeed if we acted with patience and a sense of proportion.

The Foreign Office regarded the Prime Minister's conclusion as 'not too bad' but, as Mr. Strang pointed out, the weakness of the paper as a whole was that it regarded Anglo-American relations too much in terms of Mr. Churchill's personal relations with President Roosevelt, and that Mr. Churchill's policy towards France was governed too much by these relations and by his dislike of General de

Gaulle. Mr. Churchill and the President seemed to leave out of account the damaging effect in France of the campaign against General de Gaulle. Vichy and the Germans were exploiting this campaign; we ought not to bewilder the minds of those who were resisting the invaders with such steadfastness and who, on their side, respected and admired us.

Mr. Eden did not circulate the Foreign Office memorandum, since further developments occurred within a few days. On the night

(a) of July 13–14 Lord Halifax telegraphed that he was disturbed by the position in Washington with regard to French affairs. He had little doubt that the Administration had been spreading misleading accounts of our attitude in order to disarm the increasing number of their own critics. Lord Halifax's own view was that the most satisfactory solution would be an early recognition of the French Committee by the United States and ourselves.

(b)   The War Cabinet on July 14 discussed the question primarily from the point of view of Lord Halifax's report that the United States Administration appeared to be trying to draw criticism away from themselves by misrepresenting our attitude. The War Cabinet agreed that Mr. Eden should speak to Mr. Winant on the general issues involved and ask him what reply the United States Government were likely to give to our formula for a limited degree of recognition.

(c)   Mr. Eden saw Mr. Winant later on July 14, and complained that the Administration were involving us in the American press controversy over the official policy of the United States towards the French Committee. Mr. Winant said that he was himself worried over this controversy. Mr. Eden said that we had had no reply to the Prime Minister's message enclosing our formula, and Mr. Winant, who seemed to approve of the formula, promised to telegraph on the following day to the President or Mr. Hopkins.

(d)   On the night of July 17–18 Mr. Makins reported from Algiers that General Eisenhower had told Mr. Macmillan in Tunis that, in his opinion, recognition should be given at once to the Committee. General Eisenhower thought that the Committee was now clearly established *de facto* and was carrying on the day-to-day work of administration, and that its authority was unquestioned. Recognition would be the best means of avoiding a dangerous growth of the power of General de Gaulle since delay merely increased his own prestige, and lessened that of the Committee. General Eisenhower proposed telegraphing in these terms to London and Washington, but Mr. Murphy had already sent a message to Washington covering the general's two points. Mr. Murphy was now telegraphing

---

(a) Z7816/6504/69. (b) WM(43)99; Z7869, 7880/6504/69. (c) Z7853/6504/69.
(d) Z7963/6504/69.

that General Eisenhower endorsed his recommendation in favour of immediate recognition.

The Prime Minister replied on July 18 that talk about 'recognition' was meaningless apart from a formula defining what was actually to be recognised. He asked what General Eisenhower and Mr. Murphy thought of our formula, or whether they had an alternative. Mr. Macmillan was at this time in Tunis. Mr. Macmillan saw Mr. Murphy and was told by him that our formula ought to satisfy the United States Government. Mr. Macmillan had already suggested the addition of a reference to the undertaking given by the Committee on June 3 that it would relinquish its powers to a provisional Government to be constituted 'in conformity with the laws of the Republic as soon as the liberation of Metropolitan territory permits and at the latest upon the completion of the liberation of France'. Mr. Macmillan telegraphed later that he had thought it better not to consult General Eisenhower about the formula, though he was sure that the general would approve of it. Mr. Macmillan said that he knew that General Eisenhower and Mr. Murphy had been advocating immediate recognition, and that their views had probably not been much liked in 'high circles' in Washington. He wanted therefore to avoid the possibility of an attack on General Eisenhower on the ground that he was too susceptible to British influence.

Mr. Macmillan's report that General Eisenhower and Mr. Murphy had definitely recommended immediate recognition of the Committee seems to have had considerable influence on the Prime (a) Minister. He told General Giraud on July 21, during a visit by the latter to London, that we were in favour of recognition and had sent some time ago a telegram to President Roosevelt with a formula which we proposed to employ. He had now sent a further telegram saying that, in our view, there were now practical reasons for recognition and that we would like to act in concert with the United States. Mr. Eden, who saw General Giraud later in the day, repeated our wish to recognise the Committee, and said that we had also sent our formula to the Soviet Government and asked for their views about it.

The further telegram of which the Prime Minister had spoken was a message which he sent to President Roosevelt on July 21. He (b) referred to his message of July 8[1] and said that we ought to take some action. The Foreign Office and his Cabinet colleagues were putting considerable pressure on him, and 'force of circumstances' was

---

[1] i.e. the telegram which he sent to President Roosevelt after hearing from Mr. Macmillan on July 6. See above, p. 447.

(a) Z8167/5/69; P.M.412/23/12. (b) T1077/3, No. 373 (Churchill Papers/181; Z8192/6504/69).

leading us towards a recognition of the French Committee. We needed a formula of recognition and had submitted to the President something which would meet our practical needs. Mr. Churchill had told Parliament on June 8 that the formation of the Committee with its collective responsibility had now superseded the situation created by his own exchange of letters with General de Gaulle in 1940 and that henceforward all our dealings would be collectively with the Committee. Since then we had been discussing questions on a *de facto* basis with the Committee. We were now considering with M. Massigli—who was helpful—the problems of Syria.[1] General Catroux, who was also not 'in the pocket' of General de Gaulle, was being of assistance. We should soon be transferring to the Committee all our financial arrangements with General de Gaulle. We had a number of Free French troops and establishments in Great Britain and about fifty Free French ships were doing very useful work. We had much business to do with the French colonies which had come over or were brought over to the Allied side. At present all these affairs were formally focused on General de Gaulle, but Mr. Churchill wanted to act through the Committee.

Mr. Churchill said that Mr. Macmillan's reports were to the effect that the Committee was acquiring a collective authority and that, if it broke down—as it might do if it were left without support— General de Gaulle would recover sole control except in regard to the powers exercised by General Giraud. Mr. Macmillan favoured a measure of recognition and had told us that this was also the view of General Eisenhower and Mr. Murphy.

Mr. Churchill said he was now reaching the point where he might have to take the step of recognising the Committee. In this case the Russians would also recognise it, and the position might then be embarrassing to the President. Mr. Churchill therefore asked the President whether he would accept our formula or any other formula on similar lines or whether he would object to separate British recognition. Mr. Churchill said that he was 'no more enamoured' of General de Gaulle than was the President, but that he would rather have him 'settling down to honest team work' on the Committee than 'strutting about as a combination of Joan of Arc and Clemenceau'.

(a)   This message crossed a telegram from Lord Halifax that the State Department had advised Mr. Hull that the time had come to recognise the French Committee. Mr. Hull was seeing the President about the question but had been much upset by a report that the Committee had voted a number of military reforms in the absence of General Giraud.

---

[1] See Volume IV, Chapter LIV, section (ii).

Z8146/6504/69.

A reply from President Roosevelt to the Prime Minister's message (a) was received on July 22. The Foreign Office thought at first, from the contents of the reply, that the President had sent it before receiving the Prime Minister's message, since it did not answer any of the points in the message. The President said that the Committee of National Liberation had only begun to function, and that more evidence was required of its 'complete and genuine unity'; the 'appearance of unity within the Committee' still seemed to be 'on the surface', and its members were continuing, or were ready to continue at any time 'bitter attacks on each other and on us jointly or severally'. The United States Government, however, was most anxious to join in moving 'along the line of limited acceptance of the Committee, subject always to military requirements', but it was necessary to secure that the 'plain conditions of French unity' were properly met.

The President objected to the use of the term 'recognition', since it would be distorted to imply recognition of the Committee as the Government of France when we landed on French territory. He said that the term 'acceptance' of the 'local civil authority' of the Committee 'in various colonies on a temporary basis' came 'nearer' to expressing his view. We should, however, retain the right and continue the practice of dealing directly with the local French officials in the colonies whenever there were military advantages in so doing.

The President suggested the following statement to the French Committee:

'The Governments of the United States and Great Britain desire again to make clear their purpose of co-operation with all patriotic Frenchmen looking to the liberation of the French people and territories from the oppressions of the enemy.

Arrangements have been made with the French Commander-in-Chief in North and West Africa for continuing the co-operation of the French armed forces under his control. The two Governments will co-operate with the French Committee of National Liberation in other matters of mutual interest on the understanding that the Committee was conceived and will function, on the principle of collective responsibility of all members of the Committee, for the prosecution of the war and not for the promotion of factional movements.

They desire to make clear, however, the following two conditions: (a) that the constitution and Government to established for France must be determined by the French people after they shall have been afforded an opportunity freely to express themselves. (b) that the relationship with the Committee will be subject to the

(a) T1085/3, No. 321 (Churchill Papers/181; Z8250/6504/69).

military requirements of the Allied Commanders in the prosecution of the war.'

Mr. Eden who was out of patience, in particular, with Mr. Hull's obstinacy in the matter, minuted: 'this is a petty and deplorable telegram. . . . I should like now to reply to the President: "I am sorry that this is your view. For the reasons I have already given I cannot share it, and must therefore go ahead." ' The Foreign Office agreed that the President's proposal to use the term 'acceptance' and not 'recognition' would merely anger the French, and that the Committee had already agreed to the two 'conditions' laid down in the President's proposal. Mr. Eden sent a draft reply on July 28 for consideration by the Prime Minister. The reply was in the form of a message from the Prime Minister to the President pointing out certain inconsistencies in the latter's proposals, and noting that the President's statement would be granting the Committee a lesser degree of recognition than we had given to the former French National Committee. The 'cold douche' which he (the President) proposed to administer would have a bad effect on our friends in France and on Frenchmen in Algiers who seemed to be doing their best to restore their country's good name and to assist the United Nations.

(a)   The Prime Minister replied in a minute to Mr. Eden on July 30 that he saw no reason for urgency in the matter. The question of Mussolini now occupied attention: Mr. Churchill did not want to complicate the difficult handling of this major affair by opening up another set of arguments with the President on 'recognition' or 'acceptance'. He thought that it would be a good thing that the French, who were talking so high and wanted to be the centre of world attention, should have time to see that they were in eclipse owing to their quarrels. General de Gaulle had been bitterly attacking American policy; time and goodwill were needed to undo the effect of these attacks. Mr. Churchill therefore wished to postpone the question until he could deal with it in conversation at the Quebec meeting, and meanwhile to continue our *de facto* relations with the Committee. He suggested that the Foreign Office should make another draft on more cordial lines than the President's draft, but avoiding the word 'recognition'. Mr. Churchill's aim was the recognition of the Committee in its collective capacity, and its eventual inclusion among the United Nations with the other refugee Governments. He thought that France was entitled to this status on account of the ships, troops and territory actually working with us under the French flag. The obstacle was General de Gaulle; the

(a) Z8459/6504/69.

duty of the General was to regain the confidence of the two rescuing Powers. 'If he will do his part, I will do mine.'

The Foreign Office produced another draft of the formula in accordance with the Prime Minister's instructions, but Mr. Eden (a) pointed out that we could not omit the word 'recognition' unless we reduced what was in fact 'recognition' almost to vanishing point. The Prime Minister agreed to the inclusion of the word, and the formula was telegraphed to the President. In a covering message Mr. Churchill said that he had thought at first that the President's (b) draft was 'rather chilling' and would not end the agitation for recognition. Meanwhile events had moved in our favour; General de Gaulle was now 'more enclosed in the general body of the Committee'. Mr. Churchill pointed out that the new draft included the sentence: 'The Committee will of course afford whatever military and economic facilities *and securities* in the territories under its administration are required by the Governments of the United States and the United Kingdom for the prosecution of the war.' This clause would enable us to override or break with the Committee in the event of bad faith or misconduct on their part. On August 9 the President spoke to Lord Halifax about the question. He was still (c) inclined to do nothing; in any case he thought that the term 'recognition' implied too much that we were dealing with a Government.

Meanwhile Mr. Churchill decided that a message from himself should be sent about August 7–8 (i.e. after he had left for Quebec) (d) to be given by Mr. Macmillan to Generals de Gaulle, Giraud, Catroux and Georges, and to M. Monnet and other friends on the Committee. Mr. Churchill wished them to know that he was shortly meeting President Roosevelt, and was going to try to bring about a satisfactory recognition of the Committee. Nothing would help him more in this task than a continuance of firm unity within the Committee and proofs of its determination to work in a friendly way with the two Rescuing Powers for the liberation of France and the speedy defeat of the enemy. Mr. Churchill was in favour of the Committee taking its place with the other United Nations and being consulted in those aspects of the war which were of deep concern to Frenchmen. He had been much encouraged by recent developments and felt them to be of assistance in bringing about 'what I have never swerved from, namely, the restoration of the greatness of France'.

On August 22 Mr. Eden telegraphed from Quebec that on the (e) two previous days he had discussed at length with Mr. Hull the question of recognising the Committee. In the first conversation Mr.

(a) Z8459/6504/69. (b) T1182/3, No. 399 (Churchill Papers/181; Z8627/6504/69). (c) Z8770/6504/69. (d) Z8886/6504/69. (e) Tel. Welfare 315, Z9219/6504/69.

Hull urged that there was nothing wrong with the latest American draft. He showed this draft to Mr. Eden, and said that the President had seen it but had not forwarded it to London. Mr. Hull did not know whether the President had accepted it. After reading the draft Mr. Eden pointed out that it seemed to give everything to the Committee except recognition, and that for this reason he regarded it as inadequate and was sure that it would be so regarded by the French and by the majority of people in Great Britain.

Mr. Eden argued the matter from all angles, but Mr. Hull was not to be moved. He said that if we gave recognition now we should be throwing away 'the best lever we possessed', and that for this reason we should wait until the Committee had proved its worth to us. Mr. Eden pointed out that the civilian members of the Committee —and not General de Gaulle—were pressing for recognition, and that Generals Georges and Catroux supported them though neither was especially well disposed towards General de Gaulle. Our object in recognising the Committee was to build up its collective authority; if we slighted it, we should only strengthen General de Gaulle and the wilder elements. We had recognised General de Gaulle's French National Committee and ought surely to give as much recognition to the Committee of Liberation. Finally, Mr. Eden suggested that, if they could not reach agreement, each of the two Governments should use its own formula. Mr. Hull did not reject this proposal.

At the second conversation it was clear that Mr. Hull had not receded from his position. He showed Mr. Eden the draft of a statement to be issued by the President at the time of recognition. Mr. Eden thought that the statement would not improve matters, since the French would think it unnecessarily wounding and humiliating. Mr. Eden repeated the British arguments in favour of a more complete recognition. The conclusion reached was that— however undesirable it might be—we and the Americans would probably have to 'recognise' in different terms.

(a)   The Prime Minister telegraphed to Mr. Attlee on August 22 that Mr. Hull was completely obdurate. We had therefore agreed that the Americans should publish their document and that we should publish our own document, and the Canadians a form of words which they had proposed. Mr. Churchill had said plainly to the President that the American formula would 'certainly have a bad press'; the President had replied that he would rather have a sheet anchor out against the machinations of General de Gaulle.

(b)   The British formula as finally presented to the French National Committee on August 26 and published on August 27 ran as follows:

(a) Tel. Welfare 326, Z9219/6504/69. (b) Z9382/6504/69.

'His Majesty's Government in the United Kingdom desire again to make clear their purpose of co-operating with all patriotic Frenchmen looking to the liberation of the French people and French territories from the oppressions of the enemy.

'His Majesty's Government in the United Kingdom accordingly welcome the establishment of the French Committee of National Liberation. It is their understanding that the Committee has been conceived and will function on the principle of the collective responsibility of all its members for the prosecution of the war. It is also, they are assured, common ground between themselves and the Committee that it will be for the French people themselves to settle their own constitution and to establish their own Government after they have had an opportunity to express themselves freely. On this understanding His Majesty's Government in the United Kingdom wish to make the following statement:—

"His Majesty's Government in the United Kingdom recognise forthwith the French Committee of National Liberation as administering those French overseas territories which acknowledge its authority and as having assumed the functions of the former French National Committee in respect of territories in the Levant. His Majesty's Government in the United Kingdom also recognise the Committee as the body qualified to ensure the conduct of the French effort in the war within the framework of inter-Allied co-operation. They take note with sympathy of the desire of the Committee to be regarded as the body qualified to ensure the administration and defence of all French interests. It is the intention of His Majesty's Government to give effect to this request as far as possible while reserving the right to consider in consultation with the Committee the practical application of this principle in particular cases as they arise. His Majesty's Government in the United Kingdom welcome the Committee's determination to continue the common struggle in close co-operation with all the Allies until French and Allied territories are completely liberated and until victory is complete over all the enemy Powers. During the war military needs are paramount and all controls necessary for operational purposes are in consequence reserved to the Supreme Commander of the Allied Armies in any theatre of operations. In respect of certain of the territories under the administration of the Committee, agreements already exist between the French authorities and the United Kingdom authorities. The creation of the French National Committee of Liberation may make it necessary to revise these agreements, and His Majesty's Government in the United Kingdom assume that, pending their revision, all such agreements concluded since June 1940, except in so far as these have been automatically made inapplicable by the formation of the French Committee of National Liberation, will remain in force as between His Majesty's Government in the United Kingdom and the French Committee of National Liberation." '

Mr. Eden telegraphed to the Foreign Office on August 25 that the Americans had obstinately refused to use the word 'recognition' (i.e. in the full sense of the term), but that we did not want to draw attention to the difference between their formula and ours.[1] Mr. Eden therefore hoped that the British press could be encouraged to welcome our act of recognition without making any comparisons disagreeable to the Americans. Mr. Churchill sent a message on the same day to Mr. Macmillan asking him to tell the members of the National Council mentioned in his previous telegram[2] that they would be wise 'to welcome the American declaration in most cordial terms, and not to draw invidious distinction between any of the forms in which recognition is accorded. On the contrary, the more pleasure they show at the American declaration the more value it will have for them.'

---

[1] For the American formula, see *F.R.U.S.*, 1943, II, 185.
[2] See above, p. 457.

CHAPTER XXXII

The surrender of Italy, July–September 1943

(i)

Italian peace approaches in the winter of 1942–43: differences between British and American views about invading the Italian mainland: the dismissal and arrest of Mussolini.

THE British victories in the Western Desert, the Allied landings in North Africa and the German failure before Stalingrad had an effect on the already depressed morale of the Italian army and people who could hardly fail to realise that Italy was on the losing side. A number of peace-feelers now reached the British Government from Italian sources; one of these approaches seemed possibly to have originated from Ciano. In a minute of December 2, 1942, to the Prime Minister Mr. Eden summed up the peace-feelers (a) from Italians outside Italy. Mr. Eden decided against following up any of the approaches: he thought that contacts with Italians serving the existing régime might lead to doubts about the genuineness of our declaration that we intended to destroy fascism. Anyhow, there was, as in the case of the German approaches, very great doubt whether these who made them could carry out the conditions upon which the Allies would insist.

One of these peace-feelers came through the Italian Consul-General at Geneva, and took the form of a request to establish communication between the British Government and an unnamed person in the entourage of the Italian Crown Prince; the implication behind this proposal was that the Crown Prince might be willing to bring about the overthrow of Mussolini and the Fascist regime provided that Italy were treated as an ally if Italian forces operated against Germany, and that the British Government would support the continuation of the monarchy in Italy. Mr. Eden told the Prime Minister that he had not pursued this contact because he did not think the Crown Prince capable of starting a revolution against Mussolini and because the British Government could not accept his two conditions.

The Italians in question, however, persisted in their approach. On December 12, 1942, Mr. Eden wrote a second minute to the (b) Prime Minister in which he stated that the 'unnamed person' was

---

(a) PMM/42/292; R8802/3700/22. (b) PMM/42/303, R8802/3700/22.

the Duke of Aosta.[1] The duke was represented as being prepared to lead an armed uprising against Mussolini and the regime. He was confident that he could secure the support of the Italian navy and certain elements in the Bersaglieri, though he could not depend on the army, and regarded the Italian air force as definitely Fascist.

He asked from the British Government the following guarantees: (i) Royal Air Force support to deal with the German and Italian air forces; (ii) an agreed landing by British and American troops on the understanding that they came not to conquer and occupy Italy but as allies to assist in the overthrow of the regime; (iii) no demands to be made for handing over the Italian fleet; (iv) the preservation of the monarchy in Italy. These 'guarantees' were to be given in the name of all the Allies. The duke appeared to be intending to organise and lead the rising on his own responsibility with the object of re-establishing the House of Savoy on constitutional lines and replacing the King of Italy by the Crown Prince. Mr. Eden thought that the approach was probably genuine, but that the plan was not practicable; in any case we could not be sure that the proposal for an agreed landing was not a trap. Nevertheless the prize to be won if we could contribute to an Italian collapse was very great; Mr. Eden therefore suggested that we should not refuse to listen to any further communication. The Duke of Aosta had undertaken to discuss his plan with the Crown Prince and to inform us of the result. We might await this information, and for the present do nothing more.

The Prime Minister agreed with Mr. Eden's suggestion, and on December 17 Mr. Eden informed Mr. Winant and M. Maisky of (a) the Italian approach. The Department of State, in reply, agreed with the line taken by Mr. Eden and also raised the general question of Anglo-American policy towards Italians in the service of the Fascist regime who might now wish to come over to the Allied side.

Mr. Eden replied with a statement embodying the conclusions (b) laid down in a memorandum approved by the War Cabinet on November 20, 1942. He said that the Allied aim must be to 'knock Italy out of the war' as quickly as possible. This result would be secured if Italy made a separate peace or if dissatisfaction and disorder in the country became serious enough to force the Germans to establish a full-scale occupation. In the latter event the Germans would have not only to provide troops for the occupation of Italy but for the replacement of the Italians on the Russian front, in France, and in the Balkans. We shared the doubts of the American military authorities about the value of Italy as an ally; we might well find it more to our interest that Italy should remain a member of

---

[1] Formerly Duke of Spoleto and brother of the late Duke of Aosta.

(a) R9071/3700/22. (b) WP(42)545.

the Axis, and develop into a German commitment and become, as such, an increasing drain on German strength.

We did not think that a party could arise in Italy both willing and able to conclude a separate peace until the Germans were so much weakened that they could not control Italy, and a national leader had emerged with sufficient strength to displace Mussolini. Neither of these conditions seemed likely to be fulfilled in the immediate future. In particular, there were no signs of the appearance of an alternative leader to Mussolini. Of the Italians outside Italy Count Sforza had most influence, but in our view he had been out of the country too long to count on much support.

There was little chance of the Church taking a stand against the régime. The King of Italy was regarded as a willing tool of Fascism and the Italian people appeared no longer to be looking to him as a leader. In spite of the approach by the Duke of Aosta we were extremely doubtful of the willingness or ability of any of the Royal Family to lead a revolt against Fascism. A general—e.g. Badoglio— might be able at some time to overthrow the Government, but dissatisfaction in the army did not seem as yet to have reached a stage at which a military rising would have sufficient support. The moderate members of the Fascist party also might at some time take a stand against Mussolini, but the leaders still appeared to be united, and convinced that co-operation with Germany in the prosecution of the war was essential to the maintenance of their own position.

Our view therefore was that we should not count on the possibility of a separate peace with Italy, but should aim at provoking such disorder as would necessitate a German occupation. We had considered whether we could attempt to detach the Italian people from the regime by promising them lenient peace terms, but we had decided against such a plan. The minimum terms likely to appeal to the Italian people would be a guarantee of the pre-war frontiers of metropolitan Italy, but we could not commit ourselves on this point, since it might be desirable after the war to effect frontier rectifications in favour of Yugoslavia and possibly of Austria. Our policy should be therefore to tell the Italians that they must pay the penalty for allowing themselves to become involved in the war as an ally of Germany. We should keep up heavy indiscriminate raids on Italian cities in order to cause an internal collapse which would compel the Germans to take over the defence of Italy and Italian obligations in the Balkans.

Mr. Churchill had not altogether agreed with Mr. Eden's conclusion in the memorandum of November 20 that a German (a)

(a) WP(42)546.

occupation of Italy would be to the advantage of the Allies. In any case the Germans themselves might think it better to stand on the Brenner. Mr. Churchill was also less certain that the Italians would be unable to make a separate peace. He wrote that one could not be sure what a thoroughly defeated people would do. There might be a sudden fall of Mussolini followed by a popular demand for peace. Mr. Churchill, however, accepted Mr. Eden's view, and the military decisions taken at Casablanca[1] did not extend beyond an invasion of Sicily after the Germans and Italians had been cleared out of North Africa.

The unexpected delay in finishing the Tunisian campaign meant that the operation against Sicily was also delayed. On May 13 the final enemy surrender in North Africa took place and the Allies were free to move against Sicily. They had also to decide what to do after Sicily had been won. On this subject the divergence between British and American views, which had already shown itself in previous discussions, became even more important. Mr. Churchill wanted an invasion of the Italian mainland as the easiest way of using the Allied forces already concentrated in the Mediterranean, 'knocking out' Italy, and at the same time relieving the pressure on the Russian armies by diverting German resources to the Mediterranean. This diversion was also necessary if Germany were to be weakened sufficiently to secure the success of a cross-Channel invasion. The Americans, on the other hand, were afraid that Mr. Churchill's Mediterranean strategy would delay the preparations for the cross-Channel invasion, and so postpone the attack on Japan which was the ultimate aim of the United States. They continued to suspect the British of arguing for a Mediterranean policy in order to serve their own long-range political interests. The Americans also wished to get Italy out of the war, but were more inclined to think that an offer of lenient treatment would detach the Italian people from Mussolini. Moreover, while Great Britain had suffered directly from the Italian entry into the war and from the pre-war policy of Mussolini, the Americans had no particular grievances against the Italians, and, as the President and his advisers well knew, there was a very large body of voters of Italian origin in the United States who, though anti-fascist, would be strongly opposed to a severe treatment of Italy after her surrender.

One of the chief reasons for the Prime Minister's visit to Washington in May, 1943, was that he hoped to settle these differences of view about planning.[2]

---

[1] See below, pp. 546–7.

[2] Mr. Churchill had suggested a military conference in Algiers. It has been said—with much probability—that the Americans objected to Algiers because their commanders in the Mediterranean would have taken the British view.

The decisions taken at Washington were, from the British point of view, an unsatisfactory compromise, since they did not lay down a definite plan of campaign for the Mediterranean. The proposal for a cross-Channel operation in 1943 was now given up, except in the unlikely event of a German collapse, and the target date of the proposed full-scale invasion was fixed as May 1, 1944. The Americans continued to fear that Mr. Churchill's proposals for the Mediterranean would delay the concentration of forces for this invasion, and upset the timetable. General Eisenhower was to be instructed to plan such operations in exploitation of the invasion of Sicily as (a) were 'best calculated to eliminate Italy from the war and to contain the maximum number of German forces'. The Combined Chiefs of Staff would decide later 'which of the various specific operations should be adopted'. After the Washington meeting the Prime Minister persuaded the President to allow General Marshall to cross the Atlantic with him for a further conference at Algiers. Here—at the end of May—the Americans still refused to agree in advance to (b) the invasion of Italy; General Marshall wanted only a comparatively minor operation such as the occupation of Sardinia and Corsica. On the other hand General Eisenhower was in favour of the invasion of southern Italy if the attack on Sicily had a rapid success. No final decision was taken, but General Eisenhower was now instructed to make recommendations—not merely to set out alternatives—in accordance with the progress made in Sicily.

The Prime Minister expected that events themselves would lead to what he called the 'desired solutions'.[1] This expectation was soon realised. On the night of July 9–10 British paratroops and American airborne troops landed in Sicily. Early on the morning of July 10 the British Eighth Army (including Canadian divisions) and the United States Seventh Army established themselves on Sicilian beaches. The Italian forces in Sicily offered little resistance, and the civil population welcomed the invaders. Only the Germans fought stubbornly in a retreat to the north-east corner of the island. They were not driven out until August 17, but within a few days of the landings it was clear that the way would soon be open to the invasion of the mainland. On July 16 the Combined Chiefs of Staff agreed on a plan for a double attack—across the Straits of Messina and, further north, a landing at Salerno. Furthermore, the greater part of the Allied Air Forces, which had previously concentrated on 'softening

---

[1] Mr. Churchill also thought that Turkey might be persuaded to enter the war. Neither the British nor the Americans favoured at this time extending operations to the Italian mainland in order to support an anti-fascist insurrection, since this action might merely immobilise Allied troops to no advantage.

(a) CCS. No. 2426 (COS(43)286(0), Part III). (b) COS(43)290(0).

Q

operations' in Sicily, could be used at once for targets on the mainland. Naples was bombed three times between July 14 and 17, and the first raid on Rome took place on July 19. On July 24 the Fascist Grand Council voted that the King should take command of all the Italian armed forces. On the following day the King dismissed Mussolini and ordered his detention. The King appointed Marshal Badoglio as head of a new Government. Mussolini himself was taken by surprise at this sudden action; the Fascist militia made no attempt to rescue him.[1]

The members of the new Government were, in a sense, as helpless as the personal dictatorship which they had overthrown. The general and overwhelming popular demand in Italy was for peace, but the Government could not make peace. An attempt to do so would merely reduce Italy from the status of a despised ally of Germany to that of a German-occupied country. German reinforcements had been sent into Italy in May, and now came in larger numbers. The Italian Government had no plans for resisting them, and dared not provoke them to attack. In any case the Italians would have put up little resistance. The King and Marshal Badoglio therefore tried—without success—to deceive the Germans by announcing that they would continue to fight on the side of Germany; at the same time they made secret approaches to the Allies, in the hope that the Anglo-American armies would rescue them from their absurd position.

Note to Section (i). The fall of Mussolini.

After the British victory at El Alamein and the Allied landings in North Africa, Mussolini could not but realise the desperate straits of his country and the increasing unpopularity of the Fascist régime and of himself as leader. In December, 1942, he sent Ciano (he was too ill to go in person) to see Hitler and to recommend a separate peace with Russia or at least an abandonment of the offensive and a withdrawal to a defensive line on the eastern front; the Axis forces could then concentrate on the war in the Mediterranean and the Balkans. Hitler rejected these suggestions out of hand. At the end of January, and in the hope of strengthening his own position at home by putting the blame for the Italian defeats upon the generals, he dismissed General Cavallero, Chief of the General Staff,

---

[1] See note at the end of this section.

and appointed General Ambrosio in his place. On February 5 he also dismissed most of his Ministers, including Ciano who went as Ambassador to the Vatican. Mussolini took direct control of the Foreign Ministry with Bastianini as Under-Secretary. In March, 1943, Mussolini again tried to get Hitler to agree to his proposals for peace with Russia or a 'shut down' on the eastern front. Early in April he repeated these proposals at a meeting with Hitler at Schloss Klessheim, near Salzburg. Bastianini also urged Mussolini to suggest a programme which would rally European opinion to the German New Order and counteract Allied propaganda based on pronouncements such as the Atlantic Charter. Once again Hitler would not listen.

Meanwhile Italian opinion, including that of the King, had come to the conclusion that the country could be saved from complete disaster only by the removal of Mussolini. The King was indeed waiting for an opportunity which might come with a move by leading Fascists to end Mussolini's personal dictatorship. On July 14, five days after the Allied landings in Sicily, General Ambrosio suggested to Mussolini an Italian surrender rather than the continuation of a hopeless fight. Two days later a group of leading Fascists put pressure on Mussolini to summon the Fascist Grand Council in order to give it a practical share in the responsibility of government and administration. Mussolini agreed to call the Council together, but, before it met, Hitler asked him to come to a meeting at Feltre, near Venice. Bastianini and General Ambrosio, who went with Mussolini to Feltre, wanted him to insist upon Italian freedom of action: in other words, on Italy's right to withdraw from the war and the necessity for her to do so. Mussolini, who at this time was near to physical and mental collapse, made hardly any effort to put the Italian case.

After the Feltre meeting the dissident Fascist leaders, with Grandi at their head, decided to propose at the Grand Council that the King should take command of the army and that all the Fascist organs of government should be revived. Grandi made no secret of his plan; the motion which he intended to propose was shown to Mussolini. At the same time the King told General Ambrosio that he had now decided to put Mussolini under arrest. The Fascist 'conspirators', if this term can be used of them, gave him a constitutional pretext for the action which he had long had in mind. At a lengthy and confused meeting of the Grand Council on the night of July 24–5, Grandi's motion was carried. Mussolini made no real resistance to the Grand Council, and was taken by surprise when, at a royal audience in the afternoon of July 25, the King told him that he was dismissed and that Marshal Badoglio would be the head of a new Government. Mussolini was arrested as he was leaving the Palace, and with his arrest the whole Fascist regime collapsed. The Fascist militia made no attempt to rescue him, and the Italian people accepted the fall of the regime with relief and hope that it would be followed by the withdrawal of Italy from the war. For an account of the situation in Italy, and Italo–German relations from the last months of 1942 to the fall of Mussolini, see F. W. Deakin, *The Brutal Friendship* (Weidenfeld and Nicholson, 1962).

(ii)

Anglo-American discussions on a reply to an Italian request for an armistice.

Owing to the unwillingness of the Americans to commit themselves to an invasion of Italy, the Allies also had no agreed plan for dealing with an Italian unconditional surrender. The Foreign Office and the British Chiefs of Staff had indeed been discussing for some time the terms to be imposed and the administration[1] to be set up after the Italian surrender. Towards the end of January, 1943, informa-
(a) tion had been received that Marshal Badoglio was prepared, if he had Allied assistance, to overthrow the Fascist régime and to set up a military government in Italy; he wanted to send a representative to Cyrenaica to discuss the matter with British representatives. One of Marshal Badoglio's suggestions was for recruiting an Italian military force from prisoners of war and other Italians outside Italy. The Foreign Office did not regard this suggestion as likely to be of much use; nevertheless they thought that we should receive an Italian envoy without committing ourselves to any proposals. The
(b) War Cabinet on March 18 also agreed that the envoy should be received, but that he must come 'unconditionally', and that no promises should be made to him; we should be on guard against possible political repercussions from dealing with Marshal Badoglio, who had commanded the Italian forces in Abyssinia.

Although no further communication seems to have been received from the Italians at this time the Foreign Office and the Chiefs of Staff continued their discussion of the terms to be imposed in the
(c) event of an Italian collapse or surrender. In June they sent alternative British draft proposals covering the suspension of hostilities with Italy to the United States Government. There were, however, important divergencies between the British and American views. Some of these divergencies were due to a misunderstanding of the British plan; others showed a substantial difference of ideas. The British drafts covered two hypotheses: the signature of 'articles of surrender', i.e. an armistice, with an Italian Government, or an Italian collapse, with the consequence that no Government would exist with which we could deal. The American view was that we could not sign 'articles of surrender' with any Italian Government, but that the King or the Head of the Government (at this time Mussolini) or the Italian Commander-in-Chief, or all of these, should sign a broad acknowledgment of unconditional surrender

---

[1] I have not dealt with this question in detail.

(a) WP(43)27; WM(43)9, C.A. (b) WM(43)42, C.A. (c) COS(43)296(o); R6347, 6349/6050/22; WP(43)340.

involving the abdication of the King, the removal of the Head of the Government, and the transfer of all powers to the Allies. Thereupon the Allied military commander would govern Italy, i.e. set up an Allied administration until other arrangements were made.

In a memorandum of July 12 the Foreign Office pointed out that (a) the Americans had assumed that our 'articles of surrender' would be 'negotiated' with an Italian Government. We should make it clear that we proposed unconditional surrender followed by the imposition of terms which the Italians would have to accept. The Americans also failed to realise that the rights of a military occupant, as recognised by international law and the Hague Convention, would be insufficient for us, e.g. (i) we should have no rights over Italian territory which we did not occupy and should therefore be compelled in practice to occupy the whole country; we should also have no rights over enemy property, forces or personnel outside the territory in our occupation—e.g. Italian ships in neutral ports, Italian forces in the Balkans and on the Russian front, and Italian workers in Germany; (ii) we should not have sovereign powers in the occupied territory and therefore could not carry into effect fundamental changes in the local law or system of government; (iii) the Italians would be under no obligation to co-operate with us.

The Foreign Office considered that there were very strong arguments in favour of concluding 'articles of surrender' with an Italian authority either at the time of unconditional surrender or as soon afterwards as possible. Otherwise—apart from any limitation on our powers in Italy—we should be putting an unnecessary strain on our resources by taking over the whole burden of administration and the maintenance of public order in Italy. Furthermore the Italians— before or after our invasion had taken place—might themselves overthrow the Fascist Government and set up an anti-Fascist Government which would ask for terms. It would probably suit us to accept their appeal on the understanding that it meant unconditional surrender. We should then dictate our terms, the first of which would be the right of military occupation of the area controlled by such a Government, but we might hand over to it the administration of those parts of the country which we did not need to occupy for strategic reasons.

The Foreign Office also regarded as impracticable the American proposal that an instrument of unconditional surrender should be signed by the King of Italy, Mussolini, or the Commander-in-Chief or all three. Mussolini would be unlikely to sign his own death warrant even to save Italy from further destruction; the King would probably not be willing to seal his own abdication. Similarly the

(a) DO(43)15; R6532/242/22.

Italian Commander-in-Chief could hardly take the responsibility for surrendering unconditionally on behalf of the whole nation. If, therefore, we insisted on this mode of procedure, we might delay the surrender. There was also an important political consideration. The American 'abdication' plan might be held to amount in law to the cession of legal sovereignty over Italy to the United Nations, and thus to the annexation of the country by the United Nations.

The War Cabinet Committee on Armistice Terms and Administration endorsed the view of the Foreign Office; Lord Halifax was
(a) therefore instructed on July 22 to submit these views to the United States Government, and Mr. Macmillan was instructed to inform
(b) General Eisenhower of them. Lord Halifax replied on July 24 that the question had been discussed with officials of the State Department. The Americans—at all events at this level of discussion—had agreed that it would be undesirable to force Italian signature to a document transferring sovereignty to the Allies.[1] They also agreed that it might be necessary to make use of an acceptable Italian administration. They assumed that we should not accept a Fascist administration, and asked whether we would accept Marshal Badoglio or a Government headed by the Italian General Staff, and what were our views about the Italian Royal Family.

The only remaining point of difference on procedure thus seemed to be on the question whether the Allied Commander-in-Chief should be entitled to deal on his own authority with a request for a general termination of hostilities. The Americans had hitherto regarded it as essential that, in order to avoid delay and unnecessary loss of life, the Commander-in-Chief should have such authority, and that he should also control the country until the two Governments had come to a decision about its future administration.

The Foreign Office drafted a reply dealing with this point. They suggested that General Eisenhower might be authorised to conclude comprehensive general terms of surrender with the Italian Supreme Commander. This instrument would be an abbreviated version of the full instrument of surrender for conclusion with an Italian administration. On the other hand a compromise of this kind would entail the disadvantage that no Italian civil authority would be obliged to see that essential provisions in our terms were carried out. We would therefore accept the plan only if events should make it necessary.

This draft was not sent to Lord Halifax because on the night of July 25–6 news was received of the fall of Mussolini, and of the

---

[1] Lord Halifax used this term: the term should have been 'United Nations'.

(a) R6532/242/22. (b) R6725/242/22.

formation of a new Government by Marshal Badoglio. There was at first little information about the character of this new Government. (a) The Foreign Office thought that, if the purpose of the King and Marshal Badoglio in getting rid of Mussolini had been to open negotiations with the Allies, they would probably ask us, in return for military surrender and the abolition of the Fascist régime, to protect Italy against the Germans and to recognise the continuance of the House of Savoy. We could give only one answer. We must refuse to enter into negotiations, insist on unconditional surrender, and then dictate our terms. These terms would not include a guarantee to defend Italy against the Germans, but would stipulate for the use of Italian territories as bases for our own operations. We should require the abolition of Fascism and the surrender of Mussolini. We had not come to a decision about the future of the House of Savoy.

We had therefore to consider what we should do if the Badoglio Government asked us to 'discuss' the terms which would follow their surrender. Should we discuss our terms or insist on nothing but unconditional surrender? We could sign an instrument of surrender with the King and Marshal Badoglio without being sure that they represented a satisfactory non-Fascist Government because we had explained to the Americans that we were not bound subsequently to recognise or work with a Government from whom we accepted an offer of unconditional surrender. If, however, we found that the Badoglio Government were satisfactory, we should find it difficult to resist their continuance (and that of the House of Savoy) after capitulation. We should indeed have a strong military interest in handing over as much as possible of the administration to an acceptable Italian authority.

The Prime Minister and the President exchanged messages on (b) July 26. The Prime Minister said that the changes in Italy probably meant that we should receive peace proposals; we ought therefore to consult together about joint action. The President in his message also asked for the Prime Minister's opinion. His own view was that, if we received any overtures, we should ensure that we secured the use of all Italian territory, means of transportation and airfields for the prosecution of the war against the Germans in the 'north' as well as in the Balkan peninsula. We should 'come as close as possible to unconditional surrender followed by good treatment of the Italian populace'. The 'head devil should be surrendered, together with his chief partners in crime'. The President also said that the Allied commanders in the field should not fix on general terms without his (the President's) and the Prime Minister's approval.

(a) R6774/6447/22. (b) T1113/3, No. 382; T1115/3, No. 324 (Churchill Papers/242).

This message seemed to show that the President assumed that we should effect the surrender by obtaining the signature of some Italian authority. The Prime Minister, after receiving the President's (a) message, drew up a note (entitled 'Thoughts on the Fall of Mussolini') amplifying our requirements from the Italians and also assuming that we were likely to receive an offer of negotiation from the new Italian Government. In addition to the control of Italian territory and means of transportation, we should require the immediate surrender or effective demobilisation of the Italian fleet, the surrender of Italian forces outside Italy, such disarmament of the air and ground forces as we found desirable, and the immediate liberation of British prisoners of war; the Italians must prevent the transport of these prisoners of war to Germany. There would probably be fighting between the German and Italian troops, especially south of Rome. We must demand the surrender of these Germans, and, if necessary, send assistance to the Italians for the purpose of obtaining it. We should be guided by circumstances in our decision about further action north of Rome, but we should try to seize points on the east and west coast railways 'as far north as we dare. And this is a time to dare.' We should encourage the Italian population to turn against the Germans in order that the 'new, liberated anti-Fascist Italy shall afford us . . . a safe and friendly area on which we can base the whole forward air attack upon south and central Germany'. Mr. Churchill enlarged on the advantages of this air attack, and the opportunity offered by the surrender of the Italian armies in the Balkans to send commandos and supplies into Yugoslavia, Albania, and Greece. The collapse of Italy should also 'fix the moment for putting the strongest pressure on Turkey to act in accordance with the spirit of the Alliance'. Finally, we should try—without sacrificing any military advantages—to get possession of Mussolini and his chief associates. We could then decide, in consultation with the Americans, and later with the Russians, what to do with them. Mr. Churchill wrote: 'Some may prefer prompt execution without trial except for identification purposes. Others may prefer that they be kept in confinement till the end of the war in Europe, and their fate decided with that of other war criminals. Personally, I am fairly indifferent on this matter, provided always that no solid military advantages are sacrificed for the sake of immediate vengeance.'

(b)   The War Cabinet discussed the Prime Minister's note on July 26. Mr. Eden explained that the main point of difference between ourselves and the Americans on the question of an armistice was whether any kind of Italian administration should be allowed to act. Our view was that it would be much to our advantage to have the country

---

(a) WP(43)339. (b) WM(43)103.1, C.A.

run for us as far as was possible. The general opinion of the War Cabinet was that, owing to the very great military advantage of securing a 'docile' Italy, and possibly an Italy hostile to the Germans, we should accept terms of surrender from an Italian administration now that Mussolini had been deposed and the Fascist régime broken up. On the other hand we ought to avoid any phrase suggesting the conclusion of terms of peace. With the approval of the War Cabinet, therefore, new instructions were sent to Lord Halifax on the night of (a) July 26–7 in place of the draft previously drawn up.[1] The instructions stated that, if we wished to do so, we now might be able to impose terms of surrender upon an Italian administration. We ought therefore to decide what reply General Eisenhower should give if he received a request for the cessation of hostilities. In any case the President had agreed that General Eisenhower should not have authority to conclude general terms of surrender without the approval of the British and American Governments.

We considered that we could accept either the King or Marshal Badoglio for the simple purpose of effecting a surrender and imposing our terms. We could not yet decide on the political issue of our subsequent relations with the surrendering authority. All we asked now was that the United States Government should agree on the text of articles of surrender.

Lord Halifax replied on July 27 that the State Department were (b) discussing the text and that there seemed to be some uncertainty whether the word 'surrender' referred to the cessation of hostilities by the Italian armed forces or to the complete capitulation of the country. General Marshall's view was that General Eisenhower must be able to take immediate military advantage of an offer of surrender; he could not wait while the two Governments discussed whether the offer was acceptable. He might wish, for example, to send several divisions into Rome at once, possibly by train, and even a nominal continuation of hostilities might make this plan impossible. The United States Chiefs of Staff had told Mr. Hull that General Eisenhower must have power to deal with the Italian military or civilian authorities for the surrender of the armed forces.

Lord Halifax thought that we might agree to give General Eisenhower this power, and leave the capitulation of the country as a whole for reference to the two Governments. In any case, if we had agreed with the Americans on the terms, and if we also considered that we could negotiate them through the King of Italy and Marshal Badoglio, could not General Eisenhower accept both the military surrender and the general capitulation?

---

[1] See above, p. 470.

(a) R6774/6447/22. (b) R6793/6447/22.

Q*

(a)   General Eisenhower had also telegraphed on July 27 to the Combined Chiefs of Staff giving his views on procedure in the event of an Italian request for an armistice before the Allies had invaded the Italian mainland. He outlined the military terms which we should impose. These terms included the evacuation of German land forces from the Italian mainland in stages lasting altogether not more than one month. General Eisenhower regarded it as inexpedient to require the surrender of the German forces, since we could hardly expect the Italians to turn to this extent against their former Allies. Moreover, if they did so, they would not be getting the one thing in which they were interested—i.e. peace. General Eisenhower suggested that he should broadcast the military terms at once, since they would offer the Italian people such a promise of honourable peace that no Italian Government could refuse them.

(b)   On July 28 the British members of the Joint Staff Mission at Washington telegraphed that they would soon have to discuss General Eisenhower's proposal with their American colleagues. Agreement had not yet been reached on the military terms since the matter was being discussed at a 'high level' and the United States War Department had been instructed not to agree even to the purely military terms until the political basis had been settled. The Chiefs of Staff, however, had drawn up a draft directive for General Eisenhower. This text—which the British members now telegraphed—laid down, *inter alia*, that all Italian forces should remain in barracks, camps, or on their ships, and that Axis forces other than Italian should be made prisoners of war.

These telegrams from General Eisenhower and the British members of the Joint Staff Mission in Washington were considered at once. The Foreign Office regarded them as unsatisfactory and suggested a draft reply. The draft, with some modifications, was accepted by the Defence Committee and telegraphed to Washington

(c)   during the night of July 28–9 as a statement of the British view. The statement began by agreeing that the word 'surrender' was open to misunderstanding. On the British view 'unconditional' surrender meant both military and civil surrender. The Americans, however, wanted primarily to ensure the cessation of hostilities; they had therefore proposed a procedure in two stages; (i) we should effect the actual surrender by a purely military document containing provisions for putting the Italian military machine out of action; (ii) we should then dictate our full terms to a civil administration.

The British plan was to produce our full requirements as soon as we received an Italian offer to surrender, and to say that we would

(a) NAF 302, R6793/6447/22. (b) JSM tels. 1106–7, R6793/6447/22. (c) R6793/6447/22.

not stop our attacks until these requirements had been accepted. We would agree to authorise General Eisenhower to sign our instrument of surrender (of which the Americans had copies, and upon which alone we would be willing to suspend hostilities) with the King of Italy and Marshal Badoglio or with the King alone, so that there would be no question of keeping General Eisenhower waiting while the two Governments were deciding whether the Italian offer was acceptable.

We preferred our method because it made certain from the outset that a central Italian authority would be under obligation to carry out our civil as well as our military requirements. We considered the American plan unsuitable for the following reasons: (i) once we had stopped fighting, we could not be sure of getting an Italian signature to our further terms; (ii) without such terms (i.e. on the basis of a purely military surrender) we should have to occupy and administer the whole country; (iii) since we were prepared to deal with the King and the Badoglio Government and they in turn would be able to sign and enforce civil as well as military terms, why should we not require them to do so? If they refused, their surrender would not be unconditional, and we should go on fighting. In any case, if they refused at this stage, would they accept the terms later when fighting had ceased?

General Eisenhower could conclude local surrenders with individual Italian commanders if he wished to send his troops into any given areas, but we were opposed to a general cessation of hostilities on terms not binding upon an Italian civil Government when such a Government existed and we were prepared to deal with it. We thought it inadvisable to broadcast in advance the military terms upon which we would stop fighting; it also seemed to us unwise to try to make these terms as attractive as possible to the Italian people now in order to force the hand of their Government, since we should only be increasing our difficulties later on when we came to impose the much less attractive terms in our full instrument. We therefore proposed that General Eisenhower should not make public any terms, but that he should put forward the full instrument for signature in reply to any request from the King or Marshal Badoglio for the cessation of hostilities. If signature were refused, we should go on fighting until the Italians surrendered unconditionally. In exceptional circumstances General Eisenhower alone could sign a purely military document on grounds of urgent military necessity, e.g. if the King and Marshal Badoglio's Government disappeared, and were not replaced by a central authority whose signature would be of value.

We also regarded General Eisenhower's suggested conditions as incomplete if compared with our own draft instrument. Thus he omitted to mention (i) our right to impose measures of disarmament, demobilisation, and demilitarisation; (ii) the handing over of war criminals; (iii) our right to attack and seize German armed forces and material; (iv) the obligation upon the Italian authorities to carry out the orders of the United Nations; (v) the disposal of Italian merchant shipping. General Eisenhower's own 'conditions' and the draft directive proposed by the Combined Chiefs of Staff seemed too vaguely drafted, and open to differences of interpretation. We needed, not hastily drafted instructions, but a carefully thought out document for signature by the Italians.

On July 29 General Eisenhower broadcast a message to the Italian people congratulating them on getting rid of Mussolini and calling upon them to cease at once from helping the Germans. At the request of the British Government the broadcast included a warning against allowing the Germans to take British or Allied prisoners of war out of Italy. Mr. Churchill felt very strongly on this

(a) point. He sent a message about it, through the Swiss Government, to the King of Italy on July 29 and also told President Roosevelt that, if the King of Italy and Marshal Badoglio allowed our prisoners to be removed without using force to try to prevent any such action, British public opinion would refuse to accept negotiations with the new Italian Government. Mr. Churchill also told President Roosevelt that the War Cabinet were quite clear that we should not broadcast armistice terms to the enemy. A responsible Italian Government ought to ask formally for an armistice on the basis of our principle of unconditional surrender. Mr. Churchill pointed out to the President that our draft of the terms followed the main lines of General Eisenhower's draft, but that it was more precise, and cast in a form suited to a discussion between plenipotentiaries rather than a popular appeal. Mr. Churchill added: 'There are great dangers in trying to dish this sort of dose up with jam for the patient.'

Mr. Churchill also repeated to the President the Foreign Office view that the terms should cover civil as well as military requirements, and that it would be better for them to be settled by envoys appointed by the British and United States Governments rather than by the general commanding in the field. General Eisenhower would, of course, deal with proposals for local surrender coming from troops on his immediate front.

(b) President Roosevelt's reply reached London on the night of July 29–30. The President agreed that General Eisenhower should not broadcast the armistice terms; on the other hand he thought it necessary that he (General Eisenhower) should be authorised to

(a) T1143/3, No. 387 (Churchill Papers/249/2; R6897/242/22). (b) T1148/3, No. 330 (Churchill Papers/249/2; R6959/6651/22).

state our conditions if the Italian Government asked for an armistice. The President therefore suggested that the Prime Minister should agree to allow General Eisenhower to use the terms proposed by him in his telegram of July 27[1] with the exception of the phrase that the evacuation of Germans was to be completed within a month. General Eisenhower should also tell the Italian Government that details of the military and civil requirements of the Allies would be discussed at a later date and settled by envoys appointed by the interested parties.

On receiving this telegram the Prime Minister immediately (a) summoned the War Cabinet, and, with their approval, replied in the early morning of July 30 that there was no reason to suppose that a (b) proposal for an armistice would be made to General Eisenhower, whose forces were in contact with the enemy only in Sicily, and even there with Germans and not with Italians. The Italian Government were more likely to negotiate through the Vatican, or through the Turks or the Swiss. If, however, General Eisenhower were approached suddenly by an envoy, Mr. Churchill agreed that he should have precise terms, embodying the principle of unconditional surrender, which he could use at once as a basis for granting an armistice. Mr. Churchill also agreed to accept General Eisenhower's proposed conditions subject to additional amendments: the references in the articles as drafted to German forces should be omitted, and in their place a general paragraph should be inserted to the effect that the Italians would do their best to deny to the Germans facilities which might be employed against the Allies. This change was necessary because we could not enforce any precise guarantees in the matter. In place of a paragraph requiring the acknowledgment of the overriding authority of the Allied Commander-in-Chief, there should be substituted a new clause, wider in scope, reserving for the Commander-in-Chief the right to take any measure necessary in his opinion for the protection of the interests of the Allied forces and the prosecution of the war, and binding the Italian Government to take 'such administrative or other action as the Commander-in-Chief may require. And in particular the Commander-in-Chief will establish Allied Military Government over such parts of Italian territory as he may deem necessary.' The purpose of this new clause was to establish the authority of the Commander-in-Chief over existing Italian agencies apart from the establishment of military government. Mr. Churchill also suggested the addition of provisions for (i) our full right to impose measures of disarmament, demobilisation and

---

[1] See p. 474.

(a) WM(43)108. (b) T1150/3 (Churchill Papers/249/12.)

demilitarisation; (ii) the handing over of war criminals; (iii) the disposal of Italian merchant shipping.

If, however, the Italian offer were not made to General Eisenhower, or if—as seemed likely—there were time to do so, Mr. Churchill hoped that the President would consider the 'most carefully drafted terms' which we had sent to Washington a fortnight earlier.[1] Finally Mr. Churchill said how glad he was that the President agreed that the terms should not be broadcast before an armistice had been requested or even immediately afterwards. The terms would certainly shock the Italian people and give the Germans full information upon which to act.

The Prime Minister also sent a telegram to Mr. Macmillan telling him that in the opinion of the War Cabinet General Eisenhower should not continue to broadcast appeals for peace to the Italian people, and certainly not the suggested armistice terms dressed up in popular form.

On the morning of July 30, after a discussion in the Foreign Office, Mr. Eden at first decided to suggest to the Prime Minister that he should send a further telegram to the President making it clear that we disliked the 'two-stage procedure'. The Foreign Office view was that, if we still insisted upon unconditional surrender, we must impose our full terms without discussion. The full terms, even as amended by the Prime Minister, were a good deal stiffer than the 'conditions' which General Eisenhower proposed for the first stage. Hence there was a danger that the Italian people would feel that we had trapped them into signing easy terms and then after disarming them, faced them with more stringent terms incompatible with 'honourable capitulation'. We should thus make our immediate position in Italy more difficult by stirring up popular indignation and disorder, and we should also lay up a store of resentment against us for years to come.

On the other hand if, as the President appeared to suggest, we intended actually to discuss our full terms, we should no longer be insisting upon unconditional surrender. In this case we should shape our policy accordingly, but hitherto all our arguments with the Americans had been based on the contrary assumption.

In the end Mr. Eden came to the conclusion that he would not send a minute to the Prime Minister until he had discussed the whole matter again in the Foreign Office.[2] Before this discussion took place
(a) another message from Mr. Roosevelt to the Prime Minister had

---

[1] It is impossible to discover from the documents when any terms were sent to the United States between the original draft of June 10 and the revised instructions to Halifax of July 26–7.

[2] Mr. Eden was in the country during the evening of July 30.

(a) T1156/3, No. 332 (Churchill Papers/249; R6971/242/22).

reached London. Mr. Roosevelt agreed that the Italians were more likely to negotiate through neutral diplomatic channels; he still thought, however, that General Eisenhower should be given an armistice agreement, in precise terms, which he could use if he were suddenly approached by the Italian Government. The President accepted the Prime Minister's amendments to General Eisenhower's 'conditions' and now summed them up in the following articles:

'1. Immediate cessation of all hostile activity by the Italian armed forces.

2. Italy will use its best endeavours to deny to the Germans facilities that might be used against the United Nations.

3. All prisoners or internees of the United Nations to be immediately turned over to the Allied Commander-in-Chief, and none of these may from the beginning of these negotiations be evacuated to Germany.

4. Immediate transfer of the Italian fleet to such points as may be designated by the Allied Commander-in-Chief, with details of disarmament to be prescribed by him.

5. Agreement that Italian merchant shipping may be requisitioned by the Allied Commander-in-Chief to meet the needs of his military-naval program.

6. Immediate surrender of Corsica and of all Italian territory, both islands and mainland, to the Allies for such use as operational bases and other purposes as the Allies may see fit.

7. Immediate guarantee of the free use by the Allies of all airfields and naval ports in Italian territory, regardless of the rate of evacuation of the Italian territory by the German forces. These ports and fields to be protected by Italian armed forces until this function is taken over by the Allies.

8. Immediate withdrawal to Italy of Italian armed forces from all participation in the current war from whatever areas in which they may be now engaged.

9. Guarantee by the Italian Government that if necessary it will employ all its available armed forces to insure prompt and exact compliance with all the provisions of this Armistice.

10. The Commander-in-Chief of the Allied Forces reserves to himself the right to take any measure which in his opinion may be necessary for the protection of the interests of the Allied Forces or for the prosecution of the war, and the Italian Government binds itself to take such administrative or other action as the Commander-in-Chief may require, and in particular the Commander-in-Chief will establish Allied Military Government over such parts of Italian territory as he may deem necessary in the military interests of the Allied Nations.

11. The Commander-in-Chief of the Allied Forces will have a full right to impose measures of disarmament, demobilisation and demilitarisation.'

These articles did not include a reference to war criminals. The President now thought that this question could be taken up later, and that all 'non-essential' demands should be postponed in order to avoid delay in getting Italy out of the war as soon as possible.

(a) After this message and the draft articles had been discussed in the Foreign Office on July 31 Mr. Eden drew up a minute for the Prime Minister at Chequers.[1] Mr. Eden pointed out that the President's plan still involved us in the 'two-stage' method. If we had to present something immediately to the Italians, the President's text would be adequate, though we should have liked to remedy certain omissions— e.g. there was no mention of aircraft. We could omit the reference to war criminals because our policy with regard to them had already been announced. On the other hand all the points in the President's text were more than covered by our full document. Mr. Eden thought that, as we were accepting the President's plan for an emergency, we might ask him once again to look at our text. In any case, if the President's text were used, should we not include a warning that further terms would be imposed?

Meanwhile the Prime Minister had telephoned at noon a note for Mr. Eden. He said that he agreed with the President's text, and regarded it as a 'first stage' on the analogy of the heads of a Bill agreed by the Cabinet; the second stage—the actual draft—would follow. Mr. Churchill thought that we should accept the American version as adequate for an emergency, and that we should not risk losing American goodwill by appearing to impose delay on practical action for the sake of a final legal draft.[2]

(b) The Prime Minister, however, agreed to telegraph to the President to the effect that, while we accepted the proposed text (with the addition of the words 'and Italian aircraft' after 'fleet' in article 4) as suitable for an emergency, we hoped that agreement could be reached on the full text in our Instrument of Surrender. This document included several matters not dealt with in the emergency terms and had been very carefully framed. We did not understand why the President never referred to the document since it was only

---

[1] July 31 was a Saturday.
[2] In another note of July 31 to Mr. Eden the Prime Minister said that the terms which
(c) General Eisenhower intended to offer were 'much more likely to be understood by an envoy, and thus be capable of immediate acceptance, than the legal verbiage of the Instrument of Surrender'.

(a) R6971/242/22. (b) T1162/3, No. 393 (Churchill Papers/249; R6972/242/22).
(c) PMM 544/3, Churchill Papers/249.

a more formal and comprehensive version of the emergency terms. We ought to have it, or something like it, ready as soon as possible.[1]

Mr. Roosevelt replied on August 3 that he had read the Instrument (a) of Surrender, and that, while the 'language' seemed on the whole good, he doubted the advisability of using it. He thought that the terms already sent to General Eisenhower were adequate, and saw no reason 'to tie his hands by an instrument that may be oversufficient or insufficient'.

On the day after the President's message, and before the United States Government had reached a decision upon the full text of the Instrument of Surrender, approaches were made by the Italians and, as the Foreign Office had anticipated, the Italian emissaries did not in the first instance make their way to General Eisenhower.

(iii)

Approaches from Marshal Badoglio's Government, August 4–18: Allied insistence upon unconditional surrender: presentation of Allied terms to General Castellano at Lisbon, August 19–20, 1943.

The first approach from the Italian Government came from the (b) Marquis d'Ajeta, an official in the Italian Ministry of Foreign

---

[1] On August 3 the Prime Minister wrote a minute pointing out that 'undue use' should not be made, in the text of the Instrument of Surrender, of the term 'United Nations', (c) since, in fact, only Great Britain and the United States were conducting the negotiations, and Canada (which had troops engaged against Italy) and the U.S.S.R. were being kept specially informed. Mr. Churchill thought that we should be careful that all our published documents did not refer exclusively to 'the United States', 'the United Nations', and 'General Eisenhower'. We were the 'major contributors in numbers, blood, force, ships, and aircraft-in-action' to the 'joint enterprise'.

The difference between the British and American attitude to Italy may be seen early in an exchange between Mr. Churchill and President Roosevelt about the military administration of Italian occupied territory. Mr. Churchill telegraphed to the President on April 13, 1943, his hope that, 'under the supreme direction of General Eisenhower . . . we [the British] should be senior partners in the military administration of enemy-occupied territory in that area'. The President replied on April 14: 'In view of friendly feeling towards America entertained by a great number of the citizens of Italy and in consideration of the large number of citizens of the United States who are of Italian descent, it is my opinion that our military problem will be made less difficult by giving to the Allied Military Government as much of an American character as is practicable'. *F.R.U.S.*, 1943, II, 326–7.

On July 5 the Prime Minister pointed out to the President that British public opinion would resent the insufficient recognition, in Mr. Roosevelt's proposed declaration to the Italian people, of the British contribution to the Allied force. In fact the British contribution was mentioned only once: 'all else is either United States or United Nations'. Mr. Roosevelt modified his draft to meet Mr. Churchill's request. *F.R.U.S.*, *ib.*, 329–32.

(a) T1182/3, No. 339, Churchill Papers/249. (b) Lisbon tel. 1455, R7425/242/22. (The telegrams on which sections (iii) and (iv) are largely based may also be found collected in R8567–8570/8567/22 and, to a great extent, in Churchill Papers 249 and 250.) (c) WP(43)357.

Affairs, and formerly Ciano's Chief de Cabinet, who visited Sir R. Campbell, His Majesty's Ambassador at Lisbon, on August 4. He explained that he had come on behalf of Marshal Badoglio's Government, and with the knowledge of the King and the General Staff. He said that Italy had 'turned red overnight'; there was nothing between the King, and the patriots who had rallied round him, and complete Bolshevism. The Germans were furious at what had happened. They were determined not to let the Italians out of the war. They were in full control, and had an armoured division outside Rome, and ready to march into it if there were any signs of Italian weakening. If we bombed Rome again, there would be a popular rising, and the Germans would occupy the city. Italian troops were also concentrated around Rome but had neither the weapons nor the will to resist the Germans.

In these circumstances the King and Marshal Badoglio, whose first thought had been to make peace, had no alternative other than to make a show of going on with the war. They would have to issue, on Ribbentrop's orders, a communiqué that Italy was still the ally of Germany, but the whole country wanted peace and, above all, to get rid of the Germans. Marquis d'Ajeta said that, if the Allies could not attack Germany through the Balkans, the sooner we landed in Italy the better. He did not mention any peace terms, and indeed his whole story was merely a plea that the Allies should save Italy from the Germans as well as from herself.

(a)   A second emissary, also from the Ministry of Foreign Affairs, came to Tangier on August 5. This official—Signor Berio—arrived ostensibly to take charge of the Italian Consulate-General. In fact he brought a message, which he delivered to the Acting British Consul-General, from Marshal Badoglio. Marshal Badoglio said that he wished to treat with His Majesty's Government but could not yet do so openly because he was entirely under the control of the Germans. In a few days' time he would be meeting Hitler or some other German representative, and would have to issue another proclamation that the war would continue and that the alliance with Germany could not be broken. These were neither his own views nor those of the Italian people, but it was necessary, in order to gain time, to obey the German requests.

Marshal Badoglio regarded it as essential that he should be given help to remain in power and to maintain internal order. Otherwise the Germans would seize Rome and establish a military government under a 'quisling'. Marshal Badoglio therefore asked that the Allies should refrain from air bombardment likely to cause civilian panic

---

(a) Tangier tel. 405, R7429/242/22.

and disorder; that they should create an immediate diversion by a landing in southern France or in the Balkans, and that they should meanwhile continue propaganda against him (Marshal Badoglio) in order to lull German suspicions.

Other Italian emissaries and appeals—including a message from (a) representatives of political parties hostile to Marshal Badoglio—also reached the British authorities, but the claims of these representatives to exercise any influence were more than doubtful; as far as was known, the Italian army was still loyal to Marshal Badoglio and was the most powerful factor in the country. Hence the Foreign Office considered that, without discouraging other approaches, we should deal primarily with Signor Berio. On August 7 Mr. Eden telegraphed (b) to the Prime Minister[1] suggesting tht we should insist upon unconditional surrender and that, as a first step, the Badoglio Government should notify us of such surrender. On receiving this communication we should then inform them of our terms. Mr. Eden thought that, apart from our own public declarations, any other course would involve us in long and tortuous negotiations about terms.

The Prime Minister sent a reply on August 8 agreeing generally (c) with Mr. Eden's proposals. He telegraphed a longer message on (d) August 9 after his arrival at Quebec. He suggested that our answer should be to tell Marshal Badoglio that he must state his willingness to 'place himself unreservedly in the hands of the Allied Governments who have already made it plain that they desire Italy to have a respectable place in the new Europe'. Our message should also refer to General Eisenhower's offer of the return of Italian prisoners of war taken in Tunisia and Sicily if Allied prisoners were speedily set free.

Mr. Churchill's view was that we should convey to the Italians 'the feeling that, while they have to make the formal act of submission, our desire is to treat them with consideration so far as military exigencies allow. Mere harping on "unconditional surrender" with no prospects of mercy held out even as an act of grace may well lead to no surrender at all.' The President had used the expression 'honourable capitulation'; Mr. Churchill thought that we might employ this phrase.

Mr. Eden replied that, as we had stated in public our demand for (e) 'unconditional surrender' and as Marshal Badoglio had spoken only of 'negotiation', we were bound to keep to our demand. Mr. Eden

---

[1] The Prime Minister had left Great Britain for the Quebec Conference on August 5. See below, p. 575, n. 1.

(a) Barcelona tel. 67, R7178/242/22. (b) Tels. Concrete 20, 21, 54 (Churchill Papers/249; R8567/8567/22). (c) Welfare 10 (Churchill Papers/249; R8567/8567/22). (d) Welfare 22, R7467/242/22. (e) Tel. Concrete 84, R7518/242/22.

thought that, in order to 'sweeten the pill for the Badoglio Government', we might say: 'Marshal Badoglio must understand that we cannot negotiate, but require unconditional surrender, which means that the Italian Government should place themselves in the hands of the Allied Governments, who will then state their terms. These will provide for an honourable capitulation.' We should point out to Signor Berio that the Prime Minister and the President had already said that we wished Italy to occupy a respected place in the new Europe. Mr. Eden reported his correspondence with the Prime

(a) Minister to the War Cabinet on August 11; the War Cabinet agreed that the Italians would probably try to entangle us in negotiations, and that there was an advantage in giving a reply which repeated our positive demand for unconditional surrender.

(b) The Prime Minister sent Mr. Eden's suggestion to the President (with the grim comment that at all events it would make it easier for the Italians to decide whom to double-cross). The President agreed with the proposed wording. On August 14 the reply was given to

(c) Signor Berio. Signor Berio said that he was disappointed with it, and that the continued bombing of Italy would bring only chaos and revolution, and not the honourable peace for which Marshal Badoglio was working. He asked, however, whether we expected a public declaration of surrender. He pointed out that such a declaration would lead only to an immediate German reaction.

(d) Mr. Eden, with the Prime Minister's approval, sent a reply that Marshal Badoglio must present a document offering unconditional surrender. The offer could be kept secret for the time but would be published immediately after the signature of an armistice. This

(e) message was given to Signor Berio on August 17. On August 20 he

(f) came again to the British Consulate-General to say that he had received a short telegram from Rome to the effect that the situation was unchanged, and that owing to German pressure Marshal Badoglio could not capitulate because he would be unable to carry out the conditions of an armistice. The Consul-General replied that, even with the risk of German action, Italy would gain more by immediate surrender. Signor Berio seemed afraid of a general Communist movement in Europe. He said that the members of the German Consulate-General were suggesting that, rather than surrender to the Anglo-Saxons, the Germans would throw themselves into the arms of Stalin, and form a Communist *bloc* with Russia. From this time no further exchange took place with Signor Berio because

(a) WM(43)114.4, C.A. (b) Tels. Welfare 48, Concrete 141, R7519/242/22. (c) Tel. 381 to Tangier, R7519/242/22; Tangier tels. 416–17, R7557/242/22. (d) Tel. Welfare 145; Tel. 390 to Tangier, R7584/242/22. (e) Tangier tel. 423, R7683/242/22. (f) Tangier tels. 427–8, R7887, 7888/242/22.

the Italian Government had opened a third channel of communication.[1]

The new Italian approach was made at Madrid. On August 15 (a) two Italians—one of them a General Castellano, Chief of General Ambrosio's military office—came to Sir S. Hoare at Madrid with an 'official' statement from Marshal Badoglio. The Marshal wished the British Government to know that Italy was in a 'terrible position'. Almost the whole country wanted peace; the army was badly equipped, and there was no aviation. The Germans were coming in through the Brenner and the Riviera. Anti-German feeling was intense, but the Italian Government could do nothing until the Allies landed on the mainland. In the event of an Allied landing, the Italians were prepared to join them and to fight against Germany. If the Allies agreed in principle to this proposal, General Castellano would give detailed information about the disposition of German troops and stores and also about the co-operation which the Italians could offer to General Mihailović in the Balkans. He was also authorised to concert operations with the Allies. Marshal Badoglio regarded it as essential that action should be taken at once, since the Germans were continually sending in more forces. Sir S. Hoare asked what was the Italian answer to the Allied demand for unconditional surrender. The general's answer was that the Italians were not in a position to make terms. They would accept unconditional surrender if they could join the Allies in fighting the Germans.

General Castellano was ostensibly travelling to Lisbon to carry out an exchange of Chilean diplomatic officials from Italy with the Italian Ambassador and other officials who had left Chile when the latter country broke off relations with Italy. He would have to go back to Rome with the Italian officials on August 20 or 21. Sir S. Hoare therefore said that he would ask His Majesty's Government to send a reply to the British Ambassador at Lisbon. In reporting this *démarche* to the Prime Minister on August 16 Mr. Eden pointed out that the new approach took the form of an offer of combined operations with the Italians against the Germans. The only military advantages offered thereby were unopposed landings and Italian co-operation in running railways, ports, etc. We could be reasonably sure of this collaboration even if we insisted on unconditional surrender. In view of the quality and morale of the Italian troops in the Balkans, the offer of co-operation with General Mihailović did not

---

[1] Meanwhile the Italian Government had declared Rome an open city. The Foreign Office thought it undesirable, on balance, to accept this unilateral declaration. If we (b) agreed to it, we should have to insist upon the complete demilitarisation of Rome. The Prime Minister agreed, and the Allies decided for the time to pay no attention to the declaration.

(a) Madrid tels. 1404–07; Concrete 231 (R7588, 7589, 7590, 7591/242/22). (b) Concrete 221; Welfare 147 (Churchill Papers/14).

amount to much and would give rise to political complications. In any case military co-operation would mean that the Italians retained their arms—including their fleet—and that they would probably claim, later on, Allied status and advantages.

Mr. Eden therefore thought that Mr. Churchill would wish to reply in terms similar to our answer to Signor Berio. Mr. Eden then left for Quebec but, owing to bad weather, did not arive until
(a) August 18. Meanwhile the Prime Minister informed the President of General Castellano's approach. He suggested that he and Mr. Eden should discuss the whole question with the President; his own view was that we should tell the Italians that we insisted on unconditional surrender and could not bargain with them about a change of sides or make plans with them at this stage for common action. If, however, serious fighting broke out between the Italians and Germans, a new situation would arise. We should say to the Italians that they knew we had no wish to deny Italy 'her respected place in Europe'; they should therefore resist the Germans to the best of their ability, pending the arrival of the Anglo-American armies. In particular, they should hamper the arrival of German troops by blowing up railways, roads, tunnels, etc. 'Effective action of this kind would be regarded by the victorious Allies as a valuable service, and would render further co-operation possible against the common foe.' The destruction of German lines of communication was within the power of the Italian Government, and such action would be a proof of their sincerity. They could also free and assist Allied prisoners of war, sail their fleet to ports in Allied occupation, and provide us with information about German dispositions. If the Allied armies found Italians fighting the Germans they would aid them (the Italians) to the utmost.
(b)   The President agreed in principle to this kind of reply. The
(c) Foreign Office considered that we should tell Marshal Badoglio that we could not have time limits imposed on us by his Government, or deal with two different emissaries who used different language. We should require one representative to wait in Lisbon as long as we might find necessary. The Foreign Office thought also that we should avoid any reference to 'valuable services' which the Italians would render, since we should soon have to pay for them in ways likely to involve us in difficulties with our Allies and with our own public opinion. The Russians, and possibly the French, would be suspicious of any suggestion of co-operation with the Italian Government; we might also discourage the resistance movements in Greece, Yugoslavia and Albania.

(a) Welfare 156, R7657/242/22. (b) Welfare 171, R7693/242/22. (c) Concrete 291–2, R7647/242/22.

The Prime Minister and President, however, decided, before Mr. (a) Eden's arrival, that they must answer Marshal Badoglio at once, and that the answer should be in the terms which they had already approved in principle. They considered—with the support of the Combined Chiefs of Staff—that the advantages of inducing Italy to change sides outweighed the risks. The Germans might still set up a 'quisling' administration in Rome or the whole country might drift into anarchy, but an acceptance of the Italian proposals seemed the best way to avoid these dangers. We were not making a bargain with the Italians, and after unconditional surrender they would have to 'work their passage'.

General Eisenhower was therefore instructed during the night of (b) August 17–18 to send an American and a British staff officer to report to the British Ambassador at Lisbon. The Ambassador would arrange a meeting with General Castellano. General Castellano was to be given a copy of the armistice terms previously sent to General Eisenhower and to be told that the unconditional surrender of Italy would be accepted on these military terms, and that political, economic and financial terms would be communicated later by other means. General Eisenhower was also instructed to state that the terms did not visualise the active assistance of Italy in fighting the Germans, but the extent to which these terms might be modified would depend in fact upon the amount of aid provided by the Italian Government and people during the remainder of the war against Germany. The armistice terms would take effect at a date and hour to be named by General Eisenhower[1] and the Italian Government must undertake to proclaim the armistice immediately after General Eisenhower's announcement, and at the same time to release all Allied prisoners in danger of capture by the Germans. They were also to order their fleet and as much of their merchant shipping as possible to sail for Allied ports, and their military aircraft to fly to Allied bases. Meanwhile they could do much to help the Allies without letting the Germans become aware of the proposals for an armistice.

These instructions for the meeting with General Castellano were (c) also sent through the Foreign Office to Sir R. Campbell at Lisbon on the morning of August 18; Sir R. Campbell was given the text of the military armistice terms.[2]

The War Cabinet were informed on August 18 of General (d) Castellano's approach and of the instructions sent to General

---

[1] General Eisenhower was instructed to make this notification a few hours before the Allied landing.

[2] i.e. the terms listed above (pp. 479–80) with the addition of 'Italian aircraft' to article 4.

(a) Welfare 195, R7823/242/22. (b) FAN 196. (c) Tels. 1270–1, 1273, 1279 to Lisbon, R7778/242/22. (d) WM(43)116, C.A.

Eisenhower. They regarded it as unfortunate that the full armistice terms had not yet been agreed with the United States Government, and that the short terms to be communicated to General Castellano at Lisbon would have to be supplemented later by additional conditions including political, economic, and financial terms. They also thought that the Soviet Government, which had been informed of the earlier Italian approach, should be told as soon as possible of this new *démarche*. Mr. Attlee had, in fact, already asked the Prime
(a) Minister whether he approved of an immediate communication to the Soviet Government.

The War Cabinet made one suggestion about the wording of General Eisenhower's instructions. Article 3 of the document to be given to General Castellano laid down that no prisoners or internees of the United Nations now in Italy 'may from the beginning of these negotiations be evacuated to Germany'. The War Cabinet considered that the word 'negotiations' might be quoted subsequently in support of an argument that the Italians had negotiated an agreement and had not made an unconditional surrender. The War Cabinet suggested that for the words 'from the beginning of these negotiations' there should be substituted 'now or at any time'. This proposed amendment was telephoned to the Prime Minister, and, after his approval and that of the President had been obtained, the new wording was telegraphed on the evening of August 18 to Sir R. Campbell. The Secretary of State for the Dominions was also authorised to tell the Dominion Prime Ministers of General Castellano's approach and of the instructions to General Eisenhower.
(b) On August 19 the British and American military representatives— General Bedell Smith and Brigadier Strong—with the British Ambassador and the United States Chargé d'Affaires, saw General Castellano at Lisbon. The meeting took place at the British Embassy and lasted from 10 p.m. throughout the night to 7 a.m. on the morning of August 20. General Bedell Smith said that, on the assumption that the Italian armed forces were ready to surrender, he was authorised to communicate the terms upon which General Eisenhower would agree to an armistice. These terms constituted a military armistice only and must be accepted unconditionally.

General Castellano then interposed to say that there was some misunderstanding of the purpose of his visit. He had authority, not to discuss armistice terms, but to ask whether the Allies intended to attack Italy, and, if so, to propose that Italian forces should join with them in expelling the Germans.

General Bedell Smith replied that he had come directly from General Eisenhower with the only terms which the Allies would

(a) Concrete 309, R7777/242/22. (b) Lisbon tels. 1647–8, R8569/8567/22.

accept, and that his instructions required him to make it plain that the terms must be accepted unconditionally. The question of the status of the Italian army and of the participation of the Italian Government in the operations against the Germans was one of high governmental policy of the United Nations and would have to be decided by the Heads of the two Governments concerned. The Allied forces would assist any Italian force or any Italians which fought against or obstructed the Germans. General Bedell Smith then read out the armistice terms, and the comments which he was authorised to make on them.

In spite of his initial attitude General Castellano appeared willing, and indeed eager to hear these terms. After the terms had been read and translated the British and American representatives withdrew to allow General Castellano time to consider them. On their return the General raised a number of points; he repeated that he did not wish to discuss the terms as he had no authority to do so, but he desired to have certain explanations which he could transmit to his Government. In reply to a question from him about the retention of sovereignty by the Italian Government, General Bedell Smith repeated that his instructions referred only to a military armistice, and that he had no power to discuss questions relating to the future government of Italy. He said that a military government under the Allied Commander-in-Chief would unquestionably be necessary over parts of Italian territory. General Castellano also reverted to the manner and extent of Italian collaboration against Germany. The Allied representatives explained carefully to him that they were discussing a military capitulation, not an arrangement for the participation of Italy in the war on the Allied side. General Bedell Smith pointed out that the terms of the armistice did not visualise the active assistance of Italy in fighting the Germans. He was, however, authorised to say that the extent to which these terms would be modified in favour of Italy would depend on the amount of assistance in fact received from the Italian Government and people. He repeated that wherever Italian forces or Italians fought Germans or destroyed German installations, they would receive all possible support from the forces of the Allied Nations.

General Castellano then spoke of the likelihood of German reprisals against Italy. It was pointed out to him that the Germans would be foolish to institute reprisals against the Italian population to which we could certainly reply, and that, in any case, the effect of a few days of vindictive action by the Germans would be much less serious for Italy than a long war of attrition.

General Castellano said that it would be most useful to the Italian Government to know when and where the Allied invasion would take place since it would probably be necessary for part of the

Government to move from Rome at the time of the announcement of the armistice. General Bedell Smith said that General Castellano would understand that we could not give detailed information of our military plans; we should, however, propose to announce the granting of an armistice five or six hours before our main landing. General Castellano asked for a much longer time—preferably two weeks. General Bedell Smith thought that we might agree to a longer time.

(a)   The Allied representatives considered that General Castellano and Marshal Badoglio were acting in good faith, They agreed that the general should leave for Rome on August 22,[1] and arranged for the receipt of messages from him; if no message were received from him by midnight on August 30 the Allies could assume that the Italian Government had not accepted the terms. Otherwise General Castellano would come to Sicily on August 31.

(iv)

Anglo-American agreement on the 'comprehensive terms' to be imposed on Italy, August 26: Italian contacts through General Zanussi: Italian acceptance of the Allied terms, September 1, 1943.

The 'short terms' to be used by General Eisenhower had been agreed between the two Governments before the appearance of General Castellano, but two matters of great importance were still unsettled; there was as yet no agreement either on the full terms, civil (i.e. political and economic) and military, to be imposed or on the method by which these terms should be communicated if it should prove unnecessary for General Eisenhower to employ the 'emergency' plan.

The British 'comprehensive' draft was still under discussion at Washington after the Prime Minister had left for Quebec, and at the time of General Castellano's approach. Meanwhile the text of an
(b) American draft had been received in London. The Foreign Office regarded this draft as unsuitable. It contained no specific provision for a Control Commission, or for important matters such as the release of Allied shipping, control of Italian communications, manufactures of war material, and fuel and power, or the imposition of a

---

[1] General Castellano did not return until August 25. There was delay in the arrival of the officials to be exchanged, and the general had to wait for them.

(a) NAF 333-4; Algiers tel. 1526, R8569/8567/22. (b) Concrete 358, R7867/242/22; Concrete 341, 355, Churchill Papers/249.

censorship. These matters were covered in a general clause, but the Foreign Office thought that it was desirable to avoid disputes with the Italians by laying down their obligations in more detail. They also regarded it as essential that the preamble should refer to the conditions under which the United Nations, and not merely the United States and the United Kingdom, were prepared to suspend hostilities. Italy was at war with the United Nations, and hostilities should therefore be suspended with them. The Foreign Office suggested, as a compromise, that the preamble might refer to the 'United States and United Kingdom Governments, acting on behalf of the United Nations'. This addition would be the minimum required to meet the wishes of the Dominions and other Allied Governments (including the Soviet Government) with a special interest in an Italian surrender.

On August 22 Mr. Eden telegraphed from Quebec that agreement (a) had finally been reached on the comprehensive terms, and that he and Mr. Hull had agreed to recommend to the Prime Minister and the President that it should be handed to the Italian emissaries if and when they returned for the signature of the armistice. They should be told that the document embodied the shorter terms and also covered those matters which, as they had been warned, remained to be dealt with. The comprehensive terms would thus supersede the shorter text and constitute the complete terms of surrender.

There was, however, still some delay. A message reporting the (b) agreement of the President and the Prime Minister to the comprehensive document did not reach London until August 25. This message stated that the full text was being sent to General Eisenhower. The Foreign Office arranged at once to send copies by air to (c) Sir R. Campbell at Lisbon. They heard, however, on August 26 that the text had not yet been sent from Washington to General Eisenhower.[1] They therefore telegraphed the text to Mr. Macmillan. They had already instructed Sir R. Campbell that this full text should be given to the Italians on their return, with the explanation that the text embodied the points already handed to them, and contained additional points which they had been warned to expect. Meanwhile, on August 26, a new development gave increasing urgency to the matter.

On August 26 yet another emissary came to Lisbon. The new (d) intermediary was General Zanussi, principal assistant to General Roatta, Chief of the Army General Staff. He brought with him

---

[1] The text was in fact sent from Washington on the night of August 26–7.

(a) Welfare 321, Churchill Papers/249. (b) Welfare 393 (R8570/8567/22; U3900/324/70). (c) Algiers tel. 1572, Washington tel. 3861, Tel. 1713 to Algiers, R8570/8567/22. (d) Lisbon tel. 1721, R8570/8567/22.

General Carton de Wiart who was a prisoner of war in Italian hands.[1] General Carton de Wiart had been taken to Rome from his prisoners' camp, given civilian clothes and a diplomatic passport with an Italian name, and told that he was to accompany to Lisbon and, if possible, to London, an Italian general authorised to discuss the terms of an armistice.

General Zanussi knew of General Castellano's mission and apparently was sent to Lisbon because the latter had not returned—in fact General Castellano arrived in Rome a few hours after General Zanussi left. The British Ambassador thought it undesirable, without further instructions, to see General Zanussi, but told him to stay in Lisbon until he was sure that there was no message for him to take back.

The Foreign Office, however, considered that General Zanussi's arrival might make it possible to carry out the plan which they had always supported—that is to say, the signature, at the time of the Italian surrender, of the full terms of the armistice, and not merely the short document containing the military terms.

The full text was now available for transmission to the Italian Government; General Zanussi might be able to take it back, and to get the Italian consent to it before General Castellano returned to
(a) Sicily on August 31. Sir R. Campbell and Mr. Macmillan were therefore given new instructions during the night of August 26–7. Sir R. Campbell was asked to let General Zanussi have a copy of the 'comprehensive text' and to tell him that it included both the shorter terms presented to General Castellano and the political and economic terms of which the latter had been given notice. This 'comprehensive text' represented the terms which General Eisenhower would put to an Italian emissary if the Italian Government decided to surrender. It would obviously be more convenient that the surrender should take the form of a signature of a single comprehensive document. General Zanussi should therefore go back at once to Rome with this document.
(b)   The instructions to Mr. Macmillan informed him of the opportunity of sending a copy of the 'comprehensive text' to Rome, with the possibility that it might reach the Italian Government in time for them to authorise their emissary to sign it. If this should not be the case, and if the emissary were authorised only to sign the shorter terms because the Italian Government had not received the 'comprehensive text', the British Government would agree in the case of urgent military necessity to the signature of the shorter terms, and

---

[1] Signor Grandi travelled to Lisbon in the same aeroplane, but the Foreign Office instructed Sir R. Campbell not to have any dealings with him.

(a) Tel. 1352 to Lisbon, R8570/8567/22. (b) Tel. 1722 to Algiers, R8570/8567/22.

the armistice would thus come into effect. The Italians, however, must be made to undertsand that the short terms would be replaced later by the full terms. These instructions to Mr. Macmillan were also telegraphed to Quebec; the Prime Minister and Mr. Eden (a) replied on August 27 that they agreed with them.

Sir R. Campbell carried out his instructions on the morning of (b) August 27. He gave General Zanussi until 3.30 p.m. to study the full terms, and meanwhile tried to make arrangements for sending him back to Rome, since there was no Italian air service until August 31 and the general refused to go by train. In the afternoon General Zanussi began to urge that the decision to compel Italy to make a public surrender would put the country at the mercy of the Germans and lead to internal chaos in which Communism would have free play. Sir R. Campbell cut short what appeared likely to be an indefinite discussion by saying that he was authorised only to give General Zanussi the comprehensive terms agreed by the Prime Minister and the President on behalf of their respective Governments. General Zanussi was then sent to General Eisenhower's headquarters. He would thence be flown to Sicily, where an Italian aircraft would take him to Rome.

General Eisenhower, with the support of Mr. Macmillan, did not (c) want to introduce the 'comprehensive text' at this stage of the negotiations. He felt, at first, some doubt about General Zanussi's credentials, and thought that there might be a danger of leakage to the Germans. Above all, he wanted to secure Italian assistance just before and during the Allied landing which was planned for September 3. Hence, he regarded it as necessary to accept immediate surrender in accordance with the shorter terms, if General Castellano returned with a signed acceptance of a military capitulation, and then, after these terms had been signed, to give the Italian emissary the longer document with an explanation that it contained the full terms which would be imposed by the United Nations. The President accepted General Eisenhower's view and informed Mr. Churchill of (d) it. Mr. Churchill raised no objection.

The difference between the American view—in Algiers and Washington—and the view of the War Cabinet and Foreign Office in London was thus still unsolved. A report of August 30 from Mr. (e) Macmillan gave the impression in London that General Eisenhower was deliberately neglecting the chance to carry out the British plan. Mr. Macmillan said that, after discussion with General Zanussi, it had been decided to send the latter's interpreter back to Rome with

(a) Welfare 451, R8570/8567/22; Churchill Papers/249. (b) Lisbon tels. 1732 and 1736, R8570/8567/22. (c) NAF 342. (d) Tel. R/2421, R8570/8567/22. (e) Algiers tel. 1615, R8570/8567/22.

a letter to General Ambrosio making the following points: (i) the Italian Government should decide at once to accept the short military terms given to General Castellano; (ii) in General Zanussi's view the other clauses in the full instrument of surrender dealing with political, economic and other questions, were only of relative importance.[1] The question at issue was not a matter of formulae, but of the whole Italian attitude, and, above all, the amount of practical assistance which they could provide in the war against Germany; (iii) General Castellano should therefore go to Sicily as arranged; General Zanussi would await him there. One or both of the generals would remain in Sicily in permanent touch with the Allies.

(a)   General Zanussi, in conversation, repeated his opinion that, although the authority of Marshal Badoglio's Government was accepted generally by the Italians, the Germans would have time to take over control before the Allies had completed their arrangements with Marshal Badoglio. He also thought that most intelligent Germans now believed that they could not win the war, but they were uncertain whether they would do better to surrender to the Western Powers or to Russia.[2] Hitler was trying to gain time for a *rapprochement* with Russia so that Germany could concentrate on the west, and many Germans seemed to hope that a compromise peace with the Russians was not impossible.

These arrangements with General Zanussi and, in particular, the suggestion that the non-military terms were only of relative importance, caused considerable disquiet in London. Mr. Macmillan was
(b) instructed again on August 31 that, if General Castellano signed the short terms but would not sign the comprehensive terms, on the ground that he had no authority to do so, he should be told to take the latter back to Rome and obtain authority at once for signing
(c) them. Mr. Attlee and Mr. Eden telegraphed on September 1 to the Prime Minister that they had assumed that Sir R. Campbell had arranged matters according to the instructions sent to him. These instructions laid down that when General Castellano was given the 'short terms' he was to be told that they did not include the political, economic or financial terms which would be communicated later. It now appeared that General Eisenhower and Mr. Macmillan had

---

[1] General Zanussi's interpreter did not take these terms back with him to Rome.

[2] According to General Zanussi the line of argument was that, if Germany surrendered to the Western Powers, the terms of surrender might involve the disruption of the unity of the country, in order to prevent a repetition of 1914 and 1939. This would destroy the German national achievement of the last 200 years, and might give Germanism a deep and lasting wound. On the other hand, if the Germans surrendered to Russia, they might become a Soviet Republic in alliance with the U.S.S.R. They might have to suffer bitterly for twenty years, but in the long run they would not be 'broken up' as a nation.

(a) Algiers tel. 1624, R8570/8567/22. (b) Tel. 1768 to Algiers, R8570/8567/22. (c) Tel. Concrete 685, R8570/8567/22; Churchill Papers/249.

allowed General Zanussi to tell the Italian Government that these other terms did not matter. General Eisenhower had also used the phrase 'negotiations with emissaries'. The plan at Algiers seemed to be to get the Italian signature to the 'short terms', and thus bring the armistice into effect, while leaving the question of comprehensive terms for subsequent examination. Mr. Attlee and Mr. Eden continued to think that we should meet with difficulties later, both with the Italians and with our Allies, if we did not obtain an Italian signature to our comprehensive terms or at least an agreement that these terms were an essential part of the armistice.

General Eisenhower might have in mind that, owing to increased German strength in south Italy, Italian co-operation was essential to the success of our landing, and that we could no longer afford to demand a complete capitulation but must make it as easy as possible for the Italians to get out of the war at once. The Ministers pointed out that Mr. Churchill had in fact foreseen this possibility, and provision had been made for it in the instructions[1] sent to General Eisenhower for the meeting with General Castellano at Lisbon. They suggested that it might 'ease matters' if General Eisenhower were now assured that he could develop 'to the full', in his instructions to the Italian emissaries, the kind of assistance which we required from their Government. We could also postpone publication of the full terms if they were thought to be unnecessarily humiliating to the Italian army and people. General Eisenhower appeared to think that we were planning an armistice ceremony on 'Compiègne lines' whereas the negotiations were being carried on with emissaries who had come at great risk of precipitating the seizure by the Germans of the heads of the Italian Government. We had never thought of an armistice ceremony but certain of our Allies, such as the Greek Government, who were fighting Italy, should have the opportunity to be present at the signature.

Meanwhile on August 31 General Bedell Smith, with General (a) Zanussi, saw General Castellano in Sicily. General Castellano explained that, if the Italians had been free to do so, they would have accepted the Allies' terms and announced them. They were, however, no longer free but under German control. This control was now greater than at the time of General Castellano's journey to Lisbon. It was therefore impossible to announce an armistice at the time required by the Allies (i.e. before the main Allied landing). The Italians must first be sure that the landings were in sufficient strength to ensure success and to guarantee the security of Rome where the King and Government intended to remain.

---

[1] See above, p. 487.

(a) NAF 346.

The two Italians then tried to find out the strength of the Allied forces and whether they intended to make a landing north of Rome.[1] General Bedell Smith told them that we could not discuss the question on the basis of an announcement of an armistice after our main landings had taken place, and that we could not give the Italians any military information. General Castellano then said that he must follow his instructions, and consult the Italian Government. He raised three supplementary points: (i) Could the Italian fleet go to La Maddalena rather than to an Allied port, since this concession would soften the blow of surrender? General Bedell Smith replied that no variation of the terms would be accepted.

(ii) What steps would be taken to protect the Vatican City against the Germans? General Castellano was told that the protection of the Vatican City was linked with the protection of Rome.

(iii) The Germans were bringing great pressure on the Italians to hand over to them Allied prisoners captured by the German forces in Africa. It was doubtful whether the Italian Government could resist this pressure. The Allied representatives noted this statement.

In conclusion General Bedell Smith said that the Allied terms were final; their time-limit had already expired, but would be extended to midnight, September 1–2. The Italians must say 'yes' or 'no'.

In the discussion General Castellano showed himself in fact more afraid of German strength than he had been at Lisbon and less certain of the success of an Allied invasion. General Bedell Smith told him that the Allies were determined to land on the mainland and to fight there. Nothing could prevent Italy from becoming a battlefield; the Italians could shorten their sufferings only by accepting the Allies' proposals.

As it was clear that the Italians would not sign the terms of surrender unless they were assured of an Allied landing in the Rome area, General Eisenhower decided to tell General Castellano that he would send an airborne force to this area if the armistice were signed and announced as desired by the Allies, and if the Italians would seize and hold the necessary airfields, stop all anti-aircraft fire, and fight the Germans in the Rome area. General Castellano then (a) returned to Rome. On September 1 General Eisenhower reported that a message had been received from him (General Castellano) that the Italian Government agreed to surrender on the Allied terms and that he would come back to Sicily on September 2 to arrange the remaining details.

---

[1] General Castellano was instructed to ask for a landing of fifteen divisions, mainly north of Rome. The Allied plans had envisaged a landing of three divisions at Salerno and two in Calabria.

(a) NAF 348.

On September 2 the Prime Minister[1] and the President telegraphed (a)
to General Eisenhower that they approved of his decision to land an
airborne division if the Italians accepted his conditions. The telegram concluded with the words: 'We fully recognise that military
considerations must be dominant at this juncture.'

On receiving this account of the negotations in Sicily and of the
Italian acceptance of the terms of surrender, Mr. Attlee and Mr. (b)
Eden telegraphed on September 2 that their previous message should
be regarded as cancelled, and that they agreed with the message from
the Prime Minister and the President to General Eisenhower.

The Prime Minister, however, had already replied to the earlier (c)
message from London. He pointed out the risks of the impending
invasion since, owing to our delays, the Germans might now be as
strong as ourselves, and able to build up their forces more quickly.
It was therefore not surprising that General Eisenhower should want
all possible Italian assistance. Mr. Churchill thought that we should
not worry him over minor matters such as the relative merits of the
short or long terms and details about the announcement of the
armistice. All these matters would be irrelevant if our invasion failed.
An equally unpleasant situation would arise if the Germans seized
Rome, and set up a 'quisling' government after capturing our airborne division. The overwhelming need was to win the battle, and
to get Italians to fight Germans and destroy their communications
throughout Italy.

The outstanding fact would be that the Italians had agreed to
unconditional surrender and had accepted at least the short terms.
This fact of unconditional surrender superseded all detailed terms
which would be no more than instalments of directions issued to the
defeated Power. Even in the short terms, the Allied Commander-in-
Chief had authority to give whatever orders he pleased of military
significance, and he alone could judge their interpretation.

(v)

*Signature of the armistice, and subsequent Italian attempt at delay: announce-
ment of the armistice, September 8: signature of the full Instrument of
Surrender, September 29, 1943.*

The document containing the military terms was signed on (d)
September 3, in General Eisenhower's presence, by General Bedell

---

[1] The Prime Minister was at this time in Washington.

(a) Welfare 567, Churchill Papers/249.   (b) Concrete 691, Churchill Papers/249.
(c) Welfare 577, Churchill Papers/249. (d) NAF 354.

Smith and General Castellano.[1] The British Eighth Army began their landing in Calabria at 3 a.m. on the same day, but the Allies did not require the Italian Government to carry out the agreement with regard to publication until the main landings (i.e. at Salerno)

(a) had taken place. On September 8, the day before the Salerno landings, the Italians sent a message that, owing to changes in the situation—which they described as having 'broken down'—and owing to the presence of German forces in the Rome area, they found it impossible to announce or carry out the terms of the armistice. If they were to do so, the Germans would occupy Rome, and take over the government. The Italians also were no longer able to guarantee the availability of the aerodromes near Rome for an Allied airborne force.[2]

(b)   General Eisenhower refused to accept these attempts at evasion and delay. He suspended the plan to send an airborne force, but insisted that, if Marshal Badoglio and his Government wished the Allies to retain any confidence in them, they must fulfil the obligations which they had undertaken in a signed agreement. He therefore announced their unconditional surrender, and thus compelled Marshal Badoglio at least to carry out part of the agreed programme —including the surrender of a large part of the Italian fleet. On the other hand, in their haste to leave Rome, the Government did not send adequate instructions to the small force guarding Mussolini whom they were at this time keeping in the Abruzzi. A body of German parachutists landed close to Mussolini's place of confinement on September 12, and, without meeting any serious resistance, took him away to north Italy.[3]

(c)   In view of parliamentary and press enquiries in London, a statement was issued on September 8 from No. 10 Downing Street to the effect that General Eisenhower had announced the unconditional surrender of the Italian Government; that the armistice was strictly a military instrument, signed by the military authorities, and that it

---

[1] General Castellano at first tried to argue that the signature of a document containing the terms of surrender was unnecessary because the telegram of September 1 implied Italian acceptance of the terms, and all that was now required was an arrangement for military co-operation.

[2] The Italians had in fact done nothing to try to prevent the Germans from seizing the airfields or indeed from taking any other action. On the morning of September 9 (the armistice had been announced on the previous evening), the King, Marshal Badoglio and such Ministers and senior officials who were able to escape left Rome for Brindisi in order to avoid capture.

[3] After his 'liberation' by the Germans, Mussolini was brought to see Hitler. On September 15 he set up a new 'Republican-Fascist' Government with its headquarters at Salo on Lake Garda. Mussolini was now merely a quisling, and his 'Government' of no importance. One of its acts, under German pressure, was to put to death all the Fascists within reach (including Ciano and Marshal de Bono) who had voted to deprive Mussolini of power in July.

(a) NAF 365. (b) NAF 387–8. (c) Concrete 794, Churchill Papers/249.

did not include political, financial and economic terms which would be imposed later. It was thus evident that the present position did not permit of the public announcement of the contents of the military document. Hence there would be no change in the date fixed for the meeting of Parliament, but the Prime Minister expected to be in a position to make a full statement to Parliament on its reassembly.

On September 13 the War Cabinet agreed that Marshal Badoglio (a) should now be asked to sign the full instrument of surrender. In instructing Mr. Macmillan to suggest this to General Eisenhower, Mr. Eden pointed out that the absence of the instrument covering economic and other matters was already causing inconvenience, and would create trouble with the other Allies. It was true that some of the provisions—such as the clause pledging the Italian Government to apprehend and hand over Mussolini forthwith—might seem inappropriate in the circumstances, but it had always been envisaged that parts of Italian territory would not be under Marshal Badoglio's control, and we must assume that his Government or its recognised successor would eventually be in control of a substantial part of the country and thus able to comply with our requirements. It might, however, be desirable to tell Marshal Badoglio that we realised that the terms could not at present be carried out in territory under German control. Sir R. Campbell was also instructed to take the matter up with the United States Government.

General Eisenhower agreed that Marshal Badoglio should now (b) sign the full terms, but he recommended that the original preamble of the document should be amended to take account of the fact that the military terms had already been signed. The Foreign Office agreed, and also suggested that the article about the surrender of Mussolini should read 'as soon as possible' instead of 'forthwith'.

The question of the status of Marshal Badoglio's Government[1] (c) now arose, however, and although General Eisenhower was authorised by the Combined Chiefs of Staff to obtain Marshal Badoglio's signature to the full instrument, he decided to wait until this question of policy had been decided. The War Cabinet discussed the question (d) on September 20 and approved a telegram which the Prime Minister proposed to send to President Roosevelt and Mr. Macmillan. In this telegram, Mr. Churchill said that it would make it much easier (e) for us to have the full instrument of surrender signed. Although the Badoglio Government could not now operate many of the clauses, the questions would become real as we progressed up Italy and

---

[1] See Chapter XXXIII, section (i).

(a) WM(43)127; tel. 1905 to Algiers, R8775/242/22. (b) R8837/242/22. (c) R8939/242/22. (d) WM(43)129. (e) T1364/3, Churchill Papers/250.

handed over territory to the Italians. We did not want to have to haggle over every detail with them. The longer we left it, the more difficult it would be to get the instrument signed. Mr. Churchill

(a) also told Stalin that he wanted to insist on the signature of the full

(b) terms. His telegram to President Roosevelt crossed one from the President giving the text of a directive which he proposed to send to General Eisenhower about policy towards the Badoglio Government. In this telegram General Eisenhower was asked to withhold the long armistice terms pending further instructions. Mr. Churchill con-

(c) curred in this directive, and it was sent to General Eisenhower on September 23. Stalin, however, agreed with the Prime Minister that the full instrument should be signed; he said that a reservation that certain terms would not be enforced at the present time should be only in the sense that they could not be realised on the territory occupied by the Germans. The Prime Minister passed this reply on

(d) to President Roosevelt, and on September 25 consulted the President about the terms of his answer. He suggested that the three-Power commission[1] should deal with the matter.

(e)   Meanwhile, however, Mr. Macmillan had reported that General Eisenhower and the Allied Commanders-in-Chief had welcomed the Prime Minister's suggestions on policy towards Marshal Badoglio. He asked whether the President's directive meant that the full armistice terms were to be abandoned; he believed that it would be possible to obtain Marshal Badoglio's signature in a few days, but it would be more difficult to get him to sign after a longer delay. The

(f) Prime Minister therefore sent another telegram to Mr. Roosevelt on September 25 quoting Mr. Macmillan's views and saying that he would feel much happier if the matter was clinched now, without waiting for the three-Power commission to be set up. The President agreed and instructed General Eisenhower to secure Marshal Badoglio's signature to the full terms if it could be done quickly. The full instrument with the amended preamble was therefore signed at Malta on September 29.[2]

---

[1] See below, pp. 578–80.
[2] At the time of the signature of the full armistice terms General Eisenhower, in a letter to Marshal Badoglio, stated that the terms were based upon the situation prior to the cessation of hostilities and that developments since that time had 'altered considerably the status of Italy, which has become in effect a co-operator with the United Nations'. Some of the terms were already superseded by events. The Italian Government was not yet in a position to carry out certain of the terms; their failure to do so would not be regarded as a breach of good faith. The document represented the requirements with which the Italian Government could be expected to comply when in a position to do so. The terms (and those of the short military armistice signed on September 3) could be modified from time to time if military necessity or the extent of co-operation by the Italian Government indicated such modification to be desirable.

(a) R9593/242/22; T1365/3, Churchill Papers/250. (b) T1366/3, No. 352 (Churchill Papers/250; R9594/242/22). (c) T1387/3 (Churchill Papers/250; R9595/242/22). (d) T1409/3, No. 422 (Churchill Papers/250; R9812/242/22). (e) R9110/242/22. (f) T1399/3, No. 421 (Churchill Papers/250; R9284/242/22).

CHAPTER XXXIII

British relations with Italy, September 1943–June 1944

(i)

Allied statement on Italian 'co-belligerency': the question of Allied policy towards the Badoglio Government: the return of Count Sforza to Italy.

THE interval of nearly two months between the Allied landings in Sicily and the invasion of the mainland, and the passiveness of the Italians had given the Germans an opportunity to take their own precautions. They acted with great speed, and not only secured Rome and its airfields, but were able to direct strong counter-attacks on the Allied landings at Salerno. After a difficult three days these attacks were beaten back. The Allies entered Naples on October 1; Sardinia was occupied on September 14, and the French recovered Corsica a fortnight later. The Germans, however, held the whole of the mainland of Italy to the north of the Naples area in great strength, and there was no chance of a rapid Allied advance. The bright prospects set out in the Prime Minister's 'Thoughts on the Fall of Mussolini' were unlikely to be realised without very heavy fighting.

This setback confirmed the Americans in their view that the Prime Minister's strategy—including his plans for the Aegean area—was likely to lead to a dangerous diversion of forces from the main objective—the cross-Channel invasion. The Prime Minister, who spoke in the House of Commons of the Italian campaign as a 'third front',[1] found it difficult to obtain American agreement to any important modification of the arrangements made at Quebec for the transfer of forces and—above all—landing craft to Great Britain. On October 24 General Alexander, in a report which had General Eisenhower's approval,[2] gave a warning that, with the diminishing

---

[1] The Prime Minister telegraphed to General Alexander on September 25: 'You will see that I have announced in Parliament that the Italian campaign is the "Third Front". (a) The Second Front is here in Great Britain, in potential, but not yet engaged. This form of statement should be adhered to, as it is less disagreeable to the Russians, and avoids arguing with them as to whether the Italian campaign is the Second Front or not.'

[2] General Eisenhower transmitted the report to the Combined Chiefs of Staff. The choice of May 7 as target date for the cross-Channel invasion implied a much earlier (b) date for the return of the landing craft. It was estimated that, on an average, fourteen days were required for bringing them back from the Mediterranean, four weeks for repairs and

(a) T1406/3, Churchill Papers/245. (b) NAF 486. *(continued on p. 502)*

strength of his army, he might be faced with superior numbers, and might be 'delayed south of Rome sufficiently long to enable the Germans to clear up the situation in northern Italy and then reinforce their southern front. In this case, the initiative might well pass to them.' This warning had an effect; the Americans agreed to the retention of sixty-eight landing craft until December 15. General Alexander explained that he needed them for a longer time. He finally kept most of them for the Anzio operation on January 22, 1944, but, even so, the Allied advance was held on the Garigliano–Sangro line until the spring of 1944, and Rome was not occupied until June 5, 1944.

Even with the losses and disappointments of the campaign the Allied 'third front' was a contribution of the greatest value to final victory.[1] The Germans paid a high price in Italy itself, and a still higher strategic price elsewhere in the weakening of their armies, for delaying the Allied advance. Nonetheless this stubborn German resistance added greatly to the difficulties of the political and administrative problems with which the British and Americans were faced after their landing on the mainland. The two most urgent political questions were the status of Italy in relation to the Allies, and the extent to which British and American support should be

(a) given to the King and Marshal Badoglio's Government. There was no easy solution to either question. The Allies had in their own hands the right and the power to decide upon the status of a nation which had surrendered unconditionally to them, but from a military point of view, with a difficult campaign ahead for the expulsion of the Germans from the larger and more important part of Italy, they had to consider the best method of getting the active, and not merely the passive collaboration of the Italian people—including, obviously, the Italian armed forces. These immediate military considerations

---

(*continued*)

refit, and two months for training crews and troops taking part in the invasion. Mr. Churchill rightly commented to General Marshall on April 16, 1944: 'How it is that the plans of two great empires like Britain and the United States should be so much hamstrung and limited by a hundred or two of these particular vessels will never be understood by history.' (Churchill, V, 454.) For the reasons for this shortage, see J. P. W. Ehrman, *Grand Strategy*, vol. V (H.M.S.O., 1956), especially pp. 33–8 and 49–52, and G. A. Harrison, *Cross Channel Attack* (Dept. of the Army, Washington, D.C., 1951), *passim*.

[1] The surrender of the Italian fleet was of immediate and far-reaching importance since it freed a large number of Allied ships for service in the Atlantic and the Far East. The Prime Minister, in particular, always had in mind that the King and Marshal Badoglio had done a very considerable service to the Allies in bringing about this surrender. This silent change in the distribution of naval power to the advantage of the Allies was little noticed by British and American opinion. The Soviet Government, however, were fully aware of it, and put in a claim for a share in the captured ships. (See also below, pp. 586–7.) The Italian navy suffered severe casualties in the act of surrender. The Germans made a heavy air attack on the main squadron while on its way from Genoa and Spezia to Malta; the flagship was blown up, and another battleship seriously damaged.

(a) R10098/242/22.

affected a decision on the political regime in Italy. The Allies had to secure the maintenance of order and a regular administration in the areas outside the fighting zone. They had also to take into account public opinion in their own countries and in the countries under German occupation. They did not want another 'Darlan episode'.[1]

The question of Italian status had to be settled at once. After his first meeting with Marshal Badoglio at Brindisi, Mr. Macmillan had (a) proposed the term 'co-belligerency' as a description of this status. At the meeting Marshal Badoglio had argued that the Italian Government stood for war against the Germans, and that the armed forces and the nation would not understand what was expected of them unless they were given Allied or 'quasi-Allied' status. If they received such status, Marshal Badoglio and his Government wanted to declare war on Germany.

The War Cabinet thought that a grant of Allied status was un- (b) necessary, at all events as part of the immediate programme, and that Mr. Macmillan's term 'co-belligerency' would be sufficient. On this basis we could work for the gradual conversion of Italy into an effective national force against Germany, but she would be required to 'work her passage'. In other words we would act on the principle of payment by results, and recognise useful service against the enemy by concessions in the adjustment and working of the armistice terms.[2] Marshal Badoglio would be free to declare war on Germany, and, by such a declaration, Italy would become not an Ally, but a co-belligerent.

A telegram in this sense was sent from the Prime Minister to Mr Macmillan on September 21. The Americans suggested a (c) slightly different policy. The President proposed to reply to Marshal Badoglio that, on condition that they declared war on Germany, the (d) present Government of Italy would be permitted, subject to the setting up of an Allied Commission which should be empowered to furnish guidance and instructions, 'to carry on as the Government of

---

[1] To some extent the establishment of a 'quisling' Fascist republic by Mussolini (see above, p. 498, note 3) offset any allegation that the Allied acceptance of the King and the Badoglio Government was a repetition of the policy adopted in accepting Darlan. The Prime Minister, in his speech of September 21 in the House of Commons, was able to describe the King and Marshal Badoglio as anti-Fascist and anti-quisling.

[2] The Foreign Office did not expect Italian active military collaboration to be of much value. General Eisenhower also took this view. He reported at this time that the Italians— though 'co-operative'—appeared to want to rid Italy of the Germans with the minimum (e) trouble to themselves, and the minimum amount of fighting in Italy. The Italian field army was in a bad condition, and, although the troops hated the Germans and were glad to be out of their clutches, these considerations were unlikely to raise Italian fighting value. Later experience, with certain notable exceptions, confirmed these judgments, and the Italian army was employed mainly in non-combatant services (some of which indeed were often dangerous, viz., bringing up supplies, mine-clearing etc.).

(a) Algiers tel. 1812; NAF 409–10. (b) WM (43)129. (c) Tel. 1971 to Algiers, T1364/3, Churchill Papers/250/4. (d) T1366/3, No. 352 (Churchill Papers/250/4; R9594/242/22). (e) R9609/242/22.

Italy and as such be treated as a co-belligerent in the war against Germany'. The American text thus contained an offer of co-belligerent status in return for a declaration of war, while the Prime Minister's text implied that formal recognition of co-belligerency might come at a later stage. Meanwhile, for practical purposes, the Italian Government would be treated as co-belligerent. The Prime Minister agreed that the President's text should be taken by General
(a) Eisenhower as his instructions, while the British text should serve as a commentary.[1]

General Eisenhower then suggested (September 27) that, in order
(b) to obtain the maximum effect, the President and the Prime Minister should make a joint announcement explaining the meaning and implications of co-belligerent status. This announcement would be issued immediately after the publication of an Italian declaration of war on Germany. The Prime Minister and the Chiefs of Staff agreed with the proposal, but Mr. Eden pointed out that an announcement of this kind required careful consideration, since the Russian view was that Italy should be treated rigorously as a defeated enemy. We did not share this view, but we still regarded it as of importance to emphasise the principle that Italy must 'work her passage'.

On September 30, however, the Prime Minister received from
(c) President Roosevelt the draft text of a proposed announcement in the following terms:

> 'The Governments of Great Britain and the United States acknowledge the position of the Italian Government as stated by Marshal Badoglio and accept with appreciation the active co-operation of the Italian Government and armed forces as a co-belligerent in the war against Germany. The military events since September 8 culminating in the Italian declaration of war against Germany have in fact made Italy a co-belligerent and the American and British Governments[2] will continue to treat with the Italian Government on that basis. The two Governments acknowledge the Italian Government's pledge to submit to the will of the Italian people after the Germans have been driven from Italy and emphasise that the relationship which has developed between the Government of Italy and the Governments of the United Nations is based on the clear understanding that it will not in any way prejudice the military interests of the United Nations or the absolute and untrammelled right of the people of Italy by constitutional means to decide on the democratic form of Government they will eventually have.'

---

[1] Before the receipt of the President's directive General Eisenhower had warmly approved of the terms of the telegram from the Prime Minister to Mr. Macmillan.
[2] The President proposed the inclusion of the Soviet Government if their agreement were received in time.

(a) T1381/3, No. 419, Churchill Papers/250/4. (b) NAF 422, R9813/242/22. (c) T1449/3, No. 363 (Churchill Papers/250; R9813/242/22).

The Foreign Office pointed out that this text omitted any mention of the relevant facts that the Italian Government would be held to the armistice terms, and that these terms would be regulated according to the extent of the Italian contribution to the war against Germany. Furthermore, although we had now heard[1] that the Russians would agree to allowing Italy co-belligerent status, they also wanted 'payment by results'. We ought therefore to try to get Russian participation in any statement even though the announcement would be delayed for a few days.

The Prime Minister, therefore, at Mr. Eden's suggestion, telegraphed to the President on the night of September 30–October 1 (a) suggesting that he (the President) should send the text (in a revised form) to Marshal Stalin, and ask whether he would join in the announcement. The revised text drawn up by the Prime Minister and the Foreign Office was as follows:

'The Governments of Great Britain, the United States and the Soviet Union acknowledge the position of the Royal Italian Government as stated by Marshal Badoglio and accept the active co-operation of the Italian nation and armed forces as a co-belligerent in the war against Germany. The military events since September 8 and the brutal maltreatment by the Germans of the Italian population, culminating in the Italian declaration of war against Germany, have in fact made Italy a co-belligerent and the American, British and Soviet Governments will continue to work with the Italian Government on that basis. The three Governments acknowledge the Italian Government's pledge to submit to the will of the Italian people after the Germans have been driven from Italy, and it is understood that nothing can detract from the absolute and untrammelled right of the people of Italy by constitutional means to decide on the democratic form of Government they will eventually have.

The relationship of co-belligerency between the Government of Italy and the United Nations Governments cannot of itself affect the terms recently signed, which retain their full force and can only be adjusted by agreement between the Allied Governments in the light of the assistance which the Italian Government may be able to afford to the United Nations' cause.'

The President replied later on October 1 suggesting that the Prime Minister should send the British text (which he accepted) to (b)

[1] The Prime Minister had telegraphed to Stalin on September 21 explaining the (c) British proposal for Italian 'co-belligerency'. Stalin replied on September 22 that he agreed generally with the proposal, but that the Italians must declare war on Germany. (d)

(a) T1460–1/3, Nos.427–8 (Churchill Papers/250; R9813/242/22). (b) T1473, No. 367; Tel. 1469 to Moscow (Churchill Papers/250; R9813—242/22). (c) T1365/3. Tel. 1372 to Moscow (Churchill Papers/250; R9593/242/22). (d) T1387/3 (Churchill Papers/250; R9595/242/22).

R*

Stalin. The text was telegraphed by the Foreign Office to Moscow on the night of October 1–2. Stalin replied on October 4 that

(a) he agreed with the text and would join in a declaration which could be published simultaneously in London, Moscow and Washington.

Meanwhile Marshal Badoglio had not yet declared war on the

(b) Germans. He had told Mr. Macmillan at Brindisi on September 27–8 and General Eisenhower at Malta on September 29[1] that the Italian Government could not declare war on Germany until they had returned to Rome. He argued that the authority of the Government extended over only a small part of Italy, and that under Italian law only the King could make a declaration of war. The King felt that, in the absence of an organised Government to advise such a step, a declaration of war by him would be unconstitutional.

The Foreign Office thought that there was some force in Marshal Badolgio's argument and that we ought not to push the Italian Government into a declaration of war until they felt able to make it. Meanwhile we should have to hold up the announcement of co-belligerent status, since it was illogical to grant this status until the Italians had taken at least the first step towards earning it by declaring war on Germany. Co-belligerency should be a reward, and not an inducement. The Prime Minister and the President, however, took the view that Italy ought to be made to declare war at once. On October 4—after Stalin's agreement to the declaration had been received—the Prime Minister telegraphed to the President suggesting

(c) that instructions should be given to General Eisenhower to put the strongest pressure upon the King and Marshal Badoglio. The Prime Minister said that 'there should be no nonsense about waiting until Rome is taken. It seems to us high time that the Italians began to work their passage.'

(d)   A declaration of war was the more necessary owing to leakages (apparently from American sources) that the Italians were to be

(e) offered 'co-belligerency'. Instructions were sent to General Eisenhower by General Marshall on October 5 that the President and Prime Minister agreed that Italy should declare war on Germany at once without waiting for further Allied successes, and that there was no need to delay until the occupation of Rome. On October 8

(f) the Prime Minister gave an account of these exchanges of telegrams to the War Cabinet, and obtained their approval. General Eisen-

---

[1] i.e. at the time of the signature of the longer armistice terms.

(a) T1498/3 (Churchill Papers/250; R9813/242/22). (b) R9426, 9470/242/22; R9842/5880/22. (c) T1500/3, No. 434 (Churchill Papers/250; R9746/242/22). (d) R10098/242/22. (e) JSM 1233, R9746/242/22. (f) WM(43)137, R9746/242/22.

hower acted on his instructions. On October 13 the King declared war on Germany, and the three Allies made their announcement.[1]

The tripartite declaration issued by the three major Allies after the Italian declaration of war on Germany, and the statement made by the Italian Government, had emphasised the right of the Italian people to choose by constitutional means their own form of democratic Government. The Allies had never attempted to conceal their own view that even before a full expression of Italian opinion could be obtained it would almost certainly be necessary to make changes in the Government, and probably to agree to, and even enforce, the abdication of the King of Italy whose miserable political record justified his unpopularity. The question was thus mainly one of timing. The British Government were in favour of postponing any important political changes at least until the occupation of Rome, for the obvious reasons that a Government chosen earlier would not represent a wide circle of opinion and would have little chance of establishing itself, and that the resulting political confusion would have an embarrassing and even dangerous effect on the conduct of Allied military operations. The Foreign Office, and even more strongly the Prime Minister, took the view that the retention of the monarchy would be desirable, since it could still be regarded as a unifying factor, but this view did not imply the retention of the King. The King's early abdication, indeed, was essential if the monarchy were to survive.

The difficulty of broadening the basis of the Badoglio Administration was that parliamentary government had been in abeyance for so long that the opposition leaders were either elderly survivors[2] from the early 1920's without any organised support in the country, or academic figures—such as Croce[3]—without much practical political

---

[1] The United States Government had also proposed that the King or Marshal Badoglio should issue a statement at the time of the declaration of war. The final American draft of a 'directive' on this statement to Marshal Badoglio contained the phrase: 'and make it clear that Italy no longer is at war with Russia or any of the United Nations'. The Foreign Office pointed out (i) that Italy would still be technically at war with the United Nations even after she had declared war on Germany, (ii) a separate reference to Russia might suggest that the U.S.S.R. was not one of the United Nations. The text was corrected accordingly. (a)

[2] Of the leading figures Count Sforza was 71, Signor Croce 77, Signor Bonomi 70. The Communist leaders were much younger: Signor Togliatti was 50. King Victor Emmanuel was 73 and Marshal Badoglio 72.

[3] Signor Croce was living in a villa at Sorrento at the time of the Allied invasion of Italy. On British advice he left Sorrento for Capri on September 15, but returned to the villa on October 31. Signor Croce's attitude, as shown in his diary (B. Croce, *The King and the Allies*, transl. S. Sprigge, Allen & Unwin, 1950), took very little account of the fact that the Anglo-American forces, in driving the Germans out of Italy, were accomplishing a task which the Italians had altogether failed to do for themselves, and that the Allies had some moral right to expect leading Italians to assist in 'damping down' political activities likely to hamper the course of military operations. It is characteristic of his attitude that Signor Croce refused to move elsewhere in Sorrento when the villa he was occupying was wanted for use as a rest home for forty American nurses in Naples, and that, on November 13, 1943, he should have written in his diary: 'English policy . . . wants Italy as a battlefield, but wants to leave its people in a condition of inferiority and impotence, so as not to be embarrassed by Italy in the alterations to be made in Europe'.

(a) R9941/242/22.

experience. Furthermore, a generation of Italians had grown up without the necessary accompaniments of free and democratic government such as freedom of the press or of public meeting or of open party organisation on a large scale. The Communists could be said to provide an anti-Fascist party of considerable strength and cohesion but their cohesion rested largely on the facts that they shared many of the authoritarian features of Fascism, and that they had the secret and, from the Anglo-American point of view, unscrupulous support of the Russians. The western Allies had no wish to substitute a Communist dictatorship for Mussolini, but they needed time if they were to 'mobilise' liberal and moderate opinion in Italy, or rather if the Italian politicians themselves—outside the Communist Party—were to agree upon the support of a strong anti-Fascist coalition. Here again, however, there was a difficulty. If the western Allies forced the Badoglio Government on the Italians, they would seem to be interfering with the rights of self-government upon which they had set such importance in all their propaganda and declarations. Opinion in Great Britain and in the German-occupied European countries would underrate the complexities of the political question in Italy. The United States Government, which was especially sensitive in the matter after their experience in North Africa, could not ignore the importance in the next Presidential election of the 600,000 voters of Italian origin in the United States.

Hence there was an increasing divergence of attitude between the British and United States Governments on the question of timing and on the degree to which it was desirable or even possible to make political changes while the military campaign was in a critical phase. The military authorities—British and American—were not specifically skilled in advising or even in reporting upon political matters outside their professional competence; their local handling of the situation, and even their recommendations, often added to the difficulties, particularly on the British side.

(a)   Soon after the Allied landing in Sicily, Count Sforza, the former Italian political leader,[1] who was living in the United States, applied for permission to go to Italy. The United States Government, mainly

---

[1] Count Sforza had been Foreign Minister in Giolitti's Government of 1920–1. He was Italian Ambassador in Paris at the time of Mussolini's advent to power. He resigned his diplomatic post, but remained in the Senate until 1927 as a constant critic of the Fascist régime. In 1927 he left Italy and resided first in Belgium and then in France. In 1940 he went to the United States where he became a leading figure in the opposition to Fascism and as such had very considerable influence among American citizens of Italian origin, especially in New York State. The Administration regarded his support as an important factor in securing the Italian-American vote.

(a) R7783, 8380, 8381, 8995/242/22; R9113/131/22.

for internal political reasons, considered that it would be difficult to refuse Count Sforza's request. The Foreign Office felt at first that Count Sforza, who was strongly hostile both to the monarchy and to Marshal Badoglio, might cause trouble for the Badoglio Government if he were in or near Italy. In view, however, of the need to get support for this Government on a wider basis, the Foreign Office decided that it was necessary to encourage any leading Italians, in Italy or abroad, who were prepared to recognise and assist it. Count Sforza himself wrote on September 23, 1943, to Mr. Berle, Under- (a) Secretary at the State Department, that he had changed his view, and was ready to support Marshal Badoglio. In his letter Count Sforza referred to Marshal Badoglio's statement of September 16, 1943, that he (Marshal Badoglio) considered the defeat of the Germans and their expulsion from Italy to be his primary duty, and that all Italians should join in this struggle. Count Sforza wrote:

> 'In my view it now becomes the paramount duty of all Italians, irrespective of party or political differences, to support and assist in the struggle to crush German arms and to drive every German soldier from Italian soil. So long as Marshal Badoglio is engaged in that task and is acceptable to the Allies in devoting Italian military and material resources to that struggle, I consider it criminal to do anything to weaken his position or hamper his work in fighting for the liberation of Italy and the Italian people. I am prepared to offer my full support as long as he is thus engaged, all the more because this is the only way to destroy the last criminal remnants of Fascism.
>
> Matters of internal Italian politics can, and should be adjourned for the period of the struggle, and the activities, military and political, of all Italians who seek the freedom and the future of their Fatherland should be devoted to supporting the organised forces which are endeavouring to overthrow the common enemy. I pledge my honour to do this myself, and urge this course on my many friends and associates.'

The Foreign Office considered that, in view of this letter, they could no longer oppose the return of Count Sforza to Italy. They still had some doubt, however, whether he would keep his promise of support once he was back in Italy. Count Sforza was known to be confident and ambitious about the part which he could play in Italian politics after the collapse of Fascism. The doubts about him were strengthened by reports of public statements which he made before leaving the United States and in which he attacked the King of Italy and said that he did not intend to join Marshal Badoglio's Government.

(a) R9140/131/22.

Before the Count's arrival in England President Roosevelt had
(a) telegraphed to the Prime Minister his hope that he (the Prime
Minister would 'effectively indoctrinate him during his stop in the
United Kingdom'.[1] The Prime Minister thought that it would be a
good thing if Count Sforza's letter to Mr. Berle were published, but
the Foreign Office had no power to publish it themselves or even—
without getting Count Sforza's consent—to ask the State Department
to do so. The Prime Minister and Mr. Eden, however, saw Count
Sforza while he was in London.

(b)   The Prime Minister told Count Sforza on October 11 that he was
glad to read his letter to Mr. Berle, but that he seemed later to have
made pronouncements of an opposite kind. It was possible to say
either that the King and the Badoglio Government must be given
whole-hearted support in their attempt to throw off German
domination or that by their past connections with Fascism they did
not deserve support. It was impossible, however, to take both these
lines at once. The Prime Minister suggested that the Italian
monarchy counted for something, and that it commanded loyalty as
the one element which represented any continuity in the Italian
State and the only remaining symbol of Italy.

Count Sforza assured the Prime Minister that he stood by every
word of his letter to Mr. Berle, but he digressed continually into
reflexions on the King and the dynasty, and into complaints against
Marshal Badoglio. Nevertheless, he gave the Prime Minister explicit
assurances that he would do his best to support the King and Marshal
Badoglio though he would not join the Government. The Prime
Minister made it plain that Count Sforza would be expelled if he
said anything unhelpful. The Prime Minister's comment was that
Count Sforza seemed to him a 'foolish and played-out old man,
incapable of facing, let alone riding the storm'.

Mr. Eden's impression had also been unfavourable. He saw Count
(c) Sforza on October 8. He did not mention directly to Count Sforza
the statements which he was reported to have made in the United
States; he asked whether the Count stood by his letter to Mr. Berle.
Count Sforza said that he stood by the principles in the letter. He
would support Marshal Badoglio in a 'parallel way' though he would
not join his Government. He did not think that Marshal Badoglio
was capable of handling the political situation or preventing the

---

[1] At the same time (October 2) the President informed the Prime Minister that he
had instructed General Eisenhower to tell Marshal Badoglio that the presence of Count
Grandi in his Government would not be acceptable. (The King of Italy had wished Count
Grandi to be included in the Government.) The Foreign Office fully agreed that Count
Grandi should not be brought into the Badoglio Government, but thought it odd that the
President should have sent his message to General Eisenhower without waiting to consult
the British Government or to hear their views.

(a) T1486/3, No. 369 (Churchill Papers/250; R9596/242/22); R9540/131/22.
(b) R10165/131/22. (c) R10164/131/22.

danger of a revolution in Italy. The King and the House of Savoy generally were even less capable. Count Sforza did not want to destroy his own influence by committing himself prematurely to the Badoglio Government or any other Government.

Mr. Eden thought that Count Sforza's intention was to bide his time in the hope that eventually he would impose himself upon the Allies as Prime Minister, with or without the King. Count Sforza, however, put matters in a slightly different light by telling Mr. Law that the press report of his statements in America grossly misrepresented what he had said. Count Sforza later sent a letter to this effect to the Prime Minister.

On October 19 Mr. Macmillan telegraphed for advice on the policy to be adopted towards the King and Badoglio Government (a) after the return of Sicily, Calabria and Apulia to its authority under the supervision of the Control Commission.[1] Mr. Macmillan thought that we need not wait until the occupation of Rome before trying to get changes in the Government. The Foreign Office proposed to reply that, after the signature of a protocol amending the 'long' armistice agreement,[2] we should work for the earliest possible broadening of the Government. We need not await the occupation of Rome, since we were unlikely to find there many more persons available for inclusion in the Government.

The Foreign Office was willing to give Mr. Macmillan a free hand in making arrangements on the general understanding that the new Government should be larger, more civilian in character, and more to the Left. Marshal Badoglio would have to be retained if no suitable civilian politician were found to replace him. On the other hand, if the civilians whom we thought suitable refused to serve with him, we should have to persuade him to resign the Prime Ministership, though we should hope that he would remain in the Government. The Foreign Office doubted whether Marshal Badoglio's disappearance would cause much doubt or confusion outside Italy. There were strong objections to raising so contentious an issue as the position of the King at the present time, but, subject to this qualification, we

---

[1] The transfer of territory to the administration of the Royal Government took place, according to plan, after the areas in question had ceased to be within the zone of military operations. The Allied Control Commission thus differed from the Allied Military Government of Occupied Territory in that the latter took the place of an Italian Government and exercised direct authority over Italian affairs, while the former, though it had wide powers with regard to the execution of the armistice terms, and the use of Italian manpower and resources in the prosecution of the war, acted through the Italian Government. The words 'of Occupied Territory' were not used in the title of the Allied Military Government after the recognition of Italian co-belligerency. For the Allied Military Government and the Allied Control Commission, see R.C.S. Harris, *Allied Military Administration of Italy, 1943–5* (H.M.S.O., 1957).

[2] This protocol was signed on November 9. It made the U.S.S.R. a party to the agreement, but did not lay down any important modifications in the terms.

(a) R10434/5880/22.

should not object to the appointment of Count Sforza as head of the Government. In any case, even an enlarged Government would be only temporary, and there was no reason for us to be greatly concerned about its composition.

Mr. Eden was at this time in Moscow.[1] The draft telegram was submitted by Sir A. Cadogan to the Prime Minister. The Prime Minister wrote a minute on October 21 that he was not prepared to leave it to Mr. Macmillan to decide whether Marshal Badoglio should be asked to retire. He thought that Count Sforza was 'a useless, gaga, conceited politician whose hostility to the House of Savoy and whose Republicanism is based on the fact that he sees himself representative of the House of Milan'.[2]

The Prime Minister thought that there was no need for haste, and that we should wait until the capture of Rome. Meanwhile Marshal Badoglio was the 'only solid peg', and the military authorities were unlikely to wish to break with him. We must not be deflected by questions in the House of Commons from the simple policy of holding on to the King and Marshal Badoglio until we were masters of Rome and could see what other suitable Italians would be of (a) service. The Prime Minister therefore drafted a telegram on these lines to Mr. Macmillan.

(ii)

Negotiations over the broadening of Marshal Badoglio's Government: intrigues of Count Sforza: the Bari Congress (October 1943–January 1944).

The policy of 'holding on' to the King and Marshal Badoglio, while broadening the basis of the Government by securing the support of the moderate opposition parties, was already breaking down. This policy was indeed reinforced by the declaration on Italy issued at the Moscow Conference on November 1, 1943. The first point in the declaration was that the Allies considered it essential that the

---

[1] Mr. Eden was away from London until November 10.

(b)   [2] On October 25 the Prime Minister asked the Foreign Office whether Count Sforza was the heir to the House of Milan, and when the House of Milan was 'jockeyed out' by the House of Savoy. The Prime Minister thought that Count Sforza wanted to be King himself.

The Foreign Office pointed out that the House of Sforza, as far as Italian history was concerned, came to an end with the death of Francesco Sforza's grandson in 1535, that Count Sforza did not appear to claim descent from the Milanese family of Sforza, and that the House of Savoy was older than the House of Sforza, and had not 'jockeyed' the latter out of pretensions to the national leadership of Italy.

(a) T1701/3, Churchill Papers/243. (b) R11073/131/22.

Italian Government should be made more democratic by the introduction of representatives of those sections of the Italian people who
had always opposed Fascism.[1]

Marshal Badoglio himself was willing, and indeed anxious, to
widen his Government. So also was the King, if the 'broadening'
could take place without his immediate abdication. The King
realised that sooner or later he would have to abdicate, but he
thought that the longer he delayed, the greater were the chances of
maintaining the dynasty. The chief source of difficulty, as the Prime
Minister and Mr. Eden had expected, was Count Sforza. Count
Sforza arrived in Italy on October 18. He took the line at once that
the King should abdicate in favour of his grandson—a child of six
who was at this time in Switzerland. He was prepared to accept
Marshal Badoglio as Regent, but—in the view of Mr. Macmillan
and all the other British representatives with whom he came into
contact—his intention was to secure the Prime Ministership for
himself. He obtained the support of the Neapolitan Liberals—
including Croce—for his proposal, and also persuaded Marshal (a)
Badoglio that the King's abdication was necessary. Marshal
Badoglio had come to this conclusion after hearing from Count
Sforza and Signor Croce of their refusal to join any Government
while the King remained on the throne. Marshal Badoglio thought
that no Government could be formed without Count Sforza, and
therefore agreed to resign, and to advise the King to send for
Count Sforza who would then put to him the demand for his
abdication.

Marshal Badoglio saw the King on November 1. The King was (b)
unwilling to abdicate, and said that he would go to Naples to discuss
the whole question with the political leaders. He appears to have
seen three of them. One refused to join any government owing to
fear of reprisals on his family; the other two would not join the
Badoglio Government unless Count Sforza entered it. Count Sforza
refused to see the King.

Meanwhile Count Sforza had sent his version of the affair in a
letter to the Prime Minister. This letter, which had been given to
General Mason-Macfarlane[2] and was transmitted by him to General
Eisenhower, stated that Count Sforza had been shown a letter from
Marshal Badoglio to the King advising the latter to abdicate in
favour of his grandson—thus passing over the Crown Prince—and

---

[1] The Moscow Conference also agreed upon the establishment of an Allied Advisory
Council for Italy. See below, p. 589.

[2] General Sir N. Mason-Macfarlane was head of the Allied Military Mission to the
Italian Government. The mission had arrived in Brindisi in mid-September. General
Mason-Macfarlane was appointed Deputy President of the Allied Control Commission in
January 1944.

(a) R11048/5880/22. (b) R11100, 11290, 11757, 11971/5880/22.

to appoint the Marshal himself as Regent. The King had also asked Count Sforza to enter the Government, but he had refused.

The Foreign Office thought that the Prime Minister would not wish to become involved in correspondence with Count Sforza on the issue of the monarchy, and that no answer—other than a simple acknowledgement through General Mason-Macfarlane—should be
(a) sent to the letter. The Prime Minister agreed with this procedure. On November 7 General Mason-Macfarlane reported another letter from Count Sforza—addressed to Mr. Eden and Mr. Berle—in which he said that he had refused an offer from the King to become Prime Minister, and that Marshal Badoglio shared his view that the King should abdicate in favour of his grandson.

The Prime Minister suggested to the Foreign Office[1] that he should send a sharp reply regretting the amount of trouble which Count Sforza was causing and the damage which he was doing to the cause he had promised to uphold. Count Sforza should not expect any support from the Prime Minister; on the contrary he would be loosening the existing ties between the Allies and any Italian Government. Sir A. Cadogan wrote that at first sight 'this slap at old Sforza' gave him considerable pleasure, but he thought it better again to send nothing more than an acknowledgement of the letter. Any other reply might only enhance Count Sforza's unduly high
(b) estimate of his own importance. Mr. Eden agreed with Sir A. Cadogan, and, in fact, only a non-commital acknowledgement was sent to this second letter.
(c) Meanwhile on November 2 Mr. Macmillan had asked for instruction on our attitude towards the disputes which were taking place between the King and the politicians. At first Mr. Macmillan had been inclined to wait on events; he now felt that we could not continue a policy of non-intervention; the political crisis was indeed due partly to our desire to broaden the basis of the Government, and to the impossibility of doing so unless the King abdicated. General Eisenhower's view was that we should let the King and Marshal Badoglio carry on at present; the more politically-minded Americans, including Mr. Murphy, were afraid of another Darlan episode and would like to see the King disappear.

The Prime Minister replied on November 3 that he was sure that everything could be settled better in Rome, but we did not know when we should get there. Meanwhile it seemed dangerous to make changes. The King was nothing to us, and we had no wish to incur political unpopularity on his behalf. Nevertheless the Prime Minister inclined to General Eisenhower's view. The Prime Minister also

[1] The Foreign Office thought at first that the letter was addressed to the Prime Minister.

(a) R11408/5880/22. (b) R12286/5880/22. (c) R11048/5880/22; R11177/49/22.

sent Mr. Macmillan a note prepared by the Foreign Office on their view of the situation. They thought that the trouble had arisen largely over Count Sforza's success in rallying all the available politicians who were hostile to the King, with the result that Marshal Badoglio was now unable to get any of them to join his Government unless the King abdicated. If the Italians found a solution without appealing to us, we should have to accept it even if it meant the King's abdication and the appointment of Marshal Badoglio as Regent. We did not want to be saddled with undue responsibility for deciding what government Italy was to have. If we had to express an opinion, we should say that, in view of the difficulties of broadening the Government, the King and Marshal Badoglio should continue to carry on as at present until the Government was established in Rome and was in contact with the Italian people as a whole.

The Foreign Office favoured this course because they doubted Count Sforza's qualities as a leader. He was jealous of Marshal Badoglio and would probably try to discredit him as Regent in order to take his place, not necessarily as Regent but perhaps as some sort of republican dictator. In any case it was difficult to believe that Count Sforza and Marshal Badoglio—two representatives of past and discredited régimes—would be allowed to hold power for very long, since there would soon be numbers of younger politicians eager for office after twenty years of repression. There was also the possibility of intervention by the military clique which favoured the Crown Prince. In fact the King's abdication might well open the way to troublesome problems from which we should be unable to dissociate ourselves.

This message to Mr. Macmillan crossed a telegram from him in which he put forward further points for consideration if Allied (a) intervention were necessary to settle the political crisis. He thought the arguments for and against securing the immediate abdication of the King were evenly balanced. Public opinion in Great Britain and the United States—especially in the latter—would be more satisfied with the King's abdication and the formation of a broadly based Government; this plan would also be in harmony with our basic war aims. On the other hand we could not be sure that all Italy would share the known views of the intellectuals of Naples and the alleged views of the politicians in Rome. We were also uncertain of the effect of the King's abdication on the Italian army and on the fleet which was collaborating well with us. Another argument in favour of delaying any change was that we were just about to set up the Allied Control Commission for Italy, and that it would be wiser not to decide on a vital point before consultation with the French and the Russians.

(a) R11182/5880/22.

Sir A. Cadogan wrote a minute to the Prime Minister on November 5 that he saw no reason for changing the policy which we had outlined to Mr. Macmillan. We should have to meet with bitter criticism from Count Sforza and Signor Croce and others who would be disappointed at not getting office. We could argue that the refusal of Count Sforza and Signor Croce to join a Government unless the King abdicated, and the refusal of the King to abdicate had produced a deadlock which only the Italian people could resolve. At a time when two-thirds of Italy was in German hands the Italian people had no means of expressing an opinion. We had not departed at all from the Moscow declaration, but the refusal of the anti-Fascists at present available to join a Government under the King and the refusal of the King to abdicate left us with no alternative but to accept the present situation until we had reached Rome and the Italian people were better able to express their wishes. We could take this line in our public statements and try to persuade the Americans to support it.

(a) The Prime Minister agreed entirely with this suggestion. He had sent a personal message to Mr. Macmillan on the night of November 4–5 warning him to beware of 'breaking down' Marshal Badoglio or even the King lest we should weaken the obedience of the Italian forces, and especially of the fleet. He thought that Italian politics could wait for a few weeks. On November 6 he sent a message

(b) to the President on similar lines and adding that he understood General Eisenhower to incline generally to the same view. He ended his message with the words: 'Surely we should stick to what we have got till we are sure we can get something better, and this can only be ascertained when we have Rome in our possession. I do not believe that Sforza counts for anything that will make men kill or die.'

(c) The President replied on November 9 that he was so far removed from first hand knowledge of Italian conditions that he was asking for recommendations from 'people on the spot'. He made a contemptuous reference to the King of Italy, but considered that—unless he were advised otherwise—the best plan might be to keep the House of Savoy under the King's grandson and at the same time to bring all parties into the Government as soon as possible. Mean-

(d) while on November 8 the War Cabinet had endorsed the Prime Minister's view that the balance of advantage lay in maintaining the existing Government and in giving up the attempt to broaden the basis of it before the capture of Rome. General Eisenhower told

---

(a) T1851/3 (Churchill Papers/243; R11292/242/22). (b) T1875/3, No. 495 (Churchill Papers/243; R11345/9506/22). (c) T1913/3, No. 415 (Churchill Papers/243; R11688/5880/22). (d) WM(43)151; R11559/5880/22.

Mr. Macmillan on November 9 that he was in complete agreement (a) with the Prime Minister's policy.

A new turn of events also seemed to justify the refusal to give way to the demands of Count Sforza and his fellow politicians. Shortly after the King's return from Naples a message arrived from Signor (b) Bonomi[1] on behalf of the leaders of the six opposition parties in Rome, which at the time of the armistice had formed a Committee of National Liberation (including the Socialists and Communists),[2] that they were prepared to support a political Cabinet in which Marshal Badoglio would be military but not political chief on the two conditions that the question of broadening the Government should be postponed until the occupation of Rome, and that the final decision on a future régime should be left to an elected assembly after the liberation of the country. This messsage did not mention Count Sforza, but showed that the politicians representing, or claiming to represent the six parties did not want him to set up a Government without including them.

The King now asked Marshal Badoglio to withdraw his resigna- (c) tion. Marshal Badoglio agreed to continue in office until the occupa- tion of Rome. He decided to give up the attempt to broaden the political basis of his Government, and instead to try to improve it administratively by bringing a number of experts into it in order to work effectively with the Allied Control Commission which was set up on November 12.

Marshal Badoglio was unable to get Count Sforza's support for this temporary arrangement. Count Sforza, having failed to obtain the Prime Ministership for himself, refused his collaboration with the 'government of technicians'. This refusal clearly meant that, in spite of his pledges before coming to Italy, he would continue to stir up opposition not only against the King but against Marshal Badoglio.

The next development of importance on the opposition side was an attempt to bring about a conference of such Italian political (d)

---

[1] Signor Bonomi had been a right-wing Socialist politician before 1914. He had supported Italian intervention in the 1914–18 war, and had served in the army. He became a Minister in 1919, and was Prime Minister of a Coalition Government from June 1921 to February 1922. In 1920 he had received the Collar of the Annunziata for his services in negotiating, together with Count Sforza, the treaty of Rapallo with Yugoslavia. He had lived in retirement from open political activities during the Fascist régime.

[2] One of these parties—the so-called Party of Action—was new; its programme was 'liberal-republican', with an emphasis on social reform, but it was viewed with certain suspicion not unmixed with jealousy by the leaders of the older parties. The other five were revivals of the opposition parties whose activities had been suppressed by the Fascists. The parties had been attempting secretly to organise themselves for some time before the fall of Mussolini. The Roman Committee of National Liberation was in touch with similar committees in Naples and the more important northern cities.

(a) R11622/5880/22. (b) R11425, 11757, 11889/5880/22. (c) R11409/5880/22; R11643/ 242/22. (d) R13580/5880/22.

leaders as could be brought together in Naples. The Foreign Office were not well informed of the early stages of this plan, or of the attitude of the military authorities towards it; the reports received from the news agencies in liberated Italy were in fact fuller than those sent by the military authorities.[1]

After a first refusal on the grounds that political action on such a scale was undesirable at a place as near as Naples to the area of battle, the military authorities agreed to allow a conference to be held at Bari. The Bari 'Congress', as it was called, opened on

(a) January 28. The Prime Minister had suggested to the War Cabinet on January 24 that Mr. Macmillan should try to secure the cancellation, or at all events the postponement, of the Bari meeting. The Anzio landings in Italy had introduced a new factor since the meeting had been arranged, and all energies were now concentrated on the battle for Rome. We could argue that postponement would give the Italian politicians a much better meeting place at the cost of a very short delay.

(b)   Mr. Macmillan and the British military authorities in Italy, however, considered that a second postponement would be most undesirable. The occupation of Rome still seemed a long way off, and the Americans and Russians on the Advisory Council would oppose interference with the meeting. British public opinion also exaggerated the importance of the congress, and failed to realise that there was little foundation in its claims to be representative. The Foreign Office, though they would have preferred the postponement of any large political demonstration until the occupation of Rome, agreed with Mr. Macmillan's view. No action was taken therefore to prevent the holding of the meeting.

After considerable discussion the congress accepted on January 30

(c) a programme demanding the early formation of a government with full powers, and including representatives of the six parties, the abdication of the King, and the summoning of a constituent assembly as soon as hostilities ceased. The congress also established an executive committee or Giunta[2] of representatives of the parties with the task of realising the programme. This arrangement was a compromise; the left-wing parties would have been more explicit about

(d) the future of the monarchy. Count Sforza claimed credit for the

---

[1] Mr. Macmillan, who was British High Commissioner and representative on the Allied Advisory Council, remained at this time as Minister Resident with the Allied Headquarters at Algiers. He visited Italy only three times between January and April 1944. The reports from British and American journalists in Italy were of some embarrassment to their respective Governments, since the journalists were closely in touch with the leaders of the Opposition, e.g. Signor Croce, and inclined to support Opposition views especially on the question of the monarchy.

[2] Usually spelt, in British documents, in the Spanish form Junta.

(a) WM(44)10; R1192/29/22. (b) R1435/29/22. (c) R1646/29/22. (d) R1937/29/22.

moderation of the congress, but his own part in the proceedings confirmed the British distrust of him. He spoke in abusive and insulting terms about the King and the Government, and said that failure to get rid of the King would be an embarrassment to Italy at the Peace Conference when the Italians rose 'to defend the sacred borders of the fatherland and our old and honoured colonies'.

Mr. Eden noted this statement as a forecast of the attempt which the Italian so-called democrats would make to escape from the penalties of the armistice. Mr. Macmillan's view of the congress was (a) that the moderates—the Liberals and Christian Democrats—had at least avoided a demand (supported by Count Sforza) for the elimination of the Crown Prince and the establishment of a regency; they had merely asked for the abdication of the King and, although they had not committed themselves to the succession of the Crown Prince, their statement was so framed as to make this solution possible. The report was thus not welcome to Count Sforza whom the Communists had described privately to the British authorities as 'a trimmer and an egoistical windbag'.

The British view was thus that the congress was both untimely and (b) unrepresentative, and that there was no reason to accept the demands which it put forward—or even to assume that the Junta would be of any lasting importance. The Junta was not an impressive body, and did not command complete authority over the parties from which its members were drawn. The Americans, on the other hand, were more inclined to take the proceedings at Bari as conclusive evidence of Italian opinion in general, and to regard the British view as due to the Prime Minister's liking for monarchy, and the intention of the British Government to 'keep Italy down' after the war in the interest of British predominance in the Mediterranean.

(iii)

Anglo-American differences of view on Allied policy with regard to the demands of the Junta: Russian proposals for broadening the basis of Marshal Badoglio's Government: the King's announcement of his abdication: formation of a new Government under Marshal Badoglio (February 1–April 21, 1944).

At the end of January it was unfortunately clear that the surprise attack at Anzio was not bringing the results hoped from it. The heaviest German counter-attacks had not yet been made, but the Allies were unable to make a rapid advance from their bridgeheads

(a) R1886, 2318/691/22. (b) R2582/29/22.

or to the south to break the fierce enemy resistance in the Cassino area. In this situation the British and United States Governments had once again to consider whether it was expedient to continue their policy of refusing to disturb the existing political regime until the matter could be decided in Rome.

(a)   On the night of February 1–2 Lord Halifax telegraphed that the State Department had shown to a member of the British Embassy a copy of a telegram sent to the United States representative on the Advisory Council. This telegram (which Sir A. Cadogan regarded as 'amazing') said that the State Department had come to the conclusion that the reconstruction of the Italian Government could not be delayed now that the fall of Rome was not likely to take place for some time, and that the 'liberal' forces in Italy should be allowed to set up a representative regime. No political reconstruction seemed possible under the present King, and there was no likelihood that he would abdicate voluntarily.

(b)   Lord Halifax had reported earlier (January 26) that the State Department favoured the early abdication of the King, and his replacement by his grandson. Mr. Eden at first was inclined to regard this plan favourably. He thought that, on balance, there were advantages in retaining the monarchy, but that the Crown Prince would be no better than the King. Mr. Eden said, however, that he

(c) had not made up his mind. The Prime Minister, on the other hand, remained strongly in favour of making no change until the Allied armies had entered Rome. The Foreign Office also inclined to this view. Sir A. Cadogan thought that the Bari Congress had not been followed by any demonstration of public opinion in support of its conclusions, and that, as matters stood for the time, the best plan was to leave matters alone. We could not say what we would do after the capture of Rome, since we had no idea what the state of Italian opinion would be when we arrived there.

On February 12 Mr. Eden wrote a minute generally accepting this policy, and adding—as an additional complication—that we could not forecast even approximately when we should reach Rome.

(d) The Prime Minister had already (February 3) sent a telegram to the President expressing his hope that no change of regime would be made before the capture of Rome. A disturbance of such authority as remained in the Italian State, and an attempt to form a new authority out of political groups with no real backing, would add greatly to our difficulties. A new government formed out of these groups, in its effort to get the support of the Italian people, would try to assert Italian interests much more strongly than the King and

---

(a) R1764/691/22. (b) R1446/691/22. (c) R1895/691/22. (d) T201/4, No. 564 (Churchill Papers/243; R1895/691/22).

Marshal Badoglio dared to do. Marshal Badoglio's disappearance would therefore be a misfortune and, according to our reports, action against the King might affect the Italian navy. The Prime Minister felt most strongly that, in view of the heavy fighting, we should give weight to military considerations. Six days later the (a) Prime Minister sent another message to the President that he was much opposed to an attempt to work with Count Sforza and the Italian Junta at a critical moment in the fighting. Count Sforza had completely broken his undertaking to the Allies. The Prime Minister asked once again that no decisions should be taken without consultation with us, and without an effort by the President and himself to reach agreement.

The President replied on February 11 that he had instructed the (b) State Department to take no action towards effecting a change in the existing Government in Italy until the military situation had improved sufficiently to 'warrant risking the disaffection of those Italians' who were 'now assisting the Allied forces'. The President added: 'I think though that you and I should regard this only as a temporary reprieve for the two old gentlemen'.

Before this message was received Lord Halifax had telegraphed (c) that the policy of the State Department in favour of getting rid of the King and Marshal Badoglio was becoming known, and if this policy were not put into effect public opinion would conclude that British opposition was the reason. The State Department might assist the public in reaching this conclusion. They might be glad to have an opportunity of appearing more 'liberal' than the British Government, and of taking a line which would appeal, not only to the Left wing in the United States, but to the Italian Americans whose votes were of importance in the presidential election.

The Prime Minister considered that we should nonetheless hold to our view. He had been confirmed in his judgement by a telegram (d) from General Wilson[1] to the effect that he did not want anything done which might increase internal difficulties or political unrest during the battle for Rome of which he had good hope of success. The Prime Minister therefore replied to the President on February 13 (e) that he fully agreed about the desirability of reviewing the whole political situation after the capture of Rome. Meanwhile the existing régime was the legal Government of Italy with whom we had concluded an armistice. As a result of this armistice the Italian navy and

---

[1] General Sir Henry Maitland Wilson had succeeded General Eisenhower as Allied Supreme Commander in the Mediterranean after the latter's appointment to the command of the Expeditionary Force for the cross-Channel invasion.

(a) T263/4, No. 573 (Churchill Papers/243; R2233/691/22). (b) T287/4, No. 464 (Churchill Papers/243; R2304/691/22); R1976/691/22. (c) R2192/691/22. (d) R2415/ 691/22. (e) T299/4, No. 577 (Churchill Papers/243; R2392/691/22).

some of the army and air force were fighting on our side. The Italian Government were completely in our hands, and were obeying our directions far more readily than any other Government we might constitute. This Government also had more power over the fleet, the army, officials, etc. than would be exercised by an authority chosen from the débris of the political parties, none of which had the slightest title by election or prescription. A new Government would have to make its reputation with the Italian people by standing up to us, and would probably try to wriggle out of the armistice terms.

The Prime Minister reminded the President that he had given strong support to the State Department over Darlan. The Department seemed now to regret the Darlan episode, but the Prime Minister still considered the action then taken as right. 'Several thousand British and American soldiers are alive today because of it, and it got us Dakar at a time when we could ill have spared the large forces needed for its capture.'

The Foreign Office thought it desirable to fall in with the view of the State Department that Anglo-American discussions should begin at once on the regime which would ultimately take the place of the existing arrangement with the King and Marshal Badoglio. The

(a) position was, however, further complicated by a joint message of February 10 from Count Sforza and Signor Croce to the Allied Governments. This message, which followed the lines of the proposal recommended to the Allied Governments by the Junta,[1] was to the effect that the Junta had sent a letter to the King asking him to abdicate in favour of the Crown Prince Umberto and requiring also that the latter should then delegate all his civil and military powers to an extraordinary Government or to a Lieutenant-General of the Realm (who should not be a member of the Royal Family or a soldier) until a constituent assembly had decided upon the future régime of the country. Count Sforza and Signor Croce asked the Allied Governments to put pressure on the King to abdicate and the Crown Prince to accept this programme. The general suggestion was that the moderates could not hold the political situation in Italy unless the Allies agreed to these proposals.

(b) This message was forwarded by General Mason-Macfarlane and received in London on February 15. In spite of his instructions to avoid discussions with the Italian political leaders General Mason-Macfarlane had seen Count Sforza and had persuaded him to tone down his original draft. General Mason-Macfarlane thought that we must either warn the political leaders that we would not allow

---

[1] See above, p. 518. No answer was sent to the letter from Count Sforza and Signor Croce.

(a) R2489, 2490, 2503, 2515, 2540/691/22; R3070/29/22. (b) R2489/691/22.

any interference with General Badoglio's Government until we had reached Rome, or we must persuade the King to abdicate. General Mason-Macfarlane's own view was in favour of the latter course.

The Prime Minister telegraphed to General Wilson on February (a) 16 that he had read with much concern the telegrams in which General Mason-Macfarlane shows signs of 'wobbling' on the question of the King's abdication. The Prime Minister had reached a definite agreement with President Roosevelt that the existing régime should be maintained until the capture of Rome. He thought that, if we built up now an Italian Government on a broad basis, we should merely be preparing 'a rod for our backs' because such a Government could establish their position with the Italian people only by standing up to us. The Prime Minister also telegraphed to General (b) Mason-Macfarlane that he was advocating a policy different from that to which the British Government were committed, and to which also President Roosevelt had agreed, namely the support of the King and Marshal Badoglio until we were in occupation of Rome. The Prime Minister pointed out that the Italians had surrendered unconditionally, and that there could be no question of changing our policy because we were afraid (in General Mason-Macfarlane's words) of the 'action of less responsible elements'. The Prime Minister told General Mason-Macfarlane to read Count Sforza's letter to Mr. Berle—on the strength of which he had been allowed into the Italian theatre of war—and to see how grossly Count Sforza had broken the undertakings which he then gave on his honour.

On the night of February 17–18 the Foreign Office telegraphed (c) to Mr. Macmillan that, as a result of an exchange of messages between the Prime Minister and the President, the latter had instructed the State Department that they should do nothing to bring about any change in the Italian Government 'pending such an improvement in military situation as would warrant risking disaffection of Italians who are now assisting Allied forces'. Hence there would be no Anglo-American initiative at this stage towards making any change or dealing with the question of the King's abdication.

At this point the Allied position seemed clear. The President had accepted, at least for the time, the British view that it would be a mistake to upset Marshal Badoglio's Government, which was fulfilling its pledge to collaborate with the Allies and to meet the requirements of the Commander-in-Chief. Unfortunately the Commander-

---

(a) T326/4, Churchill Papers/243. (b) T325/4, Churchill Papers/243. (c) R2725/691/22.

in-Chief himself now made suggestions out of harmony with the
(a) policy of the British Government. He telegraphed on February 18
that the political situation was changing very rapidly, and that the
tactics of the Italian Opposition might dislocate the civil administration. After consultation with the British and American authorities
in Italy, he was convinced that a decision on the political question
could not be delayed. The six parties had agreed upon a programme
to permit the accession of the Crown Prince provided that he would
delegate his powers to a Lieutenancy of a single individual or of a
group until the meeting of a Constituent Assembly after the war.
The six parties had asked for Allied assistance in carrying out this
programme, and had added that, unless it were put into effect, they
could not guarantee the actions of 'less responsible elements'.

They had themselves put out an appeal to all Italians in the
Service of the State to regard the King and the Badoglio Government
as rebels, and to take no part in such rebellion against the Italian
people. The Allied authorities had stopped—as far as was possible—
the circulation of this appeal, and had warned the Junta that action
of this kind would not be tolerated.

General Wilson considered that the attitude of the Opposition
threatened to interfere with Allied military operations more seriously
than any likely repercussions to the abdication of the King or a
change in the Government. If we arrested, or allowed the Italian
Government to arrest the members of the Junta, we should raise a
storm of protest, but we could hardly avoid a measure of this kind
if we continued to support the Government.

We had therefore to choose between putting pressure on the King
to abdicate in favour of the Crown Prince whose succession in legal
form ought to ensure the loyalty of the Italian armed forces, or
informing the Opposition that we should suppress any change in the
political situation or any attempt to interfere with the Badoglio
Government before the occupation of Rome. In either case our
intervention was necessary. General Wilson favoured the former
course and, indeed, recommended that, after his succession, the
Crown Prince should summon the chosen representative of the
Opposition to form a Government. Two days later (February 20)
General Wilson forwarded his comments on the Opposition programme.[1] This programme had already been put forward in the

---

[1] General Mason-Macfarlane—according to General Wilson—had telegraphed the
programme to London on February 19. This telegram had not reached London, and the
Foreign Office took steps—on receiving General Wilson's telegram on February 20—to
obtain the text. General Wilson sent a copy of General Mason-Macfarlane's telegram on
February 21.

(a) NAF 622, R3079/29/22.

letter from Count Sforza and Signor Croce. General Wilson thought that the proposals were as moderate as anything we were likely to get from the Opposition. If our answer were long delayed, or if we insisted upon waiting until we had occupied Rome, the Opposition parties might take action to enforce their demands. Some of the politicians might even welcome arrest as a means of securing 'martyrdom' for themselves.

General Wilson sent his telegrams of February 18 and 20 in the first instance to the Combined Chiefs of Staff and the British Chiefs of Staff. The British Chiefs of Staff at once telegraphed to the British (a) Joint Staff Mission in Washington that the Italian political situation was being considered at the highest level between the Prime Minister and the President, and that General Wilson's telegrams should not be dealt with by the Combined Chiefs of Staff. The American Civil Affairs Division and the State Department, however, had already received copies of the telegram—and had drafted a reply approving of General Wilson's recommendations that the King should abdicate and that the Badoglio Government should be replaced. This draft was accepted by the President on February 22.

In this somewhat absurd position the Prime Minister telegraphed at once to General Wilson and, on February 21, brought the matter before the War Cabinet. The Prime Minister told General Wilson (February 20) that he much regretted that he (General Wilson) had (b) put forward proposals which he knew to be contrary to the policy of His Majesty's Government. The kind of Government which General Wilson was proposing to set up as a result of pressure would most probably be a great hindrance to the Allies. The President had agreed with our policy not to make any changes until we were in Rome. Now, owing to this surrender to threats from a 'handful of unrepresentative political leaders', everything was likely to be thrown into uncertainty. If General Wilson could not control the politicians at a time when they were weak, and out of office, what would he do when 'flushed with success, they are formed into a Government whose first need it must be to make capital with the Italian people by standing up to the British and Americans'?

The War Cabinet, on hearing an account of the situation, took the (c) view that we could not feel confidence in any alternative Italian Government established at the present stage, and that it would be much better—in the absence of really important pressure on us to the contrary—to keep to our policy of maintaining the present régime until after the capture of Rome, and to inform the Italian politicians accordingly.

(a) COS(W)1162; R3080/29/22. (b) T350/4, Churchill Papers/243. (c) WM(44) 23.3, C.A.

On February 22 the Prime Minister made a statement on Italy in the House of Commons.[1] He said that the Italian armistice was signed, on the basis of unconditional surrender, with the King and Marshal Badoglio, who were, and had continued to be, the legitimate Government of Italy. The Prime Minister was not yet convinced that any other Government which could be formed at present would command the same obedience from the Italian armed forces. The best occasion for the formation of a more broadly based Government would be after the occupation of Rome. The Prime Minister could not tell whether such a Government would be as helpful to the Allies as the existing Government; it might try to establish its position with the Italian people by resisting Allied demands. The members of the parties represented at the Bari Congress were eager to become the Government of Italy, but they had no elective authority and would have no constitutional authority until the King abdicated, or until he or his successor invited them to office. It was by no means certain that they would secure effective authority over the Italian armed forces now fighting with us. The policy, therefore, to which we had agreed provisionally with the United States Government, was 'to win the battle for Rome, and take a new view when we are there'.

(a)   Mr. Eden fully agreed with this policy. There was no means of knowing how far the group of self-appointed politicians of the Junta represented Italian opinion, and if we gave way to their blackmail— the threat that they could not prevent disorder if their proposals were not accepted—we should lose control of the situation. We should avoid criticism at home and disagreement with the French, Russians and Americans if we took the line of least resistance, but in the long run our acquiescence might cause us the greatest trouble.

(b)   Mr. Eden suggested, in a minute of February 24 to the Prime Minister, that he (the Prime Minister) should send a message to the President that General Wilson's information and recommendations had not altered his view that we should make no change in the Italian administration until our armies had reached Rome. The Prime Minister might also say that a warning ought to be given by the Allied Advisory Council to the Opposition leaders in southern Italy and Rome that the Allies would not tolerate interference with the political arrangements until the occupation of Rome.

(c)   The Prime Minister therefore telegraphed to the President on February 25 that he had made his statement in Parliament in the light of the President's earlier message. The statement had been well received and the Prime Minister was committed to it. Meanwhile the President had authorised a favourable reply to General Wilson's

---

[1] *Parl. Deb. 5th Ser., H. of C.*, Vol. 397, cols. 690–2.

   (a) R3082/29/22. (b) R3080/29/22. (c) T396/4, No. 593 (Churchill Papers/243; R3144/29/22).

suggestions. The Prime Minister had been surprised by these suggestions and did not agree with them. He thought that it would be very dangerous indeed to give way to the threats of people who had so recently surrendered unconditionally. The Prime Minister hoped that the President would allow matters to stand as they were before General Wilson's telegrams. If the fall of Rome were unduly delayed, we could reconsider the position, but we must not allow the Italian parties to think that they could play one of the Allies against the other.

The President replied on February 27 that he had never intended (a) to approve of the proposed reply to General Wilson without obtaining the Prime Minister's agreement, and that the reply would not be sent. Meanwhile the King of Italy had asked General Macfarlane (b) on February 21 to tell the Allied Governments that his position had become impossible because the Allied authorities had allowed him to be openly discredited and attacked through the Psychological Warfare Branch[1] headquarters and through lax censorship. The King therefore proposed to withdraw from public affairs and nominate the Crown Prince as Lieutenant of the Realm with full powers. He would announce the fact at once, but the lieutenancy would not come into operation until Rome had been reached. The King wanted to enter Rome himself, and thought that the Crown Prince could more easily form a new Government there. The King put forward this proposal on the understanding that no more publicity would be allowed to attacks on him. If he were compelled to abdicate at once he would not permit the Crown Prince or his grandson to succeed him, and the House of Savoy would come to an end. Mr. Makins reported later that Count Sforza and Signor Croce (c) were said to be willing to accept the King's proposal.

The Prime Minister replied to the information about the King's (d) plan that it would be considered, but that there was no need for hurry. The military authorities were responsible for keeping order behind the lines among Italians who had surrendered unconditionally. The Prime Minister could not understand why there should be so much fuss or why we should have to make 'some great political gesture. What we have to do is to win the battle and maintain order, and for this ample forces are available.'

The whole situation was discussed with Mr. Macmillan on a visit of the latter to London. Mr. Eden wrote a minute to the Prime (e) Minister on February 28 that—having received the President's

---

[1] This organisation included a large number of journalists.

(a) T405/4, No. 483 (Churchill Papers/243; R3144/29/22. (b) R2892/691/22. (c) R3084/691/22. (d) R3094/29/22. (e) R3070/29/22.

agreement that no change should be made in the Italian administration until we had reached Rome—we should try to agree upon a policy with the State Department. As a first step we should warn the Italians through the Control Commission that we would not tolerate agitation likely to disturb the military situation and that we would study the various plans and suggestions before settling the political problem at the appropriate time. For this purpose we would use the Advisory Council since we could thereby bring in the other Allied Governments.

Mr. Eden thought that the best plan ultimately would be the appointment of the Crown Prince as Lieutenant of the Realm, or the abdication of the King in favour of the Crown Prince. The former plan would involve less risk to the monarchy which we wished to preserve as a unifying factor. In spite of the apparent willingness of Count Sforza and Signor Croce to agree with the plan, we should be wiser not to put it into effect at once since we did not know whether the political parties in Rome would accept it. Mr. Eden assumed that Rome would be captured within three months. He thought that, if this assumption turned out to be wrong, we might have to change our procedure.

The Prime Minister agreed that Lord Halifax should be instructed to suggest this plan to the United States Government. The Prime Minister, however, still thought that it would be a pity to lose Marshal Badoglio and that the emergence of Count Sforza or Signor Croce as Prime Minister would be disastrous.

(a) Lord Halifax carried out his instructions in a memorandum of March 6 to the State Department. On the following day the President
(b) telegraphed to the Prime Minister that, according to information from Italy, the political situation there was rapidly deteriorating and immediate action was required to break (*sic*) the *impasse* between the Government and the six Opposition parties. General Wilson had found it necessary to forbid a strike called by three of the anti-Fascist parties in the Naples area. The President was afraid that we were moving towards a situation in which we might have to use force against the anti-Fascist leaders and groups. The President wanted to give the Government and Opposition an indication of our policy towards their respective plans. He said that the American view favoured the programme of the six Opposition parties for the abdication of the King and the delegation of the powers of his successor to a Lieutenant of the Realm acceptable to the six parties. They would probably choose Signor Croce. General Wilson and his advisers had recommended that we should adopt this programme,

(a) R4088/691/22. (b) T481/4, No. 490 (Churchill Papers/243/8; R3973/29/22).

and were awaiting our approval. The President thought that we ought to get the co-operation of the liberal political groups by bringing them into the Italian Government.

The Prime Minister replied on March 8 that he was much con- (a) cerned by the President's message. On the strength of the President's telegram of February 11[1] he had made a statement in Parliament. Our own information was that no new facts of importance had appeared and that the Allied forces were capable of maintaining order in the regions they had occupied as the result of the unconditional surrender of Italy. It would therefore be a very serious mistake to give way to agitation and the threats of groups of office-seeking politicians. We might find that we had set up an administration which would not get the support of the Italian armed forces but which would try to establish its position with the Italian people by standing up to the Allies. We should thus have a more intractable version of the Gaullist committee. Meanwhile in the midst of a heart-shaking battle we were to get rid of the 'tame and helpful' Government of the King and Badoglio which was doing its utmost to work its passage.

The Prime Minister thought that the course recommended by the President would be more popular and bring a transient success, but that it would be unfortunate for the victorious conquerors to have their hands forced by sections of the defeated population, and for the two Governments to be openly divided on an important question of policy. The Prime Minister again reminded the President that he had given him, and the State Department, loyal and vigorous support over the Darlan affair.

The Prime Minister was willing to consider now proposals for making the Crown Prince Lieutenant of the Realm, but he had no confidence in Signor Croce[2] or Count Sforza for the post. Count Sforza had definitely broken the undertakings given in his letter of September 23 to Mr. Berle. The Prime Minister hoped that the President would discuss the matter on the basis of Lord Halifax's instructions. He was most anxious to see a broadly based Government in Italy, but the Allies ought not to establish such a Government under duress, and could set it up with more chances of success when they were in Rome.

The President replied later the same day that his message of (b) March 7 had been sent with a view to meeting the difficult situation

---

[1] See above, p. 521.

[2] The Prime Minister's comment on Signor Croce was as follows: 'Macmillan tells me Croce is a dwarf Professor about 75 years old who wrote good books about aesthetics and philosophy. Vyshinsky who had tried to read the books says they are even duller than Karl Marx.'

(a) T486/4, No. 160 (Churchill Papers/243; R3973/29/22). (b) T492/4, No. 494 (Churchill Papers/243; R4120/29/22).

reported by General Wilson. He now asked the Prime Minister to let him have the British proposals for dealing with this situation. He wanted most strongly to work in harmony on the matter with the Prime Minister. They might differ on timing, but they were in agreement on the 'big objectives like self-determination'.

Mr. Eden thought that the President had not seen the instructions sent to Lord Halifax, and that the Prime Minister might refer to
(a) them in his reply. The Prime Minister sent an answer in this sense on March 13 to the President. He said that he was entirely at one with the President on the question of self-determination, and that all he pleaded for was 'timing'. He did not believe that the 'ambitious wind-bags' now agitating behind our front to become the Government of Italy had any representative standing; if we drove out the King and Marshal Badoglio, we should merely have complicated the task of the armies. The Prime Minister pointed out that the Soviet Government also held this view, though their aim might be a Communist Italy. British policy aimed at the reconstruction of the Government on a broad basis by taking into account the opinion of the democratic north of Italy. If we could not get to Rome for several months, we should have to act earlier, but without the favourable conditions open to us once we were in possession of the capital.

(b)   This message crossed a telegram from the President that he had not meant at any time to give the impression that he agreed to postpone all political decisions until after the occupation of Rome. The political situation had been developing rapidly, but the capture of Rome was still remote The President did not want to use stern measures against our friends in Italy. At present General Wilson and his British and American advisers recommended immediate support for the programme of the six Opposition parties. We need not do more than tell the Junta of our support, and leave it to them to present their programme to the King and work it out among themselves. The President could not understand why we should hesitate to support a policy admirably suited to our common military and political aims. American public opinion would never understand our continued tolerance and apparent support of the King.

The Prime Minister replied on March 14.[1] He said that the
(c) Russians had announced that they were sending a fully-accredited Ambassador to the present Italian Government with whom we were still technically at war. The Prime Minister did not think it wise,

---

[1] The Prime Minister does not seem to have consulted the Foreign Office about the terms of this reply.

(a) T545/4, No. 618 (Churchill Papers/243; R4120/29/22). (b) T547/4, No. 498 (Churchill Papers/243; R4121/29/22). (c) T554/4, No. 619 (Churchill Papers/243; R4121/29/22).

without further consideration, to accept the programme of the so-called six parties, and demand the immediate abdication of the King and the installation of Signor Croce as Lieutenant of the Realm. He proposed, however, to consult the War Cabinet upon what the President had rightly called 'a major political decision'. He pointed out that our war with Italy had lasted since June 1940; we had suffered 232,000 casualties in men as well as heavy losses in ships. The Prime Minister felt sure that the President would give consideration to our views, and would remember that he (the Prime Minister) had committed himself in public after the President's earlier message.

The first stage of the Russian action to which the Prime Minister (a) referred had been reported by General Mason-Macfarlane to General Wilson on March 8. He said that the Soviet representative on the Allied Advisory Council in Italy had told the Italian Government that the Soviet Government were willing to establish diplomatic relations with the Italian Government and to exchange representatives who would have the privileges and rights of Ambassadors and a status equal to that of the Allied representatives with the French National Committee. The Italian Government had felt that they must accept this offer.

The Prime Minister sent a minute to Mr. Eden that he was glad the Soviet Government were taking the sensible step of establishing diplomatic relations with Marshal Badoglio's Government. The (b) Foreign Office also thought it satisfactory that the Soviet Government appeared to be willing to work with the Badoglio Government and the King at least until the occupation of Rome, but they found serious objections in the establishment at this stage of direct diplomatic relations between the U.S.S.R. and Italy. In the normal course the exchange of diplomatic representatives with the Italian Government would not take place while the Allies were still at war with Italy. If the other Allied Powers also appointed Ambassadors, the status of the Advisory Council and the Control Commission would be undermined. In any case it was extraordinary that the Russians had acted without previously mentioning their intention to us. Their action would give rise to all sorts of unfortunate conjectures in Italy.

The Prime Minister was convinced by Mr. Eden at least to the extent of approving instructions to Sir A. Clark Kerr to enquire (c) from M. Vyshinsky whether the Soviet Government really intended to establish diplomatic relations with Italy, and, if so, to represent to them the disadvantage of such action, and to ask them to allow the British and United States Governments time to consider the question in all its aspects.

(a) R4238/51/22. (b) R3880, 3881/51/22. (c) R3880/51/22.

(a)   The Foreign Office instructed General Mason-Macfarlane on March 13 to tell the Italian Government that they should not issue any communiqué on the matter since it was under consideration
(b) between the British and Soviet Governments. This message did not arrive in time to prevent an announcement. M. Bogomolov[1] tried to
(c) 'play down' the Soviet action, and M. Vyshinsky said that there was no question of the establishment of diplomatic relations or the appointment of diplomatic representatives. The Soviet Government merely wished to enter into direct relations with the Badoglio Government.
(d)   The United States Government also protested at the Russian action.[2] The Prime Minister did not object to these protests, though he told Mr. Macmillan again on March 17 that the Russian action was an advantage to us in relation to our policy of retaining the King and Marshal Badoglio until the occupation of Rome. The Foreign Office were, however, dissatisfied with Marshal Badoglio's behaviour
(e) in the matter, and instructed Mr. Macmillan to tell him (and also M. Bogomolov) that the Italian Government were not entitled to enter into any engagement with a foreign Power, Allied or neutral, unless they had obtained the consent of the Supreme Allied Commander. The Foreign Office had also heard from General Mason-Macfarlane that Marshal Badoglio was intending to ask for Allied status. Mr. Macmillan was instructed that we were inclined to reject out of hand any proposal of this kind.

(f)   The Prime Minister put the general question of policy to the War Cabinet on March 15, and, with their agreement, telegraphed
(g) later in the day to the President. In this telegram the Prime Minister said the War Cabinet had asked him to assure the President that they agreed fully with his wish to establish a more broadly based government in Italy, and that the future form of government of the Italian people could be settled only by self-determination. They also agreed that the point to consider was the timing. They were sure that it would be better to keep the King and Marshal Badoglio until we had occupied Rome because it would then be easier than at present to construct a more representative and solidly based administration. The War Cabinet felt that nothing could be worse for the joint interests of Great Britain and the United States and for the future of Italy than to set up in Italy a weak democratic

---

[1] Soviet representative at Allied Force Headquarters.
[2] One of the first American conclusions was that the Russians probably had in mind considerations of Balkan policy, i.e. they were hoping to secure a base of operation in the Adriatic in order to bring to bear the maximum Soviet influence in Yugoslavia during and after the war. *F.R.U.S.*, 1944, III, 1040–1.

(a) R3982/51/22. (b) R3983/51/22. (c) R4019/51/22. (d) R4194, 4246, 4281/51/22. (e) R4547/51/22; R4637/691/22. (f) WM(44)35. 1, C.A. (g) T564/4, No. 621 (Churchill Papers/243; R4121/ 29/22).

Government which would subsequently collapse. Even a settlement reached in Rome could not be final because we should have to review it after the liberation of the northern provinces and great industrial centres like Milan and Turin. The War Cabinet did not regard the six parties as representative in any true sense of Italian democracy or of the Italian nation.

The War Cabinet had of course considered General Wilson's views, and disagreed with them. We should, however, be ready to discuss the suggestions proposed in the memorandum communicated by Lord Halifax; we also recognised that if the capture of Rome were delayed for two or three months, we should have to review the question of timing.

The Prime Minister said that the War Cabinet had also asked him to put to the President the great importance of not exposing to the world any divergencies of view between our two Governments especially in relation to the action which the Soviet Government had taken. The President replied on March 18 that he fully agreed about (a) the importance of making no public statement of our divergence of views, but that he still felt that circumstances might make it desirable for us to support the programme of the six parties.

On March 21 Mr. Macmillan sent to the Prime Minister a note (b) on the Italian situation. His general conclusion was that we ought to give some answer to the King and to the Junta. We could say that the political question must remain in abeyance until the occupation of Rome, or we could tell the Junta that the King had a plan to suggest to them, and the King that he would be well advised to put his plan to the politicians. Both the King and the Junta had moved from their original positions, and we might get an agreed settlement from them which would give us some internal stability until the end of the war, and be more favourable to the preservation of the monarchy.

Mr. Macmillan's note was sent before he knew of a proposal—put forward by the Russians—for broadening the basis of the Badoglio Government. This plan was proposed in a memorandum of March 19 from the Soviet Government in support of their action in exchang- (c) ing diplomatic representatives with Italy. The Foreign Office thought that the Soviet arguments on this latter aspect of the matter were extremely weak. On the other hand, the general line taken in the memorandum was satisfactory. The Soviet Government were pre-pared to accept the British and American view that for the time it was inexpedient to get rid of the Badoglio Government and to

---

(a) T588/4, No. 502 (Churchill Papers/243; R4666/29/22). (b) R4999/53/22.
(c) R4485/51/22.

support the demand for the King's abdication. Since, however, the three Allied Governments were in agreement on this point, Marshal Badoglio must guarantee to do everything possible for the unification of the democratic and anti-Fascist forces in Italy, and must therefore take some steps to meet the wishes of the Junta. The Soviet Government therefore proposed a reorganisation of Marshal Badoglio's Government to this end. They were in fact using their influence in this direction.[1]

(a)   The United States Government sent a formal reply on March 27 to Lord Halifax's memorandum of March 6. They denied the existence of an agreement between the British and United States Governments to preserve the status of the King and the Badoglio Government until after the liberation of Rome. The United States Government had agreed only to wait before making any change until the military situation had sufficiently improved to warrant risking the disaffection of those Italians who were aiding the Allied forces. The United States Government now favoured the Junta proposal for the immediate abdication of the King and the delegation of all or some of the powers of his successor to a 'Lieutenant'. The President, however, had noted the recent decisions of the War Cabinet and had agreed that the two Governments should not permit their divergency of view to become publicly known. Nevertheless it was essential to reach a decision; the preservation of the *status quo* favoured one party in Italy, and was being interpreted by the opposition parties as an active support of the King and his Government. The British and American Governments must avoid the policy of suppressing normal political activity outside the military area and the use of force against anti-fascist leaders. The State Department therefore thought that the matter should be discussed on the Allied Advisory Council.

Mr. Eden instructed Lord Halifax to represent to the State Department that the proposal to put in force the plans of the Junta ignored later developments in the situation. The memorandum did not refer to the King's plan which was apparently acceptable to Count Sforza and Signor Croce or to the Russian plan for broadening the basis of the Badoglio Government or to the willingness of the Communist party (as a result of Soviet prompting) and probably of other parties represented on the Junta to enter the Badoglio Government without conditions. The Junta itself might be disintegrating. The British view was that it would be unwise and dangerous to revert

---

[1] Signor Togliatti, the Italian Communist leader, was sent from Moscow at the end of March to put the Russian views to the parties of the Left. The Communist decision to join a reorganised Government made it impossible for the other parties to keep out of it.

(a) R4924/29/22; R5517/691/22.

to the original Junta plan, but that the Advisory Council might well study the Russian proposal.

It was soon clear, however, that, while the United States Govern- (a) ment preferred the Junta plan to the King's plan, they were willing to consider the proposal for broadening the Badoglio Government, and indeed would accept this plan as better than the Junta plan if it led to an agreement between Marshal Badoglio and the six parties. The Prime Minister now thought that, as a result of the Russian (b) 'lack of decorum' (in the appointment of an Ambassador to Italy), we could secure almost everything for which we had asked, and that all might be well if we could 'keep that old trickster Sforza out or in a minor position'.

Mr. Macmillan was in fact able to telegraph to the Prime Minister (c) on the evening of April 7 that a new Italian Government was likely to be formed on an all-party basis without interference on our part and without prejudice to the position of the monarchy. We wanted to be sure that the new Government would accept the two sets of armistice terms and other obligations accepted by the Badoglio Government, and that Count Sforza would not be Prime Minister or Foreign Minister. It was improbable that Count Sforza would be invited to become Prime Minister, but he might well be offered the post of Foreign Minister. The Advisory Council was meeting on the after-noon of April 8. Mr. Macmillan asked the Prime Minister to approve the resolution which he intended to move (i) welcoming the develop-ments leading to the foundation of a broadly based Government, (ii) stating that the interests of the Allies required that Marshal Badoglio should continue in such a Government to hold the offices of Prime Minister and Foreign Minister, (iii) emphasising that the new Government must be made to declare its willingness to accept all the obligations of the old Government, and (iv) insisting that the new arrangements must be regarded as binding until the Italian people as a whole could be consulted.

The Prime Minister replied to Mr. Macmillan that he strongly approved of his action, and did not mind very much whether the King retired now or waited until the liberation of Rome as long as the Crown Prince became Lieutenant and Marshal Badoglio re-mained at the head of the Government. The Prime Minister hoped that Mr. Macmillan would be able to secure that Count Sforza was kept out of any important office. Before the meeting of the Advisory Council Mr. Macmillan had discussed the whole question with Mr. (d) Murphy, who had just come back after three months in Washington

---

(a) R5220/51/22.   (b) R7039/30/19; R5574, 5644/691/22.   (c) R5690/29/22.
(d) R7415/691/22.

to resume his post as American diplomatic representative at the Allied Headquarters. Mr. Murphy explained the President's attitude and spoke of the considerable importance of the Italian vote in a difficult election year in the United States. Mr. Murphy therefore wanted a compromise between the King's plan and the Junta plan which would secure the immediate appointment of the Crown Prince as Lieutenant.

(a)　The Advisory Council passed a resolution on April 8 in the terms suggested by Mr. Macmillan. Mr. Macmillan and Mr. Murphy, with Sir Noel Charles[1] and General Macfarlane, called on the King on April 10. Mr. Murphy told the King that in the interest of the monarchy he should abdicate at once or agree at least to the immediate appointment of the Crown Prince as Lieutenant. Mr. Macmillan supported this plan. The King showed considerable skill in pretending surprise (though he knew the purpose of the visit) and in trying to get delay. After much discussion the King agreed to announce the appointment of the Crown Prince at once, though the formal transfer of power would not take place until the entry of the Allied troops into Rome. Mr. Murphy argued for an immediate transfer of power, but Marshal Badoglio (who thought that in any case the industrial north would turn against the monarchy) supported the King's proposal on the ground that it was better to 'space out' the concessions, and to give the Crown Prince an opportunity for appointing a new Government on arrival in Rome. Mr. Macmillan felt bound to support Mr. Murphy, though he did so without enthusiasm since he was in favour of the King's plan, and knew that the British Government favoured it. At last, on April 12, a further compromise was arranged. The formal transfer of power was to take place on the Allied entry into Rome, but the King was to announce the appointment at once in terms stating that he intended to withdraw from public affairs, and that his decision was 'final and irrevocable'.

(b)　Marshal Badoglio hoped, on the basis of this announcement, to form a broadly based Government. He succeeded in doing so, and in keeping at least numerically a balance between the six parties. He remained Minister for Foreign Affairs as well as Prime Minister, and took in the five most prominent political leaders—including Togliatti, Croce, and Sforza—as Ministers without portfolio. The new Government gave the undertakings required of them by the Allies that they would accept the obligations undertaken by the

---

[1] Sir Noel Charles had been appointed as High Commissioner and British member of the Allied Advisory Council to succeed Mr. Macmillan as Minister Resident. He was not accredited as Ambassador to Italy.

(a) R5809/691/22. (b) R5809/691/22.

previous Government, and that they would not reopen the institutional question[1] until the Italian people as a whole were able freely to express their views.

(iv)

The question of further concessions to Italy: the fall of the Badoglio Government (April 29–June 17, 1944).

The Prime Minister had sent instructions to Sir N. Charles on (a) April 20 that our general policy was to support Marshal Badoglio and the monarchy until the capture of Rome, when the King would retire and the Crown Prince become Lieutenant of the Realm. We were likely to get Russian backing for our policy, since the Russians were 'realists in these matters'. On the other hand, the French and American representatives on the Advisory Council might try to help Count Sforza to obtain control. The Prime Minister had no confidence in this 'vain and ambitious old man' who had been out of Italy for twenty years. He had asked Sir N. Charles to give Marshal Badoglio all possible assistance in forming a new Government and in preventing the six Parties from trying, in spite of their agreement, to intrigue themselves into an undue share of power.

The Prime Minister was most satisfied with the new Government (b) on its appointment, but within a week he—and the Foreign Office— began to be less sure of the prospects of 'finality'. On April 28 Sir N. Charles reported that Marshal Badoglio had agreed to a proposal (c) by Signor Croce for the establishment of a consultative body in liberated Italy. The Prime Minister telegraphed to Sir N. Charles (d) on April 30 that it would be better to do one thing at a time. The new Government had just been formed; we ought to see how Signor Croce was behaving in it before giving him a Consultative Council on which Count Sforza would doubtless try to recover his position. We had a great battle ahead of us and had taken much trouble to keep Marshal Badoglio in office. The Marshal had no need to fritter away his position in an attempt to get untrustworthy support.[2]

Sir N. Charles replied on May 4 that Marshal Badoglio was not at (e) all alarmed by the plan for a Consultative Council, and thought that

---

[1] The Italian term for the 'constitutional' question.
[2] Mr. Eden agreed with this draft, and told the Prime Minister that he had proposed to send a message in the same sense to Sir N. Charles.

(a) R6396/29/22. (b) R6575/15/22. (c) R6706, 6852/15/22. (d) T1013/4, Churchill Papers/243. (e) R7160/15/22.

—though it would not be elected and therefore could not be taken as representative of public opinion—the Council might help to spread the views of a broadly based administration. The Foreign Office thought that Marshal Badoglio might equally well use the Council as a means of putting pressure on the Allies. Mr. Eden indeed commented somewhat angrily on Sir N. Charles's telegram that Marshal Badoglio was 'living in a fool's paradise about Italy, and so are we. We appear to know nothing and do nothing there.'

The anxiety of the Foreign Office over the Italian political situation was soon justified. On May 3 Marshal Badoglio made a
(a) fervent appeal to Sir N. Charles that Italy should be given Allied status. Mr. Macmillan and Sir N. Charles were in favour of making more concessions to Italy, partly to support the new Badoglio Government, and partly to avoid the drift in Italy towards Communism and the possibility that the Russians might take unilateral action which would increase their prestige and damage the position
(b) of the British and Americans with the Italian people. Sir N. Charles argued in favour of the immediate grant of Allied status to Italy. Mr. Macmillan thought that we might persuade Marshal Badoglio to withhold a formal request for Allied status by telling him that after the occupation of Rome and the formal assumption of power by the Crown Prince we would negotiate a preliminary[1] peace treaty with Italy.

Sir O. Sargent wrote on May 11 a long minute on the situation and on possible lines of policy. He pointed out that we had three main objectives: (a) to check the spread of Communism in Italy; (b) to recreate an efficient, prosperous, and friendly Italy which would look to us in the future rather than to Germany or Russia; and (c) to mobilise further Italian resources and manpower for use in the war. The first objective was momentarily the most important; the third was probably impracticable in any case. We ought to be on guard against a certain element of blackmail in Marshal Badoglio's demands for more concessions. Marshal Badoglio was a convenience to us, but he was not indispensable, and could do nothing to check the spread of Communism. We were unlikely to get much positive return from making more concessions to him, though, if we allowed his Government to fall, we might find the political confusion an embarrassment and the Russians might exploit our inaction by supporting Italian claims.

What concessions could we make? The acceptance of Italy as an Ally would cause difficulties with our own public opinion, and with

---

[1] Mr. Macmillan used this term. The Prime Minister and the Foreign Office also used the term 'partial' treaty.

(a) R7379, 7202, 7203/691/22. (b) R7308, 7334/691/22.

the French, Greeks and Yugoslavs; it would also be extremely troublesome to us at the peace settlement. Anyhow we could not change our relationship with the Italian Government and people to this extent while we were carrying on military operations. We should therefore have to refuse Marshal Badoglio's demand for Allied status, but for this reason it was the more necessary for us to make some concessions elsewhere if only to forestall unilateral action by the Russians. We might offer Italy a preliminary treaty of peace. We should thereby commit the Italians at once to the loss of their colonies, fleet, etc. instead of postponing these demands to a later time when we might find it more difficult to enforce them. We should, however, have to give Marshal Badoglio something to satisfy Italian opinion in return for the losses and there was little doubt that he would ask for Allied status. Furthermore we should be requiring the Badoglio Government to pledge the whole of the Italian people to a peace treaty at a time when they could speak only for the least important third of the nation. We might limit our concessions to economic matters such as allowing the Italian Government to enjoy the benefits of Lend-Lease and to share in U.N.R.R.A.,[1] or we might bring back some of the Italian prisoners of war in India. In any event we ought to attempt the difficult task of checking inflation in Italy.

Sir O. Sargent proposed that we should try to get American and Soviet agreement to a policy on the following lines: (i) we should refuse even to consider giving Italy Allied status during the war; (ii) we should tell Marshal Badoglio that we were prepared to abolish the armistice régime and to conclude a preliminary treaty as soon as the military position allowed us to do so, and the Italian Government had sufficient authority to speak on behalf of the nation as a whole; (iii) we should do our utmost to improve the economic situation in Italy.[2]

---

[1] Sir O. Sargent had also suggested earlier that, as a gesture of goodwill and confidence, Italy might be allowed to adhere to the Atlantic Charter. Mr. Eden's comment on this suggestion was: 'Please not this one.'

The Italians had already asked at the end of 1943 that they should be allowed to adhere to the Charter. Mr. Eden had instructed Lord Halifax to suggest to the United States Government that the Italian Government should be given a tactful and informal answer that their application might be misunderstood by Allied opinion. The United States Government was not willing to take this action. At the end of March, 1944, Mr. Eden again asked Lord Halifax to ask Mr. Hull whether he would send instructions to the United States representative on the Allied Control Commission in Italy which would allow agreed action to be taken to dissuade the Italian Government from publicly proclaiming their adherence to the principles of the Charter. Mr. Eden had already stated in public that the clause in the Charter relating to territorial changes did not apply to enemy countries. He thought it most inexpedient to do anything which would give even the appearance of creating an obligation to maintain Italian territories intact. The United States Government replied on May 13 that instructions on the lines proposed by the British Government had been sent to the American representative on the Control Commission. *F.R.U.S.*, 1944, III, 1111–1112).

[2] Mr. Makins, who was in London at this time, agreed with Sir O. Sargent's proposals.

Mr. Eden agreed generally with Sir O. Sargent's suggestions. Lord Halifax was therefore instructed on the night of May 20–1 to speak to the State Department on the lines of these suggestions and to ask whether the United States Government would accept them. The Prime Minister, however, commented unfavourably on Lord
(a) Halifax's instructions. He wrote to Mr. Eden on May 22 that 'it is said about Foreign Office minutes that if you read the odd paragraph numbers and the even paragraph numbers in series, you get both sides of the case fully stated. Why should it not be sufficient to say both to the United States and Russia "We are not in favour of giving Italy Allied status at this stage?"' The Prime Minister[1] thought that the telegram to Lord Halifax ended with a highly questionable and unexpected conclusion that 'a partial peace treaty should be arranged with Italy as soon as conditions permit'. It might well be that 'even when all the Governments meet together, there will be no peace treaty after the fall of Hitler, but only a prolonged armistice'. The Prime Minister thought that a shorter and simpler indication of our position would carry more weight.

(b) Mr. Eden replied to this minute on May 26 that we could merely tell Marshal Badoglio, when he asked the Italian Advisory Council to give Italy Allied status, that we did not agree. It would, however, be difficult to maintain this negative attitude, or to prevent the Russians from making capital out of it by posing as the only real friend of Italy. Hence the 'unexpected suggestion' that we might compromise by offering the Italians a partial peace treaty.

We had already found it awkward in our dealings with Italy to reconcile the legal and practical anomalies of her position as a co-belligerent and also as a defeated enemy. These difficulties were likely to increase. As co-belligerents the Italians would claim lenient treatment at the final peace settlement; the longer this settlement was postponed, the harder would it be to enforce unpopular measures such as depriving Italy of her colonies and her fleet. Thus there was something to be said for concluding a partial peace treaty containing these unpopular clauses, and offering the Italians at the same time

---

[1] On May 24 the Prime Minister made a statement on Italy in the House of Commons. He reminded the House of his previous expression of opinion (February 22, 1944) that it would be better for the King and, 'above all', for the Badoglio Government to continue in authority until the occupation of Rome, when a general review of the position would take place. This policy had entailed differences of opinion among Allied Governments, but, after various changes of circumstance, the situation had turned out according to the Prime Minister's suggestion. There was now a new and broadly based Government, and the King had decided to retire in favour of his son. The Prime Minister expressed his confidence in the new Government. He said that it would require further strengthening as we came into contact with the industrial north of Italy, and that after the Germans had been driven out, the Italians should be given a free opportunity of deciding upon the form of democratic régime which they desired.

(a) PMM 602/4, R8515/15/22. (b) PM/44/377, R8515/15/22.

the advantages of an end to the state of war and the resumption of normal relations.

We had explained this proposal to the Americans at some length because they had as large a stake as ourselves in Italy. We need not go into such detail with the Russians. If the Americans agreed with our plan, we ought to consider putting it into effect on the understanding that no treaty would be signed until we were satisfied that the military position was satisfactory, and that the Italian Government could speak on behalf of the whole nation.

The Prime Minister replied on May 27 that he saw no reason for (a) concluding a 'partial peace treaty' with Italy, and that questions of this kind should not be raised until we were in Rome and driving the enemy northwards. He had made the greatest effort in support of the Badoglio–Victor Emmanuel combination, but there was no reason for constant change just to meet Italian whims and 'try-ons'. Marshal Badoglio was lucky to be where he was; the King would be lucky if he got away to retirement, and we should be lucky if we never had anything worse than the present Italian Government to deal with.

Mr. Eden answered this minute on June 6. He said that he had (b) not proposed to conclude a treaty in a hurry with the Italian Government. He wanted merely to tell the Italians that we would be prepared to conclude a preliminary peace treaty in certain circumstances. He did not want to change the existing political arrangements in Italy, but to maintain them, and to give Marshal Badoglio some encouragement without offering Italy Allied status.

Meanwhile on June 1 Lord Halifax had telegraphed that the (c) State Department wanted further details about the scope of a 'preliminary peace treaty' with Italy. Lord Halifax was sent further instructions about our views, but the situation changed once again by a sudden and wholly unexpected development. The Allied armies entered Rome on June 4. The King carried out his promise to make (d) the formal appointment of the Crown Prince as Lieutenant of the Realm. Marshal Badoglio then resigned, and was invited by the Crown Prince to choose a new Government which would include some of the liberated leaders in Rome. Marshal Badoglio and the leaders of the parties represented in his former Government were brought to Rome on June 8 in order to consult the politicians there. There was no intention—on the Allied side—that they should reject Marshal Badoglio as head of the Government. On their arrival General Mason-Macfarlane addressed them in general terms about

---

(a) PMM 634/4, R8512/15/22. (b) PM/44/411, R8512/15/22. (c) R8619/691/22. (d) R9122/15/22.

the importance of unity. After discussion among themselves they
demanded that a new Government should be formed not by Marshal
Badoglio but by Signor Bonomi. The Crown Prince—as Lieutenant
of the Realm—and Marshal Badoglio gave way to their demand;
General Mason-Macfarlane took no steps to tell them that they could
not act as they had done without obtaining the assent of the Allies.[1]
General Mason-Macfarlane then left Rome on the afternoon of
June 9, in company with Marshal Badoglio.[2]

(a)   The Prime Minister and the Foreign Office were astonished at this
turn in events which obviously put an end at least for the time to all
discussion about buttressing the Italian Government by the offer of
a preliminary peace treaty. The Prime Minister telegraphed to Sir
N. Charles on the night of June 10–11 that he could not understand
why he (Sir N. Charles) had left the arrangements in Rome to
General Mason-Macfarlane who seemed to have been helpless in the
matter.[3] General Mason-Macfarlane had no right whatever to con-
nive at the transfer of power from Marshal Badoglio. We had never
admitted the right of the Italians to form any Government they
pleased. Italy was a conquered country and the Italian Government
were administering territory assigned to them under strict Allied
control. Before a change of Government, the Allied Advisory Council
should have been consulted, and the War Cabinet should have been
given time to receive information, deliberate on it, and consult
the Americans and Russians.

The Prime Minister said that Mr. Eden agreed with his comments.
On June 11 the Foreign Office telegraphed in equally strong terms
to Sir N. Charles[4] pointing out that General Mason-Macfarlane ought
to have told the Italian politicians that they were acting beyond

---

[1] General Mason-Macfarlane, however, told Signor Bonomi that the Allied Governments
(b) would disapprove of the appointment of Count Sforza as Foreign Minister. He reported
this statement in a telegram to General Wilson which was repeated to the Combined
Chiefs of Staff. The State Department at once instructed Mr. Murphy to protest to
General Wilson, and Mr. Winant to protest to Mr. Eden, that General Mason-Macfarlane
had no right to speak for the United States Government. The State Department wished
General Wilson to tell Signor Bonomi that the United States Government had no ob-
jection to Count Sforza's appointment. Mr. Murphy had telegraphed to Washington on
June 10 that he was strongly in favour of Count Sforza's appointment.
The Foreign Office view was that the Control Commission, including General
Mason-Macfarlane, inclined to forget that General Wilson was an Allied Commander-in-
Chief, responsible to the Combined Chiefs of Staff, and that the Commission itself was acting
on behalf of all the United Nations. Count Sforza was not, in fact, given the Ministry of
Foreign Affairs but was again appointed Minister without Portfolio.
[2] General Mason-Macfarlane was ill, and now came home on sick leave.
[3] Mr. Eden explained to the Prime Minister that General Clark had not allowed Sir
N. Charles to go to Rome, and that the communications between Rome and Naples were
very bad. Mr. Eden thought, however, that, Sir N. Charles should have appealed to
London against General Clark's refusal to let him go to Rome.
[4] The Foreign Office telegram seems to have been drafted by the Prime Minister, and
approved by Mr. Eden.

(a) R9121, 9122, 9289/15/22. (b) R9616, 9764, 9777, 9862/15/22.

their powers. Sir N. Charles was instructed to make it clear that the British Government would not recognise the new Government until the War Cabinet had considered the matter, and that the transactions in Rome had no validity. The new Government might indeed be recognised, but not until the United States, Russia, and Great Britain had agreed upon the change. In any case we could not consider recognition until after the new Government had fully subscribed to all the terms imposed upon Italy as part of her unconditional surrender.

The Prime Minister had sent a message to the President on June 10 (a) that he regarded as disastrous the replacement of Marshal Badoglio by 'a group of aged and hungry politicians'. He had thought that the Marshal was to continue in office at least until we could bring in the democratic north of Italy and secure a thoroughly sound Italian Government. The Prime Minister said that he was 'not aware, at this present time, that we had conceded to the Italians who have cost us so dear in life and material the power to form any Government they chose without reference to the victorious Powers and without the slightest pretence of a popular mandate'. The Prime Minister also (b) telegraphed to Stalin that we had lost the only competent man with whom we could deal, and that the 'present cluster of aged and hungry politicians' would naturally try to push Italian claims and might cause us the greatest possible inconvenience. The President replied on June 11 that before forming an opinion (c) he would like a recommendation from the Italian Advisory Council and General Wilson. The Prime Minister replied that he agreed (d) entirely with this view. He also asked Mr. Eden to see that the Advisory Council met as soon as possible. Stalin replied on June 11. (e) He said that he too had been taken by surprise at the Italian action without the consent of the Allies, and that there would be no objection on the Soviet side if the British and Americans thought it necessary to get rid of the Bonomi Government.[1]

On June 13 the Prime Minister explained the situation to the (f) War Cabinet. The War Cabinet considered that there might be something to be said for a change of government at this stage, and that in any case Marshal Badoglio might insist on resigning, but they agreed with the despatch of instructions to Sir N. Charles that Signor

---

[1] It was characteristic of Stalin that this reference to the affairs of Italy should have formed the first paragraph of a telegram congratulating the Anglo-American Allies on the successful landing in France.

(a) T1247/4, No. 699 (Churchill Papers/249; R9246/53/22). (b) T1248/4 (Churchill Papers/249; R9246/53/22). (c) T1260/4, No. 588 (Churchill Papers/249; R9246/53/22). (d) T1261/4, No. 701 (Churchill Papers/249; R9746/51/22). (e) T1265/4 (Churchill Papers/249; R9747/51/22). (f) WM(44)76; R9466/15/22.

Bonomi's Government should not take office until we had been able to consider the matter fully in consultation with our Allies and that for the present Marshal Badoglio's Government should continue to function.

(a)   The instructions sent to Sir N. Charles were that Italy was a conquered country, and, although a co-belligerent, was living under an armistice régime which subjected her to direct control or the indirect supervision of the Allied Control Commission. The Advisory Council for Italy had also been set up to make recommendations on Italian affairs to the Governments represented on it and to the President of the Allied Control Commission. We and the other Allied Governments concerned had a right to be consulted before agreeing to a change of government in Italy, and the Advisory Council should be in a position to give advice about it. We therefore wished to have a recommendation from the Council on the question whether the Allies should permit the substitution of a government under Signor Bonomi for the government of Marshal Badoglio. In our opinion the two prerequisites of the acceptance of any such administration would be that it should, formally and in writing, express its readiness to accept all the obligations entered into by previous Italian Governments since the armistice, including the 'long armistice terms', and that every member of the administration should know the terms of all such obligations, and that the new Government should undertake not to reopen the institutional question without the prior consent of the Allied Governments.

The United States Government and the Soviet Goverment were informed of these instructions, and invited to support them. Stalin
(b) replied on June 15 agreeing with the proposal that the Advisory
(c) Council should meet to discuss the matter. President Roosevelt answered on June 16. He said he had come to the conclusion—while regretting Marshal Badoglio's withdrawal—that it would be a grave mistake for us not to permit the prompt installation of Signor Bonomi's Government. Apart from allaying criticism at home and abroad of our Italian policy, we should find it an advantage to associate Italian obligations under the armistice with an anti-Fascist Cabinet containing the most representative Italians now available. The President understood that the new Government had pledged themselves on the lines laid down in our instructions to Sir N. Charles. He said that we had long foreseen the broadening of the Government after Rome had been reached. The negotiations had been held with the approval of the Allied Control Commission and in constant consultation with its Deputy President (General Mason-

---

(a) R9246/53/22. (b) T1298/4 (Churchill Papers/249; R9609/15/22). (c) T1293/4, No. 562 (Churchill Papers/249; R9661/15/22).

Macfarlane) and his British and American political advisers. The parties were divided about serving under Marshal Badoglio, but Signor Bonomi was their unanimous choice. Interference at this late moment with the establishment of what appeared to be a representative Government would have serious repercussions at home and in Italy and would be to the detriment of the military situation as well as in violation of our announced policy to let the Italian people choose their own Government.

The Prime Minister now came to the conclusion that we should (a) have to accept the *fait accompli* of the Bonomi Government—subject to the assurances which we required—and that it was not worth while attempting to restore Marshal Badoglio. After consulting the War Cabinet, the Prime Minister telegraphed on June 17 to this (b) effect to the President and Stalin. Sir N. Charles was also instructed to recommend to the Advisory Council the immediate recognition (c) of the new Government. In addition to the President's message, the Foreign Office received a telegram from Lord Halifax giving the views of the State Department.[1] The State Department were prepared to go even further than the President, and to recognise the new Government before it had given any written assurances.

The Advisory Council met on June 17, and passed a resolution accepting Signor Bonomi's Government; they added that 'they must, (d) however, insist that the new Government express their readiness in writing to accept all obligations towards the Allies entered into by former Italian Governments since the armistice, and that every member of the Government should be personally acquainted with the terms of the obligations. The new Government was also required to undertake not to reopen the institutional question until Italy had been liberated and the Italian people were free to express their views.[2]

---

[1] i.e. in answer to an *aide-mémoire* in which Lord Halifax had asked that the State Department should instruct Mr. Kirk, United States representative on the Allied Advisory Council, on lines similar to the instructions sent to Sir N. Charles. The telegram reporting this answer was despatched on June 16, at 9.55 a.m., and not decyphered until 9.37 a m. on June 17. The file copy has a note by Sir O. Sargent that he was making enquiries about the reasons for the delay, but the answer to his enquiry is not in the files.

[2] This requirement was met by the Italian Decree Law No. 151, of 25 June 1944, Article 1 of which read: 'After the liberation of the national territory the form of the constitution shall be decided by the Italian people who to that end will elect by universal (e) direct and secret suffrage a constituent assembly to deliberate on the new constitution of the State'.

(a) PMM 725/4, R9962/15/22. (b) WM(44)79; T1302/4; T1303/4, No. 705 (Churchill Papers/249; R9661/15/22). (c) R9246/53/22; R9524/15/22. (d) R9566/51/22. (e) R12308/15/22.

CHAPTER XXXIV

Anglo-Russian relations in 1943: British attempts to secure Russian co-operation on current and post-war questions: Russian demands for a second front in France: North Russian convoys: Foreign Ministers' conference in Moscow: the Teheran Conference.

(i)

Anglo-American decisions at Casablanca in January, 1943, with regard to military operations in Europe: British attempts to secure Soviet co-operation on current and post-war questions (January–May, 1943).

IN his message of December 3, 1942,[1] supporting the President's invitation to Stalin to a tripartite meeting in North Africa, the Prime Minister had said that a decision must be taken 'at the earliest possible moment' on 'the best way of attacking Germany in Europe with all possible force in 1943'. Stalin had refused the invitation to a meeting, but had referred in his answer to the (a) question of establishing a second front in western Europe in 1943. About ten days later Stalin repeated to President Roosevelt his confidence that the 'promises about the opening of a second front in Europe' given by the President and the Prime Minister 'in regard to 1942, and in any case in regard to the spring of 1943 will be fulfilled, and that a second front in Europe will be actually opened' at that time by Anglo-American forces.

The Russians thus continued to regard 'a second front in Europe' solely as a front established by an invasion of northern France. The military decisions taken at Casablanca did not give much support to the Russian hopes that such a front would be opened in 1943. These decisions were based on the resources which would be available after taking account of the essential needs of the Far Eastern war. The first task of the Allies was to defeat the German submarine war which was causing increasingly serious losses to shipping. After this vital defence of the Allied supply routes, the choice lay between a cross-Channel operation and further action in the Mediterranean to

---

[1] See above, pp. 386–7.

(a) T1726/2, Churchill Papers/333.

exploit the North African successes. Notwithstanding their anxiety to avoid diversions which might delay the Cross-Channel plans the Americans had agreed to an attack on Sicily, after North Africa had been cleared, in order to secure Allied communications in the Mediterranean and to help in 'knocking out' Italy to the extent of compelling the Germans to send troops for the defence of Italy and of the areas held by Italian forces in the Balkans. The Conference made no definite plans for a full-scale re-entry into France in 1943, except in the case of a sudden German collapse. The Allies might attempt to seize a bridgehead in the Cotentin peninsula. This operation also depended on a reduction of the German resources in the area; plans for it were soon abandoned as impracticable.[1] The Prime Minister and the President sent a message to Stalin on (a) January 26 summarising somewhat optimistically the conclusions reached at Casablanca. They said that the proposed Anglo-American operations in the first nine months of the year might 'well bring Germany to her knees in 1943'. They explained that they were intending to clear the Germans and Italians from North Africa, and to carry out large scale amphibious operations in the Mediterranean. They were also concentrating in the United Kingdom a strong American land and air force which, in combination with the British forces, would be prepared 'to re-enter the continent of Europe as soon as practicable'. On his return to England the Prime Minister was more definite and at the same time more guarded in a statement[2] (b) to Stalin that we hoped to 'destroy or expel' the 'quarter of a million Germans and Italians in Eastern Tunisia . . . during April, if not earlier'. We then intended in July, or earlier, to seize Sicily, with the hope of clearing the Mediterranean and promoting an Italian collapse. We were 'pushing preparations to the limit of our resources' for a cross-Channel operation in August, but shipping and assault craft would be limiting factors. If the operation were delayed by weather or other reasons it would be prepared with stronger forces for September. The timing of the attack, however, would be 'dependent upon the condition of German defensive possibilities across the Channel'.

Stalin replied on February 16 that the delay in the completion of (c) the Tunisian campaign—the estimated date of February was now put forward to April—was 'disappointing'. He was also disappointed that the establishment of the second front, 'in particular in France', was envisaged only for August or September. He thought that 'the

---

[1] See above p. 464 and below pp. 553-4.
[2] This statement was sent also on behalf of President Roosevelt whom Mr. Churchill had consulted about a request from Stalin on January 30 for more detailed information. (d)

(a) T74/3, Churchill Papers/333. (b) T125/3, Churchill Papers/333. (c) T192/3, Churchill Papers/333. (d) T257/3, No. 271; T265/3, No. 262, Churchill Papers/333.

(a) blow from the west' should be delivered in the spring or early summer of 1943. Owing to his illness[1] the Prime Minister did not send a full answer to this message until March 11. He then explained to Stalin the reasons why the Tunisian campaign had taken longer than had been estimated. He gave details about the total resources available for an attack upon Europe 'across the Mediterranean or the Channel'. He said that there were 38 divisions under British command 'spread across a distance of some 6,300 miles from Gibraltar to Calcutta'. All these forces had 'active and definite tasks' assigned to them for 1943. There were 19 'formed divisions',[2] four Home Defence Divisions and four drafting divisions in the United Kingdom. Sixteen of these divisions in the home area were being prepared for a cross-Channel operation in August. There was no possibility of increasing these numbers. In July 1942, the United States Government had planned to send 27 divisions, each of 40–50,000 men, to the United Kingdom for the invasion of France. Seven divisions had gone to North Africa, and three were to follow them. There was only one American division—and a strong air force—in the United Kingdom. 'This is no disparagement of the American effort. The reason why these performances have fallen so far short of the expectations of last year is not that the troops do not exist but that the shipping at our disposal and the means of escorting it do not exist.'

The Prime Minister then said that we wished to be 'in the general battle in Europe' as soon as possible, but with all our other commitments we had 'eaten, and are eating, into reserves'.

'However, in case the enemy should weaken sufficiently we are preparing to strike earlier than August, and plans are kept alive from week to week. If he does not weaken, a premature attack with inferior and insufficient forces would merely lead to a bloody repulse, Nazi vengeance on the local population if they rose, and a great triumph for the enemy. The Channel situation can only be judged nearer the time, and in making this declaration of our intentions there for your own personal information I must not be understood to limit our freedom of decision.'

This telegram did not disclose in so many words the Prime Minister's own judgment, in contrast with his optimism of the previous autumn, that, except in the event of a German military or political collapse (for which 'weakening' was too mild a term) a cross-Channel invasion at any time in 1943 was most improbable.

---

[1] The Prime Minister was taken ill with pneumonia on February 16.
[2] The Prime Minister explained that the total strength of a British division was about 40,000.

(a) T277/3, Churchill Papers/333.

On the other hand the statement was sufficiently clear and, in spite of his later assertions,[1] Stalin's reply showed that he did not mis-understand the Prime Minister's warning. In a message of March 15, (a) he complained again about the postponement of operations in North Africa. He realised the importance of the Sicilian plan, but pointed out that it could not 'replace the second front in France'. He reminded the Prime Minister that he had 'admitted the possibility of such a front already in 1942, and in any case not later than the spring of 1943'. Stalin realised the difficulties set out by the Prime Minister, but felt bound to add:

> 'Notwithstanding all that, I deem it my duty to warn you in the strongest possible manner how dangerous would be from the view-point of our common cause further delay in the opening of the second front in France. This is the reason why the uncertainty of your statements concerning the contemplated Anglo-American offensive across the Channel arouses grave anxiety in me, about which I feel I cannot be silent.'

For the next two months there was a deceptive lull in the Russian demands for the opening of the second front, and in the Russian complaints that the British in particular were not taking their full share in the war. At the beginning of January M. Maisky had (b) referred to these complaints and suspicions in conversation with a member of the Northern Department of the Foreign Office. M. Maisky said that, while he and others who knew Great Britain realised that such suspicions were not 'altogether justified', a number of highly placed persons in the U.S.S.R., especially in the army— perhaps not the highest placed—believed them to be well-founded, and were able to prevent a true picture reaching the Russian people.

After his return to Moscow from leave in the latter part of February Sir A. Clark Kerr was instructed to take an opportunity of saying to Stalin that he (Sir A. Clark Kerr) had found astonishment in England that the Soviet Government were so badly misinformed about the British attitude towards the war, and that suspicion of us was still given currency in the controlled Soviet press. Sir A. Clark Kerr was instructed that his conversation with Stalin might serve to throw light on reports that an influential party in the U.S.S.R. was opposed to his (Stalin's) policy of co-operation with the democracies in general and with Great Britain in particular.

Sir A. Clark Kerr did not have a chance of raising the matter (c) with Stalin until April 12.[2] Stalin then said that there were people

---

[1] See p. 555.

[2] Sir A. Clark Kerr had not received these instructions when he saw Stalin on February 24.

(a) T317/3, Churchill Papers/333. (b) N872/66/38. (c) N2227/66/38.

at the front and behind it who had the impression that it was a simple matter to open a second front by landing an army in Europe; these people drew the conclusion that we were not pulling our weight in the war. They were, however, mainly people with a 'negative understanding of military matters'. The Soviet Government and the army leaders did not underrate our achievements, though a few Russians were enemies alike of their own country and of Great Britain and were working for Hitler by putting about anti-British views.[1] Sir A. Clark Kerr was struck at this time by Stalin's

(a) friendly and expansive attitude; in a later telegram he reported that there was a real improvement in the Russian appreciation of our war effort and of the difficulties which we had overcome, and that the Kremlin had given orders to the press to treat us better.

Meanwhile, Sir A. Clark Kerr, in accordance with the policy of trying to establish friendly relations and remove Russian suspicions, had also been instructed to try to open a general discussion with the Russians on post-war policy. The fact that we ourselves had not reached a settled policy on many major questions of post-war policy was no reason for delaying a general exchange of views. There were indeed advantages in trying to consult the Soviet Government when we were raising questions of policy with the United States; we might even do something to assuage Russian susceptibilities if on some matters—e.g. the future of eastern Europe, or reparations—we opened discussions with the Soviet Government before approaching the United States.

(b) Sir A. Clark Kerr was therefore instructed[2] to ask for an interview with M. Molotov and to point out the measure of agreement shown in recent speeches by Mr. Eden, Mr. Sumner Wells and Stalin. These speeches showed a desire for the continuation of an Anglo-American-Soviet coalition after the war. Mr. Eden and Mr. Welles had said explicitly that the three Powers should settle, in advance of an armistice, the main lines of a peace settlement. Although Stalin had not made a public statement to this effect, his agreement with it was implied in his speech of November 6, 1942. We had been too much occupied with the prosecution of the war to reach any definite conclusions on major post-war problems, but we had done much preparatory work on the economic side; we had already consulted the Soviet Government on many of the matters under consideration,

---

[1] Stalin said that some time ago he had done his best to dispose of these people who had been working for Hitler. He had been fairly successful, but had not been able to stamp all of them out. He added—with a laugh—that he seemed to remember that he had been taken to task by us when he was at this work of 'stamping out'.

[2] These instructions, in the form of a despatch, were drawn up on February 4 while Sir A. Clark Kerr was still in Great Britain.

(a) N2377/66/38. (b) U321/67/70.

and proposed to do so on others as soon as we were able to make suggestions.

We wished now to ask whether the Soviet Government could supplement the general indications which Stalin had given to Mr. Eden at Moscow in December 1941,[1] and those arising out of the negotiations in London in May 1942[2] leading to the conclusion of the Anglo-Soviet treaty. There were, for example, two points in Stalin's speech of November 6, 1942, which neeed elucidation. Stalin had said: 'It is no more possible to destroy Germany . . . than to destroy Russia, but to destroy the Hitlerite State is possible and necessary. Our first aim is the destruction of the Hitlerite State and the men who inspire it.' Later in the same speech Stalin had said: 'It is not our aim to destroy all organised military force in Germany, for every literate person will understand that it is not only impossible in regard to Germany as it is in regard to Russia, but it is also inexpedient from the point of view of the future. But Hitler's army can and should be destroyed.'

Did the first statement mean that Stalin had modified the views which he had expressed to Mr. Eden in December 1941, when he proposed the restoration of Austria as an independent State, the detachment of the Rhineland from Prussia, and possibly the constitution of an independent State of Bavaria, the transfer of East Prussia to Poland, and the return of the Sudetenland to Czechoslovakia? How was the second statement to be reconciled with Article 6 of the Atlantic Charter—to which the U.S.S.R. had subscribed—providing for the disarmament of aggressor nations? We assumed that Stalin's statement was made with a view to its propaganda effect upon the Germans, and especially upon the German army, and that he was not in favour of allowing Germany to retain armed forces other than those necessary for police purposes and the maintenance of public order.

Sir A. Clark Kerr was told that he might say that, although we had not made up our minds on a definite plan, we considered that an occupation of Germany would be necessary for some time after the war. If there were general agreement on this point, we should have to settle the mode of exercising inter-Allied control; we might even find that in the chaos after defeat no central Government would emerge in Germany and that the Allies themselves would have to constitute such a Government.

The main theme of Sir A. Clark Kerr's *démarche* would be to point out the desirability of an agreement on policy between the three major Allies. Otherwise, if one of the three Powers attempted to run a policy of its own in opposition to, or behind the backs of the others,

---

[1] See above, Chapter XXVI, sections (i) and (ii).
[2] See *ib.*, section (iv).

there would be no hope of establishing a European order after the collapse of Germany. An assurance from M. Molotov that the U.S.S.R. accepted the principle of joint action would therefore be of great value as a first step.

We should also have to deal with the inevitable collapse of administration in the enemy-occupied territories of eastern and south-eastern Europe after the withdrawal of the Axis forces. It was in our joint interest to prevent a collapse into chaos; here also we should begin to concert plans well in advance of the end of the war. In relation to such plans we wanted to know how far, and for what reasons, the Soviet Government were opposed to proposals for Polish-Czechoslovak and Graeco-Yugoslav confederations, in spite of their statements that they approved such confederations in principle.

(a)   Sir A. Clark Kerr saw M. Molotov on the night of February 20–1 and found him in a friendly mood. He was pleased by our intention to consult the Soviet Government on post-war arrangements, but said that the Soviet Government had not yet gone beyond the merest preliminary study of such matters. He was unwilling, however, to commit himself to any interpretation of Stalin's pronouncements and appeared uncomfortable at Sir A. Clark Kerr's questions. Sir A. Clark Kerr said that he would put his questions in a private

(b)   letter to M. Molotov. On February 24 Stalin gave Sir A. Clark Kerr a letter in reply to his communication to M. Molotov. The reply was not in very friendly terms. Stalin did not think that the method of written enquiries would lead to anything but fruitless and lengthy correspondence. He considered that the only correct way of dealing with matters such as the disarmament of Germany would be through a meeting of British and Soviet official representatives and the conclusion of a binding agreement. He had proposed this method during Mr. Eden's visit to Moscow in December 1941, but without success. He would agree, however, to a meeting on the question of Germany or other countries, if the British Government so wished.[1]

(c)   The Foreign Office thought that, in spite of the usual acerbity of tone, Stalin's reply was not unhopeful. M. Molotov had also said, in a somewhat rambling way, that the Soviet Government would not object to three-Power conversations. It seemed best, therefore, for the time, to take no further steps, since it would be premature to hold an Anglo-Soviet meeting about Germany with the object of securing a binding agreement. Sir A. Clark Kerr was therefore instructed not to answer this suggestion, but to tell Stalin, if necessary, that, in accordance with the terms of the Anglo-Soviet treaty, we

---

[1] The Prime Minister's comment to Mr. Eden on reading Stalin's reply, was: 'Please tell me what has happened to bring all this stuff up.'

(a) U811/67/70. (b) U888/67/70. (c) U888/67/70.

were always ready to discuss with the Soviet Government matters of common interest to Europe. We did not want to bind them, as we would not bind ourselves, to particular solutions at this stage; on the other hand we would welcome a frank exchange of views in order to clear our own minds and to avoid future misunderstanding. In continuation of this policy of consulting the Soviet Government the (a) Foreign Office gave instructions on March 10, 1943, that they as well as the United States Government should be informed of peacefeelers received from the minor German satellites in Europe.[1]

(ii)

Anglo-American decisions at Washington, May 1943: Stalin's charges of bad faith with regard to the opening of a second front in France: the Prime Minister's messages in reply: President Roosevelt's invitation to Stalin to meet him in Alaska (June–July, 1943).

Apart from the difficult and unsuccessful negotiations over the Soviet-Polish question,[2] there were no other discussions with the Soviet Government on matters of common European interest during the spring of 1943. On the other hand at the beginning of June Russian resentment at the Allied decision to postpone the opening of a second front in France until 1944 flared up in angry messages from Stalin.

The proposals at Casablanca for a landing on the Cotentin peninsula had appeared impracticable to the British staff primarily because there seemed no chance that sufficient landing craft would be available. In March and April it was evident—as the Prime (b) Minister had pointed out to Stalin—that, apart from the question of landing craft, the Casablanca plans had been based on an overoptimistic estimate of the shipping position; that the number of American troops in Great Britain during the late summer and autumn would be far fewer than had been expected, and that there would be hardly enough landing craft even for training purposes. Once again, therefore, a meeting between the Prime Minister and the President was necessary, not merely to consider the cross-Channel plans but to decide upon the whole course of Allied strategy now that the Tunisian campaign was coming to an end. This meeting

---

[1] See Volume V, Chapter LXVII.
[2] See below, Chapter XXXV.

(a) C2652/155/18. (b) Hist.(F)4, Nos. 194, 210, 212.

(a) took place at Washington from May 12 to May 25. As at Casablanca, the discussions were primarily military; neither the Foreign Office nor the State Department was represented.

The Washington meeting did not decide to abandon preparations for a large-scale landing in 1943, in the event of a German collapse, but such a collapse now seemed unlikely, and with the Allied landing craft in the Mediterranean and still only one American division in the United Kingdom, the chances of seizing a bridgehead were most improbable. The meeting, however, agreed to undertake the large-scale invasion (employing twenty-nine operational divisions) in 1944 and fixed May 1 as a provisional date. Meanwhile the immediate Anglo-American objectives would be the exploitation of the North African victory by a landing in Sicily and such further action as might be necessary to eliminate Italy from the war and contain the maximum number of German forces.[1]

The Prime Minister and the President agreed upon the terms of a (b) message to Stalin. This message was sent on June 2 through the United States Ambassador in Moscow.[2] The text stated that the 'over-all strategy' of the Allies was based upon decisions: (a) to give first priority to the control of the submarine menace and to employ every practical means to support Russia, (b) to prepare the ground for the active or passive participation of Turkey in the war, (c) to maintain unremitting pressure against Japan, (d) to keep China as an effective Ally and as a base for operations against Japan, (e) to prepare the French forces in Africa for active participation in the invasion of Axis-controlled Europe. The measures for the support of Russia were an intensification of the air offensive in Europe (details were given of the increasing Anglo-American strength), an effort to drive Italy out of the war, and the concentration of forces in England for full-scale invasion of the Continent in the spring of 1944, with the possibility of taking advantage earlier of any sudden German weakening in France or Norway. After mentioning the shortage of landing craft, the message concluded: 'We have found that the undertakings listed utilise our full resources. We believe that these operations will heavily engage the enemy in the air and will force a dispersion of his troops on the ground to meet both actual attacks and heavy threats of attack which can readily be converted into successful operations whenever signs of Axis weakness become apparent.'

---

[1] See also above, p. 465.

[2] The message was drafted by General Marshall and telegraphed to the President by the Prime Minister on May 26 after he and General Marshall had left Washington for North Africa.

(a) COS(43)286(o). (b) Churchill Papers/333.

Stalin addressed his reply, on June 11, to President Roosevelt, but (a)
sent a copy to the Prime Minister. He complained that the President
and the Prime Minister had promised an operation across the
Channel for August or September 1943, and that they had now
decided on postponement until the spring of 1944—just as, in 1942,
they had postponed the operation until 1943. Stalin said that this
decision created 'quite exceptional difficulties' for the Soviet Union,
and would make a 'painful impression' on their people and army
which would 'again be left without serious support on the part of the
Anglo-American forces'. He ended his message with the words: 'As
far as the Soviet Government is concerned, it cannot join in this
decision, which may have grave consequences for the further course
of the war and which moreover was taken without its participation
and without any attempt to consider together the question of such
tremendous importance.'

On June 13 the Prime Minister telegraphed to the President the (b)
draft of a reply to Stalin. The Prime Minister said that he would like
to see a copy of the message which the President would doubtless
be sending, but the President replied that he agreed with the Prime
Minister's draft and had sent a message to Stalin 'heartily' con-
curring in it.

Meanwhile Sir A. Clark Kerr, who had received from the Foreign (c)
Office a copy of Stalin's message, telegraphed on June 14 that the
restraint in the tone of the message should not lead us to think that
Stalin was not feeling 'real concern and resentment' or that his faith
in our intentions had not been severely shaken. He was not over-
stating the impression which this fresh disappointment was bound to
make upon the Russian people and army.

> 'It is impossible to foresee what a man so unpredictable as Stalin
> might be moved to do, but his last paragraph seems . . . to contain
> [a] dictum of a kind which we should be unwise to disregard. It
> is true that we could make a case for a reply to his objection that
> he was not consulted . . . but I should not recommend that we
> should attempt to do so. His peculiar position in this country makes
> it impossible for him to leave it, and there is clearly no one he could
> send of the calibre needed to represent him in debates with such
> men as the Prime Minister and the President. . . . Thus we find
> ourselves in the unhappy position of being in fact unable to consult
> him and at the same time of provoking his anger because we have
> failed to admit him to our counsels on a question of tremendous
> importance and because we are obliged to convey our intentions to
> him in the form of a "decision" in the taking of which he feels he
> should have had a voice.'

(a) T792/3, Churchill Papers/333. (b) T795/3, No. 309; T803/3, No. 310; T847/3,
No. 289 (Churchill Papers/333). (c) Moscow tel. 500 Prisec.

Sir A. Clark Kerr hence thought it urgently necessary to arrange a meeting between the Prime Minister, Stalin and the President.

(a)   The Prime Minister replied to Sir A. Clark Kerr that he was sending a soft answer to Stalin, but that no apology was 'called for from us'. Our strategy and offensive in the Mediterranean were probably the reasons for the delay of the German offensive against Russia. The Prime Minister thought that Sir A. Clark Kerr should 'adopt a robust attitude to any further complaints'.

> 'They themselves destroyed the second front in 1939 and 1940 and stood by watching with complete indifference what looked like our total obliteration as a nation. We have made no reproaches and we did our best to help them when they were in turn attacked. Nothing will induce me in any circumstances to allow what at this stage I am advised and convinced would be a useless massacre of British troops on the Channel beaches in order to remove Soviet suspicions. I am getting rather tired of these repeated scoldings considering that they have never been actuated by anything but cold-blooded self-interest and total disdain of our lives and fortunes. At the proper time you might give Stalin a friendly hint of the dangers of offending the two Western Powers whose war-making strength is growing with every month that passes and who may play a helpful part in the Russian future. Even my own long-suffering patience is not inexhaustible.'

(b)   The Prime Minister sent his message to Stalin on June 19. He said that he understood Stalin's disappointment, but was sure that we were doing the only thing 'physically possible in the circumstances. It would be no help to Russia if we threw away 100,000 men in a disastrous cross-Channel attack.' Mr. Churchill agreed with the view of all his military advisers that, even if we got ashore, we should be driven back into the sea by superior numbers. A great British defeat might 'cause the utmost ill-feeling here if it were thought it had been incurred against the advice of our military experts and under pressure from you'.

> 'You will remember that I have always made it clear in my telegrams to you that I would never authorise any cross-Channel attack which I believed would lead only to useless massacre. The best way for us to help you is by winning battles and not by losing them. This we have done in Tunisia.'

The Prime Minister spoke of the effect of the Tunisian victory on the Axis defensive system in the Mediterranean, and of our hope of driving Italy out of the war before the end of the year. We were already holding in the west and south of Europe the larger part of

---

(a) T851/3, Tel. 740 to Moscow (Churchill Papers/333). (b) T852/3. Tel. 741 to Moscow (Churchill Papers/333).

the German air forces, and our superiority was increasing. The Prime Minister said that he had never asked for 'detailed information about the strength and disposition of the Russian armies because you have been, and are still bearing the brunt on land'. Our view was that the unexpectedly rapid defeat of the Axis Powers in North Africa had dislocated their strategy and delayed their plans for an offensive against Russia. 'It is no doubt too soon to pronounce decidedly on all this, but we should be very glad to hear what you think about it.'

Mr. Churchill then dealt with Stalin's complaint that he had not been consulted about our recent decisions. He understood the reasons which prevented Stalin from coming to meet the President and himself in January, but the need and advantages of a meeting were very great. Mr. Churchill was ready to go anywhere for this meeting. He suggested Scapa Flow as 'the most convenient, the safest, and, if secrecy be desired, probably the most secret' meeting place.

On the evening of June 24 Mr. Harriman told the Prime Minister of a proposal made by the President to Stalin for a meeting (without the Prime Minister) in Alaska.[1] The Prime Minister telegraphed to the President on June 25 that it would be 'a pity to draw U.J. (a) 7,000 miles from Moscow for anything less than' a tripartite meeting at which military staffs as well as the political chiefs would be present. If the invasion of Sicily were successful, and if the Germans did not open an offensive against Russia, a meeting at the end of July or the beginning of August would be desirable in order to make sure that the Russians attacked in full strength in October.

> 'We shall probably be able to show that our Mediterranean strategy, of which he [Stalin] approved, has in fact gained Russia the respite of this summer, and has in fact achieved all he hoped for from a cross-Channel second front. This is therefore one of the cardinal moments. I consider that a tripartite meeting at Scapa Flow, or anywhere else on the globe that can be agreed, not only of us three, but also of the Staffs, who will come together for the first time, would be one of the milestones of history. If this is lost, much is lost.'

The Prime Minister said, frankly, that enemy propaganda would make use of a meeting between 'the heads of Soviet Russia and the United States at this juncture with the British Commonwealth and

---

[1] There is no evidence that the Prime Minister or the Foreign Office had any previous knowledge of this proposal. The President had sent Mr. Joseph E. Davies to Moscow in May with a letter suggesting a meeting. Admiral Standley told Sir A. Clark Kerr that Mr. Davies had said that he did not know what was in the President's letter, or in Stalin's reply, but that he (Admiral Standley) could not believe this to be the case. See below, p. 560, n.2.

(a) T885/3, No. 328, Churchill Papers/471.

Empire excluded. It would be serious and vexatious and many would be bewildered and alarmed thereby.' The Prime Minister explained that his own visit to Moscow with Mr. Harriman in August 1942 was 'on altogether a lower level and at a stage when we had only to explain why no second front' could be opened in that year.

(a)   On June 25 M. Maisky communicated Stalin's reply to the Prime Minister's message of June 19. This reply—which was unusually long—recapitulated all the previous messages about a second front. Stalin did not quote at the same time the Prime Minister's warning that all the plans for a cross-Channel invasion were contingent upon the existence of conditions which would allow them a good chance of success. He said, however, that 'all the conditions necessary for opening of a second front' had considerably improved, and that in these circumstances the Soviet Government 'could not think that the British and American Governments will change the decision on the invasion of Europe in 1943 taken at the beginning of this year'.

'On the contrary the Soviet Government had every reason to expect that the Anglo-American decision will materialise, that the necessary preparations were being carried out, and that the second front in Western Europe at last will be opened in 1943. Therefore when you are writing now that "it would be no help to Russia if we threw away 100,000 men in a disastrous cross-Channel attack", I have only to remind you on the following. First, on your memorandum of June 1942, in which you talked of the preparation of invasion involving not 100,000, but 1,000,000 men in the first instance. Second, on your February message in which you mentioned the great preparatory measures for invasion of Western Europe in August–September of this year. It seemed obvious that this operation had to be carried out, not with 100,000 men but with an adequate number of troops.'

Stalin did not 'desire to dwell on the fact that [your] last responsible decision on the cancellation of your former responsible decision . . . was taken by you and [the] President without [the] participation of [the] Soviet Government and without any attempt to invite its representatives for talks in Washington, although you could not be unaware of the fact that the rôle which the Soviet Government is playing in the war against Germany and its interests in the question of the second front are not inconsiderable. It goes without saying that the Soviet Government cannot put up with such disregard of the most vital Soviet interests in the war against the common enemy.' Stalin said that the matter was not merely one of disappointment on the part of the Soviet Government, but of confidence in their Allies. 'One should not forget that on all this depends the possibility to save millions of lives in the occupied regions of Western Europe and

(a) T891/3, Churchill Papers/333.

Russia and reduce the colossal sacrifices of the Soviet armies in comparison with which the losses of the Anglo-American troops could be considered as modest.'

The Prime Minister's first inclination was to send no answer to this message. He decided, however, that it would be better to reply to it. He therefore sent a message to Stalin on June 26. He said that (a)

> 'at every stage the information I have given you as to our future intentions has been based upon the recorded advice of the British and American Staffs, and I have at all times been sincere in my relations with you. Although until June 22, 1941, we British were left alone to face the worst that Nazi Germany could do to us, I instantly began to aid Soviet Russia to the best of our limited means. . . . Therefore the reproaches which you now cast upon your Western Allies leave me unmoved. Nor, apart from the damage to our military interests, should I have any difficulty in presenting my case to the British Parliament and nation.'

The Prime Minister said that the views of the Staffs had been continually modified by events. It had not been possible to transport the American army to Great Britain according to the programme proposed in June 1942. Instead of twenty-seven American divisions being in Great Britain in April 1943, there was only one division in June 1943, and there would be only five by August. The war against Japan, the shipping shortage, the shortage of landing craft, and the demands of the North African campaign were the reasons for the delay. The Prime Minister repeated that the enemy's uncertainty where the forthcoming attack in the Mediterranean would be delivered seemed to be delaying and might prevent altogether an offensive in the East. Thus

> 'not only on the one hand have the difficulties of the cross-Channel attack continually seemed greater to us, and the resources available have not been forthcoming, but a more hopeful and fruitful strategic policy has opened to us in another theatre, and we have the right and duty to act in accordance with our convictions, informing you at every stage of the changes in our views imposed by the vast movement of the war.'

The Prime Minister sent to the President on June 29 copies of (b) what he called the 'very unpleasant' message from Stalin and his own reply. He said that 'this has its bearing on your proposal to meet him alone, and I shall not seek to deter you if you can get him to come'. The Prime Minister thought it 'curious that he should have recalled Litvinov, Bogomolov, and now Maisky to Moscow. There is also the cessation of the German offensive on the Russian front

---

(a) T894/3, Churchill Papers/333. (b) T905/3, No. 338, Churchill Papers/333.

which is not necessarily due only to our Mediterranean activities.'
Mr. Eden and the Foreign Office were, however, 'definitely of the
opinion that no decisive *volte-face* is impending in Russia'. The Prime
Minister himself thought a '*volte-face*' impossible 'having regard to
the deeds done between the German and Russian masses and to what
would appear to be the Russian interest in the future world'.[1]

(a)   The Prime Minister's telegram crossed a message of June 29 from
the President that he had not suggested a meeting with Stalin alone,[2]
but that the latter had told Mr. Davies that he assumed the meeting
to be only with the President, and that he agreed 'that we should not
bring Staffs to what would be a preliminary meeting'. He had
intimated that he would bring only a total of four or five people and
'on this assumption I would propose to take only Hopkins and
Harriman'. The President thought there would be advantages in a
preliminary meeting of this kind: (i) without Staffs there would be
no military collisions in regard to demands for an immediate cross-
Channel operation; (ii) Stalin would not think that we were asking
for a Russian offensive this summer if the Germans did not attack;
(iii) Stalin would be more frank in giving his views on the offensive
against Japan 'now and later'; he might also be more frank in regard
to China, the Balkan States, Finland and Poland.

The President said that he wanted to 'explore his [Stalin's] thinking as fully as possible concerning Russia's post-war hopes and
ambitions'. He would 'cover much the same field with him as did
Eden for you a year ago'. Mr. Roosevelt asked whether the Prime
Minister would consider coming over 'soon afterwards' for a meeting
with him in Quebec.[3] Stalin had given no definite dates but had
suggested tentatively the end of July or early August. The President
did not expect to hear anything further from him until about July 15.

(b)   [1] The Foreign Office, in fact, received fewer rumours of Soviet-German contacts in
1943 than in 1942. There were, however, two main sets of such rumours. The first came
from good Turkish sources in April 1943, and reported (a) that secret Russo-German
peace conversations had recently taken place in Bucharest, (b) that a 'satellite' diplomat
had said that Germany might have to come to an understanding with Russia. The Foreign
Office—in accordance with their practice of passing on rumours of this kind—informed
M. Molotov of them. M. Molotov said that no approach had been made to the Soviet
Government, and that, if any agent of Germany were to make such an approach, the
Soviet Government would 'send him to all the devils'. The second batch of rumours of
Russo-German contacts came from Stockholm in August 1943, and was of even less
substance. The Foreign Office thought the Swedes were trying to cause trouble between
the British and the Russians.
    [2] Mr. Roosevelt had in fact proposed to Stalin a meeting 'between you and me', and
had excluded Khartoum as a meeting place because it was in British territory, and Iceland
because 'quite frankly' it would be 'difficult not to invite Prime Minister Churchill at the
same time'. The President suggested meeting at one side or the other of the Bering Straits.
F.R.U.S., 1943, *Conferences at Cairo and Teheran*, p. 4.
    [3] Mr. Roosevelt said that he was sure that the Canadian Government would welcome
them, and that Quebec was a much better meeting place than Washington at that time
of year.

    (a) T904/3, No. 297, Churchill Papers/471. (b) N2249/78/38; N2405, 2516, 2564, 5230,
5231, 5348/75/38.

If Stalin confirmed his date, the President would be back from Alaska about August 15. He would spend a week in Washington, and could be in eastern Canada by August 25. The President agreed that a 'full-dress meeting' with the Russians should be held later in the autumn; for this reason he thought of his own proposed meeting with Stalin 'as a preparatory talk on what you rightly call a lower level'. Mr. Davies had also said that Stalin's colleagues did not like the idea of his flying over Finland, Sweden, Norway and the North Sea to Scapa, especially at a time of year when there was practically no darkness. The President concluded: 'I have the idea that your conception is right from the short point of view, but mine is the right one from the long point of view. I wish there were no distances.'

The Prime Minister replied at once on June 29 repeating that if (a) the President and Stalin could meet, he would 'no longer deprecate it. On the contrary . . . I think it important that this contact should be established.' The Prime Minister said that he would be 'very glad to arrange for a meeting between us and our Staffs about the end of August in Quebec which I am sure Mackenzie King would welcome'.

Stalin did not answer the President's proposal until August 8, in spite of a reminder on July 16.

The Prime Minister also telegraphed on June 29 to Sir A. Clark (b) Kerr asking 'what he could gather' of the reactions to his 'patient reply to Stalin's offensive message'.

'Naturally the sentence beginning "The Soviet Government will not put up with such treatment" etc., as well as the elaborate marshalling of all the grounds of complaint raises anxious questions in experienced minds. . . . Personally I feel that this is probably the end of the Churchill-Stalin correspondence from which I fondly hoped some kind of personal contact might be created between our countries. There is certainly no use in making it a vehicle of re-crimination. As you were the first to suggest my visit to Moscow, I should be most glad to hear what you think.'

Sir A. Clark Kerr sent a long answer on July 1. He said that so (c) far there had been 'no detectable reactions to the last two messages exchanged'. The only disquieting symptoms had been a reference in *Pravda* (which Sir A. Clark Kerr had already reported) and 'a fresh chattering among those who were employed to chatter a year ago'. Sir A. Clark Kerr then explained that, although the reasons for our decisions were compelling, 'as seen from Moscow there is a weakness in our case'. This weakness lay 'not in our inability to open this

---

(a) T907/3, No. 336, Churchill Papers/471. (b) T903/3, Tel. 786 to Moscow (Churchill Papers/333). (c) T922/3, Moscow tel. 550 (Churchill Papers/333).

T

second front but in our having let [Stalin] believe we were going to. He has picked upon this weakness and has expressed himself in very forthright terms. I do not think he meant to be offensive.' Sir A. Clark Kerr thought that the Prime Minister was also disappointed about the inevitable postponement of a second front, but Stalin's disappointment was bound to be 'a hundredfold keener' because he thought the second front vital to Russia and within his reach. 'It is melancholy to reflect that we must willy-nilly co-operate with this man not only in the beating of Hitler but in the years that will follow, and that upon this co-operation depend millions of lives and to a large extent the future of the world.' It was therefore essential to hold his confidence, but he suggested that we had lost it just when we seemed to have won it. 'God knows what tricks he will be up to if you let him get out of your hands. I can therefore only urge you to expand your much-tried patience with the old bear and to deal with him as with the bear he is. Honey and bits of meat and the stick when he deserves it. . . . I fear, however, that now he does not see himself wholly in the wrong.'

Sir A. Clark Kerr did not think that the Prime Minister's message would be 'the end of the Churchill-Stalin correspondence'. The
(a) Prime Minister, however, told M. Maisky on July 2[1] in answer to a question whether he (the Prime Minister) had any message for Stalin, that he was 'getting rather tired of being scolded, and did not see much use in keeping up a personal correspondence' if it became only a vehicle for recrimination. M. Maisky spoke of the suffering and losses of Russia, and said that Stalin was harsh in his manner, and that the Prime Minister ought not to attach importance to the tone of the messages. Mr. Churchill told M. Maisky how greatly he desired to work with Stalin, and to take the weight off Russia in the war, and how much he hoped from the twenty years' Anglo-Soviet treaty of mutual aid. Mr. Churchill also said that our Mediterranean strategy appeared to have succeeded in gaining a valuable breathing-space for Russia; the Germans might well not attack on the eastern front in 1943 on any large scale.

From this time there was a revival of the agitation in the Soviet press for the immediate opening of a second front. Sir A. Clark Kerr
(b) reported on September 6 on the increasing volume and intensity of this press campaign. The peak was reached in an article of August 1 in *The War and the Working Class*, reproduced in full on August 6 in *Pravda* in order that it might have wider publicity. The article stated that never before had the conditions for victory over Hitler been so favourable, and that, if the existing opportunity were missed, the

---

[1] M. Maisky was leaving for Moscow.

(a) N3894/66/38. (b) N5489/172/38.

war might drag on and result in enormous numbers of unnecessary victims. The members of the anti-Hitler coalition had undertaken to carry on a common war against a common enemy. It was therefore to be expected that they would make a common attack with their united forces but for more than two years the Soviet Union alone had borne the burden of the struggle with the principal forces of the enemy. In June 1942 two official communiqués on the conversations between M. Molotov and the British and American authorities had stated that full agreement had been reached about the creation of a second front in Europe in 1942. No such front was established, but it was explained that in any case a second front would be opened in the spring of 1943. After the Casablanca meeting Mr. Churchill had spoken of an Allied plan of action which would be carried out in the course of the following nine months. The nine months had passed, but there was still no second front in Europe.

The article then contrasted the immensity of the Soviet front with the limited scale of Anglo-American operations against Germany. A second front, diverting some sixty German divisions and a score of divisions belonging to Germany's allies, would give the Soviet forces numerical superiority over the Germans and thus lead to the defeat of Germany in 1943. The old excuses for not opening a second front—the strength of the Atlantic wall, the shipping shortage, and the risks of an invasion of the British Isles—were no longer valid. It was true that a few limited circles—e.g. armament firms—did not want to shorten the war, but the Allied successes in the Mediterranean, which had been rendered possible largely by the heroic efforts of the Red Army, were hastening the military and political disintegration of the enemy; the opening of a second front in 1943 would show that the anti-Hitler coalition would not allow the war to be prolonged at the cost of further sacrifice.

Another article which appeared on August 15 in *The War and the Working Class* complained that the Anglo-American conferences, of which the Quebec Conference[1] was the sixth, had not led to the fulfilment of the basic Anglo-American obligation to open a second front; the Soviet Government would welcome a three-Power conference only if it settled the principal question of preventing a prolongation of the war. The war could be won in 1943, but a refusal to open a second front would prolong it.

During a conversation with Mr. Eden on August 31,[2] M. Maisky, (a) who had come back from Moscow, repeated the familiar complaint that the Russians, whose losses were so much greater than our own,

---

[1] See below, p. 575, n. 1.
[2] See also p. 596.
(a) N4977/66/38.

felt that we did not show sufficient determination in bringing the war to an end as quickly as possible. This feeling was stronger against Great Britain than against the United States, partly because there was evidence of American help in the lorries circulating near the front and the food supplied to the Russian troops. Mr. Eden pointed out that the reason why we had not sent food to Russia was that we had none to send, and that the Soviet Government were themselves partly responsible for the attitude of Soviet opinion towards us, since they did nothing to explain our war effort. M. Maisky, for example, had made no reference to our bomber offensive against Germany, in which we had dropped over 48,000 tons of bombs and lost 761 aircraft during the months of June, July and August. The Russians always spoke exclusively in terms of divisions, as though the air factor were of no account. They never explained that, with a population of only 46 million, and a large navy and air force, we could not make an effort on land comparable with that of the U.S.S.R. whose population was 200,000,000. The Soviet Government did not even publish our explanation of the reasons why we could not invade France at once.[1]

(iii)

The question of the North Russian convoys: the treatment of British personnel in North Russia (February–December 1943).

The convoys to North Russia which had been suspended in July,[2] were begun again in September 1942; they were suspended again in October and November when all available naval forces were needed for the North African expedition. A convoy sailed in December. The
(a) whole question of these convoys was discussed at the Casablanca Conference in January 1943. The British and American Chiefs of Staff said that the Russians themselves gave very little assistance to the convoys even when they had means available to do so.[3] It was also difficult, owing to Russian secretiveness, to know whether they

---

[1] In a talk with Sir A. Clark Kerr in Moscow early in August M. Maisky complained
(b) that the British Government did not make sufficient allowance for what he called the 'inferiority complex' of the Russians. 'We made them feel like country cousins and they minded because they knew that they were ... We expected them to be as grown up and as metropolitan as ourselves. They were not, and we should remember that, for it was very important.' Sir A. Clark Kerr pointed out that, 'if there were anything in this theory, it belonged to the past'. M. Maisky, however, claimed that 'we were still not treating his people as equals, as, for instance, we treated the Americans'. Sir A. Clark Kerr wrote: 'Again I protested, but in my heart I felt that he was right. I feel that we are still holding these people at an arm's length.'
[2] See Chapter XXVII, section (ii).
[3] The British Chiefs of Staff gave instances of the Russian failure to provide assistance.
(a) COS(43)33(o). (b) N5158/66/38.

actually needed supplies in the volume now being sent to them. The Americans estimated that, if the existing rate of supply were maintained throughout 1943, the movement of American troops to Great Britain might have to be reduced by as much as 100,000 men, but that the advantages of furnishing aid to Russia were such that this reduction should be accepted, though it might be impossible to carry out the full programme of deliveries during the operations against Sicily.

The President thought that at the renewal in 1944 of the protocol[1] defining the amount of aid to Russia we should repeat the safeguarding clause that the provision of supplies could not be continued 'at prohibitive cost to the United Nations effort'. The Prime Minister felt that we should do our utmost to continue aid to Russia. He said that the Chiefs of Staff had been enquiring whether sixteen destroyers would be available from the United States in order to reduce the 'turn around' time of the convoys. The American naval authorities, however, said that they had no destroyers to spare, and that it would be necessary to stop the northern convoys to Russia from about June 14 until after the Sicilian expedition had been carried out. General Marshall also thought that we should not allow the chances of success in Sicily to be hazarded by losses in the northern convoys, and that these losses did as much harm to Russia as to the United States and Great Britain.

The Prime Minister agreed that the convoys must be stopped if their passage were prohibitive in cost; and that, while we should try to continue them throughout the summer, we should make no promises to Stalin. The President and the Prime Minister, therefore, in a telegram to Stalin, safeguarded themselves by saying that they would do their best to supply material assistance to Russia by every available route, but that it would not be in the Russian interest to send it at a cost which would cripple our own capacity to carry out a continued offensive in order to relieve pressure on the eastern front.

In January and February 1943, two more convoys, of forty-two ships in all, sailed to North Russia; six Russian ships sailed independently. Seven ships out of these forty-eight had to turn back owing to damage in exceptionally bad weather, and one was sunk. Forty-one ships—out of which five were lost—sailed homewards from Russian ports. In order to facilitate the protection of the convoys to North Russia the British authorities considered it necessary to base Royal Air Force squadrons on North Russian territory. The Russians were therefore asked whether they would find accommodation for 400–500 Royal Air Force personnel for the operation of the

---

[1] See below, p. 569.

squadrons. They agreed to the proposal, but raised objections when the Air Ministry found that larger numbers would be needed.[1] Mr. Eden explained the position fully to M. Maisky on February 15. M. Maisky promised to do what he could to help. On February 24,

(a) 1943, however, he wrote to Mr. Eden that the Soviet Government had come to the conclusion that housing difficulties at the North Russian bases made it difficult to accommodate even the numbers first suggested. These difficulties had lately become worse owing to enemy air action. In these circumstances the Soviet Government thought that it would be better to cancel the whole arrangement and not to bring any British air unit to North Russia. The Soviet air force would undertake the protection of the convoys; they could do so more effectively if the British Government would transfer to them the aeroplanes intended for Royal Air Force use in North Russia.

Mr. Eden told the War Cabinet on February 25 that he intended to say to M. Maisky that we could not accept the Russian proposals. He would explain to him the difficulty of operating the air protection of convoys, and the technical reasons—e.g. close co-operation with the British naval authorities—which made it impossible to put into effect a plan under which the Russians worked the aircraft. He would also give M. Maisky a full statement of our losses in the convoys, and say that we must retain the responsibility for their protection. Mr. Eden would press his request for the grant of facilities in North Russia and would say that, if the facilities were withheld, we should have to consider whether we could continue the convoys.

(b) Meanwhile the Russian authorities, without previous consultation with the British naval authorities, had entered the British wireless station at Murmansk and closed down special radio equipment installed to interfere with German wireless signals giving the position of our convoys. The Russians also issued instructions for the closing down of essential wireless transmitters at Archangel and Polyarnoe. The Chiefs of Staff complained very strongly of these and other less important acts of obstruction, and commented that, although our own handling of the Russians in early days might have been more tactful, 'their truculent disregard of our needs has now passed all bounds'.

(c) Mr. Eden gave M. Maisky a memorandum on February 26 stating our requirements with the comment that we found it impossible to believe that the Soviet authorities could not find accommodation for 760 officers and men. He also asked for the immediate

---

[1] In September 1942, the Soviet Government had ordered the closing down of the British naval hospital at Vaenga (Murmansk). This hospital had been set up to look after merchant seamen. The Prime Minister had sent a protest to M. Molotov, but had received a stony answer. Mr. Eden also protested against the Soviet action.

(a) WM(43)35; WP(43)85. (b) N1159/408/38. (c) N1168/408/38.

withdrawal of the Soviet ban on our use of special radio equipment and wireless transmitters, and, in accordance with his statement to the Cabinet, warned M. Maisky that, unless the Soviet Government were able to meet our requests, we might have to give up sending convoys. Mr. Eden pointed out that in the service of the convoys we had lost in killed—apart from wounded and prisoners—1,000 officers and men of the Royal Navy and over 500 officers and men of the Merchant Navy, in addition to two cruisers, ten destroyers, six other warships, and seventy-four merchant ships.

Sir A. Clark Kerr was instructed to make similar representations in Moscow. He spoke to M. Molotov on February 27, but the latter (a) had not heard from M. Maisky, and was not at all helpful in the matter. On March 4 M. Molotov gave Sir A. Clark Kerr a written (b) answer. The Russians maintained their refusal to take the air squadrons, but gave way about the special radio equipment and the transmitters. They began a long argument about the minor acts of obstruction. The Prime Minister inclined at first to send an answer suggesting that the Russians themselves should undertake the task of convoying supplies by the northern route, and that for their assistance we would hand over ten ships—to be manned by Soviet crews. We would also escort their convoys as far east as Bear Island and give the Russians all our plant, special radio equipment and Hudson aircraft at present in Russia. He proposed also to say that we could not send the March convoy since the Russians would not allow us to provide satisfactory air cover for it, and that our convoys would soon have to be suspended temporarily owing to the naval and other shipping requirements of our Mediterranean plans.

The Chiefs of Staff and the Foreign Office thought it undesirable to send this message, since in any case, owing to weather conditions in northern waters, we should not be able to give air protection to the March convoy. They also thought that it was unwise at this time to give Stalin the information about the cessation of the convoys during the period of the Mediterranean operation. Furthermore, the undertaking to send supplies[1] was a joint Anglo-American commitment, and any message about it should be sent jointly from the Prime Minister and President Roosevelt. The Prime Minister therefore decided not to send his message, and to allow preparations for the March convoy to continue.

---

[1] Under the second protocol dealing with supplies to Russia, the British and United States Governments undertook to provide shipping 'necessary to lift that part of the programme for which U.S.S.R. ships cannot be made available'. The two Governments, however, were under no obligation to ensure the arrival of the ships. The meaning of the Chiefs of Staff appears to be that since the supplies were provided by the Americans as well as ourselves, consultation with the President was desirable.

(a) N1175/408/38. (b) N1359, 1414/408/38.

In addition to the much greater hazards of the period of long daylight, two new factors now affected the position. The increase in U-boat attacks on the Atlantic convoys (these attacks reached their maximum in March) made it essential to divert to the Atlantic the flotilla of twenty-seven ships and one aircraft carrier employed in protecting the convoys to Russia. At the same time the Admiralty learned in mid-March that the Germans had concentrated a strong naval force in northern Norway. It would thus be necessary to send capital ships as escorts for the convoys into the Barents Sea. The British authorities had always regarded sending capital ships of the Home Fleet east of Bear Island as an unacceptable risk. Hence they decided that the sailing of the March convoy to North Russia must be postponed.

(a)   The War Cabinet approved of this decision on March 22. The Prime Minister then said that he had asked Mr. Eden[1] to consult President Roosevelt about the postponement; the President had agreed that it was necessary. Meanwhile the March convoy was being kept loaded, and Stalin would be told of our decision. In any case it was now clear that we could not safely continue the convoys to Russia by the northern route during the summer months and that after May we should have to wait until August or September before we could resume them without too great risk. We should also need all our escort vessels for the Sicilian expedition, and would have only a minimum number in the Atlantic. President Roosevelt had regarded it as undesirable to let Stalin know at once of this summer postponement, but the Prime Minister thought that we should inform him without delay. The Prime Minister therefore asked Mr. Eden to show the President the draft of a message which he proposed to send

(b) to Stalin. The President accepted the Prime Minister's view, and the War Cabinet considered the draft on March 29. The latest reports at this time were that most of the German warships which had been concentrated at Narvik had left Narvik Fjord; the Admiralty believed that they had been moved only to Alten Fjord in the northern area. Hence, subject to any detailed changes with regard to the location of the German battle fleet, the War Cabinet agreed to the draft.

(c)   The Prime Minister sent the message to Stalin on March 30. He explained that, as he had told Stalin in July 1942, we could not risk the Home Fleet in the Barents Sea while the *Tirpitz* and other large units of the German battle fleet remained in action. The Prime Minister and the President had therefore decided that it was impossible to provide adequate protection for the next convoy; without

---

[1] Mr. Eden was at this time in Washington. See Volume V, Chapter LX, section (iii).

(a) WM(43)44.2, C.A. (b) WM(43)46.2, C. A. (c) T404/3, Churchill Papers/393.

such protection there was 'not the slightest chance' of any of the ships reaching their destination 'in face of the known German preparations for their destruction'. We should hope to resume the sailings early in September if the disposition of the main units of the German fleet made it possible for us to do so, and if the situation in the North Atlantic allowed us to provide the necessary escorts and covering force; meanwhile we and the Americans were doing our utmost to increase supplies by the southern route and through Vladivostok. The message brought a bleak reply from Stalin that this 'unexpected (a) action' would mean a 'catastrophic diminution of supplies' which could not 'fail to affect the position of the Soviet troops'. The Prime Minister answered on April 6 with an assurance that he would do (b) everything possible to improve the passage of supplies.

On June 9, 1943, the British Government communicated to the (c) Soviet Government the draft of a protocol—the third of its kind—for the delivery of supplies to Russia during the twelve months from July 1, 1943 to June 1944.[1] The two previous protocols had been signed in Moscow and Washington; it was agreed that the third protocol—which was concluded with the Governments of the United States and of Canada—should be signed in London. A clause in the protocol allowed the British and United States Governments to reduce their aid in furnishing ships to take the supplies to Russia if a reduction should be necessary owing to shipping losses, lack of escorts, the necessities of other operations, or 'the exigencies of the situation'. This provision was particularly relevant to the question of the convoys from Great Britain to North Russia.

On August 4 Sir A. Clark Kerr telegraphed that the Russians (d) would be asking whether we intended to resume the convoys, and that they were counting on them. Sir A. Clark Kerr hoped that he might be authorised to tell the Russians that the convoys would run again. This telegram was forwarded to the Prime Minister at Quebec. He replied on August 11 that, owing to the extension of our opera- (e) tions in the Mediterranean, there was no question of our being able to resume the convoys in the near future. We could explain these

---

[1] For the first two protocols, see above, p. 264, note 2. The protocol was not signed until October 19. The Russians put forward large amendments to the draft, but the final text (f) was substantially that of the draft of June 9, especially with regard to the clause about the provision of shipping. Owing mainly to the closing of the northern route, deliveries in 1942–3 had fallen short of the programme by 34 per cent, and the total sent by the northern route was only about a tenth of the estimated amount to be shipped on that route. Between one fifth and one sixth of the supplies sent by the northern route were lost owing to enemy action. By far the greater part of the supplies to Russia were American and the largest quantity reached the U.S.S.R. via the Pacific route.

(a) T441/3, Churchill Papers/393. (b) T460/3, Churchill Papers/393. (c) ASE(43)56, N3528/45/38. (d) N4409/408/38. (e) Tel. Welfare 29 (Churchill Papers/393; N4724/408/ 38). (f) N6306/45/38.

T*

considerations to the Russians and also point to the great increases in the deliveries through the Iranian route and through Vladivostok.

(a)   The Russian Embassy in London sent a note on August 25 to the Foreign Office from the Soviet Government requesting the renewal of the convoys and complaining that the increase in supplies through the other routes had not reached the amount which had been expected. The note stated that, while in 1942—when the naval position was more unfavourable—there were only three-monthly intervals between the convoys, the interval in 1943 was six months: 'this cannot but have serious reflection on the efforts to meet the requirements of the Soviet front'.

The Russian figures about the supplies through Iran and Vladivostok were inaccurate, and the note took no account of the Prime Minister's reference in March to the disposition of the main units of the German fleet. Sir A. Clark Kerr was instructed to point out these facts if M. Molotov referred to the note, and to explain that for operational reasons we could not resume the convoys early in September or indeed come to any decision about them for the time being, but that we regarded their resumption as of great importance.

Meanwhile during the summer months the Russians continued to enforce very troublesome and hampering regulations of a minor kind on the British service and merchant navy personnel in North Russia. In the last week of July, after further complaints from the (b)   British naval authorities, the Prime Minister thought that we should consider the withdrawal of our men on the ground that they were unwelcome and that we did not want to open causes of friction. The Prime Minister considered that the Russians would then give us better treatment because they would realise that the withdrawal of our personnel would put an end to the Arctic convoys.

The Chiefs of Staff, however, informed the Foreign Office that the real reason for keeping the British naval personnel in the North Russian area was that the Admiralty were planning an operation in September against the German warships in northern bases and for this purpose required the maintenance of the present technical facilities (wireless etc.) in North Russia at least at their existing level.[1] The Chiefs of Staff also pointed out that there were twenty-four Allied merchant vessels in North Russian waters which could not be brought home without a major escort operation. If we withdrew our service personnel, the crews would be left without hospital services and communications with Great Britain. The Foreign Office

---

[1] The naval establishment was about 200. In addition there was a small air establishment and a base unit of about 120–130 men.

(a) N4851/408/38. (b) N4395/4013/38.

had previously known nothing of the proposed operation against the German warships. They considered that this factor altered the whole situation, and that the Russians should be told about it at once.

Sir A. Clark Kerr was therefore instructed on August 8 to inform (a) M. Molotov of the reasons why we wanted to keep the establishment in North Russia, and to ask that our men should receive better treatment, and that we should be allowed to send the reliefs which the Soviet authorities had previously refused to sanction. The Russians showed great interest in the proposed action against the (b) German fleet, but Sir A. Clark Kerr was not able to get much more than promises from them with regard to the removal of the vexatious restrictions on our naval personnel. They continued to put forward an argument—which seemed to the Foreign Office irrelevant—that there should be reciprocity in the sense that the number of British personnel in North Russia should be no greater than that of Soviet personnel in Great Britain. No definite reply was received from the Russians before the Prime Minister left for Quebec. On September 5 (c) the Prime Minister telegraphed from Quebec that in his view we should tell the Russians that, as soon as we had carried out our operation against the German fleet, we would withdraw all our personnel, but that in such case we could not send any more convoys by the northern route. Mr. Eden replied that we should probably need more than a single operation to put out of action all the German main units in northern waters, and that as long as strong enemy naval forces were concentrated in these waters, we needed operating facilities at the bases nearest to them. Furthermore, unless we had put all the main German ships out of action, we could not bring back our merchant ships until late November. It therefore seemed better, until we had carried out our attack on the German ships and had come to a decision about the convoys, to do no more than ask Sir A. Clark Kerr to make another attempt to remedy our grievances. The Prime Minister agreed that a decision could wait until his (d) return from Quebec.

On September 21 M. Molotov again spoke to Sir A. Clark Kerr (e) about the convoys. He said that the naval position had improved; the Italian fleet had surrendered and German submarines had left the North Atlantic. The Iranian supply route was inadequate, and the Soviet Government had received less than a third of the supplies sent in the previous year. They therefore 'insisted' upon the immediate resumption of the sailings.

(a) N4397, 4500/4013/38. (b) N4567, 4583/4013/38. (c) Welfare 628; Concrete 800 (Churchill Papers/400; N5956/45/38). (d) Welfare 676 (Churchill Papers/400; N5956/45/38). (e) N5568/408/38.

The Admiralty remained doubtful of the practicability of providing the escorts, but the Prime Minister considered that an attempt should be made to send a convoy monthly between November and March. On September 29 the naval position improved owing to a successful attack on the *Tirpitz* by British midget submarines. The ship was badly damaged, and likely to be out of action for some months. Since the Germans had already sent the *Lützow* to the Baltic, the defence of the convoys against heavy surface attack was now less hazardous.

The Prime Minister now decided to tell Stalin that we intended to resume the convoys, and at the same time to refer to our com-

(a) plaints about the treatment of British personnel. The Prime Minister sent his message to Stalin on October 1. He refused to answer the controversial points raised by M. Molotov. He said that we had done our best to help the Russians and that we had made the fullest acknowledgement of the advantages which had come to us from the Russian victories. We had now been planning the resumption of our convoys. We had to meet great difficulties. The Battle of the Atlantic had begun again, and the Germans were using with effect a new kind of acoustic torpedo. We were at full stretch in the Mediterranean and were trying to exploit the Italian collapse in the Aegean islands and the Balkans. We also had to provide for our share in the war against Japan.

Nonetheless we hoped to send a convoy of thirty-five ships—British and American—monthly from November to February, but we had to state that we were not making a 'contract or bargain, but rather a declaration of our solemn and earnest resolve' on the matter. We also wanted, in giving this information about our intentions, to bring before Stalin personally certain representations about the difficulties which we had met in North Russia with regard to the Soviet refusal to give visas for men to replace those long overdue for relief, and about the troublesome and unnecessary restrictions upon our personnel. Mr. Churchill gave a list of these restrictions, e.g. no one from a British warship—not even the British Admiral in charge— could go alongside a British merchantman without giving previous notice to the Soviet authorities. The imposition of so many unnecessary restrictions made a bad impression upon our officers and men, hampered them in the performance of their duties, and was harmful to Anglo-Soviet relations. The effect would be extremely bad if the facts were known to Parliament. No such restrictions were placed upon Soviet personnel in Great Britain.

(b) No answer had been received to this message by October 12. Mr. Churchill then asked Sir A. Clark Kerr to press for a reply, and to

---

(a) T1464/3 (Churchill Papers/393; N5746/4013/38). (b) N5746/4013/38.

say that we must have an answer on the question of our personnel if the cycle of convoys were to be resumed in mid-November. Stalin replied in a message of October 13. The message was surly and, as the (a) Prime Minister described it to Mr. Eden, 'offensive'.[1] Stalin said that our communication of intentions lost its value owing to our statement that we were not binding ourselves; in other words, we were free to give up our plan 'regardless of any influence it may have on the Soviet armies'. Our 'posing of the question' was 'a refusal of the British Government to fulfil the obligations it undertook' and 'a kind of threat' addressed to the U.S.S.R. He then turned to the Prime Minister's complaints about the treatment of British personnel. He denied that there was any need to increase the numbers of British service men in North Russia; he complained about cases of misbehaviour, and said that Mr. Churchill's reference to formalities and restrictions was based upon inaccurate information.

The Prime Minister first thought of replying that the British (b) Government must 'remain the judge of whether any particular operation of war to be carried out by their forces is in fact practicable or not', and that, in view of the efforts and risks involved in running the convoys, we should be glad to be relieved of the task if the Soviet Government did not attach much importance to them. If we were to run them we must obtain the Soviet consent to our demand with regard to the 'relief and small increases in the few hundreds' of British service men in North Russia. We would, again, be glad to withdraw all these men, and would do so as soon as we were assured that it was 'not the desire of the Soviet Government to receive the convoys under the modest and reasonable conditions' which we considered necessary. Mr. Churchill told the War Cabinet on October (c) 18 that he felt it to be right, in the interests of the war effort, to send the convoys if we could manage to do so. He had therefore asked Mr. Eden to deal orally with the matter while he was in Moscow for the Conference of Foreign Ministers.[2] Meanwhile he had seen the Russian Ambassador[3] and handed back Stalin's telegram with the statement that he refused to receive it and that Mr. Eden would discuss the matter orally in Moscow.[4]

---

[1] In sending a copy of Stalin's message to President Roosevelt the Prime Minister described it as 'not exactly all one might hope for from a gentleman for whose sake we are (d) to make an inconvenient, extreme, and costly exertion . . . I think, or at least I hope, this message came from the machine rather than from Stalin, as it took twelve days to prepare. The Soviet machine is quite convinced it can get everything by bullying, and I am sure it is a matter of some importance to show that this is not necessarily always true.'

[2] See below, section (v).

[3] M. Gusev succeeded M. Maisky as Soviet Ambassador in London in September 1943.

[4] During this discussion the Prime Minister said that it would be a great advantage if the Russians delivered their messages in Russian, and let us arrange for their translation. The Prime Minister felt sure that the translations were often very crude, and did not give the tone of the original message.

(a) T1625/3, Churchill Papers/393. (b) N6096/45/38. (c) WM(43)142.3, C.A. (d) T1640/3, No. 459, Churchill Papers/393.

(a)   To his surprise Mr. Eden found M. Molotov most helpful. At their first meeting on October 19 M. Molotov said that the Soviet Government greatly valued the convoys; he promised to arrange a meeting with Stalin for the discussion of the matter. This meeting took place

(b) on October 21. The talk covered a number of matters, but Mr. Eden began with the question of convoys. He explained the British intentions, the scale on which protection had to be provided for the convoys, and the reasons why the Prime Minister could not give a binding promise to send them. Stalin replied that his differences with the Prime Minister were not about the character of the operation but on the question whether the British Government were pledged to it. Stalin suggested that the Prime Minister's attitude was that the convoys were a gift. Mr. Eden said that this was not the Prime Minister's view; Stalin then said that he had not intended his message to cause offence.

Mr. Eden explained that we must have a minimum of naval personnel in North Russia for working the convoys. Stalin still refused to increase the number of men in North Russian ports. He said that there were already too many British sailors in North Russian ports with nothing to do, and that they got into trouble with Russian sailors. He made the significant comment that if the British treated the Russians as equals, the trouble would not arise, and we could have as many men there as we pleased. After further discussion, however, Stalin agreed that Mr. Eden should meet M. Molotov again on October 22 with a list of the British requirements.

M. Molotov then said that the required visas would be granted, and that formalities would be reduced to a minimum. He suggested that 'someone would whisper to someone' in such a way as to ensure that British sailors would treat the Russians as equals. M. Molotov raised the question of reciprocity and proposed that each side should fix a 'desired maximum' number of men which they would find it desirable to maintain in the other country.[1] Mr. Eden gave M. Molotov a memorandum setting out our requirements and suggesting what might be done to secure efficiency, and asking for an assurance that any proposals which we might make for dealing with particular grievances would be examined sympathetically. Mr. Eden offered not to increase the present number of 383 British personnel (including a hospital unit) by more than 10 per cent without Soviet agreement, and to reduce this number when the convoys were suspended in the spring. The Russians gave a favourable reply.

---

[1] As earlier, the Admiralty did not regard the 'maximum' solution as suitable. Their view was that the only criterion should be the duties which had to be carried out.

(a) N6164/408/38. (b) N6261/408/38.

(iv)

Anglo-American decisions at the Quebec Conference: exchange of messages between the Prime Minister, the President and Stalin with regard to a conference of Foreign Ministers and a tripartite meeting (August 7–September 14, 1943).

On August 17 the Prime Minister, the President, and their respective Chiefs of Staff met in conference at Quebec to settle more definitely their plans for 1944. The military situation was even more favourable than at the time of the Washington meeting in May. The German submarine successes against Allied shipping had been greatly reduced. Sicily had been captured; Mussolini had fallen and the anti-Fascist government formed by Marshal Badoglio was asking for an armistice. The Russians were advancing on their front between Smolensk and the Sea of Azov. The British and Americans could therefore reaffirm their choice of May 1, 1944, as the target date for a cross-Channel invasion as the first step toward striking at the heart of Germany. This invasion would be the primary Anglo-American effort in 1944, and action in the Mediterranean would be directed to its support, i.e. to assist in securing the conditions—a limitation in the numbers of German divisions and air force units in France—necessary for a successful landing. In these circumstances relations between the Western Allies and Stalin were likely to become easier.

After the sharp exchange of messages in June, the Prime Minister had not continued during the next few weeks his personal exchanges with Stalin. A message of August 7, therefore, informing Stalin of (a) the forthcoming resumption of the Anglo-American discussions held at Washington in May, was sent in a note from the British Government. The message stated that the work of a joint Anglo-American staff considering future operations in the Mediterranean, the preparation of the cross-Channel invasion, and long-term plans against Japan had now reached a stage at which the Combined Chiefs of Staff, the President and the Prime Minister had to meet to review it. The Soviet Government would be kept informed of all conclusions affecting the European theatre in which our 'supreme and unchanging' objective was 'to engage the enemy, as soon and as closely as possible, on the largest scale'.[1] The message went on to say that the Prime Minister still hoped for a meeting between the three

---

[1] The first Quebec Conference (August 9–17, 1943) met to settle definitely Anglo-American strategy for 1943. The Conference confirmed previous decisions that the chief operation would be a cross-Channel invasion, followed by an advance into Germany, and that the 'target date' for the invasion would be May 1, 1944.

(a) Tel. 1049 to Moscow, Prisec.

Heads of Governments. He understood that Stalin

'was unable to leave Russia for a meeting à deux with the President, which the President proposed and which the Prime Minister would have welcomed. The Prime Minister repeats his willingness to go to any rendezvous. . . . In spite of the fact that it has not been possible yet to arrange any tripartite meeting, the war affairs of the United Nations have prospered on all fronts. Nevertheless very great advantages might be gained by a discussion between the three principals, and he still hopes that this desirable end may be achieved.'

(a)   Stalin replied on August 9, through the Soviet Embassy in London, to the message of August 7. He agreed that a meeting of the Heads of the three Governments was most desirable, but said that he was unable to leave the battle front even for a week, and therefore could not come to Scapa Flow or any other 'distant point'. He suggested, however, that a meeting of 'responsible representatives' of the three States should be held to decide upon the time and place of a meeting of Heads of Governments, and that there should be a preliminary agreement on the scope of the questions to be discussed and on draft proposals for acceptance. Finally Stalin congratulated the British Government and the Anglo-American troops on their successes in Sicily which had already caused the downfall of Mussolini.

(b)   Mr. Churchill sent an answer to Stalin from Quebec on August 11. He congratulated the Russians on their victories, and said that he understood Stalin's inability to leave the front at a critical time when he was actually directing the victorious movement of the Russian armies. He agreed that a meeting of 'responsible representatives' of the three Powers should take place in the future; he said that he would put Stalin's suggestion to President Roosevelt.[1] He mentioned the great successes in the U-boat war and pointed out that they would facilitate the establishment of the largest-scale Anglo-American fronts against the Germans which were indispensable to the shorten-

(c)   ing of the war. Meanwhile Stalin had also telegraphed on August 8 to President Roosevelt, explaining that he could not leave the direction of action at the front during the summer and autumn and therefore could not fulfil his promise, given through Mr. Davies, to meet the President.[2] He thought it desirable, however, that there should be a meeting of the 'responsible representatives' of the two countries, and suggested Astrakhan or Archangel as a meeting place. If Mr. Roosevelt found this proposal inconvenient personally, he might send representatives. Stalin had no objection to the presence of Mr. Churchill at the meeting.

---

[1] Mr. Churchill also told Stalin that he was sending him a stereoscopic machine with a number of slides showing the damage done to German cities by Allied bombing.

[2] See above, pp. 557–8.

(a) T1213/3, Concrete 81, Churchill Papers/136 and 172. (b) T1221/3, Welfare 44, Churchill Papers/136 and 172. (c) Welfare 209, Churchill Papers/136.

The Prime Minister and President Roosevelt decided to send a joint message to Stalin. A copy of the text was telegraphed to London on August 18. The message opened by accepting Stalin's reasons for (a) remaining on the battle front; the President and the Prime Minister, however, emphasised once more the importance of a tripartite meeting. They did not think Astrakhan or Archangel suitable places, but suggested Fairbanks (Alaska). If Stalin could not accept their suggestion, they would agree to a meeting of representatives on the 'Foreign Office level'. Such a meeting could be only 'exploratory' in character, since final decisions would have to be reserved to the three Governments.'

On August 25 the Soviet Chargé d'Affaires in London delivered (b) Stalin's reply. Stalin once more agreed that a joint meeting was desirable, but again said that he could not leave the Russian front for so distant a place as Fairbanks. He insisted that the Soviet armies were still carrying on the struggle against the main forces of Hitler, and that new German divisions were being moved to the Russian front.

Stalin accepted the proposal for a meeting of 'representatives in charge of foreign affairs' on condition that this meeting was not merely exploratory; he wanted the meeting to prepare for 'definite decisions', and therefore maintained his request that the scope of the questions for discussion should be 'defined in advance', and that draft proposals should be prepared. He said that he approved of the terms laid down for the Italian surrender, but repeated his demand for the establishment of a 'military-political' commission.[1]

Mr. Churchill kept the War Cabinet informed of these exchanges with the Russians. The War Cabinet felt that Stalin's proposal for a (c) commission should be accepted. The proposal implied a recognition on the Russian side of the importance of the Mediterranean campaign, and established the principle of reciprocity. If we rejected the proposal, the Russians would have an excuse to deal independently with Germany and Eastern Europe.

[1] On August 24 Sir A. Clark Kerr telegraphed that M. Molotov had told him that Stalin was preparing an answer to a further message of August 19 from the Prime Minister (d) and the President about the negotiations with Italy. Stalin in fact sent a message on August 22. The tone and terms were far from cordial. Stalin made exaggerated complaints about delays in the transmission of the armistice conditions to be imposed on Italy,* and said that he could no longer tolerate a situation in which the Soviet Union, as a passive third observer, merely received information about the results of agreements made by Great Britain and the United States. He asked for the establishment in Sicily of a 'military-political' commission of representatives of the three countries to consider questions concerning negotiations with the different Governments dissociating themselves from Germany.

* The delay concerned only 17 words and was due to a mistake in cyphering and to errors in transmission.

(a) T1241/3, Churchill Papers/136. (b) T1251/3, Concrete 569, Churchill Papers/136 and 172. (c) WM(43)119.1, C.A.; Concrete 570, Churchill Papers/241. (d) Moscow tel. 803, Churchill Papers/241; Welfare 217 and 402, T1250/3, Churchill Papers/249.

It was however, desirable to obtain the immediate approval of the Soviet Government to the final instrument of Italian surrender. A

(a) message was therefore sent to Stalin on August 26 giving him the text of the instrument; the message explained the urgency of the matter, and pointed out that it was not an answer to the proposal for the

(b) establishment of the commission. M. Molotov told Sir A. Clark Kerr on August 27 that the Soviet Government approved the terms and empowered General Eisenhower to sign on their behalf. They did not think it necessary to send a representative to be present at the signature.

(c)   On August 31 Mr. Attlee and Mr. Eden (who had meanwhile returned to England) telegraphed to the Prime Minister that in their opinion the three-Power military-political commission should be set up as soon as possible. They would accept Sicily as a place of meeting if Stalin insisted upon it, but they thought Algiers, as an Allied head-quarters, a better centre. Furthermore, since Stalin wanted the Commission to deal with other satellite States detaching themselves from Germany, they recommended an early move to London from Algiers. They were doubtful about adding a representative of the French Committee of Liberation, since the Americans would not like it and the Russians might suspect it as a move to upset the balance of the Commission to their disadvantage. Representatives of the French Committee and of other European Allies should, however, be called in when necessary, and the representation of the Dominions should also be considered.

(d)   The Prime Minister, however, found that neither the President nor Stalin objected to the inclusion of French representation. He telegraphed to Mr. Eden on September 3 that he did not see any reason against the Commission starting work in Sicily, with a move later to Algiers or Casablanca. He would not try to get it to London, since it would be better to keep London available for a more important body.

The Prime Minister had also discussed with the President a possible meeting place for the Conference of Foreign Ministers. The President was not opposed to London but thought it better to choose some other place in Great Britain where the press could be kept at a distance. The Prime Minister suggested Edinburgh.[1] The Prime Minister thought that the Conference should not discuss the military situation. The Russians would bring a single general who would not

---

[1] The Prime Minister thought that Holyrood House might be available. Windsor was suggested later as a possibility.

(a) Tel. 1182 to Moscow (Churchill Papers/249). (b) Moscow tel. 833; Concrete 615, Churchill Papers/249. (c) Concrete 665, Churchill Papers/241; WM(43)120.4, C.A.; WM(43)122.2, C.A. (d) Welfare 582, Churchill Papers/241.

be allowed to do anything except ask for a second front. Any discussion of this question should take place between the Allied staffs, and the Russians must have the patience to listen to the argument about the sea, the air, landing craft, transportation, etc.

The Prime Minister and the President had considered some of the general questions for the agenda, e.g. if we won the war, what should we do about Germany? Was it to be divided, and if so, how? Should there be spheres of influence or should the Anglo-Americans and the Russians work jointly in every field? The Prime Minister thought that the latter plan would be better, but that as we and the Russians had signed a twenty-year treaty, we should be always helping each other. There could be no question of our disinteresting ourselves in any part of the world, since out of such a policy might easily come the cause of a new war.

The Prime Minister's telegram seems to have crossed a telegram of September 2 from Mr. Eden recommending London as the (a) meeting place for the Conference. Mr. Eden understood from M. Maisky that M. Molotov would come to London if we agreed with the Soviet Government about the agenda for the meeting. Mr. Hull also seemed willing to come to London but could not be expected to go to Moscow. Moreover if the meeting were held in Moscow, Stalin might stay away from it on the excuse that he had to remain at the front.

M. Maisky had also told Mr. Eden that the Soviet Government (b) much wanted to know how they would stand after the war in relation to their western Allies. Mr. Eden suggested that we might agree upon the need for collaboration and even come to firm decisions about carrying out a policy. M. Maisky then asked about frontiers. Mr. Eden said that we could not be expected at this stage to make a detailed delineation of frontiers. It would be better to agree now to work together after the war and to set up some form of international organisation for this purpose, but we could probably say that we understood the anxieties of the Soviet Government for the security of the western frontiers of the U.S.S.R. The United States might also make a similar declaration.

On September 5 the Prime Minister sent to London three tele- (c) grams (subject to the approval of the War Cabinet) for immediate transmission to Stalin. The first dealt with the establishment of the proposed military-political commission in Sicily or at Tunis or Algiers. The second telegram dealt with operations in Italy, and the

(a) Concrete 692, Churchill Papers/172. (b) N5083/3666/38. (c) Welfare 604, Churchill Papers/172; Welfare 605, Churchill Papers/241; Welfare 606, Churchill Papers/249; Welfare 613, Churchill Papers/172.

third with the Conference of Foreign Ministers. Mr. Churchill
suggested a meeting in Great Britain (as a midway point) outside
London and hoped for a date early in October. He pointed out that
the conference could not supersede the authority of the Governments
concerned, but that a personal meeting of Heads of Governments
ought to take place later, and for this purpose Mr. Churchill was
willing to go to Moscow. If Stalin wanted the Russian representative
to enquire why we had not yet invaded France across the Channel
and why we could not do so sooner or in greater strength than was
now proposed, Mr. Churchill would welcome a separate technical
military mission.

(a)   Mr. Roosevelt also sent a message to Stalin. He said that he would
accept Great Britain for the meeting of Ministers but thought that
a remoter place—e.g. Casablanca or Tunis—might be better. The
President did not want the meeting to develop at this stage into a full
Combined Staff Conference. He would have wished Mr. Hull to
attend, if Mr. Eden and M. Molotov were coming, but Mr. Hull
could not undertake a long journey; Mr. Welles and Mr. Harriman
would therefore go in his place. The President also proposed a joint
meeting with Stalin and Mr. Churchill between November 15 and
December 15, possibly in North Africa. For constitutional reasons
he could not be away from the United States for more than about
twenty days.

(b)   Stalin sent a reply—dated September 8—through the Soviet
Embassy in London on September 9. He complained about the delay
in setting up the military-political commission, but accepted the date
proposed by Mr. Churchill for the Foreign Ministers' Conference.
He suggested Moscow as a meeting place, and insisted once again
upon previous agreement about the agenda. He consented to a
meeting of the three Heads of Government in November or December, and wanted the meeting place to be in a country where all three
States had representatives—e.g. Iran. He qualified his acceptance by
saying that the time must depend on the military situation on the
Soviet western front.

(c)   The Prime Minister replied to Stalin on September 10. He agreed
to set up the military-political commission at once, and named Mr.
Macmillan as the British representative. He said that in the British
view the commission would receive full information, and would be
expected to report to and advise the three Governments, but that it
could have no independent executive powers. The Prime Minister

(a) Welfare 614, Churchill Papers/241. (b) T1307/3, Concrete 810, Churchill
Papers/241. (c) T1313/3, Welfare 681, Churchill Papers/241.

reminded Stalin that in Great Britain Parliament was supreme and would not consent to alienate its authority.

Mr. Churchill deferred to Stalin's wish that the 'Conference of Foreign Office representatives' should meet in Moscow. He was also willing to go to Teheran to meet Stalin, though he would have preferred Cyprus or Khartoum. He spoke with great emphasis of the importance of the meeting not only for the military purpose of shortening and finishing the war but as an opportunity for making 'those good arrangements for the future of the world which will enable the British, American and Russian nations to render a lasting service to humanity'.

The President also telegraphed to Stalin explaining that Egypt (a) would be much more convenient for him than Iran as a meeting place. On September 14 Mr. Churchill suggested meeting in a ship (b) at some port in Egypt or the Levant. He offered Stalin the use of a British ship.[1] The offer was not accepted; the Foreign Office indeed were sure that the Russians would be much too suspicious of hidden microphones to accept it, and that Stalin would not go to any place where he could not stay in a Soviet Embassy. Stalin, in fact, refused Egypt on the ground that the U.S.S.R. had no diplomatic representation there.

(v)

The Foreign Ministers' Conference in Moscow, October 19–30, 1943.

The agenda proposed by the Foreign Office for the Moscow Con- (c) ference covered a very large number of questions relating to the war and to certain important post-war problems, such as the treatment of Germany and other enemy countries in Europe, upon which an Allied agreement was desirable. The American proposals were less detailed, but even wider in scope, since they included the proposal for a four-Power declaration, which the United States Government had already put forward at the Quebec Conference, providing for consultation and co-operation in the maintenance of world peace after the war. The Soviet Government informed the Foreign Office on September 29 that their main proposal for the agenda was the (d) consideration of measures for shortening the war against Germany and her Allies in Europe. It was obviously impossible to launch an

---

[1] President Roosevelt thought this plan an excellent one, and supported it in a message to Stalin.

(a) Welfare 683, Churchill Papers/241. (b) Welfare 731, Churchill Papers/136. (c) WP(43)434. (d) N5779/3666/38.

invasion of northern France in 1943, but the Soviet Government stated their view that 'urgent measures taken in 1943' by the British and Americans to secure the invasion of Western Europe across the English Channel, together with the action of the Soviet armies against the main German forces would lead to a German collapse.

Mr. Eden replied to the Soviet statement on October 1 in a letter to the Soviet Chargé d'Affaires in London. He referred to the information given to the Soviet Government at the end of the Quebec Conference and to the Prime Minister's offer[1] in his message of September 5 to Stalin. Mr. Eden said that this offer remained open.

(a)   The War Cabinet discussed the agenda for the Conference on October 5 and 8. The Prime Minister thought that the Conference would give us an opportunity of ascertaining the views of the Russians, and that we ought not to define or try to reach definite conclusions on the questions likely to come up for discussion. Mr. Churchill had also drawn up a short ten-point statement for Mr. Eden's use. This document, which was approved, with some changes,[2] by the War Cabinet, summed up the policy of the British Government on matters—especially in relation to the Russian claims in Europe—where there was a divergence of view between Great Britain and the U.S.S.R. The statement represented what might be called the programme of maximum Anglo-American-Soviet co-operation for which the British Government hoped at this time.

(b)   The Moscow Conference, which opened on October 19, 1943, and closed on October 30, was not intended to do more than to prepare for the subsequent meeting between the Prime Minister, President Roosevelt and Stalin. The Conference was a success—partly indeed because the most controversial post-war questions, e.g. frontiers, affecting the Soviet Union were not discussed, and partly because the Soviet Government appear to have been satisfied with the military information given to them in confidence during the meetings.[3] In accordance with the Soviet proposals for the agenda M. Molotov brought forward the consideration of measures to be adopted for the shortening of the war. He asked whether the Anglo-American promise to undertake the invasion of northern France in the spring of 1944 remained valid. He also proposed that the three Powers should ask Turkey to enter the war and that they should ask

---

[1] i.e. the offer that Stalin should send a technical mission to London.
[2] For this statement, see Volume V, Chapter LXII, section (i).
[3] Mr. Eden was accompanied by General Sir H. Ismay and Mr. Strang. The chief American representatives were Mr. Hull and Mr. Harriman, and the chief Russian representatives, MM. Molotov, Vyshinsky and Litvinov.

(a) WM(43)135. 3, C.A.; WM(43)137.4, C.A.; WP(43)447 Revise; C12155/696/62.
(b) N6921/3666/38.

Sweden to place at their disposal air bases for the bombing of Germany.

The Soviet military questions were answered on October 20. Mr. Eden and Mr. Hull said that the Anglo-American statements with (a) regard to an invasion of northern France in the spring of 1944 remained valid, and had been reaffirmed by the Prime Minister and the President at Quebec. The plan was, obviously, subject to certain military conditions; there was every hope that these conditions would be fulfilled. General Ismay, on behalf of Great Britain, and General Deane, on behalf of the United States, explained that the scale of the initial assault depended on the number of assault ships and landing craft available, and upon the facilities for maintaining the expeditionary force before French ports were available. The recent successes in the anti-submarine campaign had enabled Great Britain and the United States to take the risk of turning over a larger part of their shipbuilding capacity to the construction of these assault ships and landing craft.[1] They also hoped to solve the problem of 'beach maintenance' in the tidal waters of the English Channel by the construction of two 'emergency ports'. General Deane gave some figures to show the magnitude of the task of organising the invasion. He said that 400 voyages by transports and 1,000 by cargo ships would be necessary during the next 7–8 months in order to bring a million men and their supplies from the United States to Great Britain; that 3,300 assault ships and landing craft would be needed for the landings, and that 100 new airfields were under construction in southern England.

General Ismay said that, apart from the question of 'maintenance', the invasion would be practicable only if there had been a substantial reduction before the spring of 1944 in the German fighter force in north-west Europe, and if the German mobile land forces and reserves available in northern France amounted to not more than about twelve divisions (excluding coastal, training and air force divisions) at the time when the expedition was launched, and could not be increased by more than about fifteen first quality divisions within two months. It was hoped that these conditions would be fulfilled as a result of the continuous Allied bomber offensive (of which the Russians were given full details), and of pressure in Italy and landings in southern France simultaneous with the northern

---

[1] The peak of German successes in submarine warfare was in March, 1943, when nearly 700,000 tons of shipping, British, Allied and neutral, were sunk. From this time there was a rapid improvement in the Allied means of defence. 28 German submarines—nearly a third of the number actually at sea—were destroyed in May. Only 19 Allied ships were lost in June, and only 3 in August. In September nearly all the German U-boats were withdrawn from the Atlantic.

(a) COS(43)704(0).

landings, guerrilla operations which would keep German troops in the Balkans, and, above all, Soviet attacks in the East.

The Anglo-American assurances were embodied in a 'most secret protocol' signed by Mr. Hull, Mr. Eden, and M. Molotov. The Prime Minister was, however, much disturbed by the Russian insistence upon an invasion of northern France by a given date without regard to the military situation elsewhere, and especially in Italy.

(a) On October 20, 1943, he telegraphed to Mr. Eden that the Anglo-American plans for 1944 were 'open to grave defects; neither the force built up in Italy nor that which will be ready in May to cross the Channel is adequate for what is required'. Twice in his correspondence with Mr. Eden at Moscow he referred to 'lawyers' agreements' made in good faith but persisted in without regard to changes

(b) in the military situation. He sent Mr. Eden—for repetition to Stalin —the warning given on October 24 by General Eisenhower and General Alexander on the situation and prospects in Italy.[1] He thought that Mr. Eden ought to warn Stalin that the assurances— which were themselves subject to certain specified conditions—about the cross-Channel invasion might have to be 'modified by the exigencies of the battle in Italy'. There was no question of abandoning the invasion, but it might have to be postponed until July: 'It is no use planning for defeat in the field in order to give temporary political satisfaction.'

(c)   Mr. Eden and General Ismay had a long talk on the question with Stalin and M. Molotov on the evening of October 29. Stalin asked whether we considered that we should have to postpone the invasion, and, if so, for how long—one month or two months. Mr. Eden could give no definite answer: he said that we would do our utmost to carry out the operation at the earliest moment at which it had reasonable prospect of success. He also repeated that, in view of the whole situation, a meeting of Heads of Governments ought to be held. The military plans for the cross-Channel invasion were discussed without the participation of the representatives of the Foreign Office and the State Department who accompanied their political chiefs. These representatives took part in the consideration of the

(d) other Russian proposals for shortening the war. On the question of the entry of Turkey into the war[2] the Foreign Office already knew that the Soviet Government were dissatisfied with Turkish neutrality, and regarded it now—whatever might have been its advantages in

---

[1] See above, pp. 501–2.
[2] For the discussion on Turkey, see below, Volume IV, Chapter LI, section (ii).

(a) T1677/3, Tel. 1663 to Moscow, Churchill Papers/342. (b) Tels. 142–3 Extra to Moscow, T1737–8/3, Churchill Papers/344. (c) T1766/3, Moscow tel. 108 Space, Churchill Papers/344. (d) N6921/3666/38.

the earlier part of the war—as of benefit only to the enemy. They were also suspicious of our supplies of arms to the Turks on the ground that we might be providing them for ultimate use against the U.S.S.R. Mr. Eden therefore explained at the Conference that in our view Turkish participation in the war was most desirable but that we should have to consider what inducements we had to offer. The Turks would certainly ask for immediate assistance in the defence of Constantinople against air attack by the Germans. In view of our commitments elsewhere we could not provide even a fraction of the 25 squadrons which we had promised to Turkey as a first instalment of assistance. We might, however, ask for the use of Turkish airfields in south-west Anatolia in view of the importance to us of capturing Rhodes.[1] We should thereby not only secure military advantages but also bring Turkey from neutrality to non-belligerency and facilitate the next step, i.e. from non-belligerency to active participation in the war. The United States Government did not think it advisable to induce Turkey to enter the war; we were already straining our resources in personnel, shipping and supplies in our Mediterranean operations and in preparations for a cross-Channel invasion. Mr. Eden also did his best to remove Russian suspicions, at which M. Molotov had hinted, about our reasons for promising to send arms to Turkey.

The British and American Governments were even more unwilling to put pressure on Sweden. Mr. Eden pointed out on October 20 that Swedish opinion would be influenced to some extent by the Soviet attitude to Finland. The chance of success would therefore be greater if the Soviet Government could indicate their intentions regarding the independence of Finland. M. Molotov said that an extension of the discussion to Finland would prevent a study of the question of Swedish entry into the war. It was then agreed that Mr. Eden and Mr. Hull should consult their Governments. As a result they put in memoranda a week later. Mr. Hull's memorandum stated that the United States Government did not favour building up air bases in Sweden since it would mean a diversion of resources from the build-up of the cross-Channel invasion. The grant of facilities for the landing, refuelling, etc. of aircraft would be useful, but these questions could be taken up later. Mr. Eden's memorandum said that we did not need air bases in Sweden, and that the Swedes would certainly ask for air support which we might find it difficult to provide. He suggested that the Conference might consider (a) what inducements we could offer the Swedes to come into the war;

---

[1] On this day the Chiefs of Staff told the Prime Minister that these airfields (in fact, landing strips) were essential if the island of Leros (which British forces had captured and were holding precariously) was to be defended. See below, Volume IV, ibid.

(b) what commitments these offers would involve, and how we could meet them, and (c) whether the commitments would outweigh the advantages.

M. Molotov accepted the British and American statements with the comment that the two Soviet proposals for shortening the war seemed to have little support from Great Britain or the United States.[1] He thought that if we really put pressure on Turkey to come into the war at once she would have no option but to do so.[2] On the other hand the Soviet Government were not forthcoming over Mr. Eden's proposals with regard to Allied policy towards the two resistance movements in Yugoslavia. Mr. Eden explained that British policy towards Yugoslavia was to maintain the unity of the triple Kingdom of Serbs, Croats and Slovenes. We had representatives with General Mihailović and also with the Yugoslav partisans, and were sending supplies to both groups. We wanted General Milhailović to carry out two operations, the destruction of the Bor copper mines and the cutting of the Nish–Belgrade railway. We had made it clear that if General Milhailović did not carry out these operations—for which he had the necessary resources—we should withhold further supplies and reconsider our general attitude towards him. In any case we wished to avoid local war between the two Yugoslav groups, and therefore hoped that the Russians would agree to advise the two groups accordingly.

M. Molotov gave no immediate reply; later, at Mr. Eden's suggestion, the question was taken out of the Conference agenda, and kept for discussion between the British and Russian representatives.[3] M. Molotov also brought forward a Russian claim to a part of the Italian fleet. He asked for a battleship, a cruiser, eight destroyers, and four submarines, and for 40,000 tons—more than a quarter of the tonnage immediately available—of Italian merchant shipping. Mr. Eden was in favour of granting this Russian request but the War Cabinet considered it better to postpone a decision until the meeting

---

(a)   [1] The Prime Minister telegraphed to Mr. Eden on October 23 that there were great advantages in the entry of Turkey into the war 'on her own initiative', and without insistence on air support which we could not provide without detriment to our main operations in Italy. Similarly, the Allies, and particularly the Russians, would gain from Swedish entry into the war. On October 25 the Prime Minister repeated his view that we ought not to 'discourage the Russian desire that Turkey and Sweden should of their own volition become co-belligerents or actual Allies. The Russians should not be put in the position of arguing for this, and we of simply making difficulties. We should agree in principle and let the difficulties manifest themselves, as they will certainly do, in the discussion of ways and means. They may well be overcome or put in their proper place and proportion. Anyhow, we ought not to begin by crabbing everything.'

[2] On the question of Sweden the Conference agreed that the views expressed should be reported to their Governments (from whom, indeed, they originated) with a view to further study. No such study seems to have taken place.

[3] See Volume III, Chapter XLI, section (iii).

(a) Tels. 106, 132 Extra to Moscow (Churchill Papers/446; R10557/55/44).

of the three Heads of Governments. They pointed out that the (a) Italian ships were unsuited to work in Arctic waters, and modifications would take several months. We had only nine Italian destroyers; it would be unreasonable to give the Russians eight of them; we had also to keep in mind the claims of the smaller Allies, particularly the Greeks. The transfer of the Italian ships to the Russians would seriously affect Italian co-operation with us and the Americans: the Italian ships which we were using might be scuttled or sabotaged, and we might lose the use of Taranto dockyard. The Prime Minister telegraphed the views of the War Cabinet to Mr. Eden on the night of October 28–9. He added later on October 29 (b) that, provided the Americans agreed, there would be no objection to telling M. Molotov that in principle we agreed that the Soviet Government should have a share of the Italian ships, and that the proportion asked was not unreasonable (though the battleship should be of the *Cavour* class, not of the *Littorio* class). Details and dates of delivery would be settled later, taking into account operations and the probable effect on the Italians.[1] Mr. Eden gave this message to (c) M. Molotov. He did not mention the claims of the Greek and Yugoslav Governments.

The main political discussions at the Conference were about the proposed four-Power declaration,[2] Allied policy in Italy and the establishment of a European Advisory Commission in London to deal with matters requiring current and close collaboration.

Mr. Hull (whose chief interest in the Conference was to secure some general statement of 'principles' regarding post-war co-operation) introduced the four-Power Declaration on October 21. The draft which he proposed had been amended slightly since it had first appeared; it also differed in a few points from the draft accepted by the British and Dominion Governments. M. Molotov at first wanted only a three-Power Declaration on the ground that no Chinese representative was present and that the signature of the document might be delayed. Mr. Hull and Mr. Eden, however, pointed out that it would be possible to get the Chinese approval of the terms before the end of the Conference. The question was left open in the first stage of the discussions, but a decision was finally taken to include China forthwith in the Declaration; the Chinese Ambassador therefore signed the Declaration with the British, American and Soviet representatives on the last day of the Conference.

---

[1] The ships would be handed over for use during the war, without prejudice to their ultimate disposition by the United Nations.
[2] See Volume V, Chapter LXII, section (i).

(a) WM(43)147.2, C.A.; R10783/17/22. (b) Extra 171, 181, R10957/8717/22. (c) R12225/8717/22.

The preamble to the Declaration stated the determination of the four Powers 'to continue hostilities against those Axis Powers with which they respectively are at war until such Powers have laid down their arms on the basis of unconditional surrender'. The four Powers declared (i) that 'their united action, pledged for the prosecution of the war against their respective enemies', would be 'continued for the organisation and maintenance of peace and security'; (ii) that those of them at war with a common enemy would 'act together in all matters relating to the surrender and disarmament of that enemy', and (iii) that they would 'take all necessary measures to provide against any violation of the terms imposed upon the enemy'. (iv) They recognised 'the necessity of establishing at the earliest practicable date a general international organisation, based on the principle of the sovereign equality of all peace-loving States, and open to membership by all such States, large and small, for the maintenance of international peace and security'. (v) 'For the purposes of maintaining international peace and security, pending the re-establishment of law and order and the inauguration of a system of general security', they would 'consult with one another and', as occasion arose, 'with other members of the United Nations, with a view to joint action on behalf of the community of nations'.

The four Powers agreed also that, after the termination of hostilities, they would not 'employ their military forces within the territories of other States except for the purposes envisaged in the Declaration, and after joint consultation', and that they would 'confer together and with other representatives of the United Nations to bring about a practical general agreement for the regulation of armaments in the post-war period'.

M. Molotov proposed during the Conference that a committee of representatives of the three Powers might be set up to work out the questions relating to the establishment of the general international organisation envisaged in the Declaration. Such a committee would work in Washington, London or Moscow, and could later include representatives of the smaller States. Mr. Eden agreed with the proposal; Mr. Hull also accepted it, but thought that the work should be done at first informally, and without bringing in the small nations. Mr. Hull later spoke again on the need to keep the matter at an informal stage; otherwise there would be too much public controversy over it. An agreement was therefore reached for an informal exchange of views by representatives of the three Powers.

The establishment of a European Advisory Commission was proposed by Mr. Eden. The suggestion arose out of the earlier Soviet proposal for a military-political Commission to deal with Italy and later with other Axis satellités wishing to dissociate themselves from Germany; the Soviet Government also thought that the Commission should direct and co-ordinate the work of the various organs of control in Italy.[1]

Mr. Eden explained the difficulties in the way of the last suggestion but considered that, apart from Italian problems, the Commission should have very wide terms of reference and act as a 'clearing-house' for European problems of common interest to the three Governments, e.g. the future of Germany, and Allied policy in liberated territories.

M. Molotov accepted the proposal, and suggested that the Commission should be kept distinct from the politico-military Commission dealing with Italian questions. The Conference agreed that the Commission should be established in London; its terms of reference were to study, and to make joint representations upon European questions connected with the termination of hostilities which the three Governments might refer to it. The establishment of the Commission would not preclude other methods of consultation, e.g. there might be tripartite discussions in London, Washington or Moscow between the Head of the Foreign Ministry and the diplomatic representatives of the other two Governments.

On the question of Italy the Conference agreed to set up an Allied Advisory Council to watch the operation of the machinery of control, advise the Commander-in-Chief on general policy connected with the work of control, and ultimately—when it was possible to bring to an end direct military control of the administration—take over the supervision of the Allied Control Commission.[2] The Conference also accepted a declaration by the three Governments that their policy in Italy would continue to be based upon the fundamental principles that fascism in all its aspects should be destroyed and that the Italian people should be given every opportunity to establish governmental and other institutions of a democratic kind. It was, however, recognised that it might remain impossible to allow full effect to these principles while active military operations were taking place in Italy.

The Soviet Government had suggested a declaration of this kind, and, in order to remove their suspicions of Anglo-American policy in Italy, Mr. Eden explained fully the steps which the Anglo-American control had already taken to get rid of fascist influence. Mr. Eden and Mr. Hull gave the Russians a memorandum on Anglo-American policy and on the instructions to General Eisenhower at the time of the planning of the operations against Sicily.

---

[1] See above, pp. 577–80.
[2] The Council in fact did not often meet, and was of little importance.

This memorandum showed that the successful measures for the extirpation of fascist influence in Sicily had been extended to the mainland and that Allied policy in the matter had not been altered by the decision to accept Italy as a co-belligerent. Mr. Eden said that Marshal Badoglio would soon cease to be Prime Minister, and that if a good anti-fascist could be found, he might become Prime Minister, but that after twenty years it was difficult to find anti-fascists of standing and authority. Mr. Eden had not been favourably impressed by Count Sforza.

In view of the Russian distrust of Anglo-American intentions in Italy it was necessary also to make clear the policy which the British and United States Governments proposed to adopt for the adminis-tration of France after the liberation of the country. Here again Mr. Eden submitted an agreed Anglo-American memorandum to M. Molotov explaining that, subject only to military considerations, i.e. the defeat of Germany, the object of the Allied forces in France would be to bring about conditions in which a democratically consti-tuted French authority would be able to take over the administration and the French people would be free to choose their own form of government. We should have no dealings or relations with the Vichy regime except for the purpose of liquidating it; we should not retain or employ in office anyone who had wilfully collaborated with the enemy or acted deliberately in a manner hostile to the Allied cause. In order to achieve our eventual purpose of securing for the French people a free choice of government we should try to 'hold the scales even' between all French political groups sympathetic to the Allied cause, but one of our first tasks would be to establish relations with the Resistance groups within France and to secure their co-operation in civil matters.

Mr. Eden explained to the Russians that our main difficulty was that there was no recognised French Government. The French Committee of National Liberation had not been recognised even as the Provisional Government of France and had indeed made no claim to such recognition. We regarded the Committee as making an important contribution to victory, especially in conjunction with the Resistance movement in France. On the other hand we could not foresee what its position would be after the liberation of the country. Mr. Eden suggested that the Conference should approve of the memorandum and send it to the European Advisory Commission who would then work out the details. After some questioning, M. Molotov agreed to this suggestion.

Mr. Eden also circulated to the Conference a British memorandum on the principles which should govern generally the liberation of

Allied territory in Europe. The memorandum was drafted in the form of a declaration, since the British Government hoped that the three Powers would encourage and reassure the peoples concerned by a public announcement of Allied policy. Mr. Eden suggested, however, that the draft should be sent to the European Advisory Commission. The draft was in general terms to the effect that the three Governments desired the restoration of self-government as soon as possible in all Allied territory in Europe liberated from enemy occupation. Their policy would be to facilitate the resumption of authority over liberated territory by the Allied Government concerned, or, where no such Government existed, by the appropriate authority recognised as capable of exercising governmental powers pending the formation of a freely elected constitutional Government.

For military reasons, however, there would be a first phase in which the commander-in-chief of the Allied forces of liberation would have to exercise supreme authority in the areas where he was conducting operations. During this phase, the conditions of modern warfare and the confusion likely to prevail in liberated territory would make it necessary for the commander-in-chief to exercise his authority in civil as well as in military affairs, but these temporary measures would be without prejudice to the two principles that responsibility would be transferred as soon as military considerations allowed to the appropriate Allied authorities, and that the reorganised administrative and judicial services in liberated territory should be conducted as far as possible by citizens of the Allied country in question who had shown their loyalty to the Allied cause.

This declaration would have had a less easy passage if the Conference had dealt otherwise than in generalities with the critical question of Polish-Soviet relations during and after the liberation of Poland.[1] The differences of view between the British and Soviet Governments were less 'papered over' in the discussion of post-war federations. Mr. Eden, in raising the latter question, referred to M. Maisky's remark to him, at the end of August, that the three Governments should agree that each of them had an interest in all parts of Europe.[2] With this consideration in mind the British Government had suggested a draft declaration by the three Powers affirming the principle that each people was free to choose for itself its form of Government and way of life provided that it respected equally the

---

[1] For the short discussion on Poland, see below, p. 644.
[2] For the British attitude toward a proposed Soviet-Czechoslovak treaty, and the general question of separate agreements between the Great Powers and the smaller Allies, see note at the end of this section.

rights of other peoples. All States were therefore free 'to associate themselves with other States in order to increase their mutual welfare by the establishment of institutions on a wider scale' than each could separately maintain, provided again, that such associations were not directed against the welfare or stability of any other State, and that they were approved by the proposed general international organisation. The three Governments would regard it as their duty and interest to assist other European States to form associations 'designed to increase mutual welfare and the general prosperity of the Continent'. The three Governments also declared that they would not 'seek to create any separate areas of responsibility in Europe' and would not 'recognise such for others, but rather affirm their common interest in the well-being of Europe as a whole'.

Mr. Hull said that the United States Government was glad to accept the principle that there should be no 'special areas' of responsibility, but that he would leave the European question for discussion by Mr. Eden and M. Molotov. Mr. Eden then said that he was prepared to give the paragraphs referring to freedom of choice of Government and to the disclaiming of 'separate areas of responsibility' a general application and to include them in the main four-Power declaration. He thought that joint responsibility for Europe was a matter of great importance; he was less concerned with the proposal for federations, and would be guided largely by the Russian view. M. Molotov then read a statement setting out this view. The statement suggested that the establishment of federations would be a premature step if it were taken before the smaller countries had been allowed time to readjust themselves. The creation of such federations by *émigré* Governments which, owing to their special situation, could not be closely in touch with their peoples, might be interpreted as imposing on the peoples concerned decisions which they did not want. The statement also pointed out that some of the plans for federations reminded the Soviet people of the policy of the 'cordon sanitaire' formerly 'directed, as is shown, against the Soviet Union'.

Mr. Eden then said that he thought the matter might wait for consideration at a later time. On the last day of the Conference, however, he referred once more to the two general points (freedom of choice of government, and the disclaiming of 'separate areas of responsibility'). Mr. Eden thought that it would be a good thing to include a mention of these two points in the published documents of the Conference. The Russians again brought forward arguments against any special statement with regard to areas of responsibility. The three Powers had already agreed to work together for the general organisation of peace; it was therefore hardly necessary to make a negative declaration. If any of the Allies had suggested that they should have special areas of responsibility it might have been desirable to refute the idea, but except in certain newspapers there had been no such suggestion. Mr. Eden said that there was some suspicion that the British were interested in western Europe and the Russians in eastern Europe. He would not, however, press his proposal. M. Molotov stated that the Soviet Government had never given expression to the ideas which Mr. Eden's declaration was intended to refute. Why was the declaration to be confined to Europe? Mr. Eden explained that the problem was more acute in Europe, and that he wanted to reassure the smaller Powers and to counter enemy propaganda. He suggested, however, that the proposal might be left over for the next Conference.[1]

On the other matters also the Russians were unwilling to commit themselves. Mr. Hull brought forward a memorandum on the treatment of Germany, which was concerned mainly with the period immediately after German unconditional surrender but also raised the question of the future status of the country.[2] The memorandum suggested that some form of decentralisation would be desirable, and reserved for the peace settlement the question of frontiers. Mr. Eden said that the British Government would like Germany to be divided into a number of separate States, and, in particular, to see the separation of Prussia from the rest of the country. They were unable as yet to assess the prospects of imposing a solution of this kind by force, and would be glad to know the Soviet view. M. Molotov said that in all measures calculated to make Germany harmless as an aggressor state he agreed with the British and American view. He repeated the words 'in all measures', but would not give a definite answer when Mr. Eden also repeated his question. M. Molotov explained that the Soviet Government were 'somewhat backward' in a study of the matter probably because of the military preoccupations of their leaders. He thought that the question of forcible dismemberment could not be excluded, and that some sections of Soviet opinion might consider that Mr. Hull's proposals were not drastic enough. Mr. Eden and M. Molotov, however, said that there could be agreement that Germany must go back at least to her frontiers before the 'Anschluss' of 1938.

The public communiqué issued at the end of the Conference included in addition to the four-Power declaration, and two statements with regard to the establishment of a European Advisory Commission and an Advisory Council for matters relating to Italy,

---

[1] For these proposals, see note to this section.
[2] For a fuller account of this memorandum see Volume V, Chapter LXII, section (i).

U

two other declarations affirming the attitude of the three Governments in favour of re-establishing democracy in Italy, and announcing their purpose to restore the independence of Austria. The Conference also published a document drawn up at the Prime Minister's suggestion and signed by him and by President Roosevelt and Stalin, condemning German atrocities and warning German officers and men and members of the Nazi Party who had shared in the commission of these crimes that they would be taken back, at the time of the Armistice, to the countries in which the crimes had been committed and punished according to the laws of the countries concerned.[1]

(a)   At the end of the Conference Mr. Eden telegraphed to the Prime Minister his impression that the Russian representatives really wanted to establish relations with Great Britain and the United States on a footing of permanent friendship, and that they had done their best to meet British and American views on a number of points. Mr. Eden said that the Prime Minister's action with regard to the resumption of convoys had made a deep impression;[2] he suggested that an encouraging message to the Russians about their desire to be allocated a small share of the Italian fleet would have a psychological effect out of all proportion to the value of the ships.

Sir A. Clark Kerr also considered the Conference to have been a (b) success. He reported favourable comments in the Soviet press—including the *Soviet War News*—and attributed the favourable comment and the success of the meetings largely to the fact that the Russians felt that they had been admitted freely and on terms of complete equality to the most intimate Anglo-American councils from which, as they saw matters, they had hitherto been excluded to a large extent. The Soviet delegation were clearly surprised at the candour with which we and the Americans put our problems before them. Sir A. Clark Kerr thought that Mr. Eden had been outstandingly successful in winning the confidence of the Russians. Even when we had to disagree with some of their suggestions for shortening the war, the Soviet representatives had shown disappointment but not resentment. M. Molotov had evidently resolved to make the Conference a success, and had conducted the proceedings with sustained tact and skill and growing good humour.

---

[1] Mr. Churchill regarded this principle of 'localisation of judgment' as likely to have some deterrent effect on German terrorism.

[2] See above, p. 572.

(a) N6353/66/38. (b) N6575/3666/38.

Note to Section (v). Proposals for an Anglo-Soviet 'self-denying ordinance' with regard to treaties with the smaller Allies: British attitude towards a Soviet-Czechoslovak agreement (June 1942–October 1943).

While M. Molotov was in London in June 1942, Mr. Eden had spoken to him of the wish of the British Government to reach an understanding (a) with the Soviet Government for joint discussion and agreement before either party concluded a treaty with any of the smaller Allies. Mr. Eden explained that our main reason for this suggestion was that we wanted to avoid an undignified competition among the smaller Allies to make treaties covering the post-war period with one or both of our Governments before we had ourselves reached a basic understanding on post-war arrangements. M. Molotov undertook to discuss this suggestion with his colleagues in Moscow. On July 14, 1942, M. Maisky had referred in con- (b) versation with Mr. Eden to what he called our proposed 'self-denying ordinance'. He said that the Soviet Government agreed with us, and were willing to accept the plan. Mr. Eden therefore assumed that there was an understanding in the matter with the Soviet Government.

In May 1943, however, Dr. Benes informed the Foreign Office that he (c) had been engaged for some time in conversations with the Soviet Government with the object of obtaining a guarantee that the latter would respect the territorial integrity of Czechoslovakia and would not interfere in Czechoslovak domestic affairs. He had also discussed the question of a Soviet-Czechoslovak-Polish pact with a view to preventing German expansion eastwards. On June 16, 1943, Dr. Benes, who was about to go to Moscow, told Mr. Eden that during his visit he intended to conclude (d) a treaty with the Soviet Government.

Mr. Eden then explained to Dr. Benes the Anglo-Soviet 'self-denying ordinance' and said also that, apart from this arrangement, we objected to his proposed treaty on the ground that it would further exacerbate Czechoslovak-Polish relations and make the restoration of Polish-Soviet relations even more difficult. On July 2 M. Maisky brought a message to Mr. Eden from M. Molotov which amounted to a denial of the existence (e) of any 'self-denying ordinance'. M. Maisky asked that we should not stand in the way of the proposed Soviet-Czechoslovak treaty; the treaty would not affect the Polish situation, and the Soviet Government might be willing to make it clear that they were prepared to transform the treaty into a tripartite agreement including Poland.

The War Cabinet agreed on July 5 that Sir A. Clark-Kerr should be (f) instructed to tell M. Molotov that we would prefer to maintain the 'self-denying ordinance', but that, if the Soviet Government insisted on concluding a treaty with Czechoslovakia, we hoped that they would draw it up in a form allowing the inclusion of Poland at a later date. We also hoped that there would be no more exceptions to the 'self-denying ordinance'.

(a) N3000/62/44. (b) R4693, 5031/1990/92. (c) C5228/525/12. (d) C7084/6009/12; C7363, 7493/525/12. (e) C7700/525/12. (f) WM(43)93; C7810, 7700/525/12.

Before these instructions were sent to Sir A. Clark-Kerr the Foreign
(a) Office learned that on July 7 Dr. Benes had spoken to M. Bogomolov[1]
about the position arising out of his (Dr. Benes's) conversation with Mr.
Eden. M. Bogomolov had replied that the Soviet Government would not
wish to pursue the matter of the treaty in view of the misgivings which
it had aroused. They also felt that, if no treaty were to be concluded, Dr.
Benes might well postpone his visit to Moscow until the autumn.

(b)   On July 26 M. Sobolev, the Soviet Chargé d'Affaires,[2] gave Mr. Eden
an *aide-mémoire* stating that in his interview of July 14, 1942, M. Maisky
had said that, while the Soviet Government agreed in principle to our
suggestion for a 'self-denying ordinance', they desired to receive a definite
proposal on the matter from us. They had not received any such proposal,
and therefore concluded that the matter had not gone beyond the
preliminary exchange of views. The note pointed out that there was no
provision in the Anglo-Soviet treaty providing against the conclusion of
separate treaties with other Allies but that the Anglo-Soviet treaty might
be taken as a basis for an agreement on the matter.

(c)   It was not clear at first to the Foreign Office whether there had been
a genuine misunderstanding on the Russian side about the 'self-denying
ordinance' or whether the Russians were merely trying to ignore the
agreement. The Foreign Office thought it best to assume that the Soviet
Government now accepted the British interpretation of the agreement.
The Russian note of July 26, however, required an answer. Mr. Eden
(d) told M. Bogomolov that he did not remember any statement by M.
Maisky in July 1942, to the effect that the Soviet Government wanted to
receive a definite proposal in the matter. Sir A. Clark Kerr was also
instructed on August 2 to tell M. Molotov that we had understood the
Soviet Government to have accepted our proposal but that we would
be ready to submit it again if M. Molotov so desired.

(e)   Sir A. Clark Kerr carried out his instructions on August 23. A week
(f) later the Soviet Chargé d'Affaires presented another *aide-mémoire* to Mr.
Eden stating that His Majesty's Government had not yet presented
'concrete proposals' and suggesting that they should submit a draft
(g) agreement to the Soviet Government. On August 31 (after his return
from Moscow) M. Maisky told Mr. Eden that our attitude over the
proposed Russo-Czechoslovak treaty had caused resentment in Moscow.
Mr. Eden said that he saw no reason why this should be the case; we
merely wanted Russia, Czechoslovakia and Poland to be united in
resistance to future German aggression. M. Maisky then said that the
Soviet Government had the same desire; would we therefore waive our
objection to the proposed treaty if it were accompanied by a declaration
signifying that it was open at any time for the signature of Poland? Mr.
Eden said that he was prepared to consider this suggestion.

M. Maisky hoped that the suggestion would be accepted, since its
acceptance would do much to remove Russian suspicions. He was afraid

---

[1] Soviet representative with the exiled Governments in London.
[2] M. Maisky was absent in Moscow.

(a) C8016/525/12. (b) N4280/66/38. (c) N4006/66/38. (d) N4280/66/38. (e) N4843/
66/38. (f) N5015/66/38. (g) N4977/66/38.

that owing to the 'unhappy past' these suspicions were easily aroused, and that his countrymen were apt to scrutinise all British or American actions to see whether a slight was intended. The Russians wished to be treated on a basis of absolute equality. Mr. Eden said that we were treating them in this way. M. Maisky continued that there were two possible methods of organising Europe after the war; we could divide it into a Russian sphere in the east and an Anglo-American sphere in the west. M. Maisky did not think this plan a good one, but, if it were adopted, we should be at liberty to exclude the Russians from French affairs, the Mediterranean and so forth, and the Russians would claim a similar freedom in the east. If, however, as the Soviet Government hoped, the three Powers could agree that all Europe was one, each of us must admit the right of the others to an interest in all parts of Europe. If we were concerned with Czechoslovakia and Poland, and the United States with the Baltic States, we must understand Russian concern with the Mediterranean. Mr. Eden replied that we already admitted these conclusions, and hoped that we might find a form of words for them at the forthcoming meeting of Foreign Secretaries.

The Foreign Office considered that we should submit a draft 'self- (a) denying ordinance' to the Soviet Government. From the point of view of securing post-war collaboration between the three Powers in all parts of Europe we wished to avoid special bilateral agreements. If we could not persuade the Soviet Government to give up their proposed Czechoslovak arrangement, we should try to make it as anodyne as possible. Our main objection to the treaty—apart from making any exception to the 'self-denying ordinance'—was that it would be regarded as directed against Poland. This difficulty could not be met by stating that Poland was free to accede to a Russo-Czechoslovak agreement, since the Polish Government were unable to do so until the Soviet Government condescended to resume diplomatic relations with them; in any case a bilateral Russo-Czechoslovak agreement would have no special interest for Poland. The best plan, therefore, if we could not prevent the conclusion of a bilateral Russo-Czechoslovak agreement, would be for us to suggest at the Conference of Foreign Ministers, if the atmosphere of Polish-Soviet relations were favourable, that, while maintaining our objections to a separate Russo-Czechoslovak agreement, we should be prepared to collaborate in trying to arrange the conclusion of a tripartite agreement between the U.S.S.R., Poland and Czechoslovakia.

The Foreign Office view at this time was that Great Britain should participate in the arrangement, since otherwise there was little chance of reaching a satisfactory solution for eastern Europe generally. We were bound by our alliance with Poland; although we had refused a Polish request in June 1942 to negotiate a new Anglo-Polish treaty, we had then told the Polish Government that we should consult with them in good time before the expiry of our existing treaty in August 1944, in order that our two Governments might 'consider how best to maintain and prolong' the 'effects' of the treaty. We had added that we should prefer

---

(a) N5752/66/38; WP(43)423; WM(43)135. 3, C.A.,; C12053/7497/62.

this consultation to take place 'when the future was clearer, and when the two Governments could also consider *inter alia*, how best Anglo-Polish relations could be fitted into a regional or general system of security'. We had also informed the Polish Government in April 1942 that we intended to 'uphold the interests of our Polish Ally, as of our other Allies, to the fullest extent to which we were capable, and that, for this purpose, we would accept our full share of responsibility for the establishment and maintenance of peace in Europe after the war'. We might therefore merge our existing agreement with Poland in a new four-Power treaty.

(a)   An *aide-mémoire* containing the draft of a 'self-denying ordinance' was given to the Soviet Chargé d'Affaires on September 29; Sir A. Clark Kerr was also instructed to suggested to the Soviet Government that the general question should be discussed at the forthcoming meeting of Foreign Secretaries in Moscow. Before this meeting took place there was a somewhat sharp exchange of notes between His Majesty's Government

(b)   and the Czechoslovak Government in London. The British note complained that Dr. Benes had authorised the issue of a statement misrepresenting the British view and giving an inaccurate account of the course of the discussions over a Russo-Czechoslovak agreement.

It was, however, clear that the Soviet Government set much store on the signature of the treaty, and that further opposition to it would cause distrust and suspicion. M. Molotov informed M. Eden in Moscow of the

(c)   proposed terms of the treaty; he said that the two parties proposed to add a protocol providing for the adherence of any third party bordering on the U.S.S.R. and Czechoslovakia which had been the object of German aggression during the war. Mr. Eden said that the British Government saw no objection to the conclusion of a treaty in this form; he did not raise the question of transforming the treaty into a four-Power arrangement including British and Polish participation.

Mr. Eden also said that, although we considered the 'self-denying ordinance' a good idea, we did not intend to go on with it in view of the changed circumstances. The Soviet Government had in fact stated that they could not accept the British proposal without making an exception in the case of agreements between the United Kingdom or the U.S.S.R. and border States. The Foreign Office regarded an agreement on these lines as of little value, since under it the Soviet Union would be free to make arrangements not only with Czechoslovakia but with countries such as Iran and China, whereas we should not be able to come to any agreement e.g. with Greece. Mr. Eden told M. Molotov that anyhow we could not accept a phrase in the Soviet statement referring to Czechoslovakia and the U.S.S.R. as 'bordering States', since the term implied a recognition of the Soviet claim to eastern Poland.

(d)   M. Molotov, in a letter of November 2 to Mr. Eden, wrote that the Soviet Government agreed with the decision not to proceed with the 'self-denying ordinance'. Mr. Eden had said that nonetheless the British

---

(a) N5015/66/38. (b) C11655/525/12. (c) C13005/525/12; C12530/7159/98; N6921/3666/38. (d) C13709/258/55; C14009/525/12.

Government considered that they and the Soviet Government should consult together about any treaty or agreement which they proposed to make with a minor European Ally. M. Molotov stated that the Soviet Government continued to hold that they had a right to make agreements on positive questions with 'neighbouring' Allied Governments without consulting the British Government or seeking their approval.

(vi)

The Teheran Conference: Russian and American opposition to the Prime Minister's Mediterranean strategy: the Prime Minister's conversation of November 30 with Stalin (November 28–December 1, 1943).

The meeting of the three Heads of Government took place at Teheran between November 28 and December 1. The absurd choice of place—due to Stalin's refusal to go elsewhere—made a long stay impossible. The subjects for consideration were primarily military. Apart from the Polish question, and the discussions on Turkey, the talks on political subjects were somewhat vague, and gave little direct indication of Russian intentions.[1] The Prime Minister had thought it essential that an Anglo-American agreement should be reached on the invasion plans and the relation between them and the operations in the Mediterranean and, as a corollary, the plans for operations against Japan before the defeat of Germany. Mr. Churchill considered a full discussion to be necessary because the American insistence upon the Quebec time-table and therefore upon moving seven divisions and a number of landing craft from the Mediterranean was seriously endangering the success of the Italian campaign and making it impossible to regain control of the Aegean or to bring Turkey into the war.

The American military authorities did not want to reopen, or rather to continue the argument with Mr. Churchill. The President was also unwilling to risk arousing Russian suspicions by holding lengthy Anglo-American discussions before the meeting with Stalin. He hoped at this stage to get Russian collaboration in the war against Japan, and in his somewhat vague plans for post-war security. He even suggested to the Prime Minister that a Russian representative should be invited to attend any Anglo-American military meetings held before the conference. The Prime Minister pointed out the difficulties of an arrangement of this kind. The Russians did not

[1] For the discussions on Poland, see Chapter XXXV; for those on Turkey see Volume IV, Chapter LI; for those on post-war questions see Volume V, Chapter LXII.

invite British and American representatives to take part in the planning of the eastern campaigns; there were no Russian troops on the Italian front and there would be none in the expeditionary force to be landed in northern France. Nevertheless the President invited

(a) M. Molotov and a Russian military representative to meet the Combined Chiefs of Staff at Cairo on their way to Teheran. On the timetable proposed for these meetings there would have been practically no opportunity for separate Anglo-American discussions.

The President's plan fell through because he was also insisting on a meeting in Cairo with General Chiang Kai-shek. The Russians refused to be represented at this meeting since they were not at war with Japan. The President, however, made the Prime Minister's position more difficult by a promise to General Chiang Kai-shek of an amphibious operation in the spring of 1944 for the recapture of the Andaman Islands. This operation would have to be carried out mainly by British forces, and the diversion of ships and landing craft to the Indian Ocean would add to the difficulty of carrying out the Prime Minister's plans for the Mediterranean.

(b)   At the Conference the Russians supported the American military views against those of the Prime Minister. They wanted the cross-Channel invasion as early as possible; they regarded the Prime Minister's Mediterranean proposals as likely to cause more delay, if not indefinite postponement. They suspected that Mr. Churchill would welcome such postponement. They also now gave up their previous emphasis on plans to bring Turkey into the war. This change of policy was probably due to their realisation, after the discussions at the Moscow Conference, that Turkish belligerency—and the opening of the Straits—could be secured, if at all, only at the price of military and air assistance which might impede the preparations for the cross-Channel invasion, and delay the date on which it would be carried out. Moreover, they could not fail to realise that, if the western Powers were occupied with the Germans in north-west Europe, the Russian armies would be able to advance into all the countries of south-east Europe (except Greece); for this reason also they did not view with favour a proposal made somewhat casually by the President—and supported by the Prime Minister—for an expedition to assist Marshal Tito.

The Prime Minister's position at Teheran was therefore not easy. He has written[1] that he could have persuaded Stalin if the President

---

[1] Churchill, *The Second World War*, V, 305–06. The President's isolation from the Prime Minister at Teheran was increased not merely by his refusal to meet the Prime Minister in a private conversation but by the fact that he was actually living in the grounds of the Russian Embassy where the conferences were held. He had moved from the United States Legation (some two miles away) after the Russians had produced reports of an alleged plot to assassinate him on his way to or from the meetings.

(a) Churchill Papers/136. (b) COS(43)791(o).

had not been 'oppressed by the prejudices of his military advisers', and had not 'drifted to and fro in the argument'. Whether, in fact, the Prime Minister would have succeeded must remain a matter of doubt, since Stalin knew the American military view, and this view coincided with the Russian demand for a binding commitment to the cross-Channel invasion at a definite date. At the first plenary session Stalin promised the entry of Russia into the war against Japan as soon as Germany had been defeated. This announcement was not unexpected, but it inclined the Americans to be more eager to begin discussions on the problem of Russian-American co-operation in the Far East than to reopen the questions of European strategy which they had regarded, in their own judgment, as settled.[1]

The Americans and Russians were therefore united, and the Prime Minister's attitude seemed deliberately obstructionist. Stalin indeed at times lost patience with the Prime Minister's persistent advocacy. After one of these long speeches he asked 'How long is this Conference going to last?'[2] On November 29, when the argument was going against the Prime Minister, Stalin put to him the direct question whether he and the British Staff really 'believed in' the cross-Channel invasion. In order to make his case clear Mr. Churchill asked for a private interview with Stalin. This interview (a) took place on the morning of November 30. From the point of view of Anglo-Russian relations the result was satisfactory.[3] The Prime Minister began by explaining that he was himself half-American and was not intending to disparage Americans, but that he was bound to explain the British view of the situation. We had twice or three times more troops in Italy than the Americans. We wanted to use all these troops 'all the time'. The difference of opinion with the Americans was not merely whether we should keep to the date of the invasion or press on with operations in Italy. The Americans also wanted an amphibious operation in the Bay of Bengal, and this plan rather than the Mediterranean operation would delay the invasion. In fact, owing to the American insistence on a definite date for the invasion we had been sending back divisions from Italy in preparation for it. Our army in Italy was

---

[1] It should be remembered that at this time the American military and air staffs regarded Russian—and Chinese—co-operation in the Far East as essential to the shortening of the war against Japan.

[2] J. R. Deane, *The Strange Alliance* (Viking Press Inc., New York, 1947), 44. The Americans, who (with the exception of Mr. Harriman) were meeting Stalin for the first time, were agreeably surprised at his intelligence and quickness, and seemed to welcome him as a 'counterweight' to the Prime Minister. See Volume I, Introduction, p. xli, note 2.

[3] On December 17, 1943, Dr. Benes told Mr. Harriman that Stalin liked and respected Mr. Churchill, 'particularly as a fighting man', but realised that he (Mr. Churchill) found it difficult at times to throw off British nineteenth century imperialism. In addition there were more specific 'historical issues between Russia and Britain still to be solved'. *F.R.U.S.*, 1943, III, 729–30.

(a) WP(44)9.

U*

'somewhat disheartened' by this withdrawal, and we had been unable to take full advantage of the Italian collapse. On the other hand the withdrawals showed that we were serious in the fulfilment of our obligations.

The Prime Minister then said that it was necessary to get an early decision on the appointment of the commander-in-chief of the invading force. Until August the arrangement had been that the commander should be British. At the Quebec Conference Mr. Churchill had agreed to the appointment of an American while we should hold the supreme command in the Mediterranean, where we had a predominance of numbers. As soon as the President nominated his commander-in-chief Mr. Churchill would nominate the Mediterranean commander-in-chief and other commanders. The President had delayed his nomination for domestic reasons, but Mr. Churchill was urging him to come to a decision before leaving Teheran.

The Prime Minister then explained the difficulties about landing craft, and the American refusal to take any of these craft from the Pacific to help in the first invasion 'lift' or in the proposed operation in the Andaman Islands. The Prime Minister had told the Americans that, with the Russian promise to enter the war against Japan after the German surrender, they could count on an earlier defeat of the Japanese and could therefore give us more help. The Prime Minister then referred to the British plans for the invasion. By May or June 1944 we should have available sixteen divisions, totalling with their corps troops and landing-craft troops slightly over 500,000 men. The British navy would transport them, and the British metropolitan air force of about 4,000 first line planes would be in continuous action. Up to the present the Americans had sent over mainly air troops and army stores; the transport of their invasion force was only now beginning, and would have reached a figure of 700–800,000 by May. Mr. Churchill was in favour of an attack in the south of France at or about the same time as the main invasion.

Stalin's answer was to warn the Prime Minister that the Red Army was depending on the success of the invasion of northern France. If there were no invasion in May 1944, the Soviet army would think that the operation was not to take place at all during the year. Unless, however, there were a big change in the European war in 1944, the Russians would find it very difficult to carry on. They were war-weary, and a feeling of isolation might develop in the army. For this reason Stalin had been enquiring whether the invasion would take place at the promised time. Otherwise he would have to take steps to prevent bad feeling in the Soviet army. The Prime Minister said that the invasion certainly would take place if the Germans did not bring into northern France larger forces than the British and Americans could put there. The Prime Minister had no doubts about the actual invasion; he was thinking of the thirtieth or fortieth or fiftieth day after it. If the Germans had thirty or forty divisions in France,[1] he doubted whether the force which we were going to put across the Channel would be able to hold on. On the other hand, if the Red Army engaged the enemy, and if we held them in Italy, and 'perhaps the Yugoslavs, and possibly the Turks, came into the war', Mr. Churchill was hopeful that we could win and that Germany would not have enough troops. Stalin's reply was that, if he knew the date of the invasion, he could organise decisive blows against Germany, and that the Germans would have no troops to spare for France.

Meanwhile the Combined Chiefs of Staff had recommended, and (a) the President had agreed to a compromise whereby the date would be sometime in May, and not necessarily May 1;[2] the offensive in Italy would be continued as far as the Pisa–Rimini line, and the landing craft required for the Italian operations would be retained until January 15, 1944. The Prime Minister accepted this arrange-ment, and hoped also that he would be able to persuade the President to withdraw his promise to General Chiang Kai-shek with regard to the operation in the Bay of Bengal.[3]

Thus the conference ended in a general atmosphere of cordiality. It is impossible to judge whether this cordiality was not bought at too high a price, or even (in the absence of documentary evidence on the Russian side) to estimate the effect of the military controversy on Anglo-Russian relations. The Prime Minister's personal explanation clearly had some effect on Stalin and at least the question of a 'second front' was no longer a cause of suspicion and dissension. On the other hand the Russians were able to see that their own tactical position in inter-Allied discussions was greatly strengthened by the two all-important facts that in the case of Anglo-American diver-gencies of view, the Prime Minister had ultimately to give way to the President, and that the President was closer to his military than to his diplomatic advisers, and that the former often failed to take adequate account of the political consequences of their own military decisions.

---

[1] According to the record of this informal conversation Mr. Churchill used the words 'thirty or forty divisions'. It would appear from the record of the meetings of the Con-ference, that he was thinking of divisions in terms of the size of a British division.

[2] Owing to the need for certain tidal and lunar conditions, the date could not have been May 1, and, if (as was implied in the Teheran decision) the Allies were no longer com-mitted to the first possible days in May, they were bound to postpone the operation until June 5, 6 or 7.

[3] The President withdrew this promise while at Cairo on his way home from Teheran, but only after the military estimate of the force required for the operation was much larger than he (and the Prime Minister) had expected.

(a) COS(43)791(o).

(vii)

The Russian demands with regard to the Italian fleet: British and American objections to an immediate transfer: the Prime Minister's proposal to lend British ships to the Russians: final agreement with the Russians (December 1, 1943–April 2, 1944).

(a)   The question of the disposal of the Italian fleet was not discussed in the formal meetings of the Teheran Conference, but at a lunch at the Soviet Embassy on December 1, M. Molotov asked for a reply to the earlier Russian request.[1] Mr. Churchill said that he was in favour of handing over some ships, but that we and the Americans would need time to arrange matters with the Italians so that there should be no mutiny and no scuttlings. He suggested that a battleship

(b)   and a cruiser should be handed over about the end of January. On December 21, however, President Roosevelt informed the Prime Minister that he had told Mr. Harriman that it was his intention to hand over one third of the Italian ships in our hands to the Russians at the beginning of February. The Prime Minister was at this time ill

(c)   in North Africa. The Foreign Office telegraphed to Mr. Balfour in Moscow on December 22 that they hoped Mr. Harriman would say nothing to M. Molotov, but that if he felt obliged to make some communication he should take account of two points which the President seemed to have disregarded, viz. the fact that the Italian ships were unsuited to the Arctic, and the risk that we should lose Italian co-operation if we informed them too abruptly of the decision. They also asked Lord Halifax to mention these points to the President.

(d)   At the same time the Prime Minister telegraphed to Mr. Eden that he did not understand why the President had spoken of one third of the Italian ships, since he thought a specific number had been agreed to at Teheran. He agreed with the instructions to Mr. Balfour. The

(e)   Chiefs of Staff replied that they were taking the matter up with the Combined Chiefs of Staff; they thought that, given time and a tactful diplomatic approach, a transfer of ships would be possible, but any sudden action was likely to have a most serious effect on the Italians. The Foreign Office also pointed out to Mr. Balfour that the President's statement about one third of the ships was not in accordance with the agreement at Teheran.

(f)   Mr. Harriman was equally aware of this latter fact, and told Mr. Balfour that if M. Molotov asked what was happening he would

---

[1] See above, pp. 586–7.

(a) WP(44)8. (b) T2044/3, No. 422, Grand 730 (Churchill Papers/240; R13651/8717/22). (c) R13652/8717/22. (d) Tel. Frozen 792, 839 (Churchill Papers/240; R13653/8717/22). (e) Grand 776 (Churchill Papers/240; R13655/8717/22). (f) R13656/8717/22.

merely say that the matter was under discussion. He would not raise the question himself until the Combined Chiefs of Staff had come to a decision, but he suggested to the President that, if it were (a) not now considered desirable to hand over the ships by February 1, he should be instructed to discuss the matter with the Russians as soon as possible; otherwise they might be suspicious about the firmness of other commitments made at Teheran.

The Combined Chiefs of Staff now recommended that the ships (b) should not be handed over for some months. They pointed out that if we lost Italian co-operation it would mean replacing the Italian ships being used as escorts in the Mediterranean, at the expense of the build-up of the British fleet in the Far East. We might also lose the use of Italian dockyards. We only had one large Italian merchant ship, which was in use as a hospital ship; the rest were in poor condition, but were being fully used in the Mediterranean. The trouble might spread to the Italian army. It would take months to refit the ships for the Russians, and Italian spares and ammunition were short.

The Foreign Office thought that, since the agreement at Teheran provided only for the transfer of a battleship and a cruiser, and not for the whole of the original Russian demand, the arguments brought forward by the Combined Chiefs of Staffs were somewhat exaggerated. We had the means—e.g. food supplies—to compel the Italians to co-operate to some extent. The effect on Stalin of going back on a promise made at Teheran would be very bad; in order to preserve the feeling of confidence established there it would be worth losing the use of one or two warships. Mr. Eden telegraphed in this (c) sense to the Prime Minister on December 31. The Admiralty, who were more impressed with the consequences of losing Italian co- (d) operation, suggested on January 1 that we might tell the Russians that we were ready to hand over certain specified ships, but that we should explain the dangers and ask them to wait until after the landings in Normandy and the south of France.

This telegram to the Prime Minister crossed one from him with the text of a message which he proposed to send to Mr. Roosevelt. In this (e) message he pointed out that nothing had been said at Teheran about one third of the Italian fleet; we had promised to meet the Russian claim to one battleship, one cruiser, eight destroyers, four submarines and 40,000 tons of merchant shipping. We must not disappoint Stalin, but the difficulties raised by the Combined Chiefs of Staff were 'very solid'. The Prime Minister suggested that he and the President should tell Stalin of these difficulties and promise to

---

(a) JSM1369, R13959/8919/22. (b) JSM 1372, R13960/8717/22. (c) Grand 925 (Churchill Papers/240; R13960/8717/22). (d) Grand 972 (Churchill Papers/240; R31/ 31/22). (e) Frozen 1031, 1077 (Churchill Papers/240; R453/31/22).

transfer the ships at the earliest moment possible 'without endangering our triple interests'. He was not anxious to get rid of the King of Italy and Marshal Badoglio; he would not mind, therefore, if they acquired some merit in the Russians' eyes by being helpful over the ships. The Prime Minister also suggested to the Chiefs of Staff that we could lessen the risk of trouble with the Italians by having the ships sailed to the refitting ports without saying anything about their future. The crews could then be repatriated. The Chiefs of Staff

(a) proposed on January 6 that the joint message to Stalin should say that we thought it necessary to delay an approach to the Italians until the loss of their co-operation would no longer be so important from the operational point of view (i.e. until after the Normandy and Riviera landings). Meanwhile we should offer the Russians technical discussions about refitting, etc.

The Prime Minister, however, agreed with the Foreign Office that the most important aspect of the question was to keep our promise

(b) to Stalin. He telegraphed to Mr. Eden on January 7 that it was 'far more important to convince Stalin that when we say a thing we mean business than to study the frills and flounces of the Italians'. He was particularly concerned to keep this promise because he might need 'some easement' over the date for the invasion of France, and also wanted friendly consideration from the Russians over Poland. 'Handing over these ships is an issue plain and square and we ought to do it even though it causes disproportionate inconvenience.'

(c)   The President now (January 9) telegraphed again to Mr. Churchill asking for his views on the Combined Chiefs of Staff's objections to the transfer, and adding: 'I think you will agree that we must not go back on what we told Uncle J.' The Prime Minister replied the same day

(d) that he entirely agreed and hoped shortly to send Mr. Roosevelt a draft message to Stalin on the subject. Next day he suggested a new

(e) idea to the Foreign Office and Chiefs of Staff: if we decided that it was too risky to take the ships from the Italians before the invasion of northern and southern France, might we not meanwhile lend the Russians one of our battleships laid up for lack of manpower, and also perhaps a cruiser, though we might suggest that the Americans should provide one. We could not spare any destroyers. We could withdraw our ships and send the Italian ones to the Black Sea when it was open.

(f)   Mr. Eden and the Chiefs of Staff replied on January 11 to the Prime Minister's telegrams of January 7 and 10. As regards trans-

---

(a) Grand 1205 (Churchill Papers/240; R453/31/22). (b) Frozen 1155 (Churchill Papers/240; R455/31/22). (c) T39/4, No. 437, Grand 1252 (Churchill Papers/240; R455/31/22). (d) T45/4, No. 543, Frozen 1190 (Churchill Papers/240; R455/31/22). (e) Frozen 1209 (Churchill Papers/240; R455/31/22). (f) Grand 1304 (Churchill Papers/240; R455/31/22).

ferring Italian ships, they thought we might minimise the repercussions on the Italians, which were more important than one or
two ships, by making a secret agreement with Marshal Badoglio:
the ships could then be sailed to an Allied port and there taken over
by the Russians for refitting. On the other hand the Admiralty saw
definite advantages in the Prime Minister's new proposal, which
would give us more time to deal with the Italians and would help us
to explain to the Russians the objections to handing over the Italian
ships before the summer. They suggested that the Prime Minister
might put the proposals to the Russians as alternatives; Mr. Eden
thought that the new proposal by itself would not meet what he
believed would be Stalin's chief need—prestige accruing from the
acquisition of Italian ships.

The Prime Minister accepted this suggestion and on January 12 (a)
telegraphed a message which he proposed to send to Mr. Roosevelt.
He suggested that until Italian ships could be transferred without
prejudice to military operations we should lend the Russians a
battleship (H.M.S. *Royal Sovereign*) and four submarines. We
could find a cruiser, but would be relieved if the Americans could
provide it. We could not supply destroyers. We could provide half
the merchant shipping tonnage. The Admiralty suggested dropping (b)
the offer of submarines, since we should have to take them from
operational duties and the Russians semed to have plenty. The (c)
amended telegram was sent to President Roosevelt on January 16.

The President replied on January 19 with a further amended draft (d)
message to Stalin. The offer would now consist of a secret arrangement with Marshal Badoglio to provide all the ships or, alternatively,
the British battleship *Royal Sovereign*, an American light cruiser,
40,000 tons of merchant shipping provided in equal shares by the
British and Americans, and an attempt to get eight destroyers and
four submarines from the Italians. Mr. Roosevelt thought the
Italians might not object to sharing with us in providing ships for the
Russians; but if this did not prove possible he suggested providing
eight destroyer escorts from American production on British account.

The Chiefs of Staff thought this proposal undesirable, as it would
again involve approaching the Italians. Moreover there were no
American-built escort vessels awaiting British crews, and every
American-built frigate to be completed before the invasion of France
was earmarked for the invasion or for the North Atlantic. The
Prime Minister therefore suggested to Mr. Roosevelt that they should (e)
simply offer to make the Italian destroyers and submarines available

(a) Frozen 1245 (Churchill Papers/240; R718/31/22). (b) Grand 1364 (Churchill
Papers/240; R718/31/22). (c) T63/4, No. 545 (Churchill Papers/240; R718/31/22).
(d) T83–4/4, Nos. 444–5 (Churchill Papers/240; R1077/31/22). (e) T100/4, No. 550
(Churchill Papers/240; R1237/31/22).

as soon as conditions allowed; his idea in proposing the offer of British and American ships had been to avoid an immediate approach to the Italians and so to escape the dangers stressed by the Combined

(a) Chiefs of Staff. The President accepted this last amendment and the
(b) message was telegraphed to Moscow in the early hours of January 23. Mr. Balfour delivered the message at once: he had already been asked what arrangements were being made for the transfer of the Italian ships. Mr. Dekanosov[1] had reminded him on January 20 that the date envisaged at Teheran had been the end of the month.

Stalin received the offer ungraciously. He replied on February 1
(c) that he had thought the matter completely settled at Teheran, and had not imagined that it would be reconsidered, or that we should not have approached the Italians. He would accept the *Royal Sovereign*, the American cruiser, and the merchant shipping, but said that they would have no significance without destroyers and submarines. Since we had control over the whole Italian fleet, it should not be difficult to carry out the Teheran decision, but he would agree to take over a similar number of British or American destroyers and submarines; the question must be settled at once and the ships handed over without delay.

(d) The Prime Minister told Sir A. Clark Kerr that he was 'deeply discouraged' by Stalin's tone. It would be folly to take British and American destroyers away from the invasion fleet or the Russian convoys, since the Russians would not be able to use them for months. It would be almost equally foolish to risk provoking a mutiny in the Italian fleet. The Prime Minister was disinclined to
(e) make any further effort in the affair. On February 3, however, he telegraphed to President Roosevelt that while we might now revert to the idea of asking the Italians for the destroyers and submarines, this demand might easily cause a mutiny in the Italian fleet and the resignation of Marshal Badoglio: he was 'so often being told that he is to be kicked out as soon as we get to Rome, he does not seem to have much to lose'. In the circumstances therefore the British Government would be prepared to make available eight old but serviceable destroyers. He hoped the United States Government might be able to find the submarines.

(f) The President again suggested asking the Italians for the submarines, or simply taking them; he could not spare any American
(g) ones. Mr. Churchill however still thought it would be a mistake to

---

[1] V. G. Dekanosov was Soviet Vice-Commissar for Foreign Affairs, 1939–47.

(a) T106/4, No. 447 (Churchill Papers/240; R1291/31/22). (b) R1238, 1053/31/22. (c) T183/4 (Churchill Papers/240; R1919/31/22). (d) T193/4 (Churchill Papers/240; R1918/31/22). (e) T202/4, No. 565 (Churchill Papers/240; R1919/31/22). (f) T206/4, No. 456 (Churchill Papers/240; R1920/31/22). (g) T217/4, No. 567 (Churchill Papers/240; R1918/31/22).

raise the whole issue with the Italians for such a small return; he therefore told the President that we would provide four modern submarines for six months; at the end of that period, when we should need them for the war against Japan, it should be possible to take the Italian ships. He instructed Sir A. Clark Kerr on the night of (a) February 5–6 to tell Stalin at once that we would provide the destroyers and submarines: a joint message from the President and himself containing the offer would follow.[1] Stalin should be warned that the destroyers were old.

Sir A. Clark Kerr was not able to deliver the messages until (b) February 23, as Stalin was away at the front. Stalin was still not satisfied. He replied on February 26 that 'it seems to me that it (c) could present no difficulties for the British and American fleets to allot if only a half of this number of eight destroyers in modern, instead of old destroyers'. He told Sir A. Clark Kerr that since the (d) outbreak of war the Red Fleet had lost thirty-two destroyers, and pressed strongly for four modern ones out of the eight.

Before any reply could be sent, the President, in reply to question- (e) ing about the Italian fleet at his press conference on March 3, said that discussions for transferring to the Russians one third of the Italian fleet or its equivalent were 'about half completed'. Since Italy had surrendered to the United States, Britain and the Soviet Union it seemed advisable to divide the Italian fleet roughly into three equal shares. This statement caused much embarrassment in London: it was likely to bring about the trouble with the Italians which we had been at such pains to avoid, and it also reverted to the idea of one third of the Italian fleet, which was more than the Russians had asked for.[2] The Italian reaction was immediate: (f) Marshal Badoglio sent for General Mason-Macfarlane on March 4 and said that the President's statement made his position impossible: he would have to resign, and the King might abdicate. General Macfarlane said that neither he nor the United States representative had had advance notice of the President's statement; he hoped Marshal Badoglio would take no action until some explanation had been received. Mr. Roosevelt's statement also brought a protest from the French Committee of National Liberation.[3] (g)

---

[1] The message was sent on February 7. (h)
[2] Mr. Churchill pointed out to the President on March 4 that one third of the Italian ships in our hands would amount to: 1.7 battleships, 2 6-in cruisers, 0.7 5.3-in cruisers, (i) 3.3 destroyers, 7.7. torpedo boats, 6.7 corvettes, 7.3 submarines.
[3] The French Committee and the Greek Government had laid claim to a share of the Italian fleet at the time of the Italian surrender in September 1943.
(a) T219/4 (Churchill Papers/240; R1918/31/22). (b) R2815, 2893, 3030, 3212/31/22. (c) T410/4 (Churchill Papers/240; R3267/31/22). (d) R3285/31/22. (e) R3495/31/22. (f) R3533, 3615/31/22. (g) R3519, 3971/31/22. (h) T244A/4 (Churchill Papers/240; R2169/31/22). (i) T454/4, No.) 602 (Churchill Papers/240; R3495/31/22).

(a)   The War Cabinet discussed the new situation on March 7 and agreed that our case in regard to the disposal of the Italian fleet should be put to the President. It was equally important to leave no room for misunderstanding with the Russians, and to reassure Marshal Badoglio. The Prime Minister therefore telegraphed to

(b) Mr. Roosevelt that he had never been asked to agree to a division of the Italian fleet into three shares. The Russians had never been promised one third: other countries at war with Italy would have claims, but we could not agree to an equal division of the fleet among them. We held very strongly that account should be taken of actual losses in the war against Italy, of which we had borne the whole weight from 1940 until the landings in North Africa. We were now providing thirteen of the fourteen warships for Russia and half the merchant tonnage. However it was important now to reassure the Italian Government: although we were entitled to dispose of the fleet, the Italians were now fighting at our side and had earned a status different from that of prisoners of war. The Prime Minister proposed to make a statement in Parliament that it was not intended to hand over Italian ships to the Russians.[1] He would not mention that we were supplying ships instead. The text of the statement was

(c) also telegraphed to Algiers and General Mason-Macfarlane was instructed to communicate it to Marshal Badoglio, who was entirely satisfied by it. The Italian fleet had remained quiet throughout.

In order to clear up any possible misunderstanding with the Russians, and also to answer Stalin's demand for modern destroyers,

(d) a joint message from the Prime Minister and the President was telegraphed to Moscow on March 9. The message emphasised that the eight British destroyers were perfectly serviceable for escort work and that we could not spare any new ones; we had lost two during the previous week—one on a Russian convoy—and our destroyer forces were fully extended, in the Atlantic, on convoys to Russia, on commitments for the invasion of France, and in the Pacific. Only seven of the Italian destroyers in our hands were fleet destroyers; the remainder were old, or only torpedo boats. All the Italian ships were unsuited to northern waters without extensive alterations.

(e)   Stalin accepted the position on March 17. Before his message was

(f) sent M. Vyshinsky had already spoken to Sir A. Clark Kerr about the transfer of the ships: he hoped they would be delivered to north Russian ports, on account of the difficulties involved in sending Russian crews to British ports for several months for training. The

---

[1] The statement was made in the House of Commons on March 10.

(a) WM(44)28.2, C.A. (b) T478/4, No. 608 (Churchill Papers/240; R3813/31/22). (c) R3615, 4024/31/22. (d) T502/4 (Churchill Papers/240). (e) T600/4 (Churchill Papers/240; R4580/31/22). (f) R4107/31/22.

United States Government were prepared to send the cruiser (a)
Milwaukee to north Russia, but the Admiralty were very reluctant to
agree to M. Vyshinsky's request. It was equally difficult for us to
send large numbers of technicians to Russia, and conditions there,
and the risk of incidents, made it undesirable to leave the men there
for months. The War Cabinet agreed on March 27 that we should (b)
not agree to sail the ships to Russia, and Sir A. Clark Kerr was so (c)
informed on April 2. M. Vyshinsky took the decision badly, but had (d)
to accept it, and Russian crews came to Great Britain to take over
the ships.

(a) R4406/31/22. (b) WM(44)40. (c) R5312/31/22. (d) N2126/25/38.

CHAPTER XXXV

Great Britain and Russo-Polish relations from the German attack on Russia to the end of 1943[1]

(i)

Russo-Polish relations from the German attack on the U.S.S.R. to the end of 1942.

(a)   ONE of the greatest obstacles to Anglo-Russian collaboration in the post-war settlement of Europe was the question of Russo-Polish relations. The underlying causes of Russo-Polish differences went back to the eighteenth and nineteenth centuries, and indeed earlier, since the partitions of Poland were attempts to destroy an already strong Polish nationalism in the interest of the three partitioning Powers. The attempts failed, in spite of the harshness with which Prussia (and later, Germany) and Russia had treated their Polish subjects. The restoration of a Polish National State after the first World War had been disliked by the Bolsheviks as much as by the Germans, and the Poles themselves had pressed their claims dangerously far in the frontier line enforced upon the Russians in the Treaty of Riga in 1921. The Russo-German agreement of 1939, as far as concerned Poland,[2] was a return to the cynical policy of Frederick of Prussia and Catherine of Russia a century and a half earlier. It was followed, in the areas occupied by Russia, by savage measures of administrative repression, including the deportation of large numbers of Poles, under the harshest conditions, to Soviet territory.

In 1941, however, after the German attack on Russia, there were obvious reasons for a sudden change in Soviet policy. The British Government used the opportunity to bring about a Polish-Soviet *rapprochement*. A Soviet-Polish treaty was signed in London on July 30,

---

[1] The two volumes (and especially vol. II, May, 1943, to August, 1945) of *Documents on Polish–Soviet relations, 1939–45* (General Sikorski Historical Institute, Heinemann, 1961 and 1967) contain important material, though in some respects not complete, for the study of Anglo-Polish relations and their bearing on Anglo-Soviet relations.

[2] See Volume I, Chapter I, section (ii).

(a) N3670/3670/38 (1943).

1941.[1] In this treaty the Soviet Government recognised that the
Soviet-German agreements of 1939 with regard to Poland were no (a)
longer valid, and the Polish Government declared that they were
not bound by any agreement with a third Power directed against
the U.S.S.R. The two Governments also agreed to resume diplomatic
relations, and exchanged promises of mutual aid and support in the
war against Germany. The Soviet Government consented to the
formation of a Polish army on Soviet territory under a Polish
commander, appointed with the consent of the Soviet Government,
and subordinate, in matters affecting operations, to the Supreme
Soviet Command upon which, however, the Polish Command would
be represented. In an addendum to the treaty, and again as the
result of British pressure, the Soviet Government granted an amnesty
to all Polish citizens detained in Soviet territory as prisoners of
war or on other sufficient grounds. At the time of the signature of the
treaty the British Government gave the Polish Government an
assurance that, in conformity with the Anglo-Polish treaty of 1939,
they had not entered into any undertaking with the Soviet Government affecting Polish-Soviet relations and did not recognise any
territorial changes effected in Poland since August 1939.

The treaty thus provided for the re-emergence of Poland as an
independent sovereign State, but the omission of any positive statement about frontiers was significant. The Russians tacitly maintained
their decrees of November 1939, by which large areas of Polish
territory had been annexed by the Byelorussian and Ukrainian
republics of the Soviet Union. The Poles—with the exception of a
small Communist minority—maintained their right to all territory
which they had occupied at the outbreak of war with Germany. A
military and political agreement between two governments with
such conflicting claims over 'metropolitan' territory was a paradox
made possible only because the disputed areas were in enemy
occupation. The Polish position, however, was weaker than the
Russian from every point of view. Without the defeat of Germany
there was no chance of an independent Poland; after a German
defeat the Russians were unlikely to make territorial concessions to
the Poles. The Russians might be exhausted by the war; the exhaustion and weakness of the Poles would be even greater. The
Russians were more likely than the western Powers to regain
physical possession of eastern Poland whatever the intervening
military situation might be. Furthermore the Poles were not in a
strong moral position with regard to a large part of their claims.
The British view at the time of the treaty of Versailles had been that

---

[1] A Polish Government in exile had been established in London. General Sikorski, the
Prime Minister, was also Commander-in-Chief of the Polish forces.

(a) C8958/3226/55.

these claims were unwise, and the proposed frontier—known as the Curzon line[1]—suggested by the British Government in 1920 had assigned to the U.S.S.R. most of the territory annexed by the Russians in 1939.

For a while these large and difficult problems could remain in suspense, while Polish-Russian relations, on what might be called a 'day-to-day basis', were fairly satisfactory. A large number of Polish men and women were released from prison, labour camps, or exile, and either joined the Polish army or auxiliary services or assembled in centres where Polish organisations could register them and care for them. The stories told, however, by those Poles who were released showed that hundreds of thousands of other Poles were still detained in various parts of the Soviet Union from the Arctic to the borders of Afghanistan.[2] The Polish Embassy made enquiries about them; the Soviet answer was that orders had been given for all Poles to be released and that all Poles must therefore have been released. There was also evidence that those Poles who were in fact released were sometimes sent off on long journeys without food or money, and, as winter drew on, died of cold and hunger. Others were left where they were without means of subsistence. A particular cause of complaint was that many Soviet officials were believed to have told the Poles concerned that their misfortunes were due to lack of interest or to obstruction on the part of the Polish Government and Embassy.

Difficulties also arose over the formation of the Polish army. The Soviet military authorities maintained that the Poles had agreed to a limit of 30,000 men; the Polish military authorities said that this figure applied only to the first formations. The Soviet authorities were also reluctant to supply arms, equipment and rations, or to allow the transfer to the Polish force of Poles who had been enrolled in the Soviet army or Soviet labour battalions.

As a result of all these troubles an increasingly sharp correspondence developed between the Polish Embassy and the Soviet Government. In December 1941, there was a certain improvement after the visit of General Sikorski to the U.S S.R. Before this visit the Polish Ambassador—with British support—had asked the Soviet Government (i) to accelerate the release of Polish citizens; (ii) to facilitate the employment in the Polish forces of all Poles fit to serve, including those in Soviet labour battalions; (iii) to concentrate the Polish army

---

[1] See note at end of this chapter. It is impossible to say whether an offer by the Polish Government as early as July 1941, or soon afterwards, to accept the Curzon line would have saved Polish independence. The Poles did not take this view, and in any case a Polish Government in exile could hardly have made the surrender of territory, especially when the declared policy of the British Government was to reserve all territorial questions for settlement at the Peace Conference.

[2] A large number of Poles had been sent in 1940 to Siberia and Central Asia; the Soviet Government apparently intended that they should be settled there permanently and should become merged in the populations of these regions.

where the British authorities could most easily arm and feed it (the British authorities had undertaken to do so to the best of their powers in view of the declared inability of the Soviet Government to fulfil this task);[1] (iv) to allow 15–20,000 Polish troops already recruited to leave for the Middle East as reinforcements for the Polish forces fighting in that area.

The Soviet replies were somewhat evasive, but Stalin agreed to the transfer to the Middle East and promised that the amnesty to Polish citizens should be unconditional and general, and that the Polish army might raise seven or more divisions. In his discussions with General Sikorski Stalin fixed at 30,000 the number of Polish troops to be moved permanently from the Soviet Union. He refused —with the comment that 'the world would laugh at him if he let all these troops go'—to allow the remaining troops to be moved to Iran or India until they were ready to fight on the Soviet front, but he agreed that they should be transferred from the region of Kuibyshev to the milder climate of the Central Asian Republics, where also British arms and equipment could reach them more easily. The Soviet Government would provide rations and allow recruiting for five to seven divisions. Polish civilians would also be concentrated in the Central Asian Republics; the order for the release of all Poles was again affirmed, and the Polish Embassy was allowed to send more 'delegates' (some had already been permitted) to look after the Polish population in the centres of assembly.

At a banquet given to General Sikorski Stalin raised with him the question of the Russo-Polish frontier; the General replied in Stalin's own phrase that 'the world would laugh at him' if he agreed to frontier changes while on his visit. Stalin took this reply in good humour, and said that there were no difficulties which could not be overcome at the Peace Conference. Stalin made a friendly speech at the dinner, and the Soviet press published a later speech by the general in which he quoted Stalin as saying that after the war Poland would be strong and greater than before. Finally a joint declaration was issued on December 4, 1941, confirming the intention of both parties to work together during and after the war.

The hopes raised by this visit were not fulfilled. There was never anything like a general release of Poles. In particular the Polish Embassy were never able to get information about the fate of the greater part of over 8,000 Polish officers and some 6,000 other ranks known to have been prisoners of war in the early months of 1940 at various Soviet camps including Starobielsk, Kozielsk and Oshtashkovo. The Russians also raised difficulties about the evacuation of

---

[1] The Soviet Government had supplied two divisions with rifles; they were unable to provide the heavier artillery, tanks, anti-tank and anti-aircraft guns, etc.

the 30,000 Polish troops to which Stalin had agreed. The whole of the Polish forces were moved to Tashkent and other southern areas in January 1942. The Russians then made various excuses for delay, e.g. they alleged that the British authorities had not informed them about the reception arrangements for the troops in Iran.

On March 15, 1942, the Polish Command were told that henceforward they could not draw rations for more than 26,000 men although their forces (including those leaving for the Middle East) already numbered 60,000 and were being recruited up to 100,000. In this situation General Anders, Commander-in-Chief of the Polish Army in Soviet territory, asked to see Stalin and secured his agreement to an increase in the ration strength to 44,000 and to the evacuation of all Polish troops above this number. The evacuation was completed in April, and included 31,000 soldiers and 12,000 civilians—mostly dependents of the soldiers. The excuse made by the Soviet Government for cutting down the ration strength was that they had not received a large quantity of wheat promised to them by the United States; the numbers of the Polish force were, however, relatively so small that this excuse could not have been valid.

Meanwhile a new difficulty had arisen in regard to the Polish civilians. The first of these to be released had been of various races including Ukrainians, Lithuanians, White Russians and Jews as well as Poles. In November 1941, the Soviet Government had refused to recognise certain Polish Jews as nationals of Poland, and, in a note of December 1 replying to a protest from the Polish Embassy, had claimed as Soviet citizens all persons who on November 1 and 2, 1939, (the dates laid down by earlier Soviet decrees on the subject) were on Polish territory occupied by Soviet forces and annexed to the U.S.S.R. The Soviet Government maintained that their willingness to recognise as Polish citizens persons of Polish race thus situated on November 1 and 2, 1939, was an act of grace and a proof of Soviet goodwill.

The Polish Embassy pointed out that Polish law did not distinguish between Polish citizens of different races; that the juridical frontier between Poland and the U.S.S.R. was that of the Treaty of Riga of 1921 until it was changed by a valid international instrument to which Poland was a party, and that, even if such an instrument had become or would become effective, it would nevertheless be in accordance with international practice to allow the inhabitants of any transferred territory to opt for their former, i.e. Polish, nationality. These arguments did not move the Soviet Government. During the following months they extended their claim to regard as Soviet nationals Ukrainians and all other citizens not of Polish 'race' to persons who had been in the occupied territories only by chance on the dates in question.

A section of the Polish press in Great Britain, under the stress of this treatment of Polish nationals and of the Polish army, now began to attack the Soviet Government, These attacks only aggravated Soviet ill-will; the Soviet Government protested against them in April and May 1942, and on May 14 refused to allow further recruitment of Poles even for transfer to the Middle East above the 44,000 to which Stalin had agreed in the previous March. On June 16 the Polish Command was told that no further evacuation would take place.

A fortnight later Stalin suddenly offered the three remaining Polish divisions to the British Government. He said that he knew that the Prime Minister would always be glad to have more Polish troops and that, in view of the military position on the Egyptian frontier, he thought it right to offer them. He believed that the offer 'would not be unwelcome to the Poles'. Stalin's motives were uncertain. He may had decided that, in view of the delay in the receipt of British equipment for these troops, his best plan was to get rid of them. In any case the Poles and the British Government welcomed the plan. The Polish Embassy failed in efforts to secure the resumption of recruiting, a further search for the missing officers, and the evacuation of 50,000 children; they were more successful in persuading the Soviet authorities to allow civilians attached to the Polish forces to leave with them. Thus 44,000 troops and 26,000 civilians left Soviet territory between August 5 and August 23.

Stalin's offer of the Polish divisions was followed, however, within a few days by a series of arrests among the Polish 'delegates' in the provinces. At the end of July most of these delegates and their staffs were in prison, and their relief work at a standstill. Some of the delegates had been recognised by the Soviet authorities as members of the Polish Embassy and therefore as possessing diplomatic privileges. The 'diplomatic' delegates were released, after strong protests to the Soviet Government, on condition that they left Russian territory. On October 16 the Soviet Government stated that fifteen of the remainder would be released, sixteen would be brought to trial, and seventy-eight, although *prima facie* guilty of infractions of the law, would not be tried but merely expelled from Soviet territory. At the same time the Soviet Government explained that they did not object to the continuance of Polish relief work if it were carried out by officials in whom they and the Polish Embassy had confidence. In fact the Soviet authorities continued to make great difficulties, not so much about the importation of relief stores and their transport to depots throughout the country as about their distribution from the depots to the Poles.

On November 1, 1942, the Soviet Government communicated to the Polish Embassy a note recapitulating a whole series of complaints about the course of Polish policy since the resumption of Polish-Soviet relations, and bringing charges, from espionage to minor offences, against the arrested delegates. Later in the month the Soviet authorities made more arrests; this time they turned against the so-called *hommes de confiance*, i.e. the Poles who acted as intermediaries between the 'delegates' in the main centres and the various Polish committees in the area allotted to each delegate.

(ii)

Increased Soviet ill-will towards the Polish Government: the question of the Katyn massacres: Soviet decision to break off diplomatic relations with the Polish Government (January 1–April 26, 1943).

(a)

M. Romer, the Polish Ambassador to the U.S.S.R., came to London at the end of December 1942 to consult the Polish Government in London. Before he left Moscow, he was assured by M. Vyshinsky that there would be no 'surprises in his absence'. On January 16, 1943, however, the Soviet Government informed the Polish Embassy that they must withdraw their 'concession' of December 1, 1941, exempting persons of Polish race from the decree of 1939 enforcing Soviet citizenship upon all persons resident in Polish territory occupied in that year by the Soviet forces. Since nearly all the Polish citizens in the U.S.S.R. had been deported from the occupied area, this decision would mean, in practice, depriving them of the relief which they were receiving through the Polish organisation, i.e. the Soviet Government would argue that as Soviet citizens they no longer required special help.

Count Raczynski, Polish Ambassador in London, complained to Mr. Eden on February 2 of the Soviet action. He pointed out that the result of it must be that these unfortunate people—many of whom were the families of Polish soldiers serving in the Middle East—would starve if they were deprived of relief. The Ambassador thought the Soviet Government were seeing how far they could go, and that, if no protests were made by the British and American Governments, they would close down the relief organisations. The Polish Government believed that one reason why the Russians wanted to take this step was their fear of the evidence provided by the actual relief supplies. The tinned food, for example, distributed as Polish relief

(b)

was better than anything which Soviet citizens could normally obtain and might suggest to them that conditions in capitalist countries were not as bad as Russian propaganda described them.

(a) C1279/258/55. (b) C2281/258/55.

Mr. Eden told the War Cabinet on February 8 that he was (a) considering whether we should consult the United States Government about supporting the protest which the Poles would feel bound to make against the Russian action. On February 9 General Sikorski (b) wrote to the Prime Minister asking for British intervention at Moscow on behalf of the 'fundamental rights of allied Poland to protect and succour her own citizens in their dire need'. General Sikorski enclosed with his letter a memorandum stating the facts of which the Polish Government complained. The Prime Minister replied that Sir A. Clark Kerr had already been asked to consider what representations he could make 'on a personal basis at a high level'. General Sikorski also wrote to Stalin in moderate terms, and (c) received a polite message in reply. On February 26 M. Romer had (d) an interview—described by Sir A. Clark Kerr as 'very satisfactory'— with Stalin at which the latter withdrew from a strict interpretation of the Soviet note of January 16 and agreed that the whole question should be made the subject of negotiations. These negotiations might begin at once, and might cover such questions as the evacuation of orphans, families, etc.

It was clear, however, that behind the change in the Russian attitude generally towards the Poles were the facts that the Russian military position had improved, and that the Soviet Government could give more consideration to future policy. Inevitably, therefore, the frontier question came more into the foreground. The Russians now had less reason for giving up any of their claims. Nevertheless, after eighteen months' experience of Russian methods of 'collaboration', the Poles were even less willing to make any important territorial concessions. The Polish press in Great Britain stated this attitude too often in provocative terms, but from information which reached the Foreign Office there was no doubt that the Polish Underground movement would withdraw their support of General Sikorski's Government if he ceded territory to the U.S.S.R. The view generally held in Poland was that the Soviet Government did not want a strong and independent Polish State after the war; that they were encouraging the small Polish Communist Party to act solely in the Soviet interest, and that territorial or other surrenders would merely encourage the Russians to push on with the policy of dividing and ultimately destroying Poland.

General Sikorski asked Mr. Eden on January 22, 1943, whether, (e) if he (General Sikorski) went to Moscow in an effort to get a new treaty of friendship with the U.S.S.R., the British and American

---

(a) WM(43)26.   (b) C1559/258/55.   (c) C2025/258/55.   (d) C2222/258/55.
(e) C910/258/55.

Governments would support the Polish claims with regard to their eastern frontier. Mr. Eden gave him no encouragement to expect such support. Four weeks later Count Raczynski, who was Acting (a) Foreign Minister in the Polish Government, as well as Polish Ambassador in London, told Mr. Eden that the Polish Ambassador in Washington had spoken to the President about Soviet policy towards Poland and that a suggestion had been made that the United States and Great Britain should issue a joint statement refusing to recognise as valid any changes made unilaterally by force during the war. Count Raczynski knew that we had given no guarantee of Polish territorial integrity, but a declaration on the lines suggested would be of great help to the Polish Government. He did not know whether the suggestion had come from the President or from the Polish Ambassador in Washington. Mr. Eden doubted whether the moment was favourable for a declaration, since the British and Polish Ambassadors had just arrived in Moscow and were consulting with the American Ambassador about taking up with Stalin directly the whole question of Polish-Soviet relations.[1]

(b)   On February 25 the Polish Government issued an official statement denying all propagandist charges made against them of hostility, direct or indirect, towards the U.S.S.R. and repeating their wish to co-operate with the Soviet Union during and after the war. The statement also repudiated alleged Polish claims to move the frontiers of Poland eastwards, and used the following terms with regard to the existing frontiers:

'The Polish Government, which represents Poland in the boundaries in which Poland, first among the Allied nations, took up the fight imposed on her, has from the moment of the conclusion of the Polish-Soviet Treaty of July 30, 1941, maintained the unchangeable attitude that so far as the question of frontiers between Poland and Soviet Russia is concerned, the *status quo* previous to September 1, 1939, is in force, and considers the undermining of this attitude, which is in conformity with the Atlantic Charter, as detrimental to the unity of the Allied Nations.'[2]

---

[1] At this interview Mr. Eden spoke to Count Raczynski about the Polish intention to give the name *Lwow* to the cruiser *Dragon* which the British Government were transferring to the Polish Navy. Since the city of Lwow was in the disputed Soviet-Polish frontier area, Mr. Eden said that the Russians would certainly regard this choice of name as provocative; he suggested that the Poles might name the ship after some other Polish city—e.g. Gdynia. On March 3 Mr. Eden made this suggestion to General Sikorski who refused it and said that he would rather not accept the ship if he could not give it the name *Lwow*. General Sikorski, however, agreed later to name the cruiser *Gdansk*.

[2] The Polish National Council, on February 26, announced a resolution affirming in stronger terms the integrity of Polish territory within the frontiers of September 1, 1939.

(a) C1983/258/55. (b) C2281/258/55.

The Soviet Government replied in a statement to the press (a)
accusing the Poles of refusing to recognise the historical rights of the
Ukrainians and the White Russians to national unity; the statement
also maintained that before 1939 Poland, under M. Beck, had
adopted a pro-fascist policy of collaboration with Germany and of
hostility to the Soviet Union. The Polish Government issued another (b)
statement on March 4 again denying that they claimed Russian
territory or that they had ever accepted German proposals for
collaboration against the Soviet Union. They pointed out that, until
the German-Soviet agreements of 1939 for the partition of Poland,
the Soviet Government had accepted the frontier clauses of the
Treaty of Riga. The German-Soviet agreements of 1939 were cancelled by the Polish-Soviet agreement of July 1941; the question of
a return to the German-Soviet frontier line of that year therefore
required no further comment.

On the day before the issue of this statement, Mr. Eden had a (c)
conversation with General Sikorski and Count Raczynski. Mr. Eden
suggested that it would be wiser for the Polish Government not to
continue a public argument with the Soviet Government, but
General Sikorski said that his own authority would be undermined
if he did not contradict the Russian allegations. He thought that the
Russians were trying to see how far they could go in anti-Polish
measures, and that silence on the Polish side would lead only to an
increase in the brutality of the Soviet treatment of the Poles. General
Sikorski thought it necessary, in the interest of Great Britain as well
as of Poland, that the Polish Government should formally rebut the
Soviet statements and dispute the propriety of Soviet policy, and
that the British Government, and, if possible, the United States
Government should give a covering approval by reaffirming publicly
their opposition to any alterations of frontiers or national status
effected unilaterally during the course of the war.

Mr. Eden explained to the Polish Ministers our own difficulties
not merely in general co-operation with the Russians but even in
delivering them the supplies for which they made urgent requests.
In these circumstances Mr. Eden did not think it politic to re-
emphasise our previous statements about unilateral alterations of
frontiers or national status. He again advised the Polish Government
not to issue their proposed statement.

Before Mr. Eden left on his visit to Washington[1] M. Maisky (d)
asked for an interview with him in order to state the Soviet point of
view on the international situation. M. Maisky said that he was
speaking without instructions, but that he felt fairly sure that he was

---

[1] See Volume V, Chapter LXI, section (iii).

(a) C1983/258/55. (b) C2468, 2510/258/55. (c) C2468/258/55. (d) N1605/499/38.

expressing the mind of his Government. It was indeed clear to the Foreign Office that he would not have ventured to give an opinion on a number of important questions if he had not been told to do so by the Soviet Government.

M. Maisky said that the Soviet Government wanted to see Germany 'broken up', though they would not exclude some kind of federal union. The Soviet Union would also claim reparations, not in money but in kind. They regarded the question of the inclusion of the Baltic States in the Soviet Union as already settled. They desired pacts of mutual assistance with Roumania and Finland, with the use of bases on Finnish and Roumanian territory. They would be willing to make a separate peace with Finland, but would not pay a high price for it.

The Soviet attitude towards Poland was unchanged. They agreed that Poland should be given East Prussia, and wanted her to be strong and homogeneous, i.e. without foreign minorities. The Curzon line, with minor adjustments, might be taken as the Soviet-Polish frontier. Western Ukraine and White Russia would have to be included, as autonomous republics, in the Soviet Union. If the future Polish Government were 'democratic and prepared to be friendly', Polish-Soviet relations should be good. If, however, the Government were of the same character as the pre-war regime, and if the Polish attitude was that of a number of *émigrés* in Great Britain (M. Maisky excepted General Sikorski and Count Raczynski), there would still be an independent Poland, but Polish-Soviet relations would be bad.

M. Maisky said that the Soviet Government were not enthusiastic about the plan of federation which the British Government was encouraging.[1] In answer to a question from Mr. Eden he admitted that there would be something to be said for a Polish-Czechoslovak federation if Poland were intending to be friendly to the Soviet Union, but not otherwise; the difficulty from the Soviet point of view was that they did not know 'what Poland is going to be'. M. Maisky thought that the Soviet Government wanted, after the war, a *bloc* of the United Nations to be led by themselves and Great Britain; within this *bloc* there might be a number of groupings of economic units, but not political units. All the various nations of Europe should not have equal voices in the *bloc*, e.g., Albania should not have a vote equal to that of Great Britain.

(a)   While in Washington Mr. Eden discussed with President Roosevelt the Russian demands as put forward by M. Maisky. He found that the President was willing to accept the Russian claim to the Baltic

_____

[1] See *ib.*, note to section (i).

(a) N1748/499/38.

States and also the Curzon line, with the allocation of East Prussia and perhaps some Silesian territory to Poland. The President asked Mr. Eden whether he agreed with Mr. Bullitt's view that the Russians wished to see Communist States everywhere in Europe after the war and to overrun the Continent themselves. Mr. Eden said that it was impossible to give a definite view; he thought that, even if Mr. Bullitt's forecast were correct, we should not make matters worse by trying to work with Russia and by assuming that Stalin really meant to fulfil his treaty with us.

On March 26, 1943, Count Raczynski informed the Foreign Office (a) that the negotiations with the Soviet Government over the Polish relief organisation had reached a deadlock. The Russians had agreed that Poles domiciled in western Poland who had chanced to be in eastern Poland at the time of the occupation should continue to be regarded as Polish citizens, but in all other respects they had destroyed the relief organisation. Count Raczynski asked that the British Government should intervene in order to try to persuade the Russians to release from the U.S.S.R. orphan children and other Poles who had relatives outside Russia able to take care of them. Count Raczynski also wished us to enquire whether the Soviet Government would allow an international body to take over the relief work.

The Foreign Office were willing to give as much help as possible, but they had to take account of the risk that British intervention might do more harm than good. In any case they thought it desirable to secure American co-operation. Sir A. Cadogan, in Mr. Eden's (b) absence, suggested that the Prime Minister might speak to M. Maisky or send a message to Stalin, explaining our interest in Polish-Soviet relations, and asking whether the Russians could not revert to the position at least as it was at the end of December 1942. Sir A. Cadogan thought that the Russians were trying to force the Poles to accept the Curzon line under the threat of working against General Sikorski's Government, and of making the position of the Poles in Russia impossible. General Sikorski could not accept such a frontier settlement now, and we and the Americans could not advise him to do so. The Russians therefore were merely playing into the hands of German propaganda by stirring up disunity among the United Nations, encouraging anti-Soviet feeling in the United States and undermining the morale of the Polish fighting forces.

The Prime Minister thought that, in view of his message to Stalin about the suspension of convoys,[1] the moment was unfavourable

---

[1] See above, pp. 568-9.

(a) C3386/258/55; C3742/335/55. (b) C3386/258/55.

for intervention and that it would be better to await Mr. Eden's
(a) return. On April 9, after Mr. Eden's return from Washington, Count
Raczynski repeated his appeal. He said that the relief organisations
had cared for about 260,000 people, of whom one half were Polish
Jews and the other half 'racial Poles'. They included a number of
orphans and of close relatives of Polish troops and of other Polish
citizens, most of whom were in Great Britain or in the Middle East.
Count Raczynski hoped that we and the Americans would receive
these categories of Polish citizens—some 50,000 in all—and request
the Soviet Government to allow them to leave the U.S.S.R.

Mr. Eden said that he would consider the Polish appeal with
sympathy, but he had to point out that the Soviet Government had
always refused to allow international organisations to function in the
U.S.S.R. Mr. Eden said also that the reception of 50,000 more Poles
in Allied territory would raise difficulties which needed careful
examination. Count Raczynski asked for an early decision, since, if
no solution were found, the Polish Government would probably be
compelled by Polish opinion to issue a statement placing responsibility
for what had happened on the Soviet Government.

(b) Mr. Eden asked the Prime Minister to reconsider his decision not
to intervene. The Foreign Office considered that the Prime Minister
overlooked the real grievances and anxieties of the Polish troops and
that, in view of the further steps taken by the Russians against the
Polish relief organisations, Count Raczynski was justified in saying
that it would be impossible for the Polish Government to avoid
publishing their own version of the treatment given to their compatriots in the Soviet Union. Unless, therefore, we were able at least
to bring about a *détente*, the situation would only get worse. Mr.
Eden mentioned to the Prime Minister that, in spite of our representations to M. Maisky, the *Soviet War News*, issued by the Soviet
Embassy in London, was repeatedly reproducing thinly veiled attacks
upon the Polish Government by a Soviet-sponsored Polish Communist
paper in the U.S.S.R.[1] The Soviet Government in their own press
and broadcasts to Poland were inciting the Poles to premature
revolts and trying to discredit the more cautious policy upon which
we and the Polish Government were agreed.

(c) The Prime Minister, with the approval of the War Cabinet,
decided to send a message in general terms to Stalin and to instruct

---

[1] This newspaper *Wolna Polska* ('Free Poland') first appeared in Moscow on March 1,
1943, as the organ of the Communist Union of Polish Patriots. The paper was largely
directed by a Mme. Wanda Wasilewska, a Polish Communist, married to a Ukrainian
author, M. A. Korneichuk. On March 23, 1943, M. Korneichuk was appointed Deputy
Commissar for Foreign Affairs. In February 1944, he became Commissar for Foreign
Affairs in the Ukrainian Government.

(a) C4020/258/55. (b) C3386/258/55; C3742/335/55. (c) WM(43)52.

Sir A. Clark Kerr to ask for an interview with Stalin at which he could explain the British view. Sir A. Clark Kerr had suggested to the Foreign Office that they might propose the substitution of an (a) international relief organisation for the Polish organisations. He was now to be instructed to put this proposal to Stalin, although there would be difficulties in finding the necessary personnel, and also to say that we would be prepared to consider relieving the Soviet Union of the care of Polish orphans and young children and of those Poles who had close relations in the Polish army or among Polish civilians in territory under our control if the numbers were not too great and if suitable practical arrangements could be made for their evacuation. The Prime Minister and the War Cabinet also agreed with the Foreign Office view that we should ask for American co-operation in our intervention.[1]

The Prime Minister saw General Sikorski on April 15. In reply to (b) the general's renewed appeal for intervention, Mr. Churchill said that he was about to discuss with the United States Government what could be done in the matter. We were, however, not in a strong position at the moment for putting pressure on the Soviet Government.[2]

Before the terms of the Prime Minister's message to Stalin and of the instructions to Sir A. Clark Kerr were finally agreed, and American co-operation had been secured, a new crisis in Polish-Soviet relations had made it impossible to limit British intervention merely to a friendly *démarche* with a view to a settlement of the questions of Polish relief organisation and the status of refugees.

At his meeting with the Prime Minister on April 15 General (c) Sikorski spoke of German statements about the discovery in a common grave near Smolensk of the bodies of large numbers of Polish officers and other men. General Sikorski gave the Prime Minister a note about Polish officers and men missing in Russia. The Prime Minister said that the German statement was an obvious move to

---

[1] A telegram was sent to Lord Halifax to this effect on April 20.

[2] Mr. Eden considered at this time whether it might not be the best policy to try to get a general settlement of the Russo-Polish frontier question, in spite of our previous unwillingness to commit ourselves to territorial changes during the war. The reasons for considering this reversal of policy were (i) that the real motive of the anti-Polish policy of the Soviet Government seemed to be their desire to secure the Polish-Soviet frontier of 1941, (ii) Mr. Roosevelt's remark to Mr. Eden on March 16 about the Russian claims (see above, pp. 622–3). Apart, however, from doubts whether Mr. Roosevelt would be able to commit himself publicly to these Russian claims, the difficulties and disadvantages of accepting them at this stage were insuperable. In any case the serious developments in the Soviet-Polish dispute after April 15 ruled out the possibility of a friendly discussion of the frontier question.

(a) C4081/258/55. (b) C4230/258/55. (c) C4230/258/55.

sow discord between the Allies, but his own comment, after the meeting, was that 'the facts are pretty grim'.[1]

The Polish note stated, *inter alia*, that it had been impossible to discover the whereabouts of 7,000 to 9,000 officers known to have been prisoners of war in Russia. Most of these officers had been sent to three special camps[2] from which they were evacuated in the spring

(a) of 1940 to an unknown destination. On April 17 the Polish Ministry of National Defence issued a communiqué on the subject of the missing officers and of the unsuccessful efforts made to trace them. The communiqué referred to the usual lies of German propaganda, but claimed that an investigation of the German allegations was necessary, and stated that the Polish Government had asked the International Red Cross Committee in Geneva whether they would be willing to make the investigation. On April 20 the Polish Government once again asked the Soviet Government for information as to the whereabouts of the officers and other prisoners evacuated from the three camps in the spring of 1940.

(b) The Soviet Government replied on April 26 with an angry note breaking off diplomatic relations with Poland and accusing the Poles of connivance with the enemy in launching a campaign against the Soviet Union in order to exercise pressure for the purpose of obtaining territorial concessions at the expense of the Soviet Ukraine, White Russia, and Soviet Lithuania. The Polish Government answered on April 28 with another denial that they had ever claimed Soviet territory or that they had failed to discharge their obligations under their agreements with the Soviet Union. They aimed at a friendly understanding with the Soviet Union on the basis of the integrity and full sovereignty of the Polish Republic. They stated that, in view of

---

[1] The number of bodies found in the graves was about 4,510—not 10,000 as the Germans alleged in their statement of April 13, 1943. An investigation of the responsibility for these mass executions at Katyn near Smolensk is outside the scope of this History. It may be said that among the facts established beyond doubt are that the victims were Polish and that they were killed in the spring of 1940—almost certainly about March and

(c) April of that year. In a long report of May 24, 1943, examining the evidence then available, Mr. O'Malley, British Ambassador to the Polish Government, considered that the evidence led to the conclusion that the responsibility for the executions lay with the Soviet Government. The Foreign Office had at first inclined to think that, as the Prime Minister had said to General Sikorski, the German statements were propagandist lies. They agreed later with the conclusion reached by Mr. O'Malley. In spite of the report of a Russian Special Commission of Enquiry in January 1944 (after the Russian reoccupation of the Katyn area) the weight of opinion has continued to attribute the responsibility to the Russians. It should be added that, in view of the fearful atrocities committed by the Germans against the inhabitants of Poland, the British and United States Governments had good reasons for thinking, at first, that the Germans had carried out the mass executions at Katyn. Indeed at the time when the Germans announced the fact of these massacres, they were themselves engaged in exterminating the Jews of the Warsaw Ghetto, and—two months earlier—had killed some thousands of these Jews whom they had lured out of the Ghetto.

[2] See above, p. 615.

(a) C4761/258/55. (b) C4840/258/55. (c) C6161/258/55.

facts known to all the world, they had no need to defend themselves against any suggestion of contact or understanding with Hitler. They appealed in the name of the solidarity of the United Nations and of elementary humanity for the release from the U.S.S.R. of Polish orphans and of relatives of the Polish forces, and also of Poles of military age who could join these forces, and for the continuation of relief work among the Polish citizens who would remain in the (a) U.S.S.R. Two days later the Polish Government announced that the International Red Cross Committee had explained the difficulties in the way of complying with their request for an investigation. In fact they could act only if all the parties invited them to do so. The Soviet Government were not represented on the Committee, and had not invited them to undertake the investigation. The Polish Government therefore said that they regarded their application as having lapsed.

(iii)

British attempts to secure a resumption of Russo-Polish relations: death of General Sikorski: proposals for an Anglo-American approach to the Soviet Government (April–August 1943).

During this exchange of notes the British Government had done their best to try to bring about a *détente*. On April 21 Stalin had sent a (b) message to the Prime Minister bitterly attacking the Poles and announcing the 'interruption' of Polish-Soviet relations. M. Maisky left this message with the Prime Minister on April 23. The Prime Minister replied on April 24 that we should oppose an investigation (c) by the International Red Cross or any other body in territory under German control. Mr. Eden was asking General Sikorski to withdraw all countenance from an investigation under Nazi auspices. On the other hand Mr. Churchill hoped that the Soviet decision to 'interrupt' relations with the Polish Government was to be read in the sense of a final warning and that the decision would not be published. Mr. Churchill said that General Sikorski's position was very difficult;

(a) C4919/258/55. (b) Churchill Papers/354; C4586/258/55; WP(43)175. (c) T580/3, Churchill Papers/345.

he was not pro-German, but a number of Poles thought that he had not stood up sufficiently for the Poles against the U.S.S.R.

Mr. Churchill added that he had drafted a telegram on the previous day asking Stalin to allow more Poles and Polish dependents to go into Iran. In view of Stalin's message he had held over this
(a) telegram. On April 25 Mr. Churchill sent another telegram to Stalin saying that General Sikorski had clearly not synchronised—as Stalin had alleged—his appeal to the Red Cross with a statement put out by the Germans. General Sikorski had told Mr. Eden that he had raised the question of the missing officers several times with the Soviet Government and once with Stalin personally. He had now accepted our strong recommendation that he should not press for a Red Cross investigation, and that he should prevent the Polish newspapers from attacking the Soviet Government.

Mr. Churchill said that in these circumstances he hoped that Stalin would give up the idea of any interruption of Polish-Soviet relations and that he (Mr. Churchill) would now be sending Stalin the telegram about getting the Poles and their dependents into Iran.
(b) Stalin, however, replied on the same day to Mr. Churchill's first message that the decision to interrupt Polish-Soviet relations had already been taken, and must be published. The decision had been necessary owing to hostile propaganda in the Polish press and the deep indignation of Soviet public opinion at the 'ingratitude and treachery of the Polish Government'.[1]

(c)   The Polish note of April 28 had been modified at the suggestion of the Prime Minister and Mr. Eden—who saw General Sikorski on April 27 and 28—and the British Government had taken steps to
(d) request the Polish press to avoid provoking the Russians and the British press not to emphasise or take sides in the Russo-Polish dispute. One difficulty, however, was that the *Daily Worker* took a strong pro-Soviet anti-Polish line. The *Soviet War News*, of which Mr. Eden had previously complained, was equally provocative. Mr. Eden told the War Cabinet that he would speak to M. Maisky on the question of press polemics.

(e)   On April 28 the Prime Minister sent another message to Stalin, but at Sir A. Clark Kerr's suggestion the terms were altered mainly to include a reference to the bad impression which the Soviet action

---

[1] Sir A. Clark Kerr, had also tried to persuade M. Molotov to delay a public announce-
(f) ment of the Soviet decision at least for a few days in order to give the British Government time to seek for a solution. The American Ambassador at Moscow made a similar un-successful attempt to secure postponement of the decision.

(a) T581/3 (Churchill Papers/354; C4668/258/55). (b) T593/3 (Churchill Papers/354; C4667/258/55). (c) WM(43)56; WM(43)59; WM(43)62. (d) C4798/258/55. (e) T606/3 (Churchill Papers/354; C4909/258/55). (f) C4646, 4647/258/55.

had made on British and American public opinion. Sir A. Clark Kerr thought that Stalin set much store on opinion in Great Britain and the United States and that it was desirable to let him see that he had now gone too far, and that the faith of this public opinion in Russian collaboration had been severely shaken.

The revised message—which was telegraphed on April 30—thus opened with an expression of disappointment that Stalin had broken off relations with the Poles without giving the Prime Minister time to inform him of the results of his approach to General Sikorski. The Prime Minister said that he had hoped that, in the spirit of the Anglo-Soviet treaty of 1942, there would always be mutual consultation about such matters especially when they affected the combined strength of the United Nations.

The Prime Minister then said that he and Mr. Eden had pointed out to the Polish Government that the resumption of friendly or working relations with the Soviet Government was impossible while they—the Polish Government—were making insulting charges against the U.S.S.R. and appearing to countenance Nazi propaganda. It was still more impossible to countenance enquiries held by the International Red Cross under Nazi auspices and dominated by Nazi terrorism. The Polish Government had accepted this view, and wanted to work loyally with the U.S.S.R. They asked that the dependents of the Polish forces in Iran and in the U.S.S.R. should be allowed to go to Iran. This request was surely a matter admitting of discussion. We regarded it as reasonable if made at the right time and in the right way, and we thought that President Roosevelt agreed with us. We hoped therefore that Stalin would consider the matter 'in a spirit of magnanimity'. The Prime Minister made it clear that we intended to have 'proper discipline' in the Polish press in Great Britain. He also mentioned that the Germans were suggesting that the U.S.S.R. would now set up a Polish Government on Russian soil, and deal only with them. We should be unable to recognise such a Government and would continue our relations with General Sikorski who was far the most helpful man whom we or the Russians could find. We expected the Americans to take a similar view. The Prime Minister thought that the Poles had 'had a shock', and that, after an interval, the relationship established on July 30, 1941, should be restored. 'No one will hate this more than Hitler and what he hates most is wise for us to do.' The Prime Minister concluded with the words:

> 'We owe it to our Armies now engaged, and presently to be more heavily engaged, to maintain good conditions behind the fronts. I and my colleagues look steadily to the ever closer co-operation and understanding of the U.S.S.R., the United States of America and the British Commonwealth and Empire not only in the deepening

X*

war struggle, but after the war. What other hope can there be than this for the tortured world?'

(a)   Mr. Eden saw M. Maisky on April 29. M. Maisky complained about the reference in the Polish note of April 28 to the integrity of the Polish Republic. He asked whether the British Government endorsed the Polish claims to their frontiers of 1939. Mr. Eden said that the Poles were repeating a claim which they had previously made to their territories as they were before they were invaded. The note was a Polish note; although we had assisted in drafting it, our own position had not changed since we had stated it at the time of the Soviet-Polish treaty of July 1941.[1] M. Maisky then went on to attack the Polish press and the Polish Government. Mr. Eden complained of Soviet press attacks against Poland. Mr. Eden said that neither he nor the British Government accepted M. Maisky's view of the Polish Government; that we intended to stand by General Sikorski and that we should regard as extremely serious any step taken by the Russians to set up an alternative Polish Government. M. Maisky regarded such a step as unlikely.

(b)   The Prime Minister sent for M. Maisky on April 30 to protest to him against an article in the *Soviet War News* headed '*Emigrés* and the People'. This article, which was reproduced from the Soviet newspaper '*Izvestia*', alleged that the Polish Government did not represent the Polish people, was unable and unwilling to lead them in the struggle against Hitlerism, and occupied itself mainly in bargaining for frontiers. Mr. Churchill pointed out to M. Maisky that we could hardly continue to curb the Polish press if such charges were made against the Polish Government in material sent out under the auspices of the Soviet Embassy. We should continue to deal with General Sikorski; the Soviet Government ought to see that they were lucky to have him at the head of the Polish Government. Mr. Churchill spoke very plainly to M. Maisky; he reminded him that the '*émigré*' character of General Sikorski's Government was 'not unconnected with a double occupation of Poland'. Mr. Churchill also took up M. Maisky very sharply when the latter spoke of Poland as a country of 20 million inhabitants next door to a country of 200 millions.

In the course of the discussion M. Maisky said that the Soviet Government did not intend to set up another Polish Government on Soviet territory, but that they would not renew relations with the existing Government. In reply to a question M. Maisky admitted that his Government did not wish to replace General Sikorski or Count Raczynski, but that a 'reconstruction' would be necessary.

---

[1] See above, p. 615.

(a) C4778, 5015/258/55; WM(43)62. (b) C5136/258/55.

On May 3 Mr. Eden told the War Cabinet that the Russo-Polish (a)
tension had lessened. The Russians had agreed to postpone the date
of the departure of the Polish Embassy from Kuibyshev: they had
not attacked by name members of General Sikorski's Government
and apparently did not intend to set up a rival Polish Government.
Three days later M. Maisky brought to the Foreign Office a message (b)
from Stalin in reply to the Prime Minister's message of April 30.
Stalin repeated his allegations against the Polish press and hinted
that the British Government must have known about the Polish
intention to start an anti-Soviet press campaign. He denied reports
that the Soviet Government were intending to establish a new Polish
Government in Russia, but suggested that Great Britain, the United
States and the Soviet Government might take immediate steps to
'improve the composition' of the existing Polish Government. He
also denied that the Soviet Government had put obstacles in the way
of Polish subjects—including the families of Polish soldiers evacuated
to Iran—who wished to leave the U.S.S.R.

Mr. Eden told M. Maisky that Stalin's reference to the evacuation (c)
of 'Polish subjects' was not clear. After considerable questioning
M. Maisky admitted that on the Soviet interpretation the term
applied only to Poles living west of the Russo-Polish frontier established after the Polish defeat in 1939. Mr. Eden pointed out that this
definition had not been adopted when the Polish forces were first
recruited in Russia; he hoped that the new decision would be
modified since otherwise the number of Poles able to leave the
U.S.S.R. to join their compatriots would be small. M. Maisky
thought that the matter might be discussed after the resumption of
Soviet-Polish diplomatic relations. Mr. Eden did not have a good
impression of M. Maisky's attitude. M. Maisky was unwilling to
accept the fact that there was a Polish as well as a Russian point of
view; he also tended to criticise the British Government as too
tolerant of Polish feelings. Mr. Eden had to remind him that we had
gone to war on account of Poland.

Five days later M. Maisky was less unfriendly in a conversation (d)
about Poland, but there was no improvement in the acts of the Soviet
Government. They announced the conscription of Poles in the
U.S.S.R. to join a Polish division which would serve as part of the
Soviet Army—a measure which the Polish Government regarded,
with justice, as an infringement of their sovereign rights; they continued their press attacks on the Polish Government, and secured
publicity in Great Britain for these attacks not only by printing them
in the *Soviet War News* but also by their reproduction in the *Daily*

(a) WM(43)63. (b) T656/3 (Churchill Papers/354; C5138/258/55. (c) C5138/258/55.
(d) C5295, 5367/258/55.

Worker and as leaflets for distribution by British Communist organisations.[1]

(a)   Meanwhile Sir A. Clark Kerr had carried out on May 7 instructions sent to him to speak to Stalin. He said that His Majesty's Government were unhappy over the effect of the Soviet action on Allied unity and thought it unwise to drive General Sikorski out of office. Stalin said that he was willing to accept our assurances about General Sikorski's loyalty, but he felt that the general was politically weak and did not resist 'pro-Hitler people about him'. Sir A. Clark Kerr asked Stalin how Polish-Soviet relations could be restored. Stalin answered that a reconstruction of the Polish Government was necessary. The present members of the Government did not want to live at peace with Russia, and were trying to play off one Ally against the other. They thought themselves clever tacticians, but 'God had given them no brains'. There were, however, plenty of capable Poles whom the Prime Minister could employ to replace the 'abnormal' men surrounding General Sikorski. Stalin was in no hurry about the matter, and was not greatly concerned with the interruption of relations.

Sir A. Clark Kerr then raised the question of the Poles in the U.S.S.R. Stalin said that, in his message to the Prime Minister, he had stated that no obstacles would be put in the way of those who wished to leave the U.S.S.R. He understood that some of the soldiers' families did not want to go. Sir A. Clark Kerr reported that Stalin seemed unwilling to discuss the matter further, and that he did not raise the frontier question.

(b)   Mr. Eden had already suggested to General Sikorski on May 6 the possibility of a reconstruction of the Polish Government. General Sikorski had promised to consider the suggestion. He wrote to Mr. Eden after M. Vyshinsky's attack on the Poles that he could not now
(c)   make any changes in his Cabinet. On May 12 the Prime Minister sent a message to Stalin that he would try to get changes in the Polish Government as soon as possible but that General Sikorski could not make them under foreign pressure. The Prime Minister also referred

---

[1] On May 6 Stalin had told *The Times* correspondent in Moscow that the Soviet
(d) Government unquestionably wanted a strong Poland and good Polish-Soviet relations after the war, and were prepared to offer Poland an alliance providing for mutual assistance against Germany. General Sikorski replied on the following day that the Polish Government desired such an alliance and would give a positive reply to any Soviet initiative coincident with the interests of the Polish Republic, but that there were limits to the concessions which Poland could make. In spite of this more friendly exchange, M. Vyshinsky, Soviet Deputy Commissar for Foreign Affairs, issued a statement on May 7. Although M. Vyshinsky said that the Soviet Government did not intend to set up a rival Polish Government in Moscow, he alleged that the Polish army had refused to fight on the Russian front, and that a number of Poles engaged in relief work had been found guilty of espionage and connivance with the Germans. The Polish Government at once replied by a denial of all these charges.

(a) C5189/258/55. (b) C5139, 5179/258/55. (c) T689/3 (Churchill Papers/354; C5138/288/55). (d) C5585/258/55.

to Stalin's promise not to oppose the withdrawal of Polish subjects from the U.S.S.R. and said that he would communicate later with Stalin on the subject.

The formation of a Polish division in Russia as part of the Red Army, and the publicity given to this action in the Russian press and the *Soviet War News*, added to the anxiety of the Poles. General Sikorski found it difficult to restrain the Poles from replying to the Russian press attacks (which, as before, were reproduced in the *Daily Worker* and distributed in leaflet form by Communist organisations in Great Britain). General Sikorski proposed to send a protest to the (a) members of the United Nations against the formation of a Polish division by the Soviet Government. He regarded this act as an infringement of Polish sovereign rights and as a breach of the Soviet-Polish agreements.

Mr. Eden secured the postponement of the issue of this protest and (b) also, on May 18, discussed the situation with M. Maisky. He said that he was afraid that the Soviet Government, though not setting up a Polish Government in Moscow, were establishing some 'authority' which might in the end amount to the same thing. M. Maisky denied that the Soviet Government intended anything more than the formation of a division to fight the Germans.[1] M. Molotov took a similar line when—on instructions from the Foreign Office— (c) Sir A. Clark Kerr spoke to him about the matter, and about M. Vyshinsky's press statement. M. Molotov said that the recruits for the Polish legion would be drawn largely from men formerly living in the Western Ukraine and Western White Russia who, although Polish by 'nationality', were now Soviet citizens. He affirmed strongly that the Communist 'Union of Polish Patriots' in the U.S.S.R. was not being treated and would not be treated as a 'competent and united Polish authority'. M. Molotov also made it clear that the Soviet Government intended to maintain their definition of Polish citizenship, and thus greatly to restrict the numbers of Poles likely to be evacuated from the U.S.S.R.

In view of the Soviet insistence upon changes in the Polish Government as a necessary prelude to the restoration of Polish-Soviet diplomatic relations, and of the impossibility of getting General Sikorski to make such changes under obvious Soviet pressure, the Foreign Office considered at the beginning of June that for the time

---

[1] In mid-June, however, at a meeting of the Union of Polish Patriots in Moscow, Colonel Berling, the Commander of the Polish Division, declared that it would 'serve as the foundation of the future Polish army'. Berling, who was promoted on August 11, 1943, to the rank of major-general in the Soviet army, had deserted from the Polish army under General Anders in 1942. See also below, p. 641, note 2.

(a) C5367/258/55. (b) C5624/258/55. (c) C5602, 5652/258/55.

we could do nothing except to try to moderate press polemics and to solve any practical questions capable of solution apart from the main political issues.

(a)   In a long and unusually 'forthcoming' conversation with Mr. R. A. Butler on June 1, M. Maisky said that he thought we ought to come to an understanding about the frontier question with the Soviet Government during the war. The Russians would advance to their 1941 frontiers and stay on them; hence it would be wiser for us to make a concession on the matter now. The Foreign Office, however, thought it impracticable to raise this larger matter. They decided

(b) to take up the question of the evacuation of Poles from the U.S.S.R. as a question which would be discussed irrespective of the restoration of Polish-Soviet diplomatic relations. They hoped to get American co-operation in this limited field, but found that the United States Government wanted to discuss the broader questions, including the definition of Polish citizenship. The American view was that we could not look for any success on the question of evacuation until we had settled the question of citizenship, since the Soviet Government might say that there were now no Polish citizens in the U.S.S.R. and that therefore no problem of evacuation existed. In any case the Soviet Government should be made to realise our determined opposition of principle to arbitrary unilateral action whereby one member of the United Nations deprived of their citizenship a large number of the people of another member.

The Foreign Office pointed out that we could not raise the question of citizenship without involving ourselves in a discussion of the future Polish-Soviet frontier. We might approach this difficult subject at a later stage, but we wanted to secure without further delay the evacuation at least of certain categories of Poles. Stalin could hardly reject out of hand an appeal on the basis of his own assurances to the Prime Minister, whereas, if we also insisted on a settlement of the citizenship question, we might have a refusal.

The Foreign Office were troubled over the long delay in arranging joint action with the United States. The two Governments had not reached complete agreement before the tragic death of General Sikorski in an aeroplane accident on July 4 while returning from a visit to the Polish forces in the Middle East. The Polish President appointed the Deputy Prime Minister, M. Mikolajczyk, as Prime Minister, M. Romer as Minister for Foreign Affairs, and General Sosnkowski as Commander-in-Chief. The Foreign Office had doubts about the latter appointment, owing to General Sosnkowski's anti-Russian views, but there was no suitable alternative.

(a) N3547/315/38. (b) C6725, 7000, 7187, 7491/258/55.

By July 12 the British and United States Governments had agreed (a) upon the terms of a common *démarche* in which the American Ambassador would deal with the citizenship question, while Sir A. Clark Kerr would concentrate mainly on the problem of evacuation. The two Ambassadors were instructed to approach Stalin as soon as possible, but were unable to do so for some time owing to his absence at the front.

On July 26, before Stalin had received the Ambassadors, Mr. (b) Churchill had a general talk with the President of Poland and Count Raczynski on Soviet-Polish relations. The President explained the reasons for Polish anxieties, and the difficulty of coming to an understanding with the Russians in the absence of a reciprocal wish on the Russian side for an understanding. Mr. Churchill did not disagree with the Polish fears, but strongly emphasised two points. In the first place he said that he was determined, as far as he could do so, to secure that Poland after the war should be independent and strong; he could give no assurances at present about frontiers. Secondly, it was essential that the Poles, like His Majesty's Government, should do their utmost to secure Russian confidence and goodwill. Mr. Churchill spoke of our own difficulties with the Soviet Government. We could not foresee their future policy; their present policy was often difficult to explain. Nevertheless Stalin did not seem indifferent to foreign opinion. It would therefore be foolish to despair of success. In any case, any hope of peace or stability in Central and South-Eastern Europe after the war depended largely on Russian policy just as the destruction of the German army depended largely on the Russians.

(iv)

Anglo-American approach of August 11 to the Soviet Government: Soviet reply of September 27: the question of the Polish-Soviet frontier: discussions with the Polish Government (August 11–October 8, 1943).

On August 11, 1943, Sir A. Clark Kerr and Admiral Standley, the (c) United States Ambassador in Moscow, had their interview with Stalin and Molotov. They appealed to Stalin on behalf of their Governments both as co-belligerents with the U.S.S.R. and Poland and as members of the United Nations. Sir A. Clark Kerr said that the British Government had already been imposing and would continue to impose a control upon foreign newspapers published in

(a) C7933, 7971/258/55. (b) C9006/258/55. (c) C9284, 10042/258/55.

Great Britain, and were hoping thereby to put an end to discussions in the press of controversial issues affecting inter-Allied relations. He then mentioned the assurances given by Stalin, in his message of May 6 to Mr. Churchill, that the Soviet Government had not put obstacles in the way of Polish subjects leaving the U.S.S.R. The British and American Governments had therefore decided jointly to suggest the evacuation of certain categories of Poles to the Middle East; they would later be taken from the Middle East to destinations where they could be suitably accommodated or employed in the common war effort. The categories were as follows: the families of Polish soldiers; Polish orphans; the families of Polish civilians at present outside the U.S.S.R; certain Polish technicians and the personnel of the former Polish welfare organisations. Sir A. Clark Kerr said that the Australian Legation in Moscow, which had undertaken to represent Polish interests[1] in the U.S.S.R., would deal with detailed questions. He also suggested that the Soviet Government would be well advised to consider the evacuation of Polish nationals coming from western Poland whose nationality was not in dispute.

The United States Ambassador supported Sir A. Clark Kerr and put forward proposals for the establishment of relief work by Soviet organisations in view of the unwillingness of the Soviet Government to allow an international organisation to function in Soviet territory. He also said that the question of Polish citizenship would have to be settled before any just or lasting resumption of diplomatic relations could be brought about. The United States Government suggested that all 'non-racial Poles' in the U.S.S.R. should be allowed to opt for Polish or Soviet citizenship, and that all 'racial Poles' in the U.S.S.R. who were domiciled in Poland on September 1, 1939, should be recognised by the Soviet Government as Polish citizens, i.e. they should not be called upon to opt.

Sir A. Clark Kerr did not refer to the question of the post-war frontiers. The United States Ambassador said that his Government felt that controversies over future boundaries should not be allowed to develop at a time when the United Nations ought to be concentrating their energies upon winning the war. The United States Government therefore considered that the liquidation of difficulties with respect to boundaries should await the end of the war and be included in the general post-war settlement.

---

[1] i.e. until the resumption of diplomatic relations between Poland and the U.S.S.R. The Polish Government had asked the British Government to undertake this representation, but the Foreign Office considered that, since we were trying to find a way out of the Soviet-Polish dispute, we should find it very difficult to protect Polish interests on Soviet territory without prejudicing all chances of our successful mediation. The United States Government were also unwilling to take over the representation.

(a)

(a) C4926, 4927, 5066/258/55; WM(43)63.

The reception of this appeal was not encouraging. Sir A. Clark (a) Kerr reported that Stalin and Molotov listened in complete silence, and that the former 'appeared to be glum'. When the Ambassadors suggested discussion, Stalin said that he could not give an answer until he had studied their proposals. In reply to a proposal from Sir A. Clark Kerr for another meeting, Stalin said that he expected to spend most of his time at the front, and could therefore make no promises; if he were unable to see the Ambassadors, he would convey his reply through M. Molotov.

Neither Stalin nor M. Molotov met the Ambassadors again for a discussion. M. Molotov did not send a reply until September 27. He (b) then communicated a formal answer in a letter stating that the breaking off of diplomatic relations with Poland was due to 'the general hostile tendency of the Polish Government's policy with regard to the U.S.S.R., which found its specific expression in the attempt of the Polish Government to make use of German-Fascist provocation about the Polish officers killed by the Hitlerites in the Smolensk area with the object of forcing the Soviet Union to make territorial concessions at the expense of the interests of Soviet Ukraine, Soviet Belorussia, and Soviet Lithuania'.

The note then dealt with the Anglo-American proposals. The Soviet Government maintained that they had given the widest possible assistance to the organisation of Polish relief, and that the Polish agencies, which included members of the former Polish Embassy in Moscow, 'had responded to all these measures of the Soviet authorities with base ingratitude by embarking on intelligence activity hostile to the Soviet Union'. The American proposal that Polish relief should be carried out by Soviet organisations was based on 'insufficient information', since in fact aid to Polish citizens was actually organised in this way.

The Soviet Government refused the suggestion for a settlement of the question of Polish citizenship. They maintained that the inclusion of the former east Polish territories in the Soviet Union was the result of a free plebiscite. The Soviet Union could not allow that all persons of Polish nationality, formerly Polish citizens, in the Soviet Union should be recognised as Polish citizens in virtue of the fact that they formerly lived in Poland. In justification of their refusal the Soviet Government said that the United States Government did not recognise as Polish citizens Poles formerly resident in Poland but now residing in the United States and that the British Government did not recognise as French citizens 'Frenchmen resident, for example, in Canada'.

For the rest, the Soviet Government denied that the proper care of Polish children could not be ensured in the Soviet Union or that

_____

(a) C9284/258/55. (b) C11378, 13460/258/55.

obstacles had been placed or were being placed in the way of the departure from the U.S.S.R. of Polish citizens and the families of Polish soldiers evacuated to Iran. Finally the note doubted the efficacy of the measures of control placed upon foreign newspapers in Great Britain and complained of the continuance of a Polish press campaign against the Soviet Union.

(a) As the weeks passed without any move from the Soviet Government towards a resumption of relations with Poland, and as the attempt to 'isolate' the question of evacuation had failed, Mr. Eden considered that it might be necessary after all to take up the most fundamental problem and to let the Soviet Government know what were the British and American views about the western frontier of Russia. The Soviet Government might be more amenable on Polish and other questions if they understood that, while maintaining their decision not to recognise during the war any territorial changes, the British and United States Governments were prepared to accept a large measure of the Russian claims. The British view was that Poland should be given Danzig, East Prussia, and the Oppeln district of Upper Silesia, and should agree to the Curzon line[1] with an adjustment to include the city of Lwow in Polish territory; that the 1941 Soviet-Finnish and Soviet-Roumanian frontiers should be retained, and that the Soviet Union should be allowed to absorb the Baltic States. Mr. Eden believed that President Roosevelt agreed with the British view. They therefore suggested that the two Governments should approach the Soviet Government. They would not propose an agreement, written or unwritten, but would merely state confidentially to Stalin their willingness to advocate at the Peace Conference a frontier settlement on the proposed lines. The British Government had special obligations to the Polish Government; we should tell them of our views and advise them to base their policy on the assumption that we should support a solution at the Peace Conference in accordance with these views. In taking these steps, we should be acting contrary to the Atlantic Charter, but there was no other way of securing Soviet collaboration after the war or securing an improvement in Polish-Soviet relations.

Mr. Eden suggested that Lord Halifax should be instructed to discuss the whole matter with President Roosevelt. No decision, however, was reached in the matter before the Quebec Conference.

---

[1] The line was more favourable to the Poles than the line of Russian occupation in 1939, since it included in Poland the Bialystok area which was inhabited by 'racial Poles'. In a later statement of the British view Mr. Eden suggested that the frontier settlement should be accompanied by a transfer of population, especially in Eastern Galicia.

(a) N4905/4069/38.

At this Conference Mr. Eden, with the Prime Minister's approval, (a) gave Mr. Hull on August 23 a statement of the British view. Mr. Hull said that the proposal raised difficult questions, and that if we were intending to make considerable concessions to the Soviet point of view, we must ask something from them in return. We might say that our concession on the frontier question depended on the general agreement of the Soviet Government to our ideas of a post-war settlement. It appeared from Mr. Hopkins that the President himself accepted the British view, and that he had said as much to MM. Litvinov and Molotov.[1]

No decision was reached on the matter at Quebec. Mr. Eden (b) thought, however, that the meeting of the Foreign Ministers in Moscow might result in a deadlock if we could not show the Soviet Government that we did not intend to oppose their frontier claims at the Peace Conference. The question was also becoming more urgent with the approach of the Soviet armies to the former Polish-Soviet frontier. On October 5, therefore, Mr. Eden submitted a memorandum to the War Cabinet. He explained that the Polish- (c) Soviet frontier was the core of the problem. The Polish attitude was that they could not accept during the war any surrender of Polish territory without losing the confidence of the Polish people at home and the Polish armed forces in the field. We ourselves could not enter into any agreement with the U.S.S.R. involving the surrender of Polish territory since we were bound by the assurances which we had given to the Polish Government in 1941 and 1942.

There were, however, signs that the Polish Government did not wish to postpone consideration of the position until the Soviet armies had crossed the pre-war Polish frontier. They had to decide soon on the attitude of the well-organised Polish Underground forces to the Russians. The question of the resumption of Polish-Soviet diplomatic relations would then become urgent, but we should find no solution unless, without abandoning our principle of not recognising during the war any territorial changes, we made it clear to the Soviet Government that we did not intend to oppose their main territorial claims in the West.

Mr. Eden then suggested that we should accept the Curzon line, but try to secure for Poland the city of Lwow. The Poles also wanted Vilna. We did not regard this claim as realisable, though we could use it as a bargaining counter in our efforts to secure Lwow for them. The Soviet Government had always favoured the transfer to Poland

---

[1] The Foreign Office considered that the President and his advisers could not disregard the large Polish vote in the United States.

(a) N5060/499/38. (b) N6004/499/38. (c) WP(43)438.

of Danzig, East Prussia, and Upper Silesia; these changes might involve large transfers of population.

Mr. Eden summarised the comments made by Mr. Hull and Mr. Hopkins at Quebec. He said that he was not at all sure that the United States Government would endorse the President's views. Mr. Hull, who was going to the Moscow Conference, was especially likely to refuse any commitment on the issue. The Moscow Conference was, however, merely to prepare the way for a meeting between the Prime Minister, the President, and Stalin. Mr. Eden therefore suggested that he might explore the position with a view to subsequent discussion. He would ask what the Soviet Government would do if the Poles were willing to accept our proposals. He would say that we would not oppose the Soviet claim at the Peace Conference, but that, if the Polish Government agreed to it, we should expect the Soviet Government to show a real willingness to co-operate in post-war matters in Europe and to show their goodwill by resuming relations with the Polish Government, and by co-operating with us and the Polish Government in finding a satisfactory solution to problems concerning Polish Underground resistance, the position of the Poles in the U.S.S.R., and the further problem of Soviet support of a rival Polish army and parties in the U.S.S.R. hostile to the Polish Government. Soviet action on these lines would go a long way to remove Polish fears that the U.S.S.R. was less interested in frontier questions than in turning Poland into a puppet State. Mr. Eden said in his memorandum that he would feel bound to inform the Poles that we intended to explore with the Soviet Government the question of Polish-Soviet relations, not excluding the frontiers. He also referred to other Soviet frontier questions. He pointed out that the Soviet Government would certainly not abandon their claim that the Baltic States had already voted themselves into the U.S.S.R.; we had already admitted this claim in our discussion in 1942 at the time of the signature of the Anglo-Soviet treaty.[1]

(a)   Mr. Eden also circulated to the War Cabinet on October 5 a memorandum on the problem of the relations between the Soviet forces and the Polish Underground movements in the event of an advance of the former into Polish territory. He pointed out that the problem was an urgent one, since fighting might break out between Soviet and Polish guerrillas in east Poland which each party regarded as its own national territory. Furthermore the Russians would expect

---

[1] When M. Molotov was in London in May 1942, the British Government expressed their willingness to sign a treaty containing a form of words which would constitute British recognition of the Soviet claim to the Baltic States. The draft treaty then under discussion was not in fact signed, since it was superseded by the Twenty Years Treaty in which nothing was said about frontiers. See above, Chapter XXVI, sections (iii) and (iv).

(a) WP(43)439.

more active measures on the part of the Polish Underground forces to harass the Germans; we and the Polish Government would therefore find it difficult to continue our policy of discouraging premature risings, especially if Russian operations continued through the winter.

We had also to consider the question of arming the Polish Underground forces—estimated at some 65,000 men. Hitherto we had done nothing to arm them; the Combined Chiefs of Staff had rejected on September 17 an appeal from the Poles for equipment and had decided for the present only to send material necessary for sabotage and intelligence purposes. Their reasons were primarily military— shortage of aircraft and the need to give priority to the Balkans—but they might have been influenced by political considerations.[1]

The Russians were strongly opposed to the supply of arms to the Polish Underground forces.[2] If we armed them without consulting the Russians, the Soviet Government would protest to us and to the United States that we were equipping a force which would be used against the Soviet Union. There was indeed little doubt that the Polish army would resist Russian encroachment on the pre-1939 frontiers of Poland. On the other hand the Poles themselves were vitally interested in the equipping of this secret force. It was for them their main army, and, if it were given the necessary arms, might take a decisive part in the liberation of Poland and the subsequent maintenance of order in the country. Finally there was the risk that if, in the near future, the Polish Underground movement came into the open in response to Russian appeals, the Russians might take the opportunity, when they entered Poland, to break up the organisation and seize the leaders.

Mr. Eden's view was that the only satisfactory way of dealing with the immediate question—the response of the Underground movement to a Russian appeal—was to discuss it frankly at the Foreign

---

[1] There is no evidence to show why the Foreign Office were not more fully informed of the views of the Combined Chiefs of Staff in this matter or, indeed, why the latter had not consulted the Foreign Office and the State Department on the political aspects before taking their decision.

[2] The Poles—who had a long tradition of underground resistance against desperate odds—had organised not only an underground army known as the Home Army, but a regular apparatus of government. This military and civilian organisation was based on the co-operation of the four principal Polish parties, the Peasant Party, the Socialists, the National Democrats, and the Christian Democrats, and was in close and continuous contact and co-operation with the exiled Government in London. If, therefore, the Russians wanted to prevent the revival of Poland as an independent State and to impose, after the liberation of the country, a government under their control, they had to do much more than disown the Government in London. Hence their efforts (while taking temporary advantage of the anti-German activities of the Home Army) to weaken its organisation by attempts to build up a rival underground military force—the People's Army—and a rival political organisation. At a suitable time this organisation could be brought into the open, and its legitimate rival liquidated by force. It is not clear from the British documents whether, at all events in the years 1942 and 1943—and even after the Warsaw revolt— Mr. Churchill fully understood the significance of the Russian attitude towards the non-Communist Underground movement.

Ministers' Conference as part of the whole Polish problem. We might say that a general uprising in Poland against the Germans during the coming winter would be premature, and would lead only to the destruction of the Polish organisation. We therefore thought that the Underground forces should not attempt more than an intensification of the sabotage and other work which they were already carrying out to good effect.

Mr. Eden suggested that we might find it desirable to advise the Polish Underground forces to withdraw altogether from operations in eastern Poland. He thought, however, that they ought to declare themselves to the Russians. We and the Americans might have to tell the Polish Government that we should use our influence with the Russians to prevent any victimisation of the Polish Underground leaders. The supply of arms to the movement was a less urgent matter, but we could not settle it satisfactorily unless we were able to reach an agreement with the Soviet Government about the Polish-Soviet frontier before the Russian armies entered Poland.

(a) On October 7—before Mr. Eden's proposals were discussed in the War Cabinet—Count Raczynski brought to the Foreign Office a statement of Polish policy drawn up by the Polish Government. The statement was made because the Polish Government were now afraid that they might have Soviet forces in Polish territory before they had been able to safeguard their fellow countrymen in Poland from complete Soviet control and from a return to the deportations and general policy adopted by the Russians against the Poles in 1939. The Polish memorandum of policy suggested *inter alia* that the aim of Russian policy might well be the complete subjection of Poland to the U.S.S.R. in order that the Soviet Government might use the country as a jumping-off ground for the establishment of Soviet predominance in Central Europe and Germany as well as in the Balkans. The best way of testing Russian intentions would be to revert to the Anglo-American *démarche* of August 11 and to press firmly for the resumption of Polish-Soviet diplomatic relations; the most urgent questions could thus be settled at once by direct Polish-Soviet contact, and the frontier differences left over for future settlement.

The note affirmed that the Polish Government were determined to stand by the integrity of the eastern territories of Poland. The Polish Government were also opposed even to a temporary and partial occupation of Polish territory by Soviet forces. If, however, such an operation were a necessary consequence of military operations against Germany, it should be preceded by a Polish-Soviet agreement following the resumption of mutual relations. Otherwise

(a) C11657/231/55.

the Russians might attempt to impose a Communist régime and to exterminate or deport the leading elements resisting this attempt. The result would then be a desperate popular rising. If, however, the entry of Soviet troops followed the conclusion of an agreement, the Polish sovereign Government and its agents would be solely entitled, according to the rulings of the Quebec Conference,[1] to take over the administration of the country. The Polish Government, assisted by the Polish Underground movement, were already in a position to fulfil this task; they would desire the presence of Anglo-American military detachments and military commissions in order to prevent Polish-Soviet friction and in particular to protect the population against possible Soviet repression.

In commenting upon the memorandum the Polish Ambassador said that various acts of Soviet policy for some time past had been consistent with the intention to set up a seventeenth Constituent Republic of the Soviet Union or a puppet Communist State in Poland. If, as the Polish Government feared, the Soviet Government had such a plan, they would not be deterred from it by the surrender of any Polish territory, but would make a concession in the matter the basis for further demands. If Poland were to agree to territorial concessions, she must have firm guarantees that they would not be followed by the absorption of the Polish State into the Soviet system. Hence the Polish Government attached great importance to the resumption of Polish-Soviet relations as a sign that the Soviet Government were not intending to disrupt the Polish State. Mr. Eden said that he understood the difficulties in the way of territorial concessions by an *émigré* Government but that the Polish Government would not get far, even in the direction of a resumption of relations, with the Soviet Government unless they showed some willingness to consider the territorial question.

The War Cabinet discussed on October 8 the two questions—the (a) Soviet-Polish frontier and the position of the Underground movement—raised in Mr. Eden's memoranda. Mr. Eden said that the

---

[1] The reference is to a proposed declaration about handing over the civil administration of their liberated territory to the Allied Governments as soon as possible. The proposal was designed to reassure the European Allies that Allied Military Government would not be applied to them; it was not issued, either after the Quebec Conference or after the Foreign Ministers' conference in Moscow in October, owing to failure to reach an agreement with the Americans and Russians on a form of words, and the whole question was then referred to the European Advisory Commission. Nothing was said officially to the other Allies at this time about the declaration, but a press statement at Quebec explained that the Conference had considered the question, and had recognised that the system applied in Italy could not be used in countries where there was already a legitimate Government on friendly terms with the British and United States Governments. Mr. Eden also said in the House of Commons on September 22 that we intended to hand over the administration of liberated territory to the national authority as soon as the military situation made it possible to do so. (U3980, 4036, 4132, 6145/3646/74; Churchill Papers/ 328(A)/6; F.R.U.S., 1943, (Cairo and Teheran Conferences), 382 n.)

(a) WM(43)137.4, C.A.

Poles had now definitely asked him not to discuss the frontier question at Moscow. The Prime Minister—with the approval of the War Cabinet—said that, while we would welcome a settlement on the lines suggested by Mr. Eden and would recommend the Poles, in their own interests, to accept it, we could not force them to cede territory to the U.S.S.R. The War Cabinet also thought that we might inform the Russians of the considerable extent to which their own military operations had been assisted already by sabotage and other activities carried out by the Underground movement. We should not, however, disclose the names of the leaders or members of the movement to the Russians if—as appeared certain—the Poles were unwilling for us to do so.

(v)

Further Anglo-Polish discussions: Mr. Eden's proposals of November 22 for a general Russo-Polish settlement: the Polish question at the Teheran Conference (October 9–December 1, 1943).

In view of the Polish refusal to agree to a discussion of the frontier question at the Moscow Conference, and of the policy of the United States Government not to consider frontier questions until after the end of hostilities, no progress was made at the Moscow Conference (a) towards a Polish-Soviet settlement. The subject was discussed directly only once, and at the end of the Conference. Mr. Eden and Mr. Hull said that they hoped for a resumption of Polish-Soviet relations. Mr. Eden raised the question of sending arms to the Polish Underground movement. M. Molotov's answer was that arms could be given only into 'safe hands' where they would be of use. He asked whether there were any 'safe hands' in Poland. M. Molotov said that the U.S.S.R. wanted an independent Poland, and was ready to help her, but the Poles must have a Government with friendly intentions towards the Soviet Union; the present Polish Government did not show a friendly attitude.

Meanwhile on October 26 the Polish Government informed the Foreign Office in confidence that they had decided to instruct the Polish Underground movement to avoid at all costs a clash with the Soviet forces when the latter crossed into Polish territory. The Polish Government were still afraid that if their Underground leaders showed themselves they would be deported or killed by the Russians; but they (the Polish Government) felt that they must rely on British

(a) C13335/258/55.

and American justice and friendship for their protection rather than on their own limited power of self-defence.

On November 12, after his return from Moscow, Mr. Eden saw (a) M. Mikolajczyk, M. Romer and Count Raczynski. He told them that, in accordance with their request and with the policy of the United States Government on frontier matters, the Polish-Soviet frontier had not been discussed at Moscow; that he and Mr. Hull had spoken strongly of their wish to see the resumption of Polish-Soviet relations, and that M. Molotov had not committed himself beyond saying that the Soviet Government wanted an independent Poland and would help Poland if the Polish Government showed friendly intentions towards the U.S.S.R.

M. Mikolajczyk repeated his fears that the Russians did not want an independent Poland. He was afraid that when they entered Polish territory they would set up a civil administration and act throughout Poland as they had done in 1939. The Poles would look to Great Britain, as their Ally, and to the United States for protection. M. Mikolajczyk asked whether it would be possible to establish some form of inter-Allied administration which would save Poland from such treatment by the Russians.

Mr. Eden said that he had found no evidence that the Soviet Government were planning to absorb Poland; they had not disagreed with the suggestion that Poland should be given East Prussia and Upper Silesia. The question of the administration of Allied territories was already being examined as an inter-Allied problem; the situation in Poland therefore would be entirely different from that of 1939 since we and the Americans would now be discussing Eastern European questions with the Russians. Mr. Eden asked whether M. Mikolajczyk would consider meeting Soviet objections to the existing Polish Government by the co-option of one or two of the pro-Russian Moscow Poles. M. Mikolajczyk refused on the ground that action of this kind would soon result in making the Polish Government a mere puppet of Moscow.

In answer to Polish questions whether the British Government still accepted the idea of federations as a basis of the post-war organisation of Europe and whether they now approved of the proposed Soviet-Czechoslovak Treaty,[1] Mr. Eden said that we still accepted the idea of confederations against Germany. The Soviet Government disliked the idea of a 'cordon sanitaire', but did not refuse the plan of confederations against Germany, though they thought it too soon to

---

[1] See above, Chapter XXXIV, note to section (v).

(a) C13543/231/55.

make definite arrangements. Mr. Eden said that the British Government found nothing objectionable in the terms of the proposed Soviet-Czechoslovak treaty, and that this treaty would be open to the accession of other neighbouring States. Count Raczynski explained that Poland did not wish to become a part of the *Lebensraum* of the U.S.S.R. but wanted to maintain her relations with the Western Powers. He asked whether Great Britain would become a party to the treaty. Mr. Eden said that he had never agreed to this suggestion, and that in our view a tripartite agreement (i.e. Poland, Czechoslovakia and the U.S.S.R.) directed against Germany would be a satisfactory arrangement. It was agreed to hold a further discussion in a few days' time. Meanwhile, at Mr. Eden's suggestion, M. Mikolajczyk said that he would talk to Dr. Benes before the latter left on a visit to Moscow.

Mr. Eden's comment on the interview of November 12 with the Polish Ministers was that they seemed to have learned nothing, and to expect the British Government to solve their difficulties without (a) making any contribution of their own. On the other hand Mr. Eden told M. Gusev, the new Soviet Ambassador, on November 17 that the Poles seemed less rigid in their attitude towards a discussion of territorial questions. It was difficult for them, as a Government in exile, to propose concessions even though they might be willing to make them under pressure from their friends.

(b) Mr. Eden spoke in this way because on November 17 Count Raczynski had brought to the Foreign Office a memorandum from the Polish Government explaining once again the Polish point of view, and the reasons why they were unwilling to discuss territorial concessions in the absence of effective Anglo-American guarantees. In presenting the memorandum Count Raczynski said that it was not M. Mikolajczyk's 'last word'. The Polish Government could not suggest concessions affecting the future of the Polish State while they were in exile and without the support of the Polish Parliament, but a new situation would arise if the friends of Poland were to tell her that she must accept such and such a settlement in order to safeguard the future of the country. This settlement would have to be guaranteed by Great Britain and the United States; the Poles would also wish to discuss its terms before it was formally worked out.

The Polish memorandum emphasised the urgency of safeguarding the rights of the Polish Government to assume the administration of the country immediately after it was liberated from the Germans. They pointed out once more that the situation on the eastern front made it likely that the Soviet armies would soon enter the country; the presence of a limited number of British and American liaison

---

(a) C13641/258/55. (b) C13615/231/55.

officers would not be sufficient to protect the interests of the Polish population if the administration were in the hands of a Soviet commander-in-chief. The Polish Government therefore appealed to the Prime Minister to intervene with Stalin with a view to the restoration of Polish-Soviet diplomatic relations.

M. Mikolajczyk wanted to go to the Middle East in order to put the Polish case to the Prime Minister before the latter left for Teheran, but Mr. Eden told him on November 19 that he and the (a) Prime Minister thought that a mission of this kind would certainly be misinterpreted. It would be said either that we and the Poles were concerting action against the Russians or that M. Mikolajczyk was trying to prevent Mr. Churchill from sacrificing the interests of Poland. Mr. Eden said that it might be feasible—in British as well as Polish interests—to try at the Conference to break the Russo-Polish deadlock even though a solution involved the question of frontiers. Mr. Eden did not ask the permission of the Polish Government to raise the frontier question; he asked merely that they should not refuse to agree to the issue being raised. Count Raczynski said that it was difficult for the Polish Government to give an answer. Mr. Eden said that he did not want an answer; he would assume Polish acquiescence unless he heard to the contrary. He added that the American attitude was not yet clear; Mr. Hull had stated on November 18 once again that the United States Government were opposed to any discussion about frontiers during the war.

On November 22 Mr. Eden went over the situation again with (b) M. Mikolajczyk and Count Raczynski. M. Mikolajczyk said that he would have liked an opportunity to speak to the Prime Minister about the arming of the Polish resistance groups, the instructions which the Polish Government should send to their Underground movement at home, and the general question of Polish-Soviet relations. He understood that this last question would be discussed at the forthcoming conference. Mr. Eden explained that the conference was being held for the discussion of Allied military plans for 1944, and that the question of Polish-Soviet relations was not on the agenda though he hoped for an opportunity to raise it. M. Mikolajczyk said that he understood the position and did not wish to dissuade Mr. Eden from discussions which would cover the whole range of Polish-Soviet problems, and would be undertaken with a view to a renewal of relations and a settlement of the frontier question. He wished to be assured that the discussions about frontiers would cover Polish claims in the west and that the Polish Government would be enabled to express their views on the result of any

(a) C13768/258/55. (b) C13865/258/55.

exploratory talks. M. Mikolajczyk would give these views after consulting their Polish Underground movement. Mr. Eden said that we were still very far from a decisive stage. All that we could hope for in the near future was that the Soviet Government might say that they were in favour of accepting the Curzon line as the Polish-Soviet frontier with compensation for Poland in the west. We should then take note of this proposal without committing ourselves or the Polish Government to it.

M. Mikolajczyk asked what could be done to reassure the Polish population. The Polish Government were afraid, in view of recent statements—especially one by Mr. Cordell Hull—that all liberated territories, including Poland, would be administered by the Allied military authorities; Poland would thus be treated like Italy, and the Poles would have no safeguard—other than the presence of a few British and American officers—against Soviet action.

Mr. Eden said that he would discuss the Polish question with the Prime Minister. He assured M. Mikolajczyk that he had no intention of disinteresting himself in the Polish case and that he did not forget the part which Poland had played in the war, but that the Polish Government must not expect too much from the Conference. Finally M. Mikolajczyk said that, although the Conference was primarily on military matters, the Polish problem also had a military aspect, since the Polish Government wanted at the right moment to arrange a rising in Poland against the Germans.

(a)   On the day of this interview with the Polish Ministers Mr. Eden circulated another memorandum to the War Cabinet setting out the possible lines of a Russo-Polish settlement. He repeated his previous views on the frontier question and referred to the Polish fears that the future existence of an independent Poland and not merely the frontiers was at stake. The Poles were afraid that the Russians wanted to set up a puppet government in Warsaw and turn Poland into a Soviet republic. To this end they would provoke disorders on the entry of their forces into Polish territory. It would then be impossible to maintain the present instructions of the Polish Government restraining the Polish population from taking action against the Russians; the latter would reply by destroying all the leading resistance elements in Poland.

Mr. Eden thought, therefore, that in return for a British undertaking to impose on the Poles the frontier settlement which we suggested, we should have to secure from the Soviet Government assurances that they would resume diplomatic relations with the Polish Government; that arrangements would be made for the return of the Polish Government to Poland (just as other European

---

(a) WP(43)528; C14592/258/55.

Allied Governments would return to their respective countries) and for their association with the administration of the country as soon as military circumstances allowed; that the Polish Government would be allowed to submit themselves to the approval of the Polish people, and that the latter should be free to choose their own government without any outside pressure. We should also ensure the immediate accession of Poland to the Soviet-Czechoslovak Treaty. We and, if possible, the United States Government would formally approve these arrangements and associate ourselves with them through a public declaration, or through our own participation in the Soviet-Czecho-slovak Treaty or by a plan to be worked out by the Allied politico-military commission in London.[1]

There were, however, serious difficulties in the way of these proposals. The Soviet Government might insist on changes in the personnel of the Polish Government, though they would have no valid reason for interference since the Polish Government was a coalition of all parties from the Centre to the Left. The real Soviet objection was to M. Raczkiewicz and General Sosnkowski (who were, in fact, behaving very 'reasonably'). The Polish Government could not be expected to change their President at Soviet orders. If General Sosnkowski were removed from his post as Commander-in-Chief, and if—as was likely—the Russians objected to General Anders as his successor, the morale of the Polish army would be seriously affected. We must therefore refuse to allow a change of this kind. In informing the Soviet Government of our view, we could say that we were not arming the Polish resistance groups on any large scale; that these groups were under the control of the Polish Government, and not of General Sosnkowski, and that the former, in close agreement with us, were preparing for a rising in Poland against the Germans before or at the moment of the entry of the Soviet armies.

It was essential to reassure the Poles that we should not throw them into the arms of the Russians, and then abandon them. The Poles had the Munich precedent much in mind. We ought to make it wholly clear that our proposed settlement differed from that of Munich in that the Poles would receive adequate compensation in the west for their losses in the east, and an effective gurantee of their future security from the Western Powers as well as from Russia. General declarations of approval would not be enough. We might therefore have to reconsider the suggestion—already made by the Foreign Office, but not accepted by the War Cabinet—that we (a) should accede to the Soviet-Czechoslovak treaty in which Poland

---

[1] i.e. the European Advisory Commission set up at the Moscow Conference.

(a) WP(43)423; WM(43) 135. 3, C.A.

would be included. Our own agreement with Poland would thus become merged in a new Four-Power Pact and a regional plan of security.[1]

(a)   The Prime Minister raised the Polish question with Stalin at the opening of the Teheran Conference on November 28. He said that we had declared war on behalf of Poland, and that the future of the country was therefore of importance to us, though we had given no pledges about frontiers. We also realised the Russian need for security on the western frontier of the U.S.S.R. The U.S.S.R. would be overwhelmingly strong after the war, and would have a very great responsibility in any decision with regard to Poland. The Prime Minister suggested that the three Heads of Government might agree on a frontier policy which we could advise the Poles to accept. Stalin had already said informally in conversation that the Poles could go west as far as the Oder. The Prime Minister and Mr. Eden also thought that Poland might move westwards.

There was a longer discussion about Poland on December 1. President Roosevelt opened this discussion by saying that he hoped for a resumption of diplomatic relations between the Polish and Soviet Governments. Stalin alleged that the Polish Government and their friends in Poland were in contact with the Germans and were killing the Partisans.[2] The Prime Minister repeated his previous statement about our interest in Poland, and our wish to achieve the security of the Soviet western frontier and to prevent an attack by Germany in the future.

Stalin interrupted the Prime Minister to say that the question of Soviet relations with the exiled Polish Government was different from that of the security of the frontiers of the U.S.S.R. Russia was in favour of the reconstruction, development and expansion of Poland mainly at the expense of Germany. Stalin had broken with the Polish Government because they had joined with Hitler in slanderous propaganda against Russia: if they would give up killing Partisans and fight the Germans, he would be glad to renew relations with them.

The Prime Minister said that it would be a great help if we knew the Russian views on the frontier question. Stalin claimed the '1939 frontier' as ethnologically correct. Mr. Eden asked whether Stalin meant the 'Ribbentrop–Molotov line'. M. Molotov said that this line was generally called the 'Curzon line'. Mr. Eden pointed out that there were important differences between the two lines, but

---

[1] The War Cabinet did not discuss Mr. Eden's memorandum.
[2] i.e. the 'People's Army'. The Poles described the so-called 'Partisans' as merely Russian agents.

(a) WP(44)8.

M. Molotov denied that these differences were essential. The Prime Minister then produced a map showing the Curzon line, the 1939 line (i.e. Ribbentrop–Molotov), and also the line of the Oder. Mr. Eden suggested that the Curzon line was intended to run east of Lwow, but Stalin maintained that the Prime Minister's map was wrong, and that he would produce a Russian map showing that Lwow should be on the Russian side of the line. Stalin also said that he did not want any Polish population, and that if he found any district inhabited by Poles he would gladly give it up.

President Roosevelt asked whether East Prussia and the territory east of the Oder approximated in size to the eastern provinces of Poland. Stalin said that he did not know. The Prime Minister suggested that the value of the land to be assigned to Poland was much greater than that of the Pripet marshes. It was industrial land, and would make a much better Poland. We should like to be able to tell the Poles that the Russians were right, and that they (the Poles) had had a fair deal. Stalin repeated that if it were proved to him that any district were Polish, he would give it up. He made some marking on the map, mainly west of the Curzon line and south of Vilna, of an area which he admitted to be mainly Polish.

The Prime Minister said that he liked Stalin's proposal, and that the Poles would be foolish not to accept it. He also said to Mr. Eden, with some emphasis, that he was not going to 'break his heart' over the cession of parts of Germany to Poland or over Lwow. Mr. Eden thought that the Curzon and Oder lines might serve as a basis of discussion. The Prime Minister repeated that the Poles would be wise to take our advice; that he was not going to make trouble about Lwow, and that he did not think that we and the Russians were very far off in an agreement on principles. In answer to a question from President Roosevelt, Stalin said that a transfer of population on a voluntary basis could probably be arranged.

The frontier question was mentioned again at the end of the meeting on December 1, after the three Heads had discussed the future of Germany. The Prime Minister said that he was not asking for any agreement, nor was he convinced in the matter himself, but that it would be desirable to draw up some formula. He suggested words to the effect that 'it was thought in principle that the home of the Polish State and nation should be between the so-called Curzon line and the line of the Oder, including for Poland East Prussia and Oppeln; but the actual tracing of the frontier line required careful study and possibly disentanglement of population at some points'. Stalin said that the Russians wanted Königsberg, but otherwise would accept the Prime Minister's formula. The Prime Minister asked about Lwow; Stalin merely repeated that he would accept the Curzon line.

(vi)

Further British attempts to bring about a Russo-Polish reconciliation: the Polish *aide-mémoire of December 30, 1943.*

On his return from the conferences at Teheran and Cairo Mr. Eden had interviews with Count Raczynski on December 17 and with M. Mikolajczyk, M. Romer and Count Raczynski on December 20.

(a) Before these meetings Count Raczynski had told Sir A. Cadogan that the Polish Ministers were anxious to know whether Stalin had said anything definite at Teheran about the resumption of Polish-Soviet relations, or about his attitude towards the Polish Government. The Poles also wanted to discuss what was to happen when the Soviet troops entered Poland. The German terror in Poland had been intensified in recent weeks, and there was a danger that, when they were being forced out of Polish territory, the Germans would act with still greater violence. In such an eventuality a general rising against the Germans would be all the more necessary. For this purpose the Poles needed arms, and the Polish Government must send appropriate instructions to the Polish people. The Polish Prime Minister was thinking of preparing a statement which he would make at the moment when Soviet troops crossed the frontier. He hoped that His Majesty's Government would issue at the same time a declaration assuring the Polish people that Russian troops were entering Poland on behalf of the United Nations in order to drive the enemy from Polish territory.

(b)   At his interview with Count Raczynski Mr. Eden said that he had hoped that the Prime Minister, who had conducted on our side most of the discussion at Teheran about Poland, might have been able to speak about it to M. Mikolajczyk, but that owing to the Prime Minister's illness, he (Mr. Eden) would give a preliminary account of what had taken place. Mr. Eden then summarised the main points of the discussion. He began with Stalin's allegations against the Polish Government, and said that we had denied them, but that Stalin seemed to be convinced of their truth.

Count Raczynski said that owing to severe German reprisals the Poles had latterly restricted themselves to action against the worst members of the Gestapo, and had not conducted indiscriminate war against all Germans in Poland. On the other hand the Soviet Government had dropped a number of agents all over Poland; the activities of these agents had brought down reprisals on the Polish inhabitants. General Sikorski had tried from the early days of the Russian campaign to discover from the Russians what their agents

---

(a) C14799/39/18. (b) C14935/258/55.

were instructed to do, but the Russians had never told him. Obviously there was some feeling among the Poles against the Russian Partisans with whom they had no means of co-operating, and whose acts involved them in trouble. There was also a danger that these Russian agents might penetrate the Polish Underground movement, and consequently that this movement might be broken up when the Russians entered Poland. Nevertheless Count Raczynski thought that it might be possible to reach some agreement with the Soviet Government about co-ordinating at a high level the activities of the Russian agents and of the Polish Underground organisation. He said that the Polish Government could draw up a statement which we should be free to pass on to the Soviet Government refuting Stalin's allegations and proposing co-operation. M. Mikolajczyk might also authorise us to inform Stalin of his proposed declaration to the Polish people on the entry of Russian troops into Poland.

Mr. Eden agreed with this line of approach, and said that he would like to have the proposed statements when he saw M. Mikolajczyk. Count Raczynski then asked about the frontier question. Mr. Eden gave him a general outline of Stalin's view, including the suggestion that the Polish frontier might be moved as far west as the Oder. Mr. Eden said that we had not committed ourselves in any way, but that it seemed clear that Stalin did not wish to incorporate Poland in the U.S.S.R.

On December 17 Count Raczynski communicated to the Foreign (a) Office documents explaining why the Polish Government were so much afraid of what the Soviet authorities would do when they came into Poland. The documents described the attempts already being made by the Soviet agents in Poland to undermine popular confidence in the leadership of the Polish Underground movement, to destroy its cohesion, and to weaken its forces. There was evidence that the Soviet agents betrayed Poles to the Gestapo, that they carried out depredations against the Polish population, and particularly against the larger land-owners and more prosperous peasants, and that they had murdered a number of soldiers and members of the Underground movement. In eastern Poland they worked for the union of the area with Soviet Russia, and in western Poland they emphasised the need of reliance upon Russian aid and alleged that the United States and Great Britain were selfish imperialists caring nothing for Polish interests and treating the Polish Government as a helpless puppet.

The Foreign Office considered that the few independent reports of our own confirmed the Polish charges against the Russian agents, but that the only thing we and the Poles could do was to try to

---

(a) C14816/258/55.

emphasise the Polish resistance to the Germans and their readiness to integrate their plans with Allied strategy and therefore with Russian military requirements.

(a)   M. Mikolajczyk, at his interview of December 20, told Mr. Eden that he had prepared a draft communication which might be shown to the Soviet Government, but that an anwer to Stalin's points must bring in the frontier question, and that a communication on these lines might not be the best mode of approach. M. Mikolajczyk said that General Sikorski had made a verbal agreement with Marshal Zhukov for the co-operation of the Polish Underground movement with the Russian Partisans. This agreement had not been formally recorded in writing. It might be possible to revive it, but it laid down that all activities on Polish territory would be under the orders of the Polish Home army, and this condition again raised the frontier question.

Mr. Eden said that, apart from the frontier question, there did not seem to be much that separated the Polish and Russian views. The Russians wished the Poles to fight the Germans, but this was what the Poles themselves wished to do. The Russians had been urging action in disregard of reprisals, whereas the Polish Government had thought it wise to wait for the right moment for a general rising; this divergence was also narrowing with the Russian approach to the Polish frontier. Mr. Eden said that he wanted a statement indicating that there was no co-operation between the Poles and the Germans and indicating the broad outline of the Polish plan of campaign and their readiness to discuss it with the Russians directly or through British mediation.

M. Mikolajczyk said that of course no Poles had co-operated with the Germans. He hesitated even to make a statement to this effect, since the Polish people would feel outraged at the suggestion that it was necessary. Mr. Eden said that he might make it in a positive way by recapitulating all that the Poles had done against Germany. M. Mikolajczyk then asked about the frontier question. Mr. Eden repeated what he had previously said to Count Raczynski. He said that the Prime Minister considered that a basis existed for agreement on Russian-Polish issues generally. The Prime Minister was most anxious to try to bring about such an agreement, and had accepted as 'something to work on' the suggestion that the future territory of Poland would be between the Curzon line and the Oder or as near to the Oder as the Polish Government were inclined to extend their frontier, with the district of Oppeln.

M. Mikolajczyk objected that the Curzon line gave both Lwow and Vilna to Russia. He said that the compensation promised in the

(a) C14981/258/55.

west would not be sufficient to justify such a surrender. Mr. Eden suggested that the Polish Ministers should think over the matter, and see him again. Mr. Eden reported these interviews to the War (a) Cabinet on December 20. He asked whether he should tell the Poles that the War Cabinet endorsed his advice to them to accept a settlement on the lines suggested. The War Cabinet agreed that he should speak in this sense.

The Prime Minister had telegraphed to Mr. Eden on December 20 (b) suggesting that he should discuss the frontier question with the Poles, and press them strongly to accept the offer of what he described as a 'magnificent piece of country.' He recommended acceptance even if the Poles did not secure Lwow. The Prime Minister thought that the Poles should be advised to 'put themselves in the hands of their British and American friends to try to turn this plan into reality'. If they refused, it was difficult to see how we could press for anything more for them.

Mr. Eden replied with a summary of the conversations of Decem- (c) ber 17 and 20. He saw MM. Mikolajczyk and Romer and Count (d) Raczynski again on December 24. He urged them very strongly to produce a statement of their plans for anti-German operations in Poland and an indication of their willingness to co-operate with the Russians on Polish territory. Mr. Eden telegraphed after the meeting (e) to the Prime Minister that it was difficult to make the Polish Ministers understand the realities of the situation with regard to the Russian frontier claims. M. Mikolajczyk said that all his information from Poland showed that, as a reward for their sufferings and fighting, the Polish people were expecting to emerge from the war as victors with their eastern provinces intact and their western provinces increased. M. Mikolajczyk was not satisfied with the offer of large areas of German territory which a weakened Poland could not easily absorb. Mr. Eden did not mention to the Poles the Soviet demand for Königsberg. He thought that this demand would only confirm Polish suspicion of Russian plans for their encirclement. Mr. Eden's own view was that if the Polish Government were willing to open discussions on the basis of the Curzon line we should press the Russians to give up the Königsberg demand.

Mr. Eden also found that M. Mikolajczyk had been invited to pay (f) a visit to the United States. The Foreign Office were somewhat disturbed about this visit at a time when we were trying to secure a Soviet-Polish agreement. They considered that M. Mikolajczyk would become the centre of Polish enthusiasm in the United States,

(a) WM(43)172.2, C.A. (b) Frozen 762 (Churchill Papers/355; C15105/258/55). (c) Grand 782 (Churchill Papers/355; C14981/258/55). (d) C15353/258/55. (e) Grand 783 (Churchill Papers/355; C15353/258/55). (f) C15251, 15267/258/55.

and that this enthusiasm would be anti-Russian, and produce statements which would greatly damage the Polish cause with the Russians. The Foreign Office thought that General Sikorski's visit a year earlier had had this unfortunate result. Mr. Eden wanted the Polish Prime Minister at least to wait until he had been able to see Mr. Churchill. Mr. Churchill therefore telegraphed to President
(a) Roosevelt suggesting a postponement, and giving his reasons. The visit was postponed for about a month.

(b)   On December 30 Count Raczynski brought to the Foreign Office an *aide-mémoire* on the lines suggested by Mr. Eden. The *aide-mémoire* included a general statement of the work done by the Polish Undergound movement in spite of the terrible reprisals carried out by the Germans. The *aide-mémoire* denied that Communists were being murdered in Poland at the orders of the Commander of the Polish Home Army and of the Polish Government. Such orders had never been given, in spite of the fact that the Polish population was being exposed to reprisals arising in some cases out of the activities of Soviet Partisans.

The Polish Government had repeatedly made efforts to reach an agreement with the Soviet authorities for co-operation and consolidation of effort against the common enemy. The *aide-mémoire* mentioned the scheme put forward by General Sikorski to Marshal Zhukov in December, 1941; these and later attempts to secure co-operation, however, had failed.

The Polish Government, with the participation of General Sosnkowski, had already in October, 1943, prepared and sent to the Polish Underground movement instructions assuming, in agreement with the Allies, the issue of an order for a general rising. These instructions required that the proposed operations should be brought within the framework of the strategic plans of the Allies.

In view, therefore, of the approach of the time when the rising would take place, the Polish Government declared to the British Government their readiness, jointly with the participation of the Soviet Government, to 'adjust political and military co-operation in the war against Germany'. The Polish Government therefore proposed, in conformity with their decision of October 25, 1943, that Polish armed action should be included in the general strategic plans of the Allies, and that details should be agreed jointly by the representatives of the Polish, Soviet, British and American General Staffs.

Mr. Eden told Count Raczynski that he would look at the *aide-mémoire* from the point of view of using it with the Soviet Government as a basis for bringing about talks between the Polish and Russian military authorities for the purpose of co-ordinating joint action

---

(a) T2063/3, No. 523 (Churchill Papers/355; C15251/258/55). (b) C190/8/55 (1944).

against the Germans. Count Raczynski pointed out that the Polish Government felt that such talks could reach a satisfactory conclusion only if the Soviet Government were to resume diplomatic relations with the Polish Government. Otherwise a breakdown in the talks might make matters worse. Mr. Eden said that if we acted as intermediaries between the two Governments, there was a good chance that the military talks might prepare the way for a resumption of diplomatic relations. Mr. Eden asked Count Raczynski whether the Polish Government had received any hints from the Russian side showing a wish to enter into direct discussions with the Polish Government. Count Raczynski said that there had been 'nothing on which we could build', though there had been personal contacts between the Polish Ministers in Algiers and Berne and the Soviet representatives.

Note to Chapter XXXV. The Curzon Line.

The Curzon Line was an attempt to find a reasonably close approximation to an ethnographic eastern frontier for Poland in 1919–20. In 1919, the principal Allied and Associated Powers welcomed the occupation by the reconstituted Polish State of all territories with an indisputably Polish majority. In March of that year, the Supreme Council in Paris asked its Commission on Polish Affairs to recommend a 'minimum' eastern frontier, within which the new State, i.e. the Republic of Poland, should be authorised to organize a permanent administration. The request was made in accordance with the thirteenth of President Wilson's Fourteen Points of January 8, 1918: 'An independent Polish State should be erected which should include territories inhabited by indisputably Polish populations and which should be assured a free and secure access to the sea . . .' Later, Article 87 of the Treaty of Versailles empowered the Peace Conference to determine the eastern frontiers of Poland.

Among the many difficulties in drawing the frontier in 1919 were the hostility between the principal Allied Powers and the Soviet Government, and between the Poles and the Soviet Government, and the refusal of the Government of the new Polish Republic to agree to any consultation of the wishes of the local population about these frontiers. The problem of deciding on a new eastern frontier affected former Russian territory (both in and east of the Congress Kingdom of 1815) and also former Austrian territory, i.e. Galicia. The new republic of Austria could not resist Polish claims, but this fact did not mean that the Polish Republic could take over without resistance the whole of Galicia. In Eastern Galicia, a

(a)

(a) C14829/551/55 (1943); C1672/140/55 (1944).
Y*

Ukrainian majority of the local population was already fighting the Poles in order to assert its own claim to independence.

There was also the difficulty caused by the uncertain future of Russia, where a counter-revolutionary movement might supersede the Soviet regime. A declaration by the Russian Provisional Government on March 30, 1917, had recognised the creation of an independent Polish State composed of 'all territories where Poles are the majority of the population'; this State would be 'bound to Russia in a free military alliance'.

In these circumstances, the Allied Governments in 1919 proposed (a) to support the Polish Government in their occupation of any territory where a stable Russian Government later on could hardly refuse to recognise Polish claims, (b) to refrain from supporting any eastern extension of Polish territory beyond the somewhat blurred and confused ethnographic line, (c) to render assistance to the Polish Government (if desired by them) to oppose attempts by the Soviet Government to encroach on what was ethnographically Polish territory.

For six months the Commission on Polish Affairs considered the eastern frontier problem. They issued their recommendations in a series of reports, of which the first (March 12, 1919) dealt with the Polish-German (a) frontier. A second report (April 22, 1919) proposed a frontier running from the border of East Prussia as far south as a point on the River Bug in the latitude of Chelm. This frontier, with its southern extension to the Carpathians across the former Austrian Crownland of Galicia, subsequently became known as the Curzon line. At its northern end, the line divided the Suwalki province between Lithuania and Poland—a relatively simple task owing to the existence there of a clear-cut racial division. Then it ran with a moderate westward bulge from Grodno to the Bug at Brest-Litovsk, leaving both these towns outside Poland, but replacing in Poland the town of Bialystok and adjacent areas ceded by Prussia to Russia in 1807.

The Commission based its recommendation of April 22 on the following facts and principles:

(1) the declaration by the Provisional Government of Russia on March 30, 1917.

(2) the omission from the Polish State of areas where there were doubts about the ethnological character and wishes of the population.

(3) the postponement of a final solution of the question until the establishment of a Russian Government with which the Great Powers could negotiate on this question.

(4) a delimitation on the basis of geographical, strategic and economic interests (including communications) of the frontier between Grodno and Brest-Litovsk 'somewhat east of the limit of the area in which it is recognised that Poles form a compact majority ethnologically'.

(a) Confidential General 177/3 (Commission on Polish Affairs), p. 130.

The Commission did not propose a boundary for the southern section
of the Polish eastern frontier, owing to a decision of the Council of (a)
Foreign Ministers of March 19, 1919, that Polish and Ukrainian representatives were not to be heard before the end of hostilities between
Polish and Ukrainian troops. Meanwhile, the frontier was not drawn
south of the latitude of Chelm, because the British delegation considered
that the line south of this point could only be determined in connexion
with the frontier of Eastern Galicia.

This report was considered by the Supreme Council on April 26, 1919. (b)
While suspending judgment on the line so far proposed, the Council
authorised the Commission to consider the frontier to be assigned to
Poland in Eastern Galicia, and to hear the views of individual Russian
personalities regarding the whole Russo-Polish frontier.

On June 17, 1919, the Commission presented a third[1] report dealing (c)
with Eastern Galicia. The Commission considered first the status of the
area. There were four possible solutions:

(i) Independence (the Commission did not recommend this plan).

(ii) Autonomy for a limited period (followed by a plebiscite) (a) under
the administration of the League, (b) under a mandate held by a
Great Power, (c) under a mandate held by a neighbouring Power.

(iii) Attachment to Poland (a) with autonomy under a mandate from
the League,[2] (b) with local autonomy or on a federal basis, (c)
annexation (the Commission did not recommend this plan).

(iv) Immediate plebiscite.

In the view of the Commission the frontier line on the north, east, and
south would be that of the former Crownland of Galicia. A decision on
the western frontier—i.e. dividing Eastern Galicia from the rest of
Galicia—would vary according to the decision with regard to status.
Two different lines, known as A and B, were suggested. Line A ran just
east of Przemysl, and gave Poland 744,000 Ruthenes, and—according
to the language figures in the Austrian census of 1910—3,513,000
Poles. Line B ran east of Lwow, and included also in Poland the oil
bearing area of Drohobycz. This line gave Poland an additional 770,000
Ruthenes and 632,000 Poles. The Ruthene majority in the area between
lines A and B was thus not large; most of the Ruthene population was
east of line B in the provinces of Tarnopol and Stanislavov which the
Poles obtained later in the treaty of Riga.

The Commission was divided on the frontier question in the event of
the acceptance of solution (i). The British Delegation recommended
line A, and the French, Italian and American Delegations line B. In the

---

[1] A fourth (supplementary) report was issued on June 20, 1919.   (d)
[2] This solution differed from that envisaged under (ii)(a) in that no plebiscite would
be held.

(a) B.C.53, Council of Ten, *Foreign Relations of the United States: the Paris Peace Conference*, Vol. IV (Washington 1953), pp. 404–12. (b) F.M.9, Council of Foreign Ministers,
op. cit, Vol. IV, pp. 624–6. (c) *Documents on British Foreign Policy 1919–1939*, Ser. I, Vol.
III, No. 699. (d) *ibid.*, No. 701, Annex A.

case of solutions (ii) and (iv) the British Delegation again recommended
line A and the French and Italians line B, while the American Delegation
reserved their decision. In the case of solution (iii) the four Delegations
recommended line A.

The Commission's report of June 17 reached the Supreme Council at
the moment when the Polish armies had defeated the Ukrainian army
(a) and had almost overcome their opposition. On June 25, therefore, the
Supreme Council decided to authorise the Polish armies to occupy the
whole of Eastern Galicia, on the understanding that this action would
not affect a territorial settlement. At the same time, the Council requested
the Commission to prepare a project of autonomy for Eastern Galicia
within the Polish State.

The Commission's recommendations were made in a fifth report on
(b) August 23, 1919. It was approved by the Council and embodied in a
draft treaty adopted on November 21, 1919. This treaty accepted Line A
as the boundary between an autonomous Eastern Galicia and territory
that was to be under direct Polish rule.

(c)   A sixth report, dealing particularly with Chelm, was presented by the
Commission on Polish Affairs on September 1, 1919. The British objection
to the line of the Bug being followed as far south as the Galician
border had now been withdrawn. The Commission unanimously urged
that the Bug should be followed on the grounds that

(a) it was the boundary of the Congress Kingdom;

(b) it was geographically the best frontier line;

(c) the local Ukrainian population on the west bank of the Bug had
always been at peace with the Poles;

(d) part of that population had emigrated since the war and been
replaced by Poles;

(e) the area had been part of Poland for 600 years except for the
Tsarist Government's innovation of 1912,[1] and the period of the
Treaty of Brest-Litovsk in 1918;

(f) it was economically linked with Poland.

The same report reaffirmed the Commission's view that the Supreme
Council should declare its recognition of the line which the Commission
had now completed from the southern frontier of Eastern Prussia to the
northern border of Galicia. The areas east of the line suggested on
April 22, 1919, and now completed as far south as Galicia were mostly
occupied by Polish troops fighting the Russians. By an agreement between

[1] In 1912 the Imperial Russian Government cut off part of the Polish ('Congress
Kingdom') provinces of Lublin and Siedlce near Chelm and incorporated it into Russia
on the ground that the population was Ukrainian.

(a) Council of Four, C.F.92, *Documents on British Foreign Policy 1919-1939*, Ser. I,
Vol. III, Nos. 701-02. (b) *Id.*, Ser. I, Vol. I, No. 61, Appendix C; Vol. II, No. 27,
Appendix I and No. 28. (c) *Id.*, Ser. I, Vol. I, No. 64, Appendix L.

Admiral Kolchak and the Supreme Council, the definite sanctioning of (a) the Russo-Polish frontier was to be deferred until the convocation by Admiral Kolchak of a Constituent Assembly. The Commission pointed out that it was impossible to foresee when a regular Russian Government could be formed. The participation of such a Government was necessary for the definite fixing of the eastern frontier of Poland. The Commission therefore asked the Supreme Council to declare that the line described in its second and sixth reports marked a boundary to the west of which the Polish Government could thenceforth legally exercise all rights of sovereignty.

This proposal was approved by the Supreme Council. In the form of a (b) Declaration, it was signed by M. Clemenceau as Chairman of the Council on December 8, 1919. The Council had thus completed the definition of a minimum eastern frontier for Poland through former Russian territory; in the north with the new state of Lithuania: then from Grodno as far as the northern border of Eastern Galicia with Russia in whatever form she might re-emerge.

The line thus drawn with its extension through Eastern Galicia along Line A was the line to which Lord Curzon proposed to the Soviet Government that Polish troops should retire in July 1920, when they were being pursued westwards by Soviet armies. This British proposal was a sequel to M. Grabski's appearance on July 9, 1920, before the British and French (c) Prime Ministers at Spa to appeal for the intervention of the Allied Governments. On July 10 M. Grabski signed an agreement defining the (d) conditions on which aid should be given by the Allied Governments to Poland. Among the conditions, the Polish Government consented to negotiate an immediate armistice on the basis of the Polish Army retiring, on the sector north of Eastern Galicia, to the line defined in the Supreme Council's declaration of December 8, 1919, and standing in Eastern Galicia on the line they had reached on the date of the armistice. Once the Polish Government agreed to the conditions, Mr. Lloyd George undertook to put a proposal for an immediate armistice to the Soviet Government.

On July 18, however, the Bolshevik Government declined the proposal of mediation. They preferred direct negotiation with Poland. In a Note, they expressed their 'willingness to agree to a territorial frontier more favourable for the Polish people than the frontiers indicated by the Supreme Council in December last, and proposed once more by the British Government in its ultimatum of July 12'.

The Russo-Polish war pursued its course, and the British proposal had no results—except that the projected minimum frontier worked out through six months of the Peace Conference became known as the Curzon Line. It was referred to under this name by the Polish Government when, in September 1920, it invited the League of Nations to urge

(a) C.F.37, *Documents on British Foreign Policy 1919–1939*, Ser. I, Vol. III, No. 233, Appendix I; No. 255, Appendix II. (b) H.D.60, *Id.*, Ser. I, Vol. I, No. 64; Vol. II, No. 32 and Appendix E, and No. 34. (c) I.C.P.126B, *Documents on British Foreign Policy 1919–1939*, Ser. I, Vol. VIII, No. 55. (d) I.C.P.128A, *Ibid.*, No. 59.

the Lithuanians to withdraw their troops who had advanced into Polish territory west of the line.

A final settlement of the Russo-Polish war was reached in the Treaty of Riga in 1921. The line fixed by this treaty corresponded generally with that of the Second Partition. It lay very much further to the east than the Curzon Line, or the modification of it in Poland's favour suggested by M. Chicherin on behalf of the Bolshevik Government.

Between 1920 and 1939, the eastern frontier of Poland was midway between that of 1772, i.e. before the First Partition, and the Curzon Line. The additional area beyond the Curzon Line acquired by Poland amounted in former Russian territory to 46,000 square miles with a population of 4,000,000, of whom $1\frac{1}{4}$ million were Polish-speaking according to the 1921 Polish census, and in the former Austrian territory of Eastern Galicia to 18,000 square miles, with a population of 4 million, of whom $1\frac{1}{2}$ million were Polish speaking according to the same census.

The Russo-German line of 1939 ran further to the west than the Curzon line, and included in the U.S.S.R. purely Polish territory in the north and a mixed area in the south.

The Poles laid especial claim to Lwow and Vilna as historic cities of Poland. Furthermore, they claimed that the whole area between the Treaty of Riga frontier (the frontier from 1921 to 1939) and the Curzon Line had always contained an important Polish minority, and had been Polish in culture since the Middle Ages. This area contained nearly one-half of the Polish territory within the 1921–39 frontiers and was, in the Polish view, necessary to Poland for strategic and economic reasons. On the other hand the Lithuanians claimed Vilna as their historic capital. The White Russians and the Ukrainians claimed the right to be united with the rest of their respective peoples. The Russians claimed that both White Russians and Ukrainians were Russian peoples, and that the Soviet annexations of 1939 rightly restored the unity of the two peoples within the framework of a Soviet Union which reunited them both with the Great Russians. They claimed also that the wishes of these people were expressed in the votes taken after annexation.

From the ethnographic point of view, which was the chosen basis for demarcation of the Curzon Line, the eastern frontier region of Poland was a much disputed area. The *mélange* of racial minority groups was complicated by historical, cultural, religious, strategical and economic considerations, leaving a confusion and a heritage of claims and counter-claims. After the outbreak of war in 1939 deportations, first by the Russians and then by the Germans, and other changes had the effect of markedly diminishing the Polish population in the areas east of the Curzon line.

APPENDIX

Text of the Anglo-Russian treaty of May 26, 1942.[1]

Treaty of Alliance in the War against Hitlerite Germany and her associates in Europe and of Collaboration and Mutual Assistance thereafter concluded between the Union of Soviet Socialist Republics and the United Kingdom of Great Britain and Northern Ireland

His Majesty The King of Great Britain and the Presidium of the Supreme Council of the Union of Soviet Socialist Republics;

Desiring to confirm the stipulations of the Agreement between His Majesty's Government in the United Kingdom and the Government of the Union of Soviet Socialist Republics for joint action in the war against Germany, signed at Moscow on the 12th July 1941, and to replace them by a formal treaty;

Desiring to contribute after the war to the maintenance of peace and to the prevention of further aggression by Germany or the States associated with her in acts of aggression in Europe;

Desiring, moreover, to give expression to their intention to collaborate closely with one another as well as with the other United Nations at the peace settlement and during the ensuing period of reconstruction on the basis of the principles enunciated in the declaration made on the 14th August 1941, by the President of the United States of America and the Prime Minister of Great Britain to which the Government of the Union of Soviet Socialist Republics has adhered;

Desiring, finally, to provide for mutual assistance in the event of an attack upon either High Contracting Party by Germany or any of the States associated with her in acts of aggression in Europe,

Have decided to conclude a treaty for that purpose and have appointed as their Plenipotentiaries:—

[Here follows a mention of Mr. Eden and M. Molotov].

Who, having communicated their Full Powers, found in good and due form, have agreed as follows:

PART I

Article I

In virtue of the alliance established between the United Kingdom and the Union of Soviet Socialist Republics the High Contracting Parties mutually undertake to afford one another military and other assistance and support of all kinds in the war against Germany and all those States which are associated with her in acts of aggression in Europe.

---

[1] The treaty was ratified at Moscow on July 4, 1942, and published as Cmd. 6376 (Treaty Series). This Command paper includes not only the English and Russian texts but reproductions, at the end of the Russian text, of the signatures of Mr. Eden and M. Molotov.

Article II

The High Contracting Parties undertake not to enter into any negotiations with the Hitlerite Government or any other Government in Germany that does not clearly renounce all aggressive intentions, and not to negotiate or conclude except by mutual consent any armistice or peace treaty with Germany or any other State associated with her in acts of aggression in Europe.

PART 2

Article III

(1) The High Contracting Parties declare their desire to unite with other like-minded States in adopting proposals for common action to preserve peace and resist aggression in the post-war period.

(2) Pending the adoption of such proposals, they will after the termination of hostilities take all the measures in their power to render impossible a repetition of aggression and violation of the peace by Germany or any of the States associated with her in acts of aggression in Europe.

Article IV

Should one of the High Contracting Parties during the post-war period become involved in hostilities with Germany or any of the States mentioned in Article III (2) in consequence of an attack by that State against that Party, the other High Contracting Party will at once give to the Contracting Party so involved in hostilities all the military and other support and assistance in his power.

This Article shall remain in force until the High Contracting Parties, by mutual agreement, shall recognise that it is superseded by the adoption of the proposals contemplated in Article III(1). In default of the adoption of such proposals, it shall remain in force for a period of twenty years, and thereafter until terminated by either High Contracting Party, as provided in Article VIII.

Article V

The High Contracting Parties, having regard to the interests of the security of each of them, agree to work together in close and friendly collaboration after the re-establishment of peace for the organisation of security and economic prosperity in Europe. They will take into account the interests of the United Nations in these objects, and they will act in accordance with the two principles of not seeking territorial aggrandisement for themselves and of non-interference in the internal affairs of other States.

Article VI

The High Contracting Parties agree to render one another all possible economic assistance after the war.

Article VII

Each High Contracting Party undertakes not to conclude any alliance and not to take part in any coalition directed against the other High Contracting Party.

Article VIII

The present Treaty is subject to ratification in the shortest possible time and the instruments of ratification shall be exchanged in Moscow as soon as possible.

It comes into force immediately on the exchange of the instruments of ratification and shall thereupon replace the Agreement between the Government of the Union of Soviet Socialist Republics and His Majesty's Government in the United Kingdom, signed at Moscow on the 12th July, 1941.

Part I of the present Treaty shall remain in force until the re-establishment of peace between the High Contracting Parties and Germany and the Powers associated with her in acts of aggression in Europe.

Part II of the present Treaty shall remain in force for a period of twenty years. Thereafter, unless twelve months' notice has been given by either Party to terminate the Treaty at the end of the said period of twenty years, it shall continue in force until twelve months after either High Contracting Party shall have given notice to the other in writing of his intention to terminate it.

In witness whereof the above-named Plenipotentiaries have signed the present Treaty and have affixed thereto their seals.

Done in duplicate in London on the 26th day of May, 1942, in the English and Russian languages, both texts being equally authentic.

(L.S.) ANTHONY EDEN   (L.S.) V. MOLOTOV

INDEX

Abe, General Noboyuki: 86, 89
Abetz, Otto, German Ambassador to Paris: 78
Adana (Cyprus): 418n
Afghanistan: 11 57–8
Africa: *see* North Africa *and* West Africa
Ajeta, Marquis d': 167, 481–2
Alanbrooke, 1st Viscount: *see* Brooke, General Sir Alan
Albania: 222, 472, 486
Alexander, A. V.: 323, 325
Alexander, General Harold: 421n, 434, 501–2, 584
Alexandria, French squadron at: 308–19, 353
Alfonso XIII of Spain, ex-King: 193–4
Algeria:—administration: 435n, 438; and Gt. Britain: 354, 403, 408; population: 360–1; *see also* North Africa, French
Algiers: 73, 360, 362, 387, 418n, 578
Allied Advisory Council (Italy): 535, 544, 589
  mentioned: 526, 528, 531, 534, 543, 545n
Allied Control Commission (Italy): 511n, 515, 517, 531, 544, 589
Allied Military Government of Occupied Territory (Italy): 511n
Alsace–Lorraine: 301, 447
Alten Fjord: 568
Ambrosio, General Vittorio: 467, 494
Anatolia: 585
Andaman Islands: 600, 602
Anders, General Wladyslaw: 616, 633n, 649
Anfa: *see* Casablanca
Anglo–Japanese Treaty of Commerce 1911: 139
Anglo–Polish Treaty 1939: 613
Anglo–Russian Treaty, May 1942: 246–52, 255, 551, 640
  text: 663–5
Anglo–Russo–Iranian Treaty, 1942: 27, 56–7
Anglo–Thai Non-Aggression Treaty, 1940: 142
Anglo–Turkish Treaty, 1939: 20–1
Annet, Armand: 327n, 330, 331
Anzio: 502, 519
Aosta, Duke of: 462
Apulia: 511
Archangel (*mentioned*): 17, 34, 47, 49, 262, 265, 566, 576, 577
Argenlieu, Admiral Georges Henri Thierry d': 332
Arita, Hachiro: 89, 91, 93, 102, 103n
Asama Maru incident: 89–90
Astrakhan: 577
Atherton, Ray: 287, 296, 425, 444, 445
Atlantic Charter:—Gt. Britain and U.S.S.R.: 30, 209, 220, 221, 225, 231, 255–6, 551; Italy: 539n; U.S.A. and U.S.S.R.: 240; Churchill on Points 3 and 4: 207–8; Foreign Office views: 203–6; inter-Allied meeting, 24.9.41: 208–10; preparation and publication: 198–203; *mentioned:* 2, 40, 216, 228, 245, 246
Attlee, Clement:—and de Gaulle: 433; policy towards Japan: 144; Surrender of

Italy: 488, 494, 495, 497; and three-power military–political commission: 578; *mentioned:* 216, 235, 458
Attolico, Sr. Bernardo: 191
Auboyneau, Captain Philippe Marie: 323, 325
Augusta: 199
Australia: 112, 113, 124, 140, 141, 636
Austria:—and Curzon Line: 657; Post-war policy and: 189, 190, 222, 223, 463, 594; 'Axis' agreement (Tripartite Pact): 109, 111–12, 125, 127–8, 150

Badoglio, Marshal Pietro:—composition of his government: 507–37 *passim;* and Gt Britain: 536, 538–9, 540, 590; *see also* Italy; and Italian fleet: 606, 607, 610; and Italian status after surrender: 503, 504, 505, 506; and the King's abdication: 536; terms of Italian surrender: 468, 471, 482–5, 498, 499, 500; his governments: 466, 467, 471, 536–7; replaced as Prime Minister: 542–5; U.S.S.R. and: 532, 533–4, 535, 536; *mentioned* 463, 470, 473, 475, 476, 502n, 507n, 509
Bagallay, Lacy: 6, 19, 387, 388
Baku: 11
Balfour, J.: 604, 608
Baltic States and post-war policy: 226–34, 237–45, 247; *see also* Union of Soviet Socialist Republics—and Poland
Bandar Dilam: 26
Bandar Shah: 26
Bari Congress: 518–19, 520, 526
Barré, General G.: 363n
Bastianini, Guiseppi: 467
Bataille, Commandant Gaston: 317, 318, 319
Bavaria: 551
B.B.C. and de Gaulle: 405, 430n
Bear Island: 263
Beaverbrook, 1st Baron, and Moscow Conference, September 1941: 35–6, 39–40, 45, 46; *mentioned:* 7, 49
Beck, Jozef: 621
Belgium:—and post-war policy: 222, 247; appeal for peace: 184
Benes, Dr. Edvard: 448, 595, 598; *mentioned:* 601n, 646
Berio, Sr.: 482, 483, 484
Berle, Adolf A.: 215, 216, 218, 509, 510
Berling, Colonel Zygmunt: 633n
Bessarabia:—post-war policy for: 223, 237
Béthouart, General Marie Emile: 360, 376, 396
Bialystok: 638n, 658
Bidault, Georges: 431n
Bir Hacheim: 336
Bismarck, Prince Otto von: 167n
Bizerta: 66, 73, 74, 77, 78, 79, 421n, 447
Bland, Sir Nevile: 186
Bogomolov, A.: 532, 559, 596

Halifax—*contd.*
declaration: 213, 215, 216, 217, 218;
U.S.A.:—*policy towards:*—
France: 63n, 64. 68, 71, 285–96
passim: 298, 307, 338, 339; National
Committee of Liberation: 443, 444,
452, 457; Italian fleet: 604; Italian
government: 520, 521, 528, 534, 545n;
Italian peace treaty: 540, 541; Italian
surrender terms: 470, 473; Japan: 97,
122–3, 130–43 *passim:* 148, 149, 150,
155–77 *passim;* North Africa: 352–3,
356, 378, 405, 419; Spain: 356;
U.S.S.R.: and post-war policy: 237–8,
239, 243; U.S.S.R.: and North Africa:
387; *mentioned:* 71, 84, 94, 178, 241,
255, 365, 369, 370, 373, 403, 406, 533,
539n, 638
Han Li Wu: 100
Hanoi: 108
Harriman, William Averell:—Foreign Ministers' Conference, Moscow, October 1943:
580; North Africa: 269; second front: 270,
271; supplies for U.S.S.R.: 33, 35, 39;
U.S.S.R. and Italian fleet: 604; *mentioned:*
266, 557, 558, 560, 601n
Harwood, Admiral Sir Henry, and Admiral
Godefroy: 309–15
Helleu, Jean: 437
Herriot, Edouard: 320n, 338
Hess, Rudolf: 277, 278, 280
Hirahuma, Baron: 86
Hitler, Adolf:—France: 70, 71, 76, 78–9;
Göring: 185; Japan: 129n, 133n; Mus-
solini: 466, 467; 'New Order' in Europe:
197–8; peace proposal: 192, 193, 194, 195;
Russian campaign: 2, 3, 256, 466;
German opposition to: 182, 183n, 188, 189,
190, 191n; *mentioned:* 70
Hoare, Sir Samuel: 59, 356, 485
Home Army (Poland): 641n, 654; *see also*
Poland
Hong Kong, Japanese threat to: 92, 93, 95,
96, 97, 105
Hoover, Herbert: 61–2
Hopkins, Harry L.:—and de Gaulle and
Giraud: 414, 416n; Japan: 122–3, 170;
Poland: 640; second front: 257n; suggests
U.S.–Anglo-Russian meeting: 30n; *men-
tioned:* 215, 243n, 266n, 391, 409, 560, 639
Horne, Admiral Frederick Joseph: 307
Hull, Cordell:—Admiral Darlan: 365, 378–9;
Atlantic Charter: 206–7; four-Power
Declaration, October 1943: 587–8;
France: 74, 83; Free French movement:
83, 84, 320, 342, 421–2, 425n, 426;
Gt. Britain: 303, 339. 404–6, 421–2;
National Committee of Liberation:
451, 454, 457–8;
German peace feelers: 196n;
Gt. Britain and Japan:—(1939–40): 91,
95–6, 100n, 108, 110, 112–14; (1941):
123, 124–5, 130–5, 145–52 *passim:*
155–70 *passim:* 176;
Gt. Britain and U.S.S.R.: 589–90;
Italian surrender: 473, 491; Italy and
Atlantic Charter: 539n; Poland: 639, 640,

644, 645, 647, 648; post-war Europe: 592,
593; second front: 583, 584; Sweden: 585;
war crimes: 278 *mentioned:* 106, 443n, 580,
645
Hungary:—and British declaration of war:
47, 48, 54; and post-war policy: 222, 223
Huntziger, General Charles: 70

Ichang: 90
India:—Afghanistan: 57; independence: 207;
Iran: 55; Japan: 113; United Nations
declaration: 213, 214, 215
Indo-China:—American policy: 146, 160,
163, 170, 171, 172, 173; Gt. Britain: 121,
127, 157, 160, 161–2; Japanese invasion:
139–40; Japanese policy: 107, 108, 127,
154, 157, 158–9, 176; Thailand: 120
Iran:—and Germany: 23–7; British policy
towards, and Turkey: 21–2; British policy
towards, and U.S.S.R.: 11, 21–2, 23–7, 41,
43, 54–7
Iran, Shah of: 23, 24, 26–7, 54, 55
Iraq: 23, 69–70, 76, 77
Ismay, General Sir Hastings: 36, 39, 45n,
582n, 583–4
Italy:—air force: 462; Allied military-
political commission: 588–9; and Germany
see Germany
peace treaty with Britain: 540–2; request
for Allied status: 538–40; British
policy towards: (December 1942–
September 1943): 462–5, 468–500
passim; (September 1943–June 1944):
501–45; peace-feelers: 461–2 ;
relations with Japan: 89, 109, 167n;
North Africa: 79, 290;
American policy towards (May 1943–
February 1944): 464–5, 468–97 *passim:*
500, 502–8 *passim:* 516, 520–22, 523;
(February–June 1944): 525, 527, 528–
31, 534, 536, 544–5 ;
U.S.S.R.: 531, 532, 589–90 *see also under*
Union of Soviet Socialist Republics;
Army: 462, 463, 483, 503n; Communist
Party: 508, 519, 534n; Junta: 518, 519,
522, 524, 526, 533, 534–5; Navy: 462,
502n, 516, 586–7, 604–11; status after
surrender: 471, 502–8, 540 ;
Anglo-U.S. discussion of surrender terms:
468–97; signature of instrument of
surrender: 497–500, 578 ;
see also Badoglio, Marshal Pietro; Musso-
lini, Benito; Sforza, Count Carlo; *and*
Victor Emmanuel III, King
I Was There (Leahy): 320n
Izvestia: 630

Japan:—Policy towards China: 86, 87–8, 90,
107, 111, 131, 158, 159; War with China:
85, 115; German policy towards Japan:
127n, 129n, 132–3n, 136, 137, 152, 153,
167n; Japanese policy towards Germany:
89–91, 102, 109, 120, 129n, 132–3n, 153,
167n; Japanese need of supplies: 98 ; and
Burma Road: *see* Burma Road;
Plan to exclude British from Tientsin:

Dd. 151957 K33 6/71 Ed (5949)